Gender in Amazonia and Melanesia

Gender
in Amazonia
and Melanesia

An Exploration of the Comparative Method

EDITED BY

Thomas A. Gregor and Donald Tuzin

UNIVERSITY OF CALIFORNIA PRESS

Berkeley   Los Angeles   London

University of California Press
Berkeley and Los Angeles, California
University of California Press, Ltd.
London, England
© 2001 by
The Regents of the University of California

Library of Congress Cataloging-in Publication Data

Gender in Amazonia and Melanesia : an exploration of the comparative method / edited by
Thomas A. Gregor and Donald Tuzin
p. cm.
Includes bibliographical references and index.
ISBN 0-520-22851-0 (cloth : alk. paper) — ISBN 0-520-22852-9 (pbk. : alk. paper)
1. Sex role—Amazon River Region. 2. Sex role—Melanesia. 3. Gender identity—Amazon River
Region. 4. Gender identity—Melanesia. 5. Sex differences—Amazon River Region. 6. Sex differ-
ences—Melanesia. 7. Kinship—Amazon River Region. 8. Kinship—Melanesia. 9. Amazon
River Region—Social life and customs. 10. Melanesia—Social life and customs. I. Gregor, Thomas
A., 1940– II. Tuzin, Donald F.
GN564.A47 G45 2001
305.3'0981'1—dc21

00-047947

Printed in the United States of America
08 07 06 05 04 03 02 01
10 9 8 7 6 5 4 3 2 1

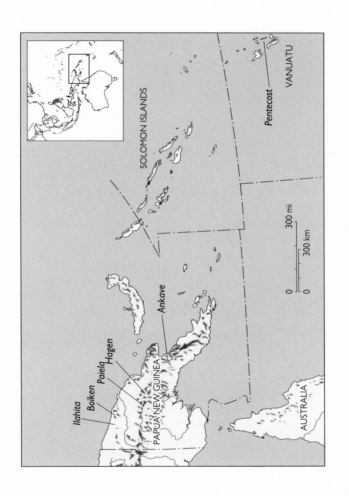

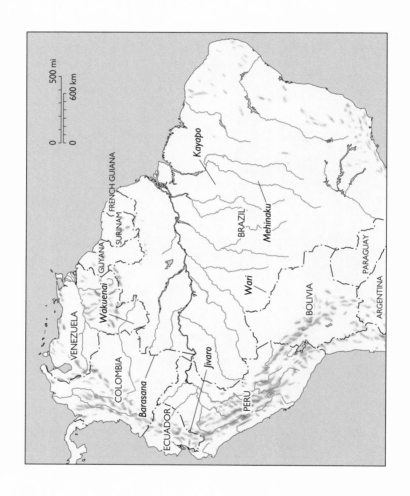

CONTENTS

ACKNOWLEDGMENTS

You are holding in your hand the first book to systematically compare the cultures of Melanesia and Amazonia and to consider the remarkable parallels and illuminating differences that exist between them. That this book exists at all is due to the confidence and financial support of the Wenner-Gren Foundation for Anthropological Research, which sponsored an international symposium in Mijas, Spain, in September 1996. The conference engaged eighteen scholars from five countries in an intense week-long meeting that examined the culture of the regions in question, with particular reference to gender issues and the nature of the comparative method. That conference, which was a model of participant conviviality and professionalism, was the inspiration for this book.

We express our gratitude to the Wenner-Gren Foundation and especially to its then-president, Sydel Silverman, who not only supported the conference but also quite actively collaborated in its conceptual and practical design. In preliminary discussions and in extended planning meetings prior to the symposium, she helped us refine the intellectual issues, held the project to the highest intellectual standards, and assisted in the selection of the participants. She added immeasurably to the conference in her several roles of organizer, advisor, and discussant. The symposium, and hence this book, which derived from it, is a project in which Sydel was an indispensable partner.

At a more personal level, we are especially appreciative of the way in which Sydel and the Foundation facilitated our collaboration as organizers and editors by providing us with opportunities for meetings and otherwise enabling us to form a partnership that sustained this complex, rather ambitious project—more than sustained: for us, the quality of our collaboration was the key to a remarkably balanced, intellectually delightful, and ultimately seamless enterprise.

We also express our gratitude to the staff of the Foundation, especially Laurie Obbink and Mark Mahoney, who with unfailing skill and good humor coordinated the submission of papers, schedules, travel arrangements, and other logistics associated with the symposium.

For technical assistance, we thankfully acknowledge Vanderbilt University reference librarians Paula Covington and David Carpenter, who compiled massive bibliographies on gender in Amazonia and Melanesia, which were an invaluable resource for the participants, and Guy Tapper, of Montpelier, Vermont, who prepared the maps of Amazonia and Melanesia.

For all this, we are deeply grateful.

Thomas A. Gregor
Nashville, Tennessee

Donald Tuzin
La Jolla, California

August 1, 2000

ONE

Comparing Gender in Amazonia and Melanesia: A Theoretical Orientation

Thomas A. Gregor and
Donald Tuzin

INTRODUCTION

Approximately one hundred years ago anthropologists identified what was to become an intriguing, enduring mystery of culture history: the question of the sources and the theoretical implications of remarkable similarities between societies in Amazonia and Melanesia. A world apart and separated by forty thousand or more years of human history, some of the cultures in the two regions nonetheless bore striking resemblances to one another. In both Amazonia and Melanesia, the ethnographers of the period found societies organized around men's houses. There the men conducted secret rituals of initiation and procreation, excluded the women, and punished those who would violate the cult with gang rape or death. In both regions, the men told similar myths that explained the origins of the cults and gender separation. The resemblances were such as to convince anthropologists of the day, including Robert Lowie, Heinrich Schurtz, and Hutton Webster, that they could only have come about through diffusion. Lowie flatly declared that men's cults are "an ethnographical feature originating in a single center, and thence transmitted to other regions" (1920, 313).

The diffusionist school of anthropology waned soon afterward, and for a long period so did interest in the puzzling resemblances of specific societies in the two regions. Nonetheless, during this period anthropologists continued informally to remark upon the similarities in regions that were separated by such a vast gulf of history and geography. The parallels included not only men's cults but also similar systems of ecological adjustment; egalitarian social organization; flexibility in local- and descent-group composition and recruitment; endemic warfare; similar religious, mythological, and cosmological systems; and similar beliefs relating to the body, procreation, and the self. So striking were such resemblances that, at times, as we review them today, they overshadow obvious differences between the regions and obscure the fact that not all subregions or societies lend themselves to this comparison.

In September 1996, in Mijas, Spain, the Wenner-Gren Foundation for Anthropological Research convened a week-long international symposium to examine similarities and differences between Amazonian and Melanesian cultures. This volume is based on that inquiry. Our intention is to examine some of the many dimensions of the Amazonia-Melanesia comparison by focusing on gender, which is perhaps the most noticeable area of resemblance between cultures of the two regions. The authors, all accomplished Amazonianists and Melanesianists, contribute to this goal by examining specific questions that derive from their own research and, above all, by comparing their findings with those drawn from societies in the other cultural region. That is to say, comparativism informed the collective enterprise and its component studies from their inception. This feature of the project distinguishes it from anthropology's long tradition of edited volumes in which, for the most part, contributors describe and theorize about a given topic in a particular ethnographic context, with little regard to cross-cultural comparison per se (e.g., Lambek and Strathern 1998; but see Strathern and Stewart 1998 in the same volume). By contrast, through argument or example, each author in the present volume examines larger theoretical issues of method and epistemology that are suggested by Amazonia-Melanesia comparisons.

THE COMPARATIVE METHOD AND ITS PREDICAMENTS

Our focus on Amazonia and Melanesia is explicitly comparative. But at its most basic level, *all* anthropology is comparative. There is no way to talk about other cultures and their institutions without, at least implicitly, comparing them to other cultures. When we speak of a society as having "men's cults," for example, we have in mind similar organizations in other societies. For all its centrality to anthropology's disciplinary identity, however, the comparative method has had a troubled history. A brief review of that history situates the present volume within the debate and provides a broader theoretical context for the specific comparisons that are the substance of our project.

Let us begin with the influential essay "The Limitations of the Comparative Method of Anthropology," published by Franz Boas (1940 [1896]) exactly one hundred years before our conference. A watershed in American anthropology, the work defined what was wrong with the "comparative method" of the preceding era and set the course for what anthropology was to be, all the way to the present. American anthropology entered a new age with Boas's essay, but it was to be an age of turbulence. Through it all eddied the dilemma of anthropology's perennial, century-long "crisis" regarding the comparative method (Barnes 1987, 119).

Boas's famous complaint with the so-called comparative method was that its Victorian practitioners assumed, without warrant, that in human affairs like effects spring from like causes, and that the occurrence of similar traits in different cultures implies participation in a universal, orthogenic, evolutionary process. Not so, wrote Boas. Rather, similar phenomena can arise from quite dissimilar processes: "The identical result may have been reached on . . . different lines of development and from an infinite number of starting points" (1940 [1896], 274). Without clear delineation of the underlying processes, without knowledge of cultural and historical particularities, comparison between cultures is impossible—except, perhaps, when the cultures being compared possess known historical affinities and occur within the same geographical vicinity.

In other words, Boas did not object to comparison per se but to comparison that is uncontrolled, uninformed, preconceived, and prejudicial. Certain laws do exist, he averred (p. 276), "which govern the growth of human culture, and it is our endeavor to discover these laws." Ultimately, a mature anthropology would have to be a blend of history and science, a harmony of the particular and the general; but "for the moment," priority had to be given to "the study of specific sequences in delimited areas" (Harris 1968, 259). Boas concluded his essay with a clear message for our discipline (1940 [1896], 280). "The comparative method," he charged, "notwithstanding all that has been said and written in its praise, has been remarkably barren of definite results, and I believe it will not become fruitful until we renounce the vain endeavor to construct a uniform systematic history of the evolution of culture, and until we begin to make our comparisons on the broader and sounder basis [of documented cultural-historical processes]. Up to this time we have too much reveled in more or less ingenious vagaries. *The solid work is still all before us*" (emphasis added).

In the century since this was written, much of that "solid work" has been done, in the form of fine-grained ethnographic description and analysis. And yet, although good ethnography necessarily entails classification, and hence comparative assumptions, the specific enterprise of comparison remains shadowy and even a bit disreputable, and its results, according to Evans-Pritchard (1965, 27), are meager and controversial. "When anthropologists generalize, they do so on the basis of cross-cultural comparison, but the rationale of their use of comparative data seldom bears close examination" (Leach 1968, 344).

LIVING WITH THE PREDICAMENT

Generally speaking, there have been two types of comparison. The first is broad or even universal in scope, such as one finds in the works of J. G. Frazer, Sigmund Freud, Ruth Benedict, Claude Lévi-Strauss, George Peter Murdock,

Leslie White, and their respective followers. Whether idealist or materialist, these approaches seek to account for traits and processes common to all humanity, or they appeal to an aspect of human nature (e.g., psychic unity of mankind) to justify a global sample in the testing of very general propositions. Although this type of comparison pursues some of the most interesting questions of all, its practitioners sometimes draw fire for their imperial attitude toward cultural evidence: decontextualizing, overselecting, teleologizing, and taking a generally dogmatic view of things. More technically, as Evans-Pritchard put it in a still vital essay (1965), broad comparisons fail to ensure that "the units of comparison" are of equivalent value. "Are 'monogamy' among the Veddahs of Ceylon and 'monogamy' in Western Europe units of the same kind?" he asked (1965, 19). If not, how can we compare them?

In a more recent article, Hobart argues that what passes for comparison is woefully simplistic: that the objects compared are prejudged as to their similarity and that there are no standards for declaring them equivalent. He makes the claim that even what appear as cultural universals are, when examined closely, culturally unique. Hence he asks: "Everywhere animals and people eat. Is this not a universal which underwrites all translation?" (1987, 39). It is not, says Hobart—who then proceeds to show that there are at least eight terms for "eating" in Balinese, and that the terms and the concept of eating vary with caste, politeness, personal health, whether the eater is known or a stranger, and so forth (1987, 39).

To an extent, this critical view of comparison rests on a concept of culture in which institutions and symbols are inseparable from their context, or at least difficult to tease apart. For example, in *Patterns of Culture*, Ruth Benedict famously argued that the diversity of culture results from "a complex interweaving of cultural traits. The final form of any traditional institution . . . depends upon the way in which the trait has merged with other traits from different fields of experience" (1959 [1934], 37). She went on to examine the guardian spirit complex in North America and concluded that when looked at closely its forms varied so much from one another that there was no "single" guardian spirit complex. Rather, the complex took different forms "according to the other traits of the culture with which it was most closely associated" (p. 39). How could one isolate comparable units if they were so embedded in local traditions? Benedict's resolution of this dilemma was to compare not single cultural traits but deeper essences or patterns (such as the "Dionysian" and the "Apollonian") that were said to be characteristic of cultures and cultural regions.

For Boas and Evans-Pritchard, the solution to the dilemma of comparable units was to limit the scope of comparison to a small number of well-studied, mutually related cultures in a local region. Its success, while perhaps modest and seemingly parochial to the region (e.g., Nadel 1952; Eggan 1950; Watson 1963; but see Tuzin n.d.), is due to methodological controls over the manipulation of variables and constants—controls made possible by historical and geographical proximities. And yet, by its very controls this method begs the question that has vexed anthropology from the start: how does one account for similarities between cultures that are historically and geographically unrelated?

In recent years, the plight of comparison has worsened. Poststructuralist critics now challenge the ontological validity of ethnographic findings and the very possibility of positive knowledge in the human sciences (Clifford and Marcus 1986; Hobart 1987; Holy 1987). If cultures are islands unto themselves or "texts" composed in the imaginations of pseudo-observers, if all classification and generalization are nothing but the exercise of Western hegemony and arrogance, if, in short, all is vanity, then comparison would be at best impossible and at worst immoral. This nihilistic rhetoric, though extreme, is not entirely new. As sober and reasonable an anthropologist as Evans-Pritchard questioned whether cultures could be compared at all, or even if they could, whether there was anything to be learned that was not fatuous or tautological. Should we not question, he wondered, "whether the basic assumption which has so long been taken for granted, that there are any sociological laws of the kind sought; whether social facts, besides being remarkably complex, are not so totally different from those studied by the inorganic and organic sciences that neither the comparative method nor any other is likely to lead to the formulation of generalizations comparable to the laws of those sciences" (1965, 33).

Despite this quote, which catches Evans-Pritchard at his most querulous, few anthropologists would be willing to carry the argument, especially the position of the postmodernists, to its logical conclusion of radical cultural relativism. To do so would mean the end of anthropology. It would even mean the end of ethnography; for, *pace* Holy (1987, 3), who exaggerates the distinction between "description" and "generalization," all description employs classes of ideas external to the phenomena, beginning with the words we use. It is an inductivist fallacy to see generalization as always and necessarily proceeding from description, rather than as the dialectical process it is. The fact is, clarifying our comparative methods and assumptions could not fail to improve our descriptions.

By its nature, the present volume challenges the more extreme assertions of poststructuralism, as well as those who would argue that comparison is futile. Balinese "eating" and other curiosa notwithstanding, the human experience is sufficiently similar to make comparison possible. The diversity that Benedict finds in the guardian spirit complex is real enough, but the various expressions subsumed by this diversity are nonetheless comparable. Indeed, by pursuing such a comparison, she learns more about the cultures in question and the way their institutions are interwoven. With respect to local context, then, and to the definition of phenomena, there is much to be learned in the process of

comparison. The editors and contributors concede, however, that the epistemological criticisms of the comparative method properly test the mettle of
anthropology, as regards its claim to scientific seriousness. The issues these
criticisms raise intrude upon our project by way of problematizing the ontological status of ethnographic description, regional classification, and cross-
cultural generalization (Holy 1987; Fardon 1990; Strathern 1990). The fact remains, however, that the poststructuralists, although modish and with
theoretical agendas of their own, are but the latest players in the century of
turmoil surrounding the comparative method in anthropology.

Amazonia, Melanesia, and the Comparative Method

In addressing the substantive and theoretical issues associated with comparison, this volume stands on an unusually solid foundation of scholarship. To
begin with, the quality of ethnographic coverage in both Amazonia and
Melanesia is of a very high order, sufficient even to Boas's stringent standards.
In addition, each region has produced a sizable literature of areally and top-
ically focused collections. In Amazonia, one notes David Maybury-Lewis
(1979) on "dialectical" societies, Peter G. Roe (1982) and Jonathan D. Hill
(1988) on myth and history, Hames and Vickers (1983) on ecology and adaptation, Peter Rivière (1984) on basic structural models among lowland societies, Kenneth M. Kensinger (1984) on marriage systems, Greg Urban and
Joel Sherzer (1986) on native discourse, and, most recently, a series of comparative works under the general editorship of Kenneth M. Kensinger, entitled *South American Indian Studies* and *Working Papers on South American Indians.*
Melanesia has produced similar studies, including distinguished collections on
sex and gender (Brown and Buchbinder 1976; Herdt 1982, 1984), ritual and
cosmology (Lawrence and Meggitt 1965; Stephen 1987; Gewertz 1988; Herdt
and Stephen 1989; Stewart and Strathern 1997), social organization (Watson
1964; Glasse and Meggitt 1969; Cook and O'Brien 1980), leadership (Godelier and Strathern 1991), and regional culture (Lutkehaus et al. 1990; Strathern and Stürzenhofecker 1995). The historical dimension of Amazonian and
Melanesian societies, so central to Boas's critique, is also increasingly accessi-
ble (e.g., Hill 1988; Ferguson and Whitehead 1992; Gewertz 1983; Gewertz
and Errington 1991; Knauft 1993). Thanks to this vigorous work, Amazonian
and Melanesian data are extraordinarily rich, and their value to wider ethnological questions has been enormous. In short, we know much about Amazonian and Melanesian cultures in context.

The "solid work" of ethnography and ethnology in Amazonia and
Melanesia has established the informational base that is necessary for testing
methodological principles and criticisms. This is a crucial precondition of the
enterprise of this volume, for it enables the contributors vastly to enrich their
own ethnographic descriptions with insights drawn from a rich, reliable, and

relevant literature. The stage is thus set for the kind of informed comparative study that Boas called for and would approve.

The strategies of comparison utilized by our contributors, however, would have seemed novel to Boas. In aggregate, the authors combine both the "universalist" and "localist" traditions mentioned above. Although the project shares the former's interest in similarities between historically and geographically unrelated cultures, it "controls" that comparison by favoring for attention instances that are, indeed, similar—or that, at any rate, appear to be so. This does not imply a lack of interest in differences between cultures of the two regions. As previously noted, some differences examined here are quite germane to the comparison; moreover, *systematic* differences between the regions may be construable as similarities at a higher level of abstraction, in that the relations between things may be similar, even if the things themselves are not. What our approach *does* imply, however, is that a search for differences is pointless, unless such differences occur and are made meaningful in the context of similarities. As Evans-Pritchard remarked (1965, 25), "institutions have to be similar in some respects before they can be different in others." This of course begs the question of how "similarities" are to be demonstrated and understood between unrelated cultures; hence the need for epistemology.

The contributors to the volume follow "localist" traditions of comparison as well as universalist models. For the most part, they compare richly contextualized constructs—systems, processes, and relationalities—rather than isolated traits. And instead of exploring the entire panoply of comparative possibilities, they sharpen their focus on gender, thereby to advance the methodological objectives of the project. As explained below, gender is a powerfully integrative topic that reflects the interests of many scholars who work in Amazonia and Melanesia.

In summary, comparison is the bread and butter of anthropology. It is inherent in the act of classification, by which we identify unfamiliar behaviors, describe institutions, and communicate the results of our work to others. We cannot describe one society without having others in mind, for comparison is the recurring element of our basic analytical tools. Comparison establishes and refines a common discourse among scholars working with different cultures (cf. Strathern and Stewart 1998, 251); it stimulates and provokes new perspectives on findings from particular cultures; and it allows us to search for general principles through controlled comparison. Comparison elevates the level of our work to the quest for principles of human life that transcend any one culture, even as it accepts the importance of culture in forming people's interests and the views they have of others. Without comparison, we risk miring our work in exotica and in the description of the particular: "without systematic comparative studies, anthropology will become only historiography and ethnography" (Radcliffe-Brown 1951, 16). The prospect is far worse than Radcliffe-Brown supposed. For, without comparison—without systematic observation, classification, and generalization—anthropology will become nothing at all. Hence the need to articulate and exemplify new approaches to the old problems of anthropological comparison.

SEX, GENDER, AND RELATED DIMENSIONS OF COMPARISON
In Search of "Melazonia"

One of the contributors to this volume, Stephen Hugh-Jones, has suggested that a comparative perspective on the cultures of Amazonia and Melanesia presupposes an imaginary place, a place which he felicitously dubbed "Melazonia." Within the borders of Melazonia, we would find cultures whose characteristics make their comparison useful and interesting. Clearly, there are many dimensions of comparison that would define citizenship in Melazonia, including similar environments and subsistence regimes, patterns of leadership, and shamanistic religion. For us and many of our colleagues, however, the resemblance among the societies in Melazonia that stands out most dramatically is gender. This is a useful basis for a comparative study, since gender is a topic at the forefront of anthropology. It is an inherently integrative subject, bringing together intellectual perspectives derived from such diverse areas as human biology, environmental studies, psychology, social anthropology, and the humanities. Above all, the territory of Melazonia, when its frontiers are defined by patterns of gender, seems to provoke fascinating insights about the cultures studied by our contributors and, more generally, about the human condition.

Gender-Inflected Societies

Gender is of great importance in the context of many of the small-scale cultures of Melanesia and Amazonia. Though we are wary of essentializing assumptions that lead to the stereotyping of cultural regions, the societies of Amazonia and Melanesia are arguably *gender inflected* (Lindenbaum 1987, 222), perhaps more than any other areas in the world. That is, gender roles and their attendant ideas about sexuality appear as templates for many other domains of culture. Human sexuality is projected upon nature so that flora, fauna, and natural objects have anthropomorphically sexual qualities. Ritual systems, cosmology, leadership, warfare, self-concepts and images of the human body, kinship, and perceptions of the environment are genderized: thought of and conceived in terms that are linked to masculinity, femininity, and human sexuality. Spiraling upward and away from the specific images of human sexual physiology and anatomy, sex and gender in Melazonia infuse broader worldviews about the nature of the human condition. Hence Stephen Hugh-Jones (Chapter 11), using material from the Barasana, sees the embodiment of gender identity as a meditation on the interdependence of men and women. For both, "the human body and its various parts—vocal apparatus, gut, bones and genitals—are all tubes. Through the couplings of these tubes and the passage of various substances—food, water, air, sound, semen, blood, feces, children—along their interiors, the flow of life is ensured." In both Amazonia and Melanesia "sexuality and reproduction flow into each other and are part of a broader confluence of indigenous philosophies about the cosmic sources of life, health, and growth and of decay and degeneration" (Jolly, Chapter 8).

The sexualized cosmos inhabited by many Amazonian and Melanesian cultures is by no means limited to these regions. What makes it remarkable is the degree to which it obtains there. Lawrence E. Sullivan (1988), for example, provides us with an extraordinarily detailed summary of Amazonian religious systems. In bringing together the mythology of the Amazonian region, Sullivan adduces seven basic summarizing principles, one of which is sexuality: "the mode of being human is distinguished by sex from the very beginning; i.e., the very consciousness of sex is sacred." Peter Roe, who has also attempted an integration of Amazonian symbol systems, is unequivocal. In an extended discussion of gender (1982, 265–273), he notes that "the most meaningful distinctions in these societies are those between male and female" (p. 265), and that gender is the source of most of the metaphors of social interaction as well (p. 266). It is easy to adduce specific Amazonian examples. Among the Desana and other Tukanoan peoples of the northwest Amazon, the entire cosmos is both sexualized and genderized. The Sun god's piercing rays are equated with phallic male sexuality, while the earth and a uterine paradise below it are identified with femininity (Reichel-Dolmatoff 1971).

Similar ideas shape the cosmos in Melanesia. Lindenbaum could have been referring to Amazonia when she observed (1987, 222), "Papua New Guineans live in a gender-inflected universe in which the polarities of male and female articulate cosmic forces thought to be located in the human body; indigenous theories of human reproduction contain within them an implicit recipe for social reproduction." In Melanesia, animals, plants, common objects, and sacred implements are often described as having a gender identity and even sexual motivation (Tuzin 1972, 1992a; Meigs 1984). Individuals, as well as cultures, are conceived largely in terms of masculine and feminine categories. Rituals marking puberty and the life cycle are redolent with gender imagery. Sexuality is an intense cultural focus, one often associated not only with procreation and pleasure but with illness and symbolic contamination. Female sexuality is considered by men to be dangerous and yet is imitated by them in rituals of symbolic menstruation, procreation, or (less commonly) parturition. Sex and gender in both Amazonia and Melanesia may have a dreamlike quality, in which, it would seem, the extremes of fantasy are realized in conduct.

We shall see that the contributions to this volume make the case for a Melazonian cultural universe that is redolent with all kinds of sexual imagery. Stephen Hugh-Jones (Chapter 11) describes the sexualization of foods, fauna, and flora within the symbolism of initiation. Paul Roscoe (Chapter 12), in his comparative chapter examining a broad sample of cultures in the two regions, looks at how ideological issues of sex and aggression are conflated, demonstrating that sexual prohibitions adhere to dangerous and aggressive ventures. Philippe Descola (Chapter 5) examines the gender categories that classify plants, animals, and spirits. Margaret Jolly (Chapter 8) looks at the equations of food and sexuality. Thomas Gregor and Donald Tuzin cite numerous similar metaphors from a range of cultures (Chapter 14). And Michael Brown (Chapter 9) describes how gender and sexuality may structure the process of religious transformation.

In considering the gender-inflected universes of many Amazonian and Melanesian peoples, the task of comparison must confront two fundamental questions. The first is the question of essentializing the two regions. Do *all* South American and Melanesian cultures construct their cosmos with the same single-minded attention to sex and gender? And what does it mean to the comparison of the two regions if some or many of them do not? One of the contributors to this volume, Philippe Descola (Chapter 5), argues that gender and sexuality are far less important in Amazonia than in Melanesia. In an original and challenging article, he maintains that gender is not of particular relevance to Amazonian cultures. Rather, Descola maintains, sex and gender are subsumed by more significant social and symbolic categories such as the relationship of in-laws and consanguine kin, and even the predator-prey relationship that distinguishes the perception of nature of some Amazonian peoples. These themes, he believes, are the essence of Amazonian cultures, which are thereby quite different from those in Melanesia, preoccupied as they are with sex and gender. For Descola, Melazonia is a small place indeed, and only half populated at that.

Descola's complex and rewarding article must be read in full to be appreciated as it deserves to be. We take issue with both his reading of the Amazonian ethnography and, perhaps more relevantly, the level of abstraction by which he adduces what is relevant for the people themselves. Moreover, Descola's own field research, conducted among a relatively nongenderized group, the Achuar, may have influenced his generalizations, or the Achuar may constitute a "limiting case" of the interregional comparison. In any case, as we see it, his search for essences or the "master codes" of Amazonia and Melanesia serves only one of the purposes of comparison. We also look for useful comparisons between particular societies that illuminate our own data and enlarge our thinking. It is no embarrassment to the field of Melazonian studies that some of the cultures of its constituent regions have no comfortable place within greater Melazonia.

Our interest in the sexualized worlds of Amazonia and Melanesia engages a second question that is also fundamental to comparison. How can we be sure that the apparent resemblances are meaningful rather than superficial? Are sex and gender as organizing ideas put to similar uses among the cultures of the two regions, or are the resemblances more a matter of surface appearance? The question is best answered by our contributors, who place the similarities and differences in richly detailed contexts. But we also note that in both Amazonia and Melanesia sex and gender are linked to self-concepts, suggesting that we are dealing with similar ways of thinking.

Body, Person, and Self

The Melazonian self is a cultural domain closely associated with indigenous assumptions concerning sex and gender. In both Amazonia and Melanesia, the self-concept, social identity, and the anatomy and physiology of the human body are intertwined with theories of conception, maturation, depletion, and death. Conklin and Pollock (n.d.), writing of Amazonia, note that social personhood, including gender, is acquired as if it were the product of growth, through an incremental process rather than being conferred all at once (cf. Biersack, Chapter 4). Even when social transitions are ritually marked, as is often the case with developmental statuses, the rituals are drawn out, so that the status is acquired over an extended period. Crucial to this process is the notion of shared or exchanged bodily substance: movements of physical material from the body of other individuals "via sexual intercourse, breast feeding, food sharing, physical intimacy, enemy killings [and] interactions with animals." The process rises in the mythic beginnings of men and women, who are commonly assigned radically different origins (Sullivan 1988; Brumbaugh 1990; Tuzin 1997). Moving through the life cycle, masculine and feminine identity is defined by the physical attributes of the human body, and the bodies with whom one comes into contact. Hence, the cultures of the two regions focus enormous attention on menstrual blood, semen, milk, and hair as markers of identity. Self-definition, depending as it does on an incremental process of absorbing the qualities of others, is highly malleable, thus providing an ideological basis for the flexibility of social organization that is so characteristic of both areas (Strathern, Chapter 10). The definition of kinship categories, group identity, and community membership are thereby "biologized" and embodied, and inevitably implicate notions of sex and the physical differences between men and women (Seeger et al. 1979; Turner 1980). These issues correspond to current concerns of Amazonianists and Melanesianists and their efforts to conceptualize similar mutable, sexual, and biologically represented relationships within the cultures of the two regions (cf. Herdt 1981; Poole 1981a; Strathern 1988).

When examined closely, how similar are Amazonian and Melanesian images of self and embodiment? For Conklin (Chapter 7), who looks at the parallels of warrior seclusion and pregnancy among the Amazonian Wari', the specific parallels are "so striking that when Amazonian ethnographers read the Melanesian 'body' literature, we often get that frisson of uncanny recognition described well by the American baseball player, Yogi Berra, who exclaimed: 'It's like *déjà vu* all over again.'"

Our authors examine these parallels of self-definition and gender in a series of comparative studies that emphasize ideas about the embodiment of identity in the two regions. Bonnemère (Chapter 12) and Hugh-Jones (Chapter 11), although using different theoretical perspectives, examine the sexual metaphors that frame masculinity among the Anga peoples in Melanesia and those of the Vaupes region in Amazonia. Biersack (Chapter 4) looks at the magical efforts of young men among the Melanesian Paiela to grow beautiful hair as a marker of growth, sexual attractiveness, and masculine status. Fisher (Chapter 6) finds similar patterns of body imagery among the images associated with both age and gender among the Brazilian Kaiyapo and the Yangorou Boiken of New Guinea. Finally, Jolly (Chapter 8), focusing on sexual desire as well as self-identity, finds resemblances between the northwest Amazon and New Guinea.

Procreative Imagery and Ritual

The embodiment of symbols and self that we note in the cultures of island Melanesia and New Guinea is often focused on rituals and imagery that are imitative of female reproductive physiology and anatomy.[1] The most vivid examples of this pattern occur in male initiation rituals, in which boys are symbolically gestated and birthed by men. In Australia and New Guinea, the implications of this idea are followed to their logical extreme, as in the passing of initiates through the legs of the men in a form of "anal" birth among the Wikmunkan (McKnight 1975, 94), the equations of breast milk and orally ingested semen among the Sambia (Herdt 1981), and many variant forms of "male menstruation" that occur throughout New Guinea (for example, the Wogeo [Hogbin 1970]).

In Amazonia we find the same pattern in male initiation rituals, albeit in somewhat more symbolic, abstract, but still unmistakable form. Barasana and northwest Amazon initiation, for example, make use of such imagery (S. Hugh-Jones 1979, 132), and in the Upper Xingu boys having their ears pierced (one of the major markers of adulthood) shed "menstrual" blood (Gregor 1985). Amazonia is also famous for that most literalized male procreative ritual, the couvade, in which fathers directly imitate the labor pains and assume the taboos of their pregnant wives. These beliefs and practices, unfettered as they are by the realities of human biology, are, in their way, extraordinary triumphs of the imagination (Shapiro and Linke 1996).

Our authors bring a number of very different approaches to the understanding of procreative symbolism. Bonnemère, who notes the parallels of Melanesian and Amazonian initiation, sees female reproductive physiology and anatomy as a natural symbol and an analogy for the "birthing" of boys: "The female body being 'a body capable of reproducing itself' . . . constitutes an adequate model for thinking and operating the maturation of men's bodies, which lack this capacity." In short, for Bonnemère, the imagery of initiation is based on observation, analogy, and logic.

Conklin (Chapter 7) and Hugh-Jones (Chapter 11), utilizing "relational approaches" developed in Melanesia, primarily by Marilyn Strathern (1988), see procreative imagery as suggestive of the mutual dependence of men and women. Conklin looks at the pregnancy-like seclusion of Wari' warriors who were said to be filled with the blood of their slain enemies. As a gestating women creates new life, so does the warrior transform enemy substance into vitality and power. Hugh-Jones, examining men's initiation in the northwest Amazon, also sees the procreative symbolism of the men's cult as a statement of dependence, closeness, and even anatomical resemblances. Taken together, the symbolism of the men's cult is a philosophy, "a meditation" about the mutually integrated roles of men and women.

Gregor and Tuzin use a radically different, psychoanalytic perspective, in that procreative symbolism is seen as reflective of masculine insecurity. Only rarely, they note, does women's ritual imitate male reproductive physiology (for the case of Shipibo clitoridectomy, see Roe 1982, 93, 106). Male procreative beliefs both express anxiety over ambiguous sexual identity and attempt to gain mastery over the feminine part of the male self.

We regard the alternate interpretations of procreative imagery as complementing one another. Human life is "overdetermined," and it is expectable that it can be approached from a variety of theoretical perspectives. What continues to astonish is the extent to which the cultures of Amazonia and Melanesia share a common vocabulary and language of gender.

Men's Cults

Among peoples of Amazonia and Melanesia that have formal men's societies, the attention to sex and gender may reach nearly obsessional intensities. Resemblances between the different regions are compelling and have been noted at least since the time of Schurtz (1902) and Webster (1907). Typically, men's organizations are associated with meeting grounds or men's houses, where men conduct secret initiations and feasts. The cults address similar spirit entities, conceal similar secret paraphernalia and sound-producing instruments, and punish female intruders with gang rape or death. Taken together, the pattern of spatial separation, initiations, and punishment of female intruders constitutes a "complex," or adherence of traits, that is found widely throughout Melanesia, and in at least four major and distantly separated culture regions in lowland South America. That "the men's house complex" (see Gregor 1979, 1985) obtains in both regions is noteworthy. What is even more striking is that the *details* of the cults also bear close comparison. The cults' origin myths tell of a time when the women possessed secret and powerful objects, often bullroarers, flutes, or trumpets, and used them to dominate the men. Rallying together, the men forced or tricked the women into giving up the sacred instruments, resulting in the reordering of the society and establishing of patriarchy (see Bamberger 1974, and Lévi-Strauss 1973 for summary discussions of Amazonian variants; see Gewertz 1988 for Melanesia). In both regions, the men share a strategic, potentially troubling secret: that the sounds of the trumpets, flutes, bullroarers, and other instruments associated with the cult are not the voice of spirits, as they allege, but are produced by the men themselves (cf. Metraux 1927).[2] This summary hardly does justice to the energy that has generated the array of ideas and symbolic associations linked to the cults. In their density, in their manneristic elaboration, in their fantastical departure from ordinary life, and in their raw, uncensored use of primary-process symbolism, they are among the more remarkable human creations documented by ethnography.

How are we to understand the parallels between the men's cults of Amazonia and those of Melanesia? Until now the comparative method, as applied within the Amazonian and Melanesian culture area, has been the most productive explanatory strategy, at least with respect to the general pattern of men's organizations. In each region the cults vary in the intensity of their initiation rituals, in the degree to which their boundaries are defended, and in the extent to which they shape community life. In the context of Melanesia, utilizing theoretical frameworks that could also be applied to Amazonia, men's organizations have been linked to such variables as local exogamy, warfare, descent ideology, and methods of child rearing (Allen 1967; Meggitt 1964; Whiting 1941). Robert Murphy (1959), working independently with Amazonian data prior to Allen's study, came to remarkably similar conclusions, as if he and the Melanesianists had been laboring in the same vineyard all along. Thus, Allen remarks that he had not known of Murphy's paper at the time of writing, but that the latter's "argument, derived from an analysis of a South American . . . community, is substantially the same as my own" (1967, 3n).

In the decades that have elapsed since these explanatory efforts, the data have become immeasurably richer. The detailed ethnographies of men's cults and initiation practices now available from Amazonia, especially from the Upper Xingu and Tukanoan groups (e.g., Hugh-Jones 1979, Gregor 1985; Murphy and Murphy 1985) and Melanesia (e.g., Gell 1975; Barth 1975, 1987; Tuzin 1980; Herdt 1981, 1982a, 1982b; Juillerat 1992), allow us to revisit the question in greater depth and in sharper focus. Dealing with one region alone, one might dismiss the similarities in gender roles as the result of a common origin among related cultures, or diffusion from a single source. But their appearances nearly as far apart as can be, among historically unrelated cultures, are evidence of similar underlying processes. Following this lead, the contributors to this volume examine men's institutions as a set of relationships and symbol systems that go beyond geographic areas. Bonnemère (Chapter 2) looks at the images of parturition and rebirth that mark initiation in both regions. Biersack (Chapter 4) looks at the relationship of men's cults and patriarchy. Hugh-Jones (Chapter 11), following Strathern's "relational" approach to gender, sees in the symbolism of the cults an expression of the interdependence of men and women. Hill (Chapter 3), in his discussion of the northwest Amazon, supports this perspective, and also provides a useful way of categorizing the intensity of the cults in both Amazonia and Melanesia. Finally, Gregor and Tuzin (Chapter 13) apply a psychoanalytic approach to men's institutions and examine the element of moral ambivalence that lies just behind the evident misogyny of exclusion, sexual opposition, and violence. They argue that the cults arise in Amazonia and Melanesia due to a mix of environmental and social factors that encourage the separation of men and women in gender-exclusive groups and leave the socialization of boys largely to their peers.

CONCLUSION

It has been just over one hundred years since the publication of Boas's critical paper on the comparative method. The editors and contributors believe that Boas's lessons have been learned by the discipline. This volume embodies a healthy and appropriate skepticism of comparative research that does not examine the comparability of the data it employs; it is animated by an awareness of the need for concepts and methods that are more powerful than before. We believe that Boas would approve our venture. Ours is a novel approach to comparison that goes beyond the small-scale, local-level comparisons Boas and Evans-Pritchard endorsed and yet controls for technology, level of culture, and many other factors. In pursuing this approach, the editors and contributors find, collectively, that there is no single, monolithic Comparative Method, but an unbounded set of comparative strategies—a battery of analytic devices, which, at multiple levels and in different degrees, illuminate both the phenomena we observe and the epistemological profiles of our inquiries. Through exemplifying these various strategies, the editors and contributors hope to enrich our understanding of comparative methodology, directly confront the meaning of the descriptive categories, and inspire each group of specialists with the ideas and findings of the other. To be sure, gender is the focus and content of the Amazonia-Melanesia comparison, as it is pursued here; but, in this context, gender also affords an exceptional opportunity to explore fundamental questions about the human condition and how one goes about conceptualizing and examining it.

NOTES

1. Since Hiatt's (1971) important article identifying this pattern in Australia, the literature has referred to male imitations of female gestation and reproduction in the context of initiation and other rituals as "pseudo-procreative" (e.g., Shapiro and Linke 1996). While we applaud the concept, the term itself strikes us as prejudging of the attitude of the participants and giving rise to a variety of logical problems concerning truth and falsehood (Tuzin 1995). Accordingly, we use the noncommittal "procreation," and allow the context to determine whether and to what extent it is "pseudo-."

2. In a forthcoming doctoral dissertation, ethnomusicologist Robert Reigle (n.d.) writes of the remarkably similar instruments, melodies, legends, and related practices that exist in Brazil's Matto Grosso and in the East Sepik and Madang provinces of Papua New Guinea. "Most striking," he comments (personal communication), "are the musical forms and instruments that don't seem to exist anywhere except Brazil and New Guinea."

TWO

Two Forms of Masculine Ritualized Rebirth: The Melanesian Body and the Amazonian Cosmos

Pascale Bonnemère

Pascale Bonnemère contrasts men's cults in New Guinea and in the northwest Amazon. She notes the striking parallels, which include the myth of matriarchy, the exclusion of women, and the physical ordeals for boys. The focus of her discussion, however, is the symbolism of rebirth that marks initiation rites. In both Amazonia and Melanesia there is a similar emphasis on women's reproductive abilities and on recourse to female physiological processes as a model for making boys grow. But Bonnemère is also sensitive to the differences between the regions. Among the Anga of New Guinea in particular, the human body is the model for the ritual; female reproduction and the boys' maturation are merged. In Amazonia, however, the metaphor is more abstract and the metaphors linking reproduction and initiation are less corporeal.

Bonnemère's discussion is especially welcome in that it deals directly with the "pseudo-procreative" imagery of men's cults, in which the men's ritual activities acquire the generative, reproductive power of women. This is a theme also developed in different ways by Hugh-Jones (Chapter 11), Biersack (Chapter 4), Conklin (Chapter 7), and Gregor and Tuzin (Chapter 13) in this volume.

Comparative anthropological analyses are difficult to undertake and a fortiori to complete successfully, for they require discovering certain laws that could account for similar modes of thought and symbolic structures beyond the diversity of social practices, representations, and discourses encountered. Although there is a recent trend in anthropology, stronger in the United States than elsewhere, that emits doubts concerning the possibility of making comparisons, given that cultures are so different from one another, many scholars in the discipline still share the idea that comparative analysis is part of the anthropological endeavor and even, for some, one of its main objectives.

Now that many fine-grained ethnographic descriptions and analyses exist for most parts of the world, anthropological comparison becomes even more legitimate, mainly because it meets the conditions of control (given the amount of data available), of scale (given the number of neighboring groups being studied), and thus of comparability. But there is more to say about the comparability of Amazonia and Melanesia. As Descola and Taylor wrote in the introduction to an important volume on the Amazonian contemporary anthropology, the area is "un extraordinaire laboratoire, comparable à bien des égards à la Nouvelle-Guinée, et qui combine une variation très ample, mais conceptuellement maîtrisable, d'expressions culturelles avec un nombre limité de grandes formules sociologiques dont on commence à entrevoir comment elles forment système" (1993, 14).[1] This in itself justifies a comparison between the two regions.

For me as for many other social anthropologists, making a comparative analysis implies that what is going to be compared is comparable. In other words, we have to choose, as far as is possible, a scale of comparison that offers the possibility of controlling the information that is not dealt with, but which cannot be presumed as having no influence upon the cultural configurations of elements we are focusing on.

In this chapter, I compare male cults in a specific part of Papua New Guinea and in a limited region of Amazonia. The male cults in these two areas have much in common: the elements acted out, the goals assigned to them, and the discourse people have in respect to them are quite similar. But similarity in itself does not justify the comparative project. In effect, we cannot expect a comparative analysis to tell much about the principles of human mind and human life that transcend any one culture by observing that, in the male cults of two very distant regions, there is the playing of flutes—musical instruments having originally been owned by women—physical ordeals of the same kind for boys, exclusion of women, and so forth. Because such resemblances lie on too general a level to be sufficiently relevant, I prefer to undertake a comparison on a different basis, a choice that stems, perhaps, from the ethnographic situation to which I am accustomed.

The site of my fieldwork is three small valleys in the eastern part of Papua New Guinea, inhabited by the Ankave, a group numbering about one thousand persons. They are a fraction of some seventy thousand people collectively known as Angans, who are divided into some twenty groups spread over a territory of around 140 by 130 kilometers, and who speak twelve related languages and share many cultural characteristics. Angan groups stem from a common background—their languages are more like each other than like any other neighboring language (Lloyd 1973)—and genetic stock (Seger et al., 1988). In the oral traditions of most of these groups, a single region, located in the center of the present-day Anga territory, is said to be the point from which their members originated. The Ankave, as well as several other groups now living in the southern part of the Anga region, are refugees who arrived in the area several hundred years ago after conflicts broke out in the original place.

This specific ethnographic situation offers the possibility, when attempting comparative work between Anga groups, to control important parameters, ecological and historical ones in particular. Moreover, people who have worked in the area have pursued theoretical approaches that, though they differ from each other, are not incompatible, thus facilitating comparative study.

Familiarity with such an ethnographic situation did not really help me in choosing the Amazonian context for an attempt to draw parallels with the microscale comparison of male rituals I did among two Anga groups, the Ankave and the Sambia. Things were all the more difficult because the homogeneity of the approaches found in this region of Papua New Guinea is not as evident in Amazonia. I finally decided to focus on two groups inhabiting the Vaupés area of Colombia, the Barasana, who belong to a set of people speaking Tukanoan languages, and their Kawillary neighbors, one of the few groups in the region speaking an Arawak language. For both of these groups, I had access to fine-grained descriptions and analyses of the Yurupari cults, some of which are labelled as male initiations, as well as to other ethnographic data necessary for understanding these ritual practices and their symbolic content.[2]

My discussion focuses on the rebirth dimension of men's cults, as they appear among two Anga groups and in two related societies of the Vaupés region. It will be seen that some differences in the representations underlying male maturation in the two areas may be linked to deep contrasts that exist between the representations of the origin of the world and the place of the human beings in the larger realm of all living species.

I proceed in two steps that correspond to two levels of comparative analysis. In the first place, I compare male initiation rituals in two closely related populations of Papua New Guinea: the Ankave, who inhabit the southwestern corner of the Anga territory, and the Sambia, who live more to the north and are well known from the writings of G. Herdt. This small-scale comparative analysis shows that behind different practices lies a similar emphasis on women's reproductive abilities and on recourse to female physiological processes as a model for making boys grow. In the second step, I move to a regional situation in Amazonia, which bears comparison to the Anga one, in other words, one that presents similarities *in scale* to the situation I am using as a departure point.

In the cultural area labelled northwest Amazon, two major sets of groups are present: the Tukanoans, living in the Vaupés region (Bara, Barasana, Cubeo, Desana, Makuna, Tatuyo, and so forth), and the Arawak-speaking peoples (Wakuénai and Curripaco) located further north, but with some groups located inside areas inhabited by Tukano groups, as is the case of the Kawillary, Tariana, and Yukuna (S. Hugh-Jones 1979, 19–22). In both sets, a ritual complex known as Yurupari involves musical instruments and spiritual entities to which the same name has been given. One of its performances is connected with the initiation of boys, other rituals of the same kind being held every year in connection with fruit seasons. Both involve objects associated with fertility.

THE ANGA GROUPS OF PAPUA NEW GUINEA

Five days' walk apart, the Ankave and the Sambia follow principles of social organization that are common to all Anga groups: patrilineal descent, absence of large-scale ceremonial exchanges, paramount importance accorded to war, and the existence of Great Men (Godelier 1986). Male initiations enjoy pride of place and have been considered as the key area in which male domination is expressed, learned, and instantiated (e.g., Godelier 1986, 62). This is particularly true among northern Angans, as is clearly shown in the writings of G. Herdt about the Sambia.[3] There, women are seen as depleting and polluting to men because of menstrual and vaginal fluids, and "male is the socially preferred and valued sex" (Herdt 1984, 171). Men's fear of pollution is the reason villages are divided into different zones, each associated with one sex: "women must travel only on specified female paths inside the hamlet, while initiates must travel only on physically elevated male paths" (Herdt 1987, 27). This segregation of the sexes also occurs in family houses, the interior space being divided into a female area, closest to the entrance door, and a male area (Godelier 1986, 11; Herdt 1981, 75–77). In sum, "one sees expressions of this polarization [between the sexes] in virtually every social domain" (Herdt 1984, 171), from sexual division of labor to spatial arrangements, from the system of food taboos to patterns of domestic violence.

Despite similarities in these general features of social organization, notable differences can be found between certain Anga groups, and particularly between a northern Anga group, like the Sambia, and a southwestern Anga one, like the Ankave, among whom I have been doing fieldwork since 1987. For instance, sister-exchange is the predominant mode of marriage among the northern Angans, while the Ankave marriage system is governed by negative rules with payment of a small bridewealth. Among the Sambia and the Baruya, young girls are initiated, but Ankave girls are not. Special huts are built for menstruating women in northern Anga villages, while Ankave women are not secluded during their periods. And finally, Ankave male initiations have never involved ritualized homosexuality, and the village has no permanent men's house. As a corollary, and though here it is a matter of slight differences or of nuances, fine-grained observations reveal that, among the Ankave, relations between the sexes are less antagonistic: for example, there is no systematic devaluation of women,[4] domestic violence does not frequently occur, and women and men cooperate in many daily and ritual activities in order to assure their success (Bonnemère 1996).

Differences between Ankave, on the one hand, and Sambia/Baruya, on the other hand, can also be observed in the male rituals. Both societies have a strong male warrior ethos that, even today, permeates the system of male life-cycle rituals. In both cases, these sets of rituals can be called male initiations and have as their main purpose to make boys grow and become strong. However, they do not have the same number of stages, are not organized according to exactly the same sequence, and do not use the same objects and substances.

A Single Hypothesis for Two Different Anga Male Rituals

Interpreting initiation rites as a rebirth is nothing new, given the major insight Van Gennep had nearly a century ago and the number of subsequent analyses of "rites of passage" that follow the pattern he set out (1981 [1909], 130–132).

It is no surprise then that the Ankave sequence of male rituals is altogether in the vein of those which exist elsewhere. What is interesting in this particular case is that the previous analyses of initiations among the Angans did not emphasize the rebirth dimension of these ritual elements and, more generally, did not elaborate on the reproductive imagery and symbolism that pervades them. M. Godelier and G. Herdt have insisted more on the physical and psychological violence imposed on the novices, on the long separation of the young boys from their mothers and the female realm, and on the establishment and reproduction of male domination through the initiations. The Ankave situation is valuable because they are one of the few groups in the southern part of the Anga region where male rituals are still performed today. In these groups, ritualized homosexual practices never existed; the major ritual act is the absorption of red pandanus, in whatever form.

The analysis of male Ankave rituals led me to extend Van Gennep's hypothesis and to propose that other events of female reproductive life may also provide a powerful analogy for interpreting the rituals (Bonnemère 1996, 345–352). As already stated, a total of some one thousand Ankave live in three unevenly populated valleys separated by a one- or two-day walk. These valleys are located on the southern fringe of the central cordillera of Papua New Guinea, in the northern part of Gulf province, near the borders of the Morobe and the Eastern Highlands. The Ankave territory, whose altitude ranges from 800 to 1500 meters, is for the most part (99%) covered in forest. Gardens supply the main foods: taros, bananas, sweet potatoes, and sugar cane. Besides working in the gardens, the women raise a few pigs and gather forest greens, which are eaten almost daily with some kind of tuber. The fruits of two seasonal plants—red pandanus and *Pangium edule*—are consumed in large quantities as a sauce. In spite of the surrounding forest, little hunting is done (marsupials, cassowaries, wild pigs), and the bulk of the game captured is given in exchanges between affinal groups. Eels are caught on a regular, though infrequent, basis, mainly to be distributed among the relatives of the deceased at the ceremony marking the end of mourning.

The Ankave are split into 29 patrilineal clans of very different size: for example, one clan accounts for 50 percent of the population. Exogamy usually operates at the clan level except in this particular case, where people frequently intermarry, providing they do not come from the same lineages. In principle, the residential pattern is patrivirilocal, but in practice the rule is often broken, and cases of alternate residence are frequent. Each family has a house in one of the hamlets in the valley, but household members do not live there all year round. Scattered seasonal camps are set up for various reasons: beating bark capes, trapping eels, preparing *Pangium edule*, or gathering breadfruits.

Every eight years or so, the Ankave perform male initiation rituals, which are divided into three stages. The first two bear the name of the main rite performed: nose-piercing ceremony (between 9 and 12 years of age) and red-pandanus-rubbing (several months to one year later). The third stage is held when a man expects his first child, but here I will focus mainly on those rites concerning young boys. My analysis of the rituals held in 1994 shows that the substances involved, the acts performed, the persons present, the food prohibited, and several other ritual actions recall the human gestation and birth processes.[5] Everything happens as though men and women were working together, but in separate places, to reproduce some of the events that took place before the boys were born. In brief, the main ritual sequence is as follows.[6]

It should first be noted that the expression for "piercing the nose," which gives its name to the first-stage initiation rituals, literally means "killing the child." This symbolic death is a necessary preliminary to the transformation of the boys into adult men. The interpretation of the whole set of rites occurring around this nose piercing during the first-stage initiations is somewhat delicate, but they all involve several substances and objects associated with femininity, maternity, and procreation in general. For example, the kind of vegetal cane that is introduced into the septum of the initiates following the piercing operation is precisely the kind used for cutting the umbilical cord of the newborn child. Similarly, the particular sugar cane cultivars that the initiates are given to drink are also those which have to be eaten by the parents of a first child several days after the birth.

These are examples of objects used both in the context of birth and during male initiations. But there are also several substances (mainly salt, ginger, and sugar cane) that are given to the initiates in order to heat and afterward to cool their bodies, thus engendering effects that are those which people stress when contrasting femaleness and maleness (women being cold and men hot[7]) or when speaking of sexuality. Temperature is also a pervasive theme in myths where a community of primordial women encounter men for the first time.

Myths also provide information on several objects used during the first-stage ceremonies. The awl employed to pierce the young boys' septum is made from a cassowary bone, and the initiates are beaten several times with cassowary quills. In many New Guinea societies, the cassowary is associated with women. An Ankave myth says that, once, a woman who was not a good spouse (she did not feed her husband, she defecated inside the house, and so forth) left the village to go into the forest, and there she turned into a cassowary. Simultaneously, a cassowary came from the forest and changed into a woman.

When commenting on the use of cassowary quills during the initiations, men mention this story and say that the bamboo knife the woman was holding became the quills. It is remarkable that, in this male ritual context, they make use of such objects so intimately linked to primordial femininity. Furthermore, the particular taro whose leaves are used to rub the initiates' noses is the one mentioned in the myth, relating how female sexual organs were first pierced. In sum, although I am not yet able to give a full interpretation of all the particular acts that are performed during first-stage rituals, it appears that most of the substances and objects used pertain to the realm of femininity and procreation.[8]

Throughout the period when the initiates' septums are healing, the boys' mothers are secluded in a large collective shelter and respect numerous behavioral constraints and food taboos, which, for the most part, are similar to those imposed on the initiates in the bush. Mothers and initiates alike must also soak their new bark capes in stream water every day at dawn before putting the capes on their shoulders. In the mother's case, many of the taboos are the same as those they had to obey when pregnant. Red pandanus juice is the principal food pregnant women eat to make the fetus grow and the one that makes its blood; but at initiation, it is the boys, not their mothers, who eat red pandanus juice during the first stage of the ceremonies. Moreover, when the boys eat this vegetal blood,[9] they do it in utmost secrecy.[10]

The main rite of the second stage of the initiations and the one that gives it its name (*chemajine'*) is the violent rubbing of the boys with red pandanus seeds. The initiates are put into a tiny shelter and placed beside an intense fire. This shelter is built next to the entrance of a branchy corridor to both ends of which have been attached red leaves and beaten bark dyed with red pandanus juice. Pushed by their sponsors, who are preferably real or classificatory mother's brothers, the young boys advance into the corridor being beaten all the while by men posted on the outside. And just as they emerge, a man flings onto their face and shoulders cooked red pandanus seeds, which he rubs in together with a reddish ochre.

We suggest that these two adjoining frames of foliage are metaphors for the uterus and the vagina respectively. The difficult progression of the initiates through the narrow passage—which, because they are pushed, can literally be called an expulsion—can be interpreted as their rebirth to a new state. The red elements at the entrance and exit of the corridor are metaphors of the blood that fills the uterus and of which a small amount spills out at delivery. And like a newborn whose head is the first body part to emerge at delivery, only the head and shoulders of the initiates are rubbed with red pandanus seeds.

Moreover, immediately after the ordeal, each sponsor applies the blood that flowed out of the boy's wounds and the vegetal blood from the red pandanus seeds onto his own body as well as his nephew's. Because blood is inherited from mothers, they are then both covered with a vital fluid that they share, like a woman and her child.

When this rubbing is completed, the boys go back to the village and are treated like newborn babies, in that two women coat their bodies with the yellow mud (*xwe'a' omexe'*) with which every infant is rubbed soon after birth. The

charm employed is exactly the same on both occasions. Then the initiates distribute the rats, birds, and small marsupials they have caught in the forest to
their sisters and mothers, which parallels the gift of game by the husband and
kin of a woman soon after she gives birth. In both cases, these rats are called
memi' tche' ("marsupials for a birth").

To sum up, I would say that the Ankave second-stage rituals are a reenactment of birth and the moments that follow.[11] The rites of the first stage
are less clear, but the main one (piercing the nasal septum) is like a death, and
the following rites bring together elements that are associated with fertility
and procreation or that induce physical conditions specific to sexuality and
maternity. As for the period between these two sets of ceremonies, during
which it is theoretically forbidden for the initiates[12] and their kin to eat red
pandanus juice, this is seen by the Ankave as a transitional phase that permits the boys to grow a bit before going through the red-pandanus-seeds rubbing. In effect, this second-stage ritual cannot be performed on boys who are
too young. So, when for some reason the rituals of the two stages have to be
performed in rapid succession, then only the older initiates are taken, the
others waiting for the next ceremonies, which will be held several years later.

Thus, initiation can be seen as a rebirth; but, as I have tried to show,
Ankave male rituals enact a gestation process as well. Since growth is the main
concern and goal of these rituals, and since, for the Ankave, the main agent
of growth is blood, which is provided by the mother, gestation is elected as the
most relevant metaphor to draw upon for making boys grow.

I now turn to the Sambia to show that, though Ankave and Sambia male
rituals are apparently very different, their ideas about how the growth of boys
should be enacted are quite similar.

The Sambia number about 2,400 people, living in a rugged mountain area
of the eastern highlands of Papua New Guinea. Their small hamlets are built
at an altitude ranging between 1,000 and 2,000 meters. They are subsistence
horticulturalists, who cultivate sweet potato and taro as staple foods, and yam
as a seasonal feast crop. Green vegetables are also planted, and mushrooms
and palm hearts are gathered from the forest on an irregular basis. G. Herdt
writes that "hunting is critical for two reasons: it provides most of the meat,
and it is a source of masculine prestige." Pigs are few and "pork plays only a
small role in gift-giving and feasts to mark ceremonies" (Herdt 1987, 20). As
among the Ankave, marsupial meat is given for initiations and marriage exchanges.

The Sambia population is divided into patrilineal clans, and the rate of pa-
trilocal residence is very high. Hamlets are made up of nuclear family houses,
where women and children live, and one or two men's houses, in which all initiated, unmarried males reside. Married men join them on special occasions
such as the performing of initiations.

Semen as Maternal Milk.[13] Among the Sambia, boys do not have their nasal septum pierced during initiation rituals; rather, the operation is performed in early childhood on boys and girls alike (Herdt 1987, 131). What happens during the first-stage ceremonies is the giving and inserting of a new nose plug. The main rite of this stage is the nose bleeding, done in great secrecy after the initiates have been "thrust into a green barricade and through a muddy, narrow, inner chamber that leads only one way into an even narrower cage-like . . . passageway" (p. 141). As with the similar corridor of Ankave rituals, pieces of red bark are tied into the branches of the green mass. Herdt adds that "approaching from the distance, it appears as if blood were dripping from the branches" (ibid.). Actually, the only difference in the two branchy structures is their moment of use. In Sambia rituals, the initiates are pushed into the structure by their ritual sponsors during the first stage, before any ritualized homosexual practices have begun, while in Ankave rituals, the ordeal occurs in the second stage, just before the violent rubbing with red pandanus seeds.

The nose bleeding itself takes place a moment after the corridor ordeal, near a river stream in order to let the blood flow into the water, so that "women cannot discover any signs of blood; and it also allows the boys to wash themselves off" (p. 143).

Two hours later comes the "stinging-nettles ritual," intended to "make way for the growth of a new masculine skin" and consisting of rubbing fresh nettles onto the boys' bodies (p. 144). The flute ceremony follows, which teaches about fellatio and about semen as a nourishing substance. It is also the occasion to teach the boys about the fatal consequences of breaking the secrecy of these practices.

Apart from the nose bleeding and the boy-inseminating practices, there are several other Sambia ritual events that do not occur among the Ankave. Most striking in this respect are the extreme dramatization of the separation of the boys from their mothers and the violence of the ritualized interactions between men and women, ending with the proclamation of the "mothers' harmful effects" on their sons, which engender the necessity for the male rituals. In short, women are held responsible for the painful events the boys have to endure and are therefore addressed and treated with considerable aggressivity (pp. 151–152).

The second-stage Sambia rituals are "the simplest of all collective ceremonies." Food taboos are less numerous than in the preceding stage and, in particular, red foods ("red pandanus fruit oil, red and blue yams, and many red-colored leaves") are now permitted (p. 126). Boys are told about the importance of continuing to take in male seminal substance: "The elders implore them to ingest as much semen as possible, to grow strong," writes Herdt (ibid.). The focus then is on the ingestion of semen and, although the rites "stretch over several days and are colorful" (p. 125), not many different events take place during second-stage ceremonies.

The gateway of branches with red objects attached to them, which is used during the first-stage rituals, can be interpreted, I think, the same way as for Ankave rituals: a difficult passage through a vagina and then a delivery. The flow of blood in collective nose bleeding, which immediately follows this painful progression, would consequently be similar to delivery blood, and the two events are actually considered equally dangerous (p. 140). Thereafter, the Sambia initiates are rubbed with nettles, possibly in the same way as their mothers were when they gave birth several years earlier.[14] Here we would therefore have a ritual act similar in meaning to the smearing of yellow mud on Ankave newborns and initiates.

The following lessons on semen and the necessity of fellatio taught by men during the flute ceremony become more intelligible. G. Herdt writes that the "tree sap [that the adult men must ingest to replace the semen lost in heterosexual intercourse] is symbolized as 'milky mother's sap'" (p. 164). And it is not the only time semen is equated with the maternal nourishing substance since, in the teachings concerning fellatio, men say, "If you try it [semen], it is just like the milk of your mothers' breast. You can swallow it all the time and grow quickly" (Herdt, p. 150).

I would then propose that homosexual relations among the Sambia are modeled on breast-feeding,[15] in the same way that ingestion of red pandanus juice among the Ankave is modeled on pregnancy. That would explain why the symbolic rebirth occurs respectively before and after this growth process in these societies. For some reason, the Ankave "chose" the metaphor of intrauterine growth while the Sambia "prefer" the one based on postpartum growth to make boys mature. This difference may well be related to differences in ideas concerning procreation and babies' growth.

To summarize, we can say that, for the Sambia, the boys' maturation is constructed upon breast-feeding as the focal point of reference and, as D. Elliston rightly puts it in a paper concerned with ritualized homosexuality in Melanesia, "breastmilk is [for the Sambia] a key substance of nurturance on which semen is metaphorically predicated" (1995, 858). This metaphorical maternal nourishment enacted in fellatio starts during the first stage of the initiations, just after the rebirth scene and the collective nose bleeding, and goes on in the second-stage set of rituals. It lasts as long as real breast-feeding does, that is, for several years. In the next stage, the initiates will be the bachelors from whom boys will in turn take their vital substance.

To interpret ritualized homosexuality as metaphorical breast-feeding helps us to account for the odd fact that heterosexual relations are seen as depleting while homosexual ones are considered much less so. This statement implies that the process of making a human grow, either as a fetus or as a young boy, causes depletion in one case (during pregnancy), and not in the other (during initiation).

This situation becomes easier to understand if the perspective adopted here is kept in mind. In effect, just as lactating mothers do not need to replace the milk they give to their children, bachelors do not need to ingest tree sap to replace the semen they give to the boys.[16] Homosexuality is not considered to be depleting, because it is not a sexual activity but a nourishing process (see also Elliston 1995). That view may also explain why there is no homosexuality among adults. Making a fetus grow or making a boy grow does not entail the same consequences for the man, in other words for the agent of growth. It may also be that boys' physical maturation through ingestion of semen is equated to babies' growth through breast-feeding, while feeding a fetus in a woman's body is thought of in a different way.

Married men have to consume vegetal substitutes for the seminal substance in order not to lose their *jerungdu*, threatened by sexual intercourse with women. The fact that "heterosexual intercourse is, as men see it, more draining than homosexual fellatio" (Herdt 1981, 249; 1984, 192) implies that it is not so much the loss of semen by itself that is the cause of depletion but the kind of body it enters. As G. Herdt writes (1981, 50), "It seems to be feminine bodies that cause worry." If genital sex is particularly dangerous, it is that way because it implies contact with a woman's sexual parts. Women's bodies are characterized as "consuming" a great amount of semen, thus causing depletion in the men's bodies that interact with them.

I now return to the comparison between Sambia and Ankave by underlining the symmetry of semen and blood in these two groups. Semen for the Sambia and womb blood for the Ankave have the capacity both of coconceiving and of making the fetus grow. Both substances are also used in male rituals, directly in one case,[17] and through a substitute, red pandanus juice, in the other. What differs most is the relation that these bodily substances entertain with breast milk. Among the Sambia, ingesting semen triggers the production of milk in women, while sugarcane performs the same function for the Ankave. For the latter, breast milk makes blood in children of either sex, a role that will be played by red pandanus juice later in life. Finally, it appears that the Ankave acknowledge that the major nourishing substances are female, be it blood or milk, while Sambia make semen the source of maternal milk and impute polluting effects to female blood.

Collective and Individual Nose Bleeding.   Among the Sambia, nose bleeding is performed in two different contexts: collectively during the first and third stages of the male rituals and individually in adult life. My interpretation of the blood released during the first collective nose bleeding as a metaphor for the blood that flows at birth does not appear to hold for subsequent ritual bleedings, either collective or individual. Thus, we are here confronted with a ritual act that involves more than one meaning.[18] But, as I am going to try to show, these meanings are all related to the women's reproductive cycle.

The second collective nose bleeding is performed during the third stage of the male rituals, when the boys are between the ages of 15 and 18 (Herdt 1987, 107). These rituals are the last to be held collectively, and G. Herdt qualifies them as "puberty rites . . . which transform the pubescent initiates into bachelor youths" (Herdt 1981, 242).

Subsequent nose bleedings are done on an individual basis at specific moments: when the man's young wife menstruates for the first time (fifth-stage initiation), at the birth of his first child (sixth-stage initiation), and finally at each of his wife's periods. Thus, "the final three (ego-centered) initiations carry the youth into full-blown manhood based on marriage, cohabitation with his wife, and fatherhood" (p. 242).

My interpretation of all these nose bleedings rests on the hypothesis that the growth and maturation of boys is conceived in terms of the main physiological events of menstruation and childbirth. More generally, since the Sambia consider women as "innately healthier and longer-lived than men" (p. 191), female bodily functioning is used by men as a model for the maintaining of their own good health.[19] This is not unusual in New Guinea: as Donald Tuzin wrote for the Arapesh living in the Sepik region, although a girl experiencing her first menses is secluded for a month, none of the rites performed on this occasion or for her second menstrual period are "thought to be essential to the maiden's procreative powers. Rather, they are meant to celebrate the manifestation, or unfolding, of powers that have been a part of her since birth" (1995, 299–300).

After having been reborn and having grown by ingesting semen, the initiate would then "menstruate" for the first time at puberty, during the third-stage rituals. The subsequent ritual events depend on the maturation of the young wife who has been designated as a spouse for him and is "of similar or younger age" (Herdt 1981, 39). When she has her first period, the fifth-stage rituals, which end with a nose bleeding, are held for the young man. From then on, he will have to nose bleed himself each time his wife "disappears to the menstrual hut" (Herdt 1982a, 209). "Sambia men thus engage in private bleeding for many years, till they halt coitus, or their wives undergo menopause and stop having periods" (p. 210).

The birth of a man's first child is the occasion to organize the sixth and final stage of the initiation rituals, which comprise a nose bleeding performed voluntarily by the young father himself. Then, "following this initiation, most men do not nose bleed themselves again until . . . they resume coitus with their wives following the child's breast-weaning" (pp. 208–209).

What seems clear from all these statements is that in adult life men stop bleeding themselves when their wives do not bleed (during breast-feeding and at menopause), confirming that men seek maturation and good health through the imitation of female body functioning. The Sambia say that they perform nose-bleedings in order for boys "to rid them of female pollutants that block 'male growth'" (p. 192) and for adult men to "remove female contaminants from the body" (Herdt 1987, 140). But if this were the case, we could legitimately wonder why in adult life men make themselves bleed only at the time of their wife's menses. Getting rid of female pollution need not it-self require matching the women's cycle; it can be done any time.

For all these reasons, I propose the following alternative reading of Sambia nose bleedings: men ritually accomplish what occurs naturally in women (see also Herdt 1981, 190). The female body being "a body capable of reproducing itself" (p. 193), it constitutes an adequate model for thinking and operating the maturation of men's bodies, which lack this capacity. Perhaps it is thus, as P. Hage wrote fifteen years ago, "the relation between these [initiation] rites and female physiology is based not on envy but on analogy" (1981, 272).[20]

Making Together / Making Alone: The Ankave and Sambia Models

Ankave men, too, are concerned by the menarche of their future wives and by the birth of their first child. Again, blood is the focus of the restrictions that are imposed on them in these particular circumstances. But the kind of inter-action between the sexes that underlies their behavior is of a totally different nature. An Ankave man stops eating red pandanus juice for several days when his wife has her first period. And, when a man's wife is expecting his first child, a great set of restrictions is imposed on him, among which the prohibition on eating red pandanus juice is the most important; it lasts from when the preg-nancy is known until several days after the birth. At each subsequent preg-nancy this particular taboo is imposed on him. The Ankave say that this is in-tended to prevent hemorrhage at birth.

We have here a system of representations in which the vegetal substitute for blood that someone, here a husband, eats can have an effect on the body of an-other person, here a wife, either menstruating or pregnant. More generally, the role of the expectant father, particularly in the case of the first child, is essential to the well-being of his pregnant wife. The whole set of food and other taboos imposed on him is intended to avoid any problem at birth, such as hemorrhage or the baby remaining stuck in the womb. The behaviors that husband and wife observe in this circumstance follow a complementary pattern. In effect, while the things the expectant father must refrain from doing are supposed to protect his pregnant wife from the hazards of birth, the restrictions that fall on her are all directed toward the child's welfare. Both parents play a role, then, in ensur-ing a safe delivery as well as the birth of a healthy baby. Note that this comple-mentarity also operates for conception and formation of the child's body parts, since man and woman are considered to participate equally.

The contrast with the Sambia situation is striking, for there we do not find any complementary actions on the part of husband and wife in the process of reproduction of life. Rather, what Sambia men do is, on the one hand, to stress the role of semen in the conception and growth of the fetus and, on the other hand, to secretly imitate the whole set of female physiological processes in order that they may grow and be in good health.

At first sight, Ankave and Sambia male initiations appear to be quite different: they are not divided into the same number of stages, they do not use the same substances to make boys grow, the mothers of the initiates are excluded in one case and participate in the other, and we could go on. But as soon as we look into the details of the ritual events, the differences fade, giving way to a similar overall structure.

In both cases, female physiology is used as a framework that shapes the ritual procedures used to make boys grow and mature. In the Ankave case, the metaphor is intrauterine growth, and red pandanus juice is secretly ingested by the initiates as a substitute for blood, which nourishes the fetus. Among the Sambia, the metaphor is postpartum growth, and the boys secretly absorb the semen of bachelors, as a substitute for breast milk, which nourishes babies.

Among all the rites performed, ingestion of red pandanus juice among the Ankave and fellatio among the Sambia are certainly the ones that are the most strictly concealed from women and children.[21] Boys are threatened with death if they reveal the secrets (Herdt 1982b, 61), and Ankave men are very careful to hide the red pandanus seeds left after the juice has been consumed.

Despite superficial differences, then, Ankave and Sambia initiations are both constructed upon imitation of female nourishing capacities. But in one case the substance comes from the male body, whereas in the other it is a vegetal substitute for a female-associated fluid. Does this really make a difference?

Red pandanus juice is equated by the Ankave with blood in general and women's blood in particular. That explains why blood needs during pregnancy or blood losses at menstruation and delivery are managed through the prohibition or the ingestion of this food. But in the origin myth of red pandanus trees, which is not told to women and uninitiated boys, this association between the red juice and women is denied, since the first red pandanus tree grew from the spilled blood of a male heroic figure who was killed because he had no name. So, in men's minds at least, the juice that the novices ingest during the rituals in order to grow ultimately comes from a male body. The myth illustrates the way men appropriate for themselves a female-associated substance that they use in order to grow during initiations in the same way as women make a fetus grow during pregnancy. Even if Sambia use a male substance whereas Ankave make their own, which is associated with femininity, there is in both societies an attempt to detach from women the substances that are locally considered as the most nourishing. In this case the difference between the two societies becomes even less clear-cut.

More than in the substances used, the main contrast between Ankave and Sambia male rituals lies in the degree of involvement of the boys' mothers. From the beginning to the end of the first- and second-stage rituals, the mothers of the Ankave initiates are secluded in a large shelter in the village. As already mentioned, during this seclusion, a great number of taboos are imposed on them, as on their sons in the forest. These restrictions are the same as those they respect when they are pregnant, and women clearly establish a link between these two events in their life: the birth of a son and his initiation several years later. To sum up, the mothers of the initiates are necessary to their rebirth and growth.

By contrast, among the Sambia, the rituals attended by women always end with a demonstration of antagonism between the sexes and the victory of the men (Herdt 1987, 134). The rebirth and growth of the boys are effected without the help of their mothers.

THE REBIRTH OF THE COSMOS:
THE AMAZONIANS OF THE VAUPÉS

The Vaupés region of Colombia is inhabited by several populations belonging to two or three linguistic families.[22] The most important are the Tukano, named after one particular social and linguistic group, and most of the languages spoken in the area belong to a so-called Eastern Tukano set. "The Barasana are one of some twenty Tukanoan-speaking Indian groups living in the southern part of the Colombian Comisaria del Vaupés" (S. Hugh-Jones 1995b, 50). The second main group comprises a few Arawak-speaking peoples, whose principal establishment is to the north of the Vaupés, toward the Orinoco and its affluents. The Kawillary are part of the group, but they live on the southwestern edge of the area inhabited by Tukanoan speakers.

Linguistic diversity and multilingualism characterize the area, with language functioning as "a badge of identity." Marriage rules specify that "a person should normally marry someone who speaks differently from themselves" (S. Hugh-Jones 1993, 96). Barasana individuals thus intermarry with their neighbors, some of them (regardless of their clan or sib membership) with Bara and Tatuyo, others with Makuna, Taiwano, and the Arawak-speaking Kabiyeri, or Kawillary.[23] That means that in one longhouse, or *maloca*, the residential unit, "the men and their unmarried sisters will all speak a common language, whilst their wives may speak up to three other languages" (S. Hugh-Jones 1979, 27).

While there is an "external equality of status between groups . . . each group is sub-divided into a series of clans related as 'brothers' and ranked according to the birth-order of their founding ancestors" (S. Hugh-Jones 1995b, 50). This age-based hierarchy also "determines status differences between brothers within the clan or longhouse" (p. 51).

What this author wrote about the Tukano set as a whole could be transposed intact to the Angans of Papua New Guinea: "Besides speaking languages or dialects of a common family, the Tukanoan Indians of the Vaupés share a large number of basic cultural features in common" (S. Hugh-Jones 1979, 22). These features relate to subsistence, residential patterns, kinship and social structure, rituals, and mythology. But "the structural features that unite the Vaupés Indians include non-Tukanoan speakers, [and form] an open-ended social system bound together by relations of marriage, economic exchange, reciprocal ritual interaction, etc." (p. 23). This explains why it is legitimate to compare the Barasana and the Kawillary as belonging to the same cultural area, although they speak languages belonging to different linguistic families.

In the domains that concern us directly, these two groups (among others) perform Yurupari rituals, which involve ritual specialists of different kinds (shamans, dancers, chanters, and so forth). This ritual specialization follows the hierarchical ranking of men according to the seniority of their clans.[24] The chiefs, the chanters, and the dancers are all considered to be descendants of the Anaconda, or more precisely, as F. Bourgue writes (n.d.), as transformations of parts of the Anaconda's body, while the shamans are connected to the Jaguar. Shamans play an important role in ceremonial occasions as well as in daily life, for they must treat, by blowing spells, any food to be consumed by people for the first time; this is because "all foods are ranked into a graded series of relative danger" (S. Hugh-Jones 1979, 32) and because some categories of persons (children and novices for example) cannot eat them without caution. Shamans are also the organizers and main officiants of the Yurupari rituals. Rituals are the domain of adult men, who are the only persons allowed to consume hallucinogenic substances, implying that women and uninitiated boys have no access to visionary experiences.

Gender relations are marked by opposition and complementarity (Bourgue n.d.). As S. Hugh-Jones states, the *He* House (Yurupari initiation) of the Barasana "establishes and maintains a fundamental division between the sexes . . . ; the division also expresses the complementarity between the sexes in production and reproduction" (S. Hugh-Jones 1979, 38). Among the Angans, "Though women are excluded from the rites, female attributes and values form a major element of the ritual symbolism" (ibid.).

These features constitute the grounds of my comparison between Amazonia and New Guinea. What form and content mark male initiation rituals in the two regional sets? To which reality (or realities) does "rebirth" refer? And is there some general conclusion that could be drawn from this comparison, limited in scale as well as in scope?

Reading the description and analysis of the Yurupari male initiation rituals given by the Hugh-Joneses for the Barasana and by F. Bourgue for the Kawillary, one is struck by the homogeneity of the diverse ritual acts performed during the three ceremonial days. Although some minor variations occur, there is not the kind of sharp contrasts we found between the two Anga groups (ritualized homosexuality on the one hand and ingestion of red pandanus juice on the other hand).[25] I choose not to discuss the two Yurupari ceremonies separately, as I did for the Ankave and the Sambia, but to present their common frame and to emphasize the few differences that I noticed.[26]

The fathers of several boys decide together that it is time for their sons to see the Yurupari. When a date for the ceremony has been fixed, things begin at dusk. First of all, it is necessary that the shaman who will perform the rituals address Yamatu (among the Kawillary), the ancestral shaman woman,[27] and ask her consent for the boys to give up their children's life.[28] She also has to decide on the identity of the ancestor to be reincarnated in each of the boys who is going to be reborn during the rituals. The secret name that is given to a boy depends on this assimilation between one of his ancestors and himself.

After having blown spells over tobacco, the shaman takes the boys and leads them toward the women who are going to cut their hair very short. Among the Barasana, the boys are also painted from head to toe with black paint by the women before being carried into the house on the shoulders of male elders. "They are placed standing in a line by the men's door with their little fingers linked together" (S. Hugh-Jones 1979, 77). Then, they eat *kana* berries (*Sabicea amazonensis*) to make them strong.

Among the Kawillary, once the boys have their hair cut, the shaman inserts tobacco snuff in their nostrils. The boys are drunk and sleepy; their bodies are lifeless. The shaman blows tobacco into their noses again and the boys begin "to see the world" (Bourgue n.d.). If they are not intoxicated, they will not see the world correctly. Then, in the afternoon, the hallucinogenic drink *kaapi* (called *yagé* among the Barasana) is made from the bark of the *Banisteriopsis caapi* vine, and the boys are led into the house by a man who holds the first one by the hand, the others forming a chain. The boys begin to crawl before standing up very slowly and, finally, walking very carefully (ibid.). They are followed by men who play the Yurupari instruments, and everybody enters the *maloca*.

The young boys are then helped to sit, one by one, on wooden benches, "their bodies arranged in a fetal position with their knees drawn up to their chests and their arms clasped round them" (S. Hugh-Jones 1979, 77). At this time, the Barasana boys are served the ceremonial cigar and blown coca before drinking the *yagé;* Kawillary boys receive several sips of blown *kaapi*. The men playing the flutes and trumpets move slowly inside the house, each drinking *kaapi* from time to time. "They parade in front of the initiates showing them each instrument in turn and then circle slowly round and round the house. This is the first time that the initiates see the *Hé*" (p. 78). Under the effect of the hallucinogenic drink, the boys lose their balance and the man in charge of watching them has constantly to make them sit up. This lasts about four hours.

The Barasana then perform a ritual act that is not found as such among the Kawillary.[29] It is the burning of beeswax, which they consider to be the climax of the rite. It is said that if the women smelled the smoke, they would die. After the burning, "two elders put on the full complement of ritual ornament . . . and then go out to play the long flutes called Old Macaw.[30] These two are the *Hé* spirits, fierce spirits, the ancestors of the living, and are very frightening and dangerous" (S. Hugh-Jones 1979, 79).

The Kawillary boys listen to the man who talks with the long trumpets; they learn the story of the Yurupari. The trumpets are then piled up and the *maloca* is cleansed of all the world's illnesses. Specialist chanters then continue to give the stories of the origin of the world; they transmit their knowledge, while specialist dancers dance in front of the boys (Bourgue n.d.). Among the Barasana, too, the flutes are played, but S. Hugh-Jones attends more to the substances the boys are given, such as coca, which older women behind the screen receive as well, together with blown red paint they have to apply onto their bodies (S. Hugh-Jones 1979, 80). Everybody is then whipped on the legs, thighs, abdomen, and chest, and a very long chanting follows. Afterward, "the initiates and younger men paint each other [with blown black paint] on the legs and body at the female end of the house" (ibid.). "Around midday, there is a parade of all the flutes and trumpets round and round the house" (p. 81). Then, everyone, women included, is given the snuff to prevent illness. Kawillary boys are also whipped on the waist, feet, and arms by the shaman, near the women's place (Bourgue n.d.). They spend the following night sleeping.

At dawn, the Kawillary shaman takes his gourd of blown tobacco, and the boys apply some of it to their bodies. Then, men go out with their Yurupari instruments and proceed to the river. It is also the case among the Barasana. "Once the instruments have been immersed, all, including the initiates and young men, get right into the water and bathe" (S. Hugh-Jones 1979, 82). People drink so much water that they vomit. They then go back to the *maloca*. The men play the trumpets for a final round. They represent the ancestors who are about to leave (Bourgue n.d.). The women have prepared food (ants, cassava, manioc, and so forth) that the *maloca* owner has brought back and that the shaman has to treat before everybody else eats. The trumpets are then wrapped in *pachuva* (chonta palm-tree) leaves and hidden until the next ceremony "in the mud under water," writes S. Hugh-Jones (1979, 83). The house is then swept out carefully. Everything used in the Yurupari ritual must be cleaned out. On this day, women are prohibited from entering the house, "and the initiates must be protected from their gaze" (p. 84). For five more days, says F. Bourgue (n.d.), people may consume only food that has been blown by the shaman (cassava, ants, and manioc starch). On the sixth day, after the game and fish brought back by the men, as well as chili pepper, have been treated, they can eat everything. Afterward, a small feast is held for which women have prepared beer and men have prepared coca (Bourgue n.d.).

The period following the rite itself is more ritualized among the Barasana than among their Arawak-speaking Kawillary neighbors. Besides being subjected to rigid food restrictions, the Barasana boys are secluded during a period of about two months at the end of which the black paint applied at the beginning of the rituals by the women has worn off (S. Hugh-Jones 1979, 84). Although they have to avoid certain foods as well, the Kawillary initiates are not secluded. In both groups, however, this is a period during which they are taught how to make baskets and feather ornaments and, formally, how to use the weapons of war. Moreover, each day before dawn the Barasana boys have to bathe, as well as drink a mixture of water and leaves that induces vomiting (p. 85). Everything that is hot (sun, fire, food classified as such) must be avoided. And, as among the Kawillary, every food that is consumed after having seen the *He* has to be blown first by the shaman. Moreover, "the first animal foods that are eaten after *He* House are very small insects that live in the ground and are said to have no blood in their bodies" (p. 93).

The end of seclusion is marked by a ritual called the "blowing of pepper." In the evening, two shamans dress for the ceremony and "enter a trance-like state. They become *He* people." (p. 95). They chant the stories of the origin of all the different varieties of pepper. Afterward, the initiates chew a small amount of pepper together with hot boiled manioc juice. The next day, the initiates bathe before coming back to the house and painting "their legs with black paint, this time with the intricate designs used at dances" (p. 96). Then the women come to paint the men and the initiates' bodies with red paint. This is followed by gifts of basketry, which "are seen as payments by the initiates for the services of these people" (p. 97), and a dance. The next morning they bathe and vomit before dawn. The same day a dance is held that lasts all night and the next day, during which *yagé* is served together with coca and ceremonial cigars (p. 98). The following day, the shamans blow different kinds of food and distribute them to the men. The initiates must wait "until all food has been shamanized for them" (p. 99).

Both F. Bourgue and S. Hugh-Jones interpret Yurupari rituals in the groups they study as a rebirth. Many elements support this interpretation. S. Hugh-Jones writes that the black paint applied all over the initiates' bodies, as well as the low position they have to adopt, "the extinction of fire and the taboo on contact with sources of heat during and after *He* House," and the effects of *yagé*, indicate that the initiates are symbolically dead (1979, 215). As for the Kawillary boys, they are said to be lifeless after the shaman blows tobacco into their noses.

In both groups, then, the boys must die before being born again. It is clear that "once symbolically dead, the initiates become identified with unborn children" (ibid.). Inside the house, the Barasana boys sit "with their knees drawn up to their chests and their arms clasped round them—a fetal position" (ibid.). Moreover, the *kana* berries they have to eat connect them "to the ancestral source of life by an umbilical cord, the river" (ibid.). In effect, the Barasana say that the vine that bears the *kana* fruit is related to the place where the sun comes from, to the east, which is the source of all humanity. These fruits are also given to newborn babies after having been blown by a shaman (p. 216).[31]

Among the Kawillary, in order to enter the *maloca*, the boys form a chain by holding each other's hand and crawl before gradually standing up. Finally, they walk, but very slowly. F. Bourgue writes that "it is like a birth; if the initiates were walking fast, their bones would break" (n.d.). We do not find here situations and behaviors that could be equated to a gestation, as is the case among the Barasana. The rebirth takes place early in the ritual sequence and is represented both by the slow motions for entering the house and by the careful positioning of the boys on the benches: "the man helps each boy to sit. Very slowly, he places his feet, his hands, then his head in a proper way" (Bourgue n.d.), before they are given *kaapi* to drink.[32]

Among the Barasana, the rebirth takes place at the end of *He* House, and it is the vomiting that symbolizes it (S. Hugh-Jones 1979, 217). Perhaps more than the act itself, it is what happens subsequently that permits us to characterize the vomiting as a rebirth. In effect, "soon after this [the bathing and vomiting at the port], the initiates are confined in a compartment, just as, soon after its birth, a baby is confined in a compartment together with its parents" (p. 218). And then, "at the end of the marginal period, comparable to the five-day period of confinement following birth, the initiates are taken back to the river to bathe. They then return to the house and are painted all over with red paint . . . just as a baby is painted red at the end of its period of confinement" (pp. 218–219). Although vomiting at the river also occurs among the Kawillary, it does not seem to connote a symbolic rebirth as clearly as among the Barasana, and F. Bourgue rather considers the vomiting as a purification act (personal communication). Nevertheless, the sequence in which the young Kawillary boys consume different foods after they have been blown by the shaman recalls the one that governs the diet of newborn babies and then of children. It is also true among the Barasana: "The order in which food is blown over for the initiates corresponds more or less exactly to the order in which it is blown over for a child, but whereas for initiates this blowing occurs within the space of a few months, for a child it takes place over a number of years" (S. Hugh-Jones 1979, 221). Moreover, the dialogue between *Yamatu* and the Jaguar *Hejechu* that takes place just before the ritual among the Kawillary occurs also when a child is born (F. Bourgue, personal communication).

In short, there is no doubt that the Yurupari initiation ritual in both societies operates a rebirth of the boys, which symbolically reenacts a real birth. But there is more among the Barasana because of the important role played by an object, the beeswax gourd, which, though also present in the Kawillary ritual, is not associated with female physiology. Rather, for the Kawillary, the beeswax is connected with the seminal substance of *Hejechu,* its vital principle, its *pupuchu* (F. Bourgue, personal communication).

S. Hugh-Jones spends a whole chapter trying to understand the meaning of this object. From the myths, we learn that "the gourd itself is the bottom half of Manioc-stick Anaconda's skull, created when he was burned to death . . . . The wax inside the gourd is [his] liver" (1979, 164–165). The author adds that "the wax is also likened to children inside a womb, the wax being the shadow of the children and the gourd itself being the womb" (p. 166). It is more precisely with *Romi Kumu,* the Shaman Woman, "and in particular with her vagina and womb" that the wax gourd is identified (p. 169). S. Hugh-Jones goes farther in his interpretation: the wax is identified with menstrual blood because, "when the wax is burned, it is transformed from a hard, dry substance to a molten semi-liquid and produces the smell of menstrual blood. The melting of wax is thus analogous to the 'melting' of coagulated blood (liver)[33] which produces menstrual blood" (p. 178).

This interpretation would imply that, "during initiation, an attempt is made to make the initiates menstruate in a symbolic sense and to make them periodic" (p. 184). Menstruation is sought because it is considered the reason why women live longer than men: "Through menstruation, they continually renew their bodies by an internal shedding of skin" (p. 250). It is associated both with immortality and periodicity, and "menstruation and cosmological periodicity are both compared to a process of changing skins" (p. 185). Skin changing is an important goal of the ritual, since "the application of black paint at the beginning of *He* House is designed to change the skins of the initiates, and its disappearance at the end of the marginal period signifies that this has been achieved and that the initiates are ready to receive pepper blown by the shamans" (pp. 182–183).

Although there is no emphasis on menstruation during the Yurupari initiation ritual among the Kawillary, the cyclical aspect is not absent. There, it is the everlasting cycle of life and death that is emphasized, as it appears clearly in a Yurupari ritual that is held each year, in connection or not in connection with the initiation of boys. It is said that, during this ritual, everyone's body is changed while at the same time the whole world is reborn. The ancestors, who are reincarnated in the Yurupari musical instruments, are directly involved in this generalized process of renewal. Among the Barasana, it is the Fruit House that is connected with the less frequently held *He* House. "The importance of Fruit House[34] comes partly from the fact that it is an attenuated version of *He* House and partly from the fact that it forms the preliminary stages of an extended process of initiation that culminates in *He* House" (p. 242). From reading the myths in which fruits used during the Fruit House are mentioned, he suggests that "caimo fruit is a male principle (sperm) and inga fruit a female principle and that the conjunction of these two fruits is an act of fertilization" (p. 223). In this view, the Fruit House ritual, which is held when inga and caimo fruits are ripe in preparation for *He* House, could be interpreted as "a symbolic conception of the initiates which is then followed by their birth at *He* House" (p. 224).

It is then more than a simple rebirth of the boys that the Barasana rituals accomplish. In effect, although there is no linear order—since a conception in the preliminary Fruit House is followed by a death, a rebirth, and menstruation during the *He* House—most events of a reproductive sequence are symbolically performed. This is less true of the Kawillary ritual. There too the procreative imagery is pervasive, but there seems to be no clear evidence of an enactment of conception and menstruation in the ritual acts performed.

As was the case for the two Anga groups discussed above, there exists a pattern of (minor) variations in the Yurupari rituals of these two neighboring Amazonian populations. In both regions, we have before us a system of structural transformations. In the conclusion to his book, S. Hugh-Jones speaks of the different sociolinguistic groups of northwest Amazonia as "an open-ended regional system that spreads across cultural and linguistic boundaries" and of their cultural differences as "variations on a common theme" (p. 241). Goldman made a similar statement more than 30 years ago regarding the Yurupari: "one of the striking characteristics of the entire Amazon drainage is the ready way in which form and content separate and recombine in new ways" (quoted in Reichel-Dolmatoff 1973, 202n).

Although the Yurupari ritual looks roughly the same in both groups, there are some differences which show that the Barasana have elaborated on menstruation and related themes like periodicity, skin changing, and immortality, while the Kawillary do not put much emphasis on this particular aspect of feminine physiology. The same kind of contrasts exist among the Angans: while Sambia men imitate women's periods by making their noses bleed regularly, it is to pregnancy that the Ankave refer during male initiations. Why this is so is impossible to say.

THE MELANESIAN BODY AND THE AMAZONIAN COSMOS

Initiation rituals as performed among the Angans and in the Colombian Vaupés present striking similarities: they involve the playing of musical instruments that are hidden from women and that were owned by them in mythic times; they imply the consumption of substances that are symbolically associated with reproduction; they are interpreted in a similar way, as a rebirth of the young boys into the world of men; and myths offer keys for understanding the ritual.[35]

Several major differences also exist. The most remarkable for a Melanesianist would probably be the predominant role played by the shaman, whose function, among the Angans at least, is only to cure illness. He does not intervene during initiation rituals, nor does he blow spells on food. Also absent in this part of New Guinea is the consumption of hallucinogenic drugs, which in the Tukano area is done in order to experience the world of the origin, depicted in myth, which "persists as another aspect of everyday existence" (S. Hugh-Jones 1979, 139). In the Anga groups, there is no such emphasis on visions, on the learning of the stories of the origins, or on dances. Although young Ankave and Sambia boys are told some secret myths, most of the ritual acts performed are physical ordeals intended to make the boys grow and to impart vigor to their bodies. The substances used in Anga initiations are not intended to induce a state conducive to seeing the ancestors' world and learning about the mythic past but to feed the body (see also Biersack, Chapter 4). They have this capacity as substitutes for human bodily fluids. Most of them come from the dead body of some human figures whose adventures are related in myths. These narratives are associated with the ritual acts in which the substances intervene, but there is no systematic revealing of stories of the past during the rituals.

More generally, a sharp contrast exists between what these people of Amazonia and New Guinea think concerning the effects of the diverse substances on those who absorb them during the rituals. Among the Ankave, for example, red pandanus is taken in order to act upon the initiates' bodies; as a substitute for blood, it makes them grow. As for the hallucinogenic drugs and the tobacco taken by the Barasana and the Kawillary, they indeed have an effect upon the boys' bodies—people say the whole ritual purifies and transforms their bodies—but mainly through acting upon their minds. These substances produce a disjunction from the world in which they are physically, and they transport them into the world of the origin, which they can then see. As S. Hugh-Jones writes, coca "allows men in the present to enter into communion with these ancestors in the past" (1995b, 54). This is a fundamental difference that certainly has consequences on the form the enactment of the rebirth of the boys takes in both areas.

In the two Anga groups of Papua New Guinea that I have discussed here, ritual actions are more explicitly an expression of rebirth than in the Vaupés region of Amazonia, and many elements (such as the configuration of the corridor into which the novices are pushed, the red leaves attached to its ends, the red seeds applied on the boys' bodies when they go out of it) clearly evoke a realistic delivery. By contrast, among the Barasana and the Kawillary, rebirth is suggested more than enacted: the slow motions of the young boys, their posture while sitting in the house, and the vomiting are the main signs indicating that they are being reborn, but there is nothing like an attempt to simulate childbirth. Nor are the references to menstruation among the Barasana as bloody as they are among the Sambia. In brief, the main differences in the male initiations of these two regions of Amazonia and Melanesia seem to lie in the way people refer to the physiology of birth: more metaphorically for the first[36] and more literally for the second.

In addition, while there is a strong correlation in New Guinea between the representations of procreation and of fetal development and the contents of the male rituals, there seems to be no such link in the two groups of Amazonia discussed here. In effect, in both of them, it is believed that conception occurs when the male substance, semen, mixes with the female substance, blood (F. Bourgue, personal communication; C. Hugh-Jones 1979, 115).[37]

CONCLUSION

In concluding this comparative study, I would like to suggest that contrasted ways of evoking a similar event may be related to different ideas about the world of the origins and in particular about the place of human beings amid other living species.

In the Ankave origin myths, people are distinguished from plants and animals from the beginning. Nothing is said about how the cosmos or the different living species came into being. The first men emerge from the ground at one particular place located in the middle of the present-day Anga territory, followed by a pig and a dog. Moreover, it is the human body itself that is the source of the plants having a crucial role in rituals. The first red pandanus grew where the blood of a man who had been killed by enemies spilled out, whereas the first red cordylines originated from a clot. Where the corpse of an old woman had been buried, several plants used in life-cycle ceremonies grew. In other words, on one hand, human beings are thought of as being born by themselves; on the other hand, dead human bodies are the source of plants playing a major role in rituals.

In the region of Amazonia that I have focused on, things are quite different. Among the Kawillary, for example,[38] the primordial world is the sun; from its navel fell some water drops, which slowly created a river. Through this river flowing inside the world, life passes on. The world was not yet born. Like a womb, it was closed, and water accumulated inside. The place where the world took shape is called "the foundation of the water." There a spirit emerged: it was *Yakamamukute*, a spirit who had no anus but a navel through which he was connected to the flux of life, *pupuchu*. For the Kawillary, *pupuchu* is the vine of life, the liana which connects everything to the origin. In the vegetal realm, it is the sap; in the water world, it is the river of the origin as well as the anaconda; in human bodies, it is the blood, the semen, and the bone marrow. It is also the *kaapi*, the substance that opens the way to knowledge.

Hejechu the Jaguar[39] also lived in the primordial world. He was the only completed being in the primordial world, where everything else was yet to be born.[40] He was a manifestation of the *pupuchu* vine, its first offshoot. In order to punish *Yakamamukute* for having killed his children, *Hejechu* opened him up by thrusting a stick into his anus. *Yakamamukute*'s body exploded, bringing the sky into existence. *Hejechu* carried his fragmented body to a hill where it produced clay. The other remains became the sons of *Yakamamukute*, the *Munully*. The jaguar *Hejechu* is thus the one who creates the present world by destroying the primordial unity.

Another major mythical character among the Kawillary is *Yamatu*, the Woman Shaman. Daughter of the Yurupari Anaconda, she was the one who regularly renewed the world by regulating the cycles of drought and rain, and establishing seasons. As for the first "real" woman, she is the transformation of a male Jaguar who became pregnant after having eaten fish fat and was castrated by a shaman called the woodpecker. She/he gave birth to Fruit Jaguar, who is the prominent figure of the Fruit Yurupari ritual.

There is no need to say more to realize that these representations of how the world came into being conceptualize the animal, vegetal, human, and cosmic world as closely interrelated (see also Hill, Chapter 3). The *pupuchu* vine is what all living kinds have in common. They are all considered to be segments of this liana and, contrary to what happens among the Angans, the *human* body is not considered to be the source of any plants. Rather, the first human beings were the offspring of animals (the Jaguar or the Anaconda). These representations of the *pupuchu* vine giving life to the world and to all the species that live in it are grounded in the idea that the vegetative mode of reproduction is the primordial one (see also S. Hugh-Jones 1995b, 56). It relates every living being to the origin, each originating from a segment of the *pupuchu* liana identical to the whole.

Finally, I would propose that the differences in the way the rebirth of the boys is represented during initiation rituals in the Anga and the Tukano areas may be related to differences in the ideas the respective populations have elaborated concerning the origin of the cosmos and of the living species. According to this hypothesis, if the Indians of the Vaupés make such an indirect and mild reference to a real birth in the Yurupari initiation rituals, it is because their representations of the creation of the world do not attribute to human beings an origin different from the other living beings, whether plants or animals. In other words, the primordial mode of reproduction is not sexual but vegetative, since every living being is born from a segment of the *pupuchu* vine.

By contrast, the Angans refer so explicitly to human gestation, birth, menstruation, and breast-feeding for making boys grow and come to a new life because, in their origin myths, human beings are not put on the same plane as the other living beings. They constitute an autonomous species with a mode of reproduction of its own, a sexual one, from which several fundamental plants originated. Consequently, the physiology of the human body provides a powerful model for making young boys into adult men. This is less true in Amazonia, where having the boys reborn cannot be done independently of reenacting the birth of the world, since human beings are considered to have originated from the same vine, or flux of life, as the other living species. In that sense, Yurupari rituals are not only male initiations intended to transform boys into adult men; their objective is also to renew the whole cosmos.

NOTES

I would like to thank all the participants to the Wenner-Gren Conference on "Gender in Amazonia and Melanesia" held in Mijas in September 1996, where I presented a preliminary version of this chapter. In writing this much revised version, I was greatly helped by the advice of B. Conklin, P. Descola, T. Gregor, and D. Tuzin, as well as by the enlightening comments of S. Hugh-Jones. I am very grateful to all of them. It goes without saying, however, that any shortcomings should be considered my own.

Though he did not collaborate on the writing of the paper itself, François Bourgue, who works among an Arawak-speaking group of the Colombian Vaupés and has published a paper connected to the theme dealt with here ("Los caninos de los hijos del cielo," *Revista colombiana de antropología*, Bogota, 1976), played a crucial role in the elaboration of the comparison between male initiations of the Angans of Papua New Guinea and Yurupari rituals of Amazonia. In effect, he allowed me to read his ordered fieldnotes, full of not-yet-published information on Yurupari, gender relations, and reproduction, as well as on the mythology of the Kawillary. This enabled me to draw parallels with the analyses that Christine and Stephen Hugh-Jones gave of a similar ritual complex among a neighboring Tukano group.

Bourgue's contribution to my paper, through long discussions and careful readings, deserves more than a simple acknowledgment. Nevertheless, the interpretations and general conclusions I am making are mine, and I am the only one responsible for them.

Periods of fieldwork undertaken among the Ankave-Anga since 1987 have been supported by the Maison des sciences de l'homme, the CNRS, the National Geographic Society, and the Fondation Fyssen.

1. Here could be one translation: the area is like an extraordinary laboratory, which could be compared in many ways to New Guinea, and which combines a broad variety, but which one can conceptually control, of cultural expressions of a limited number of sociological configurations that we are beginning to perceive as systems.

2. My choice was largely guided by F. Bourgue, who has collected very rich ethnographic data on the Kawillary, which opened my eyes to the possibility of comparing them in great detail to the analyses published for the Barasana by Christine and Stephen Hugh-Jones.

3. "Yet in male-female interactions, one sees terrible signs of opposition and fear, such as in men's beliefs about women's bodies. This overall tendency has been called *sexual antagonism* in New Guinea societies. [Sambia] men and women are not only different, but opposed, and even hostile in some respects. The sexes are at war" (Herdt 1987, 35).

4. "Perhaps the one thing I saw on patrol that most surprised me was the affection openly demonstrated between men and their wives. In this society [the Ankave] man still fulfills his ancient role of protector of his family. When people were coming into camp for the first time the man would stride towards me chest out and carrying his bow and arrows, his wife would usually be holding onto his arm looking frightened but he would occasionally turn to her and speak softly and perhaps caress her face. These and similar gestures I have never observed either on the coast or in other mountainous areas" (Didlick 1968–1969, 2).

5. Pierre Lemonnier witnessed the exclusively male rituals held in the forest, while I stayed back in the village with the secluded mothers and sisters of the initiates. The present analysis also relies on several male informants' accounts of past rituals systematically gathered since 1982 by P. Lemonnier.

6. For more details, see Bonnemère (1996, Chapter 7).

7. This has not always been the case. Myths depict a time when women were hot and give details about how their bodies became cold forever.

8. At this stage, it is hard to decide whether these difficulties in interpreting this part of the rituals are due to a lack of information and/or analysis, or whether we are merely confronted with the fuzziness and polysemy that, according to Bourdieu (1990, 245), underlie the "logic of practice" in the ritual domain.

9. See Bonnemère (1994, 25–27).

10. If I choose to reveal some of the secret practices of the Ankave rather than conceal them, it is mainly because of the oldest persons' concern that their culture be described as precisely and exhaustively as possible in these times of great, and probably irreversible, changes. For them, running the risk of losing limited but crucial data is clearly more serious than revealing secrets to people from another culture than their own. That explains why hidden practices and discourses are disclosed here. However, I would like the reader to respect the secrecy that surrounds some of the ritual actions analyzed in the chapter and that prevents several categories of people from having access to it.

11. See also M. Jolly (Chapter 8), who mentioned ethnographical information collected among the Sa of Vanuatu showing that "there are clearly ritual parallels and symbolic resonances between birthing babies and making men."

12. In fact, as noted earlier, they must consume some in secret.

13. From within Gilbert Herdt's rich corpus on male rituals among the Sambia, I rely on the very precise description given in his 1987 book. Because homosexual relations in New Guinea rituals are concerned primarily with growth, in a later edition Herdt dropped the vocabulary of "homosexuality" in favor of "boy-inseminating practices" (Herdt 1993a, ix).

14. This information is to be taken with caution. G. Herdt tells me that the body of a woman who has just given birth is cleansed with leaves and herbs, among which are possibly common nettles. Among the Baruya, Sambia neighbors who in many respects are culturally similar to them, I saw women rubbed with nettles several hours after having given birth.

15. G. Herdt formulates the same idea but differently: "Fellatio is likened to maternal breast-feeding" (1981, 234). Similarly, B. Knauft observes that "the use of semen from the adult penis as a 'life force' to grow boys into adulthood is a strong analogue—often explicitly stated in . . . societies [practicing ritualized homosexuality]—to the growth of infants through the suckling of mother's breastmilk" (1987, 176).

16. G. Herdt writes: "So men are taught to ingest tree saps called *iaamoonalyu*, 'tree mothers' milk,' which replaces the semen lost through *heterosexual* intercourse" (1987, 164).

17. Note that it may not be so direct, because the semen given to boys is called breast milk.

18. G. Herdt said the same thing when he contrasted collective and individual nose bleedings: "The meaning of nosebleeding thus changes with successive ritual initiations" (1982a, 192).

19. This statement should not be seen as contradictory to the Sambia beliefs on female pollution. A body can simultaneously have powerful self-growing capacities and produce substances inimical to someone else.

20. Male "envy" of feminine sexual physiology is a quite well-known expression since Hiatt's essay (1971); it was used by B. Bettelheim in his analysis of these widespread male rituals called "pseudo-procreation rites," which "enact a fantasy of male parthenogenesis" (Tuzin 1995, 295).

21. Tuzin writes that "ironically, the exclusion of women, for reasons given to them in the form of a veiled icon of the truth, is the surest sign, first, that the secret rite is procreative, secondly, that, unknowingly and at a mystical level, the women are being essentially *in*cluded" (1995, 299).

22. For more details, see S. Hugh-Jones (1979, 21–22).

23. Unlike the Hugh-Joneses, F. Bourgue, who works among them, calls them Kawillary, and I will follow his use. This scholar confirms that Kawillary sometimes intermarry with Barasana (personal communication).

24. To be exact, while it is true of three kinds of specialists, the chiefs, the dancers, and the chanters, it is not the case with the shamans.

25. Perhaps Barasana and Kawillary would correspond more closely to two Anga groups that have the same kind of ritual organization, such as the Baruya and the Sambia, or the Iqwaye and the Menye.

26. Here I am summarizing F. Bourgue's unpublished account of the Yurupari initiation as performed among the Kawillary and S. Hugh-Jones's description of the *He* House of the Barasana (1979, 72–84).

27. Among the Barasana, the ancestral Woman Shaman is called *Romi Kumu*. As among the Kawillary, she is also called upon at the beginning of the *He* House.

28. It would be more appropriate to say that this dialogue takes place between Yamatu and the jaguar *Hejechu* (see below), to whom the shaman is assimilated.

29. The burning of the beeswax also takes place among the Kawillary, but at the beginning and the end of the ritual, as a protection.

30. "Old Macaw is Manioc-Stick Anaconda's brother. . . . He is the lead dancer and he dances in the *middle* of the house" (S. Hugh-Jones 1979, 144).

31. This is also the case among the Kawillary, who consider *kana* berries as children's *kaapi*, but they are not given during the *Yurupari* ritual (F. Bourgue, personal communication).

32. Although we cannot extrapolate without caution from Barasana to the Kawillary, it would be difficult not to remark that, in the first group, "the *yagé* [= the Kawillary's *kaapi*] given to the initiates is compared to mother's milk which suckles the new-born initiates" (S. Hugh-Jones 1979, 216).

33. Remember that the wax inside the gourd is Manioc-stick Anaconda's liver.

34. Fruit House rituals are regularly held to "mark the seasons of the different wild and cultivated fruits which give their names to the major calendrical divisions of the Barasana year" (S. Hugh-Jones 1979, 35).

35. As S. Hugh-Jones writes for the Barasana, unless myth is systematically related to rite, many features of the rites remain inexplicable (1979, 6). Further, "it appears to be through ritual that the elaborate mythological systems of these people acquire their meaning as an active force and organizing principle in daily life" (p. 3).

36. As J. Jackson notes in a recent paper, there are "many forms used in the [Vaupés] region to describe giving, or reengendering, life that have no *immediately visible* connection to female reproduction" (1996, 112, emphasis added).

37. Among the Barasana, "there is actually a sense in which blood and semen as reproductive potentialities are passed on in same-sex lines: this is expressed in the theory of conception which states that girls are made from blood and boys from semen" (C. Hugh-Jones 1979, 163). This does not imply that the two substances are not necessary *to conceive* a child.

38. The following information on Kawillary mythology was communicated to me by F. Bourgue. I thank him again.

39. *Hejechu* can in fact take many appearances: although he is most often a jaguar, he can also be the Yurupari anaconda (Bourgue n.d.). Among the Barasana, anacondas and jaguars are ultimately transformations of one another (S. Hugh-Jones, personal communication).

40. As an autonomous being, *Hejechu* resembles the sisters of the Ankave myths who live in a world without men and carry out every task, even those now characterized as male.

THREE

The Variety of Fertility Cultism in Amazonia: A Closer Look at Gender Symbolism in Northwestern Amazonia

Jonathan D. Hill

The most dramatic single resemblance of the cultures of Amazonia and Melanesia are those provided by exclusive men's cults. Yet Jonathan Hill notes that the everyday interdependence of men and women in ordinary contexts stands in opposition to male separateness. The relative weighting of male hierarchy and exclusiveness in ritual and ordinary relationships has been examined comparatively in New Guinea by Harriet Whitehead, utilizing her concept of "cults of manhood" and "cults of clanhood." Hill adapts this idea to Amazonia in his analysis of "marked" and "unmarked" fertility cults. Marked fertility cults are those, as in the Mundurucú of Amazonia, where male ritual not only excludes women but symbolically preempts their generative powers, separates mothers from their children, and magnifies the contradiction between interdependence and hierarchy. Unmarked cults, such as those of the Wakuénai of the Northwest Amazon, which Hill has studied, conduct rituals associated with initiation and childbirth that link children and mothers through the reproductive process, and make use of a symbolic vocabulary that connects parents and children, and men and women.

Hill's chapter supports Hugh-Jones's perspective on men's cults and can be usefully read in connection with the different points of view provided by Biersack and Gregor and Tuzin.

INTRODUCTION

Male-controlled ritual cults provide one of the most striking points of similarity between Amazonian and Melanesian societies. Researchers in both areas (Hill 1984, 1989; Harrison 1985) have noted that constructions of male ritual hierarchy cannot be reduced to mere symbolic reflections of men's dominance over women in secular contexts. Instead, male ritual hierarchy in both regions is better understood as the construction of a "counterideology" of gender-inflected hierarchy "existing in a permanent tension with, or antithesis to, an institutional and ideological bias toward egalitarianism in secular contexts" (Harrison 1985, 424). Like small-scale, horticultural societies throughout the world, those found in Amazonia and Melanesia display forms of sociopolitical organization resulting from complex interactions between hierarchy and equality. What distinguishes Amazonian and Melanesian societies from other regions, or places them in a common set based on strong family resemblances, is that hierarchy is explicitly manifested in male-controlled ritual cults that to a large degree oppose and contradict the egalitarian quality of secular social relations. Analysis and comparison of these contradictions and the various local ways of attempting to resolve them opens up the possibility for productive comparative insights between these regions.

Within both Amazonia and Melanesia, there is a continuum of variability in the ways that specific societies have coped with the contradiction between ritual hierarchy and social equality. At one end of this continuum are societies that construct ritual hierarchies as exclusively male domains through giving maximal expression to pollution taboos and other methods of denying participation to adult females in any sacred activities. In these cases of strongly marked cults of masculinity, collective rituals redefine the boundary between the sexes through imagery and enactments of gender separation, opposition, or antagonism. At the same time, ritual activities are a process of building an oligarchic structure of "complete authority and complete submission" between adult males and young men undergoing initiation (Biersack, Chapter 4). Gender antagonism and extreme hierarchy based on age converge through ritual practices in which adult men symbolically usurp women's procreative powers as a way of taking exclusive possession over social reproduction. Because of the insistence on exclusion and an all-or-nothing hierarchy, adult men must be vigilant in enforcing the boundaries and secrecy of the cult. Supernatural sanctions against female violators are backed with threats of physical and sexual violence against women. The contradiction between gender hierarchy in ritual contexts, and cooperative male-female relations in everyday social life is not so much resolved as dramatized and magnified. In such societies it is not uncommon to find adult male attitudes of moral ambivalence, remorse, and guilt toward ritual activities that promote intimidation and violence against women and children (Tuzin 1982; Harrison 1990b; Gregor and Tuzin, Chapter 13).

At the other end of the continuum are Amazonian and Melanesian societies in which ritual hierarchy is a male-controlled domain that allows, or even requires, adult female participation in sacred activities. Women's procreativity and associated substances and bodily parts (e.g., menstrual blood, breast milk, wombs, and umbilical cords) are portrayed ambivalently as life-giving and life-taking powers that must be acknowledged rather than negated or denied in ritual performances. Collective rituals provide ways of coordinating and balancing male and female contributions to the processes of socializing children into adulthood and reproducing society through exchanges between communities. In such societies men rely less on intimidation and threats of physical violence against women, and public recognition of the interdependency of men and women is given in ceremonial exchanges and nonritual contexts. Rather than dramatization and amplification of the contradiction between asymmetry and equality of the sexes, the strategy consists of finessing the contradiction through layering and interweaving of separateness and complementarity between men and women.

My primary goal in this chapter is to demonstrate the complex interweavings of masculinity and femininity in the sacred rituals and intercommunity exchange ceremonies of the Wakuénai, a Northern Arawakan people of the Upper Rio Negro region in Venezuela, Colombia, and Brazil with whom I lived and studied in the 1980s and '90s (Hill 1983, 1993). Although many elements of strongly marked cults of masculinity are present in Wakuénai sacred myths and rituals, the dominant theme underlying ritual practices is the interdependence of men and women. Before delving into the situated particulars of ritual power and ceremonial exchange among the Wakuénai, I will briefly compare Wakuénai ritual practices with the exclusively male-controlled ritual hierarchy of the Mundurucú of Central Brazil (Murphy 1958, 1960; Murphy and Murphy 1974). Prior to the Rubber Boom of the late nineteenth to early twentieth centuries, collective rituals celebrating male activities of hunting and warfare established clear-cut separateness and inequality between Mundurucú men and women.

The purpose of comparing Wakuénai and Mundurucú ritual practices is to delineate the end points of a continuum between gender complementarity and gender polarity in Amazonian societies having male-controlled ritual hierarchies. Other Amazonian societies, such as the Mehinaku of the Upper Xingu region, have developed patterns of gender relations that are "bimodal," or located in the middle zone between the endpoints of complementarity and polarity (Gregor and Tuzin, Chapter 13). This brief comparison of Amazonian societies is limited to a single axis of power relations, that of gender, and it does not rule out the possibility that other axes of inequality may intersect with gender relations in ways that are not considered here. The Mundurucú materials, for example, suggest that a cultural emphasis on masculinity defined through activities of hunting and warfare may correlate with gender polarization in Amazonia. However, this correlation is cross-cut by other examples from Amazonia, such as the alignment of intercommunal warfare and gender interdependence among the Wari' of Western Brazil (Conklin, Chapter 7).[1]

VARIETIES OF FERTILITY CULTISM: MARKED AND UNMARKED

Following Hariet Whitehead's comparative analysis (1986a, 1986b) of ritual hierarchies in New Guinea, I refer to male-controlled ritual cults in Amazonia as "fertility cults" rather than "men's cults." As Whitehead notes, the term "men's cults" implies that ritual hierarchies in New Guinea are exclusively male organizations, and that women are uniformly prohibited from any participation in sacred activities. In fact, there are highly significant variations among both

New Guinea and Amazonian societies in the degree to which women participate in ritual constructions of fertility, and these differences are accompanied
by equally important variations in the degree of formal recognition given to
women's roles as provisioners of goods for intercommunity exchanges (Whitehead 1986b). Whitehead's term "fertility cult" encompasses the variable degrees of female participation in sacred rituals and intercommunity exchanges
by defining ritual hierarchy in terms of its explicit cultural purposes: the fertilization of nature and the regeneration of community (1986a, 80).

Whitehead draws a general distinction for New Guinea societies between
two kinds of fertility cults: "cults of manhood" and "cults of clanhood." In
the former, substances and symbols of fertility are entirely male-controlled
and are used in the production of adult men whose identities are defined primarily through this "manhood," regardless of kin-group memberships
(1986a, 84). Cults of clanhood (found mostly in highland areas of New
Guinea) employ a similar theme of making men, "but the ceremonies devoted
to it become adjunct to the celebration of agnatic group unity and ancestral
fertility" (Whitehead 1986a, 84). In these cults, women play important roles in
the ritual fertilization of nature and regeneration of community, but they
achieve ritual positions not as women per se but "through their status as
clanswomen" (1986a, 85). The distinction between cults of manhood and cults
of clanhood is one of "relative salience" of sex- versus kin-defined identities,
and "both components occur in virtually all fertility cults" (1986a, 85).

Whitehead's distinction between cults of manhood and cults of clanhood resembles the contrast that I have drawn above between more strongly marked cults
of masculinity that establish antagonistic or polarized gender relations and more
integrative fertility cults that aim at complementarity or interdependency of the
sexes. However, it is important to point out some of the differences between my
approach to variations of fertility cultism and Whitehead's theoretical orientation.
Whitehead's distinction between cults of manhood and cults of clanhood rests on
a rather simplistic functionalist sociology in which variations in religious beliefs
and practices are understood as symbolic reflections that support underlying
forms of social structure (Weiner 1988). My own approach departs from this functionalist view of religion and society by treating ritual belief and action as a
process of practical signification that can be constitutive of social and political relations. Ritual processes are not merely symbolic reflections of a preexisting social
order but are part and parcel of the processes through which people make, reproduce, and transform social relations (Biersack, Chapter 4; Hugh-Jones, Chapter 11). Given the dynamic, complex, and often contradictory interrelations between ritual processes and everyday sociopolitical relations in Amazonia and
Melanesia, it is better to approach the varieties of fertility cultism as a "complex
process whereby diverse cultural idioms creatively elaborate a range of sociopolitical affiliations" (Knauft 1993, 113) rather than as a simple reflection of an underlying sociological contrast.

In addition to the theoretical problem of functionalist divisions between ritual and sociopolitical orderings, Whitehead's distinction between cults of manhood and cults of clanhood runs into problems when tested against the empirical complexities of social and religious variations in New Guinea (Weiner 1988, 567–570; Knauft 1993, 113; Biersack, Chapter 4). In a comparative analysis of south coast New Guinea cultures, Knauft finds that the range of "ethnographic variation belies easy categorization into Whitehead's fertility cult types, and those classifications that might be posited do not correlate as one might have hoped with variations in female status" (1993, 114). In the Purari Delta area, for example, women enjoy relatively high status in everyday social life even though ritual practices emphasize exclusive male control, whereas Asmat women participate in ritual constructions of fertility but have relatively low social status (Knauft 1993, 113–114). Given the serious empirical problems and limitations of Whitehead's model in Melanesian contexts, it would be easy to overlook the model's potential strength as a preliminary attempt to develop holistic, comparative approaches to gender relations in Melanesia. However, Knauft credits Whitehead with having taken "a very important first step in initiating this kind of integrated analysis" (1993, 116) or a combined concern for cosmological dimensions of gender and "the historical patterns of power and practice through which they were actualized" (1993, 115–116).

The following comparison of gender relations and ritual hierarchy in two Amazonian societies builds upon Whitehead's distinction (1986a) between cults of manhood and cults of clanhood as well as on the refinements and critiques of this distinction that have emerged over the past 10 years. Replacing Whitehead's functionalist theoretical orientation with a more historical, constructivist approach to gender and ritual hierarchy, the distinction between cults of manhood and cults of clanhood can be retained as a useful tool for generalizing from specific Amazonian and Melanesian contexts to reach new comparative understandings of gender relations within and between the two regions. However, since much of the criticism of Whitehead's model has centered on the problem of linking specific religious forms to the social context of unilineal descent groups, or clans,[2] I find it helpful to replace Whitehead's terms "cult of manhood" and "cult of clanhood" with more neutral terms, "marked" and "unmarked" fertility cults, respectively. In marked fertility cults, ritual power is exercised in ways that define masculinity in opposition to femininity. In unmarked fertility cults there may be isolated expressions of male-female polarization, but the dominant theme is the building of male-female complementarity.

Mundurucú: Marked Fertility Cultism in Amazonia

The Mundurucú are a Tupí-speaking people living along the Cururú and other tributaries of the Tapajós River in central Brazil (Murphy and Murphy 1974). By the time of the Murphys' fieldwork in the 1950s, the majority of Mundurucú had abandoned their traditional horseshoe-shaped villages on the savannahs and become residents of riverine mission settlements. Major collective rituals focused on male activities of hunting and warfare had ceased to be practiced during the Rubber Boom (ca. 1860–1920) or shortly afterward. Nevertheless, in the few remaining traditional villages, men continued to live in central men's houses, apart from women and children, who occupied matrilocal extended-family households (Murphy and Murphy 1974). In an enclosure beside the open-walled men's house, adult men made offerings of cooked game meat to mythic clan-ancestor spirits believed to live inside sacred trumpets (*karökö*). These sacred instruments were the quintessential symbol of male separateness, and women were forbidden under penalty of gang rape from seeing the trumpets during the men's ritual performances (p. 100). According to myths, women originally possessed these sacred trumpets, but the men regained possession of them because they alone had the ability to procure wild game meat through hunting in the forests.

By the 1950s, Mundurucú religious traditions had lost much of their sociopolitical grounding, and women generally regarded the men's rituals as a sort of collective male fantasy. Moreover, women formed relatively united household groups that wielded substantial social and economic power through informal mechanisms such as gossip and through cooperative production of surplus manioc goods (Murphy and Murphy 1974). Although it may be accurate to characterize Mundurucú ritual hierarchy in the 1950s as the construction of an "all male fantasy world" (Nadelson 1981), it would be a mistake to project this later historical condition back to the Rubber Boom or earlier periods when Mundurucú men still practiced ritual head-hunting against outsiders. The purpose of these head-hunting raids was two-fold: (1) to bring back an enemy trophy head and (2) to capture enemy children. Thus male ritual practices went beyond mere symbolic opposition to, or usurpation of, women's procreative powers to the level of actually negating, or short-circuiting, women's fertility through an all-male ritual process of capturing enemy children (Murphy 1958, 1960).

Mundurucú head-hunting and associated rituals designed to renew the fertility of game animals ceased to be practiced during and after the Rubber Boom. As warfare declined in importance during the late nineteenth century, Mundurucú men lost their former role as ethnic soldiers in symbiotic alliance with Portuguese-Brazilian military campaigns against other indigenous groups (Murphy 1960, 48–49). Prior to the Rubber Boom, Mundurucú chiefs were powerful leaders who inherited their elite status through patrilineal descent. Most importantly, in the early nineteenth century Mundurucú chiefs enjoyed privileges of virilocal residence and polygyny, setting them apart from the majority of commoner, or nonelite, men who resided in men's houses in their wives' natal villages. Ritual head-hunting and warfare against enemy outsiders provided a means for constructing status hierarchies among nonchiefly males through bestowing special ritual powers on successful hunter-warriors, or "takers of the trophy head" (Murphy and Murphy 1974, 80–81). There was, however, always a gap between the acquired status of hunter-warrior and the ascribed status of chiefly leader, and this unresolved tension between elite virilocal "insiders" and commoner uxorilocal "outsiders" found expression in unceasing ritual aggression against outsiders.[3] The end of head-hunting raids and warfare greatly reduced the power of chiefs in Mundurucú society. The appointment of so-called "friendly chiefs" by rubber traders also did much to undermine the legitimacy of chiefly authority, since in Mundurucú political organization only the sons of chiefs could accede to their fathers' chiefly status (Murphy 1960, 84).

Mundurucú religion of the pre–Rubber Boom era provides the most clear-cut illustration of a marked fertility cult in all of Amazonia. Women of child-bearing age were strictly excluded from participation at any level (except perhaps as negative objects) in the ritual reproduction of social institutions. A single strand of practical signification ran through the entire triumvirate of male-controlled ritual activities. Trophy heads obtained in raids "promoted the fertility of the [game] animals and made them more vulnerable to hunting" (Murphy and Murphy 1974, 81). In turn, the game meat obtained through hunting gave to men, and denied to women, the ability to make ritual offerings to clan ancestral spirits housed inside *karökö* trumpets. For the Mundurucú, social reproduction was an exclusively male process of empowering the social order through reintroducing naturalized social being, or Otherness, into human social space in the form of trophy heads, children, and other tokens of the slain outsider-enemy. Among the Mundurucú, the taker of the trophy head was like a diseased individual who had to observe a number of severe ritual restrictions (seclusion, avoidance of any physical or *even visual* contact with women for at least *a year*, and special diet) and who underwent a series of ritual empowerments, such as hanging the enemy's teeth on a necklace. This transformation of the returning warrior from a source of pollution through contact with enemy Others into a fully adult male person within Mundurucú social organization endowed him with shamanistic powers to attract game animals to the male hunters as well as the power to socialize captured children into the group. As the "Peccary-Owner," the returning warrior initiated young men into the "Order of the Bow" and taught them how to become hunter-warriors.[4]

Hunting rituals, which ceased to be practiced shortly after the Rubber Boom, can be interpreted as a process of ritually alienating female horticulturalists from the products of their labor. A line of animal skulls was placed across the village plaza, and shamans washed these skulls with manioc gruel in order to attract *putcha si*, the mythic source of fertility in game animals. Only prepubescent girls could participate in the preparation of the ritual manioc gruel, since women of childbearing age (the actual producers of manioc) were contaminated with menstrual blood and would scare *putcha si* away from the village (Murphy 1958). Female fertility and sexuality were viewed as sources of pollution and disease that threatened the "purity" of all-male activities of hunting, warfare, and worshiping the divine ancestral powers. Menstruation was an unambiguously harmful process that must be kept well away from male-controlled powers of "making" individual hunter-warriors and regenerating the social order through engraving history into the heads of enemy Others. In effect, the procreative, life-giving powers of menstrual blood were appropriated by male rituals of shedding animals' and human-Others' blood, and through transforming these losses of blood into the power to regenerate the fertility of nature and society. The Mundurucú fertility cult translated negative reciprocity, or the exchange of violent blows and the taking of outsiders' lives and children, into a balanced, reciprocal exchange of cooked game meat and shrunken (human) trophy heads for ancestral protection against pollution by menstruating females.

Marked Fertility Cultism, Indiscriminate Violence, and Protection Rackets

The intrinsic connections between violence and exchange have garnered considerable theoretical and empirical elaboration in Melanesian contexts (Rubel and Rosman 1978; Brown 1979; Harrison 1990b). "In stateless societies, violent responses are themselves a form of exchange inseparably linked to all others. . . . In essence, the gift is the positive pole of a continuum that has at its negative pole the blow" (Whitehead 1986b, 279). Warfare and alliance form parts of a more general process of intercommunity exchange of 'gifts' (including male and female persons and labor) and 'blows' (including not only violence but also material goods intended to insult recipients). The connection between male-controlled fertility and male violence is clearest in New Guinean and Amazonian societies practicing ritual head-hunting. Among the lowland head-hunting cultures of New Guinea, "cultic symbolism often explicitly makes the trophy head (which only men can garner) an agent of fertility" (pp. 274–275). Similarly, the Mundurucú of Amazonia believed that the takers of trophy heads could gain power to renew the fertility of game animals and attract them to human hunters by following prolonged sexual abstinence and other ritual practices (Murphy 1958, 55).

Where male violence against outsiders was directly linked to the internal construction of male-controlled ritual hierarchies, there was little or no sense in which such violence formed part of an overall pattern of reciprocal giving and taking among groups. Among the Mundurucú, "enemies included every other group save the neighboring Apiacá, who were subservient to the Mundurucú and sometimes joined their war parties" (Murphy and Murphy 1974, 80). The Mundurucú carried out raids against numerous outside groups over an immense area of central Brazil—from the banks of the Madeira River eastward to the Xingu River, and from the main channel of the Amazon River southward to the Planalto of Mato Grosso (ibid.). Another measure of the degree to which Mundurucú violence against outsiders was generalized and indiscriminate was the ease with which the Mundurucú shifted to new targets as allies of the Portuguese-Brazilians during the early nineteenth century. "That they should receive axes, knives, guns, cloth, and other avidly desired items for doing what they had always done was probably an unusual boon" (p. 30). For the Portuguese-Brazilians, Mundurucú hostility toward all other indigenous peoples was a strategic tool for conquest and colonization of the Amazon Basin.

The same kind of random, indiscriminate violence against outside groups is found in some areas of Melanesia, especially lowland New Guinea. Writing about the Avatip of the Sepik River, Harrison (1990b, 586) observes that "any outsiders were suitable victims. That is, these ritual homicides were not carried out under the rubric of reciprocity but as an internal requirement of the village's male cult. . . . The rivalry was principally within the village and a man's opponents in war were simply means by which he sought prestige in the eyes of his co-villagers." Like Mundurucú men returning from raids with an enemy's trophy head, Avatip men coming back with enemy heads gained prestige within their communities but only after they had passed through a ritually restricted period during which they "could not return to their wives and children or resume their everyday subsistence tasks" (ibid.). Avatip men regarded warfare and hunting as a single domain of related activities. "Men sometimes described themselves as acting in raids as the hunting dogs of their war-magicians. . . . War was . . . represented as . . . a superior form of hunting with human beings as the quarry" (ibid.). For both Avatip and Mundurucú, the significance of hunting and warfare were inextricably intertwined. Among the Avatip, the two activities formed a metonymic pair, with warfare seen as a special kind of hunting. For the Mundurucú, warfare against outside enemies constituted a separate domain of activity that was ritually linked to hunting through metaphorical comparison.

The comparison of Mundurucú and Avatip as examples of marked fertility cults from Amazonia and Melanesia would not be complete without a consideration of gender relations. For both the Mundurucú and the Avatip, the strict exclusion of women from male ritual practices formed part of a broader pattern of male domination and gender polarization in secular contexts. Citing Whitehead's article (1986b) on intercommunity exchange in New Guinea, Harrison finds that warfare in lowland New Guinea contains "elements of a male 'protection racket' directed against women . . . and this observation certainly applies to Avatip" (1990b, 591). Avatip men would stage sham "attacks" by outside enemies in the presence of young female kin in order to frighten these young women into accepting their dependence on their male kin as protectors. "In effect, men in war were . . . using the threat of outsiders' aggression in an attempt to control women" (ibid.). Like Avatip women, Mundurucú women were kept under control through constant threats of male violence in everyday social contexts. According to the Murphys, Mundurucú women "join together for company and also to obtain protection against men. The lone woman is a legitimate sexual mark for a male; her loneness announces her availability and states that she is operating outside custody. The men are thus seen as potentially threatening in a very real, direct, and physical way. They force the women together, make them travel in bands, and actually increase their dependence on each other" (Murphy and Murphy 1974, 136). Thus, among both Avatip and Mundurucú, marked fertility cults based on tightly woven interrelations between hunting and warfare were coupled with broader patterns of gender polarization and threats of male violence against women in everyday social contexts. For the Avatip, these practices promoted women's dependence on their male kin, whereas for the Mundurucú the threat of male violence augmented women's need to rely on other women in opposition to men.

WAKUÉNAI: UNMARKED FERTILITY CULTISM IN AMAZONIA
Ethnographic Background

The Wakuénai, or "People of Our Language," are a Northern Arawak-speaking people living along the Guainía and Isana rivers and their tributaries at the headwaters of the Rio Negro in Venezuela, Colombia, and Brazil. About 1,600 Wakuénai lived in Venezuelan territory during the early 1980s, with somewhat larger numbers residing upstream along the Guainía River in Colombia (Journet 1988) and to the southwest along the Isana River in Brazil (Wright 1981). In late 1980 and early 1981, I spent several months doing fieldwork in a village affiliated with the Adzanéni ("Armadillo-Children") phratry, who spoke the Curripaco, or "Áh-han," dialect associated with the Guainía River in Venezuela and Colombia.[5] Later in 1981, I moved upstream to a village where men spoke the Curricarro, or "Óh-hon," dialect from the Negro and Isana rivers in Venezuela and Brazil. The men of this village were members of a highly ranked patrisib of the Dzáwinái ("Jaguar Owners") phratry, and they included powerful ritual specialists who were my most important sources of knowledge about cosmology, ritual, and ceremonialism.

The Arawakan phratries of the Isana-Guainía drainage area form part of a larger headwater region of ranked patrilineal societies in northwestern Amazonia. Immediately south and west of the Wakuénai live the various Eastern Tukanoan peoples, whose ritual and social organization have received extensive treatment in several recent monographs of outstanding depth and quality (Goldman 1963; C. Hugh-Jones 1979; S. Hugh-Jones 1979; Reichel-Dolmatoff 1971, 1975; Jackson 1983; Århem 1983; Chernela 1993). Throughout the region, subsistence activities center around an integrated pattern of bitter manioc cultivation and fishing, with important dietary supplements from occasional hunting and seasonal collecting of wild palm fruits.

Despite the basic socioecological similarities between Eastern Tukanoan and Northern Arawakan peoples of the Northwest Amazon region (see

Hugh-Jones, Chapter 11), there are significant differences in marriage practices and the degree to which local communities are organized into supralocal units of political organization, or phratries. Eastern Tukanoan peoples
of the Central Vaupés basin strictly adhere to the principle of language
group exogamy (Jackson 1983, 93–96), and the ranking of language groups
into larger political confederations, or phratries, is not reflected in spatial lo-
calization. Referring to these shadowy groupings of language groups as
"epiphenomenal phratries," Jackson (p. 86) finds that members of widely
dispersed communities frequently disagree about which language groups
belong to the same phratry and how they are serially ranked. Among the
Arawak-speaking Wakuénai, however, marriage is between exogamous
phratries within the same language group (albeit with significant dialect
variation), and marriage preferences are directly linked to rank within phratries. In other words, men from highest-ranked sibs must marry women
from highest-ranked sibs in another phratry, and so forth, down to the
lowest-ranked sibs. For example, in the second village where I conducted
long-term fieldwork in the early 1980s, the senior men were members of a
highly ranked sib of the Dzáwinái phratry, and their wives were members
of a highly ranked sib of the Waríperídakéna ("Pleiades Grandchildren")
phratry. Although sibs from different phratries were moving into the ancestral territories of other phratries due to missionization and various other
changes during the 1980s, there was still a strong sense that each phratry
controlled access to a discrete riverine territory along the Guainía or Isana
rivers or one of their tributaries.

Mythopoetic Context

The following discussion of Wakuénai sacred rites of passage at childbirth
and puberty condenses ethnographic information about which I have written
at length (Hill 1993). The core activity of Wakuénai ritual performances is a
complex genre of ritually powerful speech, called *málikai*. Senior male specialists known as *málikai limínali* ("master" or "owner" of málikai) are the only
individuals who can perform the spoken, chanted, and sung speeches and interpret the nuances of mythic meaning embodied in powerful spirit-names
(*nakúna*). Both the musicality of málikai and the verbal processes of spirit-
naming imbue the life cycle transitions of specific individuals and their families with meanings established in a cycle of narratives about Amáru and
Kuwái, the primordial human mother and child.

Profound transformations of the cosmos accompany the birth, death, and rebirth of the primordial human being. These changes include the original
coming-into-being of male and female sexuality; the ritual authority of specialists, elders, and initiated adults; brideservice and virilocal residence; and history,
or social reproduction, as a process of multiple movements away from and back

to a mythic center, or place of ancestral emergence. The significance of these cosmic events can only be understood in relation to the undifferentiated, pre-sexual space-time of the Trickster-creator (Iñapirríkuli, or "Made from Bone"). A cycle of narratives outlines a world of unceasing violence between Trickster and a group of affinal animal-enemies. Trickster and his brothers succeed at evading an assortment of lethal pitfalls, assaults, and deceptions. In effect, Trickster embodies a principle of strategic interaction, or the human ability to interpret underlying motives and act in ways that produce an imagined future that is different from an immediate present charged with danger and difficulty. The original space-time of Trickster establishes this principle of strategic inter-action as the raw, undifferentiated potential that prefigures the emergence of specifically human persons and social groups. The space-time of Trickster lacks cultural separateness, for there are no clear boundaries between men and women, adults and children, living and dead, humans and animals, night and day, or past and present.[6] Trickster's incestuous sexual relations with Amáru, a paternal aunt, set in motion a series of mythic events that give rise to culturally separate worlds of human persons and social institutions.

The life cycle of Kuwái, the primordial human being of myth, outlines a two-fold process of creation. In the first part of the myth cycle, Trickster and his brothers open up a birth canal in Amáru's womb, allowing the child to escape from death inside his mother to life in the external world. Because of his inces-tuous sexual origins, Kuwái is considered extremely dangerous and is taken to live in a remote corner of the sky. Nevertheless, Kuwái breaks out of this con-fined space and flies about the sky, humming- and singing-into-being the species and objects of nature. The world of Trickster's primordial village at Hípana, the place of mythic ancestral emergence, opens up as Kuwái musically names things into being ("The Powerful Sound that Opened Up the World"). The re-mainder of the first creation entails the return of Kuwái back down to the ground and inside the center of social space at Hípana as well as the internal-ization of his explosively creative musical naming power into human con-sciousness in the form of ritually powerful speech (málikai). The first creation reaches completion when Kuwái has taught the songs and chants of puberty initiation to Dzúli, a younger brother of Trickster and the first master of má-likai. The undifferentiated world of Trickster has transformed into a vertical structure of power relations between mythic ancestral beings of the sky-world and their human descendants living on the ground below. Individual human be-ings are defined in relation to these vertical power relations, which are socially mediated by a hierarchy of senior male specialists, elders, initiated adults, chil-dren, and grandchildren. The first creation is ritually constructed in the spirit-naming process called "heaping up the names in a single place," a process of gradual movement between categories of mythic being that signifies continuity (i.e., unimpeded transmission of knowledge across generations) and the power to control movements between distinct stages in the human life cycle.

The first creation comes to a dramatic end when Trickster and his brothers kill the primordial human being by pushing him into a great bonfire, causing the world to shrink back to its original miniature size. Enormous trees and vines grow from the ashes of the primordial human being. Trickster chops down these magical plants, cuts them into sections of varying length, and uses the hollowed out logs to make sacred flutes and trumpets.[7] Amáru and a group of women steal these instruments from Trickster, taking them to a place far downstream where they hold the first female initiation ritual. The world opens up for a second time as the women play the sacred instruments in new locations. Eventually, Trickster and a group of male followers regain possession of the flutes and trumpets and hold a ceremonial dance, called kwépani ("Kuwai dance"), to trick Amáru and the women into believing that the flutes and trumpets have transformed into animal species. After teaching men how to construct the massive "Jaguar-Bone" trumpets played only in male initiation rituals, Trickster leaves the world of human beings to live in a celestial paradise.

In the second creation, the closed, hierarchical ordering of a primordial human community opens up, or expands, into new social and geographical spaces away from the mythic center of the world. The struggle between men and women to control the sacred musical instruments has replaced the supernatural force of Kuwái's musical naming power as the source of life-giving ancestral power. Agency, or the ability to control social constructions of meaning, is strongly rooted in the female figure of Amáru and her powerful movements away from and back to the mythic center. However, this female agency is constrained in myth because it can only be exercised through moving away from the mythic center. Young women undergoing initiation at puberty face a similar dilemma: they are initiated into the local ancestor cult *so that* they can eventually move away to live virilocally in their husbands' villages. In myth, Amáru and the women have only temporary possession of the sacred instruments, for it is only Trickster and his male followers who share the secret knowledge of how to make as well as play the flutes and trumpets, and it is Trickster who restores them to their proper place at the mythic center.

In ritual performances of málikai, the dynamic, expanding world of the second creation is embodied in a spirit-naming process called "chasing after the names" (wadzúhiakaw nakúna). The performative enactment of this process is heavily laden with gendered meanings, deriving from Trickster's mythic acts of chasing after Amáru and the women as they moved across the landscape. Symbolic oppositions between men and women pervade both mythic accounts of the second creation and ritual contexts of male and female initiation. In the following overview of Wakuénai sacred rites of passage, I will explore some of the major dimensions of opposing male and female imagery as a broader process of building gender complementarity. Although mythic narratives portray gender relations as a relatively simple polarization in which men gain ascendancy over women, analysis of the social contexts and symbolic form and contents of sacred rituals will reveal a more complex process in which descent groups consisting of both men and women are concerned with managing the simultaneous gain and loss of female blood kin through exogamous exchange and virilocal residence.

Childbirth Rituals

Wakuénai rites of passage at childbirth consist of two elaborate performances of málikai chants. A first set of chants focuses on the tools and weapons of the newborn infant's father, and a second set aims at "cooking" a pot of hot-peppered game meat to mark both parents' return to a normal diet. Between the first and second sets of chanting, the newborn's father goes hunting in the forest, and the mother cooks the game meat prior to giving it to a master of málikai. The first set of chants is a musically dynamic process of "chasing after the names" of the infant's ancestral tobacco spirits, whereas the second set of chants is a musically stable process of "heaping up the names" of all the edible species of fish, aquatic animals, forest animals, and birds. The transition from more dynamic to more stable musical and verbal forms in childbirth rituals roughly parallels the mythic transformation of Kuwái's musical naming power into ritually powerful ways of speaking (málikai) during the first creation (Hill 1993).

Gender symbolism is explicitly important in the first set of chants. Verbal images of female birthing anatomy serve as an organizing metaphor for the process of "chasing after" the infant's ancestral tobacco spirits. Spirit-names are invoked in order to neutralize the potentially harmful effects of the father's return to everyday economic activities on an invisible, spiritual umbilical cord that connects the soft, fleshy parts of the infant's body to its skeleton. The father's activities can harm this spiritual cord in numerous ways:

- by using hot, "female" things in the Amáru category of names (shotguns, machetes, and other steel tools), the father can transmit heat to the infant and cause fever;
- by cutting long, thin objects, such as vines and palm fibers, the father can cause the infant's umbilical cord to bleed or break;
- by making loud, sharp, or other percussive sounds, the father's activities can frighten the child and cause damage to the umbilical cord;
- by experiencing frightening sights and sounds (e.g., a jaguar's white beard or the cough-like sound of a dolphin), the father's fear can spread to the infant and damage the umbilical cord.

Spirit-naming in this set of chants symbolically overdetermines the relations between a newborn infant's health and virtually the entire male repertoire of subsistence activities—hunting, fishing, gardening, gathering plants, making and using canoes, and making baskets. The "journey" along the infant's spiritual umbilical cord is also a movement from the eastern horizon, the fleshy womb of Amáru and source of heat, to the place where the sun sets on the western horizon, the cold, hard bone at the base of the infant's spine (Hill 1993). Underlying the rich variety of spirit-names is a basic contrast between "female" things, which are hot, soft, and fleshy, and "male" things, which are cold, hard, and bony (Hill 1988).

Childbirth rituals are an orchestration of contrasting sets of male and female imagery into an integrated whole of male and female bodily and cosmic "places." The social context of ritual chanting also aims at an integration of male and female qualities and activities. Both mothers and fathers of newborn infants observe the same restrictions (seclusion, fasting, and sexual abstinence) during the week after birth, and both the male activity of hunting and the female activity of cooking are required to produce the pot of sacred food for the second set of málikai chants. The general significance of childbirth rituals is that of transposing the "overly close" biological relations of newborn infants with their mothers (Lévi-Strauss 1969b, 335) into overly close spiritual and emotional connections between newborn infants and their fathers. The ritual process thus supports the infant's arrival into human society as a member of the father's patrilineal descent group. The newborn's social identity, however, is not complete until the overly close relations with its parents have been socialized, or "stabilized," through the parents' act of eating the sacred food (*karidzamai*). Much like the mythic transformation of primal (incestuous) sexual relations into imagery of fasting and eating, the second set of chants in childbirth rituals embodies the transformation of sex- and gender-based activities into those of cooking and eating. Sharing of supernaturalized food replaces the sharing of sexual substances as the social means for signifying the biological family's participation in a local community defined through ritual as a hierarchical ordering of empowering mythic ancestors, powerful chant-owners, and empowered human descendants.

Male and Female Initiation Rituals

In both male and female initiation rituals, the primary focus of málikai singing and chanting is a pot of hot-peppered, boiled meat (karidzamai). Unlike childbirth rituals, in which eating the sacred food signifies the stabilizing of parents' dynamic relationship with newborn infants, initiation rituals are contexts in which eating the sacred food embodies the more dynamic processes of "chasing after the names," and the mythic creation of an expanding world of peoples, animal and plant species, and geographic places. The second mythic creation is a dynamic transformation of the first creation, a turning inside-out and upside-down of the world created when Kuwái's musical naming power was brought down into the center of social space and implanted into human consciousness.

Power in the second creation does not reside inside the primordial human being and the first human family but in the external world of plant materials made into musical instruments and the movements of groups of women and men outside the mythic center. In a similar manner, initiation rituals are a dynamic transformation of the biological and culinary imagery employed in childbirth rituals. The significance of sacred food as a source of continuity and shared substance across generations within the local descent group transforms in initiation rituals into the embodiment of dynamic (ex-)changes and movements between local descent groups.

The transformation from internal to external relations is concretely expressed in the verbal and musical dimensions of málikai singing and chanting for the sacred food of initiates. These performances begin with a singing-into-being of the celestial umbilical cord that connects the sky-world of mythic ancestors to the navel of the terrestrial world of human descendants. The use of several different pitches is a musical construction of the celestial umbilical cord, the vertical power relations governing the transitions between developmental stages in the human life cycle, and the turning over of generational time. Chant-owners use a sacred whip to tap out a percussive rhythm on an overturned basket covering the pot of sacred food, adding yet another dimension to the movement from internal to external worlds. After naming the mythic center at Hípana, the opening song modulates into a chanted naming of plants and animals in different places. In a long series of chants, the verbal naming of places away from the mythic center is musically expressed through use of different starting pitches, microtonal rising, accelerations of tempo, and loud-soft contrasts. The final chants return to the naming of places near the mythic center, and a closing song using the exact same set of pitches as the opening song returns to the more stabilizing, vertical dimensions of power (i.e., the celestial umbilical cord). Overall, málikai singing and chanting in initiation rituals outlines a verbally and musically dynamic set of movements away from and back to the mythic center, or the musically stabilizing movements between distinct, sung pitches.

After the málikai singing and chanting are completed, the initiate(s) emerge from their place of seclusion to face the ritual advice of chant-owners and other elders. The initiates' mothers bring the pots of sacred food outside and place them on woven mats where the initiates must stand to receive the elders' advice. The initiates' senior kin, both male and female, participate in these ritually aggressive speeches. At the end of the advice, chant-owners lift a morsel of the hot-peppered food to the initiates' mouths on the ends of sacred whips before lashing the initiates' backs. In effect, the use of loud percussive sounds to signify the transformation from inner to outer worlds has reached a conclusion. The initiates' bodies, in full view of an assembled group of senior kin, have become percussive instruments that, through eating the sacred food, carry within themselves the dynamic, expanding world of the second mythic creation.

Málikai singing and chanting over the sacred food and the elders' speeches of advice form a core of activities that is common to both male and female initiation rituals. However, the social organization and symbolic meanings of the two rituals are distinctly different, or even opposing. Female initiation rituals are relatively small, localized gatherings held when an individual girl experiences her first menses. The young woman's loss of menstrual blood is associated with alienation from her ancestral dream soul, and the long set of málikai chants for the girl's sacred food is understood as a process of "chasing after" her dream soul so that she will be a healthy and fertile adult woman. Female initiation rituals are called *wakáitaka iénpiti* ("we speak to our child"), a label that highlights the significance of the elders' ritual advice as an arena for attaching sacred moral significance to the individual girl's physical maturation as a fully sexual being. Málikai singing and chanting for female initiates begins at noon and ends at sunset.[8] The naming of places in málikai chants starts at Hípana, the mythic center, moves across the major river basins in the Upper Rio Negro region, and ends at Mutsipani, the mythic home of Amáru. The chants outline a process of displacement, or movement away from the mythic center at Hípana, a theme consistent with the mythic story of Amáru's invention of female initiation rituals as well as the situation of women who have reached marriageable age in a patrilineal, virilocal social world.

In male initiation rituals, the pattern of place-naming and movements in málikai chants reverses and greatly expands upon the movements outlined in chants for female initiation rituals. Chants for male initiates begin at Amáru's mythic home (Mutsipani) and end at the mythic center (Hípana) after traversing a vast range of riverine territories throughout the Amazon and Orinoco basins. The overall effect of place-naming in the chants is to highlight movements back to the mythic center at Hípana, reinforcing the mythic story of Trickster's invention of male initiation rituals as a collective male negation of Amáru's control of the sacred musical instruments. Male initiation rituals are relatively large social gatherings in which chant-owners and elders from two or more local descent groups initiate a group of adolescent males. The name for male initiation rituals is *wakapétaka iénpitipé* ("we show our children"), referring to the period of instruction during which adult men show the group of male initiates how to make and play the sacred flutes and trumpets. Málikai singing and chanting for the initiates' food takes place on the final night of ritual activities, and the elders give their speeches of advice just before dawn.

Like childbirth rituals, male and female initiation rituals employ social and symbolic contrasts between the sexes to build an integral whole that not only includes but depends upon female as well as male participation. Ritual activities sometimes require strict separation of the sexes, particularly when adult men teach male initiates how to make and play the sacred flutes and trumpets. However, women are not excluded during performances of málikai singing and chanting, and they are active participants in the giving of ritual advice to male and female initiates. Female reproductive anatomy—wombs, umbilical cords, and menstrual blood—supplies much of the symbolic content for male-controlled activities of málikai singing and chanting. Ritual appropriations of women's reproductive anatomy do not portray women's fertility as a source of pollution that threatens an all-male realm of purity but as an ambiguously charged, life-giving and life-taking power that must be harnessed to collective processes of producing socialized persons and reproducing the interlocking social realms of adult women and men.

Pudáli Ceremonial Exchanges

The complex genre of málikai singing and chanting forms the integrative core of sacred ritual activities embodying the construction, reproduction, and transformation of a sacred, hierarchical ordering of society and history. These sacred ritual performances are concerned with the creation of cultur-ally and sexually differentiated being out of the primordial formlessness of the first world inhabited by Trickster. Although male and female genders are defined in myth as opposites of each other, analysis of ritual performances shows a complex weaving together of interdependent genders. The ceremo-nial exchange cycles, called *pudáli*, begin with collective expressions of gender complementarity and gradually tear down the symbolic boundaries between men and women as well as between humans and animals.

The socioeconomic underpinnings of pudáli were changing rapidly among the Wakuénai of Venezuela during the 1980s. Local people made *máwi* flutes and performed many of the songs and dances of pudáli as a form of enter-tainment or, in one case, as part of a political protest against the predatory eco-nomic practices of local merchants (Hill 1994). Nevertheless, by working with senior informants and key historical sources (Matos Arvelo 1912; Nimuendajú 1950 [1927]), I was able to construct a detailed description and analysis of pudáli ceremonial cycles as they had been practiced until fairly recent times (Hill 1987).

Pudáli is a two-part ceremonial cycle set in motion when a local group ex-periences a brief superabundance of fish and/or game meat. Ideally, pudáli begins during late March or early April, when vast schools of *Leporinus* fish mi-grate into newly flooded forests in order to spawn. Using weirs to block the mouths of streams, groups of men can capture enough fish to fill several large canoes in a few hours. Pudáli can also begin at other seasons of the year when large numbers of peccary or other game animals are killed.

In an opening, male-owned ceremony, a local group brings an offering of smoked meat to a host group, who are either actual or potential affines. When the guests arrive, they form large ensembles of male flute and trumpet players accompanied by female dancers. The guests display their offering of food in the cleared public area in front of the hosts' house, playing a standaradized máwi flute duet in unison and accompanied by the low rumbling sound of *kulirrína* (catfish) trumpets. During these large standardized performances in the opening stage of pudáli, hosts watch from a respectful distance and are forbidden to participate in the guests' music and dancing. Just before sunset, the guests' male-owner of pudáli (*pudalimínali*) and the hosts' headman (*pantímnali*, or "house-owner") make formal speeches of offering and accepting the gift of smoked meat. As night falls, the hosts put the smoked meat inside their house and invite their guests to come in to drink fermented beverages. The first relaxation of the social boundary between hosts and guests takes place through drinking songs (*pakamarántaka*). These songs consist of highly standardized melodies but personally improvised verses that allow men and women of the two groups to communicate a full range of emotions, experiences, and opinions. The late night, transitional period of male-owned pudáli concludes with a final performance of kulirrína trumpets in the first gray light of dawn. The guests give their trumpets to the hosts as tokens that signify the obligation to hold a female-owned pudáli several weeks later. At dawn, the hosts redistribute the smoked meat to guests and hosts alike, and individual men and women of the two groups join together to perform improvisatory máwi flute duets and dances.

In a closing ceremony, a female-owner of pudáli (*pudalímnaru*) organizes the production and exchange of a large quantity of processed manioc pulp. The ceremonial events outline the same general process of three stages: (1) large, standardized performances around the display of food, (2) drinking songs during the night, and (3) improvisatory dances and flute duets on the following day. However, in female-owned pudáli, the kulirrína trumpets are replaced by collective singing and dancing accompanied by stomping tubes (*wáana*).

Pudáli ceremonial cycles embody the principles of balance, reciprocity, and complementarity between men and women. At a general level, this gender complementarity is expressed through balanced formal recognition of male and female owners of pudáli. Smoked meat and processed manioc pulp are the quintessential products of male and female labor, respectively, and these food gifts serve as symbolic tokens, or "substitutes" (Wagner 1972), for the exchanges of male labor and wives in bride service. This ideology of gender complementarity works in tandem with a number of symbolic practices that serve to naturalize ceremonial activities. The verb used to describe dancing (*-irrápaka*) in pudáli is the same word used to describe the spawning activities of *Leporinus* and other fish species. The opening performances of male-owned pudáli are named after three different species of *Leporinus* (*táari, dúme,* and *dúpari*), and the low rumbling sound of kulirrína ("catfish") trumpets is said to represent the sound of a stream filled with migrating, spawning fish. Thus, the underlying symbolic theme of pudáli is the metaphorical transformation of natural processes of fertility and abundance into the regeneration of human society through public expressions of gender complementarity.

At a more specific level, each pudáli ceremony (whether male- or female-owned) outlines a collective process of constructing the presexual, precultural space-time of Trickster through gradually transforming gender complementarity and metaphorical comparisons of human and nonhuman reproductive behaviors into the interchangeability of men and women, humans and animals. These transformations of gender and cultural boundaries are embodied in a multitude of performance practices and other activities (Hill 1987). For example, máwi flutes are always made and played in "male" and "female" pairs. These instruments are blowpipes with palm-leaf reeds and lacking finger holes. Blowing harder or softer produces an overtone series of wider and narrower intervals. A single flute is thus incapable of producing a melody, so pairs of longer, "male" flutes are played in a hocket style (i.e., alternating M-F-M-F- etc.) with shorter, "female" flutes to make complex melodic structures. Each performance of máwi flute music is an interweaving of "male" and "female" voices, and this meaning is doubled by the fact that each pair of male flute players is accompanied by a pair of female dancers.

Kulirrína trumpets are also richly imbued with gender meanings, since women of childbearing age are forbidden to be present when the woven, resin-covered resonators are closed and attached to hollow palm mouthpieces. It is said that a woman's future unborn children could become stuck inside her womb, causing death to both mother and child, if she were to witness the sealing together of kulirrína mouthpieces and resonators.[9] In this case, the fastening of "male" palm tubes into the cavernous, womblike resonators to make kulirrína trumpets symbolically expresses a concept of ambisexuality, or the fusing together of "male" and "female" properties into a single object. This same meaning is externally enacted in the use of kulirrína trumpets as gifts from the sponsors of a male-owned pudáli that remind their hosts of the obligation to hold a female-owned pudáli at a later time.

Among the many improvisatory duets played in the final stage of pudáli, the most complete expression of presexual, androgynous sexuality is the improvisatory flute-dance called *dzawírra* (*Cicholasoma* sp., a species of small fish). In this performance, one of the male-female dance couples stands still while the other couple approaches and backs off three times. On the third approach, the flute-player who is standing still raises his instrument up high to allow the other couple to dance underneath in small, counterclockwise circles. Immediately following this sequence, the roles are reversed and the couple that had been moving around the others in small circles stands still. According to the Wakuénai, the dzawírra duet portrays a female dzawírra fish protecting a nest of eggs against an enemy. The approaching and backing-off motions of dancers are said to represent a process of asking the mother fish's permission to "dance" in a circle over her nest. Similarly, the raising of the máwi flute is said to be the mother fish's sign of giving her approval to the intruder to enter the nest. The dzawírra duet uses the sexual symbolism of the male aggressor versus the female protector to construct the idea of a natural, presexual reproductive process in which gender is reversible and exchangeable. The sexual meaning of the duet is not simply that of a juxtaposition of male and female genders in which two male flute-players alternatively play the role of male aggressor. Instead, the dzawírra duet expresses a total blurring of male and female genders by acting out the transformations of male aggressor into male protector and of female protector into female aggressor.

CONCLUSIONS

This essay has demonstrated how Harriet Whitehead's approach (1986a, 1986b) to the varieties of fertility cultism in New Guinea can, with some adjustment and refinement, be useful for interpreting the varieties of male-controlled ritual hierarchy in Amazonia. The distinction between marked and unmarked fertility cultism is not a static, taxonomic division between types of social or religious organization but a reflection of different processes of constructing male ritual hierarchies in contradistinction to everyday social relations characterized by relatively egalitarian relations between men and women. In marked fertility cultism, the strong emphasis on gender oppositions and exclusion of women from ritual activities is often backed up by threats of physical or sexual violence against women and accompanied by male guilt about acts of violence against outside enemies or inside women and children. In unmarked fertility cultism, women are ambiguously included and excluded from male-controlled ritual activities, which provide ways of coordinating male and female processes of socialization and of asserting the interdependence of men and women as agents of social reproduction.

This essay makes no claim for a simple correlation between varieties of fertility cultism and other, nonritual dimensions of social organization in Amazonia or Melanesia. The ethnographic literature on New Guinea makes abundantly clear the fact that marked and unmarked fertility cults can develop in a bewildering variety of sociopolitical contexts (Knauft 1993). Even among closely related societies, such as the Ankave and Sambia, seemingly minor differences in the symbolic weighting of masculine and feminine imagery can result in a pronounced contrast between unmarked and marked fertility cults (Bonnemère, Chapter 2). In fact, it is interesting to note that the key terms of the Ankave/Sambia contrast in New Guinea are fully accurate when applied to the Wakuénai/Mundurucú contrast in Amazonia.

Biersack (Chapter 4) suggests that fertility cults in Papua New Guinea and Amazonia can be understood as different kinds of reproductive regimes. This approach has the advantage of avoiding the pitfalls of psychologically reductionist explanations in favor of political models of the different degrees to which men and women are capable of controlling reproduction, both biological and social. Thus, marked fertility cultism among the Sambia or the Mundurucú is not reducible to male feelings of envy for women and their procreative abilities but is better regarded as an instantiation of "male potency and reproductive leverage." "By this reasoning, women's fertility becomes utterly secondary to [Sambia] men's inseminating power (first through fellatio and then through coitus)! Moreover, women never do bear men; they bear male infants who are converted into men through homosexual fellatio" (Biersack, Chapter 4, p. 80). This same phrasing can be made to fit with pre–Rubber Boom Mundurucú rituals by substituting "killing power" for "inseminating power," "head-hunting" for "fellatio," and "hunting" for "coitus." For both Sambia and Mundurucú, marked fertility cultism is a process of vehemently severing the ties between male children and their mothers so that these heterosexual bonds can be replaced by exclusively male-controlled ritual processes of biological and social reproduction. In short, fertility cultism asserts male potency and reproductive leverage over and above female fertility.

In unmarked fertility cultism, the symbolic weighting shifts from processes of cutting off (maternal bonds, enemy heads, and so forth) and replacing heterosexual ties to the building of enduring connections between parents and children and between men and women. Citing Marilyn Strathern's writings (1988) on the symbolism of gift exchange, Hugh-Jones (Chapter 11) suggests that the prevalence of male and female genitalia as symbols in myth and ritual relates to their tubular shape: penes, breasts, and umbilical cords ensure "the flow of life" through allowing passage of food, blood, semen, and other vital substances (p. 252). The umbilical cord serves as a unifying symbol for the first set of chants performed in Wakuénai childbirth rituals. In his chanted journey in search of an infant's mythic ancestors, the Wakuénai chant-owner travels along an internal, spiritual umbilical cord, connecting the newborn infant with its father and marking the transition from unborn fetus who receives nourishment inside its mother's womb to newly born child who consumes foods produced by its father. The mother's nurturing role is not denied so much as complemented and expanded to the social and economic connectedness between fathers and their children. It is significant that many spirit-names in these first chants refer to long-thin objects of the father's work activities: vines, palm fibers, leaves, and grasses, which men must cut from the forest in order to use them to tie things up, bind together housepoles, weave baskets, and make fish traps. Like these long-thin materials for binding and weaving things together, the chants themselves are long-thin strands of sound and meaning stretching across an invisible cord inside the infant's body and creating multiple connections between parents and children, husbands and wives, and mythic ancestors and human descendants.

The overriding importance of connectedness between fathers, mothers, and newly born infants is given additional expression in Wakuénai childbirth rituals through the second set of malikai chants. The naming of edible animal species over the pot of sacred food acknowledges the complementarity of the father's hunting and the mother's cooking of game meat. The protective powers of these chants are believed to pass from the mother to her newborn child via her breastmilk after she and her husband have consumed the pot of sacred food. Thus, while the first set of chants extends the mother's biological nurturing of the infant to the father's social role as provider of food, the second set of chants connects this social relationship back to the mother's post-uterine role as nourisher of the child during its first stage in the life cycle.

In initiation rituals, the Wakuénai construct a complementary pair of male-ness and femaleness as "places," or sung and chanted spirit-names. Females are the prime movers of Wakuénai society and cosmos. Like the primordial female of myth, women can only gain access to mythic ancestral power, or "reproduc-tive leverage," through moving away from and back to the center of the world. The onset of menstruation sets in motion the ritual process of searching for the girl's mythic ancestral spirits by musically going away from and back to the place of ancestral emergence. Initiation puts the young woman into a paradoxical place: she is initiated into the local fertility cult so that she can move away to her husband's village after a period of brideservice. Male initiation rituals construct the symbolic place of adult masculinity as a collective political and material process of exchange among exogamous phratries. Young adult men do not con-front an individual paradox but a collective dilemma of managing the simulta-neous inclusion and exclusion, or gain and loss, of their female blood kin through brideservice, exogamy, and virilocal residence.

In male and female initiation rituals, the construction of metaphorical con-nectedness is projected outwardly into the external world of peoples, commu-nities, species, and regions of the cosmos. The processes of exchange among ex-ogamous phratries require movements across social and cosmological boundaries that both sever and reconnect social ties for men and women alike. Male and female initiation rituals give active expression to the movements of foods, artifacts, labor, and persons across the cultural landscape, yet the ultimate purpose of all these collective exchanges is to reassert the social connection be-tween generations and between mythic ancestors and their human descendants via the celestial umbilical cord. This cosmic cord, musically sung-into-being at the beginning and ending of male and female initiation rituals, forms the pro-totypic connection that must never be severed: the sacred linkage between life-creating mythic ancestors and their human descendants, both living and dead.

NOTES

1. Bruce Knauft's regional comparative study (1993) of south coast New Guinea soci-eties demonstrates that a relatively high significance of "successful warriorhood to male prestige" tends to correlate positively with relatively high female status (1993, 107–108). This empirical finding contrasts with feminist theories, which have asserted a strong corre-lation between male dominance and warfare (e.g., Sanday 1981).

2. See Harrison (1990a) for an interesting study of clans as ideal taxonomic structures of names and titles among the Avatip of the Sepik Valley area and comparison with clans as corporate political units in the Highlands.

3. A similar pattern of chiefly political organization was widely reported among large Tupí-Guaraní chiefdoms of coastal Brazil in the early colonial period. In addition to chiefs who inherited their status through patrilineal descent, Tupí-Guaraní leaders included

councils of elders, or senior men who had distinguished themselves in warfare (Clastres 1995 [1975], ix). Also, the Tupí-Guaraní had prophets (*karai*) who led movements in search of the Land Without Evil. These religious leaders and movements provide an outstanding example of the antithetical relations between ritual hierarchy and secular sociopolitical organization in Amazonia (Clastres 1995 [1975]).

4. Symbolic linkages between ritual warfare and human fertility supported the relationship achieved through actual practices of capturing enemy children. Spirits of the dead (*kokeriwat*) were believed to help Mundurucú warriors in battles against outsiders, and these same spirits were believed to transform themselves into tiny birds that could enter the vaginas of Mundurucú women and make them pregnant (Murphy 1958, 20).

5. There are five mutually intelligible dialects of Wáku: Curripaco (or Áh-han), Curricarro, Óh-hon, Éh-hen, and Ñame. These dialect names refer to different terms for "yes" (áh-han, óh-hon, éh-hen) and "no" (currím, carrú).

6. Although the myths about Trickster are described as accounts about an earlier or previous time, this time is also continuous with human historical time, including the social present. See Hill and Wright (1988) for interpretations of how Trickster enters into indigenous interpretations of colonial and more recent historical periods.

7. Each kind of instrument has both anthropomorphic meanings, referring to parts of the primordial human being's body, and zoomorphic meanings (i.e., various bird and animal species). In addition, pairs of instruments are said to have gender meanings, with "female" instruments made longer and thicker than "male" ones.

8. Afternoon is also the only time of day when shamans (*malírri*) perform curing rituals, because the afternoon sun creates "shadow-spirits" in the eastern sky. There are extensive symbolic connections linking the mythic figure of Amáru, female initiation rituals, the underworld (*íyarudáti*) of recently deceased persons, and shamanistic curing rituals (Hill 1993).

9. This assertion implicitly evokes the mythic birth of Kuwái, the primordial human being, who was stuck inside his mother's (Amáru's) womb until Trickster and his brothers freed him to escape to life in the external world by making a birth canal.

FOUR

Reproducing Inequality:
The Gender Politics of Male Cults in the
Papua New Guinea Highlands and Amazonia

Aletta Biersack

Biersack examines some of the resemblances between Amazonian and Melanesian men's cults. She argues that the omatisia *ritual of the Paiela of the Papua New Guinea highlands must be understood as a political act of "reproduction" in which immature boys, born of women, are "reborn" as fertile adults. Women's fertility—their ability to give birth—is subordinated to the claimed "fertility" of men. By means of the ritual, boys could become husbands and, in turn, the source of their wives' fertility. In transforming infertile boys into fertile men, the ritual recreated, generation after generation, the asymmetries that mark the Paiela culture of gender.*

With its interest in body substances, procreation, and gender politics, Biersack's chapter invites juxtaposition with those of Bonnemère, Jolly, and Conklin, while its treatment of the Paiela men's cult resonates with issues raised in chapters by Gregor and Tuzin, and Hill.

If the dictates of biology were carefully adhered to, women might well find themselves still in the seat of power, for it is obvious that the biological functions of females are necessary for the continuity of any human group. No male occupation, however exalted, can compensate for the unique ability of the female to conceive, bear, and nurse the young of the species. This important contribution of women to group survival is . . . overlooked in myth. Why should this be so?

BAMBERGER 1974, 279

Arnold Van Gennep (1960 [1909]) and Victor Turner (1967) envisioned so-called rites of passage as a "time out of time" symbolically marking the transition from one status or state in the life cycle to another. "For every transition in the life cycle," Van Gennep wrote, "there are ceremonies whose essential purpose is to enable the individual to pass from one defined position to another which is equally well defined" (1960 [1909], 3). During the ritual, the participant is, as Turner's famous encapsulation expressed it, "betwixt and between," "interstructurally" suspended (Turner 1967, 93).

Turner's model assumes a rigid dichotomization of ritual and society. The one is symbolic, apolitical, and nonhierarchical (though initiators and initiates are stratified, a matter of some importance, as I shall show); the other is politico-jural and hierarchical (see the excellent discussion in Morris 1987, 246 ff. and the table on p. 255 in particular). Society is the sphere of politics and action and the condition of ritual, ritual its epiphenomenal reflector. That ritual itself might be a consequential arena of political action, a discursive instrument of social stratification, society's condition and not the other way around—these are possibilities that neither Turner nor Van Gennep—nor, for that matter, Durkheim (1965 [1915])—entertained (but see Lincoln 1989).

What strikes us today about Turner's and Van Gennep's writings are their silences. Despite the fact that for both, male initiation best exemplifies the more general type (Turner 1967, 95; Van Gennep 1960 [1909], Chapter 6), these texts think *status* but without thinking *gender* and its politics. My argument here is that so-called rites of passage—some of them, in any case—are arenas of social and political action in which gender hierarchies are engendered and reproduced (Rapp 1993). The distinctions implied by Van Gennep's and Turner's understandings of these rituals—between ritual and society and between ritual and politics—are therefore elided.

But why is ritual a structuring instrument, and what accounts for the gender politics of these rituals? While answers to the second question continue to be speculative and inconclusive, my answer to the first follows from the ritual analysis offered throughout and rests on two kinds of observations. First, the *omatisia* ritual traditionally performed by Paiela people of the Papua New Guinea highlands operated in tandem with related features of the traditional culture to appropriate women's reproductive capabilities (Biersack 1995; cf. Lindenbaum 1984, 1987; Tuzin 1995), and this appropriation must perforce be accomplished symbolically. (The reason myth might overlook women's contribution to reproduction [Bamberger 1974, 279] is that it is the purpose of myth to mask the facts of life with the fictions of culture.) Second, masculinized reproduction not only supplants but redeems the biological destiny of the species—death, which is associated with women rather than men (Bloch 1982; Bloch and Parry 1982)—and this redemption as well must be achieved symbolically.

The chapter begins with a discussion of the Paiela *omatisia* cult (Biersack 1982). The purposes of the growth procedures of the *omatisia* ritual are to assure a full head of hair, a mesomorphic body (the preferred masculine body style throughout the Papua New Guinea highlands), and, in general, the sexual allure that will enable the boys who participate in *omatisia* to court successfully. While I have never run across the well-known idiom "to make men," a phrase that summarizes the goals of male initiation in other parts of New Guinea (e.g., Jolly, this volume; Herdt 1982b), *omatisia* produces secondary sexual characteristics such as musculature, which transform boys into men, and to the extent that it does, *omatisia* makes men. In the important Sambia case, male cultic activity transforms boys into men as well (Herdt 1981, 1982b, 1984, 1987). Herdt's reporting on the multistage male initiation ritual of the Sambia provides ample cause for reconsidering the utility of the Van Gennep–Turner model. While Herdt himself does not explore this terrain, the present chapter takes up the challenge to do so in its middle section.

The similarities between some of the rituals of Amazonian and Papua New Guinea societies have been obvious for years. As if by diffusion, the two regions share ritual paraphernalia such as flutes and bullroarers as well as "sexual antagonism" and in particular men's hostility to and fear of women, and in both cases the rituals appear to be part and parcel of women's subjection. At the close I explore the parallels between the Papua New Guinea cases discussed herein—merely a sampling of the possible cases that could have been discussed (e.g., Tuzin 1995)—and select Amazonian cases. Because of the character and quality of the Amazonian reporting, I am led to consider (as neither Van Gennep nor Turner did) the metaphysical foundations of the gender politics of certain male cults (see Kelly 1993 for an insistence on the relevance of metaphysics in the Melanesian context). At the close, the essay shifts from a focus on society, glimpsed through sexual hierarchies and their production and reproduction, to religion, returning to the related matters of gender, death, and time in indigenous life philosophies (Biersack 1995, 1996, 1998, in press).

PLANTS, BAMBOO TUBES, AND THE SPIRIT WOMAN

A Paiela boy's growth is cultivated from the moment of birth in mundane ways such as feeding, including suckling, and, more exotically, magic. As a boy ages, he is removed from his mother's home and sent to live with his father, who teaches him techniques for magically growing his hair. Periodically he may go off into the forest to tap the sap of the *yuma* tree (Guttiferae, *Calophyllum* [Ingemann 1997, 85]), cook it, and apply it to his hair saying magical formulae (Biersack 1998). The boy actively seeks coldness, darkness, and invisibility—conditions of growth, so it is believed (Biersack 1998). In this he goes to some lengths, leaving his house very early in the morning, before others stir, and not returning until late at night, after the fire has died and people are sleeping. He conceals his hair by covering it with bark cloth. In applying sap to his hair, he moistens it, and moisture is also thought to be necessary for growth. Boys may soak their hair in the sap of the *yuma* tree several times before participating in *omatisia* retreats.

The Paiela cosmos divides between sky and earth. Earth subdivides between a midaltitude residential area and two bush zones, on either side. The upper bush zone is called *aiyandaka* or "beauty house" and is associated with youthfulness and all the conditions of growth. The lower bush zone is called *wapi* and is associated with the spirits of the dead as well as various dangerous spirits, and it is hot rather than cold and dry rather than moist. The alternation of the seasons, from wet (*kingi* or rain) to dry (*panyu*, which means sun time, summer, the hot, dry season), is a meteorological expression of the same

variation that the distinction between upper and lower bushes spatiotempo-
rally expresses (cf. S. Hugh-Jones 1979, 191–192).

The *omatisia* ritual takes place in the upper forest. Here adolescent males
assemble and perform magic under the ritual leadership of an older and experienced boy who, because he has not yet married, despite his relatively advanced years, is referred to as *kinambuli*, a term that signifies a person who is
old enough to have married and reproduced but who is still infertile. Travel-
ing with other boys their age or with older boys to the upper forest to plant
omatisia, boys participate in these procedures ideally multiple times before
marrying. The goal is to grow the body and to transform a boy into a sexually alluring male. While I have collected several accounts of this ritual from
knowledgeable males, I restrict myself here to summarizing the information
collected in 1993 and again in 1995 from Luke, son of Botane, who went on
14 different occasions to plant *omatisia*. On ten of these trips, he was the leader
and spellmaster of his group.

The residential area (*andaka*, "inside" or "at home") is where married men
and women live and where coitus and sexual reproduction occur. In repairing
to the upper forest, the boys withdraw from the zone occupied by mature,
married parents and enter a pure and virginal realm "where women-men do
not go" (*wanda-akali na pene nga*). It is important that no subject domiciled in
the residential area witness this journey. Men, women, pigs, and dogs, all of
whom live in the residential area and all of whom may have experienced disgusting and unseemly things, are ipso facto contaminated, and their gaze is
contaminating. As defiled and defiling seers, they should not look upon the
boys while in seclusion.

To prevent being seen, the boys not only retire to the upper reaches of the
forest but they do their cooking at night, so that residents below will not detect the smoke and discover where they are. Precautions are also taken to prevent anyone from the residential area seeing the food that the boys eat. While
staying at the *omatisia* house, the boys eat "unseen sweet potatoes" (*ulia na andene*). These tubers are harvested late at night and carried under cover of night
to the *omatisia* house, where they will be consumed during the ritual performance proper. In contrast, "seen sweet potatoes" (*ulia andene*) are carried the first
night of the retreat to a house that marks the boundary between the residential area and the upper forest, the *palipali* house. Here they are consumed the
first night, as the boys overnight on their way to the *omatisia* house, and again
on the way back. The security of the "seen sweet potatoes," harvested late in
the afternoon, when married people are still about, has been compromised
and their purity cannot be guaranteed.

Other precautions are taken to preserve the pristine quality of the ritual site.
Marking the boundary between the settlement and the forest, the *palipali* house is
not entirely pure. As they travel from this threshhold house to the *omatisia* house,
the boys are eager to purge themselves and the ritual site proper of any remain-

ing contaminants, and they say a spell (an *anda wai* spell) addressing a spirit woman who may be referred to as both the *omatisia* woman (*omatisia wanda*) and *uiyapa* woman (*uiyapa wanda*) . *Omatisia* refers to the bog iris that the boys plant to grow their hair, and *uiyapa* refers to the bamboo tubes that the boys place in the swamp to grow their skin. The *uiyapa* woman "sits" in the bamboo tubes, and the spirit woman is told in this spell to sit "behind a closed door" (*tuma tumane nga pete pe*)—in her sealed bamboo tube, her private house, that is—lest someone other than the boy who builds and repairs her bark houses for her (and who is, as I shall explain, her ritual husband) see her. Similar precautions are taken as the boys return at the end of the ritual period to the residential area. Before leaving the threshhold house, the boys decorate with the adornments the upper forest affords: leaves, nuts, reeds, marsupial furs, and flowers. To preserve the purity of these decorations and the boys themselves, the spellmaster walks out in front of the boys saying another *anda wai* spell, which tells men, women, dogs, and pigs, "all those who are thin and dirty" (and, by implication, since emaciation is a sign of pollution, sexually reproducing adults), to stand aside and avert their gaze. They should not look upon the boys: "I want to gouge out your eyes," and so on.

The ritual centers on the manipulation of two sets of objects. The one, the *omatisia* (literally "wig wood"), represents the head hair and is planted by all ritual participants; the other, *uiyapa*, is planted by boys who have already attended the ritual at least once. The boys are age-stratified. "Those who have put [*omatisia*] before" (*ba yo atene*) pass on plants and bamboo tubes as well as knowledge to "newcomers" (*wene yo atene*). The term "those who have put before" suggests seniority and experience. The age hierarchy that Godelier (1986), among others, notes as operating in initiation rituals operates here as well.

From the second visit to the *omatisia* house onward, a boy receives a fresh batch of bamboo tubes. He must place these in the swamp and group and house them; he must also repair the bark houses he made on his prior visit to the ritual site. The boys themselves must be purified before they can look upon the bamboo tubes where the spirit woman is domiciled. Every boy is "born of woman" (*wanda mane mandene*) and in that has seen unspeakable things; as a resident of the settlement below, the boy has perhaps seen genitalia that an awkward movement of apron or skirt has exposed or even a wayward drop of menstrual blood. Before looking upon these tubes, the boys must wash their eyes in running water (cf. Meggitt 1964) as the leader addresses the spirit woman, telling her to "come and make the boy good," to make the various parts of the body he mentions in his spell as strong as a tree branch or a wild pandanus tree. After the eyes are washed, each boy cleanses his inner body by swallowing some of the spring water he has used to wash his eyes, and he also spits some of the water out as the leader says a spell over him.

The tubes are divided into two lots: the "long" (*lu*) tubes are "our skin tubes" (*nanimana umbuaini pene*) in the sense that they are associated with the health and scale of the boys' skin. The single "short" (*topaki*) tube is where the spirit woman, sitting under the bark roof and encircled by bark walls, "sits." The tubes are grouped and housed using the *makua* bark (*Cunoniaceae, Schizomeria* sp. [Ingemann 1997, 44]). To prepare the bark for cutting, the various points of incision are marked on the bark with a pearl shell as the cult leader says a spell in which the boys are addressed as "wealthy men one and all" (*akali amango pitakana*). The bark is then cut using a sharp stone. The bamboo tubes given to older participants are cut the same way. A mark is first made with a pearl shell, and then the tubes are cut with a sharp stone as the spell invoking "wealthy men one and all" is said. The bark symbolizes the skin of the boys and the wealth that the boys will accumulate. Wealth "comes to the skin," meaning that it becomes integral to a person's reputation and image. The bark is used to encircle the various tubes each boy has and also to fashion a roof for them.

During the boy's absence, water will have seeped into the tubes. This water, provided it is clear, will be poured into the new tubes that have been cut and magically prepared by the ritual leader. The boy looks in the single short tube to see whether it contains a spider web and whether the water is clear. The spider web and discoloration of the water indicate that the spirit woman is menstruating and that the tube and its water are contaminated; this water should not be poured into the new tubes that the spellman has supplied. If the water in the short tube is fresh and there is no spiderweb in it, then the water from the old short tube is poured into the new short tube, which the spellman magically prepares for the old-timers.

Over the years the boy accumulates as many batches of bamboo tubes as the times he has participated in the ritual. If he wishes, a boy may pass on one or more of these batches to a newcomer. A boy receives his bamboo tubes from more senior participants in the ritual, either the spellman or another boy who has attended the *omatisia* enough times to have accumulated excess bamboo tubes. In receiving the bamboo, the boy pays the donor initially with cowrie shells and later, when he has returned home, with a pig. The spirit woman is thought to move with the bamboo tube and against the cowrie shells and the pig. The spirit woman is considered to be a "rich woman," and through her the boy hopes to accumulate wealth. In the course of purchasing the bamboo tubes and/or bog iris, the cult leader says a spell that tells the spirit woman to "get pearl shell and go to the boy," to make the boy rich. As the source of riches, she is also the source of bridewealth, which the boy must accumulate if he is to marry.

Those boys who are attending the ritual for the first time are not given bamboo tubes but are given bog iris to plant and to say spells over. These plants symbolize their hair. Newcomers receive their plants from participants, the spellman, or the old-timers. As they receive the plants, a spell is said to grow various body parts: the hair, the eyes, the shoulders. At the same time, the names of various rivers associated with the spirit woman are said. The boy's body is also the object of the spell that is said when, upon return trips, a boy weeds his bed of bog iris, saying magic that is designed to make the boy handsome, particularly when he travels to a dance or a pig feast.

> When I go to a pig kill, the people there should say that I am handsome.
>
> When I dance, the people at the dance should say that I am handsome.
>
> When I go on a long journey, the people where I am going should say that I am handsome.
>
> My hair should be beautiful.
>
> My eyes should be beautiful.
>
> My shoulders should be beautiful.

The boy may rub the leaves of the *omatisia* plant over his skin to make it grow.

A TALE OF THREE WOMEN: RITUAL, MARRIAGE, AND THE APPROPRIATION OF WOMEN'S FERTILITY

Skin and hair are viewed as sexual bait, and the purpose of all of the procedures is to make the boy handsome and wealthy enough to marry. The boy begins to court at some time in the middle of his participation in the *omatisia* ritual. When the boy journeys to a homicide compensation payment or to a pig feast or bridewealth distribution or to a courting party, as the spell just recounted imagines his doing, he should be irresistibly attractive, so much so that the girls attending the event fight over him. This is a male fantasy about the outcome of *omatisia* that I have heard more than once. Luke, the source of this information and still a handsome man with a full head of hair despite his 80-odd years, prides himself on his good looks and continued virility and attributes his comparative youthfulness to his diligence as an *omatisia* participant. To this day, when he reminisces about the heroic journeys he took in his youth, he is sure to imply that he made many conquests along the way.

The possibility of marriage is very much on a participant's mind. The plants and bamboo tubes are tended during the day, but at night the boys sit inside the *omatisia* house and practice their spells. Among the various spells that are said, "woman *kale*" magic appears to be the most popular. The purpose of saying this magic is to render one's girlfriend lovesick. The imagery of the most substantial woman *kale* spell I have collected is martial. The boy takes the bone of a flying fox and jabs a leaf (representing the girl's skin), telling the girl of his choice to say that her heart is "shot [toward him]," that she is smitten.

The goal of the ritual, to beautify the boy so that courting females will find him attractive, creates an instrumental bridge between the ritual and marriage. This bridge is embodied in the person of the spirit woman, who is like a wife but who is not a "real wife" (*wanda enekeya*). She is a "bamboo wife" (*uiyapa wetene*), the bamboo wife of each boy in whose bamboo tubes she "sits."

(The verb "to sit" is an idiom of domesticity.) In this regard, the most important spell is said when the boy receives his bamboo tubes. It is called the *uiyapa kimbu* spell. The word *kimbu* suggests continuation or extension by means of reiteration. To avenge a death, for example, is called "to strike or hit *kimbu*" (*kimbu peya*) and refers to the seriality of homicide under the payback system. The idea appears to be that the spirit woman circulates among the boys, passing from one to the other. The older boy who gives the bamboo tube to the younger boy is giving his ritual wife to the boy. "I give this woman, my wife, to you; you give me a pig and cowrie shells." The transfer of the spirit wife creates a quasi-leviratic relationship between the spirit woman and the various boys participating in the ritual.

The source of the boy's glamour—as heightened by the various and sundry decorations he will wear when he attends dancing parties (*mali*) and courts—is his spirit wife. When the boy displays himself for courtship purposes, those judging him in the audience should say, "The spirit woman sits alive." In this, the spirit woman takes on the tasks of a wife. Wives perform magic when they menstruate to protect their husband's skin, and they observe menstrual taboos toward the same end (Biersack 1987, 1995). The spirit woman is also quasi-uxorial in being the source of the boy's wealth. A wife co-owns pigs with her husband, and her kinspeople ideally share wealth with him. Through a wife and her labor and kin, a man accumulates the wealth that will allow him to garner prestige in the wider community. The spirit woman is a "wealthy" woman. When the bamboo tubes and the bark that will ring them are cut, they are first etched with a pearl-shell valuable, as the spellman says the spell that begins "wealthy men one and all." When she "goes" to the boy (together with the bamboo tubes), the spirit woman brings with her this same symbol of affluence: a pearl shell.

While the similarities between the spirit woman and the boy's eventual wife are easy to find, so are the differences. Of these the most important is that, whereas the boy will bear children through his real wife, his ritual wife remains chaste and infertile. Bridewealth buys a woman's womb. Wives are obliged through the bridewealth to become mothers. Although the spirit woman cultivates her ritual husband's beauty, this task is relatively trivial. The principal uxorial duty is to reproduce.[1] When a man gives bridewealth for a real woman, he appropriates the fruit of her womb. To give bridewealth is to "fence" a woman. A "fenced" woman is one who has been placed "in the middle of the garden" as its "sweet potato seed." This metaphorical language or *kokoli* uses the woman's fertility as a gardener as a symbol of her fertility as a mother. The "fencing" metaphor is masculine in its connotations, a reference to the fact that, while wives plant and weed gardens, husbands clear and fence them. The fencing metaphor refers to the constraint that the woman is placed under by the bridewealth payment, the obligation to reproduce as a fulfillment of conjugal duty. A man's right to make his wife pregnant is established with the prestation of bridewealth, which not only constrains his bride to conceive and "give-carrying" (*mandu mai*) children to him but makes the husband and his kin relatives of his children. Men assemble bridewealth with the assistance of their kin, and Paiela marriage is inherently a collective, masculine project. In brief, through the way in which men strategically orchestrate marriage, networks are organized, maintained, and transformed. In this project, women are the indispensable helpmates but not the main instigators. As a "fenced" wife, a woman bears children who are strategically positioned within the networks that her husband and his male colleagues shape. Through marriage men organize sexual reproduction. Despite their womblessness, then, men dominate in the reproductive sphere (Biersack 1995; see Ginsburg and Rapp 1991; Rapp 1993). They do so, if you will, by appropriating women's fertility (cf. Lindenbaum 1984, 1987), a political fact that the "fencing" metaphor neatly captures. Paiela "conception theory" employs a related image of constraint to the same effect. With ejaculation, a man's semen "wraps around" the woman's menstrual blood, keeping it from coming outside, and the woman conceives. By implication, without the man's intervention the woman would remain infertile; she would menstruate rather than conceive. Of course, this is true, but it is also true that a man's semen remains sterile without a woman's womb, a point that Paiela conception theory could have emphasized had its ideology been matriarchal rather than patriarchal.

The prelude to a man's appropriation of his wife's fertility is a related act of appropriation that occurs in the *omatisia* ritual itself. And here it is necessary to talk about the third woman in this tale: the mother. While the boy attends *omatisia*, his mother observes certain taboos on the boy's behalf—for example, burying the peelings of the sweet potatoes she has eaten to enhance the efficacy of the ritual (cf. Bonnemère, this volume). The mother's role as guardian and nurturer of the boy will soon end. The mother bore him, breast-fed and otherwise nourished him, and she probably also said growth magic over him. The skin that the boy cultivates through the assistance of the spirit woman is maternal, not only in the sense that mothers rather than fathers give birth but also because Paielas say that, whereas bone is paternal, blood is maternal. Through the ritual the boy transforms himself, mother-born, into a man who is wife-born, born by his ritual wife. The boys, ritual husbands to the spirit woman, marry through the sponsorship of older ritual participants, those who have been to the ritual before, who have already received their bamboo tubes and spirit wife, and who are, as a result, able to pass these on to other boys. In receiving the spirit wife, a boy receives a helpmate who will refashion him, son of a mother, into a husband of sorts, a ritual husband. Since the spirit wife comes to the boy through older males, maternal power is ultimately supplanted with the power of these males and uxorial power is ultimately subjugated to the power of these same males, who circulate the spirit woman among their protégés. Through the spirit woman and the older boys who circulate her, the participant re-reproduces himself, transforming himself from son to husband. The boy-husband is thus enclosed within a parthenogenetic loop generated in the asymmetric relationship between older and younger boys (cf. Godelier 1986 and the analysis in Kelly 1993, 157–174; on "pseudo-procreation rites," see Hiatt 1971; see also Conklin and Tuzin 1995). Insofar as the boy is re-reproduced as the offspring of patriarchs, the ritual concerns the reproduction of male domination.[2]

Participation in *omatisia* stops once a boy's beard is fully grown and his plans to marry have crystallized. Having left the heterosexual residential area, heartland of sexual reproduction, to engage in homosocial bonding, the boy returns for good to the residential area to take up a new life, no longer a son but a husband. Marriage "defiles" the plants, rendering them impotent, and the boy who wants to marry uproots his plants and discards them or gives them to a newcomer. A boy knows that he is ready to marry if a frog appears near his plants or bamboo tubes or if a certain bird soars overhead. These are harbingers of conjugal bliss, and, if the boy has found someone he wants to marry, their appearance makes him joyful. One boy, keen to marry his heart-throb, was so happy to see the frog that he reportedly picked it up and smothered it with kisses. He would now leave the spirit woman, a moment of sadness in any boy's life, and marry a "real woman" (*wanda enekeya*), a "real woman in the residential area" (*enekeya andaka wanda*). The *omatisia* ritual does more than "make men." It makes *husbands*, for the skin that the spirit wife grows for her ritual husband is the sexual bait that the boy will very self-consciously flaunt every time he decorates and courts (cf. Kelly 1993, 167). Marriage and childbearing promote the male to full patriarchal power, which is by and large the power of the inseminator. In marriage, wombs flow against pigs in ways that men largely control; they do so by sponsoring one another's marriages and positioning women *among themselves*, paralleling the way that they position the spirit woman among themselves in the *omatisia* ritual.[3]

SAMBIA RESONANCES AND BEYOND

One of the more dramatic moments of the series of Sambia initiation rituals that Herdt delineates occurs at the very beginning, when the boy is wrenched away from his mother (1982b, 68, 1987, 133–138). The moment is filled with menace and misogyny.

> For several minutes . . . the initiates are paraded around the decorated dance-ground. . . . This public display is the last occasion on which women can study the boys for years to come. . . .
>
> The moment the boys are out of sight, dramatic events unfold. The bloodied fern leaves (collected from the nose-bleeding ritual) are retrieved by [one of the ritual elders] from his string bag. . . . [He] holds up a handful of the leaves, silently flaunting them. . . . He says the men had to "kill" the boys to make them into men. Suddenly, without warning, two men run over to a woman seated on the edge of

the danceground. She is one of the boys' mothers. They grab hold of her and violently force some of the bloodied leaves down her throat. She is cursed and castigated and pushed away. They frantically criticize the other women too for "saying bad things" to their sons, thus stunting their growth. . . . Another younger man hysterically charges into a group of women. He holds more bloody leaves, and with bow and arrows in hand he curses the women and chases them. (1987, 151–152)

This moment must not be read blandly and apolitically, as an instance of a "rite of separation" (Van Gennep 1960 [1909]), but against the backdrop of Sambia male fears of women (e.g., Herdt 1981, 174, 1987, 144) and Sambia gender asymmetries. Indeed, the pattern others have glimpsed in male initiation—of men refashioning women's children as their own—is unmistakable here. When Sambia initiates are undergoing certain ordeals, their mothers "are told sarcastically that their sons will be killed in order to be reborn as 'men'" (Herdt 1987, 141), and it is the blood of their "slaughtered" sons that the mothers in the above scene are forced to eat. Notice that the boys are dead specifically as women's children and that they are reborn specifically (if the sarcasm is to be credited) as male-spawned men. These males, born of other males, are semen donors (initially homosexual but later heterosexual) and ultimately fathers as a result of the "ritualized masculinization" (Herdt 1982b, 74) that is Herdt's theme. Hence, the flutes displace the mother's breast, and same-sex relationships between older and younger boys displace the cross-sex relationship between mother and son, specifically within a project of the making of male offspring. The flutes, moreover, are likened to the babies that women bear (Herdt 1987, 153).

One could argue that the ritual evidences not so much male "envy" of women and their procreative capabilities, a theme most closely associated with Bruno Bettelheim's *Symbolic Wounds* (see Gregor 1985, Chapter 10), as it does *male potency* and *reproductive leverage*. Through this leverage, men subordinate women and the offspring of their bodies as their own creatures. During the fifth stage of the Sambia initiation sequence, the boy, now husband, is his wife's fellator; and the semen the boy obtains through male-male transfer eventually becomes the boy's wife's breast milk (Herdt 1981, 179). Hence, in the ritual symbolism there is a systematic conflation of semen and breast milk, the penis and the breast (Herdt 1981, 234–235; 1982b; 1987, 150), and "the act of feeding/inseminating is equivalent to the verbal category *monjapi'u,* male nursing" (Herdt 1984, 184; see also Herdt 1981, 234–235). Similarly, while women are thought to begin to menstruate on their own (Herdt 1984, 179 ff.),[4] they remain infertile without coitus; it is the male rather than the female, by this reasoning, who is the cause of conception. Despite the role the mother plays in the growth of the child as nurturer, this role is ultimately derivative, for the fetus "occurs through semen accumulation in the mother's womb" (p. 181), and the mother's breast milk originates in the father's oral inseminations. For male children, moreover, growth after weaning is attributed to homosexual fellatio. "Men believe that postmarital oral sexual contacts in cases of marriage before menarche provide a young wife's body with semen to stimulate the final 'growth' changes necessary for childbearing" (p. 182). Semen, it appears, is the all-purpose food—indeed, the *food-producing* food. Sambia men "do not recognize conception as such; instead, coitus simply builds up the fetus until birth occurs" (p. 195). By this reasoning, women's fertility becomes utterly secondary to men's inseminating power (first through fellatio and then through coitus)! Moreover, women never do bear men; they bear male infants who are converted into men through homosexual fellatio. Thus, the "masculine viewpoint tends to deride femaleness *while also denying its procreative functions*" (Herdt 1981, 193; emphasis added). A boy cannot become a man except insofar as he reproduces, and for that he requires semen: "procreation defines full adulthood for men and women" and "childless adults are not perceived as full persons" (Herdt 1984, 181). Among the Sambia, an idiom of this masculinist appropriation of female fertility is the horticultural idiom I know well from Paielas. "In men's discourse, a woman's body is likened to a garden in which her husband implants a seed that germinates in the womb" (p. 195).

Of course, a Sambia male becomes a reproducer specifically as a *pater*, and to be a *pater* he must marry. Indeed, marriage is embedded within the ritual cycle, and the entire sequel of rituals has as its end product and apparent purpose the production of legitimately fertile adults. The first two stages of the ritual guarantee (through male insemination) the boy's fertility; the third stage enables him to pass this fertility on to a younger boy; the fourth involves a marriage ceremony; the fifth occurs after the bride's menarche, when she herself becomes fertile (Herdt 1987, 108); and the sixth occurs when the male has had his first child. Any gender politics of the initiation ritual are therefore inseparable from the gender politics of Sambia marriage and reproduction. The woman-born boy becomes the progeny of the bachelors who inseminate him. Despite the fact that heterosexual reproduction is one of the goals of these Sambia rituals, the rituals' ultimate achievement is the subordination of one mode of reproduction—heterosexual, coital, and patently wombal—to another mode of reproduction—homosocial (and, in the Sambia and other cases, homosexual) and phallic. This is accomplished by enclosing the one mode within a patriarchal circuit of semen and wombs, the other mode. Through this enclosure men are "made" specifically as the products of patriarchal power and themselves as patriarchs; they are reborn as the sons of patriarchs and themselves as patriarchs, within a lineage of hegemonic masculinity; and the status of husband and father is therefore inextricable from the gender politics that makes men as husbands and fathers superior to their female collaborators, the very sources of their own fecundity.

This is more generally the case. In societies practicing homosexuality in the form of male-male semen transfers, marriage and ritual appear to be phases of a single loop in which wombs and semen circulate (see especially Kelly 1993, 454 ff.), presumably for the purpose of reproduction.

> A most striking aspect of social organization in societies with ritualized male homosexuality concerns the overlap between marriage and homosexual relationships. . . . The pattern of marriage in most cases is that of sister exchange, with no payment of bride-price. . . .
>
> Social relationships in these societies are characterized, then, by a kind of double affinity, by the return of a woman from a previously defined affinal group. This duplicated affinity is further heightened by semen transactions between actual or potential brothers-in-law. The rules of marriage and homosexuality thus combine in mutual support. (Lindenbaum 1984, 343–344; see also Lindenbaum 1987, 227–233)

In some cases—the Etoro and probably also the Sambia—"the ideal inseminator is a boy's sister's husband" (Lindenbaum 1984, 344). Thus, not only do the married sister and the boy have the same sexual partner, an observation first made by Kelly (1977, 181–183), but, since the sister's husband will presumably return a woman, the process of transforming a nonreproductive into a reproductive male first through male insemination and then through marriage is, if not in the hands of the same male, then in the hands of the same *class* of male—that is, of bride donor—a fact that produces an interweaving of heterosexual and homosexual rights (Lindenbaum 1984, 345). Over the course of this process, woman-born males become born of men and women's fertility is appropriated by men (Lindenbaum 1984, 1987).[5]

Lindenbaum draws a similar lesson with respect to certain eastern highlands societies, closer in type to Paiela society in being normatively heterosexual and in establishing conjugal relations with bridewealth rather than brideservice, among other similarities. However, even in these, as in the Paiela case, women's sons are ritually refashioned as the offspring of patriarchs. As in certain "homosexual" communities, "men lay ritual claim to the powers of female reproduction, a mystification of female 'reproductive' labor" (Lindenbaum 1987, 239).[6]

RITUAL AND THE POLITICS OF REPRODUCTION

Since this act of appropriation—documented for the Paiela, Sambia, and other so-called homosexual societies, as well as for some eastern highlands societies and the Arapesh (Tuzin 1995)—occurs ritually, the rituals that accomplish it could be called rites of appropriation. This returns us to the matter of "rites of passage" discussed at the outset.

The hallmark of the liminal period, as Turner characterizes it, is its complex negativity. Liminal personae are "no longer classified and not yet classified" (1967, 96), hence the liminal period's symbolism of death and rebirth. Participants are, on the one hand, symbolically dead and, on the other, awaiting rebirth, and all ritual symbolism expresses the participants' interstitiality. Poised betwixt and between at the structural way station that is the ritual, participants are sociologically nonexistent. The image is that of a chrysalis: the moth disappears from view—becomes, as all liminal people are, invisible (ibid.)—but only to emerge a butterfly (see Lincoln 1991; also, Bonnemère 1996, 344–352, and this volume).

Viewing the ritual as a "rite of passage" suggests some interpretations of the ritual's symbolism but not others. For example, reading the death-and-rebirth symbolism of the ritual as a reflection of liminality would mask any gender politics of reproduction that might underlie the ritual: the fact that women-born men are being transformed into patriarchal offspring. Herdt himself interprets the act of violence recounted at length above—the plunging of bloodied leaves down the throat of the initiate's mother as the boy is dragged away crying—as a classic rite of separation (see Herdt 1987, 117). But taking the Sambia boy away from his mother is more than a rite of separation: it is a dramatization of the ritual's reproductive politics, and it is itself a political act (see Bamberger 1974, 277).[7]

To the extent that Turner's death-and-rebirth scenario can be shown to signify not a time-out-of-time liminality but an appropriation of women's fecundity within an encompassing patriarchal politics of reproduction, ritual and marriage are joined in a complex, transgenerational system of reproductive practices and their gender politics. Women's fecundity is appropriated in the only way it can be appropriated: through myth, rite, and symbol (see Bamberger 1974; Gillison 1993; Tuzin 1995). Male initiation and like rituals are political arenas of patriarchal praxis in which patriarchy parthenogenetically reproduces itself. The ultimate referent of these Sambia rites is not the life cycle at all but the patriarchal system, which the rites do not reflect so much as reproduce—hence, as Turner himself observed, the characteristic oligarchic structure of male initiations. "Between instructors and neophytes there is often complete authority and complete submission. . . . The authority of the elders over the neophytes . . . is in a sense the personification of the self-evident authority of tradition. The authority of the elders is absolute, because it represents the absolute, the axiomatic values of society. . . . The essence of the complete obedience of the neophytes is to submit to the elders but only in so far as they are in charge, so to speak, of the common good and represent in their persons the total community" (1967, 99–100). Sambia and their male initiations are as artificial as any "new reproductive technology" (Ginsburg and Rapp 1991, M. Strathern 1992a); they are, as Herdt points out, *fantastical.*

REPRODUCTIVE REGIMES

In another era, "alliance" theorists jousted with "descent" theorists over competing conceptualizations of social organization. The one envisioned marriage as organizationally crucial. The other conjured an equally Durkheimian system of superordinate and self-perpetuating groups in terms of descent principles alone (Barnes 1970). Though both frameworks emphasized the continuity of groups and their relations, neither framework problematized reproduction, which was envisioned either as a structural effect, explicable in terms of detemporalized and objective organizational "principles," or as a natural process that fell beyond the bounds of ethnographic inquiry. As Evans-Pritchard stated in the famous closing pages of *The Nuer,* "By social structure we mean relations between groups which have a high degree of consistency and constancy. The groups remain the same irrespective of their specific content of individuals at any particular moment, so that generation after generation of people pass through them. Men are born into them, or enter into them later in life, and move out of them at death; the structure endures. In this definition of structure the family is not considered a structural group, because families have no consistent and constant interrelations as groups and they disappear at the death of their members" (1940, 262). For Lévi-Strauss, marriage linked groups, and in "elementary structures of kinship" these linkages were replicated generation after generation through the operation of prescriptive rules of marriage—if not in reality, then in the model of reality (Lévi-Strauss 1969a, xxx–xxxv). While consanguinity was a "natural fact," alliance was a "cultural fact" (p. 30).

In *Elementary Structures of Kinship* and *The Nuer,* French and British structuralism overlooked the body, sex, gender, and reproduction. In Lévi-Strauss's models women circulate as tokens and as gifts, *not as wombs.* His theory of "elementary structures" is a tale of *two* women, the sister and the wife, not the crucial *third* figure, the mother. The same is true of "British structuralism," which defined familial ties, particularly the mother-child bond, as extracultural, biological, and psychological at its root. In this paradigm, while politico-jural relations of descent were socially constructed, the "domestic domain was . . . seen to deal with reproduction as a *biological* necessity" and "consanguineal relations as such indicated a virtual *fact of nature,* a universalism in human arrangements" (M. Strathern 1992a, 102 [emphasis added]; see also Barnes 1970 and Collier and Yanagisako 1987). Yet it is just those factors that British and French structuralisms eclipse—sexuality, gender, and the body—that Melanesianists have been compelled, through the very character of the worlds they study, to focus upon (see Brown and Buchbinder 1976; Herdt 1982b; Knauft 1999; and M. Strathern 1988, among others). Indeed, much of the Melanesian materials indicates the biological ambitions of initiation rituals, the fact that their purpose in the first instance is to cultivate the body (Herdt 1982b, 1984; Kelly 1993, 157–174; Knauft 1999; Lutkehaus 1995a).

Bourdieu's *Outline of a Theory of Practice* is famous for its call to understand reciprocity as a practical achievement rather than as an "instantiation" of a prescription, as strategy rather than as structure (1977, Chapter 1). Surely the same can be said of reproduction. Rites such as *omatisia* or Sambia male initiation—

indeed, the entire literature on substances and their generation and flow in Melanesia as well as the now burgeoning literature on the Melanesian body (e.g., Biersack 1996; Knauft 1999; A. Strathern 1996; M. Strathern 1988)— suggest that reproduction, variable and fantastical, must be understood, at least in part, as a human achievement. Its various technologies include bamboo tubes, flutes, magically treated plants, and other extraordinary and powerful ritual paraphernalia, as well as semen and menstrual blood. These technologies and practices are metaphysically grounded and infused with ultimate meaning concerning life and death, sex and regeneration (Biersack 1995, in press; Buchbinder and Rappaport 1976; Kelly 1993; see also Bloch 1982, 1986). While marriage and descent are obviously crucial to the organizational side of sexual reproduction—accounting for who copulates with whom and how newborns are positioned in grids and networks—they do not exhaust the study of reproduction as a cultural and historical phenomenon. Only consideration of the construction of the body and sexuality in both the semiotic or discursive (e.g., Laqueur 1990; Vance 1991) and the nondiscursive meanings of the word *construction* (Foucault 1980, 1988; Dreyfus and Rabinow 1982, Chapters 6–8), in regard to "a discipline of the body supported by a discourse on the male and female body" (Ariss 1992, 143), can.

Whether or not the incest taboo is universal (Lévi-Strauss 1969b), every society regulates reproduction. It does so through sexual and gender norms and ideologies and through marriage, which legitimates reproduction. To regulate reproduction is to regulate kinship as well, which flows from heterosexual reproduction (Schneider 1980) and which rests upon rules governing whether kinspeople are or are not marriageable, and if marriageable which ones, even where there is brother-sister incest. Kinship is generated not through males and females but through paters and maters and depends upon the institutionalization of fertility that is marriage.

Focusing on reproduction and its organization and construction (in the various meanings of that word) directs our attention in novel ways, beyond an exclusive concern with descent or alliance, social organization or culture/symbol/meaning, society or ritual, to a multifaceted and heterogeneous study of what I shall call reproductive regimes. Such regimes center on the body as a natural and social reality and on the institutions, ideologies, cosmologies, and practices that account for its construction, circulation, and maintenance. As a result, sex-gender and age differentials as well as sex-gender politics and symbols become integral to the study of institutions such as kinship, marriage, and descent (see Collier and Yanagisako 1987; Ortner and Whitehead 1981; Peletz 1995; Rosaldo and Lamphere 1974; M. Strathern 1988; and Yanagisako and Delaney 1995).

A reproductive regime is a type of "nature regime" in Escobar's sense of that term: "regimes of articulation of the historical and the biological" (1999, 5), that is, culture and nature. Economistic reasoning presumes the priority of those institutional arrangements that serve the body as a producer and consumer. Reproduction and sexuality have the same *biological priority* that production and consumption have, for they, too, bear upon the body as a material entity; but they lead us beyond economics narrowly construed toward a *new* sociology, one that is sensitive to gender systems and their conceits, artifices, and politics; to society's fractures and historicity; and to nature-human articulations in all their cultural and historical variety. And they lead us back to economics itself, now "embedded," as the substantivists liked to say, in society, back to a concern with the material conditions of human existence, albeit without reductionism. Studying reproductive regimes requires the analytical strategies and insights of a range of masters, old and new: Victor Turner, but also Foucault (1988); Claude Lévi-Strauss, but also Geertz (1973) and Rubin (1975); E. E. Evans-Pritchard and Meyer Fortes, but also Collier and Yanagisako (1987) and M. Strathern (1988).

TOWARD A NEW *MYTHOLOGIQUES*

The Amazonian literature has been heavily influenced by Lévi-Strauss: his emphasis on the incest taboo, marriage, and alliance (Reichel-Dolmatoff 1971; Rivière 1969), his *Mythologiques* (S. Hugh-Jones 1979; C. Hugh-Jones 1979), and, most recently, his notion of "house societies" (Carsten and S. Hugh-Jones 1995). The literature on the Papua New Guinea highlands has a different root: British structuralism, with its focus upon descent. For all their differences, both frameworks are androcentric, gender-blind, and substantially Durkheimian in inspiration, and neither framework problematizes reproduction. To the extent that male initiation in the Amazonian region can be shown to rest upon a politics of reproduction like the gender politics uncovered in Melanesia, it would be possible to supplant these divergent frameworks with a reproduction-centered one capable of exposing real similarities and not just differences between the two regions. The similarities between Amazonian and Melanesian material, particularly in regard to male initiation, have long been noted (Bamberger 1974; Hays 1988), and it is relatively easy to demonstrate a politics of reproduction underlying them. Here I will examine the Yurupari cult practiced among the Barasana of Colombia, as described in Christine and Stephen Hugh-Jones's ethnographic analyses, which strongly evoke materials to be found in the Melanesian literature.

The ritual Stephen Hugh-Jones, in particular, examines is called *He wi* ("*He* House"), an initiation ritual involving boy initiates, young initiated males, and elders (C. Hugh-Jones 1979, 146, 147), and excluding women. The initiates are taken from their mothers and placed in a society of adult males. These men control flutes and trumpets, representatives of the ancestors, and the beeswax gourd, representative of an ancestress named *Romi Kumu*. "The flutes have a phallic aspect . . . and by using them the boys are opening their own penises"

(p. 147). However phallic, the Barasana flutes are also maternal, much like Sambia flutes. "Indians say that the instruments are like a female breast which adopts the participants like new-born babies" (ibid.). Not only is the "initiates' potential role in sexual reproduction" stressed in the ritual (ibid.) but the initiates are themselves reborn. They "are explicitly compared to newborn babies and . . . they must remain in a foetal position throughout the rite" (S. Hugh-Jones 1979, 182). Their rebirth recapitulates the rebirth of forefathers and is thus a rebirth into an unchanging ancestral world that stretches back to an aboriginal time. The initiates themselves become fertile through the ritual, and "this continuity is also [then] extended to the unborn by ensuring that the initiates themselves will be able to father children" (C. Hugh-Jones 1979, 149).

The myth that accounts for how men came to wield the *He* instruments appears to conform to the general pattern of so-called myths of matriarchy (Bamberger 1974). *Romi Kumu*, the primal ancestress, steals the *He* instruments from the men, but the men steal it back again (S. Hugh-Jones 1979, 265–266). Ever since then, men and not women have wielded the *He* instruments, the source of male reproductive power. While the flutes are predominantly masculine and phallic in their associations, the gourd of beeswax, representing the ancestress, is feminine, wombal (pp. 169, 190) and vaginal (pp. 167, 169) in its associations; but it is men and not women who ritually wield these gourds. "The beeswax gourd is even more sacred than the instruments themselves. . . . The climax of the *He wi* rites is the coincidence of the burning beeswax from this gourd with the initiates' first attempt on the [*He*] instruments. In other words, the sexual potency of the initiates is made to coincide with the release of the contents of the female womb. . . . These actions bring male and female sexual processes together. . ." (C. Hugh-Jones 1979, 154). It is this coincidence that accounts for the "change in state of the initiates" (ibid.).

Stephen Hugh-Jones concludes that "it is as if the men were trying to carry out the act of fertilisation without the women" (S. Hugh-Jones 1979, 225). The rite is "a rite in which the adult men symbolically give birth to the initiates" (p. 222). What results from the ritual conjunction of the *He* instruments and the wax gourd, masculine and feminine respectively, is "not new-born babies but reborn initiates who, as *He* People, are identified with the *He* instruments" (p. 225), which themselves represent the ancestors. Initiation instills sexual potency in the boys at the same time it parthenogenetically installs them within a lineage of men. It is the older men who preside over the ritual and wield the instruments, and those who are reborn as initiates will initiate a new generation of initiates—and on and on. As in the two Melanesian instances discussed above, boys are enclosed within a parthenogenetic loop generated in the asymmetric relationship between initiators and the initiated. Since women are excluded from initiation even as their offspring are appropriated, this lineage is not only patrilineal but patriarchal.

Again, the biological capabilities of women are symbolically supplanted by means of ritual objects wielded by men, which accounts for the salience of ritual as a structuring instrument. But is religion per se discursively crucial?

Underlying the dominion that Paiela males create in the reproductive sphere is a gender politics of temporality whereby women are associated with the life span and its processes—the very cycle that so-called rites of passage allegedly facilitate; indeed, women are associated with the organism and its physiology per se (Biersack 1995; cf. Bonnemère 1993; Kelly 1993, 159). Men, on the other hand, are associated with transgenerational processes. To organize sexual reproduction as men do is to transcend individual mortality through the continuity of the collectivity, which is shaped, monitored, and transformed through marriage (Biersack 1995). Whereas women's work culminates in death (Biersack 1995; cf. Bloch 1982; Buchbinder and Rappaport 1976), men's work culminates in endless regeneration (see Conklin, Chapter 7). Death, however, is not eradicated; rather, its harshness as human fate is mitigated. Genealogy provides a history of death but also the redemptive work of regeneration (Bloch and Parry 1982). Through sexual reproduction, parents bear those who will "take their place" when they die.

There are echoes of these themes in the Barasana ritual. According to Stephen Hugh-Jones's description, patriarchy is reproduced as an eternal, dreamtime-like reality (1979, 139). Ordinarily the succession of the generations involves a passage of time—a passage that, in the poetics of the ritual, is likened to "the leaves that pile on top of one another on the forest floor" (ibid.). The *He wi* ritual compresses time by "squash[ing] the pile [of leaves] so that the initiates, described as people of another layer . . . , are brought into contact with, and adopted by, the first *He* People" (ibid.) or "the first ancestor" (p. 249). This compression of time mitigates or redeems but does not eradicate death. Though "in each generation, the mythic order is re-established and society is created anew" (ibid.), death deposits a multi-layer residue, which may be compressed but never annihilated. Barasana "men inherit the name of a dead patrilineal kinsman in the second ascending generation, the names being those of the . . . first ancestors," and "there is an ideology of soul recycling such that new-born babies receive their souls from dead grandparents and are seen as being reincarnations of them" (ibid.). Barasana society has an inevitable two-generation depth, therefore. "Barasana myths make it clear that the continuity and differentiation of descent also imply death" (ibid.). In fact, death is the source of the social order, with its ancestors, descendants, and temporality, per se. "In myth, the death and destruction of a single source lead to the segmentation and continuity of its parts: the body of the anaconda ancestor gives rise to sons who live on through their descendants" (ibid.). The initiation rites do not guarantee human immortality so much as they constitute a way of sanctifying an inherently temporal and otherwise ephemeral and profane order.

Through his *Mythologiques*, Lévi-Strauss sought to demonstrate the workings of the human mind in the least practical—and therefore purest—of genres:

mythology. "If it were possible to prove in this instance, too, that the apparent arbitrariness of the mind, its supposedly spontaneous flow of inspiration, and its seemingly uncontrolled inventiveness imply the existence of laws operating at a deeper level, we would inevitably be forced to conclude that when the mind is left to commune with itself and no longer has to come to terms with objects, it is in a sense reduced to imitating itself as object. . ." (Lévi-Strauss 1969b, 10). I do not see the universal properties of the human mind as underlying and informing the similarities I have discovered between Amazonian and Melanesian materials. Rather, I see in these materials the operation of a religious imagination focused on mortality and the need to humanize and redeem a fate that otherwise remains biological. Regeneration presupposes death, a widespread theme (Bloch and Parry 1982; Buchbinder and Rappaport 1976; Gregor 1985, 78–79); in this context, myth and ritual are perhaps better conceived of not as the mind's communion with and reflection of itself but as a religious meditation upon ultimate matters. Yes, human beings die, but how to set human life on a different plane from other organic life? Why should death ritual "be so thoroughly permeated by the symbolism of rebirth?" Bloch and Parry ask (1982, 9), and they answer that "almost everywhere religious thought consistently denies the irreversible and terminal nature of death by proclaiming it a new beginning" (ibid.). There is in myth, as there is in the metaphorical notion of compressing a pile of leaves, a mythopoetics that may be traced across regions and continents for its variations in symbols, motifs, philosophical stance, and religious solution. To the extent that death and time are thematized and gendered, it could be argued that rituals of death and rebirth are the necessary vehicles for engendering sexual hierarchy, for ritual, whatever its possible impact upon the natural world, rests on semantic rather than biological foundations.

I would propose this new *mythologiques*, focused as it is on the body and embodiment rather than on the mind and its nature and processes, as an alternative to other transareal approaches. Here, in a nutshell, is the importance of the mother as the third figure: not as an object of oedipal desire but as an emblem of the biological realm itself, the very realm that the symbolism of the ritual trivializes and transcends.[8] Unlike the *mythologiques* of Lévi-Strauss (but like psychoanalytic approaches), this alternative *mythologiques* has sex and gender at its heart. Barasana accomplish regeneration much as Paielas do: collectively, through male interventions in the natural course of events. It is men rather than women who own and wield the various technologies of regeneration—flutes, trumpets, and gourds—and men rather than women who control fertility. Indeed, in the Paiela context, since a woman becomes pregnant only once semen wraps around her menstrual blood, retaining it in the womb, the phallus is the principal reproductive tool.

But why are the ritual politics phallocentric, even misogynistic or gynophobic? The answer to this question will always be contentious, I suspect. However, we could call upon still tantalizing texts such as Ortner's "Is Female to Male as Nature Is to Culture?" and Bloch's "Death, Women and Power" to suggest that women are associated with death because they give birth and not only bear but nurture the very bodies that inevitably die. Whatever the merits of this proposition in the explanation of cross-cultural and cross-regional comparisons, the proposition is a Paiela truism, for it is said that "everything that is born by woman dies."

Whether we could ever settle on the reasons *why* men rather than women are associated with this redemptive work, we have, in male cults from two regions, ample indication of *how* men achieve this association: the so-called rites of passage themselves, here reinterpreted as a way of transcending rather than facilitating the life cycle. Given ritual, what is born by men does not die. He who is ritually fathered will himself ritually father the sons of the next generation; masculine ancestral connections will exist in perpetuity.[9] To appropriate women's fertility is to supply the products of women's procreation with a *terminus ad quem* other than the one of the dictum "everything that is born by woman dies." Whether as father or descendant, the initiate becomes fount of the future and replicator of the past, and the life cycle, with its periodicity and disruptions, is supplanted with dynastic continuity. The argument is potentially broad in application, covering Whitehead's rituals of manhood but also clanhood (1986a, 1986b)[10] and accounting for the homosocial, androcentric character of the solidarity achieved in Durkheim's Australian Aboriginal totemic rituals (1965 [1915]; see Hiatt 1971) and other corporate ritual traditions. Placing reproduction in its political, social, and semantic dimensions at the center of analysis (see Ginsburg and Rapp 1991, 313) may inspire a new and transcontinental *mythologiques*, one focused on a ritual mythopoetics concerning not the universal properties of the human mind but the tragic nature of the human condition.

NOTES

Initial fieldwork was conducted under an NSF Dissertation Grant (1974–1976); graduate training was supported by awards from the Rackham School of Graduate Studies, the University of Michigan. Preparation of the dissertation was supported by a grant-in-aid from Wenner-Gren Foundation for Anthropological Research and an award from the Center for the Continuing Education of Women, the University of Michigan. Wenner-Gren supported my resumption of fieldwork in the Paiela valley in late 1993 and early 1995. A Fulbright Research Fellowship supported me while I continued my research in the second half of 1995. As always, I am grateful to my Paiela friends of Kolombi; Luke, Kauwambo, Nikolas, and Kongolome are the most important for the purposes of this paper. Thanks are given to Diane Baxter, Tom Gregor, Lawrence Hammar, Jonathan Hill, Ray Kelly, Don Tuzin, and Phil Young for their useful readings of a draft and for their encouragement.

1. The asexual nature of the ritual transactions resonates with the character of ritual leadership. The boys' leader is not a big man—someone who, by definition, is married at least once and has multiple children—but a *kinambuli,* a gender-neutral term that means

old enough to be married and to have reproduced but either not married or if married, then without issue.

2. Paiela women can and do perform parallel magic to grow their hair and body, but they do so individually rather than collectively and without entering into a relationship with a helpmate who is a member of the opposite sex. The individuality of the women's magic as well as the women's failure to control a spirit of the opposite sex are telling, for they suggest that women exert no special power of their sex class. If men's performances are patriarchal, women's performances cannot be said to be matriarchal (see remarks in Lincoln 1991, 117).

3. Outside the ritual context, leaders in these acts of marriage, re-reproduction, and transformation are called big men, and the *kinambuli* who leads the ritual is big-man-like in his powers and his projects. Luke, the son of Botane, was in his prime one of the most prominent leaders in the Paiela valley, a fact that suggests that the distinction between big men and great men (Godelier and M. Strathern 1991) conceals more than it reveals in the Paiela case: the crucial relationship between the ritual and its aftermath, which is marriage.

4. This point is not entirely clear. One of Herdt's male informants told him that a woman's mother tells her that if she sucks her husband's penis, her "'vagina will open quickly [precipitate the menarche]'" (Herdt 1981, 178); in another publication he reports that "oral insemination prepares a wife's body for making babies by 'strengthening' her, as well as by precipitating her menarche (if she has not already attained it)" (Herdt 1984, 179).

5. According to Hays, P. Newman was an early (if not the first) person to detect the political implication of flute symbolism in highlands male cults. According to Newman, "'the real secret of the flutes' was that 'it was not only control over reproductive power that is being exercised, it is male control over reproductive power'" (quoted in Hays 1988, 104).

6. Lindenbaum distinguishes societies in which men appropriate women's fertility—by and large "homosexual" societies—from societies in which men appropriate women's labor—by and large "heterosexual" societies (1987). The eastern highlands societies represent a mixture of the two (ibid.). Paiela society conforms more to the eastern highlands group. Men appropriate women's reproduction and women's labor. But for reasons I elaborate elsewhere (Biersack 1995), Lindenbaum's typology seems unproductive.

7. Herdt also envisions Sambia rites as a "liminal period: the social and psychological arrangements of initiation place boys outside the realm of 'normal society,' on the margins of everyday life," and as a "transition experience . . . of timelessness" (Herdt 1987, 181).

8. It may be speculated that this identification of the female with biological processes accounts for the fact that, in some eastern highlands cultures, women are thought to grow quickly and naturally (Herdt 1987; Meigs 1984), while men must, as it were, domesticate their own adolescent growth.

9. Despite Paiela's cognatic rule, apical ancestors, as well as typically the first few generations of descendants, are preponderantly male.

10. Whitehead has distinguished "manhood" and "clanhood" cults (1986a, 1986b). The emphasis in the latter is on the perpetuation of the group; the emphasis in the former is on physiologically maturing males and the promotion of their fertility. However, problematizing reproduction—for "alliance" or "[unilineal] descent" systems, or for anomalous systems such as the Paiela system—has the effect of undermining the utility of this distinction. See Weiner (1988).

FIVE

The Genres of Gender: Local Models and Global Paradigms in the Comparison of Amazonia and Melanesia

Philippe Descola

Noting that gender is less a focus of study by anthropologists in Amazonia than in Melanesia, Philippe Descola argues that gender is itself not a salient category in South American societies. Beginning with the Amazonian Achuar, where he has conducted his own fieldwork, Descola maintains that gender relationships are subsumed and embedded in kinship relationships of affinity and consanguinity, with women being associated with consanguine relationships and men with affinal roles. Moreover, "consanguinity and affinity are far-reaching and versatile intellectual templates that may be used to structure every conceivable form of mediation within the sphere of Achuar social life." Descola believes that this "encompassing" of gender by kinship is characteristic of other Amazonian societies. Alternatively, gender may be subordinated to other more symbolically prominent systems of thought, such as the relationship of humans and animals and predator and prey. For Descola, Amazonia and Melanesia "really appear to exhibit a distinctive style" and this is that in Amazonia, and indeed throughout the Americas, "the essential contrast is between human and nonhuman rather than between human (males) and human (females)."

Descola's chapter should be read in conjunction with Fisher's, who also sees significant differences between Melanesian and Amazonian systems of gender representation.

Seen from Amazonia, Melanesia stands out as a sort of anthropological wonderland teeming with a bewildering diversity of social institutions that specialists of the South American lowlands view with discreet envy. Shamanism, head-hunting, secret men's cults, cannibalism, ritualized feuding, dualist organizations, splendid feather paraphernalia, or sophisticated adaptations to tropical ecosystems—all these ethnographic features that the students of Amazonia would spontaneously consider as forming the characteristic landscape of their cultural area are also present in Melanesia, to which must be added an array of practices, cultural idiosyncrasies, and social systems that are either totally absent or barely sketched in Amazonia. As a result, Amazonianists tend to look toward Melanesia as a kind of evolutionary template, one that presents the full range of combinations between a set of structural potentialities of which Amazonia, for reasons yet to be properly understood, offers only a very partial realization. Melanesian cultures may thus be seen as an ethnographic thought experiment whereby the logical conditions for a possible structural transformation of Amazonian social systems may be identified.

My repeated use of the word "structural" is indication enough that cross-cultural comparison cannot be for me of the Murdockian type; that is, it cannot be reduced to correlating a set of reified phenomena or surface properties in order to establish universal connections between predefined typological features. Comparison is worthy only if it deals with differences rather than similarities, differences that stem from the operation of deep underlying schemata, that become analytically meaningful when considered as transformations of one another. A first step in the procedure is thus to isolate domains of contrast as starting points for the production of hypotheses that offer a guiding thread both for the comprehension of the internal diversity of a cultural area and for the intelligibility of the principles that may account for the systematic variations between two historically unrelated cultural areas. By inviting the contributors to this volume to focus their comparative approach on the topic of gender, the editors have judiciously pinpointed such a domain of contrast.

Perhaps the first symptom of a major difference between Amazonia and Melanesia in the construction of sex differences is the unequal coverage given to this theme in the ethnographic literature of the two regions. A recent review of the major questions treated by Amazonianists in the domain of gender (Bellier 1993) shows a paucity of studies when compared with the abundance of publications devoted to the same topic by Melanesianists (e.g., Herdt and Poole 1982; Strathern 1988). Less than half a dozen monographs and probably no more than two dozen articles can be said to deal exclusively with the question of the cultural interpretation or politics of sexual dichotomy in Amazonia, although, of course, there are passing references to gender contrasts in most publications, especially those dealing with kinship. There are reasons to believe that this disparity reflects the situation that anthropologists of both sexes have found during their fieldwork, rather than personal prejudices. After all, the ideological and ritual elaboration of sexual differences is so pervasive a theme in Melanesia that it was extensively discussed in earlier publications (e.g., Read 1952–1953), long before gender became a fashionable anthropological topic. By contrast, the first major study devoted to the relation between the sexes in Amazonia was Yolanda and Robert Murphy's classical monograph on the Mundurucú, published in 1974.

Invoking the difference in the cultural backgrounds of anthropologists working in these two areas as a possible source of epistemological bias is not very convincing either. It is true that the ethnography of New Guinea is an Anglo-American stronghold, while the study of Amazonia has been influenced by French and Brazilian structuralism. That relations between men and women are indeed predicated on contrasted sets of values in the Anglo-Saxon world and in Latin countries cannot be meant to imply that Amazonianists would take gender distinctions as unproblematic while Melanesianists would be acutely aware of them. The writings of French anthropologists doing field-work in New Guinea are as replete with bodily humors, female pollution, spatial segregation, and ritual inequality between the sexes as those of their Anglo-Saxon colleagues. Conversely, most American and British anthropologists working in Amazonia—some of them little influenced by structuralism, to say the least—have devoted little attention to these themes, as can be lazily ascertained by scanning the indexes of their monographs.

It thus seems that there is a major difference "out there" in the relative weight given to the cultural construction of sexual contrasts by Melanesian and Amazonian cultures—a difference that perhaps appears greater than it really is, due to a focusing of the ethnographic interest on certain areas of New Guinea where gender distinctions are taken to be at the core of social reproduction. Recent studies, such as Lepowsky's monograph on Vanatinai Island, offer a picture completely at odds with the standard New Guinea model but very evocative of gender relations in some parts of Amazonia. Thus, the people of Vanatinai form an egalitarian society, where women regularly hunt and formerly participated in warfare, where they can lead long-distance maritime trading expeditions, where their body is not considered polluting and their sexuality dangerous for the men (Lepowsky 1993). Conversely, the ideology of marked gender hierarchy and segregation displayed by the Mundurucú of Brazil is more reminiscent of the standard pattern of the New Guinea high-lands than it is of many Amazonian societies that strive to maintain a strict parity between the sexes, such as the Matsiguenga (Renard-Casevitz 1985) or the Amuesha (Santos Granero 1994).

Comparing gender relations, then, always reverts to the vexing question of whether the glass is half-full or half-empty, of whether the domination of men over women is real or symbolic, of whether formal equality is undermined by covert hierarchy or the reverse. In view of the internal disparities within Amazonia and Melanesia in this respect, it seems reasonable to consider the construction of sexual differences less as a universal tool for comparison than as a label subsuming a domain of broad contrasts between cultural areas, a domain that is itself revealing of strong differences in the ways societies in these areas constitute the building blocks of individual and collective identities. This is how I treat gender in this chapter, as a way of elucidating why it has remained a relatively minor topic for anthropologists working in Amazonia. Starting with an analysis of the role played by the sexual dichotomy in the cosmology and social organization of a particular society, the Jivaroan Achuar of the Upper Amazon, I show that their gender categories are encompassed by a wider set of relationships. I then argue that this is also the case for many other Amazonian societies and that this sharp contrast with Melanesia may help us to identify and assess relevant strategies for comparison.

ENCOMPASSING GENDER: THE ACHUAR

The Jivaroan Achuar (or Achuales as they are known in Peru) inhabit the upper area drained by the Rio Morona and the Rio Pastaza, on either side of the line of the Protocol of Rio de Janeiro, which separates the Amazonian territories of Ecuador from those of Peru. In Ecuador, the Achuar number a little more than two thousand persons, distributed within a territory of approximately 12,000 square kilometers extending on both sides of the Rio Pastaza. As among many other native groups of the Andean foothills of Ecuador, Peru, and Bolivia, the traditional settlement pattern is markedly dispersed in time of peace. Each household consists of a single, and generally polygynous, nuclear family and functions as a politically independent unit of production and consumption. Households are either totally isolated or in clusters of two or three; the distance that separates them may vary from an hour's to a day's trip by foot or by canoe. The sense of isolation that might result from such an extreme residential atomism, as from the lack of internal segmentation, is counterbalanced by discrete supralocal units that I call "endogamous nexus" (Descola 1981, 1982; Taylor 1983). A nexus is a collection of 12 to 20 scattered domestic units that intermarry regularly according to the classical Dravidian pattern, where the replication, at each generation, of a relation of prescriptive alliance replaces the lineal continuity usually ensured by a principle of descent (Dumont 1975). As social distance increases with geographical distance, marrying "close"—both genealogically and spatially—is highly valued. Such a system promotes the territorial stability of cognatic kindreds, which tend to identify themselves through a common reference to the name of a main river forming the backbone of the area inside which they regularly relocate their houses—every six to twelve years, usually.

Although the endogamous areas have no explicit borders, they are usually separated by extensive no-man's-lands; these have a tactical function as relations between neighboring nexus oscillate between covert mistrust and open hostility. When a conflict between nexus reaches alarming proportions, most households scattered within an endogamous area form a temporarily nucleated faction settled in a fortified house under the strategic command of a "great-man" (*juunt*). This process actualizes the latent tendency toward a cognatic solidarity within a neighborhood: the nexus coalesces not as a corporate group but rather as an occasional coalition more or less coextensive with the limits of a great-man's kindred. Since feuds are fairly frequent, settlements vary in size from half a dozen individuals, in time of peace, to more than seventy in the largest "war houses." In spite of the normal (and desired) state of dispersion, then, most Achuar spend part of their lives in conditions of collective residence that are comparable to those of traditional native villages or longhouses in some other parts of Amazonia.

Among the Achuar, as among many other nonsegmentary Amazonian societies, the Dravidian kinship model entails a characteristic sociological feature that

J. Overing Kaplan was the first to identify by reference to the Piaroa; kindred en-
dogamy, although structured by a symmetrical relation of alliance, is locally perceived and expressed as the product of an ideal consanguinity, this paradoxical
result being obtained by a deliberate blurring of affinal links (1975). Affinity appears endowed with a political function, both ambiguous and strategic, since it
conditions the marriage exchange necessary for the local group to reproduce itself but establishes a broad distinction, heavy with potential conflicts, between
two categories of coresidents (Rivière 1969). It thus becomes imperative to expel
this relation loaded with threatening alterity toward the periphery. In accordance
with this general pattern, the external relations of the Achuar nexus are graded
along a scale of social distance expressed by a variation of the modalities of the
affinal link, which becomes more schematic and abstract as one moves away
from the focal point, where it structures the actual marriage alliance. Distant kin
are called affines and treated as such when they live in a neighboring nexus;
Achuar enemies from other local groups are considered generically as metaphorical affines (they are often called *nua suru,* or "wife givers," an allusion to the common practice of abducting women during vendettas); finally, the Achuar themselves are treated as ideal affines in the *tsantsa* festivals held by other Jivaroan
tribes, where their shrunken heads serve as a medium to impart a new identity
to a perfectly consanguine child to be born in the kindred of the headhunters (for
more details, see Taylor 1993a; Descola 1996b).

Eduardo Viveiros de Castro has shown that such systems of graded alterity
are common to many Amazonian societies, where the apparent symmetry between consanguinity and affinity, typical of Dravidian kinship, is actually broken by a hierarchical encompassment—in Dumont's specific sense (1977)—and
animated by a diametrical structure: while affinity is encompassed by consanguinity at the level of the endogamous local group, it encompasses consanguinity in the relations between local groups and becomes subordinated to a
kind of meta-affinity in the (generally hostile) relations with the more distant
tribes (Viveiros de Castro 1993a, 1995; Fausto and Viveiros de Castro 1993).
This meta-affinity expresses itself in different forms of predation (cannibalism,
hunting for human trophies) on enemies that are conceptualized as generic
affines, the violent incorporation of whom is deemed necessary for the symbolic reproduction of the self.

Female Kin and Male Affines

By what means does affinity become encompassed by consanguinity within the
endogamous nexus? Basically by a manipulation of the gender dichotomy. In
a thorough analysis of the Achuar vocative terminology and system of attitudes, Anne-Christine Taylor has shown that affinity is shifted into the sphere
of masculine kin ties, whereas consanguinity is concentrated on the feminine
side (Taylor 1983). In brief, within the nexus, affinal relations between men are

always marked by affinal terminology and attitude, while cross-sex affinal relations are selectively consanguinealized in the vocative terminology by both
men and women, especially at the same generation level, but with a wider
range of kin categories on the side of women than on the side of men; on the
other hand, cross-generation affinal relations between women are always consanguinealized terminologically, while women affines of the same generation
address each other as such but behave toward each other as classificatory sisters. In other words, "women act on certain relations as operators or trans-
formers, whereby affinity is constantly absorbed and transmuted into postu-
lated consanguinity" (Taylor 1983, 335). A similar pattern has been described
for another Jivaroan group, the Shiwiar of the Corrientes (Seymour-Smith
1991). This manipulation of the kinship system would seem to indicate that the
Achuar associate women with the realm of consanguinity, while they place the
obligations and hazards of affinity in the men's camp. Such an interpretation
is supported by certain features of the technical and symbolic division of labor.

Gender Roles

As in many other Amazonian societies, Achuar women are mainly "trans-
formers" of raw products within the domestic sphere (horticulture, food
preparation, pottery, weaving, raising children and pets, etc.), while men are
essentially predators in the outside world (hunting, fishing, clearing gardens,
warfare, etc.). The dichotomy is not so neat, however, as women also engage
in certain activities that would be thought unfit for their condition in other
parts of the world. Hunting is one of them. Hunting dogs are owned by
women who are responsible for leading them in pack to the hunt, following
their husbands. This is by no means an exceptional occurrence, and a woman,
especially in a monogamous household, may go off hunting with her husband
several times a week. Due to the lack of privacy in polygynous households,
hunting also affords the only opportunity for sexual intercourse between
spouses in a secluded spot, so that husbands take great care to maintain a fair
rotation between their wives when they set off hunting, so as not to appear to
be favoring one of them. The qualities of the dogs and the ability to control
them are considered essential assets in hunting and are seen as the products
of the technical and symbolic skills of the women who raise them; especially
important in this respect is the women's knowledge of a wide range of magical songs, or *anent,* specifically designed to foster the pugnacity and hunting
abilities of their dogs, which they sing mentally while the dogs chase the
game. Women may also occasionally hunt game on their own, particularly
armadillos, rodents, or opossums, provided they use traps or blunt instruments that do not pierce or make blood flow. Young women may also participate in war parties as food-carriers, both in intratribal feuding raids and in
long-distance expeditions against neighboring Jivaroan tribes. Although ap-

parently subordinate, this function is taken very seriously by those to whom it has been entrusted, and in this capacity, as in the exclusively feminine war rituals known as *ujaj* (Descola 1996b), women appear to share the martial exaltation of their menfolk.

As in hunting, most Achuar labor processes are dependent on a tight gender complementarity (Descola 1994a), although women fare much better than men if they are obliged to fend for themselves. When the head of a household is away for some time—in a trading or war expedition, for instance—women manage to compensate for the lack of game by poison-fishing and collecting insects, crustaceans, and palm grubs. Provided their brothers or kinsmen help them to build a house and clear a garden, widows or divorced women manage perfectly well to live without a man. The reverse situation is harsher for men: a widower who has no daughter or sister to take care of his gardening and cooking usually has no alternative but to commit suicide. In other words, the sexual division of labor is not based on a native discriminatory theory that would rank productive activities on a scale of prestige according to whether they are performed by men or women. A good hunter certainly acquires prestige, but so does a woman who is an expert gardener, and their skills are complementary and interdependent both within the domestic economy and within most labor processes. This complementarity manifests itself as much in a sort of rivalry between men and women in their respective spheres of practice as in the need to combine skills in certain cross-gender tasks such as gardening or hunting. The husband of a reputed gardener will emulate her by providing great amounts of game, and he will make a point of clearing very large swiddens to allow her to demonstrate ostentatiously her gardening abilities. Conversely, the wife of a great hunter will strive to provide him and his male guests with a great variety of foodstuffs and huge quantities of tasty manioc beer. One of the strongest bases for a happy marriage rests on this kind of emulation between spouses, grounded in a healthy respect for the competence and hard work of one's partner.

The parallelism between hunting and gardening is all the more notable as the Achuar conceive of the latter as a hazardous and even dangerous activity, despite the effectiveness and sophistication of their horticultural techniques. A myth known to everyone recounts that, after giving the cultivated plants to an Achuar family, Nunkui, the protective spirit of gardens, cursed the humans for their ill treatment of her daughter, with the result that the plants diminished to a minute size and are now under threat of disappearing completely if the women do not take good care of them. Sweet manioc, the most ubiquitous of all cultivated plants and the main staple food, is also supposed to suck through its leaves the blood of those who approach it, particularly the women and their children who are most exposed to its contact. Special *anent* songs must be addressed to the manioc plants by the women who take care of them in order to protect themselves from this vampirical propensity and deflect the aggression

toward possible intruders in the garden. The whole process of garden cultivation could thus be defined as ensuring the presence of beings who might suddenly disappear while trying not to be killed by them before they are eaten. Although the nature of their uncertainty is symmetrically inverted around two
poles (desired presence of game versus feared absence of plants, and humans
as agents of killing versus humans as prey to the vampirism of plants), both
hunting and gardening are thought of as risky endeavors the outcome of
which is unpredictable. There is thus no ground here for a possible justification
of the superiority of male hunting over female gardening that would be based
on an exaltation of the dangers and unpredictability of the former in contrast
with the mundane, easygoing nature of the latter.

Vegetal Children and Affinal Game Animals

In spite of the effective cooperation between men and women that they entail,
hunting and gardening are strongly gendered in one respect. The Achuar do
not conceive these labor processes as mere technical operations intended to satisfy their material needs; rather, they see them as a series of repeated inter-
courses with various entities—plants, animals, and guardian spirits—that must
be charmed, constrained, or moved to pity by appropriate symbolic techniques. Most cultivated plants as well as game animals are considered as "persons" (*aents*), endowed with reflexivity, intentionality, and a social life and moral
code of their own; they possess a "soul" (*wakan*), which makes them receptive
to the messages addressed to them by humans through the medium of *anent*
(magical songs). They are also protected by a host of tutelary beings: Nunkui,
the female spirit who created the cultivated plants and takes care of them
down to the present; the "mothers of game" (*kuntiniu nukuri*), a race of spirits
who own and protect the animals of the forest; and the *amana*, the prototype
of each hunted species, described as a perfect and larger-than-life embodiment
of his conspecifics. The "mothers of game" are fearsome creatures who may
exact revenge on behalf of the animals upon excessive or disrespectful hunters,
mainly through snakebites. According to the Achuar, success in hunting and in
gardening thus depends largely on the quality of the relationships one man-
ages to establish with these various entities through a series of symbolic preconditions: magical songs, dream omens, food prohibitions, charms, sexual abstinence, and so forth. Now, each sphere of practice is governed by a specific
set of preconditions that is clearly assigned to one of the sexes according to its
purported predisposition for a particular regime of sociability.

The garden spirit Nunkui is thought of as the mother of all cultivated
plants, and the bond that a woman wishes to establish with her is basically a
relation of identification: the plants she grows are her children and her relationship with them is a double of the maternal relationship Nunkui entertains
with her vegetal offspring. This appears clearly in the rhetoric of the garden-

ing magical songs, where the singer always refers to the plants as her children and constantly identifies herself with Nunkui.[1] Hunting, on the other hand, implies a triangular relationship between the hunter, a series of go-betweens (the various "mothers of game" and the *amana* prototypes), and the individual hunted animals wherein the go-betweens are conceived as cross-generational affines (fathers-in-law), while the game is called and treated as a brother-in-law. The complex relationship of competition, negotiation, and complicity that the hunter entertains with these nonhuman affines closely resembles that which prevails in his dealings with his human in-laws: these are both privileged political allies within the nexus and potential enemies if they have kept allegiances in a neighboring nexus. While the gardening model of sociability is built around two identical relationships of consanguinity with the same object (Nunkui as the mother of cultivated plants, and the woman gardener as their, so to speak, "foster" mother), the hunting model is structured around two relationships of affinity with two separate objects (the hunter and the go-betweens, the hunter and the game animals), themselves related by blood. The Achuar sexual division of labor is thus based on the idea that each sex reaches its full potential in the sphere befitting its symbolic area of manipulation and in the kinship regime preferentially assigned to its range of social competence. Each gender deals with humans and nonhumans alike according to its particular abilities: women convert affinity into consanguinity within the nexus and treat their plants as children; men are in charge of affinal relations and treat the beings of the forest as in-laws.

The Politics of Sex

My emphasis on the symbolic autonomy and actual complementarity of the sexes should not obscure the effective, and often brutal, political domination of men over women in Achuar society. Men are the "owners" (*nurintin*) of women: fathers and brothers control the fate of their unmarried daughters and sisters, although they have to relinquish part of their authority in favor of their in-laws after marriage. A married woman is thus subjected to various and often conflicting rights of ownership distributed among her kinsmen and cross-generational affines. This may turn out to be an asset for her in the not uncommon eventuality of her being persistently ill-treated by a brutal husband. Men are said to be naturally prone to anger, so that beating their wives, sometimes very severely with machete blows on the head, is considered an unfortunate but normal outcome of this propensity when they become displeased with their wives or when they suspect unfaithfulness.

Because she still belongs partly to her kinsmen, a mistreated woman may appeal to them for their active support, except in cases of proven adultery, where she may be killed by her husband—along with her lover, if they are caught in flagrante—without her brothers' interfering. The very long period of uxorilocal residence allows a young man's in-laws to assess his character and behavior, eventually to remonstrate with him for improper treatment of his wife and thus to prepare themselves for future intervention if he shows inclination toward marital violence. Polygyny, particularly the common sororal polygyny, also allows co-wives to form a united front against a violent husband, who may be brought to heel eventually by concerted shows of bad temper or even a strike in the kitchen.

In spite of the political domination exerted by men, women do participate in public life. One reason for this is that the men do not form a community as such, which would have vested interests to defend collectively, such as in their joint control over women—a sharp contrast with many Melanesian cultures, needless to say. The anarchy of Achuar social life prevents the consolidation of an effective leadership over long periods of time and thus impedes the formation of corporate sodalities. The authority that a great-man exercises over the men of his faction is restricted to tactical decisions in times of open hostilities and is based on the recognition of his personal qualities; it does not extend to the women of the warriors who share his fate. The model for this ascendancy and for its public expression is in fact derived from the domestic authority that a man wields upon his sons and sons-in-law. The wife of a great-man, for instance, will command far more respect from the faction of her husband than a young son-in-law does, and she may intervene effectively to orient the course of a vendetta or even to convince her husband and his followers of their moral obligation to avenge a wrong. In sum, there are no collective mechanisms of mediation through which the men as a whole could decide the fate of women as a whole, as each woman falls under the authority of a restricted set of men with competing interests.

In terms of status, women have open access to most social activities except the exercise of violence in warfare, though we have seen that they can participate in raids and that their contribution to the success of arms is enacted in the *ujaj* ritual that they perform each night for the duration of a war expedition. We have seen also that they take part in hunting, and I can vouch that they are far from timid when they chase a quarry with their pack of hounds. Women commonly engage in barter, both between themselves—trading puppies, cultivars, mineral dyes for pottery, salt, and so forth—and with the men, with whom they exchange woven ornaments for small metal tools. They may also become shamans, although the most powerful among them are usually widows; contrary to what obtains among their male counterparts, full dedication to their shamanistic careers appears to be incompatible with a normal married life. Finally, women can seek an *arutam* vision, the most important self-fulfilling experience in the life course of any Achuar individual. This mighty quest requires absolute seclusion for several days, severe fasting, and drinking a powerful hallucinogenic decoction made of *Brugmansia* bark, combined with repeated absorptions of tobacco-water. Encounter with an *arutam*

vision helps one to shape or reorganize his or her destiny according to the nature of the revelation obtained; it greatly enhances a man's forcefulness, self-
confidence, and bravery, and increases a woman's longevity, strength of character, and mastery of feminine skills (see Descola 1993, 1996b; Taylor 1993a,
1993b). An *arutam* quest is not always successful, however, and a mature
woman who has met *arutam* several times will be granted far more respect
than a younger man who has been unable to do so. In sum, nothing supposedly specific in the nature of women is invoked to bar them from doing most
of what the men do, except killing humans.

The Encompassment of Gender

Achuar society is indeed gender inflected, but so are classless societies everywhere else, particularly cognatic societies that, for lack of explicit segmentary
divisions, tend to use the sexual dichotomy as a basic classificatory device.
However, one does not find among the Achuar the obsession with gender separation that is such a striking feature of Melanesia. It is true that the ideology
of segregation and hierarchy forcefully enacted in Melanesian rituals of manhood is often contradicted in practice by a remarkably egalitarian and mutually caring relationship between men and women in the domestic sphere,
sometimes coupled with ambivalent feelings on the part of the men toward
the harshness and brutality displayed in rituals.[2] Nevertheless, the contrast in
the treatment of gender difference is striking: Achuar women are never
banned from male domains because their bodies would be polluting, nor are
they deemed unworthy of sharing the cosmological and mythical lore that is
a patrimony common to all. Achuar men do not obstinately attempt to reproduce themselves and the social order through the ritualized transmission
of male substances, nor do they try to exist as an almost separate community,
bound by the shared secret of their initiation. The only *rite de passage* comparable to an initiation, the *arutam* vision quest, is entirely individual and open
to anyone, man or woman, who is willing to try it.

   Furthermore, sexual dichotomy seems to be subordinated to, and instru-
mentalized by, more encompassing social patterns and relationships. One is
the opposition between consanguine and affine that, as we have seen, structures every level of relatedness from Ego to the outer rim of the tribal social
space. Gender contrasts are subsumed under this elementary opposition in
such a way that women are first and foremost defined as signifiers and operators of consanguine links, while men are perceived as signifiers and operators of affinal links. Subjecting gender categories to wider social oppositions
goes far beyond the internal constraints of the kinship system, as sex roles acquire their full justification and meaning in relation to the type of behavior
proceeding from the preferential assignment of each sex to a specific kinship
category. In that sense, warfare or hunting are male affairs, not because men

would be stronger or braver than women, but because these activities are conceived as expressions of relationships with metaphorical affines, and fall therefore under the jurisdiction of those whose business it is to deal with affinity. Conversely, gardening or child rearing are female prerogatives, not so much because women would be naturally predisposed to produce and manage life, but because these tasks befit their aptitude at dealing with consanguinity.

This encompassment of gender difference by kinship relations is neatly expressed in a small myth recounting the origin of women: while they were bathing in a river, a man changed his *sai* (sister's husband and male cross-cousin for a male Ego) into a woman in order to satisfy a sexual drive, thus creating the first couple. In mythic discourse, gender relations are thus conceived as originating in a relation of affinity between men, a generative feature by no means restricted to the Achuar: in some Melanesian and Amazonian contexts, as Strathern convincingly argues (Chapter 10), same-sex relations may create the preconditions for cross-sex relations.

It should be obvious by now that my emphasizing the dominance of the consanguine/affine dichotomy over the cross-sex one does not mean that "gender" is an epiphenomenon of "kinship." In much the same way as gender does not refer primarily to reified sexual attributes but is constituted as a function of social positions (Strathern 1988), consanguinity and affinity cannot be reduced, in the Amazonian context, to mere labels subsuming kin terms and marriage categories. As I have tried to make clear, consanguinity and affinity are far-reaching and versatile intellectual templates that may be used to structure every conceivable form of mediation within the sphere of Achuar social life.

This is particularly evident in the daily commerce between humans and nonhumans. Since most plants and animals are viewed as persons to be coerced, seduced, or protected, the frontiers of Achuar society extend far beyond the sphere of humankind and almost coincide with the outer limits of the cosmos. As in any other society, this cosmos is gendered; assigning a sex to nonhumans, however, is not something that appears relevant to most Achuar. Most kinds of spirits, plants, and animals are said to be like humans: they are composed of two sexes and lead a conventional family life, some bordering on the incestuous, such as the dog or the howler monkey. Certain cultivated plants are female, such as the achiote, genipa, sweet potato, squash, and *wayus* (an *Ilex*), while others are thought to be male: tobacco, the banana tree, and the two species of fish poison, *masu* (*Clibadium* sp.) and *timiu* (*Lonchocarpus* sp.). Often based on superficial analogies between certain parts of the plant and human sexual organs, these metonymies are not taken very seriously by the Achuar. Two spirits are definitely gendered, however: Nunkui, the provider and protector of cultivated plants, is a female and a sort of embodiment of maternal care, while Shakaïm, a much lower personage than Nunkui, is said by some to be the husband of the latter and by others to be her brother. Shakaïm is the curator of the jungle, which he cultivates like a gigantic garden, and he sometimes appears in men's dreams to reveal the best locations for opening new swiddens in the forest. But the genders attributed to Nunkui and Shakaïm are not altogether surprising in view of their respective dominions over two domains of practice—the garden and the forest—that are preferentially, if not exclusively, associated with the sexes.

The occurrence of gender categories among plants, animals, and spirits, then, is less an indication of a fully gendered cosmos than a product of the technical and symbolic differential engagement of men and women with certain portions of their environment, an engagement that is itself conceived as a result of the predisposition assigned to each sex for successfully managing either a consanguine or an affinal relationship with humans and nonhumans alike. In that sense, being a woman or being a man appears as an overdetermination—in the classical Freudian sense—of a set of relations not primarily concerned with sexual dichotomy, rather than as a substantive attribute of personal identities mainly defined by anatomical and physiological peculiarities. Particularly striking in this respect, especially when compared with Melanesia, is the utter lack of concern shown by the Achuar as to the origin of bodily humors, their working mechanisms, and their possible compatibilities and incompatibilities: there are no specific prohibitions linked to menstruation, the postpartum taboo on sexual intercourse is rather short (until the mother's womb "dries up"), and everyone confesses ignorance as to what type of physiological substance may be transmitted by either of the genitors to their offspring. Gender categories among the Achuar thus specify classes of individuals whose characteristics stem not from the elementary components of their organic nature so much as from the range of social interactions that their initial physical idiosyncrasies open to them.

COMPARING RELATIONSHIPS: AMAZONIA

The subsumption of gender under a more encompassing set of relationships is not peculiar to the Achuar or to the Jivaroan groups. Instead of emphasizing sexual dichotomy, as in Melanesia, many Amazonian societies seem to downplay gender contrasts and subordinate them to more abstract generic oppositions. It is true that, in some regions of Amazonia, male initiations and some festivals involve the playing of a set of musical instruments women are strictly forbidden to see, as in the secret men's cults of New Guinea. Such rituals are often linked to a myth that recounts how, after an original period of matriarchy when women were the sole owners of the sacred instruments, men managed to appropriate these symbols of power, thereby establishing male supremacy and the foundations of a proper social order. There are two main foci for this ritual and mythological pattern, which appears to push to the forefront of public life a strongly gendered conception of social relations. One is found in Western Amazonia—the famous Yurupari complex of the Eastern Tukanoans (S. Hugh-Jones 1979, Chapter 11; Reichel-Dolmatoff 1996) and of some of their Arawak neighbors, such as the Curripaco (Journet 1995) or the Wakuénai (Hill and Wright 1988; Hill, Chapter 3), and the *ñá* festival of the Yagua (Chaumeil and Chaumeil 1977). The other is in Central Brazil: the Upper Xingú (see Gregor 1985 for the Mehinaku) and the Mundurucú of the Upper Tapajós (Murphy 1958; Murphy and Murphy 1974).

Amazonian secret male cults have attracted a lot of attention from anthropologists, in part because of their elaborate ceremonialism, complex symbolism, and ostentatious paraphernalia, but probably also because of their rarity in an area where little concern is shown for the ritual celebration of gender differences. The occurrence of these cults is indeed quite restricted when compared with their frequency in New Guinea. In Amazonia (an ethnographic construct including also Central Brazil, the Guianas, and the Orinoco basin), there are presently between 400 and 500 distinct native groups, depending on the criteria of ethnic definition; of these, probably less than 3% practice some form of secret male cult. I admit that the cultural importance of a phenomenon cannot be measured in statistical terms, but these may be helpful in qualifying analogies and comparisons.

In this small set of societies, the ritualization of gender dichotomy seems to be the enactment of a nondialectic dualist principle, either because a fully fledged system of patrilineal moieties (as among the Mundurucú) or a set of crypto-moieties (as among the Yagua) tends to dissociate each pair of spouses along their respective lines of descent, or because the linguistic exogamy of patrilineal sibs produces a partitioning of each local group into autochthonous males and alien females (as among the Tukanoans). A feature common to these northwestern and central Brazilian societies with secret men's cults is thus a strong emphasis on unilineal descent, in contrast to the cognatism that predominates elsewhere in Amazonia.[3] It is not impossible that the transcription of the consanguine/affine dichotomy in exogamous descent groups, that is, the reification of a dualist principle of social organization, may have fostered a parallel institutionalization of the gender dichotomy in myth and ritual. As for the Mehinaku, who are cognatic and follow the general pattern of Dravidian kinship, they also show strong evidence of an ideology of parallel succession: parents expect their same-sex children to embody their qualities and recapitulate their social careers as former selves (Gregor 1977, 270). All of these societies with secret male cults, whether they are unilineal or not, thus appear to share a marked emphasis on the same-sex transmission of material or immaterial attributes, in sharp contrast with the relative lack of interest shown elsewhere in Amazonia (except among the Gê groups) for the intergenerational transfer of objects and prerogatives.

Finally, in northwest Amazonia, at least, initiation cults, as celebrations of intraclan same-sex relations of consanguinity, entertain a close relation of complementarity with intercommunity feasts involving the ceremonial exchange of gendered food and artifacts between wife givers and wife takers (Hugh-Jones, this volume, for the Tukanoans; Journet 1995, 283–292, and Hill, this volume, for the Arawak). Although gender is obviously an important dimension of such ritual combinations, ceremonial exchange nevertheless tends to blur the massive singularity of intraclan male cults by inserting them in a wider framework where the familiar dialectics of consanguinity/affinity and center/periphery play a major role. If, as Hill suggests, Wakuénai women are affinal others who gradually become integrated into the cults of clanhood of their husbands (Chapter 3, this volume), then there is reason to believe that these cults are dealing as much with the encompassment of (female) peripheral affinity by (male) central consanguinity as with the stressing of gender distinctions.

Elsewhere in Amazonia, the construction of individual and collective identities does not result in one half of the society persistently attempting to distinguish itself from the other half through the ritual enactment, and mythical assertion, of its generic difference, if not always of its intrinsic superiority. I do not imply that sexual differences are meaningless in these processes of identity building, which would be absurd, but rather that they are combined with, or encapsulated within, a variety of other principles of social categorization that render gender distinction less conspicuous than in Melanesia. I cannot substantiate this claim with a detailed comparison, but a small ethnographic sample may help to sketch the type of encompassment I have in mind.

It may be apposite to start with societies that are internally segmented—whether the segments are institutionalized as social units (moieties, age grades, marriage sections, and so forth), in the spatial disposition of their villages (public center versus domestic periphery), or in a combination of both—and who thus present some likeness of features with those practicing secret male cults. The Gê and Panoan groups are the most obvious candidates for such a comparison. Among the Xikrin Kayapo, for instance, gender categories are embedded in age categories in such a way that social classification does not differentiate them: the complex system of age grades is the focus for social action and the basis for a definition of personal identities in terms of a community of age-set activities rather than internal sexual differences (Fisher, Chapter 6). Furthermore, in the series of parallel rituals establishing these age-grade identities, the social attributes conferred on persons of the same age are not distinguished according to their sex but are globally derived by metonymy from the characteristics of different cosmic domains (and of their nonhuman denizens); individual identities are thus paired with cosmological discontinuities at the level of the whole age group, not according to a central gender dichotomy (Giannini 1991). As for the Krahó, also a northern Gê group, they stress another discontinuity, the opposition between the living and the dead, which encompasses secondary oppositions such as between kin and affines or between Krahó and non-Krahó living persons: to be a Krahó (woman or man) is primarily not to be what a dead Krahó (woman or man) is (Carneiro da Cunha 1978, 142–146). Identity and alterity are defined as contrasted positions within the Krahó universe, not in reference to social, spatial, or sexual attributes, but as a function of eschatology.

The Panoan groups are also notable for the institutional complexity of their social organization as well as for their elaborate rituals of initiation. Among the Cashinahua, gender is packaged within a formal network of social categories where social and sexual identities are either conflated—in the marriage sections—or separated—in the same-sex moieties (Kensinger 1995). In the latter case, however, gender identity is conceived not as the primary index for moieties affiliation but rather as a product of the existence of moieties: "the division in two sexes . . . is described as a subdivision of the moieties and the specificities of both sexes as subspecificities of each of the moieties" (Deshayes and Keifenheim 1994, 93, my translation). Furthermore, this Kariera-type pattern is also affected by the tendency, within each pair of male and female moieties, to subsume the criterion of gender separation under a broader cross-sex analogy, the sibling relationship (Kensinger 1995, 95–100). Considering the central role of cross-sex siblingship as a sort of ideological matrix for the social reproduction of Cashinahua society, one could surmise that the relationship emphasizing an homology between sets of brothers and sisters is more meaningful than the gender distinction emphasized in the husband-wife relationship. The same pattern appears in Erikson's study of another Panoan group, the Matis, who exhibit a complex system of dual oppositions although they lack a formal moieties system; instead of stressing gender differences, the Matis "posit the union of the sexes as the model and the key for the resolution of all other conceivable forms of opposition" (Erikson 1996, 313, my translation).

In other parts of Amazonia, unboundedness seems to be the key word of a widespread social philosophy that defines humanity not by intrinsic properties but by its position in a whole series of contrast sets. I agree with Viveiros de Castro when he argues that affinity provides the idiom through which these contrast sets are defined, an idiom that becomes all the more flexible and adaptive as it departs from its function in the regulation of marriage alliances (1993a, 179–183). The language of affinity qualifies relations between generic categories—man and woman, insider and outsider, congener and enemy, living and dead, human and natural kind, humanity and divinity—at the same time that it establishes the frontiers of these categories, that is, their relative content. Now, each culture appears to emphasize a small cluster of these contrast sets to the detriment of others, the outcome being that the actual diversity of cultural styles is subdued by the unifying effect of an underlying system of relationships. The Jivaro, for example, privilege a combination of two dyads—human/nonhuman, congener/enemy—with resulting structural homologies such as

> consanguines : affines ::
> congeners : enemies ::
> plants : animals ::
> women : men

Peoples of the Guianas present a similar pattern, although trade replaces warfare as the dominant relationship with the outside. Also, if we follow Rivière's analysis of gender (Rivière 1984), it seems that the core relationship is between a father and his daughters, as it enables control over sons-in-law. Rather than a generic cross-sex dichotomy, the opposition would be between two cross-sex relationships:

> consanguine : affine ::
> coresident : trading partner ::
> father-daughter relationship : husband-wife relationship

By contrast, the Araweté lay emphasis in their social ontology on two other dyads—living/dead and humanity/divinity—since any individual in this Tupian society of eastern Brazil must die, be eaten by cannibal gods, and be transformed as a result into one of them in order to reach fully his or her destiny (Viveiros de Castro 1992); again, this eschatological tension may be expressed by a standard homology:

> consanguines : affines ::
> congeners : enemies ::
> living : dead ::
> human : divine ::
> women : men

The sub-Andean Arawak of the central Peruvian *montaña* (Ashaninka, Matsiguenga, Nomatsiguenga, etc.) have established a different dividing line between sameness and otherness, one that is both ontological and isometric in the sense that it separates the radically negative world of the Andes, full of predatory peoples and evil spirits, and the wholly positive world of the Arawak themselves, their higher gods and their game animals, who all share an identical essence (Weiss 1975; Renard-Casevitz 1985, 1991; Brown and Fernández 1991). In this particular ethnographic context, affinity seems to play a very subordinate role, as if its actual encompassment by consanguinity at the level of the local group has resulted in its complete obliteration at the level of the relations with the outside world. The relationship of the Andean peoples and the Arawak is one of pure predation of the former upon the latter. In this case the homology would run as follows:

> highland peoples : lowland peoples ::
> despotism : social equality (in kinship and gender) ::
> bewitching animals : game animals ::
> evil spirits : higher gods

I am quite aware that structural formulae of this kind are merely a convenient way to sum up homologies and differences in the patterning of sociocosmological relations. As such, however, they clearly indicate a specific relationship that may be as central to the understanding of Amazonian sociability as are gender distinctions to the construction of Melanesian identities: the relation of humans with nonhumans and particularly with animals. If the anthropology of Amazonia has shown little concern on the whole for the problem of sex and gender, it has devoted a great deal of intellectual energy to the question of the symbolic treatment of natural kinds; the exact reverse could be said of the anthropology of Melanesia.[4] My brief description of the Achuar's relationship with their environment could be extended to a large part of the South American lowlands (Descola 1992, 1996a). Many Amazonian cosmologies do not establish marked ontological distinctions between humans on the one hand and most species of plants and animals on the other, since they all share a common set of humanlike attributes. As a result, the multiple entities inhabiting the world are linked in a vast continuum animated by an identical regime of social and ethical rules. Their internal contrasts are defined not by any essentialist assumption as to their natures but according to their mutual relations as specified by the requirements of their metabolisms and particularly of their diets (e.g., Århem 1990, 1996; Brown 1986; Chaumeil 1989; Chaumeil and Chaumeil 1992; van der Hammen 1992; Jara 1991; Rojas 1994; Reichel-Dolmatoff 1971; Viveiros de Castro 1992).

Amazonian cultures are cosmocentric rather than sociocentric. They grant less centrality to the ritual and political reproduction of the human social order—including the domination of men over women—than to the continuous efficiency of their relations with the multiple actors of the universe. Much the same can be said of many other native American cultures, especially in Central and North America. What Ann Fienup-Riordan writes of the Alaskan Eskimos—"Just as gender may provide the 'master code' for Melanesia (Biersack 1984, 134), the relationship between humans and animals may provide a comparable master code in some parts of the Arctic" (1990, 9)—may in fact hold true elsewhere in the American continent, where the essential contrast is between human and nonhuman rather than between human (males) and human (females).

COMPARING COMPARISONS: AMAZONIA AND MELANESIA

Although somewhat provocative, the preceding remark was not meant to imply that one culture-specific master code should be replaced by another one, more appropriate to the local context. What I would like to suggest, rather, is that there are different types of comparison according to the nature and scale of the objects being compared. Many years ago, the Leiden school devised a research strategy that it labeled the "field of ethnological study" (*Ethnologisch studieveld*). Intended as a way out of the particularism of village monographs and developed in the wake of the first intensive field studies in Dutch Indonesia and the Malay Archipelago, it stressed that certain cultural areas were to be considered as ethnographic totalities within which each different society or community could be treated as a structural variation within an overall pattern. This is the type of comparison that most anthropologists now practice, implicitly or explicitly, and the one most likely to provide regional master codes such as "gender" for New Guinea, "lineage theory" for Western Africa, "hierarchy" for India, or "cosmocentrism" for Amazonia. That all societies conceptualize filiation, even in a minimal form, does not mean that an ideology of descent is meaningful everywhere. This is self-evident for the specialists of Melanesia and Amazonia, who started their theoretical *aggiornamento* 30 years ago by rejecting the application of African models to their respective fields of study (Barnes 1962, for New Guinea; Seeger, Da Matta, and Viveiros de Castro 1979, for Amazonia). The same could be said of gender. Sex distinctions are universal tools for the building of social categories, but this does not imply that societies everywhere give them the same weight in the definition of their social philosophy and elaborate them to the same degree (Héritier 1996). Because of the intellectual conservatism entailed by the reproduction of knowledge within each regional field of study, and also because each of these areas *does* really appear to exhibit a distinctive style, each of us tends to see his or her ethnographic province as focusing on a core of specific social and cultural features that constitute, as it were, spontaneous patterns of intelligibility; these, however, should be taken not as anthropological universals but as mere tools for the interpretation of geographically circumscribed groups of cultures.

Another type of comparison is the one that the editors of this volume have invited us to attempt. It proceeds from the previous stage and is thus rather difficult to implement, as context-related analytical tools are seldom interchangeable: my Amazonian monkey wrench will do as much damage to Melanesian screws as the reverse.[5] A way out of this compatibility dilemma is to treat two cultural areas that present superficial similarities as speculative springboards for assessing the logical conditions that would allow a reduction of their underlying disparities. Such a process implies considering these disparities as systematic variations of a set of basic patterns that can be shown to operate in different ways in both areas.

There are reasons to believe that the contrasted ideologies of gender relations found in Amazonia and Melanesia result from a deeper difference in the conceptualization and modes of implementation of exchange. In his lectures on Melanesian kinship, Lévi-Strauss remarked that, in this part of the world, marriage alliance seems to be separated from the consanguine-affine distinction in such a way as to constitute almost "a separate order" (Lévi-Strauss 1984, 206). Instead of being used to circumscribe the sphere and partners of exchange (as in Amazonia), the consanguine-affine distinction appears rather as an outcome of marriage alliance, since it is the faculty to enter or not into an exchange with cross-cousins that results in their being assimilated either to affines or to siblings. Now, this sociological precedence of the domain of exchange is directly linked to another striking difference between Amazonia and Melanesia, the possibility or not to substitute persons for objects. Writing on the Baruya, Godelier has shown that this society of the highlands combines two distinct principles of exchange: one is based on a strict equivalence as to the nature and the quantity of the entities exchanged—the model of which is the sister exchange within the Baruya tribe—while the other principle allows a disparity in the nature and the quantity of the items exchanged—the acquisition of wives against goods among intertribal trading partners (Godelier 1982). Although these principles coexist among the Baruya, Godelier argues, they are usually dissociated in Melanesia: either the only substitutes for humans are other humans (in marriage exchange and in warfare, where a death must be repaid by another death), or humans are systematically substituted for by nonhumans, in which case women and homicides are compensated for by material wealth (253–290). I find this distinction useful, in that it calls attention to the fact that the principle of substituting objects for persons is conspicuously absent in Amazonia: bridewealth is replaced by the brideservice to which young men are subjected during the widely distributed period of uxorilocal residence, and a violent death can never be repaid except by another violent death.[6]

Now, it seems reasonable to assume that what may account for the greater institutional complexity of Melanesia is the multiplicity of options opened up by the various combinations between what we may call "homosubstitution" and "heterosubstitution." Competitive systems of exchange (such as the *tee* or the *moka*), for instance, or the "big-man" complex, which are unknown in Amazonia, could not exist without the principle of heterosubstitution.[7] In fact, the whole range of intermediary institutions found between "big-men societies" and "'great-men societies," or between fully ascribed and fully achieved political status, may well stem, as Lemonnier convincingly argues, from the variations in the modes of compensation for, and exchange of, humans and nonhumans in war and in peace (1990). But why then is heterosubstitution absent in Amazonia? For what reasons cannot animals and artifacts stand for human persons or for parts of their bodies? Conversely, why is it that material wealth is deemed in Melanesia to be an adequate embodiment and a convenient carrier of social relations? I suspect that part of the answer lies in different ontological premises as to what constitutes a person, the process by which he or she is constructed and the links through which he or she becomes objectified.

A first clue to the nature of that difference is given by the striking contrast between the two areas regarding the treatment and domestication of animals (Morton 1984). In spite of the fact that the so-called "Ipomoean revolution"—the increase in pig production following the introduction of the sweet potato in New Guinea (Watson 1977)—was triggered by a plant domesticated in Amazonia several thousand years before, and although several species of Amazonian mammals are likely candidates for domestication, the Amerindians never transformed, say, the wild pigs they hunted into domestic pigs. I have argued elsewhere that this lack of domestication in the South American lowlands proceeds from the conceptualization of game animals as the independent and collective subject of a contractual relation with humans, thus preventing the kind of metonymical transfer that enables an animal to express the qualities and ambitions of those who possess it (1994b). Amazonian Indians do possess animals, but these are the young of the hunted species, kept as pets in the houses and never eaten; they are treated as orphaned or abducted children, not as expendable livestock. While game animals are affinal others, endowed with humanlike attributes and institutions, pets are consanguinealized when they are brought into the domestic sphere; in neither guise can animals be objectified as extensions of one's person, for they are persons in their own right. They are not seen as being created by human labor—as are pigs or yams in certain Melanesian contexts—and thus can never be fully owned or converted into exchange values. It is not that, failing pigs as currency, the Amazonian Indians had no wealth to exchange for humans—like anyone else, they do not lack trading goods—but rather that they could not conceive of animals as being subordinated to humans and thus as providing convenient substitutes for them.

There are good phenomenological reasons for conceiving a cosmos where humans and nonhumans live on a parity. On the whole, native Amazonia is characterized by low population densities, small and scattered settlements, and a great diversity of animal species; as a result, Amazonian Indians feel immersed in a vast ecological network where humans are extremely sparse. Their landscape is not one of densely populated villages, large enclosed mound fields, herds of pigs, and deep valleys crisscrossed by markers of land rights, as in the prototypical highlands of New Guinea, but one of timid encroachers in a vast sea of multiple life forms. Their social lives and individual growth do not imply producing and accumulating objects and substances that stand for relationships with other humans but rather accumulating knowledge and expertise about relationships with nonhumans and humans alike.

Another type of accumulation is not so benign, however, and plays a central role in the constitution of selfhood in many parts of Amazonia: the repeated assimilation of alien bodies and identities. It is an ontological accumulation and one that negates exchange, although it pushes the principle of homosubstitution to its utmost limits: it is because the flesh and soul of my enemy are analogous to my own that I am able to incorporate them and make the most of it, in spite of the temporary inconvenience that may result from my preying upon another self (see Conklin, this volume). Exocannibalism, hunting for human trophies, abducting women and children, and all other forms of Amazonian predation thus imply that absorbing otherness is necessary for constituting or perpetuating the self, an absorption not conceived as a replacement for a loss but as the addition of another *alter ego,* which will make me different. Ritual anthropophagy is the most obvious or literal expression of this obsessive desire to define oneself by assimilating alien identities, a drive that may take more peaceful expressions, such as in the ethno-taxonomy of the Panoans, who use the word *nawa* both as a generic pejorative term for strangers and as an affix for constructing autonyms (Erikson 1996, 77–82), or in the process of ethnogenesis of the various lowland Quechua communities who continuously absorb individuals from neighboring ethnic groups (Whitten 1976; Scazzocchio 1979). Amazonian cannibalism is thus a quite abstract metonymical operation rather than a mere incorporation of substances: it is that which I assimilate that predicates what I am.[8]

All this offers a definite contrast to the emphasis that Melanesian cultures lay on bodily substances as a medium for the construction of individual and collective identities along gender lines. Using bodily humors linked to sexuality and the reproductive process (semen, menstrual blood, milk, vaginal fluids) as literal markers of personal status is not very common in Amazonia, where people are mostly indifferent to the fear of pollution by physiological substances.

Conversely, these substances constitute adequate social emblems in Melanesia because of their convertibility in the physiology of exchange, such as salt becoming a substitute for semen among the Baruya, the pandanus nut becoming either milk or sperm among the Sambia, or pig and game meat becoming a substitute for the flesh and blood of a dead person when they are offered as compensation to his maternal relatives among the Etoro or Melpa (Bonnemère 1990). In Amazonia, there may be cases of homology between body parts or physiological substances, on the one hand, and artifacts or natural kinds, on the other, but these homologies are seldom made explicitly, as in Melanesia, and they must be uncovered through a sophisticated interpretation of symbolic discourse (see Hugh-Jones, Chapter 11; Bidou 1996). These metaphorical equivalences are usually found in societies who have secret men's cults analogous to those of Melanesia—where, for instance, the sacred flutes are seen as embodiments of ancestors' bones (see Chaumeil 1993 for the Yagua or S. Hugh-Jones 1979 for the northwest Amazon)—but these homologies seldom lead to actual processes of heterosubstitution in the construction or disposal of the person. Nevertheless, these societies do exhibit a peculiar relation to artifacts as substitutes: contrary to what prevails elsewhere in Amazonia, their sacred musical instruments are both embodied substitutes (metaphorically, of bodily substance or of certain spirits, and metonymically, of male power) and nonexchangeable against similar objects or other items. They have thus many features of Oceanian "inalienable possessions" (Weiner 1992) and may constitute an intermediary figure between homosubstitution and heterosubstitution: they alone stand for something else, and they alone cannot enter the network of reciprocity.

What would be the necessary conditions for switching to heterosubstitution? I know of only two native societies in the South American lowlands that have made that step: the Guajiros of the Atlantic coast of Colombia and Venezuela and the Araucanians of central Chile.[9] Both have bridewealth and payments to compensate for homicides; both were famed for their bellicosity and resistance to the Spaniards for several centuries; both associate personal and corporate prestige with the accumulation, display, and ceremonial exchange of material wealth, mainly pieces of jewelry and cattle; both of these societies are also exceptional in that they have domestic animals. The Araucanians and the Guajiros acquired cattle and horses by raiding Spanish settlements and adopted a pastoral economy during the colonial period, thereby establishing an entirely novel way of objectifying animals, no longer as persons and collective subjects of a social relationship but as mere signifiers of social status and detachable objects of generalized exchange. These two cases point again to the crucial role of the relationship with nonhumans, be they artifacts or natural kinds, in explaining the predominance of homosubstitution or heterosubstitution. Paradoxically, however, the conversion of the Guajiros and colonial Araucanians to pastoralism did not bring their social organization and values to resemble those of Melanesian societies more than those of the rest of the South American lowlands; in fact, they are more reminiscent of Nilotic peoples, such as the Nuer or the Dinka, with whom they share the "cattle complex" of large-scale herders. This may be a sign that there are wider differences than meet the eye between South America and Melanesia or, more simply perhaps, that once the speed of history has accelerated after the colonial encounter, the rates of divergence between societies become incommensurable.

NOTES

1. In her thoughtful comment on this chapter, Marilyn Strathern suggested that blood-sucking by manioc plants might be equated with suckling, thus implying a nurturing transmission of substance from the women to their vegetal offspring. However, Achuar women do not regard the vampirism of manioc as a legitimate feeding process; they view it, rather, as a very harmful propensity that must be deflected by magical songs and specific rituals.

Furthermore, women are less exposed to bloodsucking than are their small (human) children, whose main diet is composed of mashed manioc tubers. Gardening thus implies both a deadly competition between different kinds of children and an element of reciprocal predation between humans and nonhumans that parallels hunting.

2. A point made by Tuzin (1982) for the Arapesh and emphasized, in a comparative framework, by Gregor and Tuzin (Chapter 14).

3. In a sample of the kinship systems of 48 lowland societies, only 20 have indubitable exogamous unilineal descent groups or moieties (Hornborg 1988, 223); these have a disproportionate importance in the sample, as three quarters of them are either Gê (11)—that is, not Amazonian, ecologically speaking—or Tukanoan (4), the two strongholds of unilineality in the tropical lowlands and the areas attracting the most attention from anthropologists in the past 30 years.

4. Leaving aside the treatment of pigs and the large body of literature on cultural ecology, natural species are mostly taken into account as the metonymical components of ritual activities concerned with gender distinctions (e.g., Bonnemère 1992; Juillerat 1986). There are notable exceptions, of course, such as Ralph Bulmer (1967, 1974) and Steven Feld (1982).

5. This is at least the impression I have when I cast a look at a youthful attempt at comparing Amazonian and Melanesian shamanism (Descola and Lory 1982).

6. Hugh-Jones (this volume) mentions the possible exception of the Kalapalo, where "bridewealth payments" reputedly mark a woman's first marriage. It is doubtful, however, that the gifts given to newly married women *and* men can be considered as bridewealth, as these are immediately passed on to the elder in-laws of both spouses (Basso 1995, 16). The moral imperative of generosity and sharing is extremely strong among the Kalapalo and seems incompatible with the idea of a payment being made for the acquisition of a person (ibid.).

7. The Kalapalo "big-men" to which Hugh-Jones calls attention (this volume) are somewhat peculiar in that their status is partly ascribed and partly achieved. In order to become the ceremonial representatives of their villages in intercommunity feasts, they must belong initially to a class of *hereditary* titular chiefs. Apart from this initial condition, their ascension requires personal charisma, generosity, and physical strength, as well as perfect mastery of an elaborate formal language used in the rhetoric of political discourse and in ceremonial dialogues. They must also possess a shamanic competence so as to be able to launch accusations of witchcraft against other chiefs competing for the leadership of the village (Menget 1993). The capacity to channel wealth in the ceremonial exchanges between villages is thus only one dimension of a status that merges aspects of political positions seemingly differentiated in Melanesia between "big-men," "great-men," and chiefs.

8. See Eduardo Viveiros de Castro's illuminating discussion of the Tupian "cannibal cogito" (1992, 252–258).

9. See Picon 1983 and Perrin 1983 for the Guajiros. The "Araucanians" I am referring to defined themselves as "Reche" during the colonial period (sixteenth to eighteenth centuries), before their submission to the Spaniards and their subsequent ethnogenesis as "Mapuche" (Boccara 1996); however, the contemporary Mapuche have retained the practice of bridewealth (Faron 1969).

SIX

Age-Based Genders among the Kayapo

William H. Fisher

William Fisher argues that age and gender should not be separated, in that they are "part of the same complex of ideas." Moreover, throughout the life cycle, gender characteristics change, thereby creating an "inconstancy of gender imagery." Utilizing data from the Brazilian Kayapo and the Yangoru Boiken of New Guinea (Roscoe, Chapter 12), Fisher finds parallel patterns of maturation and gender, and in general, body imagery that is similar in both regions. Moreover, "the essential elements of personhood appear strikingly similar as well." Nonetheless, Fisher, like Descola, locates what he regards as significant differences in the way in which Amazonians and Melanesians discriminate between self and society and between culture and nature as they are revealed by gender and age roles. The two studies stand together as reminders that cultures and cultural regions do not need to be essentialized or utterly compliant with a master code in order for the work of comparison to go forward.

Where gender is associated with natural substances ingested into and emitted from human bodies, the human body appears to have distinctly different gender attributes at different points in the life cycle. Amazonian and Melanesian accounts generally concur on the *inconstancy* of gender imagery associated with the individual human body, whether male or female, throughout the life course. Relationships defining of a particular socially defined age may therefore be said to be coincident with gender distinctions. If gender is conceptualized in terms of bodily potency and agency, as appears the wont in Amazonia and Melanesia, then one must recognize that both age and gender are part and parcel of the same complex of ideas. More particularly, this means that we can regard the dimension of social action that embodies gendered potencies also to embody potencies particular to social age.

A comparison of Melanesia and Amazonia suggests that notions of gender, substance, and age are inextricable and may be articulated in a number of ways. If we follow Melanesianist authors such as Poole (1981a), Strathern (1988), Meigs (1984), and Herdt (1987), male and female bodies have no constant gender qualities at all points in their lives. At some level, male and female genders appear to be modeled on their opposites. Reproduction of sociality centers on an infinite recursivity through which attributes of one gender provide a template for social action by the opposite gender. Symbols of gestation, birth, and nursing seem to compose a founding metaphor that is likely to have both male and female versions (cf. Bonnemère, Chapter 2). Physiological fluids associated with reproduction appear to have an androgynous character: breast milk/semen, menstrual blood/body blood, for example.

Among Amazonians, however, although the creation of gendered potencies are equally focused on the creation of bodily attributes, gender organization is often mirrored institutionally in male and female reflections. Both male and female versions of the chieftaincy may exist, for example, and especially among the Gê peoples ritual inversions are frequent, whereby male and female space and activities are reversed. Full-scale battles between the sexes are frequently reported (Siskind 1973; Murphy and Murphy 1985; Gregor 1985; Fisher 1991). Sexual competition may manifest itself in other areas, such as the counterpoint of simultaneously sung female and male song forms (Seeger 1981). As will be made clearer in the chapter conclusion, Amazonians inhabit a cosmos whose sociality is self-evident. The distinctive form of human sociality within this larger social milieu involves "artificially created" social relationships that distinguish humans from nature rather than mimic natural fecundity. Age is stressed as much as gender precisely because human age grades do not mimic natural growth but are based on social exchanges with unlike bodily potencies. The refusal by Amazonians to acknowledge interactions with the ancestors appears to be the flip side of attempts to put relations between generations on a cultural rather than natural basis.

I take as my theme, therefore, the inconstancy of gender imagery throughout the life cycle in order to discuss the different ways age and gender are mutually constructed in both regions. I begin by focusing on one case of institutional "mirroring," the case of female chiefs among the Kayapo. I discuss the decisive role collective activities organized by leaders (male and female) play in creating appropriate bodily attributes of participants. I then briefly discuss a Melanesian case in which quite similar distinctions are made regarding the linked bodily potencies of age and gender. In conclusion, I suggest that different pervasive notions regarding the reproduction of human sociality in Melanesia and Amazonia help us understand some crucial age/gender contrasts despite the strikingly similar body imagery within both regions.

My starting point is the insistence I encountered among Kayapo men and women that the spouses of male leaders are female chiefs who lead groups of women. Female chiefs or leaders have been reported for the Kayapo (Werner 1980, 90; Posey 1994, 274; Verswijver 1985; Turner 1995, 102), as well as in the Xingu Park (Gregor 1985, 111). For the Kayapo, leaders of both sexes are said to perform similar functions inasmuch as their primary activity is the mobilization of groups of people to perform subsistence tasks. Informants' theoretical descriptions, however, did not easily fit with observations of village life in which male leaders by means of oratory seemed to exercise considerable influence while female leaders were comparatively low key. While I never heard female chiefs address the village as a whole, I did observe female coordination of some daily tasks carried out by groups of women classified according to social age. In the end, we are left with the flat insistence of both men and women that wives of male chiefs are also chiefs and that their leadership is essential for village life.

The fieldwork on which this analysis of gender, leadership, and collective social action is based was carried out among the Xikrin branch of the Kayapo. Further discussions with a Gavião[1] man and a rereading of ethnographic materials lead me to conclude that a widely shared understanding of the basis of sociality is common to the Northern Gê. This understanding centers on the link between collective and individual human activity and the centrality of the socially coordinated creation of bodily capabilities. Despite claims by Gê ethnographers that the female domain is opposed to the male domain as nature is opposed to culture (Maybury-Lewis 1979), arenas for the creation of bodily properties include both domestic practices and collective public activities. The following analysis suggests that one of the reasons little attention has been given to gender by ethnographers of the Central Brazilian Gê peoples is that gender is complexly packaged along with age such that categories of social classification and social action always refer simultaneously to both. Moreover, the heralded dualist worldview of the Gê proves not to be as revealing of gender relations as one might expect. I hypothesize that, among the Gê, the male/female polarity is further parceled into imagery that draws on male and female bodily potencies at different stages of the human life cycle and that social age becomes a more apt guideline to the sorts of social exchanges and avoidances necessary to create human sociality.

CIRCULATING COMPONENTS OF PERSONHOOD

Kayapo draw a basic distinction between those relatives who share physical substance, conceived of as a single living essence (*ĩ pydji*), and relatives with whom this connection is not a cause for observing behavioral or alimentary taboos for the protection of mutual health and well-being.[2] The quality of being a Kayapo, however, is not linked to this physical sharedness but with possession, "within one's head," of specific knowledge of cultural traditions. The hallmark of this knowledge (*kukradjà*) is centered around codes of conduct and health rules, as well as ceremonial knowledge, mythology, and the like. This knowledge, always transferred from different relations, concerns medicines, chants that are efficacious for certain activities or can serve as shields against various sorts of danger, and various kinds of ceremonial ornaments. With the exception of ceremonial ornaments that are associated with certain gender-specific ritual roles, valued knowledge of this sort may be passed from older persons to younger ones, irrespective of gender.

In public or semipublic retransmissions or retellings I witnessed, the relationship between the speaker and the person from whom the knowledge was obtained is usually mentioned as a validation of its truth and reliability. The general intelligence and aptitude of the original teller and his or her relation to the reteller are stressed. Gender seems irrelevant here, and, in fact, little boys and girls typically apprehend much valuable custom before falling asleep in the big bed of their grandmother or grandfather.[3] One's store of *kukradjà* originates from a number of different sources besides grandparents, and individuals who so desire may take the initiative to seek out new teachers with specific skills or knowledge well into adulthood.

Aside from *ĩ* and *kukradjà*, components of a person include an essence (*karon*) unique to each individual. The concept of *karon* is related to beliefs held by many Amerinds that one's shadow, soul, or ghost is also in some sense a "picture" of oneself without being equivalent to the total physicality of self. The *karon* is central to the understanding of illness, shamanism, and dreaming, as well as to a person's individual identity and afterlife. At birth, the *karon* is only loosely associated with a newborn's body. Later the association is stronger, and Kayapo say that the sound of thunder signals a death as the *karon* definitively disassociates from a body.

While "of the body," *ĩ* and *kukradjà* are also involved in circulation and exchange mediated by social institutions, or better, by specific alignments and activities of people. Kayapo stress particular social arrangements because they recognize that circulation of *kukradjà* and *ĩ* go far beyond the bounds of the village or territory they inhabit. *Kukradjà* is often discovered outside of the village among neighboring peoples, wild animals, or even among whites. *Ĩ*, on the other hand, is a universal source of vitality. It is obvious to the Kayapo that all living things contain *ĩ* and that it is circulated through something akin to a food chain. It is pointed out that the vegetation consumed by a deer supplies it with *ĩ* while deer meat when consumed, in turn, infuses Kayapo with new *ĩ*. At the same time, the deer also has its distinctive *karon* and, for various reasons, game is dangerous, both *ĩ* and *karon* being possible causes of illness for its human slayers and consumers.

The circulatory character of *ĩ* explains why it is continually depleted and replenished through human or animal activity.[4] A person's bodily state is a product of his personal social state,[5] and *ĩ* is central to this conception, but not because of any inevitable deterministic model of circulation. Rather, certain states of sociality, including certain activities implicated with these states, channel *ĩ* in particular ways. There is a certain reversal in the kind of causation that Westerners associate with biology. For example, old age is a condition in which an elder's *ĩ* is very weak. There are other kinds of typical manifestations of old age as well: one's head, site of knowledge, gradually hardens, and one speaks better than one listens, although, as might be expected, one's *karon* remains virtually unchanged. Diminished *ĩ* is evidenced through the flaps of skin, the looseness with which it covers the body. Formerly bursting with *ĩ*, the skin now hangs empty because old people's appetites are diminished. Old age does not directly cause a reduction of *ĩ*, rather, the physical/social state of old age is a reflection of self-actualized and collective social activity; in particular, the appetite of the elderly appears to decrease and they neglect to eat enough to replenish their *ĩ*. Similarly, the onset of pregnancy precipitously lowers the *ĩ* of both partners. Newly pregnant parents (pregnancy is a state shared by a woman and any men who have contributed to conception) are notoriously picky eaters because of the onset of nausea (*atkwadjy*) and so do not nourish themselves well. In sum, bodily being is never the straightforward result of the progressive acquisition of missing elements of full social personhood. Directed human activity or lack of activity is the nexus of social causation, including bodily state.

Therefore, while the Xikrin Kayapo acknowledge that male and female persons, equipped with penes and vaginas respectively, are opposed to one another in a larger sense, we must be careful of assumptions that make essential transcendental qualities of "maleness" and "femaleness" the basis of this opposition. By way of illustration, we may take a property such as strength, believed by the Kayapo to be associated with a surfeit of *ĩ*. It would be a mistake to assume that maleness connotes strength. Certainly, it is acknowledged that males from adolescence onward possess greater strength than females in general until the decline in strength experienced during old age. An unmarried boy faithfully observing the full range of food taboos and following a prescribed diet is thought to attain the maximum *ĩ*. After he marries, and with each additional offspring, his *ĩ* decreases. Strength, therefore, is not an essential trait of males but is specified in relationship to a series of life stages signaled by age/gender categories. Moreover, a married man will suffer a diminution of *ĩ* along with his wife during their pregnancy, which is thought to be shared by both partners. That is, his strength covaries in relationship to that of his spouse. Only by ethnocentrically assuming that a particular life stage can be made to represent a range of transformations undergone in male bodily qualities over the course of a lifetime can we talk about strength, or any other characteristic, as the quintessential abstract property of maleness. Women, it should be mentioned, are also admired for their strength and bulky physique.

Perhaps such qualities as fierceness or tameness come closest to characterizing essential qualities of gender irrespective of age. However, any person's ability to speak or act fiercely depends on bodily potency as well. Married women, particularly as they age, may aggressively berate an entire assemblage with no apparent shame, while bachelors in similar contexts are constrained to silence by their unmarried state.

Among the Kayapo, knowledge is closely associated with bodily potency in a manner not immediately apparent to Westerners who invest much significance in the difference between manual and intellectual labor. "Education" and the transmission of *kukradjà* are thought of in terms of circulation largely controlled by the dictates of kinship relations. Just as kinship is itself a sharing and controlling of certain bodily processes, the expressed purpose of most transmitted knowledge involves the control of health through medicines and other means. Thus the economy of bodiliness expressed through different forms of sociality is not opposed to ceremonial or traditional knowledge in the form of *kukradjà*. This knowledge is part of and accessory to other aspects of bodiliness. In contrast to other views of Gê culture that tout the fundamental opposition between biological continuity and social (nonbiological) inheritance (e.g., Seeger, Da Matta, and Viveiros de Castro), I suggest that both are conceived by the Gê as constituting a unitary process.

Age Organization

Kayapo are little interested in why a baby should be born a particular sex. As discussed later, various steps may be taken to produce a child with certain qualities, including gender, but there is something unique about each human birth that escapes social control. While sexual differences are apparent at birth, and everybody inquires whether a newborn is a boy or a girl, only later, with the active participation of the child itself, are steps taken to create the social qualities associated with a gender identity. To pave the way for subsequent development, a male has his lower lip pierced shortly after birth and a little girl is given a bead belt shortly after she is able to walk. Both children have their ears pierced and openings gradually enlarged, and both receive bracelets and leg bands and have their bodies and heads ornamented in identical styles (Turner 1980; Vidal 1977; also Seeger 1975 for Gê-speaking Suyá). As a precaution, both boys and girls are adorned only with plant equivalents of ornaments that later will be replaced with animal feathers when they are able to "walk firmly." At this time additional bodily ornaments appropriate for males and females will be presented.

Male and female babies are considered to be the same social age ("suckling ones," and later "little ones") until they begin to be differentiated in terms of male and female activities consciously undertaken as such. At this time, they begin to be categorized by parallel but separate age/gender terms, *me ôkre* for boys and *me prĩntire* for girls. More specialized ritual ornaments associated with same-sex mentor relations begin to be presented from this time until late adolescence, and a boy may begin to have his lower lip perforation gradually enlarged. Ultimately, the final decision as to the size of his lower lip opening will rest with each man himself. Only with the development of a facility for understanding, which includes the ability to observe food restrictions, obedience, and feel shame, are children fully differentiated into age grades[6] for which gender is specified.

Physical qualities such as toughness, running abilities, and the ability to hear implicitly refer to social abilities and potential. For example, "hearing" refers to more than the recognition of sounds through the ear. "To hear" and

"to understand" are synonymous. Learning, then, means "hearing" the counsel of elders, which is predicated on physical abilities. Hearing also makes one
able to cooperate with others. "To hear" never refers merely to proper aural
functioning in a strictly physical sense but to the social character of a person.
Bodily abilities index social transactions.

When I refer to "qualities" of the body in the course of the present discussion, I am referring to a limited number of abilities that crystallize central aspects of sociality for the Kayapo and other Gê. As abilities—to touch things,
hear, see, go without drinking water for long periods, and soft-headedness—all
are shorthand for referring to social practices emblematic of activities appropriately exercised by specific age/gender groupings. Thus when adolescent
boys are prohibited from eating certain foods because it would cause them to
not "see things," this refers to developing the ability to hunt game, which is
necessary to support a future wife and children.

Once boys and girls are recognized as being physically independent, self-
assured, and able to think for themselves, they begin to cultivate the qualities
of fierceness (*akrê*) and tameness (*uabô*) that differentiate males from females.
Boys of the *me bôktire* age grade, for example, are the only ones who may eat
jaguar meat, an *akrê* food par excellence. Girls, for their part, enter the corresponding age grade *me prĩntire*. The focus on diet and behavior as means to
shape capabilities becomes increasingly stressed as children are able to take
greater responsibility for their own conduct. At this age, children also observe
restrictions for their own siblings during times of illness or life crisis transitions. As a quality, *uabô* (tame) relates to the ability to remain placid and un-
ruffled, accepting of others' desires, and noninvolvement in the games of one-
upmanship that characterize interactions between groups of males. The
quality *akrê* (fierce) focuses on the potential for reacting with mindless rage and
frenzy.[7] The hallmark of an angry or fierce person is that they put aside all
thoughts of their own physical safety; literally, they have no desire to live—*tĩn
pram ket*. This is a socially mandated reaction when one's village is attacked or
one's kin, age-mates, or friend is killed. Indeed, the historical practice of
Kayapo warfare, according to the villagers, is to kill all men and take all
women and children captive. The idea of "domesticating" male captives is
difficult or impossible because of a male-cultivated willingness to sacrifice all
in the pursuit of revenge. As with male ferocity, female tameness is not innate
to sexual identity and must be socially instilled by harnessing the appropriate
natural qualities. Individual males or females may display behaviors characteristic of their gender opposites. For example, a girl may be fierce, as explained by a man recounting how his (*prĩntire*) sister, captured by Brazilians,
died in captivity because she refused all nourishment out of pure anger at her
captors, a typical male refusal of food when enraged and an index of the state
of being without desire to live (*tĩn pram ket*). As with all social qualities, tameness and fierceness are created through the appropriate eating and behavioral

practices that, although organizing of sociality, interact with wide-ranging propensities of individuals. Individual differences in personality and skill are recognized, although not assumed to be caused by sexual identity.[8]

Among items classified with respect to tameness and fierceness are bees, animals, and parts of animals. Bees that sting are by definition fierce, and consumption of their honey should be limited to men, while stingless bees produce (a rather vinegary) "tame" honey. A man would not want to consume too much honey from stingless bees, because it is part of a diet appropriate for tame people. Women must also avoid nonfood items associated with fierceness. A common example is the mixture of herbs, stinging ants, and urucum smeared on a dog to make it an effective and ferocious hunter.

Human qualities may also be developed through applications of herbal medicines. If a father recognizes a particularly truculent nature in his male offspring or fervently desires a fierce child, he may collect stinging ants and the right herbal concoction to bring out these qualities.[9] Any effort to shape children's qualities is dependent on the conscious adherence to a regimen of correct food and medicine consumption along with other behaviors. That is, for the Kayapo, education is central rather than auxiliary to the physical creation of social qualities through bodily states, since self-transformative actions are necessary corollaries to socially orchestrated actions performed on behalf of children, youths, and new parents.

Food and behavioral restrictions make possible the successful achievement of social activities. When asked what sorts of restrictions applied to an unwed female, one man incredulously replied, "What for? They don't do anything!" By which he meant that they are not undergoing food and behavioral restrictions in order to develop particular personal and social skills. While this is not strictly true, boys are certainly weighed down with more food prohibitions than are girls.

The sort of pollution and taboos that Gê-speakers recognize have little to do with intrinsic characteristics of a Manichaean cosmos of which gender opposition is a master symbol. Pollution is not inherent in any particular natural object. Instead, natural characteristics and qualities are used or avoided in the pursuit of the development of social qualities appropriate to different age/gender states. Avoidance and exposure, blocking and channeling, are the two symmetrical facets of a philosophy of social action that places human sociality both within and against broader cosmological processes that include the circulation of matter and knowledge.

Fabricating Adults: The Natural and the Cultural in Melanesia

We may now begin to note some similarities in Melanesia with the creation of bodily potentials that are at one and the same time biological and social. A common theme of Melanesian ethnography is the ritual creation of adult males. Such rituals are collective undertakings and may even depend on the aggregation of persons from several settlements. Ethnographers have proposed that such undertakings should not be reduced to a semiotic dimension. Rituals and most particularly initiation rites are held to be effective because they create bodily capacities of hardness, intensity, and resolve, such as manifest in the Sambia *jerungdu* (Herdt 1987) or *halinya* among the Sepik-dwelling Yangoru Boiken (Roscoe, Chapter 12). In discussing initiation procedures to make boys fierce, Roscoe remarks on the change in bodily qualities involved in the signaled social transformation. "As the Yangoru Boiken envisage this initiatory process, it is less a training or conferral of qualities on an existing male self than a literal change in the initiates' constitutions" (Roscoe, Chapter 12). Herdt also stresses that socially produced biological changes are involved but stresses that girls and boys mature in radically different fashions. Whereas boys must be initiated to "promote biological changes that finally cement the growth from childhood to manhood, . . . a girl is born with all of the vital organs and fluids necessary for her to attain reproductive competence through 'natural' maturation" (Herdt 1982b, 54).

Some underlying similarities between indigenous central Brazilians and certain Melanesians are striking. In both areas, essential social attributes of persons are not only grounded in particular bodily qualities, but social action aims to form these qualities by means of behavioral and food taboos as well as through positive injunctions to eat certain foods and cultivate certain behaviors. The creation of social relations depends on a transformation of existing bodily potencies throughout the life cycle.

The essential elements of personhood appear strikingly similar as well. The Sambia tripartite division between soul, body, and consciously held knowledge, along with the social salience of individual volition, is described by Herdt (1987). This underlying notion of personhoods appears by no means uncommon in Melanesia, as attested to by analogous ideas of spirit, life-force, and social wisdom among the Maring (LiPuma 1988, 108). However, the tripartite Gê person is embedded in a series of exchanges with differently aged persons, in contrast to Melanesians, whose prestations seem to focus on transactions with dead ancestors.

Age Alignments

Human sociality among the Gê is, in large part, a product of ordering and transforming *ĩ* derived from nature. Physically robust and healthy humans endowed with appropriate shares of distinctively Kayapo *kukradjà* are the result of coordinated actions of different gender/age grades and kin, each with its own distinct physicality or bodiliness. There is no "social" state as opposed to a "natural" state of being. Nor is any gender/age more or less social than any other. Before marriage and childbearing, Kayapo young people develop the physicality, knowledge, and social qualities needed to do men's and women's work and to have healthy offspring. After childbirth, men and women draw on previously created qualities to jointly tend a shared physical/emotional bond based on a sharing of physical substance. This entails both a radical change in their own behaviors and habits and a gradual reordering of relationships with their own parents. The birth of one's first child begins the redirecting of ĩ and knowledge circulation among one's spouse, offspring, and self, and one's own group of originating substance. Three generations are always implicated in what is seen as the central physical/social transformation configuring the field of kinship and the creation of parents, children, and social mentor relations. As part of this trigenerational transformation, elders or mentors must *also* be socially created along with parents and children. Mentors may transmit their names, perform ceremonially, and otherwise play a role in the socialization of grandchildren and children of cross-sex siblings. As with other social states, mentors in the kin field gradually develop the required qualities to become elders, defined in terms of particular behaviors for the development of the appropriate physicality and social qualities. Decreasing sexual activity helps one lose one's shame; one uses different speech and may intervene in disputes. As restrictions safeguarding the health of offspring are gradually discarded, both men and women may submit to acts such as leg scraping that identify them with grandchildren (*tabdjwỳ*). This is typified in the remark made by one man thinking about the impending birth of his own daughter, "I may as well become a *mebêngêt* (mentor) quickly." The developmental trend over an individual lifetime does not move from "natural" child to socialized adult; rather, particular sorts of natural processes are appropriately engaged at each step in order to recreate a condition of sociality that is always global and rests never with a single age/gender class but on relations between them.

After my first stay in the field, I had drawn analogies between growth of plants and animals and human beings. During my second field stint, Kayapo rejected these analogies and stressed that human growth involved transformations from one age to another. While plant growth may be described in terms of size, human growth is always described in terms of being in a particular age grade or making the transition to a subsequent age grade. Human growth is not linear or merely cumulative, because it involves changes in human bodies *linked to one another through connections of ĩ and aspects of bodiliness.* For this reason, the first birth is both most dangerous and also paradigmatic of subsequent changes: the firstborn may be referred to as the "true child" (*kra kumrẽn*). Each of the first four children in birth order may be referred to by distinct terms that are generally distinguished according to sex: firstborn (*kukamã*), second (*atãrè*), third (*konetã*), fourth (*õ'êrê*), while the last born is called *kutapure*. This reflects the fact that the trigenerational transformation of relations is affected over time, and each subsequent child requires fewer restrictions. Moreover, boys and girls (and their parents) undergo different types of restrictions while all-male groups of age-mates take on a surrogate role of nurturing boys in the period before marriage and residence with their wife's family.

A common pan-Gê outlook discernible in ethnographic descriptions is the linked quality of human age/gender status. Individual age is only comprehensible in terms of relations with people of different age. A glance at Crocker's (1990, 181) exhaustive summary of terms applying to age show that most of the terms are descriptive of actions taken on behalf of others. Such actions encompass both characteristics related to biology and sociality. For example, men of the age set averaging about 55 years are called both *"ampoo yii khên khu"* ("eat any 'bad' meat," that is, they save the good portions for others) and *"me hapal-re hapak-khre"* ("they advise nephews"). In short, I am making the claim that among Gê peoples, sociality is to be viewed primarily as a sociological order regulating bodily states that are linked to age/gender classes and kin. Food items, natural objects, and sex are social tools harboring both creative potential and inherent dangers. This seems to be the main reason that collective sex, usually in the form of exchanges between age grades or even moieties are so common among Northern Gê peoples (Crocker and Crocker 1994; Turner 1966), and group or sequential sex has also been reported during name confirmation ceremonies (Banner n.d.; Verswijver 1985).

The Use of Sexuality

In his fieldwork among the Canela, W. Crocker, more fully than other Gê ethnographers, has documented sexuality and attendant beliefs. He illustrates a common Gê focus on creating bachelors as an age set: "youths are interned in cells for about three months, where they are supposed to grow strong by avoiding 'pollutions' from consuming meat juices and contacting sexual fluids. They eat large quantities of unpolluted special foods" (Crocker and Crocker 1994, 33–34). Among the Canela, unmarried women are subjected to an analogous process for the creation of the required social/bodily state. "After their first menstruation, girls underwent similar dietary restrictions [to bachelors] and were required by their maternal uncles and their paternal aunts to have sex almost exclusively with men in their 40's to 60's to gain their physical and moral strength" (Crocker and Crocker 1994, 34). Two points are important to note. On the one hand, the mode of creating social/physiological states in females is the same as in males. On the other, sexual activity itself, far from being an activity to be avoided, is one which, as in the consumption of certain foods, circulates *ĩ* in a socially desirable fashion.

Women's monthly cycles are thought to be a result of their self-actualizing activity, namely sexual intercourse. Menstrual blood is not considered to be a danger to men because it is controlled through medicine. Isabel Murphy (personal communication) reports that from the time they are young, Kayapo girls take herbal remedies to eliminate the flow of blood associated with their monthly cycle. Consumption of these remedies, along with consumption of "tame" food, parallels boys' efforts to develop certain qualities associated with maleness. By the time a girl reaches adulthood her monthly menstrual flow is thought to stop. Werner (1984, 190–91) also reports on infrequent menstruation of Kayapo women and their interpretation of menstruation among adult women in terms of illness. While it would seem that constant treatment to staunch menstrual flow might make conception difficult, this would be to take conception itself as an inevitable and natural result of intercourse. However, Kayapo beliefs about conception are entirely consistent with notions of aging, menstruation, and temperament. Human knowledge and activity are necessary to harness natural potentials, and Kayapo women use several herbal medicines to encourage pregnancy and claim to be able to conceive only the number of children they desire.

Although beliefs about the dangers to men of emanations of women's generative powers, especially menstrual blood, are widespread in Melanesia (Keesing 1982), beliefs that adult women do not menstruate are also sometimes encountered. Townsend (1995, 169) reports that menstrual pollution is not an issue after marriage since married women and widows are said not to menstruate. Although it is not clear why this should be so, and there appears to be some sentiment that this is a fiction, married women do not restrict their activities once a month as girls do (Townsend 1990, 378). In other areas of Melanesia, as within the Strickland-Bosavi tribes, menstrual blood is not a focus of concern, and women may not observe monthly restrictions, although they do appear to menstruate (Kelly 1993). Whether an actual cessation of menstruation is involved or merely a diminishing of its frequency because of longer periods of pregnancy and lactation or other factors is an open question. Strassmann (1997) presents evidence that the number of menses experienced in a lifetime may differ greatly within different human populations.

Mature unmarried Kayapo girls form a parallel age grade to the bachelors, and both these groups are thought to be the epitome of vitality. Girls of this age grade have the reputation for maintaining frequent sexual relations, both with bachelors and with older men. As stated previously, the initiation of menarche among females of this age grade is thought to be a result of sexual intercourse and to chronologically follow defloration. Age at the time of menarche and first sexual experience do seem roughly to coincide. However, menstruation is not the basis of overriding concern among the Kayapo. No particular rites mark initial defloration or menstruation since this event is not accorded much significance, consistent with the ideology of blood flow as anomalous. However, during this period of a girl's life she may be symbolically married to a young man of the bachelor age grade in a ceremony referred to as "people of the blood" (*me kamrô*). This is also an alternative term referring to the unmarried girl's age grade. A girl and her groom are hidden together under palm mats within the bride's house, where they abstain from eating, movement, drinking, and bodily eliminations during the daylight hours, with the exception of three baths administered during the day separately by different age grades. Although no sexual union is involved, this ceremonial marriage may be the beginning of a real long-term partnership. If partners so choose, there are no obligations to one another after the ceremony.

The mat marriage symbolizes the creation of a couple as a unit jointly responsible for the health of any resulting children. This joint responsibility will continue throughout their reproductive years, extending until after the time their offspring bear children in turn. For example, after she gives birth, a woman's close relatives, including her parents, collectively undergo a period of food restrictions in order to "make her blood hard" to diminish postpartum bleeding. Although characteristic of females, vaginal bleeding is treated as an illness that responds to the same sorts of safeguards as other illnesses. Postpartum flow may originate from an individual woman, but custody and care is not the exclusive province of her or of other women. All physicality of the body is the province of the community of substance formed by the birth of a child to a woman and one or several husbands. Coordinated actions of people of different social/bodily states resurrect and maintain the field of sociality within which all proper development occurs.

It is in terms of sexual relations that male and female activity obtain vastly different effects. In brief, for males, sexual activity with women has the power to create relations with her other male sexual partners, while the corresponding activity of women results in nothing more than an accumulation of men she calls "husband" (*mied*), whose offspring with other women are not classified as her children. Institutionalized spouse exchanges are common, although not mandatory, and form an ongoing relationship between married couples. The relationship between the two husbands (*aben kadjy ari ku'ê*—together/ for/pl./grow erect) is particularly powerful. They become akin to brothers, and their offspring will actually be classified as siblings. Although never stated as such, spouse exchange relationships amount to a male-centered version of the sort of cooperation coordinated by females within uxorilocal households. In nonritual contexts, couples who have traded spouses are organized as a group of brothers and associated wives who cooperate in activities associated with raising each others' children. This effectively inverts the organization of the uxorilocal household based on groups of sisters and their in-marrying husbands. While rules regarding familiarity and avoidance instruct male in-laws, including in-marrying men, to maintain an attitude of reserve within the household, female in-laws are friendly and often joke with one another. Bonds between couples established on the basis of spouse exchange rely on female reciprocity of cultivated foods and cooking tasks and also depend on the agreement of the wives.

By taking multiple husbands as contributing fathers to her child, a woman attempts to create an infant with the qualities of the different fathers (Crocker and Crocker 1994, 84), and these fathers should observe food restrictions on behalf of her child. Through the institution of shared co-wives, however, men are able to partially escape the dictates of uxorilocality by creating a nexus of cooperation based on male classificatory siblingship.[10]

Because sexual intercourse is a mechanism for establishing relations between men, sex with older or married women is dangerous for bachelors. This is additional evidence that it is not "feminine pollution" that primarily undermines male development. Rather it is the contact through women with *other men* of different sociophysical state, particularly of the adjacent ascending age grade, that is deleterious. To engage in uncontrolled sex of this sort is life threatening. During the 1950s, shortly before they were officially pacified, the bachelor age grade suffered an epidemic resulting in many deaths. The Xikrin Kayapo attribute this to a massive breach of the taboo against sexual relations with childbearing women. On the other hand, there is no danger posed to married men who choose young unmarried women as sexual partners. There is no danger to these women either because care is always taken to separate sexual activity in space with meticulous hygiene that prevents mixing of sexual fluids. Such precautions are taken for the sake of offspring rather than sexual partners. Another crucial difference between the sexual activity of males and females is in the power of the smell or fluids from the vagina to cause illness in male sexual partners. In a myth told by the Kayapo, a woman takes a man along with her to collect firewood and water in order to show him that smelly vaginas can be a cause of sickness and death. After this time, both men and women take precautions, and concern with the ill effects of contact during sex does not seem to be very great. The reason why sexual activity is regulated should be clear. Sexual activity itself, as other forms of behaviors, is a mode of social action designed to produce certain social effects conceived of in terms of the bodily qualities appropriate for the creation of persons of different social ages. In this realm the agencies of males and females differ, but bodily qualities of both males and females are equally under the custody of close kin with whom substance (*ĩ*) is shared.

Age Grade Activities

I have suggested that age/gender grades are distinguished in terms of bodily properties that constitute social positions in relation to other age/genders. The following examples were related to me as illustrations of the social consequences of age grade organization. This is the flip side of the kinds of practices engaged in by kinsfolk on behalf of one another.

In past times the Kayapo spent much of their time trekking through the forest interior away from large watercourses. According to informants, this was a good place to see age grades in action, and it is clear that, as with other activities, trekking itself is a kind of collective production of proper bodiliness. When a group of men comes across a small stream, each age grade knows exactly what they may eat. Bachelors should not eat *kruet* (traíra), *krueti* (trairão), or *tucunaré* fish. Only older people will eat *ronhô'ô* (fidalgo) or *krã-êti* (pescado). If a bachelor ate these fish, he would dance conspicuously upright (while the rest of his fellows were moving in a low crouch). This would mark him as weak and would make him stick out from his age-mates. Although forbidden to bachelors, *kruati* is an excellent food for people with many children. On the other hand the eating of certain fish, *mydjwati, kunap,* and *tewa* (pião), conveyed desirable properties to bachelors and were recommended. *Tewa* imparts the ability to jump high while the other fish make a person slippery and difficult to catch. Each age group employs fishing techniques appropriate to the species "belonging" to them and positions itself accordingly along faster or slower current, and deeper or shallower stream depth. In short, bodily being and age/gender relations become part of a practical orientation to the natural world.

This applies equally well to hunting, which is particularly dangerous for bachelors. They principally limit themselves to the collection of land tortoises and thus avoid the dangers associated with the use of weaponry. Mammoth land tortoises, however, should not be eaten by bachelors because it would make it impossible for them to kill an enemy. Butchering of game once it has been killed is even risky for mature married men and, if at all possible, elders should be called on to perform this operation. Whenever game needs to be transported to the village, internal organs and intestines are removed carefully with a forked stick, avoiding any hand contact.

A similar logic holds in the way that wild fruit would be consumed. Some fruits are eaten by all but must be properly processed. The fruit of the bacaba palm, for example, is only eaten roasted. If it were eaten raw, game would prove impossibly elusive. The succulent flesh of the *rik* palm fruit is eaten by all, as are other fleshy fruits such as *kamôk, kamôkti,* and the ground fruit of the babassu and Brazil nut. *Rik-ti* is a large fruit that may only be consumed by elders who also were the only ones to eat the pequi (*prĩn*) fruit. Mothers would caution sons not to eat these foods because it would diminish their hunting ability and would make it difficult for them to obtain wives. Some fruits, such as *bôi rerek,* were prohibited only to those with suckling children. Not all food codes define social age, however; the seed of the pitobá (*kudjara*) is not eaten, because if one gets hit with a stick or a rock, a seedlike lump will spring up in the affected spot. Other plants, such as *kêre* or *mátkrá* (pitu), may only be used as medicine or eaten by elders. A similar though less lengthy list of rules applies to cultivated foods. Bachelors, for example, should not eat new sweet potatoes, because they will develop a sickness and their ears and skin may crinkle like a fungus.

On the other hand, pregnant couples are both considered part of a unity that is for all practical purposes a separate age/gender category (*me tujarô*— pregnant or swollen ones). That is, separate rules of behavior and diet apply, and these rules are cast in the same idiom as rules that apply to other age/gender classes. Pregnant people are assigned special places in dances in which age/gender groups are the basis for the order of dancers. They comprise a separate class based on restrictions they must observe to maintain the integrity of their body and vital essence in relation to others. Among other observances, they should bathe before everyone else, speak in low tones, refrain from striking animals or other people, and restrain themselves from farting or spitting wildly around others or wildly throwing away the remains of food such as banana peels or fishbones. The goal is a containment of self and of actions that jeopardize control of one's vital flux.

While avoiding many common foods, pregnant couples also choose foods to foster certain characteristics in their offspring. For example, they may eat *noroti,* honey, if they wish a tall child, or they may rub some paca fat on their backs in order to create a wide flat forehead. Isabel Murphy (personal communication) points out that while a couple is pregnant, a man who consumes honey from stinging bees would also take the precaution of eating an herbal antidote that would prevent any ill effects from carrying over to his wife or offspring.

STEWARDSHIP OF THE BODY AND CREATION OF SOCIALITY

While Kayapo conceive males and females in terms of differences evident in anatomy at birth (the respective terms for men and women are "penis people" and "vagina people"), these differences do not in and of themselves account for *social differences manifest in society.* Even the raw forms of sexual difference do not seem to be associated with cosmological dualisms. In short, although the sexual division of labor is thoroughgoing, sexual differences seem to be underdeployed symbolically; natural items with gendered valences, for example, those distinguished as tame or fierce, go only a short way in elucidating the important gender distinctions employed socially. This appears in stark contrast to Melanesia, where gendered attributes associated with natural species appear to provide the basis for a thoroughgoing classification of nature (Meigs 1984; Herdt 1987).

Gê peoples' creation of sociality is not a linear process accomplished by the initiation of young people into mature social adulthood. Rather, sociality is recreated in every generation by the bodily and pedagogical exchanges between persons of different sociophysiological state. The relative immobility of a woman is symbolic of her less precarious social state, while men are constantly at risk because of their mobility and their role as hunters and warriors.

The source of shamanic power illustrates by inversion the centrality of the control of bodily substance and knowledge for the recreation of sociality. A limited number of men and women learn skills associated with divination and have the capacity to diagnose and cure illnesses. They may also cause illness and, while considered socially necessary, are somewhat feared because of a tendency toward individualism. *Wayangá* (shamanic) powers are acquired by virtue of individual experience rather than instruction or apprenticeship. Decisive events are encounters with severe illness and pain in the form of snakebites and contacts with the vital essence of game animals. The *wayangá* transcends gender and age categories because he or she is initiated into contact with the natural world unmediated by kin or age associations. When the shaman views events far from the village, past and future, talks with animals and learns their secrets, this is accomplished in the form of a mobile *ĩ*. The *karon*-like behavior of shamanic *ĩ* is the exact inverse of the normal relationship between *ĩ* and *karon* in which *ĩ* is channeled to inculcate social relations while the individualized essence, or *karon*, wanders from the body and may be seen by others in dreams.

What we learn from the case of the shaman is that social control is largely a question of constraining the exchange of *ĩ* in ways that produce sociality through the agency of age grade activities and exchanges between kin. Kayapo state clearly that a shaman can be someone of any age—the age grade is irrelevant because his experience tears him from the ordering activities of society to which he remains somewhat perversely associated through his *karon*. In this capacity, he or she may introduce new knowledge into society in the form of cures, omens, ceremonial knowledge, and myths. This knowledge can only be socialized or domesticated if it is subsequently circulated according to the complementary kinship and age divisions that jointly produce sociality. Thus, as a conduit to the normally inaccessible world of the spirits, the shaman plays a social role in tandem with the rest of society. In doing so he reveals Kayapo understanding that sociality relies on an ongoing relationship with the natural world in terms that are set by the social alignment of human conduits organized in terms of exchanges between different sociophysiological collectivities arrayed in age/gender grades.

Parallel Male and Female Chiefs

In Melanesia, male and female bodily processes are modeled on one another with the seeming interchangeability of penes and breasts, semen and breast milk that seems unfamiliar to Amazonians (with the possible exception of the Northwestern portion, according to Hugh-Jones, Chapter 11). In Amazonia, divisions between the sexes in daily life may be as pronounced as those seen in Melanesia, but social institutions often come in male and female variants that closely resemble one another. Referring to Indian peoples of Brazil's Xingu Park, Gregor (1985, 111) takes this resemblance for granted and focuses instead on the subordinate position of women: female institutions "are not as dramatic, as frequently performed, or as politically and socially significant as the men's." However, standing in the light cast by comparative materials from Melanesia, the fact the Xingu women wrestle one another at all as a counterpart to male wrestling strikes us more forcefully than the fact that they do so under male direction. Even where female political influence appears neglible in Amazonia, social practices seem to appear in parallel male and female versions.

Among the Aguaruna and the Achuar, for example, the bloodthirsty manioc plants make female gardening an activity whose dangers mirror those faced by male hunters (Brown 1986; Descola 1994a). Both male and female must each make use of their own versions of magical songs, *anent*, which rely on uses of symbolism and metaphor that are analogous in every particular. Similarly, uses of dreams, of stones, and of charms suggest that, while males and females operate in parallel in different spheres, they exercise similar forms of agency. Even where such parallelism would seem to be diminished by the absence of spousal coresidence, as among the Mundurucú, the Murphys are adamant that the manioc processing should be seen as a female counterpart to the men's house (Murphy and Murphy 1985). In order to explore the significance of this Amazonian tendency, we return to the issue of parallel male and female chiefs among the Kayapo.

I have suggested that, while male and female qualities differ in content, the mode of agency through which these qualities are produced rests on notions of self-actualization, circulation of knowledge and substance, and proper alignment of collectivities comprised of differing sociophysiological states. While not social equals, males and females of different age/gender classes participate through both positive and negative injunctions in a common effort to reproduce the different bodily qualities and knowledge that make sociality possible. For the Xikrin Kayapo this common effort requires coordinated exchanges between linked but semiautonomous self-actualizing activities carried out by husbands and wives.

Only if we accept a structuralist analysis of Gê dualism that unequivocally associates femaleness with the peripheral domestic sphere and males with the central public domain does the presence of female chiefs surprise (e.g., Maybury-Lewis 1979). We have seen how the qualities of "fierceness" that qualify men for political and diplomatic preeminence are created through parallel activities in the domestic and public sphere. Male fierceness, however, provides no mechanism to compel female social participation. Rather, the complementary social and bodily attributes of women, such as "tameness," are equally created through parallel activities in the domestic and public spheres. Once public activity is understood in terms of bodily practice, the presence of female leaders appears as a straightforward consequence of the position of married couples within society and the age class from which the principal chief is drawn, namely that of *me krare*, or "people with children."

Attributes of social age as well as gender qualify a chief for leadership, and the age category from which the chief is drawn derives from a relationship with a spouse, as well as one's children and one's own parents. The social age of husband and wife is a product of their relationship, and both males and females share the same age grade designation. That both spouses share the same age class designation reflects a change from unmarried to married status, as can be seen by the fact that unmarried peoples' age grades are differentiated according to gender (e.g., male *me nõrõnyre* versus female *me kurêrê*). As a couple begin to have grandchildren they will continue to be jointly identified with one another in the *me bêngêt* age grade (people who are mentor relations).[11] When they become very old, the classification of males and females again diverges, with males being referred to as *"kubêngêt"* and females as *"abêngêt."*

Male preeminence in public social life is not framed in terms of control over females but on male ability to "make" things or "handle" things. Specifically, this refers to the extensive period of restrictions and specialized training that enables them to locate game and enemies far from the village and handle the associated physical and supernatural perils without endangering other humans. Similarly, contemporary male chiefs frame their ability to deal with outsiders in terms of acquiring necessary skills through knowledge and experience. Females, on the other hand, have undergone different sorts of restrictions. Their actions aim to control medicines and smoke cures in some cases but are primarily to control bodily processes, such as menstruation, lactation, and conception. However, the collective age activity by married females must parallel that of their husbands (and vice versa) since their bodily links with their joint offspring constrain spouses to act in coordinated fashion. Coordinated social action organized in terms of age grades can thus be seen to be action taken by one generation on behalf of another and to be analogous to parents' actions on behalf of their offspring and social protégés.

Chiefs neither represent groups of men, women, or villagers as a whole, nor is their primary function a managerial one. Rather they provide a social basis for the mobilization of age/gender groups acting in coordinated fashion. Since age and gender are associated with one another in a fashion that makes age grades, rather than an undifferentiated gender identity, the focus of social action, there simply are no ideas of an invariant transcendental maleness and femaleness lying behind and above the age grade system. An invariant gender identity would override and contradict the basis of age grade activity as a focus for social action. Chiefs are never simply "leaders" but leaders of particular age grades.[12] Since age/gender identities of "followers" are dependent on complementary coordination between both spouses, so, too, must leaders be identified as spouse pairs since the coordinating or political aspect of leaders is no more abstract and disembodied than other aspects of their social/bodily being. Male and female mirroring of social institutions among the Gê are based on the linked bodily practices of spouses.

Age/Gender Construction among the Yangoru Boiken

Melanesian comparisons help us to see how the linked practices of spouses are particularly salient in the separation of generations or age/gender states.

In his description of female initiation among the Yangoru Boiken, Roscoe (1995b) presents evidence from Melanesia that suggests an analogous form of social action to create a jointly held public identity of a married couple. The couple moves through a series of linked statuses within the ritual system of the Yangoru Boiken that is similar in many respects to the Kayapo system of age/gender grades. In contrast, peoples such as the Sambia (Herdt 1982b, 53) conduct the bachelor portion of male initiation in batches of age-mates and conduct the later stages as individually centered events, because these are associated with the "maturing femininity and life-crisis events of the women assigned in marriage to youths." The potential for an elaboration of joint male/female age classes exists but remains unelaborated because of the radical ritual separation of males and females. The Yangoru Boiken, by stressing female initiation, also stress the gender potency of parallel joint activities of males and females in a modality that approaches that of Amazonia. My observations on Yangoru Boiken initiation, therefore, center on similarities with the Kayapo age grade system rather than on the distinctly Melanesian components of ritual such as the blood payments made by agnates and sororal affines to a girl's maternal kin (Roscoe 1995b, 61).

After her first menstruation, a Yangoru Boiken girl will be initiated again upon first intercourse, first birth, passage into the kwuli grade, and passage into the suwero grade (ideally upon the first initiation of her son), and, finally, her long initiation sequence ends simultaneously with the first menstruation rites for her own daughter. As Roscoe outlines the successive stages, the coordination of male and female stages emerges as the most significant feature. Yangoru Boiken believe that these stages are imperative for a married couple to achieve renown in the politico-ritual sphere.

A central aspect of ritual involves the ingestion of certain items, such as ginger and ningi shrubs and saliva of the initiator, that confer such social qualities as oratorical flair, motivation or ability to amass wealth in men, and a predisposition to "follow the old-person's talk," i.e., perform traditional female tasks, among women. Additionally, each stage of initiation involves food taboos and behavioral prohibitions of different sorts. While first menarche involves pollution, this is dispersed by ceremonial means and, henceforth, what Roscoe refers to as "age-related" pollution becomes of more enduring concern. Such pollution appears linked to the married couple's own joint creation of offspring, being associated with the period between first intercourse and the couple's own children's move to sexual maturity. In making pollution the focus of husband/wife initiation, Yangoru Boiken simultaneously link social age and gender potency in both men and women. While such mutual pollution has a positive caste, pollution linking the couple and their offspring must eventually be staunched. Age-related pollution, therefore, results from connections of substance, such as blood, with offspring, and such ties are dangerous if proper constraint is not observed.

Parenting a first child qualifies parents for further initiation. This and the subsequent ritual stage resemble Kayapo age grades in that distinctions are made between parents of a single child and parents of several children, who move into the subsequent grade following their initiation. Rather than being performed as individual rites, as is the case for Sambia males, "similarly aged cowives of a subclan were initiated together, separately from the wives of other subclans" (Roscoe 1995b, 68), thus constituting de facto parallel age grades to their husbands. During these stages, husband and wife are interned separately for ritual purposes and initiated by their clansfolk. Finally, with the menstruation rites of their last daughter, the couple is once again secluded and separated from their daughter so as not to be polluted by her since "their blood is in her." This paves the way for the dispersion of the last vestiges of their age-related pollution. Roscoe (1995b, 72) declares that, with the rites of their last daughter, parents "become completely purified."

An act of central importance during female initiation is the viewing of various representations of a woman's clan's *wala* spirit or Tambaran. Again citing Roscoe (1995b, 73): "The power of wala displays are conceptually connected to the nature of wala spirits, the quintessential sources of power in the universe. Incarnated in certain mountains, trees, and stream pools, wala spirits are believed to be formed of a spiritual union of *kamba* or 'spirits of the dead.'. . . As unions of the kamba . . . wala spirits are considered potent beings." As products of a dangerous union themselves, what could be more representative of female initiates' own state, formed of a union of gender opposites whose mixing of substances generates both pollution and fertility and must be controlled? The wala also is an androgynous figure that, in the words of Roscoe's informants, should "mix the marks of men and women," and its potency results from the conjunction of male and female. In the context of ritual, the principle aim of the wala's menacing power is to ensure that initiates hold fast to the necessary food and behavioral prohibitions. Beyond the wala itself, heterosexual intercourse is represented in different fashions at several ritual stages, lending credence to the idea that the androgynous character of the wala, and indeed of the series of rites as a whole, references the parallel biosocial state of the husband/wife pair. Significantly, the final ritual acts aim to separate the pollution of the husband and wife from that of their daughter. A couple is cleansed of age-related pollution at the juncture where their daughter enters her own sequence of initiation rites during the course of which she acquires a separate potency from those of her parents. The cleansing of the couple's "age-related" pollution is precisely what allows them to act in certain ways within the politico-ritual realm. The separation that is obtained, however, is not only with pollution of their own daughter. At the end of initiation, a man should also avoid contact with the clothes, blankets, and eating utensils of uninitiated youths (Roscoe, Chapter 12).

As Roscoe states (1995b, 80), "If, then, male initiation is oriented to producing politico-ritually empowered males, we should expect the same of female initiation." Moreover, the initiation shows that the parallel activity of
paired male and female is distinguished according to divisions analogous to
age grades among Amazonians, namely, recognized ritual stages designed to
effect certain bodily transformations. In the Yangoru Boiken case, the male
and female ritual institutions that mirror one another also have the effect of
breaking the natural ties of substance that link generations. At this point we
return to the general question of why the inconstancy of gender imagery
throughout the life cycle has acquired such different castes within Amazonia
and Melanesia.

Making Discontiguous in a Fertile Universe

The joint age/gender attributes produced through Yangoru Boiken initiation
do not result in a full-blown organization of linked male and female age
grades as among the Kayapo. The reason for this seems to be that the ritual
potency created appears linked to the mystical auspices of the clan spirits.
Exchanges between husband and wife or between age/gender grades are
subordinated to the perpetuation of clan continuity. Strathern's (1988) language of partible selves seems apropos. In the Yangoru Boiken case, rites of
first intercourse and first birth involve the joint seclusion of the couple, while
in subsequent rites, men and women are initiated simultaneously but separately from their spouses. Thus they are ritually "placed" in a marriage, later
to be "extracted" in order to pass through initiations under the auspices of
different clans. The natural fertility of the couple is first activated and then
appropriated in the service of clan reproduction. In the final stage of initiation, that of their own daughter's first menarche, the couple is again secluded
together.

I hypothesize that when jointly created age/gender potency is subordinated
to the creation of descent groups, men and women's institutions tend not to
mirror one another, as is often the case in Amazonia. The wala tableau, rather
than being taken as a model for separate and complementary male and female
social action, for example, submerges male and female into a unified representation of the clan. Jolly (Chapter 8), Meigs (1984), and Herdt (1987), among
other Melanesian ethnographers, take the central issue of social acts associated
with ritual and initiation to be that of generating fertility and growth. Whether
persons or clans are the focus of ritual action, gender imagery is overwhelm-
ingly employed in the service of the requirements for fertility or growth.
LiPuma (1988, 96) remarks that, "As cultivation drives clan reproduction, it is
fitting, almost necessary, that Maring should represent the clan in terms of
vegetative propagation." Meigs (1984, 73) describes how feminine and masculine characteristics are defined in terms of qualities held by all plants and ani-

mals. Lineages may be described in these terms as well, denoting either "fast growth and the development of full musculature or its opposite."

In contrast, native Amazonians and central Brazilians do not equate sociality with socially generated growth or fertility. As Descola (1994a), among others, has described, humans share a self-evident sociality with nature. As he states (Chapter 5 of this volume), "Since most plants and animals are viewed as persons to be coerced, seduced, or protected, the frontiers of Achuar society extend far beyond the sphere of humankind and almost coincide with the outer limits of the cosmos." In a similar vein, Kayapo believe that villages similar to their own may be found among howler monkeys, peccaries, and even fish. Human society cannot be based on the direct appropriation of nature in the form of natural vitality or species attributes, therefore, but on the conscious creation of a distinctive human sociality that engenders well-being among its living members. Such human sociality must ultimately be based on the circulation of substance common to all nature. However, sociality is modeled not on the idea of natural growth, gestation, or birth but in the artifices that use natural vitality for its own ends as the currency for social transformations that preserve human well-being. Moreover, Amazonians do not seek to transcend limited human life spans founded in periodic births and deaths through the establishment of corporate institutions. In the instances where descent groups exist, with the seeming exception of northwestern Amazon, they seem to articulate with other ideas. The society of nature remains manifestly permanent and unproblematic as a backdrop to what is distinctly human. Rather, "artificial" tradition is made the basis of relations between people who transact either substance or knowledge between them, not in order to reenact social births, but precisely to counteract the idea that their relationships are based on a natural continuity.

Among the Kayapo, sexual opposition is created along with distinctions between social age and generation as boundaries across which significant relationships of kinship and public affiliation will be transacted. Gender differences thus emerge in the process of defining parties to an exchange. At this abstract level, this propensity seems to be shared by other Amazonians; at this level also, parties to a transaction—hunter/hunted, wife givers/wife takers—can be characterized by gender. In contrast with Melanesian perceptions, nature, as seen by Amazonians, does not appear to extrude gendered items "ready made" but must be parsed and directed into human bodies to acquire potencies associated with gender. There is no reason why cultural notions of gender should be modeled on a hypostasized unitary image of male and female rather than a more complex imagery that draws on male and female bodily potencies at different stages in the human life span.

Among the Kayapo, each generational continuity between parents and children involves the severance between generations immediately above the new multigenerational nuclear family unit. The focus is on abrupt differentiation of neighboring age grades above the level of children. Kayapo married couples act in concert, in other words, not to produce an unbroken intergenerational continuity but to sever ties with adjacent ascending generations. The underlying analogy is not with gestation and birth but with the complementarity of relations between different social ages/genders that makes possible the recycling of knowledge, names, and ceremonial roles on a nonnatural basis. Kayapo sociality, unlike Maring clans, is anything but vegetatively propagated.

Amazonians and Melanesians both use notions of substance and the creation of bodily potency to define both gender and sociality. Gender and social identity are relationally established through acts people take on behalf of one another. These include not only the transaction of substance and other social acts but also the avoidances and even celibacy observed on behalf of others. Both collective ceremonies and individual rites play a part in the activation or development of gender. In both areas, gendered attributes of individual humans change greatly throughout their lives, and these changes are a central focus of social action. Poole's (1981a, 116) statement made about the Bimin-Kuskusmin of the West Sepik interior of New Guinea could also apply to the Kayapo: "A particular construction of gender may crystallize in a particular context or at a particular moment of the life cycle only to be disarticulated and transformed into a new synthesis of 'natural' dimensions as the life cycle progresses or the context shifts."

Poole's linking of gender transformation and stages of the life cycle suggests that social age could be a particularly apt idiom through which gender transformations could be organized. This is precisely what one finds among the Kayapo with the centrality of public age organizations that mediate so many gendered transactions. Although approaching the elaboration of Kayapo age/gender distinction, the Yangoru Boiken case suggests that the preeminence of descent resulted in a gender configuration quite different from any found in Amazonia. Strathern has suggested that in Melanesia imbuing a body with the potential to act vis-à-vis another means to configure it as a single-sexed being that can be completed in its opposite. She likens the process of decomposing the androgynous body of a child to that of a male or female as "making incomplete" (Strathern 1993). This process of creating gender potency is associated with the creation of a sexual potency capable of producing persons who are not gendered but "clanned" (belonging as they must to a particular descent group). That is, the completion of identity occurs in relationships between *groups* that are prototypically descent groups.

Whereas most Amazonians do not recognize descent, the production of male and female persons involves the construction of "antinatural" ties that deny natural growth as the basis of sociality. Although sexual imagery may be used, this need not be related to the aims of fertility. One could say that rather than gender imagery which finds completeness in its opposite, Amazonians use the conjunction and separation of men and women to reconfigure natural continuity; whereas the creation of gender in Melanesia involves "making incomplete" what is naturally complete, the creation of the differented gender/age potencies in Amazonia involves "making discontiguous" what is naturally contiguous.

NOTES

Thanks to Bill Crocker, Paul Roscoe, Don Tuzin, Isabel Murphy, and Brad Weiss for discussions related to the chapter topic. Bill and Isabel also generously shared field data.

1. A Gê-speaking people living near the Brazilian town of Marabá.

2. Similar patterns have been documented among the Gê-speaking Apinagé (Da Matta 1982), Gorotire Kayapo (Bamberger 1967), and the Bororo (Crocker 1985). The Gê-speaking Canela refer to these relations as "restrictions maintaining people" and "non-restriction kin" (Crocker 1990, 235–236). The Canela term for restrictions is *"akhri,"* a close cognate of Kayapo *"angri,"* which carries roughly the same meaning.

3. Gê peoples traditionally slept in beds of slender trunks built close to the ground. While hammocks are currently available, not a single grandparent uses one for sleeping at night.

4. Kayapo seemed uninterested in how grass or trees become imbued with *ĩ*.

5. In writing this chapter, I found myself consistently using "state" where certain analytical orientations demand the term "status." This shift accurately reflects an underlying idea that Kayapo think of society in processual terms in which the life cycle consists of a series of socially mediated ethnophysiological states.

6. I use "age grade" to refer to a life stage differentiated from other life stages with respect to a unique set of physiological and social characteristics. During most of a person's life, age grades comprise an ongoing assemblage of age-mates who form a recognized social unit vis-à-vis other age grades. For some Gê (e.g., the Canela), boys (although not girls) are collectively inducted into an age grade, and such a group continues to be collectively promoted together as an age set for the duration of their lives. Among the Kayapo, a person moves through age grades based on individual life events.

7. Kayapo use these terms as "tame" and "wild" to characterize indigenous peoples who accepted tutelage of the Brazilian Indian Foundation as opposed to those who continue to live independently. On accepting contact, Kayapo chiefs characterized their new state as "uabô."

8. Although hunting is a "male" activity, women are not prohibited from engaging in it. As far as I know, every village has a few women who hunt; for example, in Txukarramãe and Stout (1990, 231), the first author, a Kayapo, claims his sister was among those women who bring in game. What is dangerous to offspring or may induce possible insanity in a woman is contact with implements such as a shotgun or bow and arrow. Small wooden clubs are the female weapon of choice.

9. Isabel Murphy (personal communication) points out that in some Kayapo villages a standard part of the boys' education is to be periodically scraped with a device made of dogfish teeth; then stinging medicine is applied to the long scratches on arms, thighs, and calves. Besides the disciplinary factor, this act is to make them strong and must be performed by an elder considered responsible for the training. Girls are not scraped.

10. The frequency of co-wives and co-husbands makes the collection of genealogies exceedingly complex, since, for example, parallel siblings have different sets of kin networks.

11. As a class, elders are often referred to as *"ngêti"* or *"kwatyi,"* which stresses their kinship status as a generalized orientation toward the village as a whole; that is to say, they become associated with the carrying of tradition for the village as a whole, and their well-being ideally becomes something of a collective concern.

12. The way that age/gender grades are organized can vary as grades are merged or mixed for some purposes. Nonetheless, the age/gender identity of participants is of fundamental importance, and the chief is considered to be from a particular age/gender grade.

SEVEN

Women's Blood, Warriors' Blood, and the Conquest of Vitality in Amazonia

Beth A. Conklin

Conklin argues that Amazonian and Melanesian personhood tends "to be associated with particular ideas about the human body, especially an emphasis on the mutability and transformability of body substances." Hence the accumulation of an enemy's blood in the abdomen of a Wari' warrior during his seclusion after a killing is "like pregnancy." When transformed through ritual disciplines, the enemy's vitalizing blood essence is passed on to the women, and the enemy spirit becomes the "child" of the warrior.

    Killing an enemy and controlling enemy blood and spirit are powerful pseudo-procreative ideas for the Wari', which are ultimately linked to male vitality and potency. Conklin thereby develops a theme that echoes those of other authors, including Hugh-Jones, Biersack, Bonnemère, and Gregor and Tuzin, in this volume. It is also apparent that in the midst of a highly masculine ritual, Wari' culture highlights the mutual dependence and cooperation of men and women and a sense that male and female define gender with a common idiom of ideas and metaphors. This is a theme that is also evident in the articles by Hugh-Jones and Hill.

One of the strongest resonances between the native cultures of Melanesia and lowland South America (especially Brazil) is a shared emphasis on the relational basis of personhood—the idea that the person "knows himself only by the relationships he maintains with others" (Leenhardt 1979 [1947], 153), and that the capacities of the self are activated through interactions with others. As Marilyn Strathern notes (Chapter 10), native peoples in both regions recognize that it is in relation to persons different from oneself that one develops creativity and vitality. Out of a conjunction of differences come generative possibilities.

One context in which native Amazonians have treated a conjoining across boundaries as a source of vitality is in rituals following the killing of an enemy. In a number of native Brazilian societies, one of the most highly valued transformations that a man traditionally could experience occurred when he killed an enemy and then underwent a ritual seclusion in which he lay in a hammock, abstained from sex, and observed stringent alimentary restrictions. In central Brazil, this complex of beliefs and practices has been reported among various Gê-speakers: the Shavante (Maybury-Lewis 1967, 282), Sherente (Nimuendajú 1967 [1942], 78–79), Apinayé (Da Matta 1976, 86–87), Krahó (Carneiro da Cunha 1978, 105), and Suyá (Seeger 1981, 167–168). Elsewhere, it has been described among the Araweté (Tupi-Guarani) of the middle Xingu River region (Viveiros de Castro 1992), the Urubú (Tupi) of eastern Brazil (Huxley 1957), the Yanomami (a linguistic isolate) of northern Brazil (Albert 1985), and the Wari' (another linguistic isolate) of western Brazil (Conklin 1989; Vilaça 1989, 1992).[1] These rituals are concerned with the killing of outsider enemies, not fellow tribesmembers.[2] With a few exceptions, most of these peoples have stopped practicing warfare; thus, I write about these rites mostly in the past tense.

Although enemy-killing and its rites were quintessentially manly activities, a number of ethnographers have noted that the South American warriors' seclusion involves cultural ideas and practices similar to those surrounding menstruation, pregnancy, or childbirth. A key link between the experiences of women and of warriors is the idea that all these processes involve blood flowing across body boundaries, and that the individual must control or deal with this blood properly. When a man kills an enemy, the blood of the slain enemy enters the killer's body. (Some native peoples believe that the victim's spirit enters the killer as well.) In some societies, the ideas surrounding the victim's blood/spirit and the ways that men deal with it parallel how women deal with reproductive blood and bodily processes of growth and development in female puberty or childbearing. Although ethnographers have noted these similarities in individual cases, there has been little recognition or analysis of this as a regional pattern. My goal in this chapter is to call attention to this complex of warriors' rituals and their relation to gender, and to consider how the beliefs and practices associated with the warrior's transformation articulate with cultural notions of fertility, growth, maturation, and human reproduction, as well as their antitheses: antivitality, death, degeneration, and decay.

The act of killing immerses the killer in an intimate encounter with the forces of death. In its "raw"—that is, unregulated, untransformed—state, enemy blood/spirit stands as a prime symbol and agent of antivitality. The Yanomami, Araweté, Krahó, and Apinayé consider the victim's blood in the killer's body to be linked directly to the rotting of the victim's corpse and its putrefying body fluids.[3] Other peoples emphasize the negative effects of an excess quantity of blood or the danger to the killer and his community of this intrusion of "bad" or alien blood.

Except among the Wari', the disciplines of the warrior's seclusion were directed toward expelling the alien blood from his body. Among the Urubú and the Gê peoples, the warrior bled himself with linear incisions that left pronounced scars on the chest, back, arms, or legs. The Suyá warrior also pierced his penis (Seeger 1981, 168). Among the Yanomami, Araweté, and some of the Gê groups, killers vomited profusely, with or without the aid of emetics. What would happen if a killer did not observe the proper ritual actions, or failed to expel the victim's blood from his body? Among the societies for which ethnographers report an answer, there is near-universal agreement: the killer's belly would swell up with blood until he died.[4]

Various Amazonian peoples gave somewhat different inflections to the meaning of the warrior's physio-ritual experience. In one manner or another, however, all saw the killer's mastery of the alien blood in his body as a way to transcend or mute the effects of mundane processes of biological degeneration (weakness, illness, aging, or death). By neutralizing, expelling, or transforming the enemy blood/spirit, a man gained some degree of immunity to decay for his own body, either in this life or after death. Xikrin-Kayapó thought that it brought long life and physical revitalization, making men "hard" (Vidal 1977, 157). Urubú thought that completing the seclusion made killers hard, strong, impervious to pain, and endowed with enhanced sexual potency and male fertility. Wari' think that it promotes physical growth, strength, courage, and health. Yanomami believe that it ensures a man's longevity and prevents cosmic disruption. For Araweté, the killer's transformation is equated not with physical maturation but with a *metaphysical* maturation that makes the warrior's body immune to decay when he dies and confers upon his soul an immortality that exempts him from being cannibalized by the gods (Viveiros de Castro 1992, 246–247).

These Amazonian rituals revolve around questions of how death is linked to life, how killing may be transmuted into regeneration, and how people can transcend or regulate biological forces of morbidity and mortality. The answer they propose is that men accomplish this through the conquest of enemy outsiders and the ritual transformation of enemy substances. This exemplifies what Bloch (1992) calls the ritual "conquest of external vitality"—the appropriation of elements from beings outside one's own groups to create in oneself a state that transcends (at least temporarily) the constraints of mundane biological degeneration. The notion of enemies as sources of transformative or generative powers—and of predation as a central trope in the construction of identity—is a theme in many lowland South American societies (Viveiros de Castro 1996). Here, I focus on the notions of body, power, and gender invoked by the enemy-killing rites in which killers turned their relationship to the slain enemy into a positive enhancement of the self and masculine agency.

The transformation of enemy blood to promote or protect male growth and health was framed in terms of women's physiology and the regulation of reproductive blood in a number of these ritual systems. While I do not claim that this was true in every society, some peoples clearly saw a connection between the experiences of women and those of warriors. Ethnographers have emphasized that specific rites or restrictions that killers observed were similar to those observed by girls during their first menstruation, among the Apinayé (Da Matta 1976, 86), Suyá (Seeger 1981, 167), and Urubú (Huxley 1957, 260). The most detailed ethnographic data on the warrior's seclusion come from Bruce Albert's work among the Yanomami and from studies of the Wari' by Aparecida Vilaça and myself. I compare these two cases, focusing on a few salient dimensions of these rich social and symbolic systems, especially the question of interactions between models of female and male physiology.

"Pseudo-procreative" imagery is, of course, a recurrent theme in initiation rituals worldwide and in men's maturation rituals in particular. The question of why this is so has long intrigued anthropologists and psychologists (especially those working in Melanesia), partly because of the "apparently conflicting idioms of exclusion and appropriation" (Strathern 1988, 103) in many male rites: female reproductive imagery is often most elaborate or explicit in rites that emphasize separating men from females and feminine influences. (See Hiatt 1971; Keesing 1982; Paige and Paige 1981, 4–18; and Roscoe 1995a for reviews of the literature on pseudo-procreation.) My intent in this chapter, however, is not to explain the existence of Amazonian pseudo-procreative imagery by picking a path through the thicket of competing theories of male envy, male anxieties related to mother-son bonds, or political-economic dynamics of male appropriation of female resources. Rather, my aim is to consider what this imagery reveals about how native people think about growth, health, and potency. A number of Amazonian themes are waiting to be rethought, especially concerning the social nature of body substances, the interdependence of female and male physiology, and how complementarity and antagonism are expressed in ritual. Many of these will seem familiar to Melanesianists, and I believe that lowland South Americanists, who generally have paid less attention to gender issues, might learn a great deal from the Melanesian literature along these lines.

My approach draws inspiration from one of the major insights that has emerged from the recent Melanesian literature: the value of looking at male and female rituals in relation to one another (Lutkehaus and Roscoe 1995). Perhaps nowhere is this more relevant than in interpreting "pseudo-procreative" imagery. When men and boys enact transformations of themselves that resemble female bodily processes such as menstruation, pregnancy, or birth, they instantiate M. Strathern's observation that the female body and processes of human reproduction are prime symbols of, and metaphors for, the social body and social reproduction.

There is a methodological point implicit in a focus on how female bodies and reproduction serve as metaphors for social reproduction. This is that men's rituals cannot be analyzed in isolation, as often has been done. Female and male rites often are interrelated, so that "analysis should focus as much on this complex whole as on its constituent parts" (Roscoe 1995a, 224). I would extend this to note that one must look not only at female rituals but at broader cultural concepts of how both sexes grow, mature, and develop their respective forms of agency. From this perspective, the question to ask is not just how men are made, but how persons are generated and how their gendered capacities are enhanced through social action.

THE BIOSOCIAL FABRICATION OF PERSONS

One of the strongest resonances between Melanesia and lowland South America (especially Brazil) is the centrality of social concerns with the fabrication of persons through the social fabrication of their bodies. A landmark in lowland South Americanist ethnologists' recognition of the role of body concepts in native social systems was "The Construction of the Person in Brazilian Indigenous Societies" (Seeger, Da Matta, and Viveiros de Castro 1979), which called on anthropologists to explore how the "ordering of social life through a language of the body" was a fundamental and distinctive characteristic of Brazilian Indian societies.

In the 1970s, this academic "discovery" of the cultural force of body concepts became a rallying point in Brazilian anthropologists' struggle for what Alcida Ramos (1995, 6) called "their conceptual decolonization by declaring their independence" from Africanist models of descent and corporate groups. (Melanesianists may hear echoes of their own "anti-Africanist" revolt.) In South American ethnology, focusing on the "absence" of lineages, clans, and corporate structures had led to the conceptual dead end of characterizing Brazilian Indian societies simply as "fluid" and "flexible." Anthony Seeger, Roberto Da Matta, and Eduardo Viveiros de Castro, in contrast, argued that "the societies of the [South American] continent structure themselves in terms of symbolic languages that—this is the difference from the symbols of Africans, Europeans, etc.—do not concern the definition of groups and the transmission of goods, but rather the construction of persons and the fabrication of bodies." Focusing on notions of corporeality and the social construction of the person promised analytic concepts that would "account for South American material in its own terms" (1979, 9–10).

> The human body and the elements that comprise it are a primary matrix of social meanings: in the majority of indigenous societies of Brazil, this matrix occupies a central organizing position. The fabrication, decoration, transformation, and destruction of bodies are themes around which revolve mythologies, ceremonial life, and social organization. A physiology of body fluids—blood, semen—and of processes of the body's communication with the world (food, sexuality, speech, and other senses) appears to underlie the considerable variations that exist among South American societies. (Seeger, Da Matta, and Viveiros de Castro 1979, 11)[5]

The "language of the body" in native Brazilian societies is largely an idiom of relationships. Corporeal elements and their analogs (especially foods, beverages, body paints, and body ornaments) are vocabularies through which individuals not only signify but also actively establish, intensify, transform, attenuate, and sever relations to others. Persons and their capacities are created, nurtured, and maintained through flows of tangible and intangible elements between living persons and between persons and other categories of beings, such as ancestors, animals, spirits, and enemies. Many of these transactions are believed to affect the composition or state of an individual's body, so that the development of new or transformed social relationships and the development of bodily capacities occur in tandem and are inseparable (Conklin 1996; Conklin and Morgan 1996).

The relational construction of bodies and persons and an emphasis on this as an ongoing process that requires repeated and periodic renewal are a major point of commonality between lowland South America and Melanesia. In both regions, notions of relational personhood tend to be associated with particular ideas about the human body, especially an emphasis on the mutability and transformability of body substances (see Biersack [Chapter 4], Hugh-Jones [Chapter 11], and Jolly [Chapter 8]). Where persons are understood to be "made" processually through interactions with other individuals, body elements often are thought of as interactive with each another and with elements that come from outside the body (from other people, ancestors, enemies, or animals, for example). Ideas about the social constitution of corporeal elements provide a conceptual framework and tangible techniques for expressing and enacting the social processes that create, grow, and develop individuals and their capacities.

In native Amazonian societies, social and political relations tend to be organized through the ritual control of symbolic resources centered on the biological and metaphysical components of individuals (Albert 1985, 676–677). In this regard, lowland South Americans resemble the peoples of Papua New Guinea's lowlands and the eastern highlands' "fringe" areas, with their "societies which are constituted and reproduced *ritually*"; they have less in common with the western highlands of Papua New Guinea, "where social relations are established through the production and circulation of *wealth*" (Liep 1991, 32). Margaret Jolly's (1991a, 49–50) observation that in the eastern highlands, dynamics of gender and power are based in control over the "procreation, nurture and flow of persons" might describe many Brazilian Indian societies as well.

In Brazil, as in eastern and lowland Papua New Guinea, one of the arenas where concerns with developing persons by ritual regulation of their body substances are most prominent is in rituals aimed at "making men" and enhancing male growth and vitality. In both areas, much of the work of man-making and man-enhancing rites is done by transfers and modifications of body substances, and these practices are grounded in broader systems of cultural ideas about the human body and the elements that compose it. As Bonnemère (1990, 102) notes for Melanesia, "indigenous conceptions about body fluids form the substratum of representations of the production and constitution of the person."

In her survey of representations of body substances in twenty New Guinea societies, Bonnemère (1990) identified a triad of symbolic relations among sexual/reproductive fluids: semen, menstrual blood, and breast milk. There has been no comparable systematic study of body substances in Amazonian societies, but even a cursory review suggests a number of parallels (and some differences) in how Melanesians and Amazonians think about and act upon specific bodily elements as components of persons and their relationships. The parallels are so striking that when Amazonian ethnographers read the

Melanesian "body" literature, we often get that frisson of uncanny recognition described so well by the American baseball player Yogi Berra, who explained: "It's like déjà vu all over again."

BLOOD, SEMEN, AND DÉJÀ VU

Among the body concepts that native Amazonians and Melanesians share in common are the idea of blood as the main agent of growth, health, and gendered capacities; the notion of semen as a growth agent; and an emphasis on the transformability of body substances. In both regions, blood is strongly associated with vitality, strength, resistance to disease, and the capacity for hard work. Blood is a key element—for many native groups, *the* key element—in the regulation of individual growth, health, and productivity. Blood also figures prominently in cultural ideas about reproductivity, especially two developmental processes relevant to the "man-making" rituals: conception/gestation and adolescent maturation.

In Melanesia and Amazonia, blood (especially menstrual blood) commonly is identified as the mother's contribution to conception or gestation. Many peoples in both regions believe that a fetus is formed from the combination of female blood and male semen. Some lowland South American peoples speak of maternal blood as nourishment for the fetus rather than the substance from which the fetus is formed, and a few assert that a mother contributes no substance to the fetus at all but merely provides a womb container. In contrast to Melanesia, lowland South American theories of conception seldom are related to notions of descent in any clear-cut or consistent way, and even within a single community there often is little consensus about precisely what goes into making a baby. Despite the lack of consensus about the precise bodily basis of mother-child kinship, the association between female blood and human reproduction is as salient in Amazonia as it is in Melanesia.

The relation between menstrual blood and female puberty is self-evident; both native Amazonians and Melanesians commonly recognize menarche (first menstruation) as a prime marker of a girl's transition to young womanhood. More specifically, many believe that when a girl develops the capacity to menstruate (and to handle her menses properly), this transforms and enhances other body-based aspects of her self, such as her growth, strength, vitality, and ability to do adult women's work. Menstruation thus is fundamental to womanly agency and female productive and reproductive capacities.

Blood is linked not only to female puberty; many native Amazonians and Melanesians also believe that male pubertal development depends on changes in a boy's blood. The blood changes in pubescent girls generally are assumed to happen more or less naturally, or as a result of experiences (such as sexual intercourse) that are normal events in girls' lives. In contrast, native people who think that male puberty depends on blood changes usually think that this requires intentional human intervention. This typically takes the form of ritual actions guided by older men who perform actions aimed at modifying boys' bodies. Older men often use some of the same techniques themselves to enhance or revitalize their own masculinity.

In Amazonia and Melanesia, there are two major variants of bodily manipulations in man-making or man-enhancing rituals: incorporation and purging. Almost every male transformation ritual uses at least one incorporating or purging technique, and many use several in combination.

Incorporating techniques aim to introduce into the male body positively valued substances that enhance masculinity and alter the composition or quality of blood or other body elements. Such techniques include the oral ingestion of particular foods, beverages, medicines, and other substances, and rubbing or painting substances on the skin. In Amazonia, a killer's appropriation and incorporation of the blood or spirit of a slain enemy might also be considered an incorporating technique.

Incorporating techniques often are associated with ideas about implanting or inscribing "culture"—societal values and normative behaviors—in the physical body. A striking expression of this among the Ilahita Arapesh of Papua New Guinea (Tuzin 1980, 113) is the practice of surreptitiously feeding certain magically treated substances to male initiates in the Tambaran cult. The practice implants in the body's essence a property that will turn against the body if the individual ever violates a cult taboo.

In New Guinea, the ingestion of semen (orally or anally) is another technique for incorporating quintessentially masculine body substance. This is one difference between Melanesia and Amazonia: I know of no Amazonian equivalent to the direct man-to-boy semen transfers of Melanesian ritualized homosexuality. If there are South American parallels, these involve using symbolic substitutes for semen. Hugh-Jones, in Chapter 11, explores the possibility that the secret flute cults of northwest Amazonia "also involve something akin to transactions of semen, albeit in a less overt manner."

Purging techniques, the second type of ritual bodily manipulation, aim to remove substances that impede the development of manly qualities. Common techniques for removing undesirable elements from the male body include inducing bleeding via the penis, nose, mouth, anus, or skin, and purging through vomiting or sweating. The substance to be removed often is blood, which in some cases is associated with mothers, breast milk, or female pollution, so that purging is seen as a mechanism of sexual purification for males (e.g., Tuzin 1982, 338).

Male bleeding practices have been identified as "male menstruation" by native peoples or their ethnographers in a number of well-known cases. In Melanesia, the widespread practices of penile bloodletting and nose bleeding—used in male initiation and afterward as a way to revitalize manliness—have been interpreted as male equivalents to menstruation (Herdt 1981, 245; Hogbin 1970, 88). Lewis (1980) emphasizes, however, that in some other New Guinea societies, penile bloodletting has cultural meanings that cannot be equated with male menstruation. In lowland South America, ethnographers have identified male menstruation in the Yurupari male initiation cult among Tukanoans in the northwest Amazon (C. Hugh-Jones 1979; S. Hugh-Jones 1979), in the piercing of Mehinaku boys' ears (Gregor 1985) and other practices in the Upper Xingu (Viveiros de Castro 1992, 138), and in Yanomami ideas that adolescent boys experience menarche and that the ritual seclusion of enemy-killers is analogous to the ritual seclusion of menarcheal girls (Albert 1985).

Besides these parallel Melanesian and Amazonian ideas about blood and its role in female and male adolescent development, another shared idea is the notion of semen as a growth-promoting substance. In most societies in both regions, semen is considered closely related to blood or interactive with blood, as in the widespread idea that blood-plus-semen is what babies are made of. Regardless of differences in cultural models of conception, almost everyone considers semen essential to create and/or nourish a fetus. In both regions, a common belief is that a fetus forms when enough semen accumulates in the womb and that conception requires repeated infusions of semen, not just a single act of sexual intercourse. Many people also believe that semen builds or nourishes the fetus as it grows during pregnancy; for example, Tukanoans in the northwest Amazon speak of a father's responsibility to "feed" the fetus in the womb (Hugh-Jones, Chapter 11). In some societies, semen's nurturant qualities are expressed in symbolic equations between breast milk and semen (see Bonnemère 1990, 105; Bonnemère, Chapter 2; and Hugh-Jones, Chapter 11).

In Amazonia, ideas about semen and fetal growth are part of a broader notion of what Eduardo Viveiros de Castro (1992, 187) calls "seminal nurture." Not only does semen "grow" babies; it also "grows" young women and their reproductive capacities. In a number of native Brazilian societies, the transfer of semen into a girl's body through heterosexual intercourse is believed to stimulate the onset of menstruation and female puberty. (As discussed below, this is a belief in several of the Brazilian groups that practiced the ritual seclusion of killers.) In the context of this notion of seminal nurture, menstrual blood cannot be considered the product of exclusively female processes. Rather, there is an explicit recognition that men contribute to the making of menstrual blood, so that female reproductive capacities are a product of cross-sex interactions.

Similar ideas of semen as a stimulant to female bodily development are present in New Guinea, notably among the Sambia, who believe that a husband grows his young wife's body and that his semen creates the breast milk that nourishes their baby (Herdt 1981, 181–182). As a corollary, the Sambia and several other New Guinea groups consider semen a necessary growth agent for boys as well. The belief that boys must take older men's semen into their bodies to mature properly and develop their manly capacities is the key idea behind the well-known complex of semen transfers in male initiation among the Sambia and some other New Guinea peoples, especially in the Mount Bosavi area (see Herdt 1982). This ideology of semen transfer, in combination with the idea that both fetuses and breast milk are formed of semen, amounts to an assertion of male parthenogenesis.

In native Brazilian rituals and models of the body, in contrast, semen has little potency on its own. Rather, semen functions as a growth agent only when it is combined with a feminine element—usually blood or an analogue of blood. This is most apparent in indigenous models of growth and conception. Moreover, complementary female and male substances are a theme in the many South American rituals in which men and women exchange foods or beverages with gendered connotations, such as meat (masculine) and manioc or maize (feminine), or fermented and unfermented beverages (Viveiros de Castro 1992, 138).

Another difference between Amazonia and Melanesia concerns the question of whether it is possible to replace or replenish body substances that have been lost or depleted. In Melanesia, a near-universal principle is that "life-giving substances are finite in quantity" (Lemonnier 1991, 13). According to Whitehead (1986b, 275–276), the idea that semen loss (in heterosexual intercourse) stunts male growth is nearly universal. New Guinea men use a variety of means to augment and conserve their semen. In Amazonia, however, the idea of a closed economy of finite body substances is less common. Amazonian men do not seem to worry as much about the quantity or adequacy of their semen as Melanesian men do; I have found male fears of semen loss reported only for the Mehinaku (Gregor 1985, 145). Irreversible blood loss also is not a widespread concern. Although a few native Amazonians do think that lost blood is never replaced (cf. C. Crocker 1985, 41 ff.; Reichel-Dolmatoff 1971), many others (including the Wari') believe that when blood is lost, the body simply produces more.[6]

In both regions, the gendered substances of semen and blood carry ambivalent meanings. Bonnemère's (1990, 108) observation that in New Guinea it is impossible to categorize certain body substances as positive and others as negative applies equally to Amazonia. Semen and breast milk are considered nourishing and growth promoting in certain contexts, but they also are seen as channels for the spread of illness agents and contamination in others. Similarly, menstrual blood is the stuff of which babies are made, but it can be dangerous to men and children and sometimes to women themselves (for example, in Amazonia it is believed that jaguars are attracted to menstruating women).[7] Like semen and breast milk, the blood that circulates in the body is both the foundation of health and a vector for illness agents. A large proportion of lowland South American rules about hygiene and food aim to protect vulnerable individuals from contamination with the harmful blood or blood analogues of certain animals and people.

In native Brazilian societies, healthy blood and a well-functioning circulatory system are the key to health, growth, and vitality for both sexes. The flip side of this is that weakness, illness, aging, death, and decay—the antitheses of vitality—also are intimately connected to blood processes such as the loss of blood, retention of excess blood, imbalance or degeneration of the blood, and incorporation of kinds of blood inimical to one's own. In the Brazilian warriors' seclusion rituals, the focus on regulating the enemy blood in the killer's body revolved around concerns with how men can exert control over the interconnected processes of death and degeneration, growth and generativity.

RITUAL TRANSFORMATION AND SECLUSION IN AMAZONIA

In both Amazonia and Melanesia, the most intense ritual efforts to develop masculine capacities typically are performed during a period of seclusion or semiseclusion in which males separate themselves from contact with females and control the flow of substances into and out of their bodies. As Paul Roscoe notes (Chapter 12), food taboos and sex abstinence are means by which the self constitutes itself as a different *kind* of self. Transformations of male bodies are transformations of male selves.

In Amazonia, one of the most widespread of all ritual practices for individuals of both sexes is seclusion at a moment of social transition. The two most common times for seclusion are after childbirth and at puberty. In some societies, individuals also go into seclusion in shamanic initiation, after killing an enemy (seclusion of the killer), in mourning (seclusion of the bereaved), and after death (when a newly dead person's spirit and/or body is believed to go through a ritual seclusion that initiates the spirit into the society of the dead).

Indigenous interpretations of Amazonian seclusion rituals—especially the seclusions associated with childbirth, puberty, and enemy-killing—consistently emphasize that their purpose is to achieve the formation or re-formation of the individual's body and of spiritual or psychological capacities linked to bodily states. Some ethnographers have noted that controlling or transforming *blood* is the focal concern in several forms of seclusion among the Wari', Yanomami (Albert 1985), and in some Gê societies in central Brazil (Carneiro da Cunha 1978, 105; Da Matta 1976, 86).

To understand what ritual bodily transformations mean for native Amazonians, it is essential to recognize that corporeal elements carry meanings that extend far beyond what Westerners think of as the organic/physical. In Amazonian societies, mind, thought, emotion, morality, and character often are seen as linked to (and inseparable from) bodily states. "Body" always exists in a dynamic relation to "spirit" (Pollock 1996). "Knowledge" (broadly conceived and manifest especially in speech, hearing, moral action, and pragmatic efficacy) is often closely related to bodily developments (Kensinger 1992; McCallum 1996) and visionary experiences (Brown 1986; Gow 1991). As Ellen Basso (1995, 97) emphasizes for the Kalapalo of the Upper Xingu, the goal of puberty seclusions is to create a physically and morally beautiful person, two aspects that are seen as inseparable from one another.

Substantive changes in the body achieved through the disciplines of seclusion almost always are related to processes of modifying other aspects of the person as well, such as personality, emotions (especially courage), spiritual powers, knowledge, morality, or capacity for self-restraint (Viveiros de Castro 1979). In all the Amazonian groups that practiced the seclusion of enemy-killers, a man's achievement of exerting ritual control to transform the enemy blood or spirit in his body traditionally was (or, where warfare persists, still is) a central element in cultural ideals of masculinity. The killer who accomplished this act of self-discipline always gained prestige and respect, and many groups considered this a prerequisite for the optimal development of masculine powers. In some cases, males could not attain the status of full adult men until they had performed the enemy-killer's seclusion.

Most forms of Amazonian seclusion stress a certain asceticism in which, as Basso (1995, 97) notes for the Kalapalo, secluded individuals must learn to consummate their physical needs (for food, sex, sleep, elimination) within strictly defined limits, hold emotions and impulses in check, and dedicate themselves to activities that promote social well-being. The various forms of ritual seclusion in Brazilian Indian societies vary in their intensity, duration, and the specific disciplines required. What they all share is an emphasis on regulating the flow of substances (such as food, medicines, and bodily substances, especially sexual fluids) into and out of the body. Concerns with regulating what enters and leaves the body are strongest in seclusions for childbirth, puberty, and enemy-killing.

Melanesian ethnologists have emphasized that male initiation rites often draw on cultural images of human reproduction and female bodily processes, especially images of initiation as ritual rebirth (Hiatt 1971; Keesing 1982; Paige and Paige 1981; Roscoe 1995a; Strathern 1988). Some enact analogies to other female bodily processes, such as menstruation, conception, and pregnancy or gestation. In her analysis of twenty New Guinea societies, Bonnemère found that "initiation is not solely a birth but also a pregnancy. Men reproduce at puberty that which occurred in the mother's womb" (1990, 111). The manipulations of blood, semen, and other focal body substances in male transformation rites are one technique men and boys use to assert their symbolic participation in something analogous to female bodily developments.

Amazonian ethnographies have tended to look at men's rituals in isolation, as same-sex transactions conducted in an all-male context, despite the resonances between female and male development recognized in Amazonian models of human physiology. The many parallels between Amazonia and Melanesia in ideas about the embodied basis of relational personhood suggest that Amazonianists might see something new if they looked through Melanesianist lenses to examine how male rituals relate to cultural ideas about female growth, development, and reproduction. The gendered themes that run through the Wari' and Yanomami enemy-killer's seclusion ritual suggest the fruitfulness of bringing together Melanesian and Amazonian perspectives.

THE WARI'

The Wari' (Pakaas Novas) live in the rain forest of western Brazil, in the state of Rondônia near the Bolivian border. They speak a language in the Chapakuran language family isolate and today number some two thousand or so people. Various Wari' subgroups entered into sustained peaceful contact with Brazilian national society in stages between 1956 and 1969. After the contact, Wari' stopped killing outsiders, stopped building men's houses, and stopped practicing the warrior's ritual seclusion. The following account reconstructs this ritual as it was practiced in the region of the Dois Irmãos River in the decades prior to 1956.[8]

Wari' traditionally are inhabitants of the interior forest (*terra firme*) who make their living by slash-and-burn farming, hunting, fishing, and gathering. Post-marital residence patterns are mixed; after a husband has fulfilled his brideservice obligations (which commonly involve a period of uxorilocal residence before and/or after marriage), couples are free to live near either spouse's relatives, and changes of residence are common. Interpersonal relations between wives and husbands are not highly polarized or antagonistic. An emphasis on gender complementarity and cooperative, balanced cross-sex transactions pervades Wari' daily life, productive activities, and rituals. The theme of cross-sex interdependence also pervades traditional Wari' notions of how adolescents mature into adults. Before the contact, both male and female maturation were conceptualized as social processes dependent on inputs from the opposite sex.[9]

FEMALE GROWTH, MATURATION, AND FECUNDITY

A pubescent Wari' girl's sexual maturation and physical growth are held to develop first out of a special relationship to the moon, whose influence is loosely thought of as a stimulus to breast development and menstruation. The second, more direct stimulus (upon which the efficacy of the first depends) is a cross-sex transfer of body fluid: the first time that a girl has sexual intercourse, the infusion of semen (a blood product) is said to transform her blood so that it increases in quantity and strength. This sparks a growth spurt: the girl grows fatter, taller, stronger and—a point that Wari' emphasize—able to do women's work in planting, harvesting, and processing food.

Not only does semen enhance a girl's capacity for productivity; it also is essential to her capacity for reproduction. Both Wari' women and men assert that semen stimulates the production of menstrual blood. Both women and men insist that only sexually active females menstruate; virgins and celibate women do not. An infusion of semen is thought to be prerequisite not only for menarche but for every menstrual period in a woman's life. Some younger Wari' admit that virgins sometimes do bleed vaginally, but they dismiss this by saying that it is "just a little blood" that "flows for no reason" (*ao ximao*). Similarly, older women admit privately that their vaginal blood sometimes flows even when they have not had sex for a long time, but they dismiss this by saying that it is not "real" menstruation.

This Wari' idea that heterosexual intercourse is a prerequisite for menstruation means that a woman's fecundity depends on her relationship with a man. Menstrual blood is a social product. For Wari', the oft-repeated idea that men are "made" but women mature naturally does not apply. Prior to the contact, girls ideally (and often in practice) married and began to have sexual intercourse before they began to menstruate. The ideal that a husband should "grow" his young wife's body is analogous to a father's responsibility to contribute semen to the growth of the fetus in his wife's womb and to contribute meat, fish, and vegetable foods to feed his children.

Wari' do not mark female puberty and menarche with any ritual, and they do not consider menstrual blood to be very dangerous or polluting to men or anyone else. Menstruating women engage in most of their normal activities, except that (because the blood attracts jaguars) they are not supposed to go to the forest or have sex (which would make the male partner attractive to jaguars). Wari' say that mature women's blood is "strong" (*hwara opa'*, connoting positive vitality and health). Men and children have weaker blood, and if they accidentally ingest menstrual blood, the more powerful blood can make them slightly sick. This risk affects only a menstruating woman's own husband and her prepubescent children, the individuals who share intimate body substance with her. Before the contact, when Wari' used body paint more than they do now, when a woman's period began, she, her husband, and their young children all painted themselves with fresh red annatto (*urucú*). The other visible markers of menstruation were small mats called *hujam*. When her period began, a woman wove several *hujam*, which she used to cover bloodstains on spots where she sat for a long time. Another context in which Wari' used *hujam* was in the enemy-killer's seclusion, as explained below.

Blood and blood-semen interactions are salient themes in Wari' ideas about pregnancy. Conception depends on a union of semen (which builds the fetus's flesh/body) and maternal blood (which is a source of fetal blood or its nourishment). The verb to describe the swelling of a pregnant woman's stomach is *munu*, which specifically means swelling with blood or serum in the abdomen. Fetuses are said to have a growth spurt (from an infusion of maternal blood) every month at the time when the mother's menstrual period would have come. The bloods of mother and infant merge during gestation, which transforms the mother's blood (Conklin and Morgan 1996). Wari' emphasize the great quantity and potency of blood in the bodies of infants and parturient women. Unlike menstrual blood, birth blood is dangerous to adult men in general. I have found no explanation for this difference; Wari' just say that birth blood is much stronger and stronger smelling. To protect others from contamination and to build the mother's breast milk and infant's blood, mother and newborn remain in their house (where the baby's father and siblings also sleep) and do not appear in public for several weeks after birth. A number of parallels to these ideas about blood's role in gestation and birth and the ways women deal with it run through the Wari' enemy-killer's ritual.

MASCULINITY AND WARFARE

In the decades before contact in the late 1950s and early 1960s, Wari' experienced frequent attacks and a number of massacres at the hands of non-Indian Brazilians and Bolivians, as well as Indians from other tribes whom businessmen in the Guajará-Mirim rubber trade hired to kill Wari'. In the more distant past, their main enemies had been Indians from neighboring tribes. It was in this context of threat and interethnic hostilities that the killing of an enemy outsider was valued so highly. The ritual seclusion following an enemy-killing was the most ritually elaborated event in an individual man's life. Vilaça (1996) emphasizes that the image of the warrior is central to Wari' notions of male identity: without it, "masculinity would be unimaginable." While this is true, it is also true that Wari' masculinity would be unimaginable without fatherhood, hunting, or shamanism. Wari' masculinity is a dynamic bundle of roles, competencies, and responsibilities to others. Without essentializing the warrior's role, one may recognize that among these masculine responsibilities, protecting one's people by killing enemy outsiders when necessary was a highly valued dimension of manhood.

Participation in the warriors' ritual seclusion was a pinnacle of male experience and achievement. Wari' from the Dois Irmãos region describe this as a requirement for full manhood status: an adolescent became *napiri*, a full adult man, when he had participated in killing an enemy *and* had experienced the abdominal swelling that marked his physio-ritual transformation. For adolescent boys, this constituted a rite of maturation that both marked and effected their becoming napiri.

Manhood and growth are conceptually fused, and the enemy blood that the boys who accompanied war parties incorporated was believed to stimulate the boys' growth and maturation in a manner identical to the effect of semen on girls' blood. The infusion of enemy blood made boys grow taller, fatter, stronger, more courageous, and capable of productive work—that is, able to actualize their masculine potential. Seasoned warriors also went into seclusion each time they killed an enemy. For an older man, each new killing brought another infusion of enemy blood/spirit that revitalized and enhanced his strength, vitality, courage, and resistance to disease.[10]

This was not a rite of gender formation per se—men were not "made"—but a rite of what Strathern has called "internal efficacy," aimed at actualizing capacities for masculine agency.[11] This is not to say that Wari' believe that boys do not become men at all now that there no longer are enemies to kill. Rather, they emphasize that males do not grow as much or mature as well. Santo André elders complain that today, men are smaller, weaker, and sicker than the tall, strong, fat warriors of the past in comparison to whom, they claim, the present generation (literally) comes up short.

Organized Wari' war parties typically traveled on foot for several days to attack enemies at sites far enough away that the attack would not draw retaliation against Wari' villages. As I have emphasized elsewhere (Conklin 1989, 386–388), during this journey, the warriors were thought to be engaged in a delicate and dangerous relationship with spirit forces that would determine the success of the attack. These spirits are associated with fire and the powers of predation, and they come from the underwater realm that is the abode of Wari' ancestors and the nonhuman forces that control human death. When angered by misbehavior in a war party, the spirits send *topo*—fierce storms that blacken the sky, inundate the earth, topple trees with raging winds, and bring illness and evil. If such a storm developed during the journey to attack an enemy, the warriors turned around and went home.

To maintain a positive relationship to these spiritual-cosmological forces, the war party observed certain behavioral restrictions, which were most stringent for the man who was the bearer of a ritual bundle of firebrands. This special fire bundle (which later would be used to light the fire to roast enemy body parts) was treated as sacred, and it was decorated and tied with the type of liana that Wari' used in funerals to tie the decorated firewood bundle over which they roasted corpses of their dead in preparation for cannibalizing them.

The multiple forms of death-related imagery in the warriors' journey suggest a symbolic interpretation of this as an encounter with the forces of death, although Wari' themselves do not speak of it in these terms. When the victorious warriors returned home from their encounter with death in the alien realm of the enemy outsider, the ritual acts with which women welcomed them and the ideas that surrounded the warrior's transformation in seclusion were replete with birth-related symbolism.

Wari' believe that when an enemy is killed, the victim's blood enters the bodies of everyone who witnessed the killing, regardless of whether or not they actually shot an arrow. Women did not shoot arrows, but if a woman witnessed a killing, she also incorporated the victim's blood and experienced effects similar to the male warriors. I heard of one girl and one woman to whom this happened.

Cannibalism of a slain enemy's body parts was a routine aspect of Wari' warfare, and Wari' ideas about incorporating enemy blood/spirit should be considered in relation to their practice of eating enemy flesh. When Wari' warriors killed an enemy, they usually took body parts (typically, the head and limbs) as trophies (Vilaça 1992, 47–130). The killers themselves did not eat any enemy flesh, but they roasted the enemy body parts soon after the kill (over a fire lit with the ritual firebrands) to preserve the flesh to be eaten at home by people who had not taken part in the killing.

A key point is that the physiologically active element acquired from the victim—the part of the enemy that affected the person who incorporated it— was the blood/spirit, *not* the flesh. Unlike many Melanesians and a few other native Amazonians, Wari' did not believe that eating roasted human flesh transferred any vital biosocial energies, personality characteristics, or other qualities from the person who was eaten to the person who ate them.

The fact that Wari' warriors did not eat their victims' flesh is consistent with a basic principle of Wari' cannibalism: that one does not consume the flesh of one's own consanguines. When the victim's blood/spirit entered the killer's body and (as discussed below) the Wari' warrior tamed and fed this alien spirit, this created a relationship between them analogous to consanguinity. Wari' say that the enemy spirit became the "child" of the killer in whose body it resided, and the spirit child was said to call the warrior "father." Just as a father does not eat his own offspring, warriors did not eat their victims' flesh.

The ones who did eat enemy body parts were people who had not participated in or witnessed the killing. Until recently, Wari' consistently have said the eaters of enemy flesh were men, especially old men. Recently, however, Vilaça (1996) reported statements from one or more elderly men in the Rio Negro-Ocaia community who told her that their women ate enemy flesh and that women's expressions of desire to eat it motivated men to go out and kill enemies. Although the individual women said to have eaten enemies deny having done so, Vilaça finds the male statement credible. On this basis, she asserts that a principle of Wari' gender relations was that enemy flesh was a male "offering to the women" parallel to the meat of animals that men hunt and give to women: "They [the women] desired enemy flesh, which represented a present, making it clear that [the women's] participation in war was fundamental, because it was through them and for them that the enemies were killed." While this interpretation of exocannibalism is uncertain,[12] the central point about warfare and women is valid: that enemy-killing was a service that Wari' women valued and desired from their men.

WARI' WARRIORS' SECLUSION

The immediate rewards for a man's success in warfare came from the women of his community. When victorious warriors returned home, the women greeted them with cries of joy and a ritual welcome replete with symbols of rebirth. As each man entered the village, women picked him up in their arms and carried him to the men's house. There, the women bathed each of the returned killers with warm water. (In other contexts, warm water baths are used to cleanse newborns, to treat the sick, and to revive individuals from states of unconsciousness analogous to death.) The women then rubbed the men's bodies with palm oil and smeared them all over with red annatto. An animated celebration followed in which the ritual fire-bearer was the first to tell the story of the expedition, and then each warrior spoke in turn.

After these festivities, the members of the war party secluded themselves together in the men's house behind palm-frond screens. Here, they reclined together in giant hammocks, in which they spent the entire period of seclusion. (This is the only context in which Wari' used hammocks before the contact.) When a man killed an enemy on his own, he lay alone in a hammock in a screened-off section of the men's house.

This seclusion was a time of relaxation and, when the killing had been a group affair, a time of conviviality and conversation. Much of the talk seems to have revolved around warfare and stories about warriors of the past. The men and boys did little except chat among themselves, play small reed flutes, and gorge themselves on pot after pot of sweet (unfermented) maize beverage, which their female kin made and passed to them through the palm screen. In contrast to the ascetic seclusions practiced in other Amazonian societies, this Wari' ritual brought intensified consumption of highly "social" elements: mass quantities of sweet maize beverage; assiduous attention to hygiene, with frequent warm baths and fresh applications of body oil and paint; and adornments and accoutrements (body paint, flutes, scarlet macaw feathers) that express Wari' notions of beauty.

For male adolescents, this was a time of intimacy with older men, a time of forging a shared masculine identity that transcended the kinship distinctions that divide Wari' men in certain other ritual contexts.[13] It also was a period of orientation during which older men instructed boys about masculine roles and ideals of manhood. Elders at Santo André told me that fathers used this time to lecture their sons about their new roles and responsibilities, as napiri, to direct their energies to socially beneficial activities: to hunt to feed their families and to control their sexuality by respecting other men's wives.

Warriors in seclusion neither spoke to nor touched women or children. When Wari' men talked about this, they emphasized that this avoidance of women and children was not because the men feared female pollution, but because of the need to protect others from the danger of the killer's touch. If a warrior touched a child, the enemy spirit could pass into and harm the child. If he touched a woman, she would be impassioned with uncontrollable sexual desire. Sexual intercourse was prohibited during seclusion because the enemy blood and fat would flow out in the ejaculation of semen. Unlike killers in other Amazonian societies, Wari' men did not want to get rid of the enemy blood as soon as possible. Rather, Wari' men tried to keep the enemy blood in their bodies long enough to absorb its vitalizing properties.

To acquire the benefits of the enemy elements that had entered their bodies, Wari' warriors drank copious amounts of sweet (unfermented) maize chicha. Maize chicha is a quintessentially "Wari'" food, and—in its "sweet" (unfermented or lightly fermented) form—it is a quintessentially feminine product that is symbolically identified with blood and the building of blood and breast milk and with consanguinity, amity, nurturance, and the reconstitution of a fragmented self.

Drinking chicha was said to affect the warrior in two related ways, one spiritual and one physiological. First, it fed the enemy spirit, satisfying its hunger and thereby taming and civilizing it. Not only did this establish kinship between the killer and his victim, it also transformed the former enemy's spirit into a Wari' spirit, with all the trappings and predispositions of Wari' ethnicity.[14] This Wari'-ized spirit would then remain in its killer's body as his companion for life and even after death. The "possession" of enemy spirits brought prestige to the killer. There are vague suggestions that it also brought enhanced spiritual power, but Wari' offer no clear statement on this.

The tangible manifestation of this spiritual transaction between the warrior and his victim was that the killer grew fat and his belly swelled. The disciplines of the ritual seclusion explicitly aimed to promote this abdominal swelling: to protect their newly acquired blood, men walked carefully to avoid stubbing a toe or cutting their feet and avoided unecessary contact with the earth or any dirty or polluting substance. They also did not touch food with their hands but ate using thin splinters like cocktail toothpicks.[15]

By all accounts, the chicha-gorged men really did grow quite fat. There was an aesthetic and erotic dimension to this, for the warriors emerging from seclusion with their plump, carefully oiled and painted physiques were considered very beautiful and were highly desired as sexual partners. The idea that everyone emphasizes is that the first time that a warrior has sex, the enemy fat passes out in his semen and into the body of his female partner, who then absorbs some of its vitality. Wari' say that as the men lost their newly acquired body fat, their wives grew fatter, stronger, and more vibrant. Thus, enemy-killings revitalized not only male bodies but also a wider collective body that included the sexually active women as well.

REPRODUCTIVE PARALLELS

For Wari' females and males, respectively, childbirth and enemy-killing/seclusion constituted the two biggest changes in social status, the experiences that made *narima* (full adult women) and *napiri* (full adult men). Wari' conceive of these in parallel terms. The ritual management of the warrior's transformation encapsulated images, ideas, metaphors, and practices related to several dimensions of female fecundity—female puberty, menstruation, pregnancy, and childbirth—in a single male ritual process.[16]

Female Puberty / Maturation

According to the oldest men at Santo André, enemy blood/spirit enters the Wari' warrior's body through his genitals. In his genitals, layers of the enemy's blood alternate with layers of the killer's semen. Blood-plus-semen is, of course, the generative combination that Wari' believe produces female pubertal maturation, menstruation, and pregnancy. Enemy blood stimulates the growth of boys in a manner identical to how semen stimulates the growth of girls. Thus, for both sexes, maturation traditionally was conceived as a blood transformation stimulated by the genital incorporation of another individual's body fluid.

Menstruation

According to Santo André elders, the warriors' seclusion ideally was supposed to last through a full lunar month, so that it would end at the second new moon after the killing. Wari' traditionally believe that women menstruate at the new moon. Menstruating women and warriors in seclusion marked their special blood states with two of the same visual markers: annatto (red body paint) and hujam (the small mats that women used to cover their menstrual bloodstains). Warriors in seclusion smeared their bodies heavily with annatto, just as a woman smeared herself, her husband, and her young children with annatto when her period began. When a warrior in seclusion left the men's house (to urinate or defecate) or stood playing a flute, he tucked a hujam under his arm. His mat was adorned with a long scarlet macaw feather, which swayed gracefully above his head.

Pregnancy and Childbirth

Male elders commonly describe the appearance of warriors' fattening bellies as "like pregnancy" (*ak ka nam wa*). *Munu* ("to swell with fluid") is a verb that describes the fattening of both a warrior's belly and, as noted, a pregnant woman's abdomen. Nourishing the blood is a focal concern in both processes, and maize chicha is considered the most important blood-building food during both pregnancy and the warriors' seclusion.

Wari' also compare to childbirth the loss of the warrior's fat belly after he has sex. As one male elder described it: "The enemy blood enters the warrior's body. The warrior gets fat. His belly swells. He gets really fat, like pregnancy. When the man has sex with a woman, the enemy blood goes out in the man's semen. It is like when a baby is born. The man gets thin. The enemy blood is gone, his fat is gone. The man gets thin, like a woman gets thin when a child is born."

Wari' thus projected a scenario of physiological changes in males similar to, but distinct from, female reproductive processes. (They say that it is *like* pregnancy, not that it *is* pregnancy.) This male transformation was procreative in its own way, for it produced the enemy spirit "children" who inhabit their Wari' "fathers." To call this parthogenesis (as Vilaça 1996 does) is to miss the point—which Wari' men make explicit—that this was not something that men accomplished on their own but a transformation that depended on a series of cross-sex transactions.

MASCULINITY AND INTERDEPENDENCE

Although the period of seclusion after an enemy-killing was the time in a Wari' man's life when he separated himself most from contact with women, this was not a rigid exclusivity. The warriors had intimate tactile contact with women as soon as they arrived home, when the women carried the killers into the village, bathed them, and oiled and painted their bodies. Even during the men's seclusion, some women (in their role as mothers) apparently entered the men's house enclosure: when adolescent boys were secluded after their first warfare experience, their proud mothers would visit them to pull on the boys' legs and arms, stretching them to encourage their growth.

When Wari' men talk about the warriors' seclusion, they openly acknowledge that its success depended on women's labor. An infusion of enemy blood/spirit alone does nothing for the warrior; only if the killer drinks quantities of chicha can he transform and retain this enemy substance in order to derive its positive effects. Seclusion, Wari' men say, would have been impossible without the chicha that women made.

Wari' consider sweet maize chicha the single most important food for building both healthy blood and nourishing breast milk. Sweet maize chicha is symbolically associated with femininity, consanguinity, social integration, and the formation and maintenance of nurturant relationships within the domestic sphere. The sweet maize chicha that Wari' warriors drank during their ritual seclusion was a thoroughly feminine substance. It was literally full of female fluid—saliva—since women sweetened it by chewing the maize (which breaks down complex starches into simple sugars) and spitting this masticated mixture into the pot.

Wari' see chicha as the quintessential product of female labor. During the warriors' seclusion, each warrior's sisters, wife, mother, and other female relatives worked long hours grinding, masticating, and cooking the maize to make the copious amounts of chicha the men required. When I ask older Wari' women why they were willing to do all this extra onerous work, and why it was so important for men to go through the ritual seclusion, they say that they considered the young men's growth, strength, health, and vitality essential to the well-being of the whole community. Napiri, they point out, were the ones everyone depended on for the hard work of clearing fields, for hunting, and, in the past, for protection against enemies.

The women's burden was compounded by the fact that with so many hunters temporarily out of action, there was little game to eat. Old people say that while the men grew fat, their wives grew thin from overwork and lack of meat. Some commented on how relieved women were when the seclusion ended and the men got back to work. One gathers that it sometimes ended earlier than the warriors would have liked because their female kin lost patience with the situation.

Understanding how Wari' see the warriors' seclusion as a cross-sex transaction brings us back to Strathern's point at the beginning of this chapter: that native Amazonians and Melanesians recognize that it is through transactions with persons different from oneself that one develops creative capacities in the self. For Wari', maturation to full adulthood for both girls and boys traditionally was thought to be stimulated by interactions with two categories of "others": first with a being external to Wari' society (the moon for girls, an enemy for boys) and second with members of the opposite sex in one's own group— with men who produced the semen or women who produced the chicha that helped transform an adolescent's blood.

This notion that one depends on others to realize capacities in the self is salient not just in Wari' thought but also in other Amazonian societies, like the Kayapó described by William Fisher (Chapter 6), who emphasize social interactivity as the basis for self-actualization. This resonates with Aletta Biersack's insight (summarized in Strathern 1988, 130–131) that the Paiela of New Guinea "locate the sources of their internal efficacy beyond themselves. The sources do not constitute some other realm or domain but another type of 'person.' For 'men' they lie in the acts of 'women.' These sources are not to be controlled or overcome but sustained in order to give perpetual evidence of this very efficacy." Like the Paiela, Wari' look beyond themselves for agency-enhancing resources. In the past, one place they found it was in enemy outsiders, whom Wari' treated as a kind of natural resource, a source of growth-promoting, revitalizing substance that one could journey out beyond the boundaries of their society to acquire and bring back home.

SWOLLEN BELLIES, DEGENERATION, AND DEATH

Wari' emphasize the individual's responsibility to maintain his or her own health and strength, especially by guarding the purity and strength of one's blood. For napiri, this means practicing proper hygiene (bathing and avoiding dirty substances such as charred meat) and not eating a long list of proscribed game and fish (most of which are excessively bloody or are thought to have slow blood circulation). The same foods are prohibited for anyone in a state of growth, and for pregnant women in particular.[17]

What happens if someone does not follow these rules? Wari' say that the individual's blood will slow and degenerate, leading to weakness, lethargy, and illness. This can end in a fatal, much-feared disease syndrome called *kup*, in which the abdomen swells up huge with serum, often accompanied by vomiting of blood and uncontrolled nasal bleeding.[18] Pregnant women and napiri are the two categories of people most vulnerable to this disease.

Wari' thus posit two contrasting images of abdominal swelling for both sexes: a positive process of growth and enhanced vitality experienced by women in pregnancy and by men in the warrior's ritual seclusion, and a negative syndrome of deadly degeneration that results from failure to take care of one's blood. A third image of abdominal swelling appears in Wari' thinking about death, in which the decay and bloating of a corpse is equated with the ritual swelling of a warrior's belly. Before contact, when Wari' practiced mortuary cannibalism, they did not roast most adult corpses until about the third day after death. Wari' say that during this period when the unroasted corpse lay rotting and swelling on earth, in the underworld the spirit body of the dead person (of either sex and all ages) was lying in *itam*, a ritual state of unconsciousness during which, some elders say, the spirit goes off to kill birds or enemies. The swelling of the corpse was a manifestation of the swelling of the belly of the dead person's spirit, now become napiri. When revived by the master of the underworld, the dead person's spirit is restored to complete health, beauty, and perfect maturity; children are grown to young adulthood and old people become young and vigorous again. Wari' see the bloating of the rotting corpse as the visible marker of a positive spiritual transformation. This inverts the negative symbolism of the disease kup, in which abdominal swelling signals deadly degeneration of the blood. It also inverts the connection that Yanomami and other native Amazonians make between the swelling of a killer's belly and the decay of his victim's corpse.

THE YANOMAMI

The Yanomami of northern Brazil studied by Albert are one of four subgroups of the larger population generally referred to as Yanomami, which is one of the largest and least acculturated native populations in South America. Like Wari', Yanomami make their living by slash-and-burn gardening, hunting, fishing, and gathering. Postmarital residence is normatively uxorilocal. In contrast to the Wari', warfare continues to be part of life in some Yanomami communities today, as violence by outsiders (especially in the recent invasion by Brazilian gold miners; see Ramos 1995) and hostilities among Yanomami themselves keep dynamics of attack and retribution in play. Thus, following Albert (1985), I write of the Yanomami killer's ritual in the present tense.

Yanomami directly equate the state of a killer who has incorporated enemy blood with the condition of a girl during her first menstruation. Menstruating females and killers with enemy blood in their bodies are called *unokai*, which Albert translates as "in a state of homicide." Yanomami describe all menstrual periods, not just first menstruation, as unokai, "the state of homicide of women" (Albert 1985, 604).

For Yanomami, blood is the fundamental vector of biological becoming, a key element in processes of growth and decay, health and illness, maturation and aging (Albert 1985, 607–608). Blood also is a privileged symbolic element in the Yanomami philosophy of time: human biological rhythms are closely linked to cosmo-meteorological rhythms. Displaced outside the body, blood becomes a factor and a sign of disregulated biological, social, and cosmo-meteorological periodicity. Uncontained, it plunges people, society, and the universe into an irreversible process of entropy that is analogous to organic degradation. The two major contexts in which this danger is manifest are menarche and homicide.

Albert argues that in physiological terms, both the body of the warrior and the body of the pubescent girl are affected by excessive biological "naturalness," in the form of excessive blood in their bodies (Albert 1985, 587). Yanomami are concerned to control this blood and to circumscribe and contain the threats posed by its flow outside the body. They accomplish this through the ritual seclusion of the blood-contaminated individual, which Albert interprets as a form of control and containment, a symbolic "cooking" of the "raw" naturalness of the blood.

Menstrual blood is considered to be dangerous, imbued with a harmful odor, and polluting to others, especially men (Albert 1985, 574). The blood of menarche is most dangerous. When a girl's first period begins, she must immediately retire to a hammock behind a screen in her home and observe a solitary seclusion involving semi-isolation, immobility, silence, fasting, and nudity. If she failed to seclude herself properly, or if she did not complete the full seclusion, she would quickly experience premature aging and become an old woman (Albert 1985, 583). In addition, if her blood were to flow uncontrolled (that is, if it were not ritually contained in the seclusion), the world would be subject to constant darkness, rain, and storms.

The second extremely dangerous form of blood is that of a homicide victim. Yanomami believe that the victim's blood enters the killer through his nose and mouth (Albert 1985, 361). As long as this blood is present in his body, the killer is considered to be unokai. Like menstrual blood, the victim's blood is associated with decay, degeneration, and the disruption of biocosmic rhythms. To control its deleterious effects, the Yanomami warrior observes a strict seclusion whose details of proscribed and prescribed behaviors are virtually identical to those practiced by girls during their first menstruation. The consequences of not following the ritual restrictions are identical disorderings of biological and cosmo-meteorological rhythms: the killer would age very rapidly into an old man, and the world would be inundated with constant rain, storms, and darkness in the daytime.

The Yanomami killer's incorporation of his victim's blood is symbolically conceived as blood cannibalism: inside the killer's body are spirits of cannibal animals and insects that devour the victim's vital image/blood. The blood processes in the killer's body are closely associated with the rotting of the victim's corpse (Albert 1985, 351). This blood gives off a putrid, nauseating odor in the killer's body. Like the Wari', Yanomami connect enemy blood to fat; they believe that it exudes out of the killer's body as grease sweated out on his forehead. The killer's seclusion lasts until the victim's corpse has rotted, the corpse fluids are gone, and the bones have become dry (Albert 1985, 362–363, 374). The killer then expels the remnant of putrid enemy elements from his body by vomiting (provoked by emetics) into running water and bathes to cleanse himself of the fat on his face.[19] If he failed to purge himself of this rotten blood, his abdomen would swell, bringing violent pain and death (Albert 1985, 375).

This equation between menstruation and the "state of homicide" recurs in two other contexts that Yanomami also call unokai: male puberty and conjugal seclusion at menarche. In the male puberty rite (which seems to be infrequent and not much elaborated), young men say that they defecate blood, which is literally conceived as male menarche (Albert 1985, 599–601). Boys defecating blood are unokai and are supposed to observe an attenuated version of the seclusions practiced for menarche and homicide.

Conjugal seclusion (with husband and wife lying side by side in a hammock) occurs when menstruation begins for a young girl who married before she had begun to menstruate. When a husband has "fed" and "raised" his young wife for some time, he participates in the bodily experience of her menarche: the husband is said to experience a fever, which Albert (1985, 592) views as a symbolic transfusion of heat and blood from the girl's body. Like his wife, the husband is unokai and must lie in seclusion with her. The odor of his wife's menses enters his nose and causes grease to exude from his forehead, just as the victim's blood did in the killer (1985, 593).

Here, menstrual blood and its dangers do not appear to be attached exclusively to femaleness but also may be associated with men. The emphasis is not on the polluting nature of women alone but on the responsibility of the individual (of either sex) to take proper action to control dangerous blood. Menstruating women, the husbands of menarcheal girls, pubescent boys, and killers all use the same ritual techniques to circumscribe, control, and neutralize their blood and channel it for purposes of promoting health, growth, and societal well-being.

DISCUSSION

One of the points that emerges from a regional comparison of the Amazonian warriors' seclusion rites is that while these share certain themes and construct manhood out of similar processes (killing an outsider, seclusion and its

disciplines, and regulating enemy blood in the killer's body), there is considerable variation among these societies in the cultural meanings and valences associated with enemy blood/spirit and the correspondences between male and
female biosocial transformations. Irving Goldman's (1963, 129) comment about
the Yurupari men's cult in the northwest Amazon, that "one of the striking
characteristics of the entire Amazon drainage is the ready way in which form
and content separate and combine in new ways," is apropos here also.

In many ways, the Wari' warriors' ritual complex appears anomalous in
comparison to the Yanomami and other native Brazilian peoples. Wari'
treated enemy blood as a revitalizing resource, whereas Yanomami and others associate it with decay and degeneration. Wari' warriors tried to keep the
victim's blood in their bodies so they could absorb its beneficial properties,
whereas Yanomami and others seek to neutralize and expel it. Wari' men actively cultivated the swelling of their bellies during seclusion, but Yanomami
and others see such abdominal swelling as life-threatening. Wari' symbolism
emphasized growth-related metaphors of pregnancy and birth; for
Yanomami, the dominant metaphor is menarche—an ambivalent state encompassing powers of both human fecundity and cosmic destruction.

Underlying the marked differences between the Wari' and the Yanomami
and others, however, is a shared conception of the warrior's ritual transformation as a means for enhancing masculine vitality and conferring long life
with some protection against illness, degeneration, or death. If the central
concern of these warriors' rites is male transcendence over biological forces
of death and degeneration, it is no surprise to find that men enact this by embodying female reproductive processes. Cross-culturally, rituals (especially
men's rituals) that are concerned with creating a transcendent order commonly project imageries of power that posit "a contrast between mortal bodies and Enduring Ones" (Shapiro 1989, 76). "Mortal" bodies are prototypically female bodies. Bloch and Parry's (1982) well-known argument suggests
that women and their sexual functions tend to be symbolically identified with
biological degeneration because women give birth and birth leads inevitably
to death, decomposition, and decay. Thus, in rituals concerned with creating
a transcendent order, "this world of biology is elaborately constructed as
something to be got rid of" (Bloch and Parry 1982, 18–27). Warren Shapiro
(1989, 74–75) has extended this insight with a provocative argument that the
"immense denigration of procreation by pseudo-procreative theorists . . .
[and] their often barely disguised misogyny" reflect men's "desperate attempts
to control and denigrate" the biological forces that women control. "Pseudo-
procreation, then, has to do with the magical conquest of the mortal implications of procreation, and, like certain other forms of such conquest known
to psychoanalytic theory, it partakes of its supposed antithesis." In Amazonia,
this interpretation applies most directly to pseudo-procreative (especially
menstrual) imagery in the classic men's cults such as those of the Mehinaku

(Gregor 1985) and Tukanoans (C. Hugh-Jones 1979; S. Hugh-Jones 1979) with their secrecy, rigorous male exclusivity, matriarchal myths, and expressions of polarized sexual politics.

In the native Brazilian warriors' seclusion rituals, however, neither secrecy nor the denigration of women and female physiology are mentioned in any of the ethnographic accounts. Rather than assume that misogyny must lurk beneath the surface, it seems more fruitful to probe the implications of what the Yanomami and Wari' systems explicitly assert: that female and male growth and physiology are parallel processes.

One dimension of this is an emphasis on relational interdependence, the idea that for both sexes, sources of vitality and potency that create gendered capacities (growth, health, fertility, productivity, efficacy in fulfilling adult roles) lie outside the individual in interactions with others (cf. Lindenbaum 1984, 356; Strathern 1988). For females, this is expressed most directly in the notion of seminal nurture, the idea that menstruation results from or is stimulated by sexual intercourse with a man. This idea is shared by the Araweté, Wari', and, among the Gê, at least the Xikrin-Kayapó (see Fisher, Chapter 6) and the Krahó (Carneiro da Cunha 1978, 106). The Yanomami and some Gê peoples also think that the blood processes of menarche affect men's bodies as well. This militates against a simplistic model of male and female substances as antithetical in these specific cultures. It also implies that notions of procreation are not associated exclusively with women; rather, there is a broader concept of nurturance as a component of masculinity as well, expressed in the nurture of fetuses and wives and (for the Wari') in the production of spirit "children" through warfare.

Just as female fecundity depends on a cross-sex transaction, the Yanomami and the Wari' traditionally saw men's bodily potency as derived from the incorporation and self-disciplined transformation of an enemy's blood/spirit. (The Wari' also considered women essential participants in the men's transformation.) It is worth considering whether conceptual parallels between male and female relational fecundity underlie the warriors' ritual complex in other Brazilian societies as well. Unfortunately, this is difficult to assess with the sketchy data now available.

The idea that procreativity, growth, and capacities in the self develop out of relationships between unlike individuals is something that Amazonia and Melanesia share in common. As Marilyn Strathern notes (Chapter 10), these are two world areas in which people actively seek to create social differences among categories of persons, to produce outsiders from whom one gains one's own identity. The rites surrounding the killing of an enemy are one of the most direct expressions of this. As the Melanesian literature has demonstrated, focusing on relationality opens possibilities to explore, compare, and find the common threads underlying seemingly disparate phenomena. It allows us to ask, for instance, whether native people see similar dynamics in the relationships between a breast-feeding child and its mother, a pubescent girl and her husband/lover, a killer and his victim.

A first step for Amazonianists is to begin to think about the regional patterning of male rituals and their variations on the themes of blood, semen, seclusion, and bodily disciplines of abstinence and consumption as technologies for enhancing agency in one or both sexes. The diverse cultural meanings associated with the enemy-killers' rites suggest that the argument developed by Jonathan Hill (Chapter 3)—that Whitehead's models of fertility cults offer illuminating perspectives on Amazonian men's rituals—might be extended considerably further. When Hill asserts that in "cults of manhood" in what he calls Amazonian "hunter-warrior" societies (which would include the Yanomami and Wari'), "substances and symbols of fertility are entirely male-controlled," this describes only one pole of a continuum. As Keesing (1982, 11), Whitehead (1986b), and others have noted, Melanesian rites of male initiation and man-making vary considerably in the degree of male exclusivity they involve. Whitehead (1986b) emphasizes that women participate in many male ritual activities; indeed, she suggests that some "cults of manhood" might more accurately be described as "man-woman" cults. Like their Melanesian counterparts, Amazonian man-making rituals run a gamut from antagonism to complementarity, from emphases on inimical physiological differences to notions of interdependence and the productivity of cross-sex transactions. The Wari' case, in particular, demonstrates that there is no single pattern of gender relations or male dominance associated with the social valuation of men as hunter-warriors and of enemy-killing as a source of masculine vitality. Men may assert their control over life-giving, procreative powers by acts resonant with feminine symbolism without necessarily diminishing or denying their women's own distinct powers and intrinsic sources of procreative agency.

If native Amazonians sometimes see male and female development as parallel, they obviously do not see them as identical. It is the *distinctiveness* of the male transformation that native Amazonians emphasize when contrasting femininity and masculinity. For Wari' women, the stimulus for fecundity is located within their own society, in members of the opposite sex, and women access this relational potency through sexual intercourse. The stimulus to male fecundity/potency, in contrast, is located outside society in the alien world of the enemy, and it is accessed by the violent act of killing. This contrast—between centripetal (female) and centrifugal (male) dynamics in the process of coming of age and coming into adult agency—is a cross-cultural pattern in initiation rites and cultural ideas about the transition from childhood to adulthood.

In the Brazilian warriors' rituals, another glaring difference between images of male and female development is that the male transformation is based on violence, on participation in an aggressive, often life-risking act that may entail intense physical exertion, anger, and fear. This reflects a more general pattern that anthropologists have noted for both Amazonia and Melanesia, in which "regenerative life-processes attach themselves to men only through violence and the dynamism of relating to or even expropriating what is strange and foreign" (Sullivan 1988, 329). This is something that the Brazilian warriors' rites have in common with the classic men's cults of the Upper Xingu, northwest Amazon, and Papua New Guinea, for in these cults male generativity also is represented as originating from an act of violence—the mythic theft of sacred instruments and the overthrow of their female owners.[20]

In locating the source of a young man's transformation in his interactions with an enemy outsider whom he kills and from whom he appropriates something that he may transform and thereby enhance his own masculine powers, the Brazilian enemy-killer's rituals resemble certain Melanesian societies noted by Whitehead (1986b, 278), in which male fertility develops through violence that garners elements of the enemy which become an ingredient in human fertility and the enhancement of human health and vitality. In both regions, this is expressed in beliefs about acquiring and incorporating (into individual or social bodies) elements taken from enemies, such as captive children (Murphy 1958), trophy heads, flesh, genitals, souls, or blood. In ways specific to each culture, these convey vitality, strength, long life, and sometimes even immunity to death or the rotting of one's corpse.

In both regions, some men have looked outward to enemy humans located beyond the bounds of the local group as a resource for self-transformation. In Strathern's terms, they have gone out searching to find what is hidden and must be brought into relation with the self. This theme is particularly elaborated in Amazonia, where the world outside human society—the domain of forest animals and human enemies—plays a larger role in self-conceptions and self-identity than it does in Melanesia.

The regeneration of Amazonian males' vitality via enemy-killing and its disciplines asserts masculine influence over the interlinked forces of body, cosmos, and time. This is a supremely cultural act, for as Lawrence Sullivan (1988) observed in his masterful synthesis of themes in South American religions, the idea of intercalating cosmic periodicity into human life is at the center of native Amazonian conceptions of culture: "The capacity to relate to things in a proper, periodic way is fundamental to the possibilities of culture" (Sullivan 1988, 262).[21] The Wari' warrior's journey in search of an enemy to kill was both an extension of self across space and an assertion of influence over temporal periodicity. An attack on an enemy inevitably provoked counterattacks that fed ongoing cycles of interethnic violence. In Wari' memories, attacks and counterattacks—the killings and massacres their people suffered and the moves they made in response—are rhythms of their historical consciousness.

Recognizing how warriors' acts of killing are implicated in temporal periodicity suggests another, prototypically Amazonian, reason why female physiology is a template for the warrior's seclusion rituals. Attuning the self to cosmic rhythms is a goal for both sexes, but males must actively construct this capacity whereas women *embody* the calibration between human and cosmic rhythms. For native Amazonians, "menstruation is the clearest image of the periodic quality of time that conditions human existence" (Sullivan 1988, 262). When they bleed, gestate, and give birth in a proper manner, women manifest their *intrinsic* identity as cultural beings and regenerators of human life. Men also embody human attunement to periodicity, but rather than being intrinsic to male bodies, this must be inscribed and continually reinscribed upon them through intentional acts.

This contrast between intrinsic female powers and intentionally constructed male powers suggests that male feelings of inadequacy may be a component of pseudo-procreative imagery. Tuzin (1995) identifies male inadequacy as a core dynamic in men's cult activities in Papua New Guinea, and Sullivan's survey of the literature on male initiation in South America reaches a similar conclusion. "Men's relationship to life processes, the regenerative processes of culture, is an uneasy one in comparison to women's," he writes (Sullivan 1988, 345). "Whereas women's relationship is part of the primordial condition of the mythic world, men's involvement in reproductive processes threatens to remain borrowed, instrumental, and ideological rather than material." Sullivan suggests that both the terms in which men perceive their inadequacy and the ritual mechanisms they use to overcome it are framed by quintessentially Amazonian concerns with the links among space, time, and body. Men's claims to powers of reproduction are tenuous, Sullivan asserts (p. 329), for there is "an apparent lack of relation in space between objects (e.g., men and the instruments of regeneration; the male body and the bodies of offspring from the female) and an apparent separation in time between distinct events (e.g., intercourse and parturition)." In the face of the resulting sense of male inadequacy and insecurity, the ritual appropriation of feminine symbolism in male initiation and rites of transformation "aims at providing men a fundamental and corporeal relationship to powers of regeneration, growth, and transformation" (p. 345).

Native Amazonians and Melanesians see the human body as a prime site for constructing relationships. Modifications of bodily processes—manipulations of blood and semen, seclusion and abstinence, control of what passes between the internal body and the external world—are technologies through which men activate their self-potential and construct their claims to generativity and cosmic attunement. The Brazilian enemy-killers' rituals are one example of how men have used the symbolic and substantive resources of women and enemies to express and enact masculine control over powers of life, death, and biological regeneration. These rituals embody the insight common to both Melanesia and Amazonia: that it is in relation to persons different from oneself that one develops creativity and draws capacities out of the self. The new perspectives generated by bringing a focus on relationality and gender into an analysis of the Brazilian warriors' seclusion rituals suggest that academic insights likewise may be born of a conjunction of differences, such as the conversations generated by the 1996 Wenner-Gren symposium in Mijas, Spain, which brought together distinct perspectives from Melanesia and Amazonia.

NOTES

1. The Kayapó (a Gê group) also believed that enemy blood enters the killer's body and must be ritually expelled (by scarification and exposure to the sun), but they did not enter seclusion to accomplish this (Vidal 1977, 156–157; Verswijver 1996, 24). Huxley (1957) and Viveiros de Castro (1992) have suggested that in the sixteenth century, a ritual seclusion may have been practiced by the Tupinambá, Tupians who inhabited coastal northeastern Brazil at the time of the European invasion. The Aché of Paraguay believed that only the victim's soul entered the killer's body (through the anus), where it ate his entrails and had to be vomited out (Clastres 1972, 259).

2. Among Upper Xingu peoples who have renounced warfare and do not valorize the image of the warrior, there is a similar belief that when a man kills a witch (a fellow tribesmember), the killer's belly will swell with the victim's blood unless this is purged through seclusion disciplines similar to those for puberty seclusion (Gregor 1985; Viveiros de Castro 1979). The nearby Suyá fear that the witch's blood that swells the killer's belly will make the killer into a witch, and witch-killers observe a semiseclusion similar to enemy-killers, but without any bleeding, scarring, or ceremony (Seeger 1981, 168). In contrast to enemy-killing, witch-killing does not enhance (and may even diminish) status and masculinity in these societies.

3. The Araweté killer with his belly full of enemy blood "dies" and is in "a state in which he actually becomes a corpse. . . . He feels 'as if he is rotting . . . and his bones become soft' in tandem with the rotting of his victim's corpse" (Viveiros de Castro 1992, 240, 247). Apinayé warriors consumed quantities of hot pepper because the heat drives away the spirit (which likes cool places) and consumes the dead person's cadaver more quickly, thereby liquidating the contaminating fluids (Da Matta 1976, 87). The Krahó sometimes burned the corpses of enemies and witches, thereby eliminating the blood so that the killer could shorten considerably the duration of his seclusion (Carneiro da Cunha 1978, 105).

4. Fatal male abdominal swelling is reminiscent of the "male pregnancy" illnesses reported among the Awa and Hua of highland New Guinea (Newman and Boyd 1982, 267; Meigs 1984, 52–55). I find no evidence, however, that native Amazonians think of the swelling of the killer's belly as negative pregnancy. On the other hand, a theme in several societies is the idea that fatal abdominal swelling (for women as well as men) results from transgressions of societal norms, especially improper cross-sex interactions. In view of widespread native ideas about blood as a key factor in pregnancy, perhaps it is worth considering whether Amazonian fears of warriors' bellies swelling and bursting might evoke negative pregnancy images.

5. All translations of texts with foreign titles are my own.

6. Some scholars have proposed that concerns with blood loss motivated warfare in certain Amazonian societies. The idea is that a motive for vengeance was a desire to recapture

the lost blood of one's relatives who had been killed by enemy outsiders, and that this created a hydraulic system in which attempts to capture and recapture blood drove cycles of attacks and counterattacks between enemy groups. The Brazilian warriors' seclusion rituals revolved around warfare and transfers of blood/spirit between killer and victim, but there is no indication that they had anything to do with such a hydraulic model of blood circulating in a closed system. With one exception, the aim always was to get rid of the enemy blood that had entered the killer's body, not to conserve it. The Wari' were the one exception. The basis for a hydraulic model would appear to be present, for Wari' believe that when an enemy outsider kills a Wari', the killer absorbs the Wari' victim's blood/spirit. But Wari' adamantly deny that this "lost" blood/spirit of the slain Wari' was recaptured when Wari' warriors killed enemies in return.

7. In most societies in both regions, native people consider menstrual blood and the blood of childbirth at least somewhat polluting or dangerous to adult men. In much of Melanesia, there are stringent taboos and prohibitions on contact between men and menstruating women. Some Amazonian groups also see menstrual blood as quite dangerous, while others treat its risks as minimal.

8. This account is based primarily on data collected in the village of Santo André in June 1985–June 1987 and May–June 1991, with supplementary data collected in the villages of Ribeirão, Lage, Tanajura, and Rio Negro-Ocaia. Fieldwork was funded by the Wenner-Gren Foundation, the Fulbright Commission, and the Inter-American Foundation, authorized by the CNPq and FUNAI, and sponsored by Júlio Cesar Melatti of the Universidade de Brasília.

9. Throughout the life cycle, Wari' conceive of individuals as developing and maturing through their engagement in flows of elements (tangible and intangible) between persons in contrasting social categories. Transformative interactions involve transfers of substance (usually blood or its analogs) between different types of Wari' persons (female/male, mother/fetus) or between Wari' persons and nonpersons (animal spirits, enemies). These latter nonpersons, however, ultimately are conceived as persons: *jami karawa*, "animal spirits," have human-form (Wari') spirits; and an enemy spirit becomes Wari' in the killer's body.

10. This applied only to the killing of outsider (non-Wari') enemies (*wijam*). The killing of a fellow Wari' tribesmember did not involve transfers of substance, nor does it appear to have been ritualized in any manner analogous to enemy-killing. Readers desiring a fuller understanding of Wari' warfare and the category of wijam should consult Vilaça (1992).

11. Biersack (Chapter 4) emphasizes how men's rites of passage reproduce gender hierarchies. In the Wari' case, gender hierarchies were not pronounced, but it is worth noting that any claims that Wari' men might make to superiority over women—such as physical strength, self-control, or the knowledge of how to handle the dangerous blood of animals or corpses—were buttressed by their claims to enhanced blood acquired through the disciplines of the warrior's seclusion.

12. I hesitate to read these scanty data as evidence of a fundamental dynamic of Wari' gender relations, especially since so many Wari' interviewed independently by five different ethnographers have represented exocannibalism as a male activity. The denial by the women who allegedly ate enemies is troubling, especially in view of the relative openness with which Wari' speak about their cannibalism practices. Vilaça's argument that it makes sense that women would have eaten enemy flesh because the men had taken part in the war party and thus were precluded from eating is unconvincing. This assumes that Wari'

war parties left women and children home alone without any adult men at all. They did not. On the contrary, Wari' emphasized to me that there always were some men (especially older men) who stayed home, unable to take part in the warriors' arduous cross-country journeys and thus eligible to eat the enemy flesh.

13. Viveiros de Castro (1992, 281–282) suggests that there is a broad Tupian (and perhaps pan-Brazilian) pattern of equating enemies with feminine symbolism and equating relations to enemies with relations to affines. Vilaça (1992) develops a complicated argument to assert that Wari' project images of affinity onto their enemies. From this perspective, oppositions between consanguines and affines are not absent from the warrior's ritual but are displaced onto Wari'/enemy oppositions.

14. The enemy spirit acquires the markers of Wari' ethnicity: it comes to speak the Wari' language, enjoy Wari' foods, and sleep on a bed (as Wari' normally do) instead of a hammock (as Brazilians and most neighboring Indians do). Vilaça emphasizes that the Wari' system does not fit Viveiros de Castro's (1992) model of the Araweté (Tupian) killer, in which the killer takes on characteristics of the enemy Other. On the contrary, the spirit of the slain enemy becomes Wari'. "The society of the [Wari'] killer does not appropriate any symbolic goods of the dead enemy: there are no songs, names, insignias. Neither does it appropriate [the enemy's] 'negative' attributes: his anger, thirst for vengeance, in sum, his position as enemy. Everything [in the Wari' system] appears to reduce to a transference of substances, to an operation restricted to the level of individual physiology, which culminates with the enemy spirit transformed into the offspring (parthenogenetic) of the killer" (Vilaça 1996).

15. Wari' use such "toothpicks" to eat meat and *pamonha* (a sort of dense, unleavened corn bread) in certain festivals and, in the past, in funerary cannibalism.

16. Vilaça suggests that some Wari' directly equate menarche and the male transformation via enemy-killing. In the Rio Negro-Ocaia community, she reports hearing the term napiri used to describe a girl after her first menstruation. Wari' with whom I worked, however, disavowed knowledge of such a usage.

17. Until old age, napiri were supposed to safeguard the enhanced blood in their bodies by strict attention to hygiene; they were supposed to bathe and apply body oil and annatto paint frequently and avoid contact with dirt and the soot on charred meat. They also were supposed to avoid eating a long list of animals and fish species that are thought to be excessively bloody or to have slow blood circulation. The same species are prohibited for consumption by anyone in a state of growth—pregnant women, young adolescents, and small children and their parents (who share intimate connections of body substance). Eating these foods is said to cause stunted growth and physical disfigurement in children and adolescents. For adults (especially pregnant women and napiri), eating proscribed animals or failing to observe the hygienic prescriptions is said to lead to weakness, lethargy, and eventually death.

18. These symptoms resemble the (biomedical) disease ascites, in which disorders of the liver, pancreas, or other organs lead to the presence of free fluid in the peritoneal cavity, gross abdominal swelling, and sometimes hematemesis and nasal bleeding as the result of ruptures of gastro-esophageal varices associated with portal hypertension.

19. A similar practice of men vomiting to rid themselves of blood after a violent encounter occurs among the Mehinaku of the Upper Xingu in central Brazil. In the Jawari ritual of contests between members of different, ethnically distinct villages, a man who is struck by a spear thrown by an opponent from another group vomits and uses medicines

to rid himself of the blood. When Xinguanos kill witches or, more rarely, outsider enemies, the killers attempt to remove the defiling blood by consuming medicines (Gregor 1990b, 116–117).

20. See Sullivan (1988, 328–329) for an extended discussion of the role of violence in men's cults and strategies of initiation.

21. Sullivan offers an evocative image of this nexus of cosmic, bodily, and social rhythms: "Throughout their lives men continue to embody the periodic rhythms to which they were first initiated in the womb: in the blood pulsing through the body or spurting from wounds in war or rite, in the tempos of the hunter's life (the periodic fasts, avoidances, and sexual abstentions), in the steady 'thump' of one's lineage as it matures and falls as the ripe fruit of a new generation or age-set during the periodic performance of initiation" (Sullivan 1988, 265).

EIGHT

Damming the Rivers of Milk?
Fertility, Sexuality, and Modernity
in Melanesia and Amazonia

Margaret Jolly

Like other authors (Hill, Gregor and Tuzin, Bonnemère), Jolly notes that in both Melanesia and Amazonia, cultures vary in the extent that they bring men and women together in creative relationships or separate them as antithetical and opposed. In Melanesian Vanuatu, this dialectic is in part mediated by mutual sexual attraction and culturally imposed continence. Continence, however, is not simply the denial of sexuality but also "generative of fertility and growth. . . . The periodic suppression of desire . . . is thought rather to heighten desire and to secure vitality, fertility, and health."

Jolly maintains that the balance of desire and restraint is linked not only to bodily substances, such as semen, blood, and milk, but also to foods, which in their associations and ritual significance are equally gendered. Hence, she notes, in Vanuatu, the same expression denotes fasting and sexual continence. Mythology links human sexuality and fertility with such foods as taro, yams, and pigs, all of which are "thought to have been generated in diverse ways from the human body."

Turning to specific parallels, Jolly looks at the cultures of the northwest Amazon, where she finds striking resemblances to Melanesia in the "stress of life and growth," which is "punctuated and perpetuated by periods of sexual separation and continence," and in the specific connections between foodstuffs and the human body. Jolly's chapter should be read in connection with the many others that focus on body and social identity (including Conklin, Bonnemère, Biersack, Gregor and Tuzin, and Hugh-Jones) but also Roscoe's discussion of masculinity and sexual avoidance.

INTRODUCTION

The metaphor in my title plays on that of Christine Hugh-Jones's brilliant ethnography of the Barasana, *From the Milk River* (1979). Through this absurd image of damming rivers of milk, I query a hydraulic[1] theory of desire and its radical separation from reproduction. As many other ethnographers have shown and as is amply attested in this volume, in both Melanesia and Amazonia, sexuality and reproduction flow into each other and are part of a broader confluence of indigenous philosophies about the cosmic sources of life, health, and growth and of death, decay, and degeneration. But implicit in my comparison of these two regions is a comparison with another position of viewing— "the West." My image of damming thus also evokes the way in which foreign influences and colonial projects challenged indigenous philosophies through the ravages of introduced diseases and through the importation of radically different notions of sexuality and fertility. These exotic imports included missionary ideals, colonial state policies, development programs, and more diffuse Western notions of gendered persons, which tend to portray reproduction, as distinct from sexuality, as the particular domain of women. This privileging of women, or rather mothers, as reproductive subjects, is patent both in earlier debates about depopulation and in contemporary global projects of population control.[2]

Many recent Western theorists proclaim the necessity of studying sexuality as an autonomous sphere—separate from gender and from reproduction, freed from the sclerotic presumptions of a constrictive, normative reproductive heterosexuality (e.g., Connell and Dowsett 1992; Herdt 1994; Vance 1991). New technologies of contracepting and assisting reproduction more forcefully separate heterosexual intercourse and making babies (see Strathern 1992a), and the conceptual autonomy of sexuality is also proclaimed to witness and to value the variety of human sexual experiences and identities—homosexual, bisexual, and transexual (e.g., Rubin 1992 [1984]; Vance 1989, 1991; but see Elliston 1995).

Le Guin has challenged such a radical rupture, observing how recent notions of "sexuality" have elided reproduction from sex and limited sex to "copulation as if it knew nothing about pregnancy, birth, nursing, mothering, puberty, menstruation or menopause" (1992, 228). She insists on meshing the sexuality of woman-as-lover with that of woman-as-mother, thus refusing a stark separation of sexuality and reproduction. This is not to marginalize nonreproductive women but rather to insist on the pleasures as well as the pains of reproducing heterosexual women.[3] But one might observe how such a radical dissociation of sexuality and reproduction also has consequences for male subjects, in separating the man-as-lover and the man-as-father. Although the collective politics of reproduction and fertility control are still saturated by masculinist values in countries such as the United States and Australia, a rupture between sex and reproduction often confers on male subjects both less responsibility for, and less interest in, reproductive "choices" as fathers. This perpetuates a common contemporary Western presumption that maternal desires and connections are stronger than paternal and that motherhood is foundational and fatherhood a more evanescent and superficial flow.[4] To extend the geological metaphor, while the notion of a sexual drive (for women and men) is often imagined in masculine mode, as an irresistible underground river gushing forth to the surface, the notion of the maternal is seen as deep but solid rock.

Such a radical separation of a masculinized sexuality and a feminized reproduction is even more problematic in Melanesia. Here desire and fertility are very intimate partners, and both homosexual and heterosexual practices are focused on conception, growth, and health. Thus, by several accounts (e.g., Ernst 1991; Herdt 1981, 1984; Knauft 1993; Wood 1982) ritual homosexual acts seem to be more about growth than pleasure, a recognition that prompted Herdt to rename them "boy-inseminating practices" (1993a, ix).[5] In "making men," sexuality and reproduction are palpably connected. But more generally we might witness how, in contrast to contemporary if not past Western practices, Melanesian men are central, even privileged, actors[6] and indeed often marginalize women in the processes of corporeal and social reproduction (Biersack, Chapter 4).[7]

Part of the purpose of this chapter is to ask how we might reimagine the relation of gender, sexuality, and reproduction in Melanesian ethnography. Their connection has been much explored in the literatures on "concepts of conception," "sexual antagonism," "pollution," male/fertility cults, and ritual homosexuality. These literatures primarily focus on Papua New Guinea (PNG) and in stark contrast with the literatures of demography and population projects still tend to privilege men as subjects or actors.[8] The writings of Biersack (1994, Chapter 4), Bonnemère (1996), Elliston (1995), Faithorn (1975), Kyakas and Wiessner (1992), Lindenbaum (1984, 1987), Lutkehaus and Roscoe (1995), M. Strathern (1972, 1988), and A. Weiner (1976, 1988) have in various ways challenged this undue focus on men and the perduring masculinist presumptions of Melanesian ethnography of sexuality and reproduction.

FERTILITY AND SEXUALITY IN SOUTH PENTECOST, VANUATU

It is in the context of these re-visions that I now discuss the perpetuation and transformation of ancestral practices of sexuality and fertility among the *kastom* (traditionalist) villages of South Pentecost, Vanuatu, as I observed it from the early 1970s. These people, along with their close neighbors in Christian villages, now number close to 1800 and still speak Sa (an Austronesian language) as well as the national lingua franca, Bislama. The archipelago is characterized by small language and cultural regions (110 languages are spoken among about 180,000 indigenes), rather small, sparse settlements, shallow genealogies, dispersed groups, based on place rather than descent, and, until recently, marriage with close neighbors. The Sa speakers, like all ni-Vanuatu, are zealous cultivators of crops and domesticators of pigs. Although they hunt and fish, the Sa speakers are less concerned with the regeneration of the deep forest or the deep sea than with their gardens and their pig herds. As will become clear, yams, taro, pigs, and coconuts are constantly brought into association with human fertility—not just through metaphoric links but through ritual practices. As in the PNG Highlands, it is gendered foods rather than the sexual substances of blood and semen that are privileged (cf. Whitehead 1986a, 1986b).

Although shared ancestry, occupation of land, and shared consumption of conjointly produced food secures identity as *manples*,[9] the identities so generated are very different from those of the Highlands. In South Pentecost there are no large male-focused clans or lineages—long lines of men stretching from the living to named male ancestors. The sense of connection rather depends on a notion of "layers" of men who are both linked and separated, agnatically connected but differentiated in terms of owing origins to different mothers (Jolly 1994a, 113). In many discussions of kinship and gender in Vanuatu, South Pentecost has been typified along with South Malakula as strongly agnatic, virilocal, and strenuously male dominant (e.g., Allen 1967, 1998). But as Layard (1942, 722–724) recognized long ago, there is a pervasive stress on *debts* to mothers—and especially for the blood shed at parturition and conferred by mothers to their offspring. This blood is not thought to be polluting, it is not imagined as something that needs to be purged from the male person, but it *is* thought to be dangerous, for women as much as men. If it is not staunched by gifts throughout the life cycle it may cause the descendants of that woman to sicken or to die. Even in those cults of fertility that seem most orchestrated by men—circumcision and initiation and the rites of the male "graded society"—debts to mothers must be affirmed and repaid.

Continence is enjoined at many stages of such rites but is here seen as *generative* of fertility and growth.[10] In privileging restraint rather than excess, such peoples do not manifest a "low energy sexual system" (Heider 1976), nor are they "repressed." Knauft has recently queried the tendency of Western observers to essentialize sexual cultures in typologies such as the "lechers" and "prudes" of early Highlands ethnographies (1994) or, we might add, his Dionysian and Apollonian modalities. Repression, prohibition, abstinence might be seen not only to produce desire (after Foucault 1978) but, in contrast to a view of sexual avoidance as an indigenous "contraceptive," to generate human and cosmic fecundity. In stressing the negativity of avoidance, analysts have thereby often assumed the viewpoint of a male subject anxious to avoid women's bloody pollution, or semen depletion. This is not to deny that in some parts of PNG men *do* view women and heterosexual relations in that way. But this construction of women as polluting or depleting is not universal in Melanesia (see Faithorn 1975; Keesing 1989; Meigs 1984). Moreover, we have to be careful in assimilating this viewpoint to our own (cf. Strathern 1988, 53 ff.).

In the *kastom* communities of South Pentecost (a tiny traditionalist enclave in a pervasively Christian country) there are still tenacious patterns of sexual segregation—exclusivist men's houses, or *mal*, separate from the household *im* and commensal separation therein, with men's and women's cooking fires. Such gendered patterns of spatiality were attacked by Christian missionaries and abandoned by most ni-Vanuatu decades ago. But even in traditionalist villages—because of young men departing as indentured and later wage laborers to plantations and towns, the intrusions of commodity values, and the influences of a colonial and now an independent state—we witness a transformed and perhaps more trenchant form of male domination (Jolly 1994a). The transcendent value of fertility in the ancestral religion persists, although it is ultimately appropriated by men as their spiritual potency (Jolly 1994a, 162, 177 ff.). But women here are not perceived by men as polluting through blood or depleting of semen. Rather there is a *mutual* requirement of avoidance—untimely sexual intimacy can cause the sickness, death, or infertility of either man or woman. The sacred power, *konan*, which both men and women accumulate in taking titles, arguably a local variant of a "fertility cult," makes that person dangerous to *any* person of lesser rank (see Jolly 1994a, 187). Moreover, women *as mothers* are accorded a sacred, if dangerous, place in both human reproduction and cosmic regeneration by the debts that descendants owe for their blood (cf. Hanson 1982; Keesing 1989). But first let me try to conjure an image of women as lovers.

Scene from a Kitchen, 1972

I am sitting cross-legged with my sisters Tsibewano and Belaku, in the *im* of Wari-Sus, in Pohurur, a small traditionalist hamlet in South Pentecost. Sali, a beautiful young man of about 18, unbetrothed, and a prospective husband to my "sisters" (and, they insist, to me), is preparing our supper. The breadfruit has already been cooked on the women's fire, its hard, green skin peeled off, its steaming yellow, yolklike flesh detached from the bitter seeds, in preparation for *u beta* (a breadfruit pudding). Sali first pounds the flesh with a huge green coconut, greased with coconut oil on the outside. He sits with legs astride, wearing only the traditional bark belt and *bipis*, or penis sheath. His exposed testicles undulate rhythmically as he pummels and pounds. Tsibewano, my more forward sister, starts teasing him, addressing him as *nak adumwan*, "my husband." He laughs and jokingly reciprocates—*nag isin*, "my wife." She continues with the usual formula of joking with potential husbands: "*ik rah ras lok ape itau nok,*" "you scrape the paste but it is not finished," a phrase rich in erotic suggestion. Her elder sister Belaku, still unmarried at 20, it is said because her breasts are still upright, "unbroken," giggles shyly.

We know he is a virgin; he has to be, to make this pudding for us. He pummels the hot sinews of flesh into a smooth yellow paste and spreads it over the deep dark wood of the *bwelarabi*, the food platter, shaped underneath with the legs and snout of a pig, the sacred animal. Meanwhile, on the women's fire, cream from another opened coconut is cooking in two coconut shells. Sali takes the tongs and thrusts hot stones from the fire into the milk, boiling it into a thick cream. He then fashions two circular wells in the breadfruit paste and drizzles the steaming cream into each. He then invites us to eat, and we do so greedily, using our right hands as a knife, cutting the paste into strips, dipping it into the cream, and langorously dribbling the creamy, golden strips into our throats. Although he has cooked for us, he cannot eat. He has already taken two titles in the *warsangul* (the men's graded society) and thus can only eat from the fire at the back, the titled men's fire.

My memory of this mundane kitchen scene encodes as densely as any Sa myth the deep associations between sexual and culinary longing, between eroticism, food, and fertility, which still pervade indigenous concepts and practices in the *kastom* communities of South Pentecost, Vanuatu. The condensation between the milk of women's breasts, the milk of coconuts, and the milk of men's bodies is here the subject of teasing and of erotic play. I offer this first scene of titillation to insist that the long periods of sexual continence for male and female persons throughout their lives are not perforce a symptom of a "low energy sexual system" (after Heider 1976), perhaps not even something we might call repression. The periodic suppression of desire—*palan*, fasting from sex and from food—is thought rather to heighten desire and to secure vitality, fertility, and health.[11]

Lo Sal—Cycles of Continence and Growth

This is no "natural" regime of fertility,[12] as imagined by some demographers, but one that emphasizes control and regulation, in making babies and in securing their health and growth from infancy to maturity. This is encoded in the vernacular notion of *lo sal* (inside the road/path), the path of regeneration connecting birth, circumcision, marriage, and death with the rites of growing crops, killing pigs, and killing men (Jolly 1991a, 1991b, 1994a). Although Western constructs tend to polarize birth and death, creating and killing, indigenous notions rather see them not just as linked phases in a cosmic process of regeneration but, until the recent past, as intrinsically connected through ritual practices (cf. Biersack 1995; Brown and Buchbinder 1976; Weiner 1976). Pigs were sacrificed to the ancestors to secure the health of the living and the growth of crops. Enemies were sacrificed in war to propitiate the ancestors, while cannibal feasting revitalized the strength not just of warriors (*bwahri*) but of all men and women in their local group. Abstinence was critical to most acts of creation/destruction.

Ni mpal—"I abstain"—the same expression is used for fasting and sexual continence. Sexual abstinence is typically accompanied by restrictions on eating certain foods (although the reverse does not always pertain), but the foods pro/prescribed differ in marking gender in different modes of same-sex and cross-sex relation (cf. Strathern 1988). Elsewhere I detail the ensemble of what are perhaps local "fertility rites"—rites of the life cycle, of agricultural fertility, of title taking, and of warfare (1994a, 141–210, 231–235). Here I focus on birth and circumcision, planting yams, and the land dive as moments when sexual continence is enjoined, and where refraining from certain foods and partaking of others is required.

Making Babies

Babies are recognized as the joint creation of male and female effort and substances, of blood and semen, although unlike some parts of the PNG Highlands these are not seen to generate different body parts, such as blood/flesh versus bone. Menstrual flows are described as *tabwian na isiniri* (the sickness of women) but, although they require circumspection on the woman's part, are not seen as defiling or as impure (see Jolly 2001b). Unlike many parts of Melanesia there is no separate house for menstruation and childbirth and women do not stop working or cooking during their periods. Menstruating women remain in their natal or their conjugal household but are careful in the use of leaves, mosses, and now cloth rags to stop the blood from flowing uncontrolled or in public view. If the woman is married, her husband can either retreat to the *mal* or remain with her in the *im*. But they should avoid intercourse lest he catch the sickness and his penis start bleeding. In the past, girls reached menarche at about 15 and were likely to be married by then or soon after. Today girls first see their periods when they are about 13 or 14, and the average age of marriage for women is now closer to 18. Although premarital sexuality is not condoned, liaisons between adolescents are quite frequent and thus the risk of unmarried mothers is greater. This is usually solved by a hastily arranged marriage.

Married couples are enjoined to have a baby soon after they wed but are then expected to space children at about three-year intervals. The child is thought to be a combination of paternal and maternal substance: the semen is seen to block menstrual blood and to fix the form of the fetus, or *walalala*, lying in the *tewung* (basket/womb). Several acts of intercourse are thought necessary to secure this, but when the blood stops flowing, sex should be avoided for fear of unsettling the baby.[13] But "fixing" the fetus is also secured by *lo sal* prestations (of pigs, red mats, and now cash) that go from the expectant father (and his "brothers") to his wife's father and brothers. These are thought to hold the fetus in the womb and to secure the milkiness of the mother's breasts. When the child is born, s/he is given titles that recognize this (*atiltilbarni, atiltilsus*). The pregnant woman and her husband are bound by a series of food and behavioral proscriptions.[14]

The baby is usually born in the mother's hut, with the father absent and with assistance from female kin and a midwife (Jolly 1994a, 145–147). The newborn child is placed on a bed of coconut leaves and a cradle of wild taro leaves, secured with four stones at the corners. Once the baby is born, certain foods are prescribed, others proscribed, for mother and child. In the past the neonate was fed with premasticated taro until the breast milk started flowing; this was seen as enhancing the baby's strength, whereas yams fed in this context would be debilitating. The mother and the female kin who remain with her eat only taro during the twenty-day seclusion, and at five-day intervals they share celebratory feasts of taro in the *im* while the father and close male kin enjoy parallel celebratory feasts of taro in the *mal.*

This seclusion is likened to the seclusion of boys after circumcision and of men in the *mal* after they have taken titles (all are *loas*—dangerously sacred). The women and the baby are dangerous to men and to other women not because of the horror of blood or the exuviae of birth but because they have come close to ancestral powers and are more vulnerable and open to spiritual influences at this time. The mother and the baby bathe in the sea[15] (again at five-day intervals), baths which are seen not to remove "pollution" but gradually to neutralize their state of sacred danger and to bring them closer to the world of daily sociality. This accords with Hanson's thesis about *tapu* in Polynesia (1982) and Keesing's revised interpretation of *abu* in Malaita in the Solomons (1985, 1989) that women at menstruation and parturition are not so much polluting or repugnant to the gods or ancestors but are attractive and open to such forces, that the uterine canal is a "path for the gods," a passage through which spiritual powers can move closer to the living.

But it is not just the mothers who are seen as responsible for the growth and the health of the infant. When the infant is about four months old, the father's sisters perform a ritual called "eating on the head." The father and his sisters collect coconuts, which are then used as a kind of tonic for growth and fertility. Each father's sister takes a coconut, describes a circle round the child's head, and hits the coconut with one of the four stones that were earlier used to secure the baby's cradle of taro leaves. This circling is repeated four times for each of these stones and then the coconut is pierced and its milk partly poured over the child's head and partly drunk. Some younger women told me this rite ensures that when the child's hair is cut for the first time it will not have a headache. Wanam Sus, an older woman, offered a more profound rationale—that the father's sister thus ensures the growth and future fertility of the child. Moreover, the father must again make *lo sal* payments to the mother's agnates—again in red mats, pigs, or cash. Such payments are thought crucial to the child's growth and health, to avert the potential malevolent influence, especially of the mother's brother.

Mother and father should both, ideally, refrain from sexual intercourse for two to three years while the infant suckles. This protracted postpartum proscription is still widely followed in *kastom* communities; in fact, some children seem to have been suckled for even longer in the past. It was alleged that one old man, in his late sixties when I first started fieldwork (and thus born c. 1905), was suckled till he was five—a fact memorialized in his first grade name Teulsus ("young green coconut suckling"). Women of his generation liked to remind him of this by continually using this rather than his later titles in addressing him.

Two rationales are offered for this protracted sexual abstinence—first that the growth of a second child in the womb while another is on the breast would threaten the life of both mother and child, and second that ingesting more semen from the husband would sour or spoil the milk of the mother.[16] Though seemingly mutual this sexual proscription does not equally constrain father and mother. Unlike early reports from Fiji (Decrease Report 1896, 145–146, and see below), polygynous men can make love with other wives without fear, and those with only one wife can take other lovers or prostitutes without risking their infant's life.

Making Men

When a boy is circumcised at about five or six, both mother and father are bound to refrain from sex completely for the period of his seclusion. The father remains sequestered in the *mal* with his newly circumcised son, and any men who remain there to provide company and solace are alike enjoined to abstain. Such abstinence is thought crucial to the healing of the wounds of circumcision. If it is broken the cuts will fester and stink. It also secures the future growth of the boy and his right to emerge not as a *wahmalmal*, a naked one, but as a *wahbo*—a boy imbued with, even personifying, the power of the male ancestor, Wahbo (see below). He must now wear a pandanus penis sheath to cover the sacred site of his circumcised penis and distinguish him from younger boys whose penes may be totally bare or covered with a mere scap of banana leaf.

The ceremony of circumcision is a small, individual affair compared with the male cults of the PNG Highlands and Sepik and entails neither a violent separation of the boys from their mothers nor a protracted seclusion in the forest or a distant ritual site. While secluded in the men's house for a few weeks at most, the boys are not subject to such corporeal punishments as nose bleeding, septum piercing, or abrading with cane, nor are they subject to psychological terror and treachery by older men.[17] Nor are the boys inseminated, despite the reports of ritual homosexuality for the Big Nambas of North Malakula and contrary to Layard's speculations about South Pentecost (Allen 1998; Layard 1942). Circumcision is still seen as an ordeal both for the boys and for the mothers who must relinquish their sons to the control of men, but the emotional tone is more benign, emphasizing the shared suffering of the boys and the assembled men and women. The stress is rather on the complementary nurture afforded by women as individual, birthing mothers and by men as collective, rebirthing "fathers."

On the morning of the operation, the *wahbo* breakfast on taro pudding. This is the last time they will eat taro during their seclusion (which is typically from two to four weeks); the boy, his father and mother, and all others abstaining must eat only yams and refrain from taro (in this context marked as "female" and therefore debilitating; see Jolly 1991b). The operation—the removal of the foreskin with a bamboo knife—is performed behind a coconut screen at the side of the *mal* away from the gaze of women. But they are proximate enough to hear the screams of the boys and the subsequent whoops of joy from the men. The assembled women, especially the mothers, wail the boys' names as they are cut and sob strenuously in a manner akin to mourning ritual. The newly created *wahbo* finally emerge, being carried like infants on the backs of boys circumcised in the last ceremony. Their fathers come forward, place four green coconuts on the dancing grounds, around which the *wahbo* circle (a circling action that echoes the "eating on the head" ritual four months after birth). Their mothers come forward with coconut leaf mats for them to sleep on during the period of seclusion, which lasts for as many weeks as the wounds take to heal. Fathers and other men stay with the boys, dressing their wounds, crooning songs to assure them they will become strong men, like the warriors of the past, and eating only yams and drinking coconut juice, not water. Mothers of the *wahbo* must maintain a similar dietary regime, and both mother and father are enjoined to abstain from sex. The breaking of either *palan* (abstention) will mean the cuts will inflame or fester.

Then, in a series of feasts and sea baths at five-day intervals (again echoing those after birth), the *wahbo* are progressively taken out of the *mal* and brought back into the world of cross-sex sociality. Night dances are held in preparation for the feast that ends their seclusion—*taltabwean*. Although taro and coconuts are also displayed in this feast, the central feature of *taltabwean* is the competitive display of long yams especially cultivated by men. Men gather in the *mal* in the middle of the night to compare their yams; the nocturnal silence is pierced by the ribald joking of men on the chronic equation of penis and yam. The man who wins has the honor of placing his largest yam last on the pile of yams. Women, too, are central in this ritual, especially as mothers and as father's sisters. The latter receive yam puddings, each of which bears the name of a *wahbo*. By eating these they ensure the boy's health and growth. Reciprocal prestations of tubers, red mats, and pigs also celebrate and reinscribe the relations between affines and in particular the debts that are owed for the blood of the mothers of the *wahbo*.

There are clearly ritual parallels and symbolic resonances between birthing babies and making men—the penis is cut with a bamboo knife akin to that used for the umbilicus; a coconut leaf screen and mats enshroud the boys just as they do the newborn; leaves of wild taro are wrapped around the penis just as they cradle the baby; the boys are piggybacked around like young infants. Rather then being mere envy or mimicry of female parturition, this is an effort at eclipsing it. Mothering has a patent value—in the blood and the milk that flow to the child. But these processes are insufficient for "making men," which requires a transcendent spiritual paternity. Layard described such operations on the penis as sacrifice (1942, 480); the act certainly renders the tip of the penis a sacred site, a site that must in public remain covered by a penis sheath, even if the testicles hang free. The removal of the foreskin places the boys in a dangerous state, concentrating in their bodies the power of the ancestor Wahbo. As with many such male cults, a woman is credited with its origin. The story of Wahbo explains why all men are now circumcised: Wahbo's wife did not like his penis, because it was too long and made her feel sick when they had intercourse; she fled into the bush and climbed a tree to escape him; he sent his long penis up toward her, but she cut it with a sharpened bamboo; he cried but she insisted that it gave her greater pleasure like that (Jolly 1994a, 150).

Making Yams

The significance of the circumcision rite goes beyond making boys into men. It is closely linked both in its timing and in its symbolism with the harvest of yams and the ritual of the land dive. The ceremony is held directly after the yam harvest, and there is a sympathetic connection between the yams and the boys' penes—if the yam harvest has been poor or the tubers attacked by insects, this augurs ill for the *wahbo*—their wounds will not heal quickly. A series of important myths link yams with male bodies. Yams are thought to have been generated from the body of the male ancestor, Singit, his various body parts generating different kinds of yams (Jolly 1994a, 66). Another myth explains the origin of death as due to the adultery between Barkulkul's wife Sermorp and his younger brother Marelul. The ensuing primordial fratricide took place in a yam garden: Barkulkul killed his younger brother and planted him like a long yam (Jolly 1994a, 163–164). Yam gardens still occasion collective fraternal effort; they are made by brothers conjointly and entail intensive communal but competitive work at every stage of cultivation. Unlike taro their cultivation is characterized by a rigid sexual division of labor—men dig the hole and plant the seed yam, women soften and sift the topsoil that forms the yam mound, a process of multiple authorship that is explicitly equated with heterosexual intercourse and procreation, in bursts of risqué joking and repartee.

Yams are seen as the more valued and sacred tuber: the cycle of their cultivation structures temporality. The year is called by the same word *dam*, and each month or *ul* (moon and coconut) is named for the phase of yam cultivation that is then ongoing. Moreover, each phase is ritually orchestrated by a senior man who by hereditary title is *loas na dam*, or priest of the yams. He initiates each phase of cultivation—clearing, firing, staking the vines, weeding, harvesting—by himself. He first performs these acts ritually, together with associated spells and chants. These acts are rendered potent by fertility stones that he buries in his garden. For yams these are Janus figurines, sculpted superbly in representation of watching ancestors (akin to slit gongs in Malakula and Ambrym). This secures the fertility of his own yams and all those who plant under his aegis. Equally crucial to each of these phases, however, is sexual abstinence on his part: for five days he and his wife refrain from sex before he dares to utter the spells, sing the chants, and perform the rites that are his *gurian* (inherited knowledge/power). Moreover, during the first days of the yam harvest, all men and women are enjoined to be sexually continent.

The Towering Body

Intimately linked both to circumcision and to the yam harvest is the creation of the body of the land-diving tower. Given the persistent popular representation of the land dive as the "Pentecost jump"—an acrobatic feat, a rite of virile daring, a tourist spectacle, and the major inspiration of bungee jumping—it is hard to recuperate the sacred character of the rite, which enshrines an intimate connection between harvesting yams and making men (see Jolly 1994a, 237–244, 1994b). But let me try.

The tower and the land dive are called in Sa *gol*—which literally translated means "the body." The tower is imagined as a human body—it has ankles, knees, a belly, breasts, shoulders, a head, even genitals; the diving platforms that jut out from the tower are conceived of as the penes, and the struts underneath as the vaginas of the tower. The tower is thus, it seems, an exuberantly bisexual body, although when a man jumps from it, the act is markedly masculine in its climax. He teeters on the edge of the struts, makes a speech or chants to summon ancestral strength, extends his arms like a hawk in flight, and then clasps them tightly together facing up and out. He thrusts into the vertiginous void from the body of the tower, plummets, and is sharply brought up with a jerk, his upturned body swinging in the swaying arc formed by his suspending, restraining lianas, his head ideally gently grazing the soft soil beneath. Other men quickly release his inverted body by cutting the ropes from his ankles. He then runs off with whoops of joyous victory, echoing those that men utter after circumcision and while taking titles.[18]

Another well-known myth explains the origin of the *gol;* like the story of the origin of circumcision this is about a woman who is unhappy with her husband, Tamlie. The several versions I was told all stressed her sexual unhappiness: that Tamlie was too vigorous in his sexual demands, and that she determined to evade these by running away into the forest. He pursued her into the forest, where she further eluded him by climbing up a banyan tree, but he climbed up after her. She leapt from the top but, being an astute woman, tied lianas to her ankles before jumping and was saved; he, being a stupid man, forgot the lianas and plunged to his death. The several men who recounted this story to me typically concluded by saying, "but now things are the right way up—we jump from the tower, and the women dance and whistle in celebration and adoration underneath!"

The technical details of the tower's construction and the meaning of the ritual are both closely related to the cycle of yam cultivation and the association between yams and men's bodies. The land dive was in precolonial times always performed in association with the yam harvest—usually sometime in April. This timing had both a technical and a ritual rationale. The construction of the tower, with its wooden platforms and the attached lianas, is best done in the drier season. It requires weeks of arduous communal labor by about twenty or thirty men, cutting down the trees for the body of the tower, clearing the site for its planting, sifting the soil of all rocks and rubble, and cutting the lianas, which in this season have the right springiness and tensility to restrain the fall of the divers. Throughout this period, the men involved should seclude themselves from women and remain sexually continent. No woman is allowed to approach the tower until the day of the diving, for to do so would be to seek the vengeance of the ancestor Tamlie who dwells within, and risk accident or the death of a diver.

Rather than being seen as a threat to the health of the divers, the jump is seen as therapeutic. A good dive is thought to enhance both the bodily health and the strength of those who dive, getting rid of aches and pains and the maladies of the wet season. It is also thought to ensure good communal health, partly through the sympathetic relation between a successful dive and a good yam harvest. The men who jump supposedly enhance their beauty and sexual appeal to women, both at the moment of diving and beyond. Their lithe, gleaming bodies are supposed to be especially alluring. Women often rush forward at the conclusion of the dive to embrace sons, brothers, or husbands, although wives should not be too vigorous in this unusual physical display, since this might prove too public a sign of enthusiasm about resuming conjugal sexual relations.

The dive is patently about male bodies and ideals of masculine strength, virility, health, and beauty, but it must be stressed that this is but one form of masculinity being celebrated. Diving is done by young men, canonically adolescents and young adults, single and married. Equally, and perhaps more important in their view, are the older men who are the ritual experts in the construction of the tower. Diving is seen as an expression of the hot, risk-taking, and aggressive powers of young men—the powers that were in the past associated with the *bwahri*, the warrior. Since pacification, this aspect of volatile masculinity has been subdued, and the salience of the land dive as a manifestation of this kind of masculinity has thus been enhanced. Moreover, although it is an ideal for all young men to dive, as it was to be a warrior in the past, those who have/had no "stomach" for it were not denigrated as cowards. On several occasions I have witnessed young men draw back, unable to plunge from their platform, but they were never castigated or humiliated for this failure. The power of older men, and especially those who have taken high rank in the graded society, *warsangul*, is thought by contrast to be cool, equable, and pacific. Killing pigs and killing men were seen in the past as antithetical domains—war could not proceed while a grade-taking ritual was in process and vice versa. The power accumulated through the exchange of pigs and mats and sacrificing pigs was thought to render a man a peacemaker (Jolly 1991a).

The land dive and the graded society, though seen as distinctly different ritual domains, both used the idioms of height and elevation to mark the power of men. The graded society was conceived as a ladder, and actual ladders were constructed successively atop household dwellings and men's huts in the rituals associated with the higher grades. When a man took a grade, he was symbolically identified as a soaring hawk, and the titles of the very highest grades evoked this soaring state. Although women also took titles in two series and thereby attained states of sacred power and danger akin to those of men, the ceremonies for these higher titles did not deploy ladders or summon up a parallel female image of a soaring hawk.[19] Images of height pervade title taking in the northern islands (Bolton, 1996), yet the land dive was confined to this tiny population in the south of Pentecost.

The land dive is not just an inherited rite—it has a history. I write elsewhere of its colonial transformations and transmutations into tourist spectacle (1994a, 1994b). Here I rather insist on the intimate link between the health and beauty of young male bodies and sexual continence, by considering a *gol* that went horribly wrong. In 1972, on the occasion of a visit by Her Majesty Queen Elizabeth II, the British colonial administration was keen to ensure an interesting itinerary during the royal tour of the archipelago. They managed to persuade the English-speaking, Anglican adherents of the Melanesian Mission at Point Cross to perform a *gol*.

The *kastom* people with whom I lived were aghast at this suggestion for several reasons. First, they noted that it was absolutely out of season in the middle of the wet, and thus the woods and the lianas for the tower would be too spongy and the lianas would not have the requisite tensility. They also doubted whether the elders at Point Cross had the appropriate skills to instruct, and the young men the necessary experience and daring, to make the dive safely. As it transpired, their worst fears came true. From a platform in the middle of the tower a young man from Point Cross plummeted. Both his lianas broke, his back was broken in the plunge, and he died in a hospital soon after. Men in the *kastom* villages were certain what went wrong—not only was it the wrong season with the participants lacking the necessary skills, but he had assumed a platform constructed for another man of different stature, weight, and spiritual potency, and, worst of all, he had broken the rules of sexual continence by sleeping with his girlfriend the night before.

Breasts, Penes, and Coconuts: History and the Mythic Moment

The Sa traditionalists persist in the face of colonial intrusion and postcolonial development to try to perpetuate ancestral order and regenerate it. The flow of life that these rites imagine and (in local views) secure have their source in

myths such as those of Tamlie and Wahbo. The primordial Sa myths of creation constantly link human sexuality and fertility with food; taro, yams, pigs
are all thought to have been generated in diverse ways from the human body.
Taro is thought to have emerged from sputum, yams from the fingernails and
then the buried body parts of the male ancestor Singit, and pigs from the testicles of Wahgere.

In previous writings (e.g., Jolly 1991a, 1991b, 1994a) I privilege this trio of
cultivated products in marking gender. The complex patterns of relation between male and female reproductive bodies and substances and the way in
which they both generate foods and are signified and transformed by them is
patent. Taro is clearly marked as feminine, associated with birth, but eaten
then by both men and women, who abstain from sex and yams. Yams are
masculine, associated with circumcision, and must be eaten on that occasion
by both men and women, who abstain from sex and taro. The bodies of pigs,
their meat, and their ivory—and especially hermaphroditic and castrated
tusked boars—can be seen to mark not just sexual difference and complementarity but ultimately the hierarchical encompassment or eclipsing of female by male values in the exchanges and sacrifices necessary to take titles.
Plaited and dyed red mats, canonically portrayed as women's wealth, signs of
their reproductive fecundity, and now affirmations of women's role in *kastom*,
have been taken rather as countersigns of female value in the rites of life and
of rank (but see Jolly 1994a, 2001b; Bolton 1996). My discussion here then is
partial, with a rather vegetal bias, focusing as it does on taro, yams, and especially coconuts.

The coconut, like the pig, marks neither male nor female, masculine nor
feminine, but in Strathern's terms (1988), "cross-sex relations," heterosexual
conjugation, and perhaps even the hermaphroditic fecundity of the cosmos. In
Sa, coconut and moon are alike *ul,* and the logic of their association is no doubt
more than that both are round. Just as the moon waxes and wanes, so coconuts
swell and ripen, fall to the ground, germinate, and generate new growth. Although they are cultivars, they require much less intervention in their cycles of
growth than do yams or taro. Their growth is certainly not attended by the elaborate sexual division of labor that pertains to cultivating yams.

As in the rites of birth and circumcision, in many myths the coconut is pervasively linked with the processes of life and regeneration, as a surrogate for,
and on occasion a brutal substitute for, the milky breasts of women. Sa narratives and songs of the deep past, like many Melanesian and Amazonian
myths, imagine a primordial moment of asexuality or male parthenogenesis.
The first creator beings were a set of male siblings, Barkulkul, the eldest, and
his brothers, who slid down a coconut palm from the sky world and who, without women, drank the milk of the young coconut in lieu of a milky maternal
breast. Whereas other foods emerged from the bodies of named ancestors, the
coconut tree preexisted the first men. The first woman, Sermorp, was created

by the castration of the youngest brother with hot chestnuts (her name means "broken chestnut"). Barkulkul's brothers each tried to entice her into a relation of commensal conjugality, but only he selected the right food and the right kinship terms and thus had the right to make her his wife. Neither his conjugal exclusivity nor his fraternal authority, however, went unchallenged. Marelul, his trickster brother, committed adultery with Sermorp, then was killed by Barkulkul and planted like a long yam. (His death is proclaimed the first one, and adultery is thus seen as the source of mortality). Melesia, another younger brother and the creator of the arts of war, engaged him in rival magical combat and in culinary competitions, some of which entailed deadly substitutions of women's breasts for coconuts.

In the rites of birth and circumcision depicted and the myths alluded to above, coconuts are signs not just of male or female substances or organs (milk-semen, breasts-penes) but of an abstract value of regeneration, which is not so much androgynous as a moment of reproductive identity, of hermaphroditic copresence of men and women. Given its central place in images of ancestral regeneration, it is ironic, even poignant, that the coconut became the most important commodity by which ni-Vanuatu were connected to the global capitalist economy. In a series of foreign and then indigenous coconut plantations, coconuts were assiduously cultivated not for food, drink, fiber, or thatch, nor as ritual artifacts, but as commodities. The nuts were lopped, and the flesh was cut out and then smoked to make copra and exported for the manufacture of soap and other cosmetic products in the factories of Europe. Unlike their Christian neighbors, the traditionalists whom I knew best were not impressed by the need to convert their subsistence cultivation to cash-cropping, because they saw "insurance" in food in the ground and feared dependence on foreign markets, since prices might fall (Jolly 1994a, 86–7; cf. Rodman 1987). As it transpired, their doomsday prophecies were fulfilled when prices for copra plummeted, begining in the late 1970s. Tourism has since supplanted copra as the major earner of foreign exchange. Today many ni-Vanuatu find the prices too low to justify the effort and cut copra only when they are desperate for cash for school or medical expenses. The coconut in most of Vanuatu today is thus less a sign of the endless regeneration of ancestral order than a sign of the failed promise of capitalist development.

HIGHLANDS, LOWLANDS, AND ISLANDS: SEXUALITY, FERTILITY, AND MODERNITY IN MELANESIA

Let me now situate this material from Vanuatu in the broader debates and discussions about sexuality, fertility, and modernity in other parts of Melanesia. There is a dual challenge here: to revision women through reinterpreting the gender relations inherent in the pervasive patterns of sexual segregation, male domination, and "male cults"; and to consider the dramatic transformations consequent on the influences of missionaries, commodity economics, and the development of states—the combination of forces that we might, after Knauft (1997), call "modernity."

We observe at the outset that for mainland PNG (as for the other islands of Melanesia)—although there is a huge and burgeoning literature on male cults and perduring concerns about womb envy and pseudo-procreation—we know little about the everyday dramas of birthing by women (but see Kyakas and Wiessner 1992; Merrett-Balkos 1998; Lukere and Jolly 2001). Perhaps, despite Marilyn Strathern's admonitions long ago (1981), we still tend to naturalize and dehistoricize maternities, while we proliferate types of "men" (big men, great men, men-men, clan-men) and culturalize and historicize paternities. The varieties of women, femaleness, and maternities are more rarely plotted and, if they are, are typically seen as derivative (cf. Strathern 1988).

Consider Harriet Whitehead's magisterial if controversial survey of the fertility cults of PNG (1986a, 1986b). She, like most recent writers, prefers to speak of "fertility" cults rather than "male" cults, since women can play a part—in complementary acts, particular ritual episodes, or their own initiatory events (see Lutkehaus and Roscoe 1995). Moreover, even in those cults where women are most violently excluded, men's ritual acts often mimic women's reproductive processes as they aspire to eclipse them. Core to Whitehead's argument is her discrimination between those cults of the "lowlands,"[20] which celebrate manhood and which occlude the diverse kinship origins of men, and those cults of the Highlands, which rather celebrate clanhood, where male identity is submerged in collectivities of agnates.

This difference is related to a second alleged difference. "Manhood" cults work on the sexed substances of the body—accumulating semen or purging blood. In the South Coast cultures of PNG (Knauft 1993) and the Papuan Plateau, boys must ingest semen given orally or anally by older men, to grow as men. On the fringes of the Highlands and in the Sepik, boys are rather purged of the "bad blood" of mothers/women by having their penes, tongues, noses, or anuses cut or abraded. "Clanhood" cults by contrast work not on bodily substances but deploy foods and other wealth objects as significations and transmutations of blood, semen, and milk. Thus, as in South Pentecost, the emphasis is rather on the shared substance of food and place: pigs and crops conjointly nurtured and consumed and imbued with the "grease" of the clan dead buried on the land. In the second part of her paper, Whitehead (1986b) plots another set of associations between women's participation in fertility rites and their acknowledgment and formal recognition in intercommunal exchanges. She discerns that in the Highlands, where women's labor is most intensive and directed toward male-centered exchanges, fertility cults are less important and clanhood rather than manhood prevails. Clearly this further set of associations derives from the first two discriminations in her model. So, despite Whitehead's efforts to embrace women and affirm their place in both fertility cults and communal exchanges, her model still confers centrality on male concerns—be it to rid themselves of contaminating female or maternal blood or to accumulate semen and vitiate the harmful effects of losing semen in heterosexual intercourse or to secure male power through collective male performances and exchanges, using "signs" rather than substances of the body.

Although Hill (Chapter 3) finds her model useful in his comparisons of hunter-warrior and shaman-farmer gender hierarchies in the Amazon, other work casts doubt not just on her separation of society and ritual, and the notion that ritual reflects rather than constitutes gender relations, but on the worth of such typological generalization (J. Weiner 1988; Biersack, Chapter 4).[21] Thus Bonnemère's work on the Ankave (1996 and Chapter 2), and her comparisons with Sambia and Baruya, suggests that differences in the cults (including the degree of women's involvement) may reflect neither principles of descent and residence nor the enchaining teleologies of a progression from low-intensity to high-intensity systems, from the circulation of bodily substances to foods and wealth objects. Not only do semen storing and blood purging coexist (Herdt 1981), so do cultic circulation of sexed substances, foods, and wealth objects. Moreover, we need to think again about how the differences and secret similarities of male and female bodies are simultaneously imagined (Strathern 1988).

Both Sambia and Ankave male rites imitate the female maternal body—in the former with a substance from the male body (semen), in the latter with a vegetal substitute for the blood of women in general and mothers in particular. This more microscopic comparison of two proximate Highlands groups poses problems for a strong distinction between cults that deploy bodily substances and those which deploy food and wealth objects as signifiers of such substances. More important in Bonnemère's view is the fact that whereas Sambia rites violently exclude the mothers and celebrate sexual antagonism and male domination, the Ankave rites rather require their presence and depend on complementary ritual acts between men and mothers. Mothers are secluded and observe restrictions like their sons (restrictions akin to those for pregnant women).

The Ankave pattern is at variance not just with the Sambia but with many other fertility cults in the Highlands, which emphasize sexual antagonism, male domination, and gender hierarchy. Thus, Biersack in her discussion of Paiela rites (1995, Chapter 4) avers that patriarchal values are here secured with a metaphysical foundation, conferring on men immortality and spiritual transcendence and on women mortality and the mire and decay of the body. In seeking an explanation to "rebirthing sons," she turns not to the variety of societies or rites but to the universal and recalcitrant fact that it is those who give birth who are associated with death. Echoing Simone de Beauvoir's discussion in *The Second Sex* (1952) and Ortner's propositions (1974, 1996) that women's reproductive biology brings them closer to nature than men, Biersack perceives women as chronically associated with mortality, decay, and death, while men appropriate to themselves the capacities of eternal regeneration, as fathers rebirthing sons.

Yet this seems to deny important differences between cults that violently exclude women and those that do not, to conflate those societies where sexual gender hierarchy is violent and oppressive to women with those where male domination coexists with more benign relations between men and women, to confuse those sites where women are seen as dirty polluters and semen depleters and those where women's procreative powers are not just acknowledged or valorized but seen to bring them closer to divine, if dangerous, forces. We need to sustain the sorts of differences Bonnemère detects between Ankave and Sambia or, on a rather larger canvas, the differences I discern between the Sa speakers and the Paiela. Further, we might compare Biersack's portrait of the Paiela with Weiner's picture of the matrilineal Trobriands, where men are reduced to mere mortal time and women are rather the source of eternal regeneration, again because they are mothers (1976). Finally, we might ask what happens when such cults are terminated or abandoned, when the disruptions of historical time compound the periodicities of generational time (Strathern, Chapter 10). This is not just a question of dating ethnographic reports but of deeper reflection on the temporality and historicity of fertility cults. Of the several examples discussed by Whitehead (1986a, 1986b) and others, some are contemporary and have persisted to the present, while others have been abandoned long ago or more recently due to missionary pressure and pacification, or successively attenuated by foreign influences and indigenous transformations.

The Malaise of Modernity

In all the valleys, plateaus, coasts, and islands of Melanesia, the effects of colonialism and development are palpable. These are not just the relentless global forces of modernity. The "modern" can be resisted, accommmodated, or actively appropriated, and the melding of ancestral and modern forms of gender relations is universal in Melanesia, if differentially realized. In a superb review, Knauft (1997) juxtaposes classic depictions of male-female relations in Melanesia and Amazonia with contemporary configurations, stressing how earlier patterns of male bonding, male insecurity, and resentment against women yield novel patterns of gender identities and gendered appropriations of modernity. He stresses how in Melanesia the quest for masculine prestige has extended to the acquisition of trade goods and money and aspirations to wealth, if not development as defined by national and global agendas. Women, for the most part, are excluded from this and have become increasingly dependent on men for cash and angry when household resources are diverted into gambling and drinking. This generates a distinctively modern male insecurity and a novel salience to questions of female sexual propriety and mobility. Men, especially husbands and lovers, increasingly fear women's alleged licentiousness. Women who travel to trade, to attend school, or to work in towns are suspect and subject to control and surveillance. Knauft suggests (1997, 239), echoing Tuzin on Ilahita Arapesh (1997), that as the old male collectivities and cults have gone, sexual antagonism has not diminished but has rather become more individuated, less a matter of public collective displays of male power and menace, more the private anguish of domestic violence.

Several other recent writers, reporting from many parts of PNG, stress that the end of male cults has not, as some earlier anthropologists predicted (e.g., Langness 1967), ended the antagonism between men and women. The recent study by Tuzin (1997) of the end of the Tambaran among the Ilahita Arapesh is a singular account of how in 1984 men abandoned the cult and exposed its secrets as lies (an act in many ways provoked by millennial and mythic expectations of his own return from America). Decades after the South Seas Evangelical Mission arrived, indeed after the last white missionary had returned to New Zealand, the cult was ended by an indigenous revival movement. This was led by women who not only exposed cult secrets and sacra but also sought to expunge those many facets of daily life that were associated with the cult—the complex and differentiated patterns of relations between men based on age grades, moieties and exchange partnerships, extended mourning and funerary rites, male oratory, yam growing for ceremonial surpluses, and even casual collective male sociality and consumption of betel nut. Yet the revelation and the associated gender revolution brought no resolution of sexual antagonisms, he suggests. Indeed, Tuzin argues, in the past the violence of the cult coexisted with domestic harmony (even in polygynous households, where he suggests a particularly ordered bliss). Today without this sanctuary of male power and a space to vent anger and frustrations men seem to be taking it out on women and vice versa, in domestic violence and court disputes. Thus Tuzin (1997) observes, like Knauft, that sexual antagonism has assumed now a more individual than a collective character. Whereas Knauft (1997) privileges the political economy of the situation—the nagging sense of insecurity that individual men have in their pursuit of goods and money in an economy where these are becoming ever more elusive—Tuzin stresses the psychological and mythopoetic dimensions of male fears. In the debates between traditionalists and modernists about the promise and the risks of the future, there is often a link between material and spiritual wealth, between abundant goods, a healthy body, and cosmic order. Hinted at in Knauft's paper and elaborated by Tuzin and others elsewhere, there is a pervasive concern in contemporary Melanesia about novel threats to the body, dangers for its health and growth in this new epoch, and nervous, deeply gendered concerns about what we may loosely call "the malaise of modernity."

Melanesian traditionalists in many sites past and present see the disruption of ancestral order, the removal of taboos and sexual segregations, the end of male cults, and conversion to Christianity as having undesirable corporeal effects. This is especially remarked in recent ethnographies of the Highlands of PNG (e.g., Clark 1997a). Past the dangerous spread of new diseases and epidemics, there are perceptions that indigenous bodies (and especially those of men) are shrinking or becoming emaciated, their skin duller and flakier, and their bodies less fertile, because the bodies of men and women are now too close.

Such diagnoses echo those in coastal and insular regions of Melanesia, subject to much earlier colonial influences and particularly missionary pressures to end cults and sexual segregation. I briefly return to the islands of Vanuatu, Fiji, and the Solomons to remember such earlier processes and the relation of indigenous and foreign etiologies of depopulation and decline. Among the Sa traditionalists of South Pentecost I heard many laments about the debilitating consequences of Christian conversion—of how the bodies of their Christian kin had become lazy and slack, like those of foreigners, how without the disciplines of ritual, men drank kava daily and were unable to work or even walk the next day. I also heard remarkable gossip that young women of Christian villages who moved from the island for education or employment were becoming promiscuous and even turning to prostitution.

One particular sad story remains in my memory. In a long conversation in 1977, Molman of Sankar explained why in the 1950s he had converted briefly to the Church of Christ. He was enmeshed in continuing disputes with the Catholic mission at Baie Barrier and decided that adhering to *kastom* had become a liability. His resolve was strengthened by alarming rumors that the Americans (a pervasive presence in the group in World War II, and in ni-Vanuatu imagination since) would be returning and shooting any man still wearing a penis sheath. He converted and took the name Joe. But like many of the new converts from the *kastom* communities of Lonbwe and Sankar he disputed with missionaries about indigenous marriage exchanges and especially about the payment of the brideprice. He reverted to *kastom* and successively married three women, the second two polygynously. His first wife died without bearing him a child, and neither his second nor his third young co-wife, Tsibeworle, ever became pregnant. Although women are here usually blamed for infertility, in this case the universal opinion was that the problem lay with Joe, not because of an imputed lack of virility but because of his preference for sleeping with his two wives, on alternate nights, on a double bed mattress. Although reverting to *kastom* and polygyny, he retained this symbol and instrument of Christian conjugality, and it was his routine nocturnal proximity to his wives that was thought to have rendered the marriages infertile.

This diagnosis echoes that of some indigenous testimonies in the famous colonial report of Fiji, *The Report of a Commission of Enquiry into the Decrease of the Native Population* (1896), more commonly dubbed the Decrease Report. This was an extraordinary document, for several reasons: its length, comprehensiveness, and influence; the zealousness with which it investigated the many

alleged causes of depopulation; the range of submissions from colonial offi-
cers, missionaries, anthropologists, and other settlers; and last but not least that
many of its recommendations were implemented (see Jolly 1998, Lukere 1997).
But perhaps most singular is the fact that the commissioners' conclusions drew
on indigenous testimony, albeit mainly from high-ranking Fijian men. Like the
foreigners, they canvassed a wide range of causes for the decrease: introduced
diseases, abortion and infanticide, the insufficiency of Fijian mothers, alcohol,
new deadlier weapons of war. They also named a cause rarely admitted by
outsiders: the deleterious effects of Christian conversion on conjugal behavior.
Monogamy was seen to promote a relation between husband and wife that was
too intimate. Husbands and wives were not only sharing a bed but were resuming sexual relations too early after the birth of a child. The commissioners
reported "the fixed belief of the Fijians that incontinence impairs the quality
of the mother's milk" (Decrease Report 1896, 145). The cohabitation of the
parents during the suckling period was thought to cause *dabe*—a sickness in the
child, signs of "attenuation," accompanied by an "enlarged abdomen and general debility" (Decrease Report 1896, 146).[22]

Thus we have the paradox whereby many Fijians, ni-Vanuatu, and
Solomon Islanders confronted the specter of their "dying out" by choosing to
convert to Christianity, while at the same time conjugal cohabitation and the
relaxation of sexual avoidances espoused by this new religion were seen as reducing their vitality and health, if not their fecundity. Christine Dureau (1993)
has suggested that the precipitous conversion to Methodism in Simbo in the
Western Solomons was a collective response to those British punitive raids
around 1900 that ended head-hunting by destroying canoes and desecrating
skulls. Her argument, baldly, is that given the beliefs of the ancestral religion
that the blessings of the ancestors were manifest in creativity and efficacy in the
world, including victory in battle, that defeat challenged the very basis of ancestral religion and its associated fertility cults (head-hunting) and thus afforded
space for a rival creator. In her analysis, Christian conjugality, although it may
have been seen to reduce the spiritual potency and health of parents and children, became a major factor in the present overpopulation of Simbo. Couples
now lived together routinely, and the earlier long periods of abstinence by both
men and women after birth and during head-hunting raids were abandoned.
Christian husbands insisted on their conjugal rights to sex and to babies.

The process of conversion in Vanuatu was hardly so precipitous; conversions wrought by the many Protestant and Catholic denominations from the
1850s were faltering and hard-won (see, e.g., Douglas 1989; Jolly 1996; Spriggs
1985). But I discern a similar centrality in the experiences of political subjugation and demographic collapse in the processes of conversion and rever-
sion. The early missionaries were seen both to kill and to cure, as the purvey-
ors of disease and as those with the sacred powers to heal; conversions often
proceeded through contests over disease and death (Jolly 1996). Indigenous

conversions to Christianity seem often to have proceeded on the assumption that ancestors had abandoned them or that a more powerful creative source of sacred power and efficacy had entered their world.

Thus Burt (1994) reports for Malaita that Christians persist in their belief in ancestral spirits, but that their power is thought to have been diminished by the coming of the Christian God and the Holy Spirit. Whereas ancestors were credited with both creative and destructive powers in the past, missionaries treated them as devils or agents of Satan. Contemporary Christian Malaitans thus view them primarily as sources of darkness, disease, and death in opposition to the Holy Spirit of light, health, and eternal life. Those who persist in *kastom,* as do the Kwaio traditionalists of interior Malaita extensively studied by Keesing, maintain the opposite view, that disorder and degeneration in the world derive from conversion and that evil emanates from Christian villages (Keesing 1985, 1989). Traditionalists, here as in South Pentecost, see their Christian kin and neighbors as slack, lazy, and dirty. Contemporary cosmic decline proceeds because they no longer adhere to the tradition whereby men secluded themselves in men's houses to communicate with ancestral spirits and women secluded themselves in menstruation and childbirth houses, alike to draw close to ancestors. Both of these states were marked as *abu* in contradistinction to the zone of everyday relations between men and women in the village and household. Keesing and Schreiner (see Keesing 1985, 1989) recorded the voluble voices of many Kwaio traditionalists, men and women, who lamented the undue proximity of Christian conjugality, the sorry state of Christian bodies, the dangers and threats this posed to themselves, their children and their gardens, and ultimately the power of indigenous *kastom* to keep on being regenerated.

We witness, then, in Vanuatu, Fiji, and the Solomons, the way in which indigenous philosophies of fertility confronted the colonial experience of depopulation, pacification, the labor trade, plantation development, and the growing power of missions and of states. We also witness a tension between traditionalists and modernists, often marked by anti- and pro-Christian postures. Although resistant enclaves of traditionalists persist in both Vanuatu and the Solomons to the present, the effects of these forces have been to introduce and promote novel ideas of sexuality, conjugality, and fertility. For instance, in the discourse of the dying race and of combating depopulation and later in the language of contraception and restricting repopulation, a novel abstract idea of "population" was promoted. This instrumentalist concept divorced human fertility from its intrinsic connections to natural fecundity and from the sacred origins of an ancestrally ordained, potentially regenerative cosmos. It also decentered men from this cosmos and increasingly privileged women as the natural subjects of state surveillance or projects of sanitation, reform, or development (Jolly 2001a). This melded with Christian messages about domesticity, which often aspired to improve the situation of women and to remake Melanesian women as good wives and mothers. In damming "the rivers of milk," colonial influences more often interpreted it as the milk of breasts, not of penes.

In contrast to coastal and insular Melanesia, the Highlands of PNG experienced "first contact" in the 1930s. Some areas of the Highlands were not pacified and brought under colonial control until the 1960s; government malfunctioning since PNG independence (1975) means that in many regions, and not just the remote areas, state influence and control is very weak (see Clark 1997b). Some view the Highlands' experience as a telescoping of colonial temporality, a compression of powerful foreign forces in but two generations, whereas those in insular and coastal regions had several generations to negotiate colonialism and development. The present epoch might be characterized as one in which the receding promise of capitalist development combines with an uncertain and fragile national independence. Yet, despite these important differences, the contemporary language of the "malaise of modernity" in the Highlands echoes that of the earlier epoch of depopulation in insular and coastal Melanesia.

Clark's depiction of the Huli (1997a) might be taken as extreme but not unique. He reports on indigenous perceptions of male and female bodies after the abandonment of the bachelor cult and conversion to Christianity. The bachelor cult in Huli has ended, or rather has been transformed into the *bisnis pati*. Men and women no longer keep apart, and the effects, some say, are woefully apparent, especially in male bodies. Their skin no longer shines, their hair is no longer lustrous, their muscles are no longer taut, their bodies are emaciated and shrinking. Women are still feared as sources of pollution, not just the pollution of their reproductive bodies but of introduced diseases (especially venereal diseases and HIV/AIDS) and the heat and dirt of money. While the "good woman" is now modeled on the Christian ideal of wife and mother (hardworking, modest, and faithful as in the past), "the bad woman" is lazy, immodest, and unfaithful. With the diminution of sexual sequestration has come greater freedom in sexual liaisons, and some women, like men, are promiscuous, and some sell sex. Yet the specter of the prostitute (*pamuk mari*) has swollen to accommodate other women who are variously seen as too flashy, too modern, or too mobile. Bad women are frequently associated with modernity and mobility. Prostitutes, in paintings by Kauage, are associated with highways, trucks, and even helicopters (a less likely locale for selling sex). As Knauft (1997) observes, merely in being mobile a woman risks aspersions about her sexual propriety.[23] This anxiety about controlling women's movement and sexuality is compounded by a sense of exclusion and estrangement from the major sources of wealth now concentrated in the capital of Port Moresby. Again, this economic alienation has a gendered, corporeal, and mythopoetic inflection. Women's bodies are thought to be hot, dry, and dangerous—like the capital city.

The shape, substance, and movement of gendered bodies are thus intensely scrutinized in the contemporary world of Highlands PNG. Moreover, these signs of decline, disarray, and disease are being linked to broader worries about the end of the world. The ancestral philosophies of some Highland groups like Duna and Huli indeed imagined that the world was in decline or entropy, a decline that could be arrested if not reversed by the actions of the living. These notions of the end of the world now meld with the millenarian thinking of Christian missions active in the area and with the doomsday prophecies of local and foreign NGOs concerned about the ecological outcomes of the extractive industries of logging and mining. As Brown (Chapter 9) has suggested more generally and Tuzin (1997) demonstrates for the Ilahita Arapesh, the millennium in Melanesia is gendered. Female prophets were few in the contexts of earlier millenarian cults in Melanesia, although male prophets often decreed dramatic transformations in the prevailing relations between men and women. As Lindstrom (1978) observed long ago, there is often decreed a marked diminution of sexual distance as male sacra are destroyed, sexual taboos ended, and men and women sit down and eat and even bathe together. In some ways these movements imitate and even exceed the way that Christian missions tried to subvert male cults and sexual segregations. What Tuzin (1997) reports for the Ilahita Arapesh is even more remarkable. The dominant *tok profet* of this revivalist movement are women, since having been excluded from the evil of the Tambaran in the past they are better placed to lead the new religion. They lead it with a ferocity and a thirst for revenge that Tuzin associates with the first woman of Ilahita myth, Nambweapa'w, who, realizing she had been kept in captivity and subjugation, recovered her cassowary skin, made an alliance with her youngest son, and murdered her husband. He perceives then perhaps not just the "death of masculinity" but its rebirth in an even more agonistic relation to a reborn, even militant femininity.

TO THE MILK RIVER?

How then do we compare the regions of the Amazon and Melanesia not just in terms of the similarities and differences in male cults or the perduring antagonisms and insecurities of male-female relations but in terms of how the perpetuation or transformation of gender relations is situated in the broader processes of colonial penetration and postcolonial development? How might we situate the scrupulous detail and attention to local meanings that have been so notable in the classic ethnographies to date in spatiotemporal coordinates large enough to scrutinize these two regions in changing global contexts? There are clearly questions here not just of scale but of partiality, in both senses. Strathern (1988, 1991), noting that similar axes of difference emerge at different scales of comparison, sensitizes us to how the starting point in any comparison overdetermines successive differences, and how they are plotted— as between the Ankave and the Sambia, the Western and the Eastern Highlands, the Highlands and the Lowlands, Melanesia and Amazonia.

I must perforce be partial in my selection of Amazonian examples, by focusing first on the Barasana/Pira-parana and in particular the twin monographs of *From the Milk River* (C. Hugh-Jones 1979) and *The Palm and the
Pleiades: Initiation and Cosmology in Northwest Amazonia* (S. Hugh-Jones 1979). The
conjunction between the books is important. In the latter, we have a compelling account of the myths and rites of *He* male initiation; in the former, the
insistence that there is an equally deep and complex notion of cosmic regeneration at work in the everyday processes of life. C. Hugh-Jones (1979) argues
that there has been undue emphasis on ritual to the exclusion of the mundane
but very important work of producing manioc, done mainly by women. The
links she draws between foods and male and female bodies are compelling—
between starch and semen, pepper and menstrual blood—and echo some of
the Melanesian materials already discussed. She also ponders the way in
which enduring soul and ephemeral body are linked in the rites of *He wi* and
menstruation respectively. The stress on life and growth is also here punctuated and perpetuated by periods of sexual separation and continence. She
shows how, in such processes of growth and fertility, the human body is linked
with collectivities and elements of this world with manifestations of ancestral
origin and power. She plots the different ways in which secular and ritual life
structure space-time and suggests associations, between cumulative horizontal
upstream cycles and patrilineal descent groups, and reversible horizontal
downstream cycles and the passage of women's reproductive powers between
groups. This in many ways seems to parallel the gendered spatiotemporality
Biersack (Chapter 4) plots for the Paiela, although among the Barasana,
women's procreative powers seem to be more positively valorized.

How might we situate this ethnography from the northwest Amazon in relation to Hill's attempt, following Whitehead (1986a, 1986b), to distinguish between the gender hierarchies of hunter-warriors and shaman-farmers? In the
first, women of childbearing age are strictly excluded from participation in
ritual reproduction, and prestige is accorded only to male hunting and warfare. Women's agricultural efforts are thus denigrated, while their products
are alienated. Women's fertility and sexuality are seen to pollute male purity,
while men arrogate the powers of ancestral regeneration by shedding the
blood of hunted animals or enemies. The Mundurucú and the Arawete are
Hill's best examples. In the shaman-farmer societies of the northwest Amazon, of which the Barasana are exemplars, women by contrast are a part of
the ritual reproduction of society, in their role as affines. Women are first initiated into the ancestral cult but then excluded from it when they leave to bear
children in other villages. Menstrual blood has a more ambiguous potency: it
both threatens and creates life.

Hill (Chapter 3) offers a scintillating description of the Wakuenai sacred rituals and the gender complementarity that pervades childbirth ritual, male and
female initiations, and *pudali* ceremonial exchanges. Whereas the myths speak

of male ascendancy, the rites seem to position men and women as partners in negotiating the flows of female blood or as interdependent, even blurred genders, their relations constituted by, rather than reflected in, song and dance. One wonders, however, whether the category of hunter-warriors also deserves some modulation, especially on the basis of Conklin's analysis of the Wari' (Chapter 7), who, although clearly hunter-warriors, do not evince the same pattern of the violent exclusion of women and the denigration of their life-giving powers.

Among the Wari', the warrior in seclusion in fact mimics the several phases of a woman's reproductive cycle—puberty, menstruation, pregnancy, and childbirth. In contrast to the Yanomami, who, after a man has killed, perceive the enemy blood as threatening to invade the warrior and portending decay and degeneration, Wari' warriors try not to expel through piercing, bleeding, or emetics but rather to retain, to cultivate swelling in their bodies through the retention of enemy blood. Like the Yanomami, the Wari' warrior in seclusion is thought to become hard and potent, and his longevity and that of the cosmos ensured, but he does this by processes that clearly use the female, maternal body as the model. Blood, including menstrual blood, is seen as the source of both life and death, but as for the Sambia of the PNG Highlands, menstrual blood is seen to be stimulated by semen in intercourse or else a transformation of it. This cross-sex relation is even more apparent in the warrior's seclusion. It is women who welcome the successful warrior home with a bath of warm water, urge him to relax, eat and socialize, and beautify his body with paint and other adornments. The warriors drink copiously of sweet maize *chicha*, a canonically feminine product seen to build blood and breast milk. The fattened bodies of men were thought to be both stronger and more sexy; their semen, enhanced by enemy fat, gave vitality to the woman fortunate enough to be his next sexual partner. Such a mimesis of the female reproductive body allows Conklin (Chapter 7, p. 168) to conclude, echoing Bonnemère on the Ankave, that "men may assert their control over life-giving, procreative powers . . . without necessarily diminishing or denying" women's separate powers.

Another echo from the New Guinea Highlands is Conklin's comment that, since Wari' warfare and warrior seclusion have ended, Santo elders complain that Wari' men are smaller, weaker, and sicklier than the tall, strong, fat warriors of old. This is precisely the language of the "shrinking man," and perhaps the portent of cosmological decline, which I earlier dubbed the "malaise of modernity" in Melanesia. Traditionalist nostalgia for the past glories of male cults seems often to assume similar shape.

Convergent or Divergent Modernities?

Hill (Chapter 3) points out not just the important ecological and ethnographic differences between Melanesia and Amazonia but the large differences in historical experience. The effects of foreign intrusion in the Amazon have no doubt been both historically deeper and more traumatic since the arrival of Europeans from the early sixteenth century—in depopulation, enslavement, and forced relocations. Contemporary fertility cults then should be considered together with the fact that Amazonia lost 95% of its precontact population. Warfare was early transformed by the introduction of rifles during the rubber boom into an internecine arms race. Indigenes today live in expansive, developing states controlled by ethnic others, with whom they have to sustain relations of patronage.

We might wonder how these contrasts impinge on the scale of differences we as anthropologists are used to. Knauft (1997) bravely attempts to relate them by enlisting comparison beyond the spatiotemporal coordinates of ethnographically grounded locales and regions. He points to the differential experiences of outsiders and the differential trajectories of modernity in both regions. One compelling difference is in the relation of these groups to states. Amazonian Indians are but tiny ethnic minorities in states controlled by outsiders, and thus the language of indigeneity is perforce a language of resistance to a national culture, controlled by ethnic others. Melanesians, though their states are culturally and linguistically diverse and subject to increasing pressures from Asian, Australian, and indeed global capital, have for the most part retained customary ownership of their land and indigenous control of their states. The national arena then is a realm of power and prestige to which men aspire (though they are often frustrated in this). Women are for the most part excluded from political or high bureaucratic power, although increasingly they are laying claim to the state's administrative and judicial agencies. Avowals of tradition and modernity in small communities are deeply gendered, but so are debates about *kastom* and development in Melanesian nation-states and in the older and especially the newer Christian churches. Perhaps, although similar modernist pressures pervade the Amazon, rendering relations between men and women more individuated and commoditized and more personally antagonistic, the way in which these are articulated in national and global fora will be different. Perhaps, as is the case with other indigenous groups in states controlled by foreigners, the need to meld female and male interests in the language of Indianist resistance to powerful strangers will more often prevail.

BEYOND COUNTRIES
OF CONVERSATION, TOWARD MELAZONIA?

During the course of our conference we gleefully adopted the term Melazonia to imagine an ideal place or zone of interregional conversation. Our regions of study, our area specialisms, are not just places on a map but imagined "countries of conversation." Strathern and others note how a particular region often becomes indissociable from a concept or a theory, for example, big men and

Melanesia and Dumontian hierarchy and India. Accordingly, when we compare gender in Melanesia and Amazonia we are comparing not just the patterns of gender relations in these two sites but also our discursive genealogies about gender, which as Biersack (Chapter 4), Descola (Chapter 5), and Hugh-Jones (Chapter 11) discern, are very different between these two regions.

Yet there was an earlier confluence in theoretical and ethnographic conversations that flowed between the Amazon and Melanesia, in discussions of "myths of matriarchy" and of male cults in the 1970s and 1980s. These comparisons seem rather archaic now, saturated as they were by a comparative language of traits and variables and displaying a rather unreflective disregard for the way in which struggles about male dominance in America and Australia were fought with the armory of the myths and rites of exotic others. Clearly, the lives of Melanesian and Amazonian peoples are connected to our own, not just in providing mirrors or moral tales where we can see ourselves anew, but by the power of a shared ethnographic and global history. If we plot not only a more reflexive anthropology into our landscape of comparison but also the divergent histories of these regions, the process of comparison becomes very much harder. But this is the sort of comparative project toward which we should be struggling. Otherwise, we might be approaching Amanesia.

NOTES

1. See Vicinus (1982) for a consideration of hydraulic theories of desire.

2. This is a veiled reference to Foucault and his arguments in *The History of Sexuality* (1978). See Stoler (1995) for a critical consideration not just of how Foucauldian theory might be applied beyond Europe but of how his theory ignored the racial and colonial character of the transformations of sexuality in Europe itself (cf. Stoler 1991, 1992). See Herdt (1993b) for a reinsistence on the need for a theory of repression.

3. The previous few sentences repeat some thoughts from the introduction to Jolly and Manderson (1997) but further develop them.

4. But see the recent work by Marilyn Strathern (1992a) and others on the new reproductive technologies, which observes how this maternal rock has been shaken by distinctions between the woman who gives the egg and the woman who supplies the womb. This has entailed a slippage in notions of the real as against the surrogate mother.

5. This is part of a more general caution about unduly assimilating past and foreign same-sex practices with the erotics and identities of contemporary gays in places like Australia and the United States. There has been much debate by Halperin, Herdt, Weeks, and others about the need to recognize the historical and cultural specificity of ancient Greek, earlier European, and contemporary non-European examples and experiences (but see Elliston 1995 for a brilliant critique of Herdt). Thus Herdt (1993b) acknowledges not just the emphasis on growth rather than pleasure, but indeed the pervasive violence and terror that the seniors inflict on the juniors in the Sambia rites. Moreover, in contradistinction to conservative Western models, same-sex practices do not here compromise gender identity of either the passive or the active partner. Inseminating boys in no way compromises but

rather secures and enhances the maleness of their bodies and their masculine identification. Indeed, it is seen to be essential not just to making them "men" but, as Biersack emphasizes (Chapter 4), to ensuring they become husbands and fathers in heterosexual marriages. Very often there is not only a discursive but a relational link between homosexual acts and conjugal and/or parental relations. In certain places the senior partner should be the husband of one's sister (Etoro) or later become so (Sambia) or be the father of the woman who should become your wife (Kamula).

6. I do not deny men's role or engagement as fathers, nor do I deny that contemporary reproduction in the West can still be seen in terms of male dominance, as is most obviously the case in the politics of abortion in the United States (Ginsburg and Rapp 1995). But individual men are less confidently endowed with patriarchal controls over reproduction than in the past, and women are more often in the United States and Australia the privileged subjects of reproductive choice or control. Of course, the situation is very different between the developing states with predominantly antinatalist policies and those developed states where pronatalism prevails, at least for those of the right ethnicity, class, and ability, where the new reproductive technologies aim to promote, not constrain, fertility for the right sort of folks who can pay. For development of these arguments, see both my introduction and later chapter in *Borders of Being* (Jolly and Ram 2001). For reflections on the stratified nature of global reproductive politics, see Ginsburg and Rapp (1995), and for a scintillating examination of the new reproductive technologies, see Strathern (1992a).

7. There are important differences and exceptions to this statement. Thus the corpus of Annette Weiner (1976, 1988) on the Trobriands suggests not only that women are central to reproduction there but that men are marginal. The same argument could be developed not just for the matrilineal societies of Melanesia but for many cognatic societies as well. But, as Bonnemère (Chapter 2) shows, the degree to which women are made central or marginal to reproduction is not just a matter of descent or residence principles.

8. Central references in this large literature include Read (1952–1953); Langness (1967); Hogbin (1970); Faithorn (1975); Tuzin (1980); Herdt (1981, 1984); Poole and Herdt (1982); Meigs (1984); and Jorgensen (1983).

9. This is an important concept in Bislama, referring both to indigenes in general as against foreigners and to local custodians of the land as against migrants. I elsewhere discuss its masculinist referent, and the way in which men and women are differently located in the language of place (Jolly 1994a, 1999).

10. Compare Roscoe's analysis of male sexual avoidance (Chapter 12), which he sees as productive in the sense of being constitutive of self. But he focuses on the male self, refraining from considering female sexual avoidance in similar detail. He notes male sexual avoidance before warfare, hunting, fishing, ritual, gardening, artistic production, and football. No doubt all of these require a potent self, but whether they all require minacity is arguable. His argument relies on a neurophysiological argument about sex and aggression, common to male and females it is claimed, and an argument about sexual relapse, which is singularly male. In Sa interpretations, I stress, avoidance produces a more vital and empowered self for both men and women.

11. Compare the insights of the late Jeff Clark apropos Huli sexuality. As well as aptly criticizing Heider (1976), he notes that for the present, the reduction in abstinence and pollution avoidance and greater sexual promiscuity are seen to endanger both health and beauty—of men in particular.

12. I allude to the extraordinary presumptions of some demographers in their analyses of "demographic transition," namely, that prior to modern mechanical and chemical contracep-

tives the world's populations were characterized by natural regimes of fertility, which they conjure as uncontrolled (see Robinson 2001 and Jolly 2001a for critiques). The evidence for most parts of the western Pacific in the pre- and early colonial period is that, beyond high rates of mortality (especially for infants and mothers), fertility was controlled by a combination of abortion, infanticide, and neglect, as well as by the techniques of abstinence highlighted here. Postpartum and other taboos on sex were often rendered easier by the sequestration of men and women in different houses. Dureau (1998) has shown superbly the links between women's sexual continence and their brothers' lives in warfare. Any hint of his sister's having sex outside marriage, or indeed any reference to her body in his hearing, justified a man's murder of her.

13. This contrasts with those places where intercourse continues since the semen is seen to feed the fetus, or where the blood is seen to be wrapped around or enveloped by the semen (Bonnemère, Chapter 2; Biersack, Chapter 4).

14. In those foods proscribed for the pregnant mother there is a sympathetic connection imagined between the food and the fetus. For example, if she ate clams, the child would cling to the womb and not come out; if she ate octopus, the child would be covered with warts. Coconut is proscribed since the fetus would split in half like the coconut shell and become twins. Such food taboos deny to pregnant women many delicious and nutritious foods. They also underline the clear substantive connections made between foods and human corporeality. As examples of behavioral proscriptions, a pregnant woman should never use a digging stick, lest the water break prematurely, and she should not walk over coral or white rocks, lest the baby be born an albino. Both parents should avoid sacred sites where ancestral spirits may be lurking. If an expectant father wants to impose a taboo on his fruit trees, he must delegate another man to cut and place the *mwil* (the cycas leaf, a sign of such an injunction).

15. The saltiness of the sea is descibed as *nkonkon*. Thinking that this might be linked to the state of sacredness, *nkon*, I probed for possible connections with several native speakers of Sa. They shrugged or laughed, so this was probably bad folk etymology on my part.

16. This is a very common and perduring notion both in the Austronesian and the Papuan-speaking regions of Melanesia, as is attested in McDowell (1988) and Marshall (1985).

17. Patterson (1981) claims for cognate north Ambrym, the island immediately south, that there were elements of both terror and trickery; Allen notes for the Big Nambas that boys were threatened with sodomy by older men (1998). Moreover, in South Pentecost the rites of *temat*, a so-called "secret society," did involve elements of violence and terror. These have been abandoned since the late 1920s, roughly coincident with the abandonment of warfare and cannibalism.

18. I thank Stephen Hugh-Jones for inviting me to detail further the diving and the way in which it might have ejaculatory overtones. It was never explicitly described to me in those terms by my local interlocutors, who instead stress male beauty and bodily therapy.

19. The higher women's titles did convey ideas of danger and destructive potential—e.g., Wohmat, loosely translated as the power of death—but successive titles were named numerically, as one, two, three, and so on. I should note that although women were not cast as hawks, they were in other contexts strongly associated with birds and with notions of flight and movement.

20. A dubious designation for the various sites of the South Coast, the Papuan Plateau, the Highlands fringe, and the Sepik River region of PNG.

21. This point is made in J. Weiner's critique (1988) and in Hill (Chapter 3) and Biersack (Chapter 4).

22. The commissioners adjudicated that, "So long as the village *bure ni sa* [the communal men's house] existed and the husband and wife lived in different houses, each under the surveillance of persons of their own sex, secret cohabitation was impracticable. It was made still less possible by the custom of young mothers of leaving their husband's house and going to live with their relations for a year after the birth of a child; but since the *bure* system has been abandoned, and an imitation of European life substituted for it, husband and wife no longer separate during the period of lactation, but rather give their parole to public opinion to preserve the abstinence prescribed by ancient custom. The health of the child is jealously watched by the other villagers for signs that the parents have failed in their duty" (1896, 146; italics added). The commissioners endorsed the practice with their own instrumental logic: given the lack of stamina of the Fijian mother, her poor nutrition, and the lack of breast milk substitutes, they perceived its benefits and satirized missionaries who saw the isolation of the nursing mother as "absurd and superstitious." But their instrumental recuperation of the practice was rendered difficult by the additional discovery that adulterous affairs by the new father could also cause *dabe*. Thus "in Namosi, where lactation was continued for three years, a man who had an intrigue with another woman" caused his child to sicken with *dabe*, or in local idiom, "alien thigh-locking" (ibid.). The commissioners ultimately concluded that "retrogression is now impossible" and that the only feasible remedy is the "use of milk from the lower animals" (p. 148)—a remedy that portended even more infant malnutrition and death.

23. This echoes the way in which women from Vanuatu and the Solomons who went as migrant laborers to Queensland in the late nineteenth century were alike sexualized and cast as prostitutes in indigenous and foreign accounts (see Jolly 1987).

NINE

Worlds Overturned:
Gender-Inflected Religious Movements
in Melanesia and the Amazon

Michael F. Brown

Noting that gender colors "nearly every aspect of social life," Michael Brown focuses on the radical alterations in sexuality and gender that may accompany millennial movements. Using data from Amazonia and Melanesia, he examines what he calls "gender revolutions" in which religious change is accompanied by remarkable alterations in traditional relations between men and women. He finds that in both areas millennial religious movements reduced separation and distance between men and women and that they brought "an explicitly political quality to female assertiveness." "Millenarian movements," Brown tells us, "open political spaces into which women may insert themselves." Nonetheless, "although the movements produced at least a temporary elevation of women's prestige and symbolic power, they seem to have done little to ameliorate women's practical subordination to men."

Brown's chapter should be read in connection with Jolly's (Chapter 8), which also looks at the historical experience of Amazonian and Melanesian peoples and its impact on gender.

INTRODUCTION

Those who survey gender regimes in a range of societies are invariably struck by their ability to color nearly every aspect of social life. As other contributors to this volume have shown, societies bring to bear powerful forces—ranging from child-rearing norms and sexual codes to the hidden messages of myth and ritual—that replicate particular gender arrangements in each new generation. The multidimensionality and pervasiveness of gender regimes make them stubbornly resistant to change.

When these sturdy configurations do begin to stir, perhaps destabilized by changes in settlement patterns, labor relations, or demographic trends, they usually do so slowly. Occasionally, however, we are startled by examples of what would appear to be gender revolutions, dramatic shifts in belief and practice that take place with great rapidity, often within the context of cargo cults or fast-moving episodes of Christian conversion. Such cases are admittedly rare, and what we know about them may be clouded by poor records and colonialist assumptions. Nevertheless, their presence in the ethnographic record is, to pilfer a metaphor from Raymond Chandler, as conspicuous as a tarantula on an angel food cake.

These cases have received less attention than one might expect, perhaps because they make scholars uneasy. By definition, religious movements, especially those of a millenarian cast, depart from established social norms, and they often appear chaotic to participants and observers alike. Because research on gender has primarily attempted to expose the unspoken rules and implicit assumptions of everyday practice, instances of radical disorder have seemed more distracting than heuristic. These movements are also likely to repudiate customary practices, thus confronting observers with a difficult quandary. On the one hand, we are inclined to applaud native assertions of agency in the face of external challenge; on the other, we mourn the loss of a particular heritage. When male religious authority collapses in the face of the emergence of female prophets working within a Christian idiom, for instance, should we be cheered that women have achieved a degree of religious equality or discouraged because men now feel lost and betrayed by their culture?

This dilemma is nowhere better illustrated than by A. F. C. Wallace's classic study of Iroquois revitalization, *The Death and Rebirth of the Seneca* (1969). Wallace presents a compelling argument that by the late eighteenth century, the power of Seneca matrilineages became a source of social disunity as men made the painful transition from itinerant warriors and traders to settled farmers. The prophetic teachings of Ganioda'yo (b.1735?, d.1815), also known as Handsome Lake, condemned the influence that mothers had over their daughters and insisted on the centrality of marriage, preferably in a nuclear family headed by a man. Although the religion inspired by Handsome Lake helped the Seneca to meet the challenge of European control, survival came at the cost of women's power. Looking at Wallace's work after three decades of feminist research, one may be uncomfortable celebrating the Handsome Lake movement as an unqualified triumph of cultural adaptation.

Complicating matters further are divergent opinions about the best way to interpret millenarian beliefs and practices.[1] In the face of growing dissatisfaction with an approach that treats millenarian movements as disruptive "outbursts," scholars such as Nancy McDowell (1988) and Nancy Lutkehaus (1995b) make a case for rigorously de-exoticizing them. Melanesian cargo cults, they assert, should be understood within the context of a group's underlying theories of history and social change. As Lamont Lindstrom argues convincingly, however, the proposed normalization of millenarian movements creates problems of its own. "Thanks to anthropology," he writes, "Melanesians now are known to be cargo cultists even when they are not actively having a cargo cult. . . . Everything is now saturated with cargoism: Melanesian worldview is cargoism; Melanesian cognition is cargoism; Melanesian psychology is cargoism" (Lindstrom 1993, 62). The conclusion that millenarian movements represent an extreme application of everyday understanding may contradict the experience of participants, often one of profound disorientation.

Equally problematic is the current tendency to link religious movements to colonialism while ignoring millenarian traditions that predate European contact. A small but growing body of evidence suggests that some Amazonian revitalization movements grafted colonial concerns onto an ancient tradition of religious renewal involving the periodic abandonment of existing social norms in favor of the utopian vision of powerful prophet-leaders.[2] Recognition that millenarian thought may have precontact roots does not diminish the value of studies that interpret crisis cults in light of colonial or postcolonial realities. It simply challenges the claim that such movements are a unique response to capitalism and to the aggressive expansion of Western social institutions.

Also undergoing revision is our understanding of religious conversion and the social dynamics of Christian missionary work. A one-dimensional and reflexively hostile view of missionaries is giving way to a more nuanced analytical approach that calls attention to differences in the conversion strategies of specific religious denominations and acknowledges the complex and creative ways that native peoples appropriate Christian ideology and institutions for their own purposes. Christian conversion sometimes creates new political spaces for individuals and groups within indigenous societies even as it opens the possibility of forging strategic alliances with transnational entities, thus countering the intrusive power of the state.[3]

For anyone interested in gender relations, then, millenarian movements and episodes of rapid religious conversion present an especially muddy field on which to play; sharply divided thinking about their origin and trajectory makes it difficult to use them as a platform for consideration of the cross-cutting (and equally vexed) subject of gender. Nevertheless, a few intrepid souls have ventured into this difficult terrain. A comparative study of Melanesian cargo movements undertaken by Friedrich Steinbauer (1979) reveals a small number of cases, amounting to about 4 percent of his total sample, in which female prophets rose to prominence, sometimes articulating the desire of women for a more influential role in religious activities. Steinbauer considers such movements "triumphal manifestations of the female element above the ancient antagonism of the sexes," leading to a situation in which "women have gained greater liberties even where no true women's movement developed" (p. 121). Writing at about the same time as Steinbauer, Lamont Lindstrom (1978) undertakes a comparison of three cargo movements with an eye toward assessing their impact on notions of "institutionalized sexual distance." Here Lindstrom refers to the complex of beliefs and practices that separate men and women by fostering fear of cross-gender pollution, the creation and reproduction of male solidarity through ritual secrecy, and the expression of outright hostility between the sexes. In each of the three movements, Lindstrom finds evidence that sexual distance was significantly de-emphasized or diminished. Traditional male cult objects were destroyed, men and women began to sit together during meetings, taboos on intercourse were abolished, and women gained prominence as agents of proselytization.[4]

Lindstrom's explanation for these common features focuses less on gender per se than on the political realities of cargo movements. Drawing on the work of Peter Worsley and other scholars who see millenarian movements as mechanisms for the creation of regional alliances, he notes that local male solidarity stands in the way of effective proselytizing, especially when the movements originate among traditional enemies. Therefore, he argues, cargo cults focus on destroying the symbolic apparatus of local male solidarity as a necessary step in the creation of supratribal alliances. "Since local level male solidarity is symbolized and associated with fears of female pollution, with bachelor purification rites and with phallic symbolic objects," Lindstrom writes, "all these things must be denied in the cult" (1978, 51). Women come to the fore because their presence tends to dispel suspicion when proselytizing delegations arrive from the villages of traditional enemies. This pattern builds on traditional affinal relations, which are intensified at the expense of male consanguinity as a strategy to promote regional integration.

Amazonian cases comparable to the Melanesian ones analyzed by Lindstrom are exceedingly rare, and the available information tends to be sketchy. Nimuendajú (1952), for instance, mentions in passing that Tukuna millenarian prophets were sometimes adolescent girls. Various ethnographers (e.g., Butt 1960; Staats 1996) note that the so-called Alleluia religion of the Circum-Roraima area, probably the most important and durable nativistic movement in lowland South America, includes women among its founders and current leaders. But little more can be inferred from the information currently available.[5]

The recent appearance of several detailed studies of gender-inflected religious movements in Amazonia and Papua New Guinea makes it possible to revisit some of the questions first posed by Lindstrom. Under what circumstances do societies repudiate male religious control and raise women to positions of moral authority? Do these revolutions produce permanent changes in gender relations, or are they merely short-term perturbations? What, if anything, might they suggest about the links between religion and what Micaela di Leonardo (1991) has called the "political economy of gender"?

THREE CASES

Canela, Eastern Timbira, Brazil

William and Jean Crocker (W. Crocker 1990; Crocker and Crocker 1994) have documented a remarkable series of incidents that took place among the Gê-speaking Ramkokamekra, or Canela, people of interior northeastern Brazil. They commenced in January 1963, when the mantle of prophecy descended on a middle-aged woman named Khêê-khwèy, or Maria, while she worked in her garden. Maria began the first of a series of conversations with her developing fetus, which identified itself as Dry Woman. Dry Woman informed Maria that Awkhêê (often spelled Auké), a key figure in the mythology of the Canela and other Eastern Timbira, would soon reappear to overturn the current world order. Joining forces with his sister Dry Woman, Awkhêê planned to banish Brazil's non-Indian population, the *civilizados*, to the forests and savannas. Indians, in contrast, would assume their rightful place as landowners, truck drivers, teachers, and airplane pilots.

Despite the modest role that women played in the regulation of traditional Canela religious life, Maria managed to convince male elders that the prophecy merited attention. She was allowed to travel to other Canela settlements to share Dry Woman's message. Maria quickly gathered around her a group of young supporters, whom she referred to as her "employees," committed to helping her organize the activities that would usher in the new millennium. These included incessant dancing in the style of Brazilian peasants and transfer of all money and valuables to Maria herself.

Maria's rapid ascent is startling in view of the complexity and durability of Eastern Timbira political institutions. At the time of European contact in the early eighteenth century, the Eastern Timbira lived in towns of a thousand residents or more. Leadership remains unusually formalized for post-Conquest Amazonia, with a male high chief and council of elders. Although descent and residence are organized around matrilineal principles, the society is cross-cut by several distinct moiety systems that recruit members according to age-set and name-set affiliations. Ritual sodalities and men's societies, the latter now somewhat attenuated in their importance, create additional links between adult men. Although William Crocker, the Canela's principal ethnographer, describes women as enjoying high status in this society, the most significant political and ritual offices were, and are, held by men. The virtual collapse of such finely tuned and elaborate social institutions in the face of the prophecies of Maria in 1963 was notable even if one takes into account the help that she received from the young men, most from high-status families, found among her "employees."

With single-minded determination, Maria set about dismantling the Canela's leadership structure. She and her followers first humiliated the principal chief by exposing his daughter's genitals during a public procession. They then appropriated a house and converted it into a place where villagers could pay homage to Dry Woman by kissing Maria's swelling abdomen each morning as she sat in state. Maria soon abandoned her husband in favor of a young man named Thunder, son of a high-status family. Their household grew to impressive proportions. Meanwhile, the Canela continued to dance and to divest themselves of material goods. As food supplies dwindled, young men began to rustle cattle from nearby ranches.

Maria's millenarian project nearly collapsed in mid-May, four months after it began, when she delivered a stillborn boy rather than the promised girl.

With Thunder's counsel, Maria announced that Awkhêê still intended to return provided that the Canela showed themselves sufficiently devout. Growing skepticism led her followers to institute punitive measures among apostate Canela, including the imposition of sequential sexual relations on men and women. Particularly significant was the punishment of men by forcing them to have intercourse with several women in the female-superior position.

Enraged by Indian cattle rustling and nervous about rumors of native unrest, local ranchers attacked Canela villages in early July. Five Indians and one rancher died in the fracas. The death toll among the Indians would have been much higher had not the Brazilian Indian Service and other concerned officials intervened and evacuated the Indians to a safe place. The Canela spent five years in exile before they were allowed to return to their homeland in 1968. Happily, their population and general morale have rebounded from the disorder of 1963. Maria resumed a life of relative obscurity in her community, and her prophecies are now little more than a fading memory for those who lived through the millenarian unrest that they unleashed.

The Canela movement represents a vivid example of what Marshall Sahlins (1985, 54–55) calls "mythopraxis," a social process that hews to a mythic template. Awkhêê, the mythical being whom Maria predicted would return with the birth of his sister, Dry Woman, was held responsible for the marked discrepancy in wealth between Indians and Brazilian settlers. What Awkhêê had ordained he could presumably reverse, and Maria led her followers to expect that he would magically transform palm-leaf bracelets into wristwatches. This theme of reversal was played out in other ways, including Maria's edict that apostate men were to be used sexually, apparently against their will, by multiple female partners, an obvious inversion of the traditional practice by which designated women served (in this case, consensually) as sexual partners for groups of men during key rituals. She also ordered followers to have sexual relations with persons in formerly prohibited categories of kin. As Manuela Carneiro da Cunha (1973, 32) observes in her analysis of the Canela millenarian movement, Gê-speakers associate incest with confusion and moments of sweeping change. Maria's encouragement of incest was part of an attempt to destroy existing institutions and thus promote a transfiguration of the world. The spectacle of a woman taking charge of religious activities in a society where this was not the norm, the invention of Dry Woman, a feminine counterpart to a male culture hero, the curious "rape" of dissident men ordered by Maria—all point to the symbolic salience of sex and gender in the Canela's efforts to institute dramatic change.

Ilahita, East Sepik, Papua New Guinea

Arguably the most detailed ethnographic study of the links between gender and millenarianism in Melanesia is Donald Tuzin's *The Cassowary's Revenge:*

The Life and Death of Masculinity in a New Guinea Society (1997). At the risk of bowdlerizing a complex work, I can summarize Tuzin's ethnography as follows. In 1984, the Arapesh-speaking people of Ilahita, a village in East Sepik Province, renounced the secret men's cult known as the Tambaran. At a Christian worship service, men revealed to the women of the congregation that the Tambaran was a fraud: spirits did not, as women had been told for generations, appear to the men during rituals. This revelation summarily destroyed the heart of the Tambaran, for if women knew its secrets, then it was no longer of any use to men, nor could it retain its power to guarantee collective prosperity. For Tuzin, a significant feature of this event was that it happened at all. If the majority of the village had already converted to Christianity, as seems to have been the case, why bother to destroy the Tambaran rather than let it quietly die of neglect?

The answer is that a series of increasingly apocalyptic visions by female prophets revealed that the community must undergo a collective cleansing if it were to participate in an imminent millenarian Event.[6] Hence the need to destroy the Tambaran and for men to confess their past sins. Precisely because women had been excluded from the Tambaran's evil secrets, they were uniquely empowered to save Ilahita from divine punishment. Religion fell almost completely into the hands of women, while the spiritual authority of men, with all its social and political implications, was thoroughly discredited. Hence the reference to the "death of masculinity" in Tuzin's evocative subtitle.

Tuzin's study devotes considerable attention to the role of mythology in providing a symbolic template for women's assertions of superiority. In particular, he stresses the extent to which Arapesh myths, as well as the obsessive secrecy associated with the Tambaran cult, came to be regarded by both men and women as evidence that male domination was a sham and, by implication, that the hoax would eventually be unmasked and women restored to their natural ascendancy. Although elements of this mythical substrate are uniquely Arapesh, many other groups in Melanesia and Amazonia share the belief that men's ritual secrets, like masculinity itself, are inherently fragile and in need of constant revalidation.

Kaliai, West New Britain, Papua New Guinea

Andrew Lattas (1991, 1992a, 1992b) describes a series of contemporary cargo cults in interior Kaliai, West New Britain, that include ideological transformations similar to those reported by Tuzin for Ilahita, but with different social implications. Lattas's principal interest is the impact of colonial domination on the people of Kaliai. He argues that their experience of subordination has induced a profound existential crisis that plays itself out in ruminations on the theme of procreation, especially the apparently vast procreative powers of whites compared to what is perceived to be the diminishing fecundity of native peoples, the latter expressed in generalized fear about "the subversion of morally ordered sexuality" (1991, 239) and the belief that everything in the native world, from human beings to taro corms, is becoming smaller. In a cult arising in the village of Metavala, creative modification of Bible stories has given rise to an ideology that repudiates the Tambaran and other elements of traditional religion focused on male fertility. Instead, woman is restored to her role as the primal generative force—and therefore as the ultimate source of cargo. Lattas quotes a woman who played an important role in the Metavala movement: "Food comes from women, from the ground. You, men, sing out for food, but we, women, food belongs to us, it comes from us, women. . . . She carries family. Cargo comes from women" (p. 243).[7] As one might expect, women gravitate to the movement, sometimes over the objections of their husbands. Their dancing and singing, according to Lattas, "is seen to be the new 'law' that will usher in the new age of prosperity and equality" (p. 244).

Although the validation of women's sacredness and generative power among the people of interior Kaliai would seem to replicate the overthrow of the men's cult in Ilahita, the political effects have been quite different. Male cult leaders either claim to embody male and female qualities (Lattas 1992b, 41) or insist that, as was the case in a myth describing the male theft of the Tambaran from its original female owners, they have now gained control over the implements of cargo magic first discovered by women (Lattas 1991, 249). Women who aspire to leadership positions in the Kaliai cargo cults have been harassed, beaten, and even raped by men, leading Lattas to conclude that the movements "represent a new symbolic means of men appropriating women's reproductive powers so as to authorize their domination of women" (p. 248). However revolutionary the symbolic changes produced by the movement, it has not resulted in the advancement of women to positions of authority.

COMPARATIVE ANALYSIS

Lindstrom's hypothesis about the reduction of institutionalized distance between men and women offers a useful point of departure for a comparative assessment of these three cases, although it proves more instructive in the Melanesian context than the Amazonian one. As a result of the Ilahita and Metavala movements, women and men worship together. Indeed, most Melanesian religious movements, whether they be cargo cults or episodes of mass conversion to Christianity, seem to lessen the extreme gender segregation associated with traditional men's cults, and in some cases (see, e.g., Kale 1985, 47) sacred places to which women were formerly denied access are converted to ritual sites where men, women, and children are now welcome.

The Arapesh case documented by Tuzin suggests that the reduction of social and physical distance between men and women may be strongly linked to the collapse or repudiation of male cult secrecy. As Marilyn Strathern (1988) and others have pointed out, secrecy allows one group to control meaning vis-à-vis another; in Strathern's words, it creates "collective privacy." Millenarian movements often have the effect of shifting the locus of secrecy from men's cults to the opaque world of Europeans and their apparently boundless wealth—in other words, to the secret of cargo. Among the Arapesh, this has created a situation in which women could gain the upper hand. In contrast, male cult leaders in Kaliai have succeeded in persuading their followers that they control the new secret of cargo. In both instances, the movement of mystery from the center of native society to its periphery has opened a political space for women, sometimes with a significant reduction of the distance that separates them from men. Still, it is worth noting the circular quality of the gender-distance hypothesis when applied to such cases. Tuzin says that the Tambaran functioned to maintain distance between men and women and to regulate relations between them. It is hardly surprising, then, that when the Tambaran collapsed, so did many traditional gender barriers. In this instance, cause and effect are indistinguishable.

The extreme gender separation characteristic of many Melanesian traditions is virtually unknown in Amazonia, although one finds examples of context-specific separation of men and women coupled with anxiety about cross-sex pollution. Even though Canela ceremonies are controlled by men, for example, they generally take place in full public view. Women serve as spectators and, to a more limited extent, as participants. The Canela express a concern with sexual pollution, and young men are urged to avoid sexual contacts until they have reached full physical development, yet the actual behavior of Canela adults is almost unimaginable from the perspective of Highland New Guinea. On major ritual occasions, for instance, several women are invited to make themselves available for formally sanctioned sequential sex with all members of a moiety or dance group to whom they are not related, leading to a situation in which a woman may have sex with as many as twenty men in a single encounter. Crocker and Crocker (1994, 143–171) insist that participation is voluntary for all concerned; it is not, in other words, a case of rape. Although recruitment to sequential sex is accomplished through steady psychological pressure, it eventually becomes voluntary and, as far as the ethnographers can determine, pleasurable for some women. It also brings important social rewards.[8] Taking these remarkable ethnographic data at face value, one can reasonably infer that over the course of a lifetime Canela men and women will have sexual relations with many, perhaps most, fellow villagers of the opposite sex with whom intercourse is not specifically prohibited by incest taboos. Given this level of sexual intimacy, the concept of reduced gender distance sheds little light on the Canela religious movement of 1963.[9]

More illuminating is an analysis that integrates a range of ideological and social factors. First among these is the symbolic calculus of the millenarian imagination. If men were dominant in the old order, then the new order logically calls for female equality or even superiority—in other words, an inversion of existing social arrangements. Among the Canela, this is readily apparent in the prophet Maria's promotion of incestuous sexuality and the "rape" of apostate men by women. Less extreme inversions are evident in the substitution of joint worship for the traditional pattern of male-dominated ritual in a highly gendered men's house.

One of the striking features of the Melanesian cases and, to a more limited extent, the Amazonian one is the degree to which they reveal an explicitly *political* quality to female assertiveness that is recognized as such by men. Among the Ilahita Arapesh, female prophets undertook a spiritual cleansing of the community based on visions that "revealed misconduct or breaches of faith and charged the perpetrators, who were nearly always men, to confess their crimes" (Tuzin 1997, 10). The Arapesh case is echoed by similar struggles elsewhere in Melanesia. Whitehouse (1995, 146–148; 187) notes that in the course of the Pomio Kivung movement among the Mali Baining of East New Britain, one woman agitated for an equal role of women in the presentation of temple offerings, expressing her hope that the cult would usher in a new millennium in which they would be equal to men. An influential female prophet in the same movement was forcibly silenced by male movement leaders, who branded her an upstart. Joan Kale (1985, 52), who analyzes a Christian-influenced movement among the Kyaka Enga in the 1970s, reports that women were the first to experience the trembling and trancing that initiated the movement, leading her to speculate that "perhaps subconsciously they saw their opportunity . . . to achieve some sort of status in the community."

Anthropologists observing such gender politics today are likely to look for their origin in the internal divisions fostered by colonialism. In both Melanesia and Amazonia there is much to recommend this approach. Changes in religious practices, settlement patterns, and networks of patronage have sometimes pushed women to the margins of public life in their communities, resulting in a loss of prestige and personal autonomy. But the reverse can occur as well. When men are forced to migrate to plantations or urban worksites, the wives they leave behind may take on symbolic attributes once claimed by men—that is, as paragons of traditional communal values. In such circumstances, Marilyn Strathern observes, "it looks almost as though women now come to stand for 'society' itself" (1988, 77; see also Herdt and Poole 1982, 18–20). Similar processes are at work in the Amazon, where "tradition" has become increasingly feminized. In South America, women are less likely to be bilingual or to receive advanced education, so they become de facto repositories of traditional knowledge in their communities. This may enhance their moral authority and give rise to demands that religious activities include them as full partners.

Still, I would argue for a more balanced view of postcolonial gender relations and, by extension, for a less romantic vision of the precolonial situation.

Both Melanesian and Amazonian ethnographies provide evidence that even prior to full incorporation into global political and economic systems women could be critical of their collective status with respect to men and rather skeptical of male claims of moral superiority. In Melanesia, Ndumba women sing that "men are the enemy" (Hays and Hays 1982, 229). In Amazonia, Robert and Yolanda Murphy (1985) found that among the Mundurucú, women were surprisingly indifferent to male-dominated rituals: "It is as if they had investigated the secret sources of the men's power—and had found absolutely nothing" (p. 167). Such cracks in the foundations of reasonably pristine societies lend support to the claim of Gregor and Tuzin (Chapter 13) that men's cults in both regions are afflicted by a degree of moral ambivalence, a subversive awareness that the ascendancy of men over women is precarious and even artificial.

When belief in the efficacy of traditional religious practices becomes difficult to sustain in the face of cultural change, women's oppositional tendencies, once held in check by notions of spiritual complementarity, begin to express themselves more publicly. This is most obvious in the Arapesh case documented by Tuzin, but one can see it as well in the sexual punishments inflicted on dissident Canela men by the prophet Maria and her followers—punishments that can be read as an implicit critique of the sequential group sex for which women had traditionally been recruited. Millenarian movements and episodes of rapid conversion to Christianity open political spaces into which women may insert themselves, creating entirely new fields of influence.[10]

CONCLUDING THOUGHTS

For all the detail offered by the three cases considered here, there are still many unanswered questions about the circumstances by which women suddenly move from background to foreground in public discourse about religion. Research in both regions emphasizes the importance of oratory, the mastery of which is typically the province of men, in assertions of political and religious power. How was it, then, that Maria convinced Canela leaders that her story of spiritual visitation was credible and in urgent need of retelling? What gifts of speech did she marshal to rally support? Or had the Canela entered into such a state of collective demoralization that traditional oratory was itself losing its power to inspire? Similar questions could be asked of the Melanesian material. We also know frustratingly little about women's specific contribution to the cauldron of ideas from which millenarian theologies emerge. To what extent, for example, did women consciously argue their own interests when they advanced alternative liturgies and theologies?

Ursula King, a prominent advocate of feminist approaches to religion, insists that religion "structures reality—all reality, including that of gender" (King 1995, 4). An appraisal of the three cases reviewed here, each of which involved at least the temporary abandonment of male-dominated rituals and the ascent of female prophets to positions of prominence, suggests that King's claim may be overstated. Although the movements produced at least a temporary elevation of women's prestige and symbolic power, they seem to have done little to ameliorate women's practical subordination to men. Lattas's account of the Metavala movement in Kaliai, for instance, suggests that it provided the pretext for further erosion of women's personal autonomy. Tuzin documents a similar shift among the Arapesh of Ilahita, despite the moral ascendancy of women after the desecration of the Tambaran and its rituals. "The death of the Tambaran, and the corresponding loss of masculine legitimacy, has driven men more into the domestic sphere, where their authority is resented and resisted," Tuzin (1997, 55) observes. The result has been far higher levels of physical violence against women and far greater contentiousness in the village court. The Tambaran cultivated an ideology that must be considered misogynist, yet its hostility was directed toward women as a category rather than toward *specific* women. Furthermore, Tuzin argues, the sanctuary offered by the men's cult provided a safe outlet for everyday male frustrations, which were therefore less likely to spill over into ordinary domestic life. Turning to the Canela, we have less to work with because the violent interruption of the millenarian movement of 1963 makes it impossible to know whether Maria's prophecy and the social changes it spawned might have led to a permanent realignment of institutions and gender roles in her society. As far as can be determined, however, gender relations returned to the status quo ante when the Canela were able to reoccupy their ancestral lands in 1968. This contradiction between a rise in women's religious power and an increase in their relative subordination illustrates what Sherry Ortner (1990, 45) has called the "multiplicity of logics" that together define each society's gender regime.

As I write, a growing number of American men and women are exploring the links between gender and religion in an attempt to implement broad social change. Thousands of men have attended mass gatherings organized by a group called the Promise Keepers, a Christian fellowship dedicated to helping men "reclaim their manhood" by accepting responsibility for their actions as husbands and fathers (Wagenheim 1995). Meanwhile, women develop new feminist theologies offering an alternative to what they feel is the patriarchal core of the Judeo-Christian tradition. Late in 1993, two thousand women gathered in Minneapolis, Minnesota, to explore the concept of Sophia, a female personification of the divine whose existence some feel is supported in biblical texts. The event caused a furor in the conservative wings of the Presbyterian and Methodist churches, which denounced the conference as an expression of goddess worship (Steinfels 1994). This controversy, with its self-conscious, polemical debates about orthodoxy and heterodoxy, democracy and "empowerment," is worlds away from the millenarian turmoil of isolated villages in the developing world. Nevertheless, it reminds us that even in societies that afford women considerable freedom and multiple avenues of self-expression, religion continues to serve as an arena in which key gender representations are contested and, on rare occasions, radically transformed. Although accounts of such contestations in Melanesia and Amazonia remain sketchier than we would like, they have much to tell us about the complex processes by which women and men rethink tradition and renegotiate relations of dominance and subordination in times of change.

NOTES

This chapter benefited from many useful suggestions offered by participants in the Wenner-Gren symposium in Mijas, Spain, and by colleagues at Williams College. Donald Tuzin and Thomas Gregor deserve special mention for their support and organizational skills and, in Tuzin's case, for his generosity in making available a book manuscript prior to its publication.

1. Space limitations lead me to sidestep the usual terminological wrangling about what is or isn't a "millenarian movement," a "cargo cult," and so on. For the purposes of this chapter, a millenarian or revitalization movement may be understood to mean a process of comprehensive social and cultural change defined by religious idioms, usually contrasting with prior social forms and practices in a self-conscious way. I am persuaded by the arguments of other contributors to this book that when considering Melanesian and Amazonian ethnography there is little point in making rigid distinctions between millenarian movements and dramatic instances of Christian conversion, many of which exhibit strong millenarian undercurrents.

2. The evidence for precontact cargoism in Melanesia is briefly reviewed in Lindstrom (1993, 65–66) and, for Amazonia, in Brown (1994) and Clastres (1995 [1975]).

3. See, for instance, the essays in Jolly and Macintyre (1989) for the Pacific and, for the Amazon and other parts of Latin America, Brown (1993), Garrard-Burnett and Stoll (1993), and Pollock (1993). Ortner (1990) presents a provocative analysis of the gender politics behind the overthrow of the Hawaiian *kapu* system in 1819.

4. The three movements compared in Lindstrom's essay arose among the western Dani in the mid-1950s, the Kamano and neighboring groups in the mid-1940s, and the Taro Enga, also in the 1940s. Other comparative studies of millenarian movements in Melanesia (e.g., Burridge 1960, 1969; Knauft 1978; Worsley 1968) have little to say about gender.

5. Some of the apparent disparity between Amazonia and Melanesia may be attributable to the nature of Amazonian colonization. Europeans used the region's great river system to penetrate the interior from the sixteenth century onward. Badly outnumbered and understandably nervous about native unrest, settlers made it a point to suppress quickly any movement that could be construed as rebellious or disruptive. Curt Nimuendajú reports that among the Tukuna, for instance, young men and women in seclusion were sometimes visited by spirits who inspired them to announce millenarian prophecies. Whenever the Tukuna gathered to see whether the prophecies were to be fulfilled, Nimuendajú declares, local Brazilian settlers would "with more or less brutality intervene to crush the movement"

(Nimuendajú 1952, 138). Relatively few such movements were allowed to develop long enough for their full ideological and institutional potential to be revealed.

Although similar repressive measures were routinely applied in Papua New Guinea, as an Amazonianist I am struck by the extent to which cargo cults were able to unfold before the colonial officials intervened. The discrepancy may reflect the relative isolation of interior New Guinea and the low probability that movements in such regions would pose an immediate threat to European settlers.

6. Biersack (1996b, 99) provides a vivid description of a similar purification movement among the Enga in the 1940s. In the course of ritual bathing, "males and menstruating women gathered together in the rivers and they looked at each other. 'The woman's blood flowed into the water; we forgot our ancestral knowledge [*mana*]; we looked at the woman's menstrual blood,' one man told me. Some claim that these men and women stood naked in the river yet experienced no shame."

7. Although Lattas asserts that Kaliai cargo cults validate the generative power of women, he also presents information that contradicts this. At one point, for instance, he notes that Christian missionary work has had the effect of undermining the traditional matrilineal moiety system, thus leading some men to speculate on whether human gestation and birth are simply "tricks" played to convince men of women's procreative power (1991, 232). Whether or not this contradiction can be completely resolved, Lattas's account demonstrates the power of religious movements to evoke gender-inflected political struggle.

8. In interesting ways, Crocker and Crocker's portrayal of the involvement of Canela women in sequential group sex parallels Herdt's (1981, 282) analysis of homosexual coercion among Sambia male initiates.

9. The Canela case may be extreme, but one can see echoes elsewhere in Brazil. The Mehinaku, for instance, exhibit social institutions often associated with the New Guinea Highlands (men's houses, sacred flutes, men's ritual secrets, and male anxiety about the threat of pollution through contact with women), yet Gregor (1985, 36) reports that adult men are carrying on an average of 4.4 sexual affairs at any one time. Extramarital relations are sufficiently widespread that the Mehinaku recognize joint paternity, an institution also found among the Canela and elsewhere in Amazonia. Such radical discrepancies between an ideology of sexual aversion and the reality of flamboyantly widespread extramarital sexuality raise interesting questions about the relationship between ideology and practice in Amazonian societies.

10. Feminist historians working with North American materials have documented several cases in which native women used new religious options offered by Christian sects to increase their sphere of influence in community life. For a comparative assessment of this literature, see Strong (1996). Specific case studies from North America include Devens (1992) and Shoemaker (1995).

TEN

Same-Sex and Cross-Sex Relations: Some Internal Comparisons

Marilyn Strathern

In this thought-provoking chapter, Marilyn Strathern explores "internal" comparisons involving relations of sex, gender, and generation. In particular, same-sex and cross-sex orientations change across the life span and, in accordance with other corporeal and symbolic bodies, and dependencies and predations, alternately enter into the cultural constitution of gender. These internal dynamics of sex and gender are in turn implicated in the continuities and discontinuities between generations, sometimes in ways that affect the course of culture history. Strathern uncovers these systemic properties by comparing ideas of body substance among the New Guinean Etoro and Hageners, among others, and by extending this comparison to the Peruvian Piro and certain groups in northwest Amazonia. The external, interregional comparison enables Strathern to identify structural similarities between the Piro and Etoro, in contrast with the Hageners. The result is a deeper understanding of all the terms—internal and external, conceptual and phenomenal—of comparison.

With its methodological focus on relationalities, Strathern's study bears comparison with those of Hugh-Jones (Chapter 11) and Conklin (Chapter 7), and with Descola's contrast between "homosubstitution" and "heterosubstitution" (Chapter 5), while its topical focus on body substance, attachment, separation, and loss are reminiscent of chapters by Bonnemère (2), Jolly (8), and also Conklin (7).

The sexes have different destinies, especially marked in the early years of marriage. A young man may leave home to find employment, perhaps returning from time to time, but expecting to travel over a wide area before eventually taking up residence at either his own place or his wife's. A young woman may stay with her parents, perhaps making visits to her husband's settlement to bear children there, lest misfortune be laid at the door of her own kin, while maintaining gardens and residence at her natal home. If later the two have a joint household, much will depend on the flow of goods between the spouses. Without the precise normative expectation "of both partners wanting to live with their own kin" or of the pressure implied in "the visiting and giving of food" to persuade people to shift residence, their accommodations could almost describe the Piro-speakers of the Bajo Urubamba River in Peruvian Amazonia (Gow 1991, 197, 221).

Piro are conscious of other alternating possibilities, as in the work they do. Thus they see themselves either as "searching for money" or "searching for food" (1991, 101). Searching apparently involves using one's knowledge to find what already exists (as in hunting or fishing); in the case of money, this means entering into relations with bosses who contract out work, and developing local enterprises. The level of consumption goods obtained by money defines people's "civilized" status, rich and poor being divided by clothes and by the kind of food they procure. But in addition to searching, there is a whole other modality of productive enterprise that Piro distinguish as "work." Work involves the physical production of something that did not previously exist and includes all agricultural labor. Piro define themselves as people who eat plantains and manioc, as well as manioc beer and game. This is "real food." Real food is thus obtained both through work (plantains) and searching (game), and through the relations of marriage. Exchanges between men (game, fish) and women (plantains, manioc, manioc beer) as husbands and wives are gendered. These days, a man also has to satisfy his wife's demands for money. There is a constant balancing, Gow remarks (1991, 128), of the claims husband and wife have on one another, and the relationship of demand is a central feature of marriage. Aspects of this description could apply as well to Mt. Hagen, in the highlands of Papua New Guinea, where people are very conscious of different economic modalities.

In Hagen money may take people away from horticultural work altogether, or men and women may work in their gardens to produce money for the market as well as food for themselves. To consume a range of commodities through money signifies an orientation to a world contrasted with that of "custom" (Melanesian Pidgin *kastom*). The way in which links are sustained with maternal kin is one explicit example of kastom. Like the real food in Piro that is crucial for kinship relations, and people's knowledge of themselves, Hagen kastom is consciously sustained through the meeting of kinship obligations. Between husbands and wives there is a high level of demand, especially for money. Opportunities to make money off the land may well be among the reasons people give for choosing where they live.

It was a present-day option in Hagen to which I was referring in the opening paragraph, although to anyone familiar with "Hagen" ethnography the description would seem perverse. There always were different destinies for men and women, but in the past it was men who routinely stayed to work their clan land while women went off in marriage. Although it was always possible for women to maintain some gardening rights with their natal kin, they did not generally expect to reside there. Moreover, while the division of labor was predicated on the differing contributions of husbands and wives, this was a matter of coproduction (spouses did not exchange "things" with one another, as brothers-in-law did). The present level of demand between spouses is an intensified or speeded-up version of the meeting of expectations that in the past unfolded over an annual cycle of garden work.

While Tuzin and Gregor (Introduction) urge that any comparative exercise must start with similarities, they would not want to conceal the contrivance this involves. I have contrived this similarity through introducing Hagen as it appeared from my reacquaintance with a few people on a brief visit in 1995,[1] and have done so in order to make a point about comparative time. Time is relevant to certain internal as well as external comparisons that I wish to consider.

The impetus comes from Melanesian materials where the kinds of dependencies that people imagine for themselves are differently distributed among close relationships. Some Melanesians seem to treat conjugality (and the combinations and separations implied in the division of labor) as they do parent-child relationships, at least insofar as the generations seem dependent on one another. Others do not. Whereas "dependency" generally seems to characterize conjugal relations, it need not—to follow an argument that Collier and Rosaldo (1981) made a long time ago—necessarily characterize relations between children and parents. And relations between the generations may or may not be perceived as continuous. Amazonian materials offer some interesting counterpoints here.

TEMPORALITIES, SEQUENTIAL AND ALTERNATING
Which Time?

If I offer Hagen as a reference point for comparative purposes, which Hagen would it be: the one I witnessed in 1995 or the one that is now lost?[2] Already I have introduced different kinds of time to this question (changing historical conditions and continuity or discontinuity between the generations). People live through historical change and generational sequencing at the same time. If Galton's original commentary on Tylor's 1888 lecture cast into historical terms a query about the extent to which phenomena were independent of one another,[3] we might re-ask that question with reference to the generations.

Hagen and Piro can appear more alike from the (highly contrived) account I have just given than does the Hagen of 1995 to that of 1965, although between the former there is no historical connection, whereas the latter concern people whose own personal histories span the two points in time. The easy comment would be that one is dealing with a common history of another kind—with the recent advent of commodity markets and other features of globalization that have forced Hagen and Piro into a comparable mold.[4] However, I follow another route; I wish to fuse the question of how we deal with what is historically lost or absent with how we might approach the temporality I am calling generational time. That "lost" Hagen is encompassed by the present and constantly visited in people's imagining of kastom.

Gow, following Overing and de Castro's view of the topological unity of indigenous Amazonian communities, argues that these cultures are variants of a single structure of relations, none of which evinces it *as* a basic structure. The Bajo Urubamba Piro regard themselves as a "mixed people" made up of but subduing the radical differentiation of earlier generations (1991, 275–276). This is, so to speak, one of many possible transformative moments. "Nothing could be less like a native community of the Bajo Urubamba than the Guianan desire for a settlement without affinity or strangeness," Gow writes (1991, 277), "but that should not mask the underlying unity of the two areas in their desire for communities where everyone is related as kin." The difference is that the people on the Bajo Urubamba see this community as something to be created, while Guianan societies see it as something to be preserved. He adds that rather than asking why one society lacks the social forms that appear so prominent in another, we should ask how societies come to produce what they do, and the answer has to be through history (p. 279). We could also see the Guianan and Piroan communities as though each were the other seen from a different *temporal* moment in its own development.[5]

Anthropological knowledge has "lost" those axes of morphology that once focused on what was present (the idea that if Hagen people did not practice initiation that was because they did not "have" it). The issue here is not a question of challenging positive knowledge (Gregor and Tuzin, Introduction) but of knowing what to be positive about. Focusing on the presence or absence of traits through logocentric analysis made it hard to grasp, indeed concealed, that second and internal "history," the indigenous creation of things absent or prior ("lost"). The point is central to the way in which generations succeed one another.

Gow provides some evidence for this with reference to mixing and separation between the generations. Consider, he says, the peoples of northwest Amazonia. Whereas the latter constantly recreate difference with each new generation of male initiates (see Fisher, Chapter 6), the Piro see each new generation as combining or mixing differences already there. He cites the work of the Hugh-Joneses for the extent to which Barasana male initiation, "operating through a heightened opposition between men and women and their reproductive capacities, brings each new generation into contact with the ancestral state and thus 'flattens' the accumulation of generations" (1991, 278, after S. Hugh-Jones 1979, 248–251; C. Hugh-Jones 1979, 107–168). If in northwest Amazon the primordial differentiation of "kinds of people" is endlessly renewed, on the Bajo Urubamba "the system is constantly expanding through continual mixing and the search for new differences" (Gow 1991, 278). Mixing is thus a derivative state in Piro, while in Barasana it is the prior state from which the primordial necessity for differentiation arose. From the Barasana figure of the original androgynous father, the primal Sun, come the two differentiations that make human society, not only between the generations (the original father becomes an ancestral father and his sons), but between the sexes (the original androgyne divides into males and females) (S. Hugh-Jones 1979, 248).[6] Mixing from the perspective of difference, and difference from the perspective of mixing, hold or fix people's preoccupations (we might say) at certain temporal moments in a cycle of anticipations: the recovery and transformation ("loss") of past positions for the future.

Let me turn to differentiation and mixing between the sexes in Kelly's (1993) study of the Papua New Guinean Etoro. He conducts a running comparison[7] with neighbors in the region, Kamula, people who are like the Etoro in their hunting and sago-collecting practices. However, whereas the Kamula division of labor between husband and wife means that the sexes separately produce and then exchange their produce at the time of consumption, that kind of mixing is, so to speak, anticipated in the Etoro view, which takes food production as a combined activity from the outset, and therefore its products are not further exchangeable between the sexes. Kamula are explicit about the fact that female-produced sago is exchanged for male-procured game (p. 103). In Etoro, by contrast, the labor of husbands and wives is mingled; sago-processing parties explicitly involve both men and women, who generally pool their resources (p. 108). Game is not in return for sago, and it is not the exclusive domain of men. Etoro distributional rights accrue to those who bring the product to completion, and women have rights over the sago they cook and give to others. As far as domestic provisioning is concerned, however, what is jointly produced is also jointly consumed (p. 109).[8] In both cases, then, men's and women's activities are distinct at certain moments while they combine the products of their work at others, although those moments of separation and combination are differently sequenced in time (cf. Damon 1983).

Now, the particular way in which Etoro finesse the joining and separation of the work of the sexes does not preclude men's and women's work being exchanged in other ways. Since men's game (and they procure by far the most) is not committed to a return for the woman's sago-producing activities, it can be committed elsewhere—not to exchanges with other men (that is the preserve of shell valuables), but to exchanges with women for something else: female childbearing. When a woman has given birth, the husband plies her with game. Kelly adds that female fecundity and male generosity act in counterpoint. Game is also a medium through which the child is animated and has life (*hame*, spirit).[9] Etoro men claim emphatic and unilateral responsibility for the growth and vitality of their children.

Were one to compare these several cases in terms of the way in which the work of the sexes was differentiated, or combined, on which temporal moment would one focus? The question also applies to men and women themselves. In Hagen at least, their relations with others as social persons put men and women in *alternating* positions, so that their gender is perceived as now in a combined or mixed state, now in a disaggregated or separated state. We might think of these alternating gender states as generations (as though they were at different moments in a developmental cycle), although they would be "generations" with the property of reversibility (between the modalities of separation and combination).[10] If so, the issue is not just to which Hagen do I refer in historical time, but to which gender in generational time.

Which Gender?

"Difference" between men and women is taken by Euro-American construc-tivists as axiomatically at the heart of gender relations ("the social construction of sexuality") precisely because of the *non*alternating nature of that construction. If we abandon the methodological objectivism (Weiner 1995, 11) of questions about the presence and absence of traits, we can abandon such formulations of gender as a reflex of sexual difference. At least in the Melanesian case, we can-not go back to an unexamined division between "men" and "women": their in-teractions assign them different gender positions. Men and women are sources of metaphors about maleness and femaleness, but in combination as well as sepa-ration, and this I take as the most interesting "relationship" between them.

To generalize from my own perspective on Melanesian materials, I would say that in terms of consequences for social action, the alternatives (the two "generations") move between disaggregated states and combined ones, that is, between orientations differently modulated in *same-sex* and *cross-sex* interac-tions. Men and women alternate between orientation toward their own sex (which separates them from the other) and orientation to the other (which combines it with their own).[11] In that framework, a person can act from either gender position (cf. Moore 1994). Where gender relations take such alternat-ing forms, it is worth adding, men's and women's sexual identity may well be socially unremarkable.

In other words, from any one person's point of view, and thus from all per-sons' point of view, relations may be conceived alternatively as own (same) sex and other (cross) sex. Social practices that elicit these different states construct an "opposition" between alternating socialities. It remains to be added that a unified sexual state (same sex) is created through shedding or detaching the ex-ogenous (other sex) element from a cross-sex relation (M. Strathern 1988). That creates the conditions for finding one's "lost" part in the opposite sex.

Werbner's (1989, 1992) commentary on Melanesian materials is relevant here. The logic of presence might lead the analyst to isolate distinctive types of action ("traits"), as one might have demarcated the Piro difference between searching and work, or consider the *ida* festival (cf. Gell 1975; Juillerat 1986, 1992) of the West Sepik a ritual by contrast with other actions. Werbner (1992, 229) suggests that it is unhelpful to think of the ida, as such, as a ritual; rather it is work ("labor") from the point of view of its oscillation between two modalities, what he refers to as high season and low season ida, a state of being always lived in one or the other of its two times. For the temporal interval indicated by the possibilities of alternation means that what one was one may become again, that one's present state is in anticipation of another, that to seek an object is to seek again what one has lost (Weiner 1995, xiv).[12] A similar dynamic lies at the heart of current reconfigurations of the division of labor in Hagen, with its novel residential arrangements and conjugal demands, and drives their sense of alternating historical possibilities, that one may act as either a past or future person in the present.

Now, history deals with what has been "lost" as well as with what is found. If I sense a loss of Hagen tradition, I am only echoing the musings of Hagen people, middle-aged like myself, that the next generation will make a radical break with the present: there is nothing to transmit. Older men point out that younger men do not take their "power" any more, do not learn by listening to their elders, and do not need their knowledge. The world seems divided between the parts that have continuity (kastom) and those that do not.

Yet this is hardly a product of politico-economic history alone. The idea of a world divided between parts that have continuity and those that do not is already there in gender. Same-sex relations imply continuity where cross-sex relations do not. We might even say that alternation itself appears as one of two alternative possibilities: cross-sex relations both alternate with same-sex relations and contain an inherent premise of alternation within.

S. Hugh-Jones (1979, 250, my emphasis) depicts two Barasana modes of creation, "one involving the *alternation* of death and life, the other [alternative] involving the continuity of life through *replacement*." Men's and women's different destinies concern what they do or do not pass on. In Gimi (Gillison 1993), for instance, men pass on to other men their lineage identities and spirits, while women pass on to women their ability to grow things and the magic they know (replacement/replication). Cross-sex interactions divert or rechannel these same-sex flows, setting up an essential discontinuity between past and present states of being (alternation/substitution). A Gimi man can see himself in his male child only if the female components of that child are detached from the child, while his daughter is detached from him when she becomes another man's woman on marriage. A woman sees her work and spirit in the body of the growing child, as she does in plants and pigs, but when the boy grows into his male world or the girl into her conjugal one, her care is overlaid by other people's. And that loss of continuity was already anticipated, repeating earlier losses. From the perspective of men's mythology, a child born of his substance has to be forcibly extracted from a woman in the first place, while, from the perspective of women's mythology, a woman has to detach herself from her father's primordial presence in her. Hageners set up similar extractions through protocols of exogamy and exchange.

The formula of same-sex and cross-sex relations allows one to integrate into a gender model those processes of reduction and augmentation or loss and recovery that seem crucial to generational transmission in many societies of Melanesia. Persons create others by shedding parts of themselves and emerge as the completed acts of others by incorporating their parts (cf. Mosko 1995).[13] One could as well say this of the groups of kin who create conjugal partners for one another as one could say it of the generations in relation to one another. However, this makes us ask what effect it would have on analysis to start with either the one relationship (same-sex) or the other (cross-sex).

Consider, for instance, that Gimi, in denying the mother a vitalizing role in procreation, also deny "the father," meaning here the woman's father, who is eclipsed by her new husband (Gillison 1993, 22).[14] Gillison suggests that one of the two "fathers" who impregnate the woman is thus rendered invisible, concealing the homosexual relationship between men (woman's father/husband) to which Gimi attribute the creation of life. What prompts me to this reference is Kelly's account of the Papua New Guinean Etoro. Put simply, *I cannnot find any Etoro mothers*—analytically speaking, they offer no starting point for analysis: I have "lost" them.

How are "mothers" to be found? Surely, there are daughters as well as sons, sisters as well as brothers, and wives as well as husbands. But there seem to be no mothers in the way there are fathers. There is the usual discontinuity set up by cross-sex relations across the generations, taking as one might expect a different course for men and for women. Thus fathers have their children snatched away to be completed by other men (sons and daughters are both inseminated by other men), and they are left holding other men's droplets of semen (cowrie shells) in compensation, over which they weep tears. Nonetheless, where men can claim that the next generation exists because of the vitality they have expended on it—as true of their daughters as their sons, married off as a brother-sister pair—women have no such claim to make. Possibly the Etoro mother is anticipated by the father's very virtue,[15] for at the moment of receiving the shells the Etoro father has become a mother. The male father receiving semen from another male becomes not only like his own children who are inseminated, but in that likeness even like his own wife (the children's mother), whom he has inseminated himself. From participating in the same-sex flow of valuables, he finds himelf being put (by other men) into the position of a recipient in what we could then read as a "cross-sex" act (between men). Perhaps the absent Etoro "mother," then, is the father in his anticipated female ("absent") form. So if I were to talk about Etoro masculinity in the context of procreative practices, a temporality that spans a lifetime, which "father"— the father who inseminates or his counterpart the wife [the absent mother] who is inseminated—would it be?

It is of course a false question, since we are asked to compare "roles" no more than "societies" or "Amazonia and Melanesia." One could have taken any point in a life cycle to find radically different worlds; all I have drawn attention to here are those eclipsed or lost or absent worlds that people may also presume. So if my own focus in the rest of the chapter is cross-sex relations, and this is where my comparisons will lie, it involves ignoring the alternative gender, same-sex relations. Within the field of cross-sex relations, my further focus on conjugality (rather than sexuality) is meant to draw attention to the division of labor and the kinds of dependencies it does or does not set up.

GENERATIONAL DISCONTINUITIES
Dependency and Predation in a Papua New Guinea Case

Speaking generally of Etoro, Kelly remarks on the absence of dependency as a modulator of relationships: "The absence of a consolidated set of dependencies invested in a single key relationship (to parents, or to agnates, or to spouse) is a general feature of the Etoro socioeconomic system" (1993, 133). This includes relations with maternal kin. Now, in terms of a person's agnatic identity, relations with maternal kin are axiomatically cross-sex. From a comparative perspective, they seem to be much attentuated in Etoro. Maternal kin are not credited with the kind of investment in their sister's children that elsewhere makes persons dependent on them for growth and health. As we shall see, the way in that conjugal relations are conceived possibly lead Etoro men (we do not know about women) to downplay the cross-sex symbolism of links to such kin.

Kelly argues the general case with reference to the fact that there are no relationships in which persons can accrue the labor of others. At the same time, there is one relationship that sets up singular obligations: between husbands and wives (p. 135). The general substitutability (homosubstitution in Descola's terms) of persons that pertains elsewhere is set aside: husbands and wives have a binding sexual commitment to each other. This extends to a limited perception of economic dependency between them; we should also note that there is an essential combination of conjugal labors in the coproduction of sago (p. 108) and children. Nonetheless, this interdependence between the sexes seems not to become a model for parent-child relations themselves.[16]

On the contrary, Kelly is explicit about the devaluation of social dependency in relations between parents and children. There is no intergenerational transmission of rights in resources, eliminating as he says (p. 133) "any potential for parental control, dependencies, feelings of indebtedness, and holder-heir conflicts." If there are dependencies they are conceived in other idioms altogether, above all through the child's dependence on the father's vitality for its growth. Women are radically dependent on their fathers, as well as on husbands and brothers, to assist them with compensation to protect their lives should they become accused of witchcraft (pp. 235–236). But Etoro men "are not indebted to their mothers in the same way as they are to their fathers" (p. 71). While payments flow between affines, there is only minimal acknowledgement of maternal kin, in a single gift given at childbirth, and no subsequent illness, injury, or mortuary payments are due them (Kelly 1974, 220–221). Kelly puts this lack of indebtedness partly down to the absence of any notion that in producing the next generation females suffer depletion in the same way that males do. A child acquires life-force as a direct consequence of the *father's* loss of it.

Kelly claims for Etoro that "it is the transmission of life-force between the generations rather than gender that is employed to conceptually order the world and the cultural formulation of gender attributes is specified in the context of this life-force ideology" (1993, 71). No wonder, given the absent mother, fathers are free, so to speak, to regulate and distribute the life-force, which (the regulation and distribution) thus appears to the anthropologist as the organizing "social force."[17] However, note that Kelly only refers to gender when the sexes are distinct as men or women and there is an antithesis of some kind between them. This is despite the fact that his account is shot through with the "fundamental Etoro opposition . . . [between] homosexuality: heterosexuality:: growth, strength, and vitality: senescence, weakness, and death," with the secondary association of homosexuality with men and heterosexuality with women (ibid.).

For all that Etoro children "depend" on their own particular fathers for life-force, however, this is not built into a sequence of further dependencies. Despite the glorification of the father's sacrifice in vitalizing his children (especially his sons), it is not a process that the father completes. The control of products lies with those who complete their production (p. 204), and in the end the father exercises no such control over his children. It is handed over to others, as we shall see. The singularity (nonsubstitutability or irreversibility) of the father's relationship with his offspring is no more carried forward than is the singularity of his relationship with his wife. And what happens to the father also happens to his whole generation. In an echo of Barasana, there are, so to speak, only two generations: the growers and the growing. While there is a kind of complementarity between the generations insofar as the one grows at the expense of the other, and that displaced growth (in the child) is also evidence of the parent generation's vitality, this sequence closes with the second generation. There is no forward effect; it cannot be carried on.

Notions of substance become relevant here. With Hugh-Jones's caveat (Chapter 11), we may refer briefly to Collier and Rosaldo's (1981) point about the expenditure of body energy in "brideservice societies" by contrast with systems where valuables represent the accumulation of labor. The Etoro material problematizes the corporeal dynamics here. For the latter system requires an analogy (on the part of the actors) between the substance of the human body and the substance of valuables/objects. In a "bridewealth" society such as Hagen, for instance, growing fat is a sign of wealth. Etoro, however, do not seem to imagine such a body; on the contrary, growing fat has quite other, negative connotations. There is, as it were, no enduring corporate body that will take forward the creativity of generations, because there is no enduring corporeal body. By *corporeal* I mean a body that transforms external into internal substance, and vice versa.[18] Etoro do not turn such things into body and cannot "body forth" things. In almost Amazonian fashion, the physical world of the Etoro is some kind of shadow realm by contrast with the real world of spirits, soul, life-force, and incorporeal bodies. The body that you see is simply a register of the state of hame. That is all that can be drawn from it.

In addition to the inert corporeal body, a person has two potent forms, both implanted by spirits, one a noncorporeal body and the other a soul (Kelly 1976). The noncorporeal body, *ausulubo,* is the vehicle that spirit mediums use to gain access to patrilineal spirits; it is also a vehicle for witches and is vulnerable to witchcraft attack. The condition of the ausulubo is evident in the visible (corporeal) body. Both bodies (corporeal and noncorporeal) are animated by hame, life-force, which imparts vitality to them and which is subject to increase and depletion. For men, hame is lost in two ways—by witchcraft, which eats it, and by their own acts of generosity, which make them bestow it on others. Etoro distinguish men from women in this regard because men's hame is concentrated in semen. This at once reifies their power and symbolizes the inevitable loss of power through its expenditure. In fact, they seem to have locked themselves into the logic of having to demonstrate their own plenitude by constant expenditure. So they pour their efforts into procuring shell valuables and inseminating youths in order to make obvious their own vitality. But they can only enlarge their demonstrated vitality by increasing the occasions on which they expend it; they increase the demonstration but lose the vitality itself.

In reifying vitality in semen and shells, Etoro men also seem to have locked themselves into an imagery of own-growth/alter-growth. For a man's own growth is best demonstrated in the extent to which he grows others. This bestowal is one-way. It would seem that it is men's ambition to make boys and women fat while keeping themselves thin. But not too fat. Witches become fat by preying on the hame of others, and, with their augmented supply, they produce fat babies known by their size as witch-children. Thus it is the hame that is augmented or depleted in acts of intercourse and witchcraft. As Kelly tells us, semen is more a source of vitality than a material that adds to flesh. It is almost as if Etoro felt compelled to inseminate boys, because the body is such an ambiguous metaphor for growth. There is a comparative point here: semen is not everywhere the same kind of body "substance."

Etoro think of starch staples as satisfying hunger but not as nourishing (Kelly 1993, 159); they do not grow people in the same way as the game hunted by men do. Meat is also held to augment the child's flesh, blood, and skin, which are provided by the mother in procreation. But women do not transmit their hame; it is already in them in diminished supply, and they have no vehicle for demonstrating it. The children they bear are animated by paternal hame, and on her marriage the daughter, who was a sign of paternal vitality, will be vitalized by another. As Kelly says, women give birth to nothing but lifeless flesh. He also says (p. 159) that, in any case, maternal blood is masculinized over time with the augmentation of game, even as maternal milk transfers essentially male nurturance (game fed to the mother) (cf. Broch-Due 1993). So why "maternal"? Why speak of maternity at all? The mother is created by her own father and husband: this is what male conception looks like—as a consequence, men would want us to think that there are no "mothers" in this system, only "fathers." So it is *not* a mother who gives birth to lifeless flesh but an emasculated *father-in-law*.

For the father (in-law) is incapable of animating the children of his children, by a double deprivation. First, in the case of sons generally, the role of their insemination is taken over by agnates and older men in the initiation lodge, and the sons do not reach the point of being able to transmit semen until they have had this nonpaternal infusion. Second, in the case of daughters and younger sons, it is the husband who will complete the father's job by inseminating brother and sister together. If mothers stand for the impotence ("absence") of fathers, daughters stand for the impotence of sons. Other men help remedy the latter where none can remedy his own.

I have rendered this material from the point of view of older middle-aged males (cf. Robertson 1996). Kelly suggests that the dominant ideological thrust in fact comes from younger middle-aged men, men "in their prime," especially after they have been initiated and turn from becoming recipients to donors of semen (1993, 186), the category from whom spirit mediums are drawn, with an interest in the circulation of semen and shells, tokens of their aspirations to virtue. Let me relate a brief encounter. The *kosa* ceremony (pp. 408 ff.) draws together hosts and guests typically related through marriage. An initial display of hostility is followed by a guest who presents marsupials to a cross-cousin or affine; in return the hosts give the guests a meal. Kosa dancers are young men, while hosts are older men: it is from older men that expressions of grief are drawn, for which they are compensated with shells. But the recipients of the shells are often the next generation—not the older men who wept, but their "sons." It is younger men who demand shells from the dancers. In short, the compensation given by junior-generation dancers is collected for the hosts by men of their own (junior) generation (p. 410). I note that while the ethnographer may refer to these items as compensation, they are not directly comparable to the kinds of payments familiar from other regimes where compensation substitutes for substance loss. Kelly insists that payments are given to assuage grief, not to counterbalance the expenditure of semen.

In the eclipsing of the senior generation[19] we perhaps see something of the way in which older Etoro men think of the junior generation as predatory

(Kelly's concept) on their seniors. Certainly, the recipient of insemination is regarded thus in relation to his inseminators. Here is the point at which relations between the generations and relations between spouses appear analogous to relations between (male) parents and children. Youth, wife, and child are all predators on male virtue, just as the witch is a predator on the healthy adult (Kelly 1976; 1993, 177). But while the witch is both predator and beneficiary, the woman is an agent of depletion without herself enjoying an enhancement of hame, and the child is a beneficiary without being an intentional agent of depletion. The debt youths owe to those who inseminate them is one they will discharge for the next generation.

There are two modes to the relationships here. From the point of view of the gender positions involved, I conclude that these relations (whether between men, between women, or between men and women) are construed as same-sex when the flow is seen as one of benefit and virtue, and cross-sex when it is one of predation and depletion. In the former, beneficiary and donor are presented as mutually masculinized (acquire vitality and virtue), while in the latter the relationship becomes asymmetrical and the *victim* in each case (the one who loses vitality) is feminized.[20] When the recipient of semen is a youth, the donor can see himself as engaging in a same-sex flow of vitality among males; but for an older man, beyond his prime, the situation becomes ambiguous. When his daughter marries, the final act of generous bestowal is the point at which most vitality is extracted from him. The donor is also victim. As the recipient of other men's shells he is "victim" to these men's predation on his children. At the same time, I have suggested that he is like his wife in that he himself is acting as an agent of depletion—receiving the shells of other men—without by this stage being a beneficiary of vitality; the shells he gains are simply treated as "surplus" to be disposed of among kin (Kelly 1993, 391).

In this comparison between different Etoro relations, as I have contrived it, it is the predatory tendencies, not the (work-based, nurturant) interdependence, of the conjugal pair that offer an analogy for cross-generational relations. Maternal kin hardly enter into the picture; at least from a man's point of view it is as though they were shielded from the full metaphorical implications of cross-sex imagery. Nurture in turn receives little metaphorical elaboration. Depletion and augmentation of the body, not its substantial composition, is the focus of aesthetic attention.

A COMPARATIVE NOTE ON SUBSTANCE

I have dwelt at length on the Etoro case for its Amazonian resonances, as will be apparent from other contributions to this book. I do not refer simply to the idiom of predation or to the significant soul life that renders the physical world so partial, or for that matter to perceptions of body depletion as extruded or actualized vitality, e.g., in Kayapo or Wari' (Fisher, Chapter 6; Conklin, Chapter 7). Rather, I refer to the absence of what Descola (Chapter 5) calls heterosubstitution. He relates this in turn to the general role that bodily substance plays in Melanesian ideas of gender difference, a point with which I would agree, although in a sense perhaps not meant by him. There is nothing self-evident about body substance. On the contrary, it is the very possibility of substitution that creates separately conceptualized body "substance," and the very possibility of heterosubstitution (as in the compensation of body growth by wealth) that creates substances as though they were detachable resources. That in turn requires a specific form of social relations: items can only be detached *from persons by persons,* so to speak.

Etoro concepts appear in a stark counterpoint to the perspective of their Papua New Guinean congenors in Mt. Hagen in terms of wealth disposition, exchange, and heterosubstitutions (compensation payments). But Etoro are by no means alone. Gell (1992, 150) has properly complained about the highlands bias in accounts of Papua New Guinea. Indeed the Sepik population of Umeda is even further removed from Hagen in having no imported shells or domesticated pigs at all, no marriage payments, child payments, or death payments, and no exchange. Rather, Umeda display an "indigenous service economy" in which "material transfers are the physical embodiment of 'service' obligations" (p. 152), morally motivated and in some cases quite onerous. It is obligation and not reciprocity that makes people behave as they do. The provisioning of children by parents and the services owed to seniors from juniors, Gell argues, put everyone into an asymmetrical relationship with others. Within a rather different constellation of relations, then, we encounter the Etoro effect: regardless of whether anyone is dependent on anyone else, or whether everyone is obliged to someone else, body imagery does not presuppose connections of substance. Marriage is the reproductive crux that produces obligations of service and provisioning (p. 157), but primarily as the relationship between male in-laws. Gell stresses the fact that it is the son-in-law who owes his own bodily energy to his parents-in-law (in "brideservice"), by contrast with "bridewealth" situations in which women not only help raise the valuables that will be given for them but perform for their in-laws the services an Umeda man performs.

I also drew on the Etoro ethnography for the precise moments at which it echoes Gow's ethnography of the Amazonian Piro: lack of emphasis on maternal indebtedness; spouses in a unique relationship of mutual demand, whereas "real kin" must passively await satisfaction (1991, 166); above all, the child as passive recipient of nurture.[21] However, the position of the Piro child is interesting. It raises again a comparative question about substance.

For the Piro, the blood that signifies personal vitality, filled up in young people and lost in sickness or death (pp. 129, 263–4), refers to the person's own origin in their parents' sexual activity. The child comes from the bodies of its parents, a physical link created through actions of the parents in eating, working, and sex. The newborn child puts a temporary stop on those activities, for the acts that defined the parents' marriage and will produce future children must now stay combined in the child just produced. Parents observe numerous restrictions on their conjugal behavior in order to protect the new child (pp. 153, 156). Apart from that, the child as coproduct of parental activity is complete. Thereafter the child will grow into a series of relationships through the food it is given by kin,[22] and it is this feeding that subsequently defines kinship, rather than any wider notions of "shared substance" (p. 263). Blood refers, Gow reiterates, not to kin ties, and certainly not to group membership, but specifically to "life" as the outcome of parental sexual activity. At the same time, Gow interprets it as very much a corporeal substance.

How is this substance realized? It is as though the prohibitions that follow birth, and momentarily disaggregate the parents from each other, displace the parents' earlier activity; the outcome can now be extruded in the child, thought of as another body. That displacement accomplished, the parents are not, as far as I know, further depleted by effort on its behalf. Instead, they eventually resume conjugal relations and work to make further children. The parents have, so to speak, "bodied forth" their vitality in the child, and once created, the child can demand no more. In short, that detachment creates a substance to be elicited from body, for the child is their bodily vitality transformed and thus in another form. At any rate, Piro seem to value fat persons.

Within the familial circle, then, persons can to some extent detach themselves from one another. As we shall see, this is the job of nurture in Hagen. It involves, as we shall also see, both severance of a kind and consumption. The process is to be contrasted with those Amazonian situations where (as Descola describes for Achuar), between hunter and prey, or gardener and plants, the very act of severance (killing or harvesting) supposes not extinction or uprooting but a counterflow of blood that jumps into the hunter's or gardener's body. Or again (as Conklin describes for Wari'), where homicide creates a bodily kinship between enemy and killer, and death requires that consanguines absorb the deceased's body, consumption does not work as an idiom of detachment either.[23]

CROSS-GENERATIONAL DEMANDS IN HAGEN

Etoro and Piro together have perhaps served to defamiliarize what Euro-Americans might otherwise take for granted: physical ties between persons as ties of substance and the dependency of children on parents, of which the archetypal case for them (Euro-Americans) is the mother-child tie.[24] The point is that versions of both are evident in Hagen, and they need explaining. The interdependencies of conjugal partners are replicated in interdependencies between parents and children, especially for a man in relation to his mother. Why is such value put on cross-sex relations?

In Hagen, conjugal dependency and the reciprocities to which it gives rise, the unmediated exchange between spouses, is refigured in parent-child relations, not only between fathers and children but also between mothers and children. So I have turned my earlier question around and, instead of asking why Etoro do not have mothers, ask why Hagen people make so much of them. Indeed I would argue that this is at the root of conditions one may witness today. From the viewpoint of the Hagen agnate, relations with maternal kin are cross-sex. Many of the economic changes evident in 1995 Hagen, including the odd residential shifts noted at the outset, make sense in terms of an inflation of cross-sex relations.[25] Cross-sex relations provide metaphors of consumption/dependency for all kinds of interactions.

Is there more to this than Gell's (1992, 162) caustic comment that the regime of reproductive gifts such as is found in Hagen must be founded on men's bad faith? Men exchange women through the products of the women's own labor (the pigs they raise), he says,[26] so that a fictitious "loss" of a daughter has to be compensated with wealth that purports to replace the loss of agnatic nurture! Certainly the extraction of valuables from cross-sex conjugal relations to circulate between (same-sex) men mirrors men's claims to agnatic continuity (extracting agnates from a cognatic matrix), while the compensation men owe their wives' kin in a cross-sex relation is like the compensation children owe the kin of their agnatically cross-sex parent. But settling debts is not the end of it.

Maternal kin figure prominently in the way Hagen people think about their overall health and success in life (some claim that attending to maternal kin is quintessential Nuigini kastom). The parent-child relationship is construed as one of interdependency insofar as a child is expected to reciprocate the care it receives when young. Conjugal relations are demand relations, although not uniquely so; they compete with other demand relations, especially between affines and between maternally related kin. Finally, children are neither predators who drain vitality nor silent witnesses to past acts. On the contrary, it is as though their own bodies augmented that of their parents. In a same-sex mode, these bodies are conceptually continuous with the parents'. The cross-sex mode implies discontinuity.

We need to focus not on (the bad faith of) reciprocity but on the mechanics of extraction. The Hagen daughter can only be extruded from the clan body, as the wealth given for her is so extruded, because body substance (nurture) is already separable from body. It is separable because of the social relations in place; there is a recipient to consume the substance. Hence killing and uprooting become metaphors/vehicles for severance, not, as in Achuar, vehicles for the absorption of the victim's blood by executor. Severance sets in train a whole series of internal comparisons.

If the value of cross-sex relations comes from the way in which relationships are shed or lost (persons "severed" from one another), then the two examples I have been dealing with throw light on the distinctiveness of the Hagen process. In the Etoro case, the tie between parent and child is analyzed by the ethnographer as a question of the child's absorption of male vitality, both directly from the father and indirectly from him through the mother's food. The father only gets rid of the child when other men take over his pro-creative (vitalizing) role. In Piro, the procreative (sexual) activity of the parents seems curtailed at another developmental point—at the child's birth; their re-lations with the child subsequently become merged with that of other kin who also feed it. In Hagen, by contrast, the detachment of the child happens *before it is ever born,* in transactions involving its parents. The transactions create an analogy between male and female parent, and their different destinies, for de-tachment from one parent is inscribed in attachment to the other. From the perspective of the agnatic clan, children of either sex are detached from their maternal kin while becoming attached to their paternal kin, and the analogy between the two sets of kin is created through the bridewealth payments that separate them.

Because that detachment is anticipated, it looks as though everything Ha-geners do subsequently is to overcome the separation (see Gillison 1993, 345). It is as though Hagen bridewealth were at a different moment in generational time from the payments Etoro make—as though it were taking place a whole generation earlier[27]—as though the weeping were already over. Hagen par-ents do not have to repeat the primal discovery of Etoro fathers, that they must lose their child. On the contrary, they have already done so and actively seek to affirm the act.

What is drained is not, from a man's point of view, life-force, but substance already externalized or reified (wealth, resources). To put it rather abstractly, a man at once augments his resources to a point of completion—in gift ex-change, they "match" the gift he was given—while in detaching them from himself he guarantees their further life in other men's hands. The model of the detached wealth (child) is there in every man's wife and sister severed by marriage from their natal clan. Is it because procreative body effort is already (anticipated as) detached from the person that body substance appears to re-produce itself? It is found as a ubiquitous outcome of procreative activity (whether from sex, work, or ritual), in the fertility of soil, the nourishment of tubers, the fat of pigs, and the size of persons. Might we then—after the Piro (and see M. Strathern 1988, 182, 278)—understand "substance" as completed vitality or capacity? Substance would then be a "product of men's and women's capacities rather than the capacities themselves" (Weiner 1995, 27), body perceived apart from life.[28]

In equally abstract terms, this holds for women and the pigs and children they rear. But there is nothing abstract about the "need" mothers have to de-tach these from themselves. Where a girl's mother looks to see her daughter well married, a boy's mother looks to see her pigs well disposed in bridewealth.

Bridewealth thus includes a special "mother's pig" that is the object of attention from women on both sides: the potential groom's mother fattens the pig with the potential bride's mother (she may be as yet unidentified) in mind. When a child shows no signs of making a (good) match, women become agitated with the thought of bridewealth going to waste. Indeed, mothers are as burdened by not being able to give it as by not receiving it.

Bridewealth is another form of payment for "body" made to maternal kin. The overt rationale is recompense for the mother's breast (milk), a source of nurture in counterpoint to the nurture derived from paternal food (from a person's clan/lineage land).[29] As in Gimi, it creates different destinies for men and women.

Maternal nurture from the lineage of a person's mother, anticipated at the transmission of bridewealth that establishes the marriage in the first place, is further acknowledged once a child is born, initially through child payments. For a man this is revived for the last time in mortuary compensation. But while at funerals a man's maternal kin are principal recipients of pig, in the woman's case it is her paternal kin. Her maternal kin have eaten her bridewealth, and it severs her from them as though, in Hagen idiom, she were dead. (As Paiela say [Biersack, Chapter 4], there is no continuity through women.) The special bridewealth pig destined for the bride's mother, along with those portions of the bridewealth that her maternal kin receive, is thus their final due. Thereafter, the girl's paternal kin become assimilated to "maternal kin" of the mother's children.[30] Maternal kin are singled out, for while the "work" that goes into making a child comes from both parents, only paternal kin reap the axiomatic benefit of the child's affiliation, and then continuously only in the case of boys. However fictitious, the idiom of "lost nurture" depicts maternal kin as already detached from the next generation. What has been detached from them is the substance whose growth they began and over which they remain a potent source of future blessing; indeed, the act of separation (recompense) may be repeated over and again. It can only be done, of course, if connections are maintained, an effort that cannot be taken for granted, but which requires further "work." The work of successful detachment is manifest in the rounded body of the baby and the stature of the adult.

Dependencies across the generations, living and dead, are evident. The investment of bodily labor in growing sweet potatoes, feeding a child, raising pigs (women), and providing the land on which this is done (men) renders analogous the division of labor between spouses and the attention parents and children should pay each other. In detaching women from the land and dispatching them to other men, Hagen men are also setting up a counterinheritance to what they pass on to their children, making children dependent on their two parents in quite different ways. Children receive dual nurture, one aspect of which is constantly lost and found in the reiterated payments made to maternal kin, finally settled for a woman through bridewealth and for a man through mortuary payments. Girls do not have to be dramatically torn from their natal kin, because their nurturance is already transferable in the work they do with their hands; boys do not have to be initiated into the same-sex company of men, because their mothers shed them when they shed the bridewealth animals.

The Hagen kind of "substance" has one interesting effect. When capacity or vitality becomes body and can be embodied in wealth items, it never really drains away. By contrast with Etoro, we might say that Hagen men are locked into inevitable aggrandizement—rather like the effects of capital (money turns into more money)—for efforts are not wasted when they become "things." Things circulate endlessly to men's credit, and credit is the enlargement of the person by these circulations. What a man sheds or gets rid of becomes lodged in other persons as an expansion of his own influence. So he cannot help enlarging his sphere of social relationships; the gifts cannot be finally given away. For all a man's heroic efforts to detach wealth, *other persons* are the repository of these efforts and in due course will return them to him. There is, logically, no place for "self-sacrifice."[31] What is true for men and wealth is also true for parents and the children they nurture, except that between the male and female parent a father's continuing relationship with his children can be mediated through clan membership and rights to land while a woman's is divided between the obligations her children owe to her natal kin and the obligations they owe to herself.

These observations are not set in a timeless present. My focus on cross-sex relations also reflects a historical shift. The whole structure of bridewealth and childwealth payments noted here, and of the creation of pigs through the joint labor of the spouses, conceals men's same-sex identification with valuables and transacted pigs and women's same-sex identification with food and the produced pigs. These same-sex relations still become the object of people's actions on other occasions,[32] but they have lost some of their rhetorical force. It was through appeal to the solidarities of same-sex relations that older men in the past put pressure on younger men to work and attach themselves to sponsors thereby. Their exhortations had an effect in part because of the men "at their back"; in the 1990s they seem less effective. It was both lineage solidarity and the mutual interests of male affines that meant that women were usually kept at the husband's place. With the eclipse of flamboyant same-sex display in ceremonial exchange has also gone women's magic for making gardens grow, and the one-to-one relationship a woman once had with her growing crops today has the appearance of the individual proprietorship of a commodity producer. The demise of separate residential arrangements for men and women should be added here. One might under these circumstances, where separations are abandoned and combinations exaggerated, expect that the character of cross-sex relations would change.

For insofar as each set of gender relations (same-sex, cross-sex) acquires its power by being bracketed off from the other, as alternating modalities of social life, the cross-sex interactions that appear to dominate aspects of contemporary Hagen life have lost some of the particularizing force they once had. In Mt. Hagen I found myself spontaneously using the Piro term for "mix" for a whole range of social configurations, from residence patterns that had people from different clans and different highlands regions living cheek by jowl, to the anonymizing congregations of evangelical gatherings, to the undifferentiated sleeping rooms in houses now that menstrual huts are gone. Daughters living on their father's land are part of this mixing.

COMPARISON BY DIVISION[33]

I have focused on internal comparisons between different types of social relations. It is not the Euro-American "difference" between male and female that has concerned me but an indigenous gender model of same-sex/cross-sex relations. In this model, each relation can come only from the other. I thus point to a Melanesian source of internal reflexivity, relations modeled on relations. This indigenous comparison has to be, so to speak, comparison by division or detachment, and is at once a conceptual and a social process.[34] Detachment as the separation of categories from one another[35] creates the conceptual possibility for modeling by analogy or metaphor. Detachment as the separation of sets of relations from one another sets up social possibilities for treating some relations as aspects of other relations. Thus the way in which spouses are merged in or separated from one another may or may not be echoed in the merging or separation of children from parents. And thus I can "compare" the extent to which conjugal and parent-child relations are metaphors for one another, and hence a source of internal reflection.

How relations between spouses come to metaphorize other relations points to different modes of bodily continuity and discontinuity. Hagen men seek to detach items from themselves as routes to enlarging their contacts with others. Traditionally attached to their land, rooted there, they always made great effort to "lose" their connections, divide themselves off from others; in exchange these others were recreated or found again as the objects of their regard (partners). Women who traditionally moved away were themselves uprooted and detached, yet kept up their contacts with their kin as best they could. This their children also did for them by stimulating the flow of maternal payments; we might say they "found" their kin again through their children. Nowadays men can overlay their attachment to land with other sources of wealth; as they move between spheres of activity, money acquires a translatable value. Women in turn are much freer to seek out their natal kin and enjoy the luxury of living there.

The analysis has some purchase for understanding contemporary Hagen relations between the generations. Continuity, like same-sex gender relations, elicits expectations of replacement. At the same time, and as an alternative position in generational time, the generations can be conceived in a cross-sex, discontinuous mode. I recall being puzzld some 30 years ago by certain enterprising youths who mounted a prestation (gifts of pork and money) from themselves as "young men" to their seniors. They turned the seniors into passive recipients. I see now that they were dividing the generations thereby, and pointing to the displacement/substitution of old times by new.

ACKNOWLEDGMENTS

My thanks to Richard Werbner, who persuaded me to turn a peripheral interest in generations into a focus, and to Peter Gow for sharing an unpublished paper on the Piro. Claudia Gross and James Leach both provided significant comments on an earlier draft. I must acknowledge the influence of James Weiner's work, and of Aletta Biersack's (1995) essay, "Homosexual Meanings: Society, Economy, and Gender among Ipilis." I also single out Beth Conklin for her extensive comments on my contribution.

NOTES

1. The field visit was funded with a British Academy research grant, which I acknowledge with gratitude. It should be clear that I am extrapolating from a short visit and limited experience. While the particular groups and settlement area where I lived may have been unusual in its occupation of fertile land that attracted incomers to startling demographic effect, the accommodations people made to this state of affairs drew on existing cultural resources. It is that cultural potential which concerns me here.

2. I dramatize for argument's sake. One could of course give a perfectly coherent account of the continuities between 1964 and 1995.

3. Some recent discussions are adumbrated in Strathern (1991, 48–51). I take it for granted that we do not "find" similarity and difference but create these axes in the process of making comparisons.

4. Gow cautions against falling into the trap of imagining that one is dealing with a people either with no history but a coherent culture or with a coherent history and no culture (1991, 291)—a sensitive point given how Piro have been denigrated for their "acculturation." Gow suggests that we take Piro seriously. They do not see their ancestral culture as heritable property but as weapons for the defense of kinship, because for them history is kinship. History is what kin tell one another; remembering is central to relations between kin and in turn constitutes a history of kinship.

5. A point I have made elsewhere. On perspective, see M. Strathern (1991, e.g., p. 54), after Werbner (1989); on modalities of time as a different view of cognatic and lineal organization, see M. Strathern (1992b, Chapter 5).

6. If life is always two generations (two sexes) deep, the primordial depth so to speak is between a potential and realized capacity for differentiation/mixing. I add that if one interpreted this as a same-sex/cross-sex oscillation (see below) also reproduced in the two perspectives, "Food House" and "*He* House," from which the house (community, cosmos) may be seen (S. Hugh-Jones 1995a), one could create several similarities with Melanesian materials.

7. This is part of a detailed consideration of several societies in the Strickland-Bosavi area, Kamula being interesting as one end of a range of recognizable variations in house design, provision for same-sex socializing, and emphasis on cross-sex domesticity.

8. At marriage, the female kin of groom and bride exchange mounds of tubers—female kin because women hold distributional rights in harvested crops; the mound from the groom's kin is topped by bridewealth shells. Kelly (1993, 464–465) suggests that these mounds epitomize the joint exchange of items coproduced through both male and female effort (the taro and sweet potato are like the brother and sister who are exchanged together).

9. Hame is immanent in both the corporeal and the spiritual body. Children are grown through "insemination" (with semen or milk), not "food." Kelly notes the Gebusi practice whereby a male child is fed semen to grow it while girls need only milk (1993, 148–149). Similarly, a witch grows large through eating the limbs of victims—not by adding substance but by enlarging his or her hame.

10. And of variable duration, from the most fleeting to an infinite fixing in certain institutions.

11. I owe the formula "own and other sex" to Roy Wagner (personal communication).

12. Comparable in scope to the Barasana alternations between life and death (S. Hugh-Jones 1979, 250).

13. Biersack (1995) draws attention to what she calls a sacrificial model of reproduction, with its emphasis on the depletion of life-force. Mosko (1995, 763–764) connects an appearance of "sacrifice" to the way in which Trobriand chiefly (paternal) agency is premised on processes of personal *reduction*, the disembodiment of the chief's (father's) person, and its incorporation by followers. This would make the reducing capacities of the chief similar to the gender construction in which an androgynous (cross-sex) subject sheds parts of itself in order to emerge in a single sex state vis-à-vis others. Mosko's work also suggests intriguing cross-generational parallels.

14. Contrast Weiner (1995, 106).

15. The male virtue of giving one's vitality to others is at the heart of the gender system that Kelly models for Etoro.

16. On women as nonnurturers see Collier and Rosaldo (1981, 275–276), and in South New Guinea, Lemonnier (1993, 141).

17. Kelly (1993, 91) refers to Etoro men's "self-sacrifice." A condition for such self-denial has to be a regime in which persons specifically cannot add to themselves by investing in others. (What kind of "self"-sacrifice can it be if a man instead enlarges his sphere of influence thereby?)

18. Following Weiner's (1995, 17) definition of embodiment as any perception that calls forth its own external bounding ("skin"), we would have to say that the Etoro body holds both life-force and the feelings or emotions that become the subject of compensation payments; both are elicited by others.

19. Younger men possess a spiritual quality older men lack (Kelly 1993, 186). If one were to track the circulation of shells, one would probably conclude that their connotations vary with the point in the life cycle at which they are given or received (cf. Robertson 1996).

20. This is perhaps why Etoro have no theory of depletion in relation to women, since I suggest that in the encounter between spouses it is the male partner who is feminized (loses vitality) in the act. By the same token, the wife is put in a "male" position without the benefits of masculinization. No wonder the mother is absent! This runs against Kelly's analysis, which takes the wife as female and, in the equation of sexual relations and witchcraft, identifies the witch as feminine.

21. The birth of a child stops conjugal relations for a while (in a set of postnatal prohibitions on both sexes), as manioc beer interrupts the flow of food and sex in daily life (Gow 1989, 1991, 156).

22. Including its parents, who establish relations with the child beyond the initial tie of substance (see below). Food giving is the principal means by which kin are lodged as memories in the child. Memories are eventually "lost"—a crucial premise for future relations (Gow 1991, 263).

23. The acts of cannibalism by which consanguines absorb the bodies of deceased relatives serve to detach them (the relatives) nonetheless from the memory or presence of the dead person.

24. Perhaps one might reexamine the axiomatic nature of the primacy given to parent-child dependency in other accounts, such as that of Fortes (1959, 78), who extrapolates Tallensi religion from such interdependencies, with the qualification that it is a society whose social organization is "based" on kinship.

25. My hypothesis is that in patrilineal regimes dominated by same-sex solidarities among men in particular, caring for maternal kin was always an area of individual expansiveness and requires special attention and energy; that energy is released under changing conditions.

26. Gell takes his "bridewealth" case from Maring, where women appear to contribute (through helping their husbands raise pigs) to their own marriage payment; in Hagen a woman contributes to her son's marriage payment, not to her husband's.

27. A relational counterpart perhaps to the anticipated harvest of future root crops from each seed corm or vine that is detached from the present harvest.

28. By contrast, Etoro *hame* can only produce *hame*.

29. On the equation between the "grease" of breast milk, semen, and fertile land, see A. Strathern (1972). A man's semen (penis grease, *kopong*) contributes to making a fetus as a woman's milk (breast grease, kopong) makes a child grow fat, along with the fat (kopong) of pig meat. All these are directly or indirectly nourished by the fertility (kopong) of the soil, which embodies the labor of ancestors. Between parent and child the physical tie may be designated as either grease (kopong) or blood (*mema*); over time both are gradually depleted (as discussed later).

30. The story of a woman who wanted to get rid of her pig (based on events witnessed in 1995) is told in M. Strathern (1998). There I refer to a man who told me that it was always worthwhile investing in daughters, because a married daughter thinks of her own parents all the time and wants to send things to them, whereas a married man must think of his parents-in-law. He had adopted two daughters, with a prospect of the flow of money that would come to him by this route. A reason why women feel they can leave their husbands with impunity these days is that they know (they say) that if they have cared for their children then their children will always seek them out, wherever they are living.

31. Hagen men and women do experience bodily "depletion" over a lifetime, and this may be specifically related to the nurturing of the next generation—an old man or woman will point to their reduced state with some pride—but it is not, I think, imagined as depletion of a "life-force." Moreover, unlike Etoro, parents finish what they begin. People thus look to children as their "replacements," so in this sense nothing is "lost."

32. Warfare and adolescent gang activities provide some contexts.

33. After M. Strathern (1995).

34. The world is made by division (cf. Mimica 1988; also McKinnon 1991). In being divided off, each part has alternating potential, creating a dual configuration of which it is an incomplete part while at the same time containing the whole within it in a fractal or holographic manner.

35. By contrast with concealment as the Etoro mother is concealed. Categorical detachment may be achieved only through great effort; see Gillison (1993, 24).

ELEVEN

The Gender of Some Amazonian Gifts:
An Experiment with an Experiment

Stephen Hugh-Jones

Noting some of the differences between Amazonian and Melanesian societies, including descent systems, bridewealth, and the absence or presence of animal domestication, Hugh-Jones points out that the two regions are also separated by different intellectual traditions—perhaps to the impoverishment of scholarship. Hugh-Jones's "experiment with an experiment" is an application of Marilyn Strathern's relational approach to gender, derived from her work in Melanesia, to the men's secret cults of the northwest Amazon. Given the striking resemblances of Melanesian and Amazonian cults, "it should follow that Strathern's critique of analyses of secret flute cults in Melanesia, in terms of men's domination over women, their appropriation of female reproductive capacities, and their need to establish an unambiguously male gender identity, might apply equally to the analyses of such cults in Amazonia."

Hugh-Jones sees northwest Amazon cults as not so much about gender differences and male domination as they are a reflection on the nature of men and women, male and female. For both men and women, the human body "and its various parts—vocal apparatus, gut, bones, and genitals—are all tubes. Through couplings of these tubes and the passage of various substances—food, water, air, sound, semen, blood, feces, children—along their interiors, the flow of life is ensured." The flutes and their attendant cults are not so much about male domination as signifying a "generalized capacity to reproduce, which men and women share."

Hugh-Jones's approach to men's cults, implicitly supported by Hill, is quite different from the point of view of Biersack, and Gregor and Tuzin. But Hugh-Jones is ultimately synthetic in his approach, maintaining that "each perspective is nuanced and enriched by the other."

INTRODUCTION

Any attempt to compare two large, internally varied, historically unconnected, and geographically remote ethnographic regions is fraught with epistemological problems. Are the apparent similarities significant and interesting, do they result from similar causes, or are they merely the product of evidence carefully selected and removed from context? Are the differences really "there" or are they simply a product of different regional ethnographic traditions informed by differences in theoretical bias?

Let us begin with what, at first sight, might look like some relatively straightforward differences. In Melanesia, descent, both matrilineal and patrilineal, is widespread; in Amazonia, patrilineal descent is rare and matrilineal descent absent. Secret men's cults are likewise relatively widespread in Melanesia, but their strikingly similar Amazonian counterparts are mainly restricted to north-west Amazonia (henceforth NWA) and central Brazil, where they are associated with some kind of descent ideology that contrasts with an emphasis on the cognatic kinship more characteristic of the region as a whole.

In Melanesia, marriage is organized sometimes by bridewealth transactions, sometimes by a principle of direct or indirect sister exchange. In bridewealth, bloodwealth, and many other transactions, objects can stand or substitute for aspects or qualities of persons. In Amazonia, a direct principle of substitution rarely operates in the context of exchange. The predominant principle is that of a life for a life, a wife for a wife, goods for goods, or food for food. "Instead" of bridewealth we find brideservice.

Finally, Amazonians are enthusiastic domesticators of young animals and birds found in the wild, but the only animals they breed are dogs.[1] Dogs are an important item of exchange, but other animals are exchanged only as meat and other products and never directly as substitutes for people. In Melanesia, by contrast, the domestication of the pigs underwrites bridewealth transactions and elaborate systems of competitive, incremental exchange that have no parallels anywhere in contemporary Amazonia.

Important and significant as they may be, to catalog differences in this way begs a series of questions. In both areas, the relevance and meaning of "descent" has been the subject of considerable debate.[2] In the Melanesian context, the contrast between bridewealth and sister-exchange masks important continuities between groups who exhibit one or another form (see Strathern 1988, 228). Likewise, to lump all Amazonians together as "brideservice societies" obscures important differences between their various marriage arrangements. Furthermore, it is not for want of raw material that Amazonians have "failed" to domesticate animals and exchange them or other valuables for people. They would have had no difficulty in domesticating wild peccaries (see Morton 1984), and their feather ornaments are another obvious potential candidate for bridewealth. The reasons Amazonians have not exploited such possibilities appear to have less to do with opportunity than with their ideas concerning substitutability and their particular conception of the proper relations between people and animals; true domestication is probably something more inconceivable than impossible (see Descola 1994b).

Leaving aside the whole issue of two quite different colonial histories, there is also the problem of two different intellectual traditions. These traditions have common roots in exchange theory, but it has been developed in two very different directions. In part, at least, these developments reflect the concrete experience of ethnographic fieldwork that has molded each one to suit local conditions. As with Lévi-Strauss and the Bororo, other anthropologists tend to harmonize their thinking with the intellectual styles and practical concerns of the peoples they study. Building on the works of Mauss and

Malinowski, the exchange theory of Melanesia has been predominantly that of gift exchange, with its emphasis on economics and interpersonal transactions. The Amazonianists' exchange theory also has Maussian roots, but, following Lévi-Strauss, this version has been largely that of marriage alliance, with its global emphasis on system, category, and classification, a version developed in tandem with a focus on mythology and cosmology, often treated in a similarly systemic, categorical, and classificatory manner. In this scheme, economics tends to be squeezed uncomfortably between structuralism and cultural ecology, often figuring as an unhappy compromise between "symbol" and "subsistence."

Marilyn Strathern's *The Gender of the Gift* (1998) belongs in the long lineage of Melanesian exchange theory, but it also signals a new departure. I cannot here summarize this complex work. Instead, I offer a brief outline of selected points based, in part, on Alfred Gell's (1999) lucid exposition of Strathern's work. Integral to her critique of the hidden realist and materialistic biases that she sees as underlying much of the Melanesian ethnography is her adoption of an idealist viewpoint. She presents the Melanesians' world not as one made up of humans, animals, and things that exist initially as independent and self-contained entities, a position from which they then enter into external or causal relations with one another, but rather as a system of meaningful signs. Because the elements of this system—people, pigs, pearl shells, potatoes—are the outcomes or products of previous relations—sex, breeding, feeding, manufacture, gifting, growing—all of which are included under an extended rubric of "exchange," they are themselves relationally constituted. Because these already relational elements enter into further relations in different contexts, their meaning or identity is not fixed or given in advance but instead relative to how they articulate with other elements at any one moment of time. It is as if people who enter into social relations already carry within them the "trace" of the relations between their two parents or as if potatoes contain the "trace" of the relations of those who grew them; as if persons and things were merely the signs or vehicles of these relations; as if it is the relations in which they engage that determine which aspect or component of their relational identity is pertinent (see also Strathern, Chapter 10).

In its formalism and its emphasis on the relational constitution of the elements involved, this Strathernian version of exchange theory shows affinities with Lévi-Strauss's structuralism and may thus offer a bridge between the two regional intellectual traditions mentioned above. But in other respects there are some very important differences, which suggest the potential for using Strathern's Melanesia-based theoretical position to challenge some assumptions that underpin the ethnography of Amazonia.

In much of Amazonian and Melanesian ethnography, in particular in most analyses of secret men's cults, "gender" is taken to be a fixed, unitary, and relatively unproblematic attribute of persons. If there is a "problem of gender," this problem is seen to lie in men's initial dependence on their mothers (which compromises their capacity to achieve a fully masculine adult identity), in their search for power over women and their envy or denigration of women's reproductive capacities, and in the fact that, in their position as in-married wives, women threaten to subvert the integrity of male coalitions and patrilineal groupings. For Strathern, the "problem of gender" lies not in gender's achievement or affirmation by Melanesian men but precisely in the analysts' assumption that gender is something fixed and unitary. In her analysis, because persons are constituted through previous relations between two parents, in their unmarked or "resting" state, they are of androgynous or mixed sex. In their marked or active state, as when they enter into relations with others, one "pole" of their androgynous identity is eclipsed so that they assume, temporarily, a single-sex identity in relation to a transactional partner who, from *their* point of view, now has an opposed, single-sex identity; from that partner's perspective, the polarities are reversed.

Let us take a concrete example: a man of patriclan X gives his sister as a wife to a man of patriclan Y. As a person, the woman is mixed sex or "male-female," but, as a sister, a part or extension of her brother and an agnatic, "male" group, she is herself also "male." By detaching a "female" bride and thus eclipsing a "female" component of themselves, this brother and his agnates constitute themselves as "male," now in an active state of potential in relation to "female" wife takers and a "female" future brother-in-law. From clan Y, the wife takers' perspective, they are collectively "male" and the husband is "male" in relation to his bride-to-be. With the transaction completed, all then return to a mixed-sex state.

The case above is an example of what Strathern calls a cross-sex or "mediated exchange": as in the classic form of gift exchange, something passes between the parties involved. But exchange may also be single-sex and unmediated, as when a mother grows a child within herself. Here the child, boy or girl, is initially a "female" extension or replication of the body of its now "female" mother. At the end of the pregnancy, a gift from the husband/father provokes the detachment of the child as a countergift, allowing the mother to constitute herself as cross-sex in relation to the child, which she now reveals as the product of her growing. As will be shown, the same logic can be applied to the crops that Amazonian women grow in their gardens, to the beer they brew in womblike containers, and to the neophytes that all-male cult groups grow in equally womblike houses or ritual enclosures.

Equally important in the context of initiation cults and ceremonial exchanges involving single-sex male groupings is Strathern's critique of the notion that such ritualized collectivities represent, or serve to misrepresent, a higher-order, all-encompassing "culture," "society," or "social structure" portrayed as the prerogatives of men, from which women and children are excluded as less than full "members," and defined in opposition to "nature," the "individual," or "domestic life." As against "top down" abstractions of this kind, Strathern begins from the other end, with a more concrete "sociality," that is, social relations, which are constituted, manifested, and modified through the ongoing play of exchange. In this view, public rituals and ceremonials and the clans and other groupings that they generate are not manifestations of "society" or "social structure" but rather one mode of sociality that is temporally constituted in relation to its complementary mode of domestic kinship and upon which it draws for rhetorical effect. By the same token, a ritual is not the playing out of a "script" that is given in advance but rather a performance that allows people to display their capacities, the outcome of hard transactional work that provides a momentary summation of their particular claims. In this it is ultimately no different from the symbolic transactional work that is effected in any of the more mundane exchanges that make up the gamut of social existence.

In his reader's guide to Strathern's study of Melanesian gender symbolism, Gell observes that the "Melanesia" of *The Gender of the Gift* is less a real place than "the setting for a sustained thought experiment" whose methodological usefulness "is not restricted to Melanesia, as opposed to Africa, America, Asia or anywhere else" (1999, 34). If this is so, then it should follow that Strathern's critique of analyses of secret flute cults in Melanesia, in terms of men's domination over women, their appropriation of female reproductive capacities, and their need to establish an unambiguously male gender identity, might apply equally to the analyses of such cults in Amazonia.[3] Following this cue, I shall attempt an experimental reanalysis of my own and others' data as if seen from the perspective of this imaginary place. In my own case, this amounts to a self-critique of two earlier works (S. Hugh-Jones 1979, 1995a), on which much of what follows is based.

Like Strathern's "Melanesia," my "Amazonia" is a semi-imaginary place. I shall be mainly concerned with NWA, an area I treat as if it were a single whole, often ignoring both differences between the peoples of its two major subregions and those between the theoretical biases of their different ethnographers. That said, I should explain that the northern part of NWA is inhabited by Arawakan-speaking Curripaco and Wakuénai and that in the southern part live some 15 exogamic groups, each speaking a different but closely related Tukanoan language. My own field research was conducted among the Barasana and their neighbors in the extreme south, but I shall also refer to the more northerly Tukanoan Desana and Wanano.

To carry out my experiment in full would require too much space. Instead, I shall attempt to knit a few Amazonian motifs into the fabric of Strathern's Melanesian net bag in return for inspiration drawn from selected elements of her work. In general, these are, first, her view of gender as a categorization of persons, objects, and events that draws on sexual imagery to make concrete ideas about the nature of social relationships, a function of particular social relations rather than an immutable attribute of whole persons (1988, ix), and, second, her extension of the concept of exchange to embrace not only "mediated exchanges"—as when one person detaches something of him/herself to give to another in the form of a gift—but also unmediated exchanges—as in the production of material goods or the reproduction of people. More specifically, I draw on her reanalysis of initiation cults among the Gimi and Sambia of the eastern Papua New Guinea (PNG) highlands, a reworking that highlights mythological and ritual exchanges of parts of persons—flutes, neophytes, bodily substances—among the participants.

Shortage of space means that I must take much of the original Sambia and Gimi ethnography and Strathern's reanalysis for granted. Relying mainly on Strathern, I ask whether her reanalysis might be used to present material "closer to home" in a new light. In particular, given other striking parallels between Sambia initiation and the secret flute cults of NWA, I want to explore the possibility that the latter also involve something akin to the semen transactions that occur between senior Sambia men and neophyte youths, albeit in a less overt manner (see also Bidou 1996). I then move on to consider NWA ceremonial exchanges, making comparative reference to the Daribi of the New Guinea highlands.

For Amazonia and Melanesia, both intra- and interregional comparisons have tended to compare like with like, flute cults with flute cults, exchange with exchange. Relative to Melanesia, the issues of gender and gift exchange have received relatively little attention in the Amazonian context (Descola, Chapter 5). Where gender has been considered at all, it has typically been treated as straightforwardly "about" men and women. Gift exchange is rarely discussed as such. More often it figures as part of "subsistence," or else it is subsumed under the more concrete and deceptively transparent rubrics of "trade" or "barter" (see Hugh-Jones 1992). A major component of *The Gender of the Gift* is the argument that the Gimi, Sambia, and other eastern highland initiation cults can be viewed as transformations of the ceremonial exchange systems of the Melpa and other western highlanders. Few if any Amazonian peoples make use of true bridewealth, the sine qua non of western highland incremental exchange, but it is nonetheless apparent that, as celebrations of intraclan relations of "descent," NWA initiation cults "make sense" in relation to intercommunity exchanges of food and manufactured items that take place between affinally related groups. If initiation cults are all-male affairs, NWA ceremonial exchanges are frequently conceptualized in terms of gendered groups and gendered products. In an earlier paper (Hugh-Jones 1995a), I explored this theme through the medium of architecture; here I build on this analysis, but now with reference to exchange, using some ethnography from the Xingu region of central Brazil as a comparative counterpoint.

FLUTES, FISH, AND MANIOC TUBERS

I begin with a brief consideration of some NWA myths that account for the origins of the flutes and trumpets used in initiation. My treatment is necessarily selective, partly because space is limited and partly because I am concerned to relate these myths to stories about the origins of manioc.[4] Manioc products—raw pulp, cooked bread, and fermented beer—figure prominently in ceremonial exchange and also play a significant role in initiation. In one story, the flutes and trumpets are made from sections cut from a palm tree that springs from the ashes of an ancestor who was burned on a fire. The flutes are the ancestor's paired bones, while his skull becomes a ritual gourd (see below). In another story, the instruments, now as protohuman ancestors, figure as the segments of the body of an ancestral anaconda who swims upstream from the Milk River in the East, his moving body giving rise to the river up which he travels, and who then vomits up his sons, one after the other. In yet another story, the burned body of this ancestor, now called Manioc-Stick Anaconda, gives rise, not to a palm tree and a set of flutes and trumpets, but to a manioc garden, his flesh as manioc and his bones as the burned logs of swidden cultivation. These stories suggest an analogy between bodily segmentation or vomiting as asexual modes of procreation and the vegetative propagation of manioc from the broken stems of the plant, manioc tubers being the analogues of children.

In various ways, the myths also suggest an equivalence between flutes and fish that reappears in several other contexts: anacondas are the "fathers of fish"; the flutes are stored underwater in rivers; a wide-mouthed fish shows the women how to play the flutes; the Barasana call some fishes and all fish swim bladders *buhua,* a term for all tubes including flutes. A further parallel is drawn between fish and male genitalia: comments on their common form and smell occur in conversation and several cases of transformation or mistaken identity occur in myths. To complete the circle there are many contexts in which manioc tubers are likened to both fish and male penes. Journet's (1995) Curripaco material is especially rich in this regard. In Curripaco myth, fishes are responsible for opening the birth canal of Amaru, the equivalent of Woman Shaman (see below); in ritual exchanges, gifts of fish are said to "call" an abundant manioc harvest; and in their daily lives, like their Tukanoan cousins, Curripaco women alternate between periods with and without fish. During menstruation and after giving birth, women abstain from sex, from eating fish, and from working with manioc; in fertile periods, when pregnant or not menstruating, sex, fish, and garden work are all recommended (Journet 1995, 266–268 and passim). The same ideas figure prominently in the Xingu area. Here, secret flutes are directly identified with fish, both flutes and fish are said to cause menstrual bleeding, fish are considered to be both phallic and vaginal, a large-mouthed fish plays a female role in the invention of sexual relations, manioc tubers are directly identified with both male genitals and fish, and the women's processing of manioc tubers has marked sexual connotations (see Bastos 1978, 173–176; Gregor 1985, 71, 80–83).

NWA peoples also tell versions of the "myths of matriarchy" that are equally thematic of male initiation in Melanesia.[5] These myths, which tell how a theft of sacred flutes led to a reversal of the current relations between men and women, also suggest an association between flutes, male and female genitals, and the onset of menstruation. In the Gimi myth, men steal flutes originally owned by women; men now have penises while women menstruate via the wound left by the removal of the flute penis (Gillison 1980, 154–156). In the Barasana myth, the theft is more convoluted. Originally male possessions, the flutes are first stolen by women and later recaptured by men. Woman Shaman, the principal thief, is herself explicitly androgynous and also the counterpart of Manioc-Stick Anaconda, with whom she is sometimes identified. Another episode of this myth reflects this androgyny and two-way transfer between men and women, inverting the story of the theft of flutes and the theme of a male ancestor as a phallic, tubular anaconda/palm trunk. Here Woman Shaman, now as a palm-tree womb, gives asexual birth, first to two manioc-tuber daughters and then to flute sons who menstruate like women. Later Woman Shaman invites these sons to eat from a gourd of beeswax and powdered coca that she keeps between her legs. Instead of aggressively recapturing flutes that Woman Shaman has stolen, the men now refuse to accept what she willingly offers them on the grounds that it is something that properly belongs to her—her genitals and the smell of beeswax that emanates from them. Their refusal means they lose the full capacity to menstruate. Later she gives the men a lesser gourd, which they now use in initiation rites along with the flutes and which underwrites their claim to be "menstruating."

As Strathern has shown for their Melanesian counterparts, as an alternative to interpreting them in terms of a zero-sum game in which one sex's gain is the other's loss, myths such as these might equally be seen as a reflection on the bodies of men and women, on the congruence between the form of their genitals, and on their respective reproductive capacities. Like rivers, anacondas, palm trunks, and flutes, the human body and its various parts—vocal apparatus, gut, bones, and genitals—are all tubes. Through couplings of these tubes and the passage of various substances—food, water, air, sound, semen, blood, feces, children—along their interiors, the flow of life is ensured.[6]

Strathern's "Melanesia" is characterized by two major constraints: that all transactions are gift transactions and that all gift transactions are gendered (see Gell 1999, 36). In this system, theft too is a gift transaction and falls under the wider rubric of exchange. From this perspective, the theft of the flutes appears in a quite different light. Rather than a capture of instruments of domination, a symbolic appropriation of female reproduction, or the invention of

culture and society as an exclusive male domain, Strathern sees it as a transaction in which women *retain* as a part of their bodies what they also give up
to men in objectified form. As total tubular persons, the self-reproducing, androgynous figures of the myths described above, and as tokens of congruent
inverted/everted body parts, the flutes signify a generalized capacity to reproduce, which men and women share. But in their detached, external, and
objectified form as men's ritual possessions, the musical instrument flutes signify a more specifically male capacity to elicit and activate the more internal
reproductive capacities of women.

The equivalent NWA myths can be considered in the same light. "Theft,"
here as a two-way transaction between men and women, is but one of several
transactions of flutes that are enacted or evoked during the initiation. Besides
teaching the neophytes a myth that is reenacted through the rite itself, the senior men show flutes to the neophytes, give them flutes to play, blow trumpets
over their exposed genitals, and "vomit" (i.e., pour) water from the flutes' hollow interiors over their heads as they bathe in the river. These and other actions add up to an understanding that young boys are being endowed with the
"flutes" that will later enable them to cause women to reproduce. At the same
time, the enactment of their "vomited" birth reminds them where they came
from in the past.

What Strathern says of the Melanesian Gimi applies equally well to the
Tukanoan Barasana. Through these myths and ritual acts, the neophyte
learns "that what he has (his genitals) are signs of encounters with women that
have already taken place" (1988, 112) and also signs of the future encounters
for which he is being prepared. They suggest that, like the ancestors, the "true
man is . . . pan-sexual and capable of reproducing himself without women"
(ibid.). They also serve to demarcate boundaries of form and function between the inherently androgynous body parts of men and women, to mark off
the limits of their respective capacities, and to recall the union of the parents
of whom they are the androgynous product. This androgyny is reflected in
the pairing of a gourd of coca and beeswax, simultaneously the womb and
genitals of a "female" ancestor and the skull of her "male" counterpart, with
musical instruments that are themselves paired as "male" and "female" and
that have "male" and "female" origins in different myths.

Strathern's work destabilizes some of the key assumptions—society/
individual, male ritual as society, male/female, nature/culture—that lie behind
previous analysis of initiation cults in Melanesia. I cannot pursue here the full
implications of her critique for analyses of their Amazonian equivalents. With
reference to gender, it is sufficient to say that the NWA material presented
above and Strathern's analysis of its Gimi and Sambia parallels both suggest
that to view gender difference simply as a fixed and naturally given attribute of
men and women does not do full justice to the richness and layered complexity of indigenous conceptions. In the NWA context, it also renders problematic

any claim that initiation cults reflect or sustain male dominance in any simple or self-evident manner. Rather than providing clear answers to the question of men's powers, the rituals and myths appear to explore a series of possibilities in something inherently ambiguous and ill-defined—what Biersack describes as "a religious mediation on ultimate matters" (Chapter 4). It is doubtless for this reason that whereas some Barasana men assert that their rituals exemplify men's superiority over women, others describe them as a pretense.

We now return to manioc and another story of theft and recuperation. A Desana (Tukanoan) story of the origin of manioc begins by describing how Baribo, the Master of Food, had a magical white stone, the source of all food, which he kept hidden under the bowl used to collect the starch and juice when manioc tubers are processed. The presence of this stone guaranteed an abundance of starch; present-day Barasana keep such stones, the stone axes of their ancestors, in their gardens and in their starch bowls. When Baribo tells his daughter-in-law not to move the bowl, she replies, "You are not a woman. Women are in charge of these things. Why meddle in my affairs?" Later, when Baribo goes fishing, she lifts up the bowl and sees the stone, which she takes and hides in her vagina. On his return, Baribo sees that his stone is gone. He casts a spell on his daughter-in-law, causing her to fall asleep with her legs apart. As she sleeps, starch seeps from her genitals. Baribo introduces his "curved stick" into her vagina and extracts the stone, picking it up from the floor where it has fallen (see Buchillet 1983, 232–237).

In Curripaco versions of the same story, the "theft" of starch is presented as a voluntary transfer. Kaaritairi, Baribo's equivalent, puts starch either directly into his daughter-in-law's vagina or into her mouth, from where it dribbles down to her genitals, to see if she will be good at brewing beer. The indirect variant recalls Curripaco female puberty rites during which starch or manioc bread is placed in the mouths of young girls to ensure their future beer-making capacities (Journet 1995, 324). Versions of this myth are common throughout NWA. Taken together, they establish clearly what was already suggested by the myths considered above, namely, that manioc is the body of a male hero, that despite being a woman's affair, manioc is also something "owned" by men, and, more particularly, that manioc starch may be identified with semen. This identification is reflected in the name Kaaritairi, which translates as "the master of white foam, semen or tree-sap," and in the belief that manioc starch is a source of male semen (Journet 1995, 241). Mingau, a ubiquitous Amazonian drink made from manioc starch boiled in water, has a glutinous texture, looks like semen, and is the subject of ribald comment.

These extended associations between the fertility of manioc and men's fecundity are counterbalanced by an equally strong association of manioc with women, with their fertility, and with their capacity to grow crops and children. Other myths identify manioc with the bodies of women: women are described as the "mothers" of their manioc-tuber "children," and their process-

ing of manioc and baking of bread is metaphorically associated with conception, gestation, and birth. Such ideas would be immediately comprehended by
the Gimi (see Gillison 1980, 148 and passim). Although cast in a more structuralist idiom, C. Hugh-Jones's (1979) and Journet's (1995, 241 ff.) works on this
topic in NWA are entirely consistent with Strathern's account of such
processes in terms of the encompassing, totalizing relationship between highland PNG women and the crops they produce in a process of unmediated,
single-sex replication or growing (1988, 250–251). The stories of the women's
"theft" of their brothers' flutes and those of a woman's "theft" of her father-
in-law's stone assert that neither flutes nor manioc can be unambiguously assigned to men or women. Each sex retains in one form, proper to themselves,
what they give up in another, the retained "portion" providing the source for
further transactions between them. Both sexes "have" manioc, but manioc
work is properly a woman's affair; both sexes "have" fish and flutes, but fish
work and flute work are the affairs of men.

BLOOD, SEMEN, AND MILK

To pursue these ideas further and to return to my theme of initiation cults, I
need to consider briefly NWA ideas concerning conception. Regional variations in such ideas—the perceived differences between the relative contributions of women and men in the creation of children and the analogies or contrasts that different peoples make between blood, semen, and milk—play a
key role in Strathern's reanalysis of the Sambia and Gimi ethnography (1988,
Chapter 9). In the NWA context, I hesitate to set too much score on the reported variations, for they appear to reflect, on the one hand, an interplay between differences of cultural dogma and differences of emphasis between
ethnographers and, on the other, uncertainties and differences of opinion on
the part of individuals due to the fact that conception is something hidden
and mysterious, not something open to direct observation.[7]

For the Barasana, several views of the process coexist. Some say that boys
come from their father's semen and girls from their mother's blood; some say
that bone (and other hard parts—hair, skin, nails) come from semen and, by
inference, that flesh comes from blood; and some say that the father's semen
alone forms the body of the child, the mother's contribution being to provide
a receptacle in which it grows (see C. Hugh-Jones 1979, 116). Also relevant is
that the terms *rií,* "blood," *rií, rií,* " flesh," *riia,* "semen, children," *riaa,* "egg,"
and *riaga,* "river," are all close cognates, and that children receive soul stuff or
spirit essence both through their fathers' semen prior to birth and through the
receipt of paternally derived names soon after.

Inconsistent though they might appear, taken overall, these ideas suggest
that blood and semen are considered to be close analogues of one another
and that they come together to form the child, a view shared by the Curripaco

(Journet 1995, 275). Menstrual blood is thus unproductive blood that is lost, as opposed to blood creatively combined with semen. Although menstrual blood is carefully avoided, Tukanoan attitudes and behavior suggest that their concern with menstrual pollution is mild in comparison with that of the Xinguanos and even more so when compared with some PNG highland groups. There is, however, a difference between blood and semen, namely that, whereas the child's blood comes directly from its mother through an unmediated relation of replication or growing, which is likened to that between women and their crops, the father's relation to his child is mediated through his semen. The Curripaco describe this relation as the father "feeding" the child in the womb through repeated intercourse and state that the mother also transforms semen into milk, which she then feeds to her child after it is born (Journet 1995, 247; see Strathern 1988, 238 on the distinction between mediated "feeding" and unmediated "growing").

The implication of these ideas is that brothers and sisters share common substance that has two gendered manifestations, semen and blood. These substances are transmitted in parallel linear flows, brothers transmitting semen to their offspring and sisters transmitting blood to theirs. To phrase it differently, one might also say that men circulate their own blood through the bodies of their sisters (see also C. Hugh-Jones 1979, 161ff.). This image of "flow" is especially apt for the Tukanoans: for them, rivers and river travel provide some of the principal metaphors used to represent procreation and lineal continuity—this is already clear in the anaconda ancestor myth mentioned above and in the close relation between *ria* and *riaga*, the terms for "children" and "river" (see also S. Hugh-Jones 1995). However, I borrow the image from Wagner's (1977) account of Daribi kinship in the PNG southeastern highlands. Although the Tukanoans and Arawakans make no use of bridewealth, in other respects there are some clear parallels between them and the Daribi (see below).

If NWA conception theories seem vague and ill-defined, they appear more coherent when set against those from the Xingu region. In NWA, male semen figures as the analogue of both female blood and milk, while in the Xingu it appears as the analogue of milk only, apparently in opposition to blood. Writing of the Kamayurá, Bastos (1978, 34–36) distinguishes between the indirect transmission of seminal substance by men and its direct elaboration by women. A man receives semen through his father, but its ultimate source is his patrilineal ancestors. A man's ancestrally derived semen is stored in a special organ and is supplemented by the fish and manioc products he eats. Semen is described as a "kind of milk," some of which is the "food of the vagina" and some of which contributes to the milk that women feed to their children. For the Xinguanos, the idea of intercourse as "eating" applies to both sexes but is considered more debilitating for men, whose bodies, organs, and substances are "consumed" by their partners (Gregor 1985, 144). Barasana men appear less bothered by this problem—it is usually they or their penes that are said to "eat." The Xinguano child's body is made entirely from accumulated semen, the mother's womb being described as the child's "house," which molds the semen and transforms it into flesh, bones, and blood (see also Gregor 1977, 261; 1985, 85–90 for the Mehinaku).

There are clear parallels between these Xinguano ideas of conception and those of the Sambia, both in general and in the specific notion of an organ for storing semen (see Herdt 1987, 77–78). In NWA, semen, blood, and milk all appear to be considered as manifestations of the "same" substance, whose different forms either complement each other or substitute for one another, in different contexts. For the Xinguanos, the affinities between semen and milk appear to be more strongly marked than they are for NWA peoples. In addition, the opposition between blood and semen appears to be manifest in the Xinguano practice of bloodletting, a practice not found in the NWA area. The Xinguanos would thus appear to conform to the pattern Strathern (1988, 245) describes for the Sambia. Xinguano men also share the Sambia concern with the risks of menstrual pollution, and like Sambia nose bleeding, they frequently have recourse to bleeding. For the Xinguanos, bloodletting from the buttocks and upper legs is particularly associated with wrestling and male puberty seclusion and forms part of a more general complex of bleeding that includes menstruation and also the ritual piercing of boys' earlobes, another practice absent in NWA. Like Herdt's interpretation of Sambia initiation, to which he refers, Gregor's view of Mehinaku male ritual is cast in terms of male gender identity, socialization, and men's anxieties concerning their identification with women. As a part of this more general thesis, he interprets ear piercing and allied themes as being linked with ambivalence concerning the feminine components of the male self and as an imitation of women's menstruation to master something mysterious and feared (1985, 198). Though coming from a less psychoanalytic point of view, parts of my earlier analysis of Barasana initiation adopted the same line (see S. Hugh-Jones 1979, 130–131, 198–200).

Tentatively, I would suggest that Strathern's reworking of the Sambia and Gimi data can place these Xinguano acts of bloodletting in a different light. It also brings out an important difference between Xinguano and Barasana "symbolic menstruation." Xinguano men do bleed themselves, but Barasana merely say that their rites are "like menstruation," never having recourse to actual bloodletting. In the Xinguano case, there is a clear lineal flow of semen as a substance coming not from the genitor himself but via him from his patrilineal ancestors, but there is no corresponding contribution from the genetrix (Bastos 1978, 35). I have found no unequivocal discussion of Xinguano ideas concerning maternal blood, but it would appear that, as in the Sambia case, it is believed that men and women share circulatory blood regarded as female in either essence or origin and that, in addition, women also have their own menstrual-womb blood. In any case, the mother's blood seems to play no role in the feeding or formation of the fetus, while menstrual blood is certainly considered antithetical to male strength in general and specifically to male semen.

For Xinguano men, partible blood, akin to the menstrual-womb blood of their mothers, is a disposable substance that they neither transmit nor benefit from. It contained them in the past but should not do so again in the future. Instead, like the Sambia in Strathern's analysis, the men appear to constitute themselves as the male containers of female blood and hence would be doing something rather different from imitating the women's menstruation— perhaps this is why Mehinaku state that ear piercing is both like menstruation and also different from it (Gregor 1985, 188). By voiding blood, the men enhance their vigor by getting rid of something debilitating and female in essence or origin, perhaps also "making room" for the ingestion of foods that build up their supply of male semen (see Gregor 1985, 86). Significantly, it is above all fish, whose penile/seminal characteristics were noted above, that are forbidden to those who are secluded and bleeding, though enjoyed immediately afterward (Gregor 1977, 235–236; Basso 1973, 70). However, bloodletting is practiced by both sexes and believed to make young girls stronger as well.[8] In the case of young girls, it could be that this "making room" relates to their present status as daughters and their future destiny as wives. As daughters they receive seminal manioc and fish from their fathers, but it is mediated through their mother's cooking; as wives such foods will come directly from their husbands and be cooked by their own hands.

In the Barasana case, where blood and semen are analogous substances that both sexes transmit, it would make no sense for either men or women to get rid of blood intentionally. Bleeding is considered to debilitate, not strengthen, the body, and people take steps to conserve their blood and enhance its supply. When a baby is born, its parents keep a small bark-cloth bag filled with a lump of red powder (~gɨdaya) that represents the child's body and life-force. When the child falls ill, the parents ask a shaman to blow spells on its paint bag to revitalize their child's body. Adults use this same powder as a face- and body-paint and apply it to their temples and umbilicus in order to revitalize themselves. Produced by women and identified with their own, or Woman Shaman's, menstrual blood, this paint also figures as an important "female" item in ceremonial exchange between affines.

SEMINAL FRUITS AND GREEN MILK

In my earlier work, I was already aware that Barasana ceremonial exchange involved relations between affinally related groups, while initiation was more concerned with intragroup descent relations, but I had assumed that initiation was the maximal expression of a common ritual pattern of which ceremonial exchange was merely a simplified and attenuated form, thus failing to see the complementary, transformational relationship between the two (S. Hugh-Jones 1979, 37–38). Like the Melanesianists whose arguments form the subject of Strathern's extended critique, I had conflated the indigenous rhetoric of the clan, as a collective male unit that is manifest in initiation, with the anthropologists' "society" or "social structure." In a more recent work (Hugh-Jones 1995a), I began to rethink my previous analysis, using the indigenous concept of the "house" as a critique of the notion of descent and as a vehicle to explore the relation between initiation and intergroup exchange.

As I have already indicated, Strathern's critique of analyses of Melanesian initiation cults and of their theoretical underpinnings could be usefully applied in the Amazonian context. Rather than recapitulate her arguments at length, I want instead to extend my own reanalysis of Barasana initiation, picking out selected bits from a complex whole and using ideas derived from Strathern's work to recast them in a form that makes them more directly comparable with Melanesian data. My earlier reanalysis was more concerned with the relatively static image of the house as a totalizing representation of the different collectivities created during initiation and ceremonial exchange (see Strathern 1988, 115, 120 on similar totalizing images of collective domesticity in Melanesia). This image is reduplicated in the identification of the house with the world on the one hand and with the human body on the other. The house itself is an androgynous production, its gender being relative to a given ritual context, "male" in the case of initiation, "female" in the case of ceremonial exchange. Bearing in mind the passage of rivers through the world and of substances through the body, I want here to shift focus to the more dynamic concerns of flow and growth. Specifically, I shall focus on some of the transactions involving vegetal substances—fruit, powdered coca leaves, cigars, tobacco snuff, yagé,[9] and manioc bread—that occur during initiation, to ask whether we can find any analogues of Sambia semen transactions.

I can give only a bare outline of the rites themselves. Initiation occurs in two stages. During the first, a set of less potent secret flutes and trumpets are revealed to the neophytes during "house where fruit is brought in," a rite that also takes place on a regular basis, independent of initiation. At the start of the rite, the men carry large quantities of wild or cultivated tree fruit into the house, accompanied by the playing of the instruments. The men remain in the front of the house with the women and children confined in the screened-off rear section. The fruits come as a gift from the spirits of the wild, who are represented by the musical instruments, and the men who play them. Inside the house, the fruit is tipped into baskets in a manner that might be taken to suggest that it pours forth from the interior of flutes and trumpets themselves. The men also throw fruit against the screen dividing them from the women, sometimes pelting the women and children directly. This throwing of fruit would seem to emphasize both the separation of the men from the women and the "masculine" quality of the fruit itself. During the day, the men play the flutes and trumpets round the house, sometimes whipping the women and children to make them grow. At nightfall, the instruments are removed from the house, the screen is dismantled, manioc beer is served, and the women join the men in dancing. When neophytes are present, the rite is extended; it is they who are the focus of the whipping, and, for the first time, they play the sacred flutes, eat coca, drink yagé, smoke ritual cigars, and have snuff blown into their noses through a bone blowpipe.

In the second stage, *hee wii,* or "house of sacred instruments," no fruit is involved. Instead, it is the neophytes themselves who are carried into the house, where a set of more potent instruments is revealed to them. This second stage follows the same basic pattern as the first, but it is much more serious and drawn out. The rite itself takes two whole days, and instead of being immediately followed by a dance, rite and dance are interspersed by a long period during which the neophytes are secluded in a special enclosure away from contact with the women. At the start of the rite they are painted from head to toe in black paint; the disappearance of this woadlike skin dye marks the end of their seclusion. During seclusion they are taught the mythological basis of the rites they have been through, and, as part of their preparation as future husbands, they are also instructed in the arts of basket making. The initial preparation of manioc gardens and the provision of the basketry used to process manioc are the husband's chief contributions to the married couple's joint production of bread, beer, and other manioc-derived foods. Baskets thus have important "masculine" connotations and figure prominently as "male" items in ceremonial exchanges.

Each day, the secluded neophytes are taken to the river, where they bathe, drink copious amounts of water, and vomit. This bathing and vomiting is designed to cleanse the "dirt" suffused throughout the neophytes' bodies, a cleansing that complements their special, pure diet. They eat only ants, termites, fruits, and *sireria,* a special bread made from pure manioc starch. The insects are considered as especially appropriate food partly because of their own seminal associations and partly because their bodies contain no blood. The special bread is supplied by a woman who acts as the neophytes' ~*basolio,* or "adoptive mother," the counterpart of an "adoptive father" (~*basoli*), who looks after them during the rite itself. The initiates' portion is but a small part of a huge supply of pure-starch bread that the women of the house prepare together during the seclusion period, under the ~*basolio*'s supervision.[10] Together with the manioc beer that the women brew, a pile of this bread forms a centerpiece of "the house of manioc bread," a major feast marking the young men's emergence from seclusion.

While the initiation itself is a predominantly intraclan affair, it is important that people from affinally related communities attend the dance that follows.

Before the dance begins, the seclusion compartment is destroyed, and the young boys, decked out in full finery, are presented to the women. The women now paint them from head to foot with red paint and present them with the newly woven knee bands they have been making. In return, the boys give them the products of their own basket making. This exchange creates a cere-monial partnership (~*heyeri*-~*heyrio*) between the boys and women that prefig-ures the adult relationship between husband and wife.

Bearing in mind that Sambia men supplement their supply of semen not only directly from others but also by drinking tree sap (Herdt 1987, 164), I begin by considering the role of the fruit in Barasana initiation. In my previ-ous analysis, I commented that their connotations of growth and periodicity suggested an identification between tree fruits and the initiate boys. Although it was clear that the fruits were closely associated with the men who typically gathered them, what I did not then notice was their specifically agnatic and seminal connotations. Tukanoan rites involving tree fruits belong to the wider category of intergroup ceremonial exchanges. However, what distinguishes these exchanges of fruit from other exchanges is that whereas the latter typi-cally take place between affinally related communities, the former occur mainly between agnatically related communities belonging to the same clan or language group (see also Chernela 1993, 116 for the Wanano).

In Barasana, tree fruits themselves are known collectively as *hee rika, hee* being "secret flutes and trumpets" and *rika* having the general meaning of "arm" or "appendage." Like flutes and initiates in relation to palm tree an-cestors, fruits can thus be considered as the detachable components of the in-struments. In the rites, it is as if both fruits and initiates spew forth from the hollow flutes as sprays of fruit and leaves emerge from the tops of palm trees growing in the forest. These parallels, which suggest the seminal character of fruit, are echoed elsewhere. *Ahe,* "seed," is close to *ahea,* "penis," and the names of several individual fruits or fruit products refer directly or indirectly to semen.[11] In addition, in a story widespread throughout NWA, the ancestor whose burned body gives rise to the secret flutes and trumpets is himself con-ceived from a caimo (*Pouteria caimito*) fruit given to his mother to eat. The gluti-nous juice of the fruit trickles from her mouth down to her genitals, making her pregnant (see, for example, S. Hugh-Jones 1979, 262).

I have never heard individual men claim that they consume fruit to supple-ment their supply of semen. Nonetheless, what all this appears to suggest is that, in Strathernian terms and in relation to a collective body, gifts of fruits between agnates and the ritual act of bringing fruit into the house can both be understood as unmediated transactions that replicate clan substance by aug-menting a supply of semen and ensuring its continued flow. The rites are said to guarantee a continuous supply of fruit, which can be understood literally as such and metaphorically as a supply of both semen and children. The fruit is taken into a house that, in this context, stands for the clan as a collective male body. Further evidence for this assertion comes from the contrast between the verbs ~*soo-* ("to take in, incorporate") and *eka-* ("to feed, give out"), which marks the contrast between agnatic exchanges of fruit and the exchange of other foods between affines, respectively *hee rika ~sooria wii*, "the house which takes in fruit," and *baare ekaria wii*, "the house which gives out food." This local contrast between "incorporation" and "giving out" matches Strathern's more general distinction between "growing" and "feeding" as, respectively, unmediated and mediated exchanges.

Other transactions involved in initiation may also be understood in this light. During the rites themselves, the men must not consume any normal food, "food" here being understood as fish, meat, or manioc products that would come from women. The substances they ingest—coca, tobacco, yagé, and manioc beer—are explicitly opposed to the normal foods of which they are analogues (see Hugh-Jones 1995b) and are served up exclusively by men. Leaving beer aside for the moment, these other "non-foods" share in common an association with semen and with the male genitals. Coca (*kahi*) and yagé (*idire* ["drink"] *kahi*) are owned by men and propagated vegetatively from cuttings, a procedure that produces an unbroken "male" line of agnatic continuity through time. The counterpart "female" line is produced by the manioc cuttings that women plant and transmit to their daughters. Both kinds of *kahi* are alike in being considered part of clan identity, and they stem from a common rootstock, which is also that of the clan itself. Both plants are also said to have come from within the hollow interior of the flutes and trumpets. They would thus be the "marrow" of the bones these instruments represent, bone marrow (*badi*) being a source or form of semen (also "*badi*").

The act of planting coca also has sexual connotations, which are amplified in a myth of the plant's origin. The daughter of Fish Anaconda, Yawira, herself both fish and manioc, asks ~Yake, the younger brother of her husband Yeba, to help carry manioc cuttings to her garden. There she seduces him, making love so enthusiastically that he dies as he ejaculates, his body giving rise to the neat rows of coca that men plant in the garden's blanket of manioc cuttings. Yawira becomes pregnant, the implication being that, *in this context*, the relationship between coca and manioc is analogous to that between "male" and "female." Finally, in a previous section of the myth, Yawira gives Yeba tobacco, a gift from her father and the source of all tobacco. It comes in the form of a cigar that is at once a fish and her own father's penis (see S. Hugh-Jones 1979, 296–298, and also 1995b).

I emphasize the contextual nature of these gender associations, bearing in mind not only Strathern's lesson but also that of the ethnography itself. I have already made clear the androgynous character of both the sacred instruments and of the bodies of those from whom they derive. This androgyny applies also to these "non-foods." If coca and yagé are "forms of" semen, they are equally "forms of" milk. Yagé is the milk of Woman Shaman, and the ancestral stock of both coca and yagé is located in the Milk River, whose waters are tinged with green (Reichel-Dolmatoff 1971, 46). Like maternal milk, coca also satisfies hunger, the former being food for the body, the latter being soul stuff and a food for the soul (see C. Hugh-Jones 1979, 228, 239 and passim). Finally, in a Desana origin myth, both coca and yagé come from the detached fingers of a woman's body (see Reichel-Dolmatoff 1971, 36–37).

Given the above it can, I think, be said that when the presiding shaman distributes the coca, snuff, cigar, and yagé on which he has blown protective spells, when the senior men circulate these substances among themselves, and when they are given to the neophytes, these exchanges can indeed be considered, in hidden, metaphorical terms, as being tantamount to transactions of semen resembling those of the Sambia and with a similar rationale. If this is so, then, following Strathern's reanalysis of the Sambia material, the gender of these substances and that of the people from whom they are detached as partible objectifications both depend on context and point of view. When the shamans blow snuff up the noses of the neophytes and other men, this act of "insemination" can be seen either as an unmediated transaction between parts of a same-sex, all-male collectivity or as a mediated, cross-sex transaction in which a "male" shaman "inseminates" a "female" neophyte with a "male" substance. Likewise, the coca that the neophytes eat from the beeswax gourd can be seen variously as a "male" seminal substance emanating from a "male" source, which grows the young men's bodies in a same-sex relation, or as that substance in its "female," milk-like form, emanating from a "maternal" shaman who stands in a cross-sex relation to the neophytes and who feeds them as her "sons." Both "readings" are consistent with ethnographic evidence that, on quite different grounds, suggests the androgynous character of the shaman (see S. Hugh-Jones 1979, 125–126) and that mirrors the explicitly androgynous status of the beeswax gourd as both male skull and female genitals (see above).

Let me now turn to the neophytes' postinitiation diet of manioc starch and the requirement that they must vomit out the "dirt" from their bodies. Given the associations between starch and semen explored above, a diet of starch can be seen as yet another manifestation of the flow of semen from seniors to neophytes, a flow that represents the clan as a collective body, extends this body via the boys, and prepares them for fatherhood as semen- and flute-endowed men. But here it might be objected that the flow now comes from an "adoptive mother"—a woman not a man. Two things suggest that this "adoptive mother" stands in a single-sex, "male" relationship to the boys. First, she is specifically an agnatic relative who stands as a father's sister to her brother's sons. She is thus a metonymic extension of the collective male group. Second, her supplying of starch bread is described not as an act of "feeding" (*eka-*) but rather as one of "growing" (*bikio*) or "adopting" (*~basoo-*). The significance of this contrast emerges more clearly in relation to pets. *Eka-* applies not only to "feeding" but also to the taming or domestication of wild animals and implies a difference of identity between feeder and fed. When human beings are adopted, the emphasis is on the identity between the two parties, which is reflected in the literal meaning of ~*basoo-*, "to make human." In conclusion, it would appear that what the ~*basolio* provides is clan "seminal" substance, but this time not in its "male" form as a "non-food" but in its female form as "agnatic food" or blood, a recognition of the agnatic blood that circulates in the bodies of clan sisters.

As Strathern shows for the Sambia and Gimi, the same act of vomiting can be seen in different lights depending on nuances of ethnographic detail and on the perspective that is adopted. Here I shall use her analysis to suggest three possible interpretations for the Barasana practice mentioned above. The "dirt" that is cleansed by vomiting is specifically associated with food; this is made clear in relationship to yagé. Yagé and food are emphatically incompatible. One must always empty one's body of food ("dirt") before drinking yagé, and the drink itself induces further vomiting. Coming from the women who process and cook it, eating food would appear to imply an equation with the maternal body—though I have never heard it stated in such bald terms. If this is so, then the men's, and particularly the neophytes', vomiting can be understood as one part of the more general process whereby the men constitute themselves as an all-male, single-sex collectivity metaphorically identified with the body of the clan and clan ancestors. This they do by detaching themselves from women. At the same time, in the neophytes' case, this vomiting can also be seen as part of the process whereby the senior men substitute themselves for the neophytes' mothers, taking over their maternal role as the suppliers of seminal (non-)foods (see above). By vomiting out their mother's food, the neophytes constitute their bodies as hollow containers ready to receive the seminal substances they are offered.

It is also possible that voiding this "dirt" can be viewed as the getting rid of bad maternal womb blood. This is suggested by the poisonous connotations of such blood. In a Curripaco myth, when Amaru gives birth to Kuai, the ancestor whose body gives rise to the sacred flutes, she puts him in a manioc sieve to separate him from the blood of the birth, an act that mirrors the culinary process in which manioc pulp is washed in a sieve to separate the poisonous juice and sedimented starch from the fibrous portion. The blood becomes a violent poison that can cause hemorrhaging in both men and women (see Journet 1995, 270). The voiding of bad blood is also implied in the gradual cleansing of black paint from the initiates' bodies during seclusion. Womb-blood is described as being dark or black, and it is likened to a black sauce made from caramelized manioc juice (C. Hugh-Jones 1979, 224). The substitution of black paint by red paint (directly identified with life-giving, circulatory blood) at the end of seclusion would thus mark the successful conclusion of this change of blood.

However, the story recounted above, in which a male ancestor detotalizes himself by vomiting his male children from his body, would also suggest that vomiting is equivalent to ejaculation. Here vomit appears not as maternal "dirt" but as paternal semen, the initiates' vomiting prefiguring their future role as husbands and fathers. More abstractly, vomiting, a reversal of the flow of substances through the gut, can also be understood as a general metaphor of potency and production. Quite apart from being a commonplace of everyday experience, the image of sound, semen, food, milk, vomit, fruits, and children spewing forth from various tubes is central to much of the mythology to which I have alluded. The myths teach that all such productions form part of the essential processes of life and that each partakes of the other. The gender of these tubes and of the substances they emit is not intrinsic but depends on the context of use and on the identity of the user.

In the closing phase of the rite, each sex reveals the abundant productions of their different containers to the members of the opposite sex. The men reveal the handsome initiates they have produced in the house body of their clan, and the initiates reveal the piles of baskets woven in their enclosure. The women too reveal the products of their own "gestations"—red paint and garters, a trough full of manioc beer, and a splendid pile of manioc bread. A panache of red macaw tails on top of this pile draws attention to the affinities between manioc starch and blood, the same substance that, in paint form, the women smear on the emerging neophytes' bodies. What each has produced as a single-sex collectivity they now display to the other, entering into cross-sex exchanges mediated by the products of their hidden work.

I could continue in this vein, applying the appropriate Strathernian vocabulary to each of these and several other transactions—of flutes, feathers, names, and neophytes—exploring in detail different cross-sex and same-sex gender perspectives from which they might be viewed. But I hesitate to do so. Having already made the point, to go on would amount to no more than an exercise of ethnographic painting-by-numbers. I also hesitate because, like all such exercises, this one can be taken too far. Barasana people would be horrified by the parallels I have drawn between their own metaphoric subtleties and the literal-minded practices of the Sambia. But, the latter aside, some of their shamans might well accept much of my rendering of the material given above precisely because it is "there"—in the myths, the ritual acts, the language, and the jokes. But putting them together and pursuing their implications depends on individual perspective, both theirs and mine. For them, such issues are shrouded in secrecy both because their implications are potent, dangerous, and worrisome and because, beyond a certain point, there are no commonly accepted dogmas, only individual speculation. Some things are better thought than said or done.

To conclude, I have said enough to indicate that, like those of the Sambia initiation cult, the exchanges in Barasana initiation can be described, in

Strathernian terms, as promoting the internal replication of lineal, clan substance through the flow of partible objects (boys, flutes, coca, yagé) between
the members of a single-sex, all-male cult group in such a way that the neophytes emerge as extensions of the clan and as signs of its internal strength
and growth. Putting the clan's genesis into reverse, the flute men constitute
themselves as the retotalized male ancestor who comes to adopt the neophytes
as his "sons," substituting himself for the neophytes' individual mothers and
incorporating them into a collective body. The value of seeing initiation in
these terms lies not in recycling old material through a new vocabulary but in
my knowledge that this kind of comparison has helped me to better understand NWA ethnography and in my hope that it will also suggest avenues for
future comparison. In addition, I would now be very hesitant to accept my
own or anyone else's claim that Amazonian secret flute cults are simply or
straightforwardly "about" men's domination of women and their appropriation or mimicking of female reproduction. If they are about that, they are also
about several other things that render this view problematic and coexist with
it in a contradictory and tense relation.

I now turn from initiation to ceremonial exchange, from clanship to kinship, shifting my focus away from the Tukanoans toward the Arawakans and,
comparatively, away from the Sambia toward the Daribi.

DANGEROUS FISH AND STERILE BEER

Ceremonial exchanges between affinally related communities occur throughout the NWA region. Overall, these exchanges conform to a common pattern.
People from one community visit their affines in another community, bringing them gifts and dancing in their house. In return, the host community prepares a large quantity of manioc beer, which is consumed during the dance.
Later, the tables are turned. The erstwhile hosts now bring a reciprocal gift to
the initial donors in their place of residence, dancing in return for the beer
supplied by their hosts. The proceedings unfold in a characteristic pattern,
which serves to transform the relationship between the two parties from one
of separation to one of mutuality. When they arrive, the guests are treated like
strangers or potential enemies and remain firmly separated from their hosts.
They do not enter the house, they dance alone on the cleared patio under the
watchful and critical eyes of their hosts, and they sleep outside in temporary
shelters.

In the morning, after presenting their gifts, the guests come inside the house
to dance but still sit apart from their hosts as a clearly separate group. The atmosphere is initially one of tense formality mixed with ambivalent sexual in-
nuendo, flirtation, and aggression, but, as the time goes by, things become
more relaxed and easygoing. Hosts and guests now sit and dance together, and
boisterous hilarity and gossiping increasingly drown out the drawn-out sessions

of formally chanted greetings and recitations of ancestral pedigree that earlier formed the main style of communication. By the end of the feast, visitors and residents form a single, undifferentiated group. They eat together as a single commensal community, and the initial gift is redistributed to hosts and guests alike (see Hugh-Jones 1995, 233). These gatherings are also marked by an emphasis on sexuality, which is manifest in jokes, in flirtations and seductions, in the form and significance of the dancing, and in the layered symbolism of the different musical performances. This sexuality promotes the fertility of humans, animals, and fishes, and of animal species, and ensures an abundance of manioc in the gardens (see also Hill 1987 and Journet 1995, 266).

Despite this common pattern, there are some significant variations as to who gives what and to whom among the peoples living in different parts of NWA. In the south, among the Tukanoan Barasana and their neighbors, ceremonial gifts between affines are almost always restricted to items of food, principally smoked fish and smoked meat—hence the expression "food-giving house." The exchanges can be viewed from two perspectives. On any one occasion, the visitors, as wife takers (WTs), bring a "male" protein gift and receive "female" manioc products—beer and bread—from their hosts and wife givers (WGs) in return. This exchange parallels the domestic exchanges of protein and manioc between husband and wife (see Hugh-Jones 1995a). It also parallels the supply of meat and fish that a son-in-law provides for his wife's father in brideservice, a parallel enshrined in myth. Yeba, an uncivilized jaguar, marries Yawira, the daughter of Fish Anaconda and the head of the Fish People. Fish Anaconda provides Yeba with the manioc and other cultivated plants that he previously lacked. The plants are themselves Yawira and her sisters. In return, at the first and prototypical ceremonial exchange, Yeba kills game animals, his own people, and gives their meat to his father-in-law. As the myth suggests, from this perspective the ceremonial exchange celebrates a particular marriage and is built around a precise set of kin relations.

However, seen from another perspective, this short-term, asymmetrical exchange is but one half of a longer-term, symmetrical and reciprocal exchange of protein items, ideally meat for fish but sometimes one species of meat or fish for another—what matters is that they should differ in some way. The reversibility of these exchanges is consistent with the fact that, given the Tukanoan preference for direct sister-exchange, in global terms each clan is simultaneously WG and WT to its affines. Thus we find, for example, that whereas the Desana consider themselves "male" in relation to their "female" Pira-Tapuyo WGs, the Pira-Tapuyo see things the other way round (Reichel-Dolmatoff 1971, 18). From this more global perspective, the exchange underscores the ongoing relationship between affinally related clan-based communities. It also allows people to disembed exchange from its kinship matrix and talk of different food items as circulating against each other in an independent sphere—like a nonincremental version of the Hagener's *moka*.

This is even more marked among the Tukanoan and Arawakan groups living further north. Here, in addition to exchanges of food, we find exchanges of manufactured goods associated with a specialized production of particular items—baskets, sieves, stools, paint, manioc graters, and so forth—by different groups. The system remains poorly understood, partly because it has been substantially affected by contact with outsiders and partly because the extant accounts tend, on the one hand, to view it from a utilitarian perspective as barter trade associated with unequal resource distribution and, on the other, to mix up a theoretical, "totemic" allocation of goods to groups with the realities of what people actually produce and exchange (see also Hugh-Jones 1992). For present purposes, it is sufficient to note that the items exchanged are "gender-marked" both as the products of men and women (as in the basketry and red paint mentioned above) and as coming from WG or WT groups. Barasana refer to such exchanges in their myths, but in practice they exchange manufactured goods on an individual basis and in nonceremonial contexts. The only exception to this rule is a ritualized exchange of feather ornaments that sets up a special relationship—*hee* ~*teyia*—between two groups. Besides "secret flutes," *hee* refers to all things connected with the ancestral state, while ~*teyia* means "in-laws" or "affines." This expression and the form of the exchange are indicative of the unrealized potential of feather ornaments as items of bridewealth.

The Wakuénai have yet another variant. Here an opening, male-owned gift of smoked fish or meat is matched by a closing, female-owned gift of processed manioc pulp. Hill suggests that the difference between this Arawakan exchange of smoked protein for raw vegetable products and Tukanoan exchanges of foods of the same kind reflects a difference in their respective marriage patterns. The Wakuénai prefer marriage with distant cousins or nonrelatives and emphasize brideservice as a compensation for the loss of female labor. Ceremonial exchange, "a loaning of the products of male labor to affinal sibs before a later repayment in the form of the products of female labor" is seen as "a symbolic enactment in miniature of the practice of brideservice, a loaning of male labor in exchange for the eventual loss of female labor" (1987, 189). In the Tukano case, a preference for sister exchange and close-cousin marriage means that "the same principle of direct, reciprocal exchange is evident in food exchange as in marriage" (1987, 190). In addition, whereas all Wakuénai affinal relations are tinged with ambiguity and contradiction, the Tukanoans polarize between balanced reciprocity with closely related affinal sibs and negative reciprocity between distant or unrelated affines. Finally, the equality of value between the male- and female-owned gifts of meat and manioc is taken to indicate that "the relative value attributed to women's horticultural products and to the status of women is somewhat higher among the Wakuénai than among their Tukanoan neighbors" (1987, 191).

This is one reading of the gender of these gifts. Following Strathern on Melanesia and Journet on the Curripaco, I want to suggest another. Superficially at least, it would appear that for both Wakuénai and Tukanoans, the difference between WTs and WGs is signaled by the gendered difference in what they exchange: male-produced, male-owned fish or meat from the WTs in return for female-produced, female-owned manioc beer from the WGs. This was the conclusion I reached in an earlier work (Hugh-Jones 1995a). However, a number of things would suggest that the issue of gender is considerably more complex. To begin with, there is the androgyny of both fish and manioc discussed above. The "ownership" of manioc and its products is also ambiguous. A woman's manioc is grown in her husband's garden, and the division of labor between them involves a set of unmediated cross-sex exchanges, their joint input into the final product. In addition, when manioc beer is distributed during the exchange rites, it is the men who distribute it, and they do so in their own name. Manioc could thus be subjected to a set of gender permutations similar to those which Strathern applies to Melanesian data. It is at once "male" as a single-sex extension of the male garden owner, "female" as something ("children") that women produce in single-sex replication, and "cross-sex" as the product of unmediated cross-sex exchanges. Finally there is Journet's report that, in addition to bringing "male" fish, the visitors at Curripaco ceremonial exchanges may also bring pottery, while the hosts may provide their guests with presents of baskets (1995, 262). As we have already seen, basketry is a "male" product; pots are made by women, and, throughout the region, much metaphorical play is made on the analogy between cooking pots and gestating wombs. Thus "male" guests may also bring "female" gifts, and "female" hosts may provide "male" countergifts.

I shall follow Journet's (1995, 253ff.) analysis in what follows. The Curripaco view ceremonial exchanges as being organized around a core set of kinship relations, namely those between a father, his daughter, and his son-in-law, as in the Barasana myth of Yeba and Fish Anaconda. The paradigmatic Curripaco exchange occurs as a man's acknowledgment and celebration of his daughter's marriage. He invites his daughter, now living in another community, to prepare manioc beer for him, promising her and her husband a gift of fish in return. Assisted by his brothers and sons, he marshals the necessary fish, while his daughter, for her part, makes the beer, sometimes counting on her co-wives and female in-laws to help out.

The daughter's role in supplying beer for her father is prefigured in the rite she undergoes at puberty. At the onset of menstruation she spends a month secluded in a compartment, eating a diet that is initially very restricted and later less so. Journet gives no details, but I think we can say with confidence that it will be like that of male Barasana neophytes: manioc starch and small, bloodless creatures but no fish. The secluded girl must keep herself very busy making decorated pottery, the counterpart of the young men's baskets and their complement in the processing of manioc. At the festival marking the end of seclusion, the girl offers her father and brothers manioc beer and pottery. In return, her father and other male agnates offer her an abundance of smoked fish.

The father's orchestration of his daughter's seclusion serves to establish his control over her menstrual cycle and thus over her fertility. His control extends to the well-being of his daughter's children. If the children should die, the daughter's husband may accuse his father-in-law of killing them out of spite. The fish that the father gives his daughter are also implicated in her fertility. Eating fish both signals and contributes to a woman's fertility. Menstruating (i.e., infertile) women do not eat fish, and fish spirits are often held responsible for menstrual problems, abortions, stillbirths, and neonatal deaths. The fish take human children in revenge for their own fish children that humans catch and eat. The fish-giving father, with power over the life of his daughter's children, is himself like a fish spirit.

If the father's gifts of fish are both sign and vehicle of his control over her blood and fertility, the daughter's gifts of beer and pottery can likewise be understood as manifestations of her capacities as a wife and mother who will transform or "cook" her husband's semen and manioc tubers into children, bread, and beer. Just as her father and his fish imply the potential to both create and destroy life, so also do she and her beer imply a potential control over life and death. Like their Melpa sisters, women in NWA are "women-in-between," caught between conflicting loyalties to their own and their husband's kin. Infanticide is both a perceived threat and a real possibility. When babies die, the father may accuse his wife of conspiring in their death; when a wife is angry with her husband or his kin, she may kill her newborn child in revenge.

Beer too stands midway between life and death. On the one hand, the production of beer evokes the metaphors of gestation and birth that surround the processing of all manioc products. Manioc tubers, the "children" of men and women, are first separated into their component parts: fibers, juice, and starch, which stand in analogical relation to bones, blood, and semen. These parts are then reassembled and cooked into different foodstuffs in a process likened to the creation and birth of children, the products of transformed semen and blood (C. Hugh-Jones 1979). On the other hand, beer itself lies at the extreme end of this culinary process. It is made from manioc bread burned to a toast, mixed with manioc juice, which is poisonous when raw, and then allowed to ferment. Curripaco are explicit in describing beer as "rotten" and are ambivalent about its strong taste (Journet 1995, 271). People also use beer as the favored vehicle for delivering poison to their enemies.

Bearing these points in mind, let us return to the parallel between puberty rites and ceremonial exchange. At puberty, a girl prepares beer from her father's manioc and gives it to him in return for his fish; on marriage, she makes beer from her husband's manioc and gives it to her father in return for his fish. The husband has thus substituted himself for the father as the source of the woman's manioc. As Journet makes clear, it is precisely this substitution that is played out in brideservice. Globally, at the level of interclan relations, women are said to be exchanged for other women, and, from the perspective of a father, the daughter-in-law he gains may be a replacement for the daughter he loses. But from the perspective of a new husband, wife and sister are not equivalent: his wife will provide him with the children, but his sister cannot. Before his father-in-law will cede his rights over his daughter's children, the husband must demonstrate his capacity to provide for her. This he does by making a manioc garden for his wife's parents and by providing them with fish and meat (Journet 1995, 238–241).

The exchange of fish for beer can thus be understood in two ways. On the one hand, seen prospectively, the exchange can be understood in terms of sexual complementarity. The new wife offers beer to her agnates as a sign of her own fertility. Like her children, the beer is a transformed, "female" form of her husband's semen/manioc. Her agnates contribute a complementary "male" substance in the form of fish. The Curripaco say that fish "call" manioc and guarantee the abundant harvests needed to supply quantities of beer (1955, 266); by implication they also call forth many children. These children will belong to the husband, as does the beer made from his manioc and distributed by him. On the other hand, seen retrospectively, the beer can also be understood as a recognition of the power that a woman's agnates still hold over her children, a power contained in the blood they share with her. In the beer they are given, they receive in "rotten," substitute form what they might otherwise claim for real: their sister's or daughter's spoiled fertility in the form of unproductive blood and stillborn children.

During the rite, the guests incarnate the spirits of the fish they bring. These fish spirits also threaten to claim their due by taking their "children"—the fish the guests have killed and now offer to their hosts as a present. For their part, the hosts incarnate terrestrial animals who offer their children in the form of manioc and beer. Each party thus offers to the other as "food" what to themselves represents their own "children." Like the delicious but potentially lethal fish offered by the guests, the hosts' beer also carries a double message: wholesome drink or vehicle of poison. Through its staged transformation of potential hostility into a relation of mutual trust, the rite enacts the creation of the good faith upon which its success depends.

The visitors at Tukanoan exchange feasts frequently vomit out the beer they are offered. In part this is an effect of the yagé they drink. Sometimes it is also the only way they can avoid losing face by failing to finish what their hosts offer them. From one perspective, this vomiting can also be understood as the voiding of a potentially lethal substance that is also tantamount to poisonous blood, but it can also be seen in a more positive light. The beer is served from a large trough hollowed from a trunk of wood in the manner of a canoe. The Desana name for the anaconda in which the ancestors traveled prior to being spewed out as human "sons," ~*pabiri gasiru* ("fermentation canoe"), suggests that this beer trough is none other than the ancestral anaconda itself. In order to enhance the fermentation of beer, the women first chew and spit out some of the ingredients, using their saliva to convert starch to sugar. If fermentation is a form of gestation, vomiting beer and spitting out chewed manioc would appear to be signs of male and female fertility that play upon beer as an ambiguously gendered substance.[12]

In conclusion, Journet's account of Curripaco ceremonial exchange is consistent with Hill's argument that Arawakan ceremonial exchange is intimately linked with brideservice. However, despite the fact that they prefer close-cousin marriage, the Barasana myth of Yeba and Fish Anaconda (and much other evidence not given here) makes it clear that this is true of the Tukanoans as well. This myth inverts Journet's account: instead of WGs who incarnate the fish they bring to their sister and brothers-in-law, with the latter as incarnations of terrestrial animals, we have a WT, Yeba, himself a terrestrial jaguar, who brings his own slaughtered kin, in the form of meat, to present to his father-in-law, Fish Anaconda, the father of the fishes. The rite and the myth, as two moments in the same process, revolve around the same set of kin relations and draw on a common natural idiom.

Instead of Hill's suggestion that the difference between Arawakan asymmetrical food exchange and Tukanoan symmetrical exchange is correlated with the former's preference for distant marriage and brideservice and the latter's preference for close sister-exchange (see above), I would rather see them as different possibilities allowed by the same overall system and seen from two different perspectives. Like symmetrical exchanges of food and goods, sister exchange represents the global, clan-based perspective of affinity. Here exchanges are all of a kind but in different spheres: food for food, goods for goods, women for women. But from a local, kin-based perspective, they appear less as affinal exchanges of food, women, or labor and more as asymmetrical transactions between particular individuals involved in the production of wives and mothers, husbands and fathers, which bring about the particular marriages around which collective affinal relations are built. To treat such exchanges through the commodity logic of "loan" and "repayment" masks a gift logic in which husbands substitute for fathers and beer substitutes for children and in which clan sisters and male semen are exchanged as the detachable components of persons. Northwest Amazonians do indeed speak of their gifts as being male- and female-owned, but, without going further into the details of their various permutations as cross- or single-sex, mediated or unmediated, I hope that I have said enough to indicate that the gender of such gifts is in fact more complex.

CONCLUSION

By way of some comparative conclusions, I turn first to Wagner's (1977) paper on Daribi analogical kinship. If Barasana initiation, as manifesting an un-mediated flow of semen within a collective all-male group, shows parallels with the Sambia flute cult, there are also clear parallels between NWA affinal exchanges and those of the Daribi. As for the Tukanoans, Daribi embryos re-sult from a double parental contribution that is manifest in the substance flow of both father's (semen) and mother's (blood) linealities. Flows of detached, partible women, meat, or shells between wife-exchanging units of different substance stand in opposition to an internal, lineal flow of common semen within the clan. Meat, as an externalized, partible equivalent of semen, is both given out and consumed to increase internal vitality. WTs represent their flow to both their own offspring and to their WGs as a flow of maleness, giv-ing the latter meat or male products. They regard the lineal flow of their WGs as a flow of female substance, and, along with wives, they receive female wealth-items from them. The WGs themselves regard their gifts of women as a lineal flow of "male" substance but represent it as "female" in the gifts they give, thus distinguishing it from the male flow that passes to their offspring. "Women [thus] emerge as the detachable objects of mediation [who] embody a male flow from their kinsmen that the husband's kin interpret as female flow. Departing from their kinsmen as metonymic gifts, . . . they present them-selves to their affines as metaphoric gifts, totalizing the identity of the mater-nal connection" (Strathern 1988, 372 n., 207–208).

Remove shells, add fish, and substitute the appropriate male and female products, and Strathern's paraphrase of Wagner's Daribi could well be a sum-mary of Tukanoan ceremonial exchange. But there are also some important differences. Unlike the Tukanoans, Daribi prefer leviratic marriage and avoid marriage with close kin, features reflected in a terminological identification between a man's sister's child and his own child. Furthermore, whereas north-west Amazonians reapply the original distinction between paternal and ma-ternal linealities (or "WTs" and "WGs") in the next generation in accord with their preference for repeated, close marriages, the Daribi pay "childprice" to set up a new differentiation between the two linealities in each generation (Wagner 1977, 641). But even here the parallel holds good. The Curripaco son-in-law's (WT) gift of beer, a detached, partible equivalent of the sub-stance flow that unites father and daughter, deflects the father-in-law's power to curse his daughter's children. If it is not explicitly recognized as such, it is nonetheless the analogue of the Daribi "childprice."

Another difference is, of course, that the Daribi "have" bridewealth, while NWA groups "have" brideservice instead. Without denying the institutional consequences that can result from this "presence," it is still true that behind this supposedly radical contrast lie some important points in common. For the

Tukanoans, as for the Daribi, women "are defined as extractable from their natal kin by virtue of being owed to another," and in both cases they "reify partible components of male identity" (Strathern 1988, 228, 229). Nowhere in Amazonia does the direct substitutability of wealth for women reach Melanesian proportions, but in NWA ceremonial exchange, both food and wealth items appear to substitute for aspects of female identity, albeit to a more limited extent. Above all, in view of the more than superficial parallels between Barasana and Sambia initiation and between NWA and Daribi ceremonial exchange, I would not accept Collier and Rosaldo's view that "the apparent commonalities among certain bridewealth and brideservice peoples—in terms of polygyny, gerontocracy and exclusive male ritual practice and so on—are . . . the product of distinctive processes in . . . radically different social formations" (1981, 280).

Wagner's essay on Daribi analogic kinship is also a critique of a descent theory that assumes that lineages are a manifestation of analytically prior or given connections. Instead, he argues that lineality must be continuously produced by limiting and constraining the analogical flow of kinship, which would otherwise render all kinship relations alike. Seen in this way, "descent groups" too appear not as "things" that some groups "have" and others lack but rather as the outcome of the same kind of contrived differentiations that, in other regimes, produce different outcomes. This critique links up with that of Strathern when she observes that, in their conflation of kinship with descent, anthropologists have swallowed the indigenous rhetoric that treats collective clan action as if it were kinship writ large rather than a specific transformation of the particularities of kinship (1988, 257). In the analysis of "secret flute cults," the conflation of collective clan relations with "kinship" or "social structure" often goes together with the argument, first proposed by Allen (1967) for Melanesia and Murphy (1959) for Amazonia, that the cults themselves are a reflection of the divisive presence of in-married women in exogamous patrilineal regimes and a ritualized manifestation of a male-dominated and male-produced "social structure." I myself argued along these lines in my original account (1979) of Barasana initiation. But I am not alone. Much of the analysis of NWA kinship has suffered from treating the mythopolitical rhetoric of collective male ritual, linguistic exogamy, and interclan relations as "social structure" rather than as being an alternative, transformed mode of domestic sociality; a later paper (Hugh-Jones 1995a) was offered as a partial corrective to this view.

As part of her comparison between the peoples of the eastern and western New Guinea highlands, Strathern suggests that whereas the collective initiation and marriage rituals of the Sambia and Gimi appear as "an adjunct to the way in which kinship produces more kinship," in the Hagen case "male collective life appears to create (political) forms of its own" (1988, 261). This distinction is allied to Gregory's contrast between restricted, balanced exchange and incremental, delayed exchange of wealth items, and to Godelier's contrast between great-men and big-men systems, which goes together with that between direct sister exchange and marriage exchanges mediated by bridewealth. Part of my aim in comparing initiation cults and ceremonial exchange in NWA has been to suggest that, despite the near absence of bridewealth and incremental exchange, such distinctions might also usefully be applied in Amazonia.

Viewed from this perspective, and inserting them into a wider, imaginary "Melanesia," the peoples of NWA might be described as falling midway between the eastern and western highland "types." If their initiation cults are concerned with the production of kinship, they are equally concerned with the production of clanship through the ritual construction of an all-male collectivity conceived of as a single male body separated from others by a rule of exogamy and by its detachable sisters. It is precisely this which underlies the unique (for Amazonia) "patrilineal" cast of NWA social systems. Furthermore, while ceremonial exchanges are built around particular marriages and here involve asymmetries between the parties involved, there is much slippage between the perspectives of kinship and clanship. As in the Hagen case, on a collective level, male affines behave as though they were equal exchange partners, and the evidence suggests that, in some contexts, the ceremonial exchange of wealth items takes on a life of its own as a relatively detached and independent sphere.

This emergence of ceremonial exchange as a self-contained sphere of collective male political activity whose goals and values are relatively independent of relations of kinship and marriage seems to be even more apparent in the Xingu area. As in the western highlands, here too the significant organizational role of ceremonial exchange goes together with the formation of larger groupings (see Strathern 1988, 47). Although not cast in the language of gift exchange, Basso's (1973) and Gregor's (1977) brief accounts of the Xinguano *uluki* ("intervillage trade ceremony, formal barter sessions") suggest something quite similar to the Hageners' ceremonial exchange. In its most prestigious form, the intervillage *uluki* is an exclusively male affair that involves bouts of wrestling followed by the exchange of valuables such as shell belts, necklaces, decorated pots, feather headdresses, bows, and guns, the specialized productions of different groups. The exchanges are sponsored and organized by factional leaders who represent their villages. These leaders, the richest men in their villages, accumulate and distribute wealth in their own right and also orchestrate the exchanges of other villagers, urging them to display the generosity that they themselves exemplify. They are "big men" not only metaphorically but also literally, as men who are physically taller and renowned for their prowess as champion wrestlers (Gregor 1977, 199). Finally, and perhaps uniquely for contemporary Amazonia, the valuables exchanged in the *uluki* also figure as the bridewealth payments that mark a woman's first, arranged marriage (Basso 1973, 88, 96).

In sum, in both NWA and the Xingu region, we find secret flute cults and systems of ceremonial exchange. In the former case, these are associated with "patrilineal descent," with both brideservice and an ideal of direct exchange of women in marriage. In the latter case, they are associated with a bilateral, cognatic emphasis, with an ideal of repeated but more distant marriage exchanges between kin groups, and with the simultaneous presence of both brideservice and bridewealth.[13] However, the lesson of these presences and absences should not be to encourage an analysis in terms of variation but rather to suggest that, as in the case of Strathern's Melanesia, these permutations are better seen as the expressions of a common underlying logic. Although space does not allow a full analysis of the Xingu data, my analysis of NWA material suggests that, there too, the logic is one of gift exchange in the extended Strathernian sense.

And that brings me to the subject of gender. Thus far, and when compared to Melanesia, gender and gift exchange have played relatively minor roles in the Amazonianists' analytic tool kit; understood in Strathern's sense, they have not figured at all. Where gender does figure, most prominently in the analysis of secret flute cults, it has been seen as an inherent attribute of whole men and women. As Descola (Chapter 5) explains, understood in this sense, gender takes its place alongside a set of other contrasts—consanguine/affine, close/distant, center/periphery, inside/outside—under which it is often subsumed. The contrast between predator and prey, which has proven so useful in the Amazonian context (Descola 1993, Viveiros de Castro 1993a), also forms part of this set. This contrast, itself intimately linked with the absence of domestic animals and with a corresponding emphasis on hunting, gives Amazonian systems a characteristic inflection that appears to be less evident in Melanesia. However, precisely in NWA and in the Xingu region, where ceremonial exchange goes hand in hand with the development of integrated regional polities, attitudes toward hunting take on a different character than those elsewhere in Amazonia (see Hugh-Jones 1996).

In an effort to move things forward, I have used Strathern's destabilization of analyses of Melanesian men's cults experimentally to destabilize my own (1979) Amazonian version. In doing this, I do not wish to imply that my previous analysis, or those of other colleagues, are wrong, merely that in looking at the same phenomena from several different angles, each perspective is nuanced and enriched by the other. Externally, the phenomena in question, men's cults and their associated mythology, display considerable variation between our two regions. Internally, each is a complex, multifaceted whole anchored within the wider historically specific culture, experience, and way of life of a given group of people. To some extent, the cults and myths are indeed formally and logically ordered—were this not so, anthropologists would not have recognized the common cultural patterns they do. But as Gregor and Tuzin (Chapter 13) make clear, they also disorder and subvert, describing or physically enacting attitudes and behavior that are simultaneously violent, aggressive, terrifying, attractive, exciting, and arousing. These emotionally charged acts are accompanied and enhanced by an overt display of sexualized oedipal themes that create an atmosphere of contradiction and moral ambivalence. To these performances, each participant, included or excluded, male or female, senior or junior, savant or fool, brings his or her own perspective, which he or she may then share, in part, with inquisitive anthropologists. Combining these tangled or interwoven perspectives with their own, anthropologists construct their analyses, each one an approximation of something that "says" and "does" many things at once and for which there can be no one true account.

Comparing data from one region with those from another within a common analytical frame, be it social structure, gender politics, personality dynamics, psychoanalysis, or any combination thereof, anthropologists have already made considerable progress in making sense of Melanesian and Amazonian men's cults. In the Amazonian context, what is interesting about Strathern's perspective is precisely that it is not the same as these other perspectives but different from them. But the issues of gender politics, sexuality, or psychodynamics are not thereby laid to rest. I am not fully convinced by, or perhaps do not fully understand, Strathern's (1988, 325 ff.) discussion of domination, and, in my view, a satisfactory squaring of her perspective with those that have gone before is work that remains to be done.

NOTES

I dedicate this piece to the memory of Alfred Gell, with whom I discovered anthropology as a schoolboy and without whose wisdom this paper would not have been written. For their comments and criticisms, I especially want to thank Aletta Biersack, Tom Gregor, and Donald Tuzin.

1. I use the ethnographic present intentionally to indicate the abstract, ahistorical, and "floating" nature of any such broadscale comparison.

2. See Hugh-Jones (1995a) for a recent Amazonian contribution.

3. See, for example, Gregor (1985), S. Hugh-Jones (1979), Jackson (1996), Murphy (1959), Murphy and Murphy (1974), and Nadelson (1981).

4. Full versions of the myths to which I allude are given in S. Hugh-Jones (1979, 262–308).

5. See Bamberger (1974) for Amazonia and Gewertz (1988) for Melanesia.

6. Despite being cast in a different idiom, there are some very obvious parallels between Strathern's analysis of tubes and containers and Lévi-Strauss's discussions of the same theme in Amerindian myth (Lévi-Strauss 1985).

7. Also relevant are Cecila Busby's remarks (1997a, 32–33) on the importance of distinguishing between intuitive, practice-based knowledge and reflexive, intellectualized discourse in relation to native theories of procreation.

8. Scarification and bleeding of women occurs only in exceptional circumstances—after an eclipse, and prior to a ritual of role reversal during which women wrestle (Gregor, personal communication).

9. A hallucinogenic drink prepared from the *Banisteriopsis caapi* vine.

10. See C. and S. Hugh-Jones (1993).

11. Thus *badi* is both "fruit of Erisma japura" and "semen, bone marrow"; ~*ree badi* is "*Mauritia flexuosa* pulp"; *siti* is both "umari (*Poraqueiba sericea*) seed pulp" and slang for "penis"; *iye* is both "fruit of *Porouma cecropiaefolia*" and "oil, grease, energy"; the pips of *toa* (unidentified) are squeezed between thumb and index finger and "shot" at private parts in a game between the sexes.

12. See also Viveiros de Castro (1992) on the ambiguous gender of Araweté beer and Butt (1958) on the fertile connotations of beer brewing in Guyana.

13. Whether they are bridewealth in the same sense as in Melanesia is a moot point. However, what these Xingu payments and the Tukanoans' use of gifts of feather ornaments to set up relations of ritual affinity both indicate is that, in two areas of Amazonia, the development of regional polities appears to go together with peoples hovering on the brink of creating bridewealth systems. I cannot explain why they went no further, but one wonders what went on in the larger-scale chiefdoms of prehistoric middle Amazonia.

TWELVE

"Strength" and Sexuality: Sexual Avoidance and Masculinity in New Guinea and Amazonia

Paul Roscoe

Paul Roscoe draws upon a large sample of Melazonian cultures in order to examine the correlation between sexual continence, abstinence, and separation, on the one hand, and masculine aggressivity and strength, on the other. Specifically, he argues that "sexual avoidances are part of the means by which males . . . temporarily or more permanently constitute themselves as 'strong.'" Examining the ideology of abstinence among the Yangoru Boiken, Roscoe shows that the essence of masculinity includes not only strength and courage but also a crucial element of "power and menace, of dangerous potency." He finds markedly similar concepts of masculinity both in New Guinea and throughout the Amazonian region, wherein aggression and self-assertive activities are associated with sexual taboos.

Roscoe's broad comparison is particularly effective in that it deals with the concept of masculinity in a well-described ethnographic context. His analytic association of aggression and sexual taboo suggests one way in which men's cults may foster exclusiveness and gender separation (see Biersack, Chapter 4) and may be partly explained by the theoretical perspective developed by Gregor and Tuzin. Although applying its own methodology, Roscoe's chapter has many issues in common with those of Jolly's chapter.

INTRODUCTION

It is often noted but less often discussed that, in many parts of the world, war and hunting are associated with sexual taboos (e.g., Frayser 1985; Hays 1964). This chapter presents data drawn from a larger set to discuss sexual avoidances in Sepik and Highland New Guinea (hereafter "New Guinea") and the Amazon.[1] The relevance of these avoidances to the study of Amazonian and Melanesian gender is the role they play in constructing a type of masculinity conceptualized in terms of "strength," where this may mean not just physical but also social and/or spiritual "strength," an active quality in which men are conceived as powerful and menacing, as being dangerously potent, in literal or metaphoric senses. This vision of masculinity is especially valued, and becomes incandescently manifest, during the activities with which these avoidances are associated.

Pursuing the comparative spirit of this volume, I shall construct this argument using a cross-cultural comparison of coded data. Unfortunately, nowadays this method risks being dismissed as dated positivism. It is difficult to identify with confidence the sources of this pejorative attitude (Roscoe 1995a,d), but it appears to arise from one or both of two related grounds. The first is cultural anthropology's contemporary turn from old-style, scientific anthropology—represented par excellence by holocultural comparativism—to embrace a more interpretative and postmodern anthropology. The pivot for this turn has been cultural anthropology's idiosyncratic notion of positivism coupled with a critique that equates science with positivism; by pointing out the obvious errors of the latter, the approach then pretends to dispose of the former (Roscoe 1995d). The problem here is the colossal error of supposing that positivism adequately describes scientific practice. Science, as most philosophers and sociologists of science (e.g., Feyerabend 1978, 31, 69–80; Latour and Woolgar 1986) have long accepted, is a thoroughly hermeneutic endeavor and, as such, indistinguishable in its essential processes from interpretative and postmodern anthropology (Roscoe 1995d, 494–497). Thus, to dismiss as somehow positivistic the kind of comparative exercise engaged in here is, in effect, to dismiss also contemporary anthropology. Clearly, if contemporary anthropology is to dispose of traditional cross-cultural comparison, then a more nuanced critique is in order.

The second ground for dismissing coded comparison is that it misleads by extracting behaviors or beliefs from their meaningful context. This point is well taken, but it is often pushed to an extreme. Grounded in an assumption that meanings are explanation, it frequently seems to presume that meanings are the *only* explanation, and this is indefensible. Meaning is surely of paramount importance in understanding many aspects of cultural difference—why initiation rites on the Papuan plateau, for example, should involve certain distinctively different practices. In considering beliefs or behaviors that are universal or quasi-universal (e.g., incest avoidance) or occur with high frequency (e.g., initiation per se in politically uncentralized communities), however, it is difficult to maintain that meanings are necessarily the only explanations—as even the most committed symbolic anthropologists have reluctantly conceded (e.g., Schneider 1976, 158–159). When similar behaviors recur in communities widely distributed in space and time, one must suppose either the workings of remarkable coincidence, the operation of multiple end-point probability, or the possibility that signification has been subordinated to other factors (Roscoe 1995a). In this chapter, I review a behavioral and ideational cluster that seems to have widespread occurrence in New Guinea and Amazonia, and I attempt to identify what some of these explanatory phenomena and processes might be.

MALE SEXUAL AVOIDANCE IN NEW GUINEA AND AMAZONIA

The ethnography of sexual avoidance is not readily apparent in the ethnographic record. Perhaps because the phenomenon has never attracted much analytical attention, its ethnography tends toward the afterthought—the footnote or skimpy aside—so it is difficult to assemble a detailed, contextualized picture of sexual avoidance either within or across societies. Tables 12.1, 12.2, and 12.3 summarize some New Guinean and Amazonian data on male sexual avoidances[2] associated with war, hunting, art, ritual, and other activities.[3] These tables suffer all of the problems that accompany codification of ethnographic data. Most problematically, they pluck sexual avoidances from the cultural context within which they are embedded. In a number of societies, for example, men do more than just avoid sexual contact with women in connection with activities such as war and hunting; they avoid all contact with women at these times. Nor do the tables indicate other sexual and nonsexual avoidances that usually accompany those listed. Postpartum sex avoidances seem to be ubiquitous, while food avoidances—especially of meat—commonly accompany sexual avoidances. Codes inevitably also denature the data, a particular problem in the "Ritual" column, where it has been necessary to collapse such disparate phenomena as pig exchange festivals (Manga, Melpa); "fertility" rites (Gahuku, Gende, Anggor); apprenticeship or participation in cults, singing, or dancing (Au, Coastal Arapesh, Maring, Melpa); taking "medicine baths" (Cuna); collecting forest medicines (Cuna); preparing narcotics (Jívaro); and ritual enactments of mythical events (Melpa).

Notwithstanding these limitations, the data do document that sexual avoidances are widely associated with hunting and warfare in New Guinea and Amazonia. Sex is commonly avoided before and/or during hunting and ritual in all three areas, before warfare and gardening in both the Sepik and the highlands, after a homicide in the Amazon, and before and/or during artistic activity and yam growing in the Sepik. Sexual avoidances before fishing, trade, canoe building, and sago processing are sporadically reported.[4]

Although male sexual avoidance is clearly widespread in New Guinea and Amazonia, it would be hazardous to assert a universal association with any specific practice. It most commonly accompanies war, hunting, and ritual—though the capacious definition of the latter category renders its prominence unsurprising. In five instances, there appear to be no hunting-related avoidances: the Bahinemo of the Sepik, the Kalam of the highlands, and the Siriono, Yanomamö, and the Upper Inuya Amahuaca in Amazonia. In the case of the Kalam, Siriono, Yanomamö, and Amahuaca, these exceptions may be related to a comparatively heavy dependence on hunting[5] and the serious disruption of reproduction and subsistence that sexual avoidance consequently would impose. The ethnographic record for a swathe of sweet-

TABLE 12.1 Male Sex Avoidances in the New Guinea Sepik Region

Society	Sex Avoided in Connection with						
	War	Hunting	Fishing	Art	Ritual	Yams	Garden
Abelam							
Eastern				Y^{bd}		Y^{d}	
Central				Y		Y^{d}	
Western						Y^{d}	
Wosera						Y^{d}	
Alamblak	Y^{b}	Y^{b}					
Ama	Y^{b}	Y^{b}					Y^{b}
Anggor		Y^{b}			Y		
Angoram		Y^{b}	Y^{b}				
Arapesh							
Balif	Y			Y	Y	Y	
Coastal	S^{p}, Y	Y, Y^{m}			Y^{m}		
Ilahita		Y^{mb}		Y	Y^{m}		
Kaboibus						Y	
Mountain						Y	
Au	Y^{b}	Y^{b}	Y^{b}		Y^{b}		Y^{b}
Bahinemo		Y^{b}			Y		
Boiken		N					
Nagum	Y^{b}, Y^{mb}	Y^{bd}, Y^{m}			Y^{d}		
Yangoru	S^{b}, Y^{b}, K	Y^{b}			Y^{da}		N
Gnau	Y^{a}	Y^{ba}, Y^{m}	y^{d}	Y^{d}	Y	Y^{d}	Y^{ba}
Iatmul	Y^{b}					Y^{ba}	
Kwanga							
Kwanga		Y^{mb}					
Mende						Y^{d}	
Tau		Y^{b}				N	
Kwoma	Y^{b}			Y^{b}	Y^{a}, Y^{b}		
Manambu	Y			Y^{d}	Y^{d}	N	
Mehek	Y	Y					
Mundugumor		Y				Y^{b}	Y

Murik		y^b				
Namia				y^b		
Sawos					Y^b	
Umeda					Y	Y^d Y^d
Urat	y^{mb}				y^{mb}	Y^d y^{mb}
Urim					Y^b	
Wogeo					Y	Y^b

ABBREVIATIONS: a = sex avoided after; b = sex avoided before; d = sex avoided during; K = sex avoided after having killed; m = sex avoided for magic associated with; N = sex not avoided; n = sex probably not avoided; Sp = sex avoided in connection with sorcery practice; Y = sex avoided; y = sex probably avoided.

NOTES: Abelam-Eastern—Forge 1966, 28; 1967, 75; 1969, 88; 1973, 180; 1990, 168; Abelam-Central—Kaberry 1940–41, 364; 1941–42, 215; Abelam-Western—Scaglion and Condon 1979, 18; Abelam-Wosera—Aufenanger 1972, 162, 315, 402, 418; Gorlin 1973, 70; Alamblak—Edmiston and Edmiston 1989, 26; Ama—Guddemi 1992b, 130, 146; Anggor—Huber 1974, 152, 261 n. 3; 1980, 48; Angoram—Apo 1986, 144; Arapesh-Balif—Macdonald 1992, 66; Arapesh-Coastal—Gerstner 1937, 967, 970, 971; Arapesh-Ilahita—Tuzin 1976, 52, 223; 1978a, 62; 1978b, 84; Arapesh-Kaboibus—Mead 1940, 449; Arapesh-Mountain—Mead 1940, 344, 449, 451; Au—Philsooph 1980, 533, 558; Bahinemo—Dye 1983, 6, 12; Boiken-Nagum—Aufenanger 1972, 170; Gerstner 1952, 179, 180, 181, 184; 1953, 432; Boiken-Yangoru—Pongiura 1993, 11; Roscoe, fieldnotes; Gnau—Lewis 1980, 128–129; Iatmul—Bateson 1932, 436; Hauser-Schäublin 1977, 153, 258; Silverman 1993, 400; Weiss 1994, 246 n. 31; Kwanga-Kwanga—Brison 1992, 191; Kwanga-Mende—Manabe and Manabe 1982, 22; Kwanga-Tau—Obrist van Eeuwijk 1992, 80, 119; Kwoma—Bowden, 1983, 102–103; May and Tuckson 1982, 218; Whiting 1941, 126; Williamson 1975, 383; 1990, 393; Manambu—Harrison 1982, 144; 1996, personal communication; Mehek—Crockett 1979, 56; Mundugumor—McDowell 1991, 118, 119; Murik—Lipset 1984, 326; Namia—Feldpausch and Feldpausch 1988, 24–25; Sawos—Schindlbeck 1980, 122; Umeda—Gell 1975, 117, 168, 253; Urat—Allen 1976, 33; Eyre 1988, 68; Urim—Luoma 1981, 1; Wogeo—Hogbin 1934–35a, 331; 1970, 75, 90, 92.

TABLE 12.2 Male Sex Avoidances in the New Guinea Highlands

	Sex Avoided in Connection with						
Society	War	Hunting	Fishing	Art	Ritual	Garden	Sago
Eastern Highlands							
Awa	Y^{bd}					Y^d	
Baruya`		Y^b, Y^m				Y^b, Y^m	
Bena Bena	Y					Y	
Binumarien							
Fore					$Y^{ma/d}$		
Gadsup	Y^{bd}				So, Y^{mb}		
Gahuku					Y^d		
Gende	Y^b				Y^b		
Gimi	Y^b						
Hua						Y^b	
Kamano	Y^b				So, Y^m		
Ndumba	Y^b	Y^b					
Tairora	Y^{bd}						
Central Highlands							
Chuave					Y^d	Y	
Western Highlands							
Enga							
Kyaka					Y		
Mae					Y		
Raiapu	N						
Gainj						Y^d	
Kalam		N N^b				Y^d	
Manga	Y^m				So, Y^d	Y^d	
Maring	Y^d, Y^m				A^d	Y^d	
Mt. Hagen							
Kaimbi					Y^d		
Melpa	Y^b	Y^b	Y	Y^d	Y^{bd}	Y^d	
Wahgi	Y					Y	

Mountain Ok					
Baktaman	Y^{bd}				
Bimin			Y^d		
Irian Jaya					
Eipo	Y^{bd}	Y^d	Y^d		
Kapauku	Y^d				
Ketengban					
Southern Highlands					
Foi	Y^d	Y^d	Y^d	Y	Y^d
Huli			So^a	Y	
Kewa	N^b, Y^b	Y^{bd}	So, Y^{bd}		
Wiru				Y	
Wola		Y^b	Y^b		
Papuan Plateau					
Etoro	Y^d	Y^d	Y^d	Y^d	Y^d
Kaluli	Y	Y	Y	Y	Y^d

ABBREVIATIONS: a = sex avoided after; b = sex avoided before; d = sex avoided during; m = sex avoided for magic associated with; N = sex not avoided; So = sex avoided in sorcery apprenticeship; Y = sex avoided.

NOTES: Awa—Boyd and Ito 1988, 54, 55, 56; Newman and Boyd 1982, 280; Baktaman—Barth 1975, 150; Baruya—Godelier 1986, 18, 44, 60; Bena Bena—Langness 1967, 173; Bimin—Poole 1981b, 131; Binumarien—Hawkes 1978, 375; Chuave—Warry 1986, 12; Eipo—Schiefenhövel 1982, 154; Enga-Kyaka—Bulmer 1965, 149; Enga-Mae—Meggitt 1957, 49–50; 1964, 210, 223 n. 11; Enga-Raiapu—Waddell 1972, 100; Etoro—Kelly 1976, 43, 45; 1993, 155; Foi—Weiner 1986, 76; 1987, 263; Fore—Lindenbaum 1979, 133; Gadsup—DuToit 1975, 81, 139; Gahuku—Read 1965, 41; Gainj—Johnson 1996, personal communication; Gende—Fitz-Patrick and Kimbuna 1983, 42, 126; Gimi—Gillison 1987, 175; 1991, 192; Hau—Meigs 1976, 402; Huli—Glasse 1968, 101; Kalam—Bulmer 1967, 15, 23 n. 17; Kaluli—Schieffelin 1976, 65, 123; Kamano—Mandeville 1979, 226, 227; Levine 1987, 63; Kapauku—Pospisil 1958, 93, 159; Ketengban—Sims and Sims 1992, 95; Kewa—Josephides 1985, 120; Macdonald 1991, 69, 70, 163; Warus 1986, 50; Manga—Cook 1969, 102; Cook and Pflanz-Cook 1988, 85; Maring—Buchbinder and Rappaport 1976, 20; Lowman-Vayda 1973, 352–353; Rappaport 1968, 134; Healey 1988, 116; Mt. Hagen-Kaimbi—Nelson 1971, 382; Mt. Hagen-Melpa—Asea 1986, 77–78; Brandewie 1981, 125; Strauss 1990 (1962), 44, 224, 321; A. Strathern 1970, 576; 1976, 148; M. Strathern 1972, 165; 1979, 253; Strathern and Strathern 1968, 196–197; 1971, 86, 104, 136–137; Ndumba—Hays and Hays 1982, 207; Tairora—Watson and Watson 1972, 405, 501; Wahgi—O'Hanlon 1989, 34, 42; Wola—Sillitoe 1979, 79; Wiru—A. Strathern 1976, 150.

TABLE 12.3   Male Sex Avoidances in Amazonia

Society	War	Hunting	Fishing	Ritual
Aché				Y^d
Aguaruna				A^d
Amahuaca				
Chumiciniá		Y^b		
U. Inuya		N^{bd}		
Arawete	B^d, K			S^b, A
Bacairi				So^b
Bororo		Y^b		
Canela		Y^d		A
Cashinahua	Y^b	Y/N		A
Cuna			Y^b	Y^b
Jívaro	Y^{mb}, K	Y^d	Y^b	A^d, Y^b
Mehinaku	W^b	Y	Y^b	Y
Mundurucú	K			Y^b
Paez				A^d
Serente	K			
Siriono	n	n	n	N
Sharanahua		N	Y^b	
Tukano				
Barí	Y^b	Y^b		Y^d
Desana		Y^b		$S^b A^{da}$
Wari'	K			
Yanomamö	Y^b?	N		A^d

ABBREVIATIONS: A = sex avoided in connection with shamanic apprenticeship; a = sex avoided after; B = sex avoided in connection with carving bow; b = sex avoided before; d = sex avoided during; K = sex avoided after having killed; m = sex avoided for magic associated with; N = sex not avoided; n = sex probably not avoided; S = sex avoided in connection with shamanic practice; So = sex avoided in sorcery apprenticeship; W = sex avoided in connection with wrestling matches; Y = sex avoided; Y/N = "purification" ritual involving sexual abstinence undertaken if hunting success is poor; Y? = men secluded from women prior to a raid, but unclear if the intent is linked to sex avoidance.

NOTES: Aché—Clastres 1972, 128, cited in Sullivan 1988, 343; Amahuaca—Carneiro 1970, 341 n. 13; Arawete—Viveiros de Castro 1992, 180, 191–192, 240, 361 n. 8, 367 n. 7; Bacairi—Altenfelde Silva 1950, 267; Bororo—Baldus 1937, 145; Canela—Crocker and Crocker 1994, 104, 147; Nimuendajú 1946, 85; Cashinaua—Kensinger 1995, 81, 185, 211; personal communication; Cuna—Nordenskiöld 1938, 344, 391, 489; Jívaro—Descola 1994a, 281–282; De Waverin 1930, 6–7, cited in Sullivan 1988, 502; Descola 1996, personal communication; Harner 1973, 81, 135; Karsten 1935, 216; Mehinaku—1977, 150, 334; 1985, 80, 145, 147, 156, 202; Mundurucú—Murphy 1957, 1025; 1958, 55; Paez—Reichel-Dolmatoff 1975, 52; Serente—Nimuendajú 1967, 78; Sharanahua—Siskind 1973, 114; Siriono—Holmberg 1969, 170; Tukano-Bará—Jackson 1983, 130, 190; Tukano-Desana—Reichel-Dolmatoff 1971, 67, 127, 145, 221, 224, 225; 1975, 77, 82, 85, 117; Wari'—Conklin 1996, 17; Yanomamö—Albert 1985, 356; Chagnon 1968, 52; Good 1991, 74; Ramos 1996, personal communication.

potato-dependent societies in the eastern, central, and western highlands of New Guinea is notable for providing almost no information on hunting-related avoidances, probably because hunting makes "little" or "negligible" contribution to their subsistence, rendering the issue moot.[6] The rarity of fishing-related avoidances in many highland communities may have a similar cause.

Although sexual avoidances are common following homicide in Amazonia, they seem, in comparison to the Sepik and the highlands, significantly less frequent *before* war. To a degree, the difference simply may be an artifact of colonial histories. Whereas in many parts of Amazonia indigenous warfare had declined or disappeared by the turn of this century, it lasted in most of the Sepik until the 1930s to 1950s, and into the 1950s or 1960s in many parts of the highlands. War therefore being a more distant feature on the cultural landscape, Amazonian ethnographers may have been less able than their Melanesian counterparts to collect data about it. In some parts of Amazonia, however, sex avoidance prior to war is absent because of people's peacefulness. The Barasana were sometimes attacked, for example, but they did not themselves launch war—nor probably did they ever—so the opportunity to practice sex abstinence prior to war did not arise (Hugh-Jones, personal communication). The same may be true of the Mehinaku and Siriono, who likewise are sometimes attacked but rarely themselves attack (Gregor 1990b; Holmberg 1969, 11, 157–160).

In New Guinea, where most societies launched war from time to time, the data contain only two instances in which men did not avoid sex prior to war. The Gainj observed no sexual avoidance prior to their occasional, small-scale skirmishes (Johnson, personal communication). Josephides (1985, 120) reports that Kewa warriors actively sought rather than avoided sex prior to battle, but both Macdonald (1991, 69) and Warus (1986, 50) report that Kewa men did avoid sex prior to war, suggesting that there may be subcultural variations in the practice.

As one might expect, sexual avoidances connected to art are most in evidence in the Sepik, long noted as among the most prolific theaters of art production in the so-called tribal world.

Tables 12.1, 12.2, and 12.3 also note, when the information is available, whether sexual avoidance is practiced before, during, or after the activity in question. Practically, it would be somewhat surprising to find sex enjoined during hand-to-hand combat or while chasing after a wild pig. On the other hand, it is less obvious why sex should be avoided during the entire period until fighting has been ceremonially concluded, as among the Gadsup (Du-Toit 1975, 81), or during a hunting trip that might last two or three weeks, as among the Canela (Crocker and Crocker 1994, 147). In some cases, moreover, the distinction between "before" and "during" is ambiguous. In the highlands, for example, where periods of active warfare can last several months,

sex proscriptions *during* this period might mean that warriors actually endeavor to avoid sex *before* skirmishes that might break out at any moment.
Where the information is available, the tables also document whether sexual
avoidance is associated with magic accompanying an activity rather than with
the activity itself.

In addition to the activities listed in the tables, sex avoidances are reported
in connection with making weapons, shields, or arrow poison (Arawete,
Melpa, Jívaro, Yanomamö); visiting warriors who have been wounded in war
(Eipo); funeral periods (Awa, Northern Abelam, Siriono, Yangoru Boiken);
sweat-house ritual (Eastern Highlands); killing and/or eating pigs (Baruya);
handling and/or cooking meat (Mae Enga); salt manufacture (Baruya, Hua,
Kamano); the pandanus nut harvest (Kalam); trading expeditions (Etoro,
Wogeo); house building (Baruya, Etoro, Mehinaku, Wola); the maturation of
sago grubs (Etoro); trying out new axes (Kewa, Melpa, Wola); making hunting nets (Nagum Boiken); making canoes (Murik, Warrau, Wogeo); carving of
slit gongs (Yangoru Boiken); handling of pearl shells (Wiru); magic to attract
wealth (Yangoru Boiken); the role of initiator (Ama, Bena Bena, Eastern
Abelam, Gadsup, Gende, Gimi, Kwoma, Wogeo, Wola); healing of pierced
ears (Canela); and narcotic preparation (Jívaro). In addition, it is sometimes
reported that one should not give food and/or tobacco to others if one has recently had intercourse (Etoro, Hua).[7]

SEXUAL AVOIDANCE AMONG WOMEN

Except in reference to pre- and postpartum observances, the New Guinean
and Amazonian literature provides little evidence that women practice sexual
avoidance to the extent their menfolk do. Since the record is so much a male-
centered document, of course, this conclusion must be treated with caution.
Nevertheless, among the Yangoru Boiken of the Sepik, the subjects of my
own field research, women's activities do emerge as less sexually circumscribed than men's. In contrast to men, women are not obliged to abstain in
connection with such quintessential female tasks as taro cultivation, firewood
gathering, portering, or caring for pigs and children. Nor must they avoid intercourse while manufacturing netbags, contributing to wealth-gathering activities, or participating in most female ritual.

And yet, neither in earlier days nor now are Yangoru women entirely relieved of sexual avoidances. On occasions when her husband has to avoid sex,
a wife is supposed to do likewise, else his projects will not succeed. By her
adultery, she jeopardizes his ability to perform on the battlefield (in earlier
days) and in the hunt (nowadays), though it is apparently not her sexual act
per se that undermines his success but rather the domestic trouble it represents. Similar restrictions are imposed on Abelam wives while their husbands'
long yams are growing and on Mehek wives for their husbands' protection

while hunting or at war. To ensure the success of her husband's trading voyage, a Murik wife must avoid sex during his absence (even though, contrarily, her husband is expected to have intercourse while he is away).[8]

In a few further instances, women are noted as avoiding sex in connection with their own, rather than their husbands', projects. In some parts of Yangoru, women used to help make pig-hunting nets and were expected to remain abstinent while they did—though, because they were usually elders, the issue tended to be moot. Like their husbands, women were obliged to avoid sex during and following the first and second stages of their initiation lest they become worthless individuals given to laziness, gluttony, and promiscuity.[9] Iatmul women observed a similar avoidance during the preparatory phase of a female initiation that apparently existed until contact, and also during dances associated with women's ceremonial. Among the Abelam, women avoided sex during taro growing; among the Rao, before picking greens; on Wogeo, before sago-leaf dying; and among the Kwoma and Barí, during pottery manufacture.[10]

THEORIZING SEXUAL AVOIDANCE

Much of anthropology's general theorizing about "taboo" will be familiar and hardly needs recapitulating here. Suffice it to say, it is an analytical commonplace that taboos are means by which social persons communicate their states or statuses. In Fortes's words, prohibitions and avoidances, be they taboos of African high office or the food, exercise, and sleep observances of the Western athlete, "serve as a means by which a person can account to himself, as well as to the world at large, for the conscientious discharge of his moral obligations" (1966, 82; see also Barth 1975, 163).

In the case of sexual avoidances, some modification of this commonplace is in order. In Melanesia and Amazonia, as in most other societies, sex appears to be among the more private of acts. Thus, the fact that a man is avoiding sex is rather easy for all but the restricted universe of his customary sexual partners to overlook—unless, of course, he publicly trumpets his abstinence, which seems uncommon both in New Guinea and Amazonia. Whatever moral accounting takes place in the case of sexual avoidance, in other words, is probably more to oneself than to the world at large. The fact that a society proscribes sex prior to or during hunting and war may well communicate something about the nature of "hunters" and "warriors" (not to mention "lovers") as *categories*, but the practice of abstinence seems ill-suited to communicating publicly the status of particular hunters and particular warriors (as well as particular lovers).

In his phenomenological reflections on a cut finger, Gell (1979) has argued that sexual and gustatory avoidances do more than just communicate status. They "circumscribe a 'hole' in the texture of shareable intersubjective reality which, privileged with respect to a specific individual, constitutes his soul, or ego, or personality. Taboo does more than express the self: it constitutes the self" (p. 137). I should like to develop these thoughts by arguing that sexual (and perhaps also food) avoidances are not just means by which the self constitutes itself but the means by which it constitutes itself as *a particular kind of self* on temporary or more permanent bases. Specifically, sexual avoidances are part of the means by which males (and, in certain contexts, perhaps also females) temporarily or more permanently constitute themselves as "strong."

I shall arrive at this conclusion from a consideration of two further aspects of sex and sexual avoidance. First, the activities in which sex is avoided are commonly described as activities in which males manifest "strength," "power," or "vitality," terms that may refer not just to physical but also to social and spiritual states and that connote a kind of dangerous potency. Second, excessive or inappropriate sexual activity is commonly depicted as a threat to this "strength," "power," or "vitality." I shall develop the argument first with reference to the case I know best, the Yangoru Boiken, and then tentatively extend it with reference to the broader literature from the Sepik, highlands, and Amazonia. Finally, I shall consider why sexuality should so often be singled out for avoidance and why it is so commonly yoked to the same constellation of activities—namely, hunting, war, art, and so on.

STRENGTH, SEX, AND SEXUAL
AVOIDANCE AMONG THE YANGORU BOIKEN

Among the Yangoru Boiken, activities subject to male sexual avoidance are all spoken of as manifesting *halinya*, the quintessential attribute of masculinity. In Tok Pisin, *halinya* is translated as "strong," and it is easy to gloss the term as "strength." But "strength" only poorly captures the semantic complexity of the term. To begin with, *halinya* means more than just physical strength. To be sure, some activities that manifest *halinya*, such as success in war and hunting, demand a degree of physical stamina and strength, but others such as trapping, art, yam growing, and learning certain magical spells require little or none. These activities manifest *halinya* because they demonstrate cognitive or psychological "strength," in the sense of mental acuity, courage, commitment, and motivation, and/or spiritual "strength," in the sense of being graced by ancestor spirits, who can bring or withhold health and success in such activities as war, hunting, gardening, pig rearing, and wealth gathering.

Second, "strength" does not quite capture an element of power and menace, of dangerous potency, that lies at the core of *halinya* (Roscoe 1995c). Masculinity in Yangoru is embodied in, and conferred by, the minacity of the spear: indeed, the penis—the sine qua non of maleness—is metaphorized as the spear, and vice versa (Roscoe 1994, 59–60). In confronting and killing enemies and wild pigs with their spears, men demonstrate their dangerous potency in direct, physical terms. When they attend a moot, they demonstrate potency in the strapping sons at their side, by the mock spear charges with which they emphasize their arguments, and by the aggressive verbal skill with which they respond to insult.

It must be emphasized most strongly, however, that *halinya* does not refer solely to *physical* violence or threat. Especially within the village, where physical violence should be suppressed, actual belligerence or threatening behavior is usually deplored and often counterproductive. In these contexts, further dimensions of *halinya* become more visible. It emerges as the manifestation, in addition, of a kind of nonviolent power and menace, a dangerous potency expressed in metaphoric rather than literal terms. It is conceptualized as a kind of general aura or bearing, a radiance of potency and danger that is not necessarily directed at anyone in particular. People describe *halinya* men as "hot," by which they mean something vital, powerful, and therefore of value, but something that can also be a danger or a threat if mishandled or mistreated. Thus, by their handsomeness and demeanor, their fine oratory, and their grand food houses, men manifest a brilliance that puts others in their shade and makes them "afraid." With startling salvos from their slit-gongs, identified as their "voices," they broadcast their assertive presence for miles across the landscape. With the pigs (and sometimes yams) they confer on their exchange partner and the shellwealth they contribute to kinship conveyances, they demonstrate an aura of political power and menace. Indeed, gifts of pigs, yams, and shellwealth are symbolically rendered as metaphoric spears thrown at metaphoric enemies (Roscoe 1989, 223–224, 1994, 60). Through the *ka nimbia* spirit houses they construct and the art they lavish on these structures, men also constitute themselves and their descent groups as *affectively* powerful and menacing presences (Roscoe 1995c).

In Yangoru, the male self is not seen as "naturally" *halinya*, nor do acts manifesting dangerous potency come "naturally" to it. Rather, to become and to be capable of manifesting *halinya*, the male self must be transformed through initiation. If males were not initiated, it is said, they would forever remain callow, soft, and weak—physically, psychologically, and spiritually. They would be *fatchik*, "rubbish men," who just wander aimlessly around the bush, their minds unfocused on the tasks of manhood and their beings unable to manifest them. With each initiatory grade, however, initiation renders them increasingly *halinya*. It makes them physically strong; it endows them with minds "clear like water" and a "strong" breath (*yamembi*)—capacities permitting them to "talk" and "organize things"; and it ensures their ardor for the masculine role by making them feel energetic and vigorous, and their limbs and bodies "light," not "heavy." In war, they would skillfully plot and set ambushes while avoiding those of the enemy. They would have the physical and psychological strength to "stand up straight" in a fight. They would be eager and able hunters, able to track pigs through the bush, avoid their snarling jaws and sharp tusks in the confrontation, and spear them with deadly accuracy. At home, they would be ready and able to manifest "strength" in the symbolic wars involving shellwealth and pigs. And they would be able to create affectively powerful carvings and paintings without hopelessly botching the work as would callow youths or women.

As the Yangoru Boiken envisage this initiatory process, it is less a training or conferral of qualities on an existing male self than a literal change in the initiates' constitutions. Initiation, in effect, produces qualitatively new men, or at least men with qualitatively new *penga*, "skins" or "bodies." It transforms them from "cold" quiescence to "hot," dangerous potency. When a Sima village woman insulted her husband's sexuality, the village councilor declared the act an offense, because the husband's body "had seen the Tambaran" (during initiation). Later, he explained that initiation had changed the husband's body, and to insult such a man is to "cut into" this body. Such an insult is called *tua haza*, literally "man cuts": it "cuts into the skin," it "breaks a man open" and "removes the flesh, so there is only a skeleton left, like a house with no roof or walls."

The bodily transformation that Yangoru initiation effects is symbolically enacted in ritual practice. First, the initiates' bodies are symbolically stripped from their bones. In the first, *sumbwi* stage, for example, each initiate enters the *hworumbo* enclosure by crawling along a muddy trench bridged by a tunnel of crossed sticks that initiators could scissor down, pressing the initiate into the mire. The contraption represents a pig's alimentary tract and, as each lad is about to enter the trench, his father calls out to the initiators, "Wild pigs! You eat! I give you this youth. I give you my child now. *You eat his skin and his flesh; leave just his bones for me*, his father!" The rites that follow—beatings, penis bleedings, ingestion of magically empowering substances, exposure to ritual *wala* tableau, and sexual avoidances—then build a new, more dangerously potent body on these bones (see also Poole 1982, 115). When all is finished, the initiate's possession of this new, stronger self obliges him to avoid the blankets and clothing of uninitiated adolescents and to avoid eating from their plates, on pain of pollution, weakness, and serious ill health.

Initiation into various magical practices is viewed in precisely the same way as male initiation: temporarily or more permanently, it creates a qualitatively new person or *penga*. In becoming rainmakers or sorcerers, for example, it is not sufficient that men simply learn the appropriate spells. The spells have efficacy only if they are uttered by a body that has been qualitatively transformed through an initiatory sequence of appropriate actions and taboos. Thus, a stone surreptitiously rubbed against a rainmaker's body can be used to cause rain because it carries his empowered sweat. Partly because their bodies, as much as their spells, incarnate evil, fully initiated sorcerers are said to smell bad. Ritual preparations for such male activities as hunting, war, art, and wealth gathering also create, albeit on a more temporary basis, qualitatively different, male selves. Through magical rites and, of course, sexual avoidance, men make their persons briefly but intensely "hot" (*yaiyi*); they become *incandescently* powerful and threatening. Among the Nagum Boiken, Gerstner reported (1953, 432), warriors were said "to have been nearly demented" once war magic had been performed on them; the Yangoru idea that warriors' ears became deaf (i.e., they were transformed into uncontrollable beings) resonates very much with this description.

To return now to the issue at hand, sexual avoidances were ubiquitous concomitants of these permanent and more temporary transformations of the male self. In the more lasting transformations of callow boys into *halinya* men, they were imposed on initiates into all male initiatory grades (for the mostly pubescent virgins entering the first grade, these impositions seem to have been less a formal taboo than a good-natured admonishment). Sex avoidances also were observed during apprenticeship into all magical powers, such as rain-making and sorcery. And, as documented in Table 12.1, they were associated with all of those activities in which males were temporarily transformed into incandescently powerful and menacing selves.

In Yangoru, the reason people give for these observances is a belief that sex has an antithetical effect on the capability to achieve and manifest *halinya*. Sex in general is considered dangerous to "strength." Indulged to excess or inappropriately, it is said to "cool" a man's blood. It befuddles him, rendering him ineffectual in male affairs—"like a woman," in fact. In northern Yangoru, men sometimes insult one another by shouting, "All you ever do is sniff around women's crotches!"— the implication being that the rival's promiscuity has "cooled" his blood, rendering him *fatchik,* a "rubbish man." Indulged in the context of ritual empowerment, the mere act of sex is catastrophic. During or in the aftermath of male initiation, it nullifies the "strength" with which these rituals attempt to imbue initiates. During magical apprenticeship, it destroys the magical powers for which a man is striving. In both cases, transgressions can also lead to sickness or death.

On the occasions when men attempt to render themselves incandescently *halinya,* sexual activity can also be disastrous. The magician finds himself unable to cause rain, attract pigs or wealth, sorcerize others, and so on. With his blood "cooled," the warrior or hunter is left dangerously befuddled and lethargic.[11] His eyes are "unclear," he finds it difficult to track game or enemies, animals avoid his traps, and he is unable to hurl his spears with force. He fails to avoid the charging hog; enemy spears, smelling his wife's sexual fluids, eagerly seek him out in battle. The killer finds himself "held" by his victim's spirit and dies. The yam grower discovers his harvest is poor and his yams fibrous. The artist notices that his carvings split before they are finished and his paint dulls as it dries. The sponsor of a new slit-gong is dismayed to hear his finished instrument echo with a dull thud rather than a sharp and resonant boom.

STRENGTH, SEX, AND SEXUAL AVOIDANCE IN NEW GUINEA

In Yangoru, in sum, masculinity is idealized as a dangerous potency. Not being born with this "strength," the callow and weak self of boyhood must be transformed into a potent and dangerous self through initiation and, on certain occasions, into temporarily and incandescently powerful and menacing selves. Sex avoidances appear to be part of the repertoire of acts through which these transformations are effected.

As in Yangoru, a masculine ideal of dangerous potency seems widespread in Sepik and Highland New Guinea. In the Sepik, what I have described as *halinya* closely resembles *ka'aw* among the Manambu. *Ka'aw* denotes the quality of "competitiveness," "aggressive potency," "fierceness, energy, fighting spirit"; "*ka'aw* represents an ideal of living life, as it were, wholly in the active voice, of the self-determining person acting upon the world but not himself acted upon." Among the Kwoma, the same quality is captured in the concept of *ow* to which men aspire. *Ow* encompasses "strength, power, might," "hardness" and "quickness to anger," "energy, force or aggressiveness of disposition." Among the Ama, the equivalent appears to be *ö*, the "term for vigor or 'fight,' the 'sine qua non of maleness,'" manifest as "the culturally validated pattern of anger/fierceness which provides prestige among men." Among the Bun, *aba* ("blood") appears to confer a similar quality. Gnau men were required to have "strength and readiness to use or face violent action, courage, steadfastness and loyalty," and ritual life sought to prepare them for this; "success in hunting and killing, health and strength are desirable in a man. . . . This is a great part of the virtue in a man." Even the "gentle" Mountain Arapesh appear to be no exception, Mead noting that the Arapesh man has "a dread of his own maleness and the aggression which it signifies."[12]

In Highland New Guinea, "strength," "vigor," "vitality," or "potency" are commonly mentioned as esteemed masculine qualities (e.g., Bimin-Kuskusmin, Etoro, Gahuku, Kaluli, Melpa, Sambia, and Tairora). As Read noted (1959, 427–428) of the Gahuku, however, the reference seems to include more than just physical strength or potency. A "strong" man need not be physically strong, and though he is usually "aggressive, a warrior," he is also "a man inclined to swagger and boast, who displays a marked awareness of his individuality and is jealous of his self-importance." Among the Bimin-Kuskusmin, "controlled anger" is the esteemed quality in men; they should be "stoic, controlled, autonomous"—men "who aggressively assert their prerogatives and actively forge what is to be made of sociopolitical relations." Among the Kaluli, there is an "aggressive," "assertive," "destructive," "dark side" to "male vitality." For the Tairora, the "masculine ethic . . . has much to do with strength, forcefulness, indifference, and hence immunity to fear or threat, and with unconcern for the normal consequences of acts involving danger." "Aggression and killing" are so much a part of the "strongest" men "as almost to resemble a reflex." Among the Etoro, a man's *hame*, his "life force," appears to have overtones of power and menace to it.[13]

Again, though, echoing the Yangoru Boiken case, "strength" can also refer to activities that manifest a metaphoric, symbolic, or spiritual, rather than a literal power, menace, or aggression. Among the Etoro, a man's *hame* is an "animating principle and vital energy" that innervates men not just physically but also "spiritually" (Kelly 1993, 147–149). A Gahuku "strong" man is not just, nor even necessarily, a physically aggressive individual. In addition, he "should be an orator, able to express himself with force and also knowledge-able in various prescriptive speeches which are required for different occasions. The ability to argue is important. In addition, 'strength' is correlated with wealth—principally in the form of pigs—which enables a man to make large contributions to marriage and funerary payments and to other group festivals" (Read 1959, 428). Indeed, though a man who aspires to leadership must exhibit the qualities and possess the skills that convey the ideal of "strength," he must be careful within the community that this behavior not overtly become aggression (pp. 433–434).

Activities associated with sexual proscription were also commonly associated with the manifestation of dangerous potency. The menacing qualities demonstrated in the male activities of war and hunting hardly need laboring, but it perhaps deserves emphasizing that the same qualities have been noted in the less obviously threatening activities of art and ritual. As might be expected, minacity often has been identified as the intent behind the art of war: the songs sung on the way to battle (Ilahita Arapesh), the paint and costumes worn (Ilahita Arapesh, Manambu, Melpa, Yangoru Boiken), and the art of the shield (Maring, Wola) were apparently all calculated to terrorize or intimidate. The same appears true of seemingly more peaceful activities such as Hagen dance decorations, which refer to "feelings of triumph, aggressiveness," and Kwoma yam-harvest sculptures, which acquire the "hard," "aggressive" "power" of *ow* (see above).[14] Manambu men's ritual aims to affect the audience's emotions and is conceived of as "a kind of violation or attack . . . an assault upon that person's Spirit." Among the Gahuku-Gama, an affectively powerful dance performance is said to "kill" the audience. Among the Kaluli, decorated dancers are physically attacked with firebrands for the powerful feelings they evoke.[15]

As in Yangoru, there is a common belief in Sepik and Highland New Guinea that the male self must be transformed to be "strong," to be dangerously potent. Male initiation is the means by which Sepik and Highland New Guinea communities create "strong" men from callow youths, and the recurrence of birthing, rebirthing, and other pseudoprocreative rites (see Bonnemère, Chapter 2) suggests that selves are being transformed into different sorts of selves in the process. The common practice of oiling, ornamenting, and

painting the newly initiated young men, unadorned when they were first inducted, symbolically underscores the emergence of a new self.

The preparations that Sepik and highland males undergo for those particular
occasions when they manifest their "strength"—war, hunting, art, and so forth—
are also viewed as transformative of the self. Having been ritually prepared for
battle, Manambu men are in "a state of dissociation in which they became capable of extreme, indiscriminate violence, a kind of trance-state in which their
thoughts were of homicide" (Harrison 1993, 95). Nowadays, a weaker form of
the same magical preparations attend the performance of certain rituals, and
men say that "their faces become strange and 'different' . . . ; their faces turn fearsome or 'bad.'. . . In other words, *they undergo a change in their social personalities*" (p.
96, emphasis added) and "speak of the aftermath of the fighting as a kind of re-
awakening or recovery of their senses" (p. 95). Lewis (1980, 56; see also 1975, 210)
notes of the Gnau that "in hunting and killing, some men go into a fierce state
of trance in which they are less aware of their surroundings and of danger to
themselves. In certain rites for hunting and killing, they seek to arouse this state
called *wuna'at gipi'i* (empty or blank consciousness) and it may be shown by some
men." Even the performance of art appears to involve a kind of transformation
of self. Tuzin (1978a, 62) notes of the Ilahita Arapesh that achieving artistic mastery requires "a comparable mastery over oneself. The rigors to which the artist
ambitiously submits himself— . . . which, as one artist put it, enhance and focus
his personal 'power'—ostensibly ensure that his hand will be steady and the design exact. But in the process he also attains that complete confidence in himself
which is the primary character trait of a New Guinea leader."

As among the Yangoru Boiken, sexual avoidances were ubiquitous concomitants of these transformatory manifestations of "strength," of dangerous
potency. This is documented in Tables 12.1 and 12.2 for those specific occasions such as war, hunting, and art on which "strength" was demonstrated.
But sexual abstinence was also commonly required of initiates into the male
cult, as for example among the Wosera Abelam and the Saniyo-Hiyowe of the
Sepik; and the Daribi, Telefol, Huli, and Wola of the highlands. (For the
Baruya and Ketengban of the highlands, it is unclear whether the initiate, initiator, or both must avoid sex. In many other instances, initiates were so young
that sexual abstinence was rendered a moot issue.)[16]

The reason sex is avoided in these creations and demonstrations of dangerous potency is commonly reported to be its deleterious consequences on
"strength" generally and its specific manifestations in war, hunting, art, and so
on, in particular. Excessive intercourse, if not the mere act of intercourse, is
spoken of as detrimental to male "strength," "potency," "powers," or "vitality" among the Bahinemo, Bun, Iatmul, and Urat of the Sepik and among the
Baruya, Etoro, Gende, Kewa, Maring, Melpa, Samo, and Tairora of the
highlands. It is spoken of as "debilitating" or "weakening" among the Abelam
and Au of the Sepik and among the Foi, Kamano, Melpa, Ndumba, and

Tairora of the highlands. As for the Wiru, sex depletes group "strength" through the intermediary of shellwealth.[17]

On the specific occasions when "strength" is manifest, the perils of sexual infraction vary with the activity. Before warfare, it is thought to weaken a warrior, deflect his arrows, undermine their power, and/or prevent his chasing or escaping from an enemy (Awa, Wahgi, Manambu, Nagum Boiken). It may weaken his ardor for battle (Mountain Arapesh, Nagum Boiken), leave him vulnerable to enemy arrows, spears, or war magic (Ama, Au, Awa, Baktaman, Gadsup, Gende, Kapauku, Kwoma, Wahgi), or endanger others of his village (Kapauku). In the Maring case, sex is avoided because the war magic performed on the warrior would endanger his sex partner.[18]

Sexual infractions in connection with hunting most commonly result in a diminished catch (Anggor, Coastal Arapesh, Etoro, Gnau, Melpa, Nagum Boiken, Sawos, Umeda). In addition, it is sometimes said that the hunter or his dog would be wounded (Ama, Au), his bones would soften (Melpa), or he would lose his ardor for the chase (Mountain Arapesh).[19] Sexual infractions related to fishing include a poor catch (Namie), failure of the fish poison to do its work (Ama), and harm to the fisherman (Au).[20] Sexual transgression related to gardening may damage crops (Ama, Bena-Bena, Foi, Gimi, Gnau, Etoro, Iatmul, Mae Enga, Raiapu Enga), induce pigs to ravage the garden (Etoro), or cause the garden spirits to bring harm (Au). Among the Abelam and Ilahita Arapesh, illicit sex has a particularly deleterious effect on their famous long yams.[21]

In Highland New Guinea, art is primarily on the skin, and sexual infractions are said to dull its colors (Melpa), cause the skin to slacken or dry (Melpa, Wahgi), or dry up the skin oil (Melpa). In the Sepik, where art is more independent of the body, artists believe they paint better following abstinence (Abelam, Ilahita Arapesh, Kwoma). Drums are also said to become "silent" (Melpa) and pots to crack in firing (Kwoma). Among the Manambu, the ritual potency required for successful art endangers a sex partner.[22] In ritual, sexual transgressions can also endanger a partner (Gnau, Kwoma, Manambu) or anger the associated spirits (Au).[23]

STRENGTH, SEX, AND SEXUAL AVOIDANCE IN AMAZONIA

In many New Guinea communities, then, the masculine ideal is that of dangerous potency, whether manifest literally or physically in contexts such as the hunt or the battlefield, or metaphorically or affectively in contexts such as art or wealth- and pig-exchange. In the Amazon, some communities seem to envision masculinity in similar terms. Among the Mehinaku, the ideal man is "big and tall," "a strong wrestler, a powerful worker, and a prominent chief"; "he inspires fear and respect in his relationships with other men." Among the Tukano-Desana, the "masculine principle" is *tulári*, "masculine energy," which includes "physical strength, intellectual capacity, and certain supernatural faculties." It "means authority, command, the power of leading," and it carries connotations of injecting as through a fertilizing sting.[24]

In contrast to New Guinea, however, some Amazon communities represent dangerous potency as but one refraction of a more complex vision of masculinity that might also encompass less threatening dimensions. Activities such as war and hunting, which presumably are seen to manifest a kind of dangerous potency, are certainly highly valued in Amazonian males. Among the Yanomamö, those who are successful warriors have greater prestige. Among the Cashinahua, hunting is intimately bound up with manhood: "a real man is first and foremost a hunter." Shamanism also manifests dangerous potency and is similarly a masculine ideal. Among the Jívaro, shamans enjoy prestige for their role in a kind of magical warfare, manifesting supernatural power and menace in the deployment of spirit helpers as "darts" and "shields." The soul of a Tukano-Desana shaman is said to "illuminate," to "shine with a strong inner light rendering visible all that is in darkness," while the effect of his "penetrating glance" is likened to "the sudden fear when lightning strikes nearby, the charge from an electric eel, the shock felt when the elbow is struck against a hard object."[25]

In at least some communities, though, dangerous potency was not always valued *outside* these roles or contexts. Among the Mundurucú, male bravery in war was highly valued, but beyond that sphere, men were not supposed to swagger or seek to dominate others. They had to be modest and unassuming, letting prestige come naturally (Murphy 1961, 57). Among the Barasana, the masculine ideal has a powerful and menacing pole, manifest particularly in hunting, but there is also a more pacific pole, epitomized by the shaman who is idealized for his sharp wits rather than sharp implements (Stephen Hugh-Jones, personal communication). A similar circumstance existed among the Cashinahua (Kenneth M. Kensinger, personal communication).

In yet other communities, masculinity has connotations of power and threat, but these are manifest in nonphysical ways. Achuar men are supposed to exercise self-mastery rather than aggression. They dominate others by what they radiate rather than by literal threat or aggression. Great men who can talk or sing are said to have an "inner force" or strength derived from visions (Philippe Descola, personal communication). Among the Sanumá, the masculine ideal, *waitili*, has less to do with physical strength and violence than with bravery, in the sense of withstanding pain and boasting of one's fierceness. It can refer also to superior capability in delivering ceremonial dialogues (Alcida Ramos, personal communication).

These complexities in the conceptualization of masculinity may stem from the relative attenuation of warfare noted earlier in some regions of Amazonia. With greater levels of ambient peace than prevail in New Guinea, concepts of masculinity may have become more differentiated, as they are in the

West. Here, the state's monopoly on force and an advanced, industrial subsistence base renders hunting and warfare relatively infrequent male activities. Consequently, the manifestation of dangerous potency in literal terms—in the manifestation of violence and aggression, the killing of game or of humans—is not highly valued and usually is devalued. Nevertheless, the symbolic manifestation of dangerous potency *is* a highly valued aspect of masculinity in certain contexts, notably athletics. These are the symbolic wars of industrial society and, concomitantly, athletes are symbolic fighters who achieve prestige for demonstrating a metaphoric power and danger. Furthermore, they remain the principal arena of Western society in which sexual avoidances are practiced prior to engagements, on the basis that sexual activity will sap the athletes' "strength" and ability to "score."

Evidence suggests that, in Amazonia, becoming "strong" is conceptualized as a transformation of the male self. Conklin (Chapter 7) states of the Wari' that "the killing of an enemy outsider and the ritual seclusion that followed was the most highly valued and ritually elaborated event in the trajectory of male maturation." By incorporating into themselves the blood of the slain enemy, boys were ritually "transformed" into adult men. For seasoned warriors, each new killing was a "ritual transformation" that "revitalized and enhanced their strength, vitality, courage, and resistance to disease." These were rites that "aimed at actualizing capacities for masculine agency." Echoing the metaphors of rebirth that recur as males are transformed through initiation into new kinds of selves, these homicides and the seclusions that followed were conceived of as parallels to female childbirth. Conklin suggests that similar homicide-seclusion complexes among other Amazonian peoples might fruitfully be analyzed along similar lines. Beyond the sphere of war, Tukano-Desana shamans appear to become different selves when they enter a drug-induced trance. They "penetrate to another existential plane"; they transform themselves into, and are referred to as, jaguars (Reichel-Dolmatoff 1971, 126, 129–130).

As in New Guinea, these transformations are commonly accompanied by sexual avoidance. This is documented in Table 12.3 for those occasions such as war and hunting in which "strength" was demonstrated. In initiation, sexual abstinence was required of male initiates among the Mehinaku, Serente, and Tukano-Barasana (for the Canela, it is unclear whether the initiate, initiator, or both had to avoid sex). And, as Table 12.3 documents and Conklin (Chapter 7) points out, sexual abstinence was part of the homicide seclusions practiced in numerous Amazonian societies.[26]

As in New Guinea, the motive for avoiding sex in these contexts was its deleterious consequences on "strength" generally and its manifestations in war, hunting, art, and so forth, in particular. Excessive intercourse, if not the mere act of intercourse, is spoken of as detrimental to male "potency," "energy," or "vital energy" among the Cashinahua, Jívaro, and Tukano-Bará, and it is spoken of as "dangerous," "debilitating," or bringing "weakness" and "sickness" among the Cashinahua and Mehinaku.[27] Sex before warfare is thought to spoil a warrior's aim among the Yanomamö. Among the Arawete and Wari', sexual infraction in connection with the rites for homicide resulted in the diminution of the warrior's strength and vitality or in his death.[28] Sexual infractions in connection with hunting most commonly result in a diminished catch (Amahuaca, Canela, Tukano-Desana). In addition, it is sometimes said that the hunter or his dog would be wounded (Jívaro, Tukano-Desana), that he would be careless of the dangers of the forest (Cashinahua), or that he would get sick and die (Tukano-Desana). Sexual infractions related to fishing include a poor catch (Mehinaku), failure of the fish poison to do its work (Jívaro, Sharanahua), or loss of "strength" in turtle fishing (Cuna). Sex during shamanic initiation is believed to nullify the shaman's power (Jívaro, Mehinaku).[29]

SEXUAL AVOIDANCE, STRENGTH, AND AGGRESSION

To summarize, we can say that sex avoidances are typically deployed in Melanesia and Amazonia in connection with enterprises that create or draw on "strength"—understood as dangerous potency. These avoidances are part of a moral or phenomenological process by which individuals seek to transform themselves into "strong" selves capable of manifesting this power and menace—permanently in the case of initiation; temporarily, but incandescently, in activities such as hunting and war.

There remains the question, though, of why *sex* (of all things) should be the means of moral accounting or of constituting the self in these activities. At an immediate remove, a relatively obvious answer is at hand. As noted, there is widespread evidence that excessive or inappropriate sex is considered antithetical to male potency, draining it away. Hence, if it is believed that, to manifest male "strength," it is necessary first to muster and then sustain or conserve it, then sex, as a drain on that "strength," will be avoided during this preparatory period. Behind this answer, however, there is a more interesting question: granting that sex is avoided because it is believed to drain "strength," why is sex so widely *believed* to drain away "strength"? Why do humans so commonly consider it antithetical to war, hunting, and various forms of ritual and art?

A number of arguments bear on this issue. Brain (1979) has argued that sexuality is widely held to be dangerous because of the proximity of the sexual organs to the anus and its associations with decay and death. Shapiro (1989; 1995) suggests that the female reproductive tract is widely conceptualized as an absorptive danger (e.g., vagina = swallower) that threatens masculinity (penis = spear) and its typically projective projects (e.g., hunting and war). Tuzin (personal communication) points out that sexual avoidance may be a cultural elaboration of difficulties in sexual performance that males encounter prior to anxiety-inducing activities such as war and hunting.

Given how primitive are the ethnographic, psychological, and neurobiological data on this complex phenomenon, it would be difficult to "test" these arguments in more than a superficial way. Instead, I should like to suggest two further theoretical possibilities. The first involves the so-called "relapse" or "refractory" period, the period of depressed physiological response that follows the male sexual act (Byer and Shainberg 1991).[30] Given a common human-male physiology, the relapse period is presumably experienced across cultures. In Yangoru, it seems to be recognized as a kind of male death. Thus, a woman might tease her lover by saying, "You're so strong; [but] after you've given me your semen, you'll die" (see also Gregor 1985, 88 for the Mehinaku). It is thus possible that the avoidance of sex prior to or during the manifestation of male "strength" might be a culturally modulated, symbolic elaboration of this potency-depleting sexual consequence.

Such an argument is in close accord with the exegesis, already noted, that sex depletes male "strength," "vitality," "energy," and so on. A possible difficulty lies in female sexual responses. Women, it appears, sometimes can manifest "strength." In the normal course of events, Yangoru Boiken women are said to be "cold," lacking in "strength" and "power." If they perform their wifely duties to perfection, however, they can be described as *halinya*, especially if their activities are recognized as contributing to their husbands' *halinya*. Among the Ama, the quality of "vigor" or "fight" is a sine qua non of maleness "but is not exclusive to men"; "successful women hunters also receive a reputation for vigor or 'fight,' which is highly valued in a wife" (Guddemi 1992a, 306). Harrison (1990a, 354) implies that Manambu women can manifest *ka'aw* in noting that it is "one of the most admired qualities an individual— particularly a man—can possess." Unfortunately, the record is mute on whether, as is the case with men, the activities through which women manifest such qualities are associated with sexual avoidance. If they are, however, this presents a problem for a sexual relapse argument, since women do not experience relapse (Byer and Shainberg 1991, 190).

There is a second explanation, however, for why sex should be considered antithetical to the manifestation of dangerous potency, one that produces a prediction that, though nonintuitive, is borne out by the available data. It is begged by the remarkable coincidence that sexual activity is not only avoided around the world before hunting and war; it is equally widely conceptualized *as* hunting and war.

I have provided evidence elsewhere (Roscoe 1994, 53–56, 59–66) that humans experience seduction and intercourse as a form of aggression, in particular as a kind of predation or war. Ethological and neurological evidence (MacLean 1962; Roscoe 1994, 53–56; Zillmann 1984, 29–35) suggests there may be a biological substrate to this association, and this certainly would explain why sex is so widely metaphorized in these terms around the world. Among the Yangoru Boiken, as noted earlier, the penis is metaphorized as a spear, and intercourse is spoken of as an act of "spearing." Preferred marriage partners, for example, cast one another as "enemies" because the husband will "spear" his bride once they are married. Similar metaphors occur throughout the Sepik, highlands, and Amazonia. The image of the penis as an "arrow," "spear," or "weapon" occurs among the Abelam, Anggor, Arawete, Cashinahua, Eastern Highlanders, Iatmul, Ilahita Arapesh, and Manambu. Among the Eastern Highlanders and Arawete, it is also a "bow." Correlatively, sex is a "shooting" or "spearing" among the Sambia, Gimi, Murik, and Umeda, and a "shooting" with "arrow" or "spear" among the Auyana, Awa, Baruya, Dani, Eastern Highlanders, Fore, and Kwoma. It is spoken of as "killing" among the Gimi, Kamano, Melpa, Tukano-Desana, and Umeda. A woman is said to "die" or be "killed" in orgasm among the Auyana, Cashinahua, and Umeda, while men are said to "die" in intercourse among the Cashinahua. Conversely, killing game is a seduction among the Tukano-Desana. Intercourse is likened to hunting among the Amanab, Anggor, Gainj, and Tukano-Desana; to fish trapping among the Mehinaku; to an aggressive "devouring" of women among the Faiwol and Mehinaku; and to "biting" or "stinging" among the Awa and Tukano-Desana. Consensual sex is "violence," "fighting," "warfare," "armed combat," or "battle" among the Eastern Highlanders, Gainj, Iatmul, Ilahita Arapesh, and Mendi. It is thought of as "aggressive" among the Bumbita Arapesh, Eastern Highlanders, and Mehinaku, and is likened also among the latter to wrestling with the crushing hold of the anaconda. Male sexual desire is described as "anger" among the Arawete, the erect penis is said to be "angry" among the Arawete, Jívaro, and Mehinaku, and among the Sambia a war leader would exhibit his erect penis as "a sign of his aggression." Intercourse is spoken of as "hitting" or "striking" among the Bena Bena, Kamano, and Melpa; and as "cutting" among the Gimi. Female genitalia are a "bow" or "weapon" among the Arawete and a venomous spider among the Tukano-Desana. Female sexual desire is likened to "homicidal rage" among the Tukano-Desana, and females are pictured as aggressively "devouring" men among the Mehinaku and Mundurucú.[31]

At some level of New Guinean and Amazonian consciousness, then, perhaps as part of the ambivalence discussed by Gregor and Tuzin (Chapter 13), sex is thought of as an aggressive or menacing act akin to hunting or war. In other words, it is conceptualized in terms of the very acts for which "strength"—power and menace—is demanded and must be created prior to the event. Thus, to indulge in sex prior to hunting, war, or ritual would be to drain away the very "strength" that needs to be created in initiation or mustered ahead of time if it is to be manifest incandescently on the battlefield, in the hunt, or on the ceremonial ground.

Because the neurophysiology of sex and aggression is common to males and females, this explanation can encompass female sexual avoidances, if these prove, like their male counterparts, to be linked to the manifestation of power and menace. In addition, it can accommodate the common occurrence of food avoidances alongside sexual avoidances prior to war, hunting, art, initiation, and so on. In addition to neurophysiological connections between sex and aggression, there is also, as Tuzin (1978a, 91) notes, some evidence that similar links exist between aggressive and oral arousal and activity, and sexual and oral arousal and activity (see MacLean 1962; Zillmann 1984). Metaphors also commonly link these arousals and activities. In English slang, for example, *to eat* means to kill or knock off; *bite* means an instance or act of coercion (Lewin and Lewin 1988, 126; Thorne 1990, 41). Enemies are equated to prey animals that one eats: in World War II, Royal Air Force pilots would be sped on their way with the comment, "Good hunting!" In New Guinea, among the Iatmul, Kwoma, Manambu, and Yangoru Boiken of the Sepik, enemies are likewise equated to game animals (Bateson 1958, 140; Bowden 1983, 110–111; Harrison 1993, 102–103). Gnau hunting rites were believed to equip men to kill both game and enemies (Lewis 1980, 168). The Abelam and Yangoru Boiken equate biting with spearing or killing (Forge 1966, 27). Metaphors equating sexual partners to food and sex to devouring are also ubiquitous (see Roscoe 1994, 70–71 nn. 3, 4, 6).

THE AVOIDANCE OF AGGRESSION, CONFLICT, AND VIOLENCE: A CONCLUDING PREDICTION

The argument that, because sex is conceived of as aggressive or menacing, it is therefore avoided before aggressive or menacing acts has the virtue of making a nonintuitive prediction. If sex is considered antithetical to becoming an aggressive self because it is conceptualized as a form of aggression, then the same should be true of nonsexualized, literal aggression. In other words, one should expect avoidance of sex to be accompanied by the taboo or avoidance of aggression, conflict, and violence.

This is indeed the case. Among the Yangoru Boiken it was believed that, if warriors or hunters became involved in aggression, conflict, or violence with anyone in the hours prior to a battle, ambush, or hunt, they would fail or be killed in their endeavor. Male initiation, pig-exchange ceremonies, and the construction of *ka nimbia* spirit houses, all occasions for creating or manifesting *halinya,* were declared times of ritual peace precisely because of a belief that violence would undermine the venture's success. Conflict among participants was considered inimical to the rituals for attracting wealth and ensuring the success of pig exchanges. At the height of the rites to restore fertility to the Earth, as at the climax of the Peli millenarian movement in

1971, shouting and even talking out loud were proscribed for several hours since they betoken discord, which was believed to destroy the effectiveness of the rituals.

Similar findings are reported from elsewhere in New Guinea and Amazonia. Among the Alamblak of the Sepik, discord prior to hunting or war was believed to bring "bad luck" to the endeavor. To prosecute war successfully in the Kaugel valley of the highlands, warriors first had to confess and resolve potential interpersonal conflict. Among the Sawos, a man embarking on a hunt should not hit or fight with his wife. Among the Sepik Wape, arguments and fights were considered antithetical to good hunting. Among the Cashinahua, bad luck in hunting might be attributed to a bad marriage and the social confusion and disruption that results.

The declaration of ritual peace prior to initiation has been noted among the Manambu, Wosera Abelam, Ilahita Arapesh, and Siane. Peace or the suppression of conflict was a necessary precursor to other forms of ritual among the Kaluli, Siane, and Northern and Wosera Abelam. A Wahgi clan's successful performance at a dance festival depended on its members first confessing and resolving wrongdoings; similarly, the Umeda *ida* fertility ritual could not be performed in "troubled times." These were all occasions when men were transformed into "strong" beings; they were all accompanied by sexual avoidance; and, as the argument formulated here predicts, they were all hedged with taboos against aggression, conflict, and violence.[32]

NOTES

For ethnographic assistance in compiling this paper, I am deeply grateful to several conference participants and to Stephen Beckerman, Simon Harrison, Patricia Johnson, Arnold Parapi, and Richard Scaglion. I owe a special debt to Terrence Hays, who kindly provided me with the contents of topics 12, 13, and 49 from his files on Highland New Guinea sexuality; depending on the subject, these files have furnished me with between about 60% and 95% of my data on highland sexual avoidances and sexual metaphors. I am grateful to Hays, Tom Gregor, Ken Kensinger, and Don Tuzin for comments on an earlier version. I am also indebted to a number of my Amazonianist coconferees for gently nudging me into recognizing that Amazonian concepts of masculinity were perhaps more complex than I had supposed.

1. Evidence suggests that sexual avoidances in the Sepik and the highlands are broadly typical of Melanesia, with the added advantage that these regions represent both sides of the common distinction drawn between "lowland" and "highland" Melanesian societies.

2. I call these sexual *avoidances* rather than sexual taboos because the latter term is semantically ambiguous, sometimes meaning an explicit cultural rule (e.g., Leavitt 1990, 984 n. 1), sometimes referring only to a behavioral avoidance, and often including both. For

the task at hand, unfortunately, the data are usually too few or fragile to reveal these sorts of cognitive and affective details, often, the most that can be safely assumed when sex is said to be "tabooed" is that its frequency is attenuated in some degree.

3. The data in Tables 12.1, 12.2, and 12.3 are drawn from a larger set that suggests sexual avoidances prior to warfare, hunting, art, and ritual are widely present throughout so-called "tribal" and "chiefdom" societies (e.g., Polynesia, Micronesia, North America, and Africa). Similar, though not always identical, avoidances are found in state-level societies, including our own.

4. In light of these data, it comes as an initial surprise to learn that Frayser (1985, 182), in a holocultural sample of 56 societies, found that in only 20% were "economic pursuits" the focus of sexual prohibitions, in only 16% were "religious occasions," and in only 5% were "military occasions." Frayser herself was surprised "that men did not reinforce their masculinity by sexually separating from women before they went into battle," suggesting that perhaps "the de facto continence implied by absence from home during war eliminates the necessity for a taboo." This might be true of industrial warfare, but it does not explain most "tribal" and "chiefly" instances, where war and home are usually close companions. Rather, Frayser's description of her coding procedures (1985, 448, 467–468) indicates that she counted as negative instances societies for which her sources contained information on some sexual prohibition (for example, a postpartum taboo) but for which there was no information about those associated with hunting, war, and/or ritual.

5. Carneiro (1970, 331); Chagnon (1992, 91–97); Holmberg (1969, 47).

6. Dani—Heider 1991, 43; Fore—Boyd 1991, 63; Gahuku—Read 1951, 155; Gainj—Johnson and Wood 1991, 71; Huli—Allen and Frankel 1991, 91.

7. SEPIK: Ama—Guddemi 1992a, 131; Eastern Abelam—Forge 1990, 168; Kwoma—Williamson 1975, 165, 383; Nagum Boiken—Gerstner 1952, 179; Northern Abelam—Kaberry 1940–41, 365; Murik—Barlow 1985, 116; Yangoru Boiken—Pongiura 1993, 23, 50; Roscoe, fieldnotes; Wogeo—Hogbin 1934–35a, 331, 332; 1934–35b, 380. HIGHLANDS: Awa—Boyd and Ito 1988, 56; Baruya—Godelier 1986, [1982] 60; Bena Bena—Langness 1967, 165; 1969, 39; 1999, 8; Eastern Highlands—Berndt 1965, 90; Eipo—Schiefenhövel 1982, 150; Etoro—Kelly 1976, 41, 43, 44, 45; Gadsup—DuToit 1975, 99, 243; Gende—Fitz-Patrick and Kimbuna 1983, 53; Gimi—Gillison 1993, 261; Hua—Meigs 1976, 402; Kalam—Bulmer 1967, 15; Kamano—Mandeville 1979, 226; Kewa—Warus 1986, 50; Mae Enga—Meggitt 1957, 49–50; Melpa—Strathern and Strathern 1971, 86, 104; M. Strathern 1972, 165; Wiru—Clark 1991, 319; Wola—Sillitoe 1979, 78, 79, 83, 95 n. 1. AMAZON: Arawete—Viveiros de Castro 1992, 180, 367 n. 7; Canela—Crocker and Crocker 1994, 108; Jívaro—Karsten 1935, 217; Mehinaku—Gregor 1985, 147; Siriono—Holmberg 1969, 170; Warrau—Wilbert 1977, 27, 36, 38, 176; Yanomamö—Lizot 1985, 9.

8. Abelam—Forge 1966, 28; Kaberry 1941–42, 215; Mehek—Crockett 1979, 57; Murik—Barlow 1985, 112–113, 117–118, 120–121.

9. The same may also have been true of the third (final) initiatory stage, but I have very few data on the subject.

10. Abelam—Kaberry 1940–41, 355 n. 33; Barí—Beckerman 1996, personal communication; Iatmul—Bateson 1958, 149; Weiss 1994, 246; Kwoma—May and Tuckson 1982, 220; Rao—Kasprus 1973, 143.

11. Claims about the deleterious effects of sex on pig hunting with dog and spear reflect ideology as much as, or more than, practice. Very often the hunt with the spear is

opportunistic. Passing through the forest, a man spots a pig or happens upon its spoor and immediately gives chase, fully anticipating success even though he has had no chance to observe sexual abstinence.

12. Ama—Guddemi 1992b, 10, 14, 306; Bun—McDowell 1975, 219–222; Gnau—Lewis 1980, 103, 167; Kwoma—Bowden 1983, 92–93, 113; Manambu—Harrison 1982, 149; 1993, 107, 109; Mountain Arapesh—Mead 1940, 345.

13. Bimin-Kuskusmin—Poole 1982, 137, 141, 150; Etoro—Kelly 1993, 147–149; Gahuku—Read 1951; 157; 1954, 22–23; Kaluli—Schieffelin 1976, 124–127; Melpa—Strauss 1990 [1962], 79–82; Sambia—Herdt 1982b, 52; 1987, 36; Tairora—Watson 1973, 267–268.

14. Gombrich (1982, 124) likens the artist to a hunter, and his description of how artists try to capture a particular effect is revealing in this context: "likeness has to be caught rather than constructed. . . . It needs the method of trial and error, of match and mismatch to trap this elusive prey."

15. SEPIK: Ilahita Arapesh—Tuzin 1976, 47; Kwoma—Bowden 1983, 93–94; Manambu—Harrison 1993, 113, 121–122; Yangoru Boiken—Roscoe, fieldnotes. HIGHLANDS: Gahuku—Read 1955, 273; Kaluli—Schieffelin 1976; especially 24, 205; Maring—Lowman 1973, 19, 31; Melpa—Strathern and Strathern 1971, 101–106, 137–138, 154; M. Strathern 1979, 246; Wola—Sillitoe 1980, 495.

16. SEPIK: Wosera Abelam—Aufenanger 1972, 314; Yangoru Boiken—Roscoe: fieldnotes; Saniyo-Hiyowe—Lewis 1988. HIGHLANDS: Baruya—Godelier 1986, 60–61; Daribi—Wagner 1972, 154; Huli—Glasse 1968, 112; Ketengban—Sims and Sims 1992, 68, 95; Telefol—Brumbaugh 1980a, 346, 347; 1980b, 367.

17. SEPIK: Abelam—Huber-Greub 1990, 283; Au—Philsooph 1980, 558; Bahinemo—Dye 1983, 12; Bun—McDowell 1975, 241; Iatmul—Silverman 1993, 401; Urat—Gell 1975, 253. HIGHLANDS: Baruya—Godelier 1986 [1982], 18; Gende—Fitz-Patrick and Kimbuna 1983, 42; Etoro—Kelly 1993, 147–149, 155–156; Foi—Weiner 1987, 263; Kamano—Mandeville 1979, 226; Kewa—MacDonald 1991, 163; Maring—LiPuma 1988, 43, 177, 275; Melpa—Strathern and Strathern 1971, 86, 136–137; Ndumba—Hays and Hays 1982, 206; Samo—Shaw 1990, 153 n. 6; Tairora—Watson 1971, 249–250; Wiru—Clark 1991, 319.

18. SEPIK: Ama—Guddemi 1992b, 130, 146; Au—Philsooph 1980, 533; Kwoma—Bowden 1983, 103; Manambu—Harrison 1996, personal communication; Mountain Arapesh—Fortune 1939, 39; Nagum Boiken—Gerstner 1953, 432. HIGHLANDS: Awa—Boyd and Ito 1988, 56; Baktaman—Barth 1975, 150; Gadsup—DuToit 1975, 81; Gende—Fitz-Patrick and Kimbuna 1983, 42; Gimi—Gillison 1987, 175; Kapauku—Pospisil 1958, 93; Maring—Buchbinder and Rappaport 1976, 20; Melpa—Asea 1986, 77; Wahgi—O'Hanlon 1989, 34, 42.

19. SEPIK: Ama—Guddemi 1992b, 130, 131; Anggor—Huber 1974, 152; Au—Philsooph 1980, 533; Coastal Arapesh—Gerstner 1937, 971; Gnau—Lewis 1980, 128; Mountain Arapesh—Fortune 1939, 39; Nagum Boiken—Gerstner 1952, 181; Sawos—Schindlbeck 1980, 122; Umeda—Gell 1975, 253. HIGHLANDS: Etoro—Kelly 1976, 43–44; Melpa—Strathern and Strathern 1968, 136, 196.

20. Ama—Guddemi 1992b, 130; Au—Philsooph 1980, 533; Namie—Feldpausch and Feldpausch 1988, 24.

21. SEPIK: Abelam—Forge 1990, 168; Kaberry 1940–41, 356; 1941–42, 215; Scaglion and Condon 1979, 18; Ama—Guddemi 1992b, 130–131; Au—Philsooph 1980, 533; Gnau—Lewis 1980, 128; Iatmul—Silverman 1993, 400; Ilahita Arapesh—Tuzin 1972,

237. HIGHLANDS: Bena Bena—Langness 1967, 173; Etoro—Kelly 1976, 43; Foi—Weiner 1986, 76; Gimi—Gillison 1991, 192; Mae Enga—Meggitt 1964, 210, 223 n. 11; Melpa—M. Strathern 1972, 165; A. Strathern 1976, 148; Raiapu Enga—Waddell 1972, 100.

22. SEPIK: Abelam—Forge 1973, 180; Ilahita Arapesh—Tuzin 1978a, 62; Kwoma—Bowden 1983, 102, 103; Manambu—Harrison 1996, personal communication. HIGH-LANDS: Melpa—Strathern and Strathern 1971, 86, 136; M. Strathern 1972, 165, 253; Wahgi—O'Hanlon 1989, 42.

23. Au—Philsooph 1980, 533; Gnau—Lewis 1980, 128–129; Kwoma—Whiting 1941, 126; Manambu—Harrison 1996, personal communication.

24. Mehinaku—Gregor 1985, 144; Tukano-Desana—Reichel-Dolmatoff 1971, 54–55, 58, 126.

25. Cashinahua—Kensinger 1995, 81; Jívaro—Harner 1973, 277; Tukano-Desana—Reichel-Dolmatoff 1971, 126, 129, 138; 1975, 77; Yanomamö—Chagnon 1992, 205.

26. Canela—Crocker and Crocker 1994, 169; Nimuendajú 1946, 174; Mehinaku—Gregor 1977, 150, 226; Serente—Nimuendajú 1967 [1942], 50; Tukano-Barasana—Hugh-Jones 1979, 85, 90, 220.

27. Cashinahua—Kensinger 1995, 79,80,81; Jívaro—Descola 1994a, 210; Mehinaku—Gregor 1977, 150; 1985, 144–149; Tukano-Bará—Jackson 1983, 190, 191.

28. Arawete—Viveiros de Castro 1992, 240; Wari'—Conklin, Chapter 7; Yanomamö—Albert 1985, 356 n. 24.

29. Amahuaca—Carneiro 1970, 341 n. 13; Canela—Crocker and Crocker 1994, 147–148; Cashinahua—Kensinger 1995, 81; Cuna—Nordenskiöld 1938, 391; Jívaro—Descola 1994a, 281–282; Harner 1973, 81, 135; Mehinaku—Gregor 1977, 150, 334; 1985, 80, 147; Sharanahua—Siskind 1973, 114; Tukano-Desana—Reichel-Dolmatoff 1971, 221, 224; 1975, 85.

30. There is an additional syndrome known as *la mort d'amour*, the fear of sudden death during intercourse (Bohlen et al. 1984). In addition, sexual folklore in England associates the relapse period with a postcoital psychological depression known as *petit mort* or *post-coital tristesse*. Unfortunately, I have been unable to locate any clinical work on such a phenomenon.

31. SEPIK: Abelam—Forge 1966, 27; 1967, 77n. 1; 1990, 168; Losche 1982, 190; Amanab—Juillerat 1986, 282; Anggor—Huber 1974, 152; Bumbita Arapesh—Leavitt 1991, 898; Iatmul—Bateson 1958, 141; Silverman 1993, 400; Ilahita Arapesh—Tuzin 1972, 243; Kwoma—Bowden 1983, 53, 117; Manambu—Newton 1987, 253; Murik—Lipset 1984, 326; Umeda—Gell 1975, 115, 249. HIGHLANDS: Auyana—Robbins 1982, 178; Awa—Loving and Loving 1975, 90, 150; Baruya—Lloyd 1992, 151, 252; Bena Bena—Langness 1999, 138–139; Dani—Heider 1976, 194; 1979, 139; Eastern Highlanders—Berndt 1962, 115, 124, 129, 148 n. 1, 170, 284; 1965, 84; Faiwol—Jones 1980, 161; Fore—Lindenbaum 1976, 56; Gainj—Johnson 1982, 242 n. 1; Gimi—Gillison 1978, 336; 1993, 202; Kamano—Mandeville 1979, 228; Melpa—Strauss 1990[1962], 233; A.Strathern 1972, 247 n. 11; M. Strathern 1972, 188; A. Strathern 1984, 16; Mendi—Nihill 1989, 78; Sambia—Herdt 1981, 178; Reddish n.d. AMAZON: Arawete—Viveiros de Castro 1992, 187, 195, 223, 363 n. 16; Cashinahua—Kensinger 1995, 36; 1996, personal communication; Jívaro—Descola 1994a, 282; Mehinaku—Gregor 1985, 32, 40, 71, 75; 1996, personal communication; Mundurucú—Murphy 1959, 95; Tukano-Desana—Reichel-Dolmatoff 1971, 58, 60, 218, 219–220, 224, 225.

32. SEPIK: Alamblak—Edmiston and Edmiston 1989, 25–26, 32; Manambu—Harrison 1990b, 91–92; Northern Abelam—Scaglion and Condon 1979, 19–20; Sawos—Schindlbeck 1980, 122; Umeda—Gell 1975, 157; Wape—Mitchell 1978, 173–174, 179–180; Wosera Abelam—Schroeder 1992, 82, 84, 164; Ilahita Arapesh—Tuzin 1996, 15–16. HIGH-LANDS: Kaluli—Schieffelin 1981, 3; Kaugel Valley—Didi 1982, 75–76; Siane—Salisbury 1962, 33–34; Wahgi—O'Hanlon 1989. AMAZON: Cashinahua—Kensinger 1995, 33, 121.

THIRTEEN

The Anguish of Gender:
Men's Cults and Moral Contradiction
in Amazonia and Melanesia

Thomas A. Gregor and Donald Tuzin

Gregor and Tuzin take as their starting point the remarkable resemblances of men's cults in Amazonia and Melanesia. The similarities include myths of matriarchy and role reversal; body imagery that merges male and female reproductive anatomy and physiology; rituals that assign generative, pseudoreproductive powers to men, who may "give birth" to initiates; hyperphallic cult objects in ritual; secrecy and constant vigilance against penetration of the cult by women and noninitiates; and terror and violence directed against those who breach the rules of the cult.

In their understanding of men's cults, Gregor and Tuzin offer a perspective that is different from Biersack, who sees the cult as reinforcing patriarchy, and from Hugh-Jones and Hill, who point to elements of cult symbolism that suggest that the cult is an expression or even meditation upon the interdependence of men and women. Rather, Gregor and Tuzin argue, the cult reflects an effort, at times desperate, to hold together an all-too-fragile masculine self.

This defensive quality of the cult explains the tremendous energy that is put into its fantastical symbolic elaborations and the secrecy, sexual antagonism, and misogynistic violence that mark it. Taken together, this latter pattern constitutes an "anguish of gender," in which men and women who may be closely related also stand opposed and antagonistic. This contradiction is the moral fault line of the cult and may lead to its rapid demise or, at minimum, to personal questioning and uncertainty. The men's cult thereby reflects on the broadest human questions of honesty, integrity, truth, and deception.

THE PROBLEM

For almost a century anthropologists have been aware of the similarity of men's secret organizations in many tribal cultures of Amazonia and Melanesia (e.g., Schurtz 1902; Webster 1968 [1907]). Typically, these organizations are associated with meeting grounds or men's houses, where men conduct secret initiations and feasts. The cults recount similar charter myths, address similar spirit entities, conceal similar paraphernalia and sound-producing instruments, and similarly punish female intruders with gang rape or death. That this combination occurs in both regions is noteworthy. More striking is that the details of the cults also bear close comparison.[1]

In both cultural regions, the men share a strategic secret: the sounds of the trumpets, flutes, and other instruments associated with the cult are not the voice of spirits but are produced by the men themselves. One source of mysterious sounds, the bullroarer, is widely used in conjunction with such rituals, both in Melanesia and Amazonia (see also Metraux 1927). We shall identify other remarkable parallels between the two regions in this paper. So similar are the cults and myths in the two regions that Robert Lowie flatly declared that men's cults are "an ethnographical feature originating in a single center, and thence transmitted to other regions" (1920, 313).[2]

Lowie, Schurtz, Webster, and others were right to note the parallels in men's institutions in Amazonia and Melanesia, but they were, perhaps, overly optimistic in attributing the similarities to diffusion. The cultures in question are separated by half a world of geography and 40,000 years or more of culture history. Even if men's cults were invented but once, why did they not evolve differently and develop beyond recognition in the two regions? The similarities of men's institutions in Amazonia and Melanesia is one of the great riddles of culture that has not received the attention that it deserves, especially from the vantage point of modern ethnology. No systematic comparison of the cults exists in the literature, and, for the most part, efforts at explanation are culture-specific rather than broadly comparative (though see Allen [1967] and Whitehead [1986a, 1986b] in the context of Melanesia).

The purpose of this paper is to contribute to the comparison by examining psychological features of the cults that we regard as especially salient. Our paper will give special attention to the symbolism of the cults, particularly the myths that form the native explanation of men's organizations in the two regions. These fanciful tales, which have been called "myths of matriarchy" by Joan Bamberger (1974; see also Gewertz 1988), are remarkable in and of themselves. Psychologically revealing, they are one of the keys to the complex of practices and symbols associated with men's institutions, so much so that we refer to the entire assemblage as *myth-cults*.

The myths tell of a time when the women discovered, invented, or possessed the cult objects, bullroarers, flutes, or trumpets that are the central symbols of the men's cults.[3] These objects permitted the women to dominate the men or at least to live apart from them (see Gewertz 1988, 111). Banding together, the men forced or tricked the women into giving up the sacred objects, resulting in their possession of the generative powers of the flutes, the reordering of society, and, in some cases, the establishment of patriarchy. Within this general scenario, there are significant variations. For example, the rule of women and the subordination of men, in an explicit political sense, is present in but a few Melanesian cultures (Hays 1988), while it is more common in Amazonia. The themes of separation of men and women and the acquisition of power from women by men, however, are more prevalent across both regions.

Despite variations, the myths show an extraordinary similarity,[4] which has provoked a variety of explanations. Some of these explanations center on the roles of men and women in societies with men's cults. Thus Terence Hays (1988), in a useful comparative study of such myths in the New Guinea highlands, interprets them as reflecting the unity of men who defend their communities while demanding labor and loyalty from wives who may originate in enemy villages. Reay (1988) shows that the myths help to maintain the social system by teaching girls and women their roles in a patriarchal society. Reversing this perspective, some authors argue that the myths, rather than directly reflecting or supporting social organization, are commentaries upon it (Gardner 1988; Errington and Gewertz 1988).[5]

Our own approach to the myth and the cult is through psychoanalysis and personality dynamics. We are hardly the first to take this path. It is explicit in the work of Roheim (e.g., 1950), developed in Robert Murphy's (1959) understanding of the Mundurucú men's cult, and amplified further in the context of Melanesia in ethnographies by Allen (1967), Herdt (1981), Hays (1988), Gillison (1993), and others. For the most part, however, the psychoanalytic approach to the myths has been focused on particular stories within particular cultures. Our own paper will suggest in broad terms what the approach can accomplish through comparing the cultures of the two regions. We will then examine two Amazonian and Melanesian myths, from the Mehinaku of central Brazil and the Ilahita Arapesh of northeastern lowland New Guinea, to explore a set of recurrent features that we regard as crucial, but which have largely been bypassed in the literature: the deception, distrust, and moral ambivalence that permeates the myth-cult.

THE MYTH-CULT

A myth is a dream that many have begun to tell.
A MEHINAKU VILLAGER, TO ONE OF THE AUTHORS

The similarity of myths and dreams, first systematically explored by Freud and Abrams, rests on the surreal, fantasy-like quality of both types of narrative. Events and characters are joined by metaphor and emotion rather than, or despite, a logically developed plot. The concepts that Freud used to understand dreams (the "dream work") is admirably suited to myth. But there are also differences. Dreams are private and idiosyncratic, made, in the words of one analyst, "to be forgotten" (Arlow 1961, 379). Myths, on the other hand, are made to be recalled and retold. They are dressed up well enough by the drama of narrative art to compel the attention of those who hear them. But they are more than entertaining: they are riveting. They express the inner wishes and fears of those who tell them and those who listen: myth "makes possible the containment of terror and impulses by the decorum of art and symbolism" (Bruner 1960, 227; also Hook 1979, 288). Finally, the myths are authentic voices of the inner self in that they are emotionally powerful and they endure over millennia (see Tuzin 1977, 220).

To an extraordinary extent, the men's cults in the two regions reflect inner psychic processes. Cult secrets and paraphernalia, rites of initiation, and other rituals associated with the institution vividly enact—or barely disguise—the conflicts and wishes associated with childhood, sexual maturation, and tension between men and women. The cults do more than this, of course: they are engaged in politics, the defense of the community, significant economic and technological endeavors, and other societal functions that constitute both the cult's institutional dimension and its overdetermined quality. That is to say, within the framework of these activities, the cults appear as virtual enactments of primary-process thought; they are waking, collective, male dreams.

The fantastical, dreamlike quality of cult imagery, while perhaps not unique to Amazonia and Melanesia, is another feature of comparative and theoretical interest. In standard psychoanalytic fare, symbolic equivalences and associations are often deeply disguised; typically, they require patience and ingenuity on the part of both analyst and analysand. In Amazonia and Melanesia, however, symbols we are accustomed to thinking of as psychologically primitive, because deeply buried, often seem to operate very close to the surface of mental life. Not only does one find ritual objects treated overtly as genital parts, but entire psychodynamic scenarios, such as the Oedipus complex, are portrayed in almost laughable undress. What does this imply about the dynamics of "public" and "private" symbols in these areas? How is one to apply Freud's topographic model, when what (in a theoretical sense) must be repressed and denied is more or less openly admitted? Finally, what contribution, if any, does this quality of symbolic phenomena make to the shared distinctiveness of Amazonia and Melanesia? Such questions are somewhat beyond the scope of the present paper (though see the discussion of the disjunction of ritual and daily life and the concept of encapsulation, below), but they are implied by our material, and we propose them for consideration by the reader.

ANALYZING THE MYTH-CULT: COMMON THEMES

The Centrality of the Myth-Cult

In both Amazonia and Melanesia the myth of matriarchy and its attendant cult are profoundly expressive of self-identity, group organization, and ritual ideology. Capturing the essence of gender relations in the cultures in which it is told, the myth accounts for the origins of the men's cult, the tension and antagonism between the sexes, and the men's need for secrecy and vigilance with respect to women. For the individual, the myth and the panoply of symbols and metaphors that surround it condense many issues of gender psychology. The myth-cult is thereby a crucial feature both for the societies in which it appears and for the individuals who compose them.

Body Imagery

Primary sexual characteristics and other portions of the human body are the major symbolic currency for the myth-cult and its associated beliefs. Male and female, rather than being different by nature, appear as permutations of one another. Genitalia, rather than being permanently rooted to bodies by nature, have a life of their own, independent of their owners. They may become detached, often violently, as occurs in myths of castration (see Gregor 1985) or in reality, as in the genital operations that are often associated with the cults in Melanesia. In myth, genitals have personalities and may actually separate themselves from their owners as a consequence of their own whims and volition.[6] The detachability of genitals from their owners anticipates their mutability as male and female organs. Penises, clitorises, vaginas, anuses, breasts, mouths, noses, and tongues are symbolic permutations, one of the other. They condense, merge, and differentiate (see, for example, Lidz and Lidz 1989; Strathern, Chapter 10). Hence, in Amazonia, the mythical "Big Clitoris Women" of the Shipibo had greatly enlarged clitorises (perceived as "penises") with which they ruled men. Historically, in the Shipibo *ana shreati* puberty rite, newly menstruating girls would be clitoridectomized (and thereby feminized, that is, castrated) prior to marriage (Roe 1982, 93, 106).[7] In other Amazonian cultures, men, while living under the mythic matriarchy, menstruated, gave birth to children, and gave milk (Barasana [S. Hugh-Jones 1979, 266]; Shipibo [Roe 1982, 164]; Mehinaku [Gregor 1985]). The fantasy of male menstruation exists in Melanesia, as well, along with a welter of images suggestive of the mutability of both gender and sex (Hogbin 1970; Tuzin 1980; Lindenbaum 1984; Bonnemère, Chapter 2; Biersack, Chapter 4).[8]

As these examples suggest, genitals and secondary sexual characteristics are key symbols, cropping up in what for us are wholly unexpected areas of world view and explanation. Thus in New Guinea, Gimi fetuses are conceived of as phalluses, with the newborn's fontanel as the urethral aperture (Gillison 1993). Sex may become a template for the entire environment, which is genderized, thought of, and conceived in terms that are linked to masculinity, femininity, and human sexuality. For the Tukanoan peoples of the northwest Amazon, the entire cosmos is sexual: the Sun god's piercing rays are equated with semen and phallic male sexuality, while the earth and a uterine paradise below it are identified with femininity (Reichel-Dolmatoff 1971).[9] The power-charged flutes and bullroarers that are crucial to gender differentiation in many of the myth-cults are themselves consciously sexualized, having simultaneously male and fe-male referents. The flutes may be both penises and nipples that provide "milk" (Herdt 1987, 188). Bullroarers are simultaneously phalluses and vaginas or, in mythology, are even seen as emerging from women's vaginas (cf. Dundes 1976, especially pp. 224–225). The sacred flutes are at once instruments of phallic ag-gression (women who see the flutes in myth are violated with them [S. Hugh-Jones 1979, 131, 266]) and vaginas (Gillison 1993). Bará (Tukanoan) mythology fuses male and female imagery associated with the flutes by asserting that the original female owners of the flutes kept them hidden in their vaginas (Jackson 1983, 188).[10]

   The mutability of both sex organs and gender suggested by these exam-ples appears to be part of a more general feature of masculine selfhood in the cultures of both regions, in which defining physical attributes of the self are not fixed (for example, as in Western beliefs about sexual biology) but are moral and social achievements dependent on behavior and rituals such as initiation. Writing of Sambia initiation, for example, Herdt (1982b, 55) notes that "underlying men's communications is a conviction that maleness, unlike femaleness, is not a biological given. It must be artificially induced through secret ritual; and that is a personal achievement." (See Roe 1982 for a simi-lar general statement in the context of Amazonia, and Gregor 1985 for spe-cific examples among the Mehinaku.) By the same token, masculinity is un-stable and must be actively maintained against an always encroaching feminine possibility.

Reproduction and Procreativity

The transformability of sexual anatomy has many functions within the sym-bolic world of the myth-cult. It at once expresses and attempts to resolve anx-iety over ambiguous sexual identity (the mutability of sex/gender vs. hyper-phallic differentiation of males through possession of cult objects) and is the basis of sadistic practices, including gang rape, terrorizing of initiates, killings, and genital operations (see below). Perhaps the most widely reported function of the symbols and their rituals, however, concerns what has sometimes been called, somewhat tendentiously (Tuzin 1995), the "pseudo-procreativity" of men—a topic that is well articulated in the literature on Australian Aborigines (see Hiatt 1971; Shapiro 1996; Shapiro and Linke 1996; note also p. 16, this volume). Thus, lacking the obvious reproductive capacity of women, men nonetheless "give birth" to initiates, as in Arunta initiation, in which the ini-tiators' subincised penises (verbally equated with vulvas) drip "postpartum blood" on the "newly born" initiates, or in the anal birth of the Wikmunkan (McKnight 1975, 94), or in the Barasana symbolism of initiation (S. Hugh-Jones 1979, 132 ff.).

More diffusely and metaphorically, the myths of matriarchy and the attendant cults are procreative in that they are about the birth of culture, in which the secrets of the men's organization are conflated with the invention of technology, law, and custom. Hence, "Gimi men claim that the continuity of society, and their own authority, rests upon the secret of the bamboo flutes" (Gillison 1993, 345; see Tuzin 1997). Similarly, among the Barasana, if women were to see the flutes, society would be replaced by "chaos during which men would fight and kill each other" (S. Hugh-Jones 1979, 128). Playing the flutes, an incessant activity in some of the cultures, ensures the well-being of the community (in the Mehinaku, Gregor 1985), the intercession of clan spirits (in the Mundurucú, Murphy 1959), and the favor of powerful female spirits (in the Sambia, Herdt 1987).

The Fragility of the Masculine Self

The irony of male procreative imagery is that the myths tellingly ascribe the origins of the cult to women. The Mehinaku version of the story is a particularly good example of its kind from Amazonia. It begins with the men in a cultureless world, suffering from the absence of women:

> The men had no women at all. Alas for the men, they had sex with each other, and they had sex with their hands. The men were not happy at all in their village—they had no bows, no arrows, no cotton arm bands. They walked about without even belts.[11] They had no hammocks so they slept on the ground, like animals. They hunted fish by diving in the water and catching them with their teeth, like otters. To cook the fish they heated them under their arms. They had nothing—no possessions at all. The women's village was very different—it was a real village. The women had built the village for their chief, Iripyulakumaneju. They made houses, they wore belts and arm bands, knee ligatures, and feather headdresses, just like men. They made the sacred flutes, the first sacred flutes: "tak . . . tak . . . tak," they cut them from wood. They built the men's house for the flutes, the first place for the Spirit. Oh, they were smart, those round-headed women of Ancient Times.

On one level the myth is an appreciation of the generative, culture-creating power of women. Without women, Mehinaku men are helpless—reduced to living like animals. But the legend also reflects the historical experience of each man, who comes into the world cultureless, as a helpless, dependent child, and is raised in a sex-dichotomized world by powerful (from the infant's perspective) women (cf. Chodorow 1978). Typically, in both Melanesia and Amazonia, the pattern of socialization is one in which infants are immersed in an embracing maternal world, until they are weaned (often traumatically) and replaced by a younger sibling. The extent of physical closeness in many cultures is difficult to overstate. Among the Mehinaku, for example, a mother and child sleep unclothed in the same hammock, and children may nurse (at least intermittently) for as long as five years (Gregor 1985). Arapesh mothers and infants are comparably close, with a lactation interval averaging three years.

The apparent psychological result is a partial merging of self-identity with the mother, which establishes a feminine side to a masculine self (see Hays's [1988] interpretations of the Melanesian myths). This notion is literalized in the idea that masculinization requires young boys to be ritually "purged" of feminine substances originating in maternal proximity and, especially, breast milk (e.g., Tuzin 1980; cf. Herdt 1981); similarly, in adult males periodic blood-letting restores masculine purity in the face of sexual and domestic contact with women (Hogbin 1970). At the deepest level, the men fear loss of self-differentiation and autonomy, and, ultimately, maternal symbiosis (Stoller 1974). Yet at the same time, they yearn for the secure maternal world they left (Gilmore 1990). The effort devoted to warding off the seductive pull of femininity produces the fantastic symbolic complexity of the cult, with its attendant misogyny, phallic sadism, sexual anxiety, procreative ritual, and secrecy.

An array of additional supporting cultural data from Amazonian and Melanesian societies, ranging from fear of menstrual blood to castration themes in mythology, documents the fragility of masculinity and the intense anxiety associated with femininity. Person-centered approaches, in which we have psychological as well as cultural data, are unusual in the literature of both regions (especially in Amazonia), but what there is suggests that the culture of male fragility is matched by the psychological concerns of individuals (for example, Tuzin 1977, 1997; Herdt 1981; Gregor 1985).

The myth, in which the men steal their autonomy from women and found it on the possession of cult objects, is a story of child development projected upon group history. But it is also a story of continuing fear of regression. Dependent boys, insecure in their own sense of their masculinity, gain autonomy by being broken free of their mothers, who stand for dependence and femininity. As men, they recall (in the language of the myth) that they claimed their masculinity from the women and continue to defend it against them. But their possession of cult objects, no matter how grandiose or hyperphallic, is not the same as inner confidence. Unlike our own beliefs that gender is based on the immutable facts of life, the myth opens the possibility for a feminine counterrevolution, loss of the powerful cult instruments, and the resubordination of men.

Secrecy

The world of the myth and the cult is factually wrong: it is based on "error" (Keesing 1982) and is objectively "preposterous" (Hays 1988). As such, the cults and their mythic charters are potentially unsteady edifices that are threatened by positive, intimate relationships between men and women (Tuzin 1982) and the openness they engender. One of the adaptations to this threat is the secrecy and deception that are at the heart of the myth-cults. The content of the secrets bears attention. At times the secrets are highly strategic, as when the men, impersonating spirits, terrorize women (the Yahgan[12] [Chapman 1982]; Ilahita Arapesh [Tuzin 1980]) or hide shameful activities from them (Sambia homosexuality and symbolic menstruation [Herdt 1987]). Just as often, however, the secret is virtually empty of strategic content and conceals mainly the details of the men's hidden rituals. Thus Valentine writes of the Lukalia men's cult of New Britain: "Yet virtually the only real secrets beneath all this elaborate cultural camouflage are the details of the internal structures of the masks and the procedures surrounding their construction" (1961, 481). In Amazonia, writing of the Mehinaku, Gregor notes that a woman who somehow slipped into the men's house would be disappointed as to how inconsequential the men's secrets actually were (1985, 98).

The often empty nature of the men's secrets in both cultural regions is especially revealing when paired with another observation that appears to apply universally to men's cults in Amazonia and Melanesia. In no case that we are aware of is the *existence* of the cult a secret, only its specific objects and activities. Invariably as well, at least some of these activities, normally the most dramatic, are held within the partial sight or sound of the women and boys who are excluded. In Ilahita, for example, some flutes are accompanied by women who sing the high harmony of the song, but only with their backs turned to the instruments. We conclude that the function of secrecy is that of social differentiation, enfolding the cult members who share it and separating them from those who are excluded.[13] Following Georg Simmel, the cult's "secret surrounds it like a boundary outside of which is nothing but . . . opposite matter" (1950, 362). The boundaries of the cults are thereby artificially buttressed, creating an apparent gulf between men and women. Ultimately, what the secrets and social boundaries screen is the frailty of the masculine self. Moreover, this screening is understood by the men to be essential to the social order. As the case of the collapse of the Arapesh men's cult (below) will show, they may well be correct.

Secret Cult Objects

The solution offered by the cult to the fragility of the masculine self is the possession of external objects imbued with masculine power. Ordinary objects will not do. They must, by their nature or by their form, be suitable as repositories of male energy. As a consequence there is a material culture of cult objects that is remarkably uniform across the dimensions of time and space in our comparison. Hence cult fetishes are hyperphallic, in that they are large and elongated;[14] they include flutes, trumpets, and bullroarers. Bullroarers, described by Haddon as "perhaps the most ancient, widelyspread and sacred religious symbol in the world" (1898, 327), are of special interest because of their remarkable association with men's cults. They show astounding uniformity in design, usage, and even symbolic interpretations across our field of comparison (see Dundes 1976, 225). Often bullroarers and the other cult objects are finely made. They are manufactured, sometimes in secret, and handled with exquisite care by respected specialists. They produce sounds, usually in deep registers, that are inherently dramatic and haunting.[15] In being heard but not seen, these objects are perhaps ideal for conveying mystery and instilling fear in the naive listener. Bullroarers, the sounds of which vary from low-pitched throb to a whine, may produce the loudest noise in a tribal environment other than thunder. Symbolically, these dramatic objects are displaced penises (the equation is often a conscious one; see the references in Gewertz 1988, 104), designed to dramatize masculinity.[16] But at a deeper level, these "prime symbols of male hegemony" (Meigs 1984, 134) are at best boys' penises in that they remain inadequate to the task put to them (Horney 1966 [1932]).[17] Were it otherwise—were cult objects in truth repositories of male power—they would be exhibited rather than hidden from the women. We can therefore understand why the most brutal punishments of all, rape and death, are meted out to women who see the flutes and bullroarers, and why the men often equate the act of women seeing the flutes with chaos and the destruction of society. If women were to see these objects, they would reach a truth about masculine frailty that the men can barely screen from themselves, and for that very reason must defend so aggressively.

Vigilance and Obsession

Defending a "loud secret," in this case literally a noisy secret, in the open setting of a face-to-face community requires vigilance. The women, who are presumed to wish to penetrate the secrets—as they are presumed to wish for the men's phallic power—must be limited in their movements and activities. Threats of violence against novices who might reveal cult mysteries keep the secrets intact. Among both the Sambia and the Yahgan an individual could be killed for revealing cult secrets. Physical barriers to the men's house, such as walls and baffles, passively serve the same function of preserving secrecy. What is of special interest is that in both Amazonia and Melanesia the men are not content to simply keep the instruments safely hidden. Rather they parade and play them in public areas such as gardens and plazas that are normally open to the women. As such, the men must be extraordinarily vigilant in sequestering the women during rituals. Among the Mehinaku, women are herded into the houses and the doors are shut before the men play the flutes on the plaza or whirl the bullroarers (Gregor 1985). In Melanesia, where the men may appropriate "virtually the whole community and countryside" for their rituals, the women and children were subject to "nightly chasing" into their houses (Gewertz 1988, 105).

Patrolling the boundaries has an endless, obsessive quality, as does the mythic character and the exorbitant ritual and symbolic features of the cults themselves. The object of the ritual activities and of the mythic charter is to shore up the self by pushing away the essence of the other, specifically, that which is feminine. More informally, negative stereotypes of women, aggressive jokes, and (in the vicinity of the men's house) public jeering may repeat the same message, namely that the men are *not* women. But as in classic obsessive-compulsive neuroses, vigilance and magical formulae will not ward off the underlying anxiety. The task is therefore endless: no amount of ritual, gang rape, myth telling, flute playing, or bullroarer whirling is sufficient to guarantee masculine identity.

Resembling clinically described obsessions (Freud 1950 [1913], 27–28), masculine anxiety in these societies is volatile and contagious and spreads to new objects, where it reproduces the same fears in new symbolic forms. Thus the most sacred objects associated with the cult, those that are most deeply imbued with masculinity, may be permeated with the essence of the rejected feminine other. Among the Gimi, the myth-cult describes how the women exacted revenge against the men who took their flutes by plugging the blowing hole of the first sacred flutes with their pubic hair. The hair took root on the faces and bodies of the men who played them. Tellingly, the Gimi say that there is now "a vagina on men's faces" (Gillison 1993, 263, 266). Remarkably parallel mythic images appear among the Mehinaku, where village boys ceremonially receive feather earrings, which are a major marker of masculine status. According to myth, the earrings were originally fabricated from the pubic hair of a woman. Moreover, during the ritual of ear piercing the boys "menstruate" from the incision in their ears (Gregor 1985). In New Guinea, a similar upward symbolic displacement occurs in the "menstrual" nose-bleeding rituals prevalent in the eastern highlands (Hays and Hays 1982, 221). In other words, despite the astonishing energy that the myth-cults put into repudiating and shouting down femininity, feminine essence adheres to both symbol and self (Tuzin 1995).[18]

THE ANGUISH OF THE MYTH-CULT:
TERROR, VIOLENCE, AND POSTTRAUMATIC STRESS

The myths and cults may be "preposterous," but they have real consequences. These are almost invariably painful for the initiates, involving systematic violations of their bodies and personal security. Examples from Amazonia and Melanesia—in general, the tribes of the latter are rougher in their treatment of initiates than the tribes of the former—include circumcision, genital laceration, nose bleeding, cane swallowing, scarification, tooth evulsion, beatings, threats of death and mutilation, whippings, exposure to stinging ants, wasps, and nettles, terrorization by masked adults, threats of death, and homosexual violation. The most violent of the cults combine many of these abuses in the course of a single ritual. Given that the initiates are as young as six years old, the psychological impact is certain to be profound. Although the literature seldom offers a psychological perspective on the experience of the initiate, the data we have are generally consistent with the implied terror of the novice and the sadism of the initiator. Thus, Herdt (1987) graphically describes the cruel jokes directed toward children who are about to be forced to fellate the bachelors among the Sambia, and their consequent revulsion and terror.

From a psychoanalytic perspective, the myth-cult bears many of the markers of posttraumatic stress.[19] The violence of the cult, especially as inflicted on children by fathers or other trusted adult males, is more than sufficient to produce the disorder, whose symptoms include reliving of the trauma, intrusive and unwanted "flashbacks," continued vigilance against events that are symbolically connected to it, and in the case of those who have been victims of violence, blind rage. The concept of posttraumatic stress was developed to understand individual pathology, such as that of the shell-shocked veterans of the world wars who continued to experience apparently random panic attacks, fear of such things as loud noises, outbursts of anger, and nightmares. We speculate that the organized fantasy world of the myth-cult allows its adherents to encapsulate the trauma of their initiation. In the course of initiating their own sons, they reexperience the trauma in a way that may help them master and control it (Crapanzano 1981; Tuzin 1992b). On occasion, the ritual actually seems scripted to ensure an intense "reliving," as when in the course of Arunta initiation the men open their old subincision wounds to drip blood on the initiates. From this perspective, initiation creates a cohort of men who evince the symptoms of posttraumatic stress in ways that are culturally legitimized. The men's obsessive vigilance against femininity, their rage directed against initiates and women, and the nightmarish ideology of the myth-cults may thereby have their roots in the experience of initiation. The paradox of the myth-cult may be that it is both pathological *and*, if not actually therapeutic, adaptive.

Phallic Aggression

The cruelty of the cults is mitigated by the fact that after their social death as children, the boys will be reborn as men. They will identify with the values and secrets of their elders—to such an extent that they will one day torment their own children. The situation is different for women who intrude upon the cult or who see the cult objects: they are subject to death and gang rape (e.g., Murphy 1959; Gregor 1990a; Errington and Gewertz 1987, 81–82; Chowning 1987, 148 n.). That both Amazonian and Melanesian cultures include phallic aggression as a penalty for violation of cult boundaries is especially significant, in that rape (both heterosexual and homosexual) is the quintessential assertion of male dominance. In many cultures (for example, Mehinaku [Gregor 1985]) the rape is a cult-authorized ritual activity, in which the spirits of the flutes rather than the men are said to be the rapists (the same idea is enacted more literally in Barasana myth, in which women who steal the flutes "have the flutes rammed up their vaginas" [S. Hugh-Jones 1979, 131, 266]). The political dimension of these practices is also evident in at least some of the myths, where women are raped to ensure that they act within their role. Toward the end of the Mehinaku myth, the men ripped off the women's belts and clothes and rubbed the women's bodies with earth and soapy leaves to wash off the gender-coded design. The men lectured the women:

> "You don't wear the shell *yamaquimpi* belt. Here, you wear a twine belt. We paint up, not you. We stand up and make speeches, not you. You don't play the sacred flutes. We do that. We are men." The women ran to hide in their houses. All of them were hidden. . . . The men shut the doors: This door, that door, this door, that door. "You are just women," they shouted. "You make cotton. You weave hammocks. You weave them in the morning, as soon as the cock crows. Play the sacred flutes? Not you!" Later that night, when it was dark, the men came to the women and raped them. The next morning, the men went to get fish. The women could not go into the men's house. In that men's house, in Ancient Times. The first one.

The political dimension of rape is also evident in that women who have acted out of the traditional feminine role may be raped even though they have not violated the taboo on seeing the flutes. (Murphy [1959] reports that Mundurucú women who attended mission schools were especially at risk.) Further, in some (though not all) of the societies with men's cults there is frequent opportunistic interpersonal rape, occasioned simply by the availability of a woman. The Murphys describe how any Mundurucú woman outside of the village was considered fair game for forced sex, and that one young man would lie in wait in a tree hoping to force himself on a passerby (see also Gregor 1990a for Mehinaku examples).

Mythic accounts of the rape and execution of women who violate the cult may reach extraordinary proportions. In myth (and sometimes in reality [Gregor 1985]), the rage and fear underlying male antagonism are so powerful that the rapists and executioners willingly violate primary kinship relations to punish transgressions. Yurupury, the mythic culture hero in the northwest Amazon, had his mother executed after she saw the flutes (Roe 1982). In a Tukuna myth, a woman who broke the taboo is quartered, smoked over the fire, reduced to mush, and force-fed to her mother and sister. Eating their daughter and sibling, however, is not sufficient: they must endorse the act. The executioners smear soot under the women's eyes so that they too may be killed if they are detected weeping (Nimuendajú 1952, 78).

Women and Projective Identification

The myths and the world they describe project a view of women as dangerous and powerful. After reviewing a wide range of Amazonian literature, Roe notes: "To put it bluntly, women are the archenemies of the social order" (1982, 230). This perspective, projected upon women by men, is powerful and persuasive, so much so that it may become part of the women's self-concept. The anguish of the myth-cult is that the women may internalize its values. The extent to which they do so varies, since the literature shows a range of adaptations. Among the Mundurucú the women confront the men with cynical and surly resistance. "There they go again" was one Mundurucú woman's comment upon hearing the men play sacred trumpets. "It is as if they had investigated the secret sources of the men's power—and had found absolutely nothing" (Murphy and Murphy 1974, 18, 141). Among the Gimi, on the other hand, the women believe fully in the men's culture and accept that their bodies and sexual physiology are dangerous to both men and themselves: "I did not find women to be subversive nor opposed to prevalent cultural norms. . . . [The women believed that] menstrual blood could indeed be fatal to their husbands, and even to themselves. . . . Women seemed to accept, and even embrace, men's characterizations of their sex as part of an ancestral order that was beyond question or doubt" (Gillison 1993, 7). There are many intermediary cases, such as the Barasana, where the women have secretly seen the flutes but are proud of them and identify themselves with the cult (S. Hugh-Jones 1979), and the Mehinaku, where the women accept current conditions but are nostalgic for the mythic matriarchy (Gregor 1985).

MORAL AMBIVALENCE IN THE ARAPESH AND MEHINAKU MYTHS AND CULTS
The Inevitability of Moral Ambivalence

If there is one overriding characteristic attributed by psychoanalysis to the human condition it is that of ambivalence, "the simultaneous existence of contradictory tendencies, attitudes or feelings in relationship to a single object—especially the coexistence of love and hate" (Laplanche and Pontalis 1973, 26). In psychoanalysis, conflict derived from ambivalence "is a constitutive part of the human being" and is the basis of the internal dynamic of opposed feelings, drives, and prohibitions. The analysis of conflict and its associated repressions, resistances, and defenses is the basis of analytic therapy and theory as well as an inevitable part of the human estate.

If ever there was an organization that appears to contradict the analytic assumption of the universality of ambivalence, it is surely the men's cult. In its unremitting misogyny, in its obsessive vigilance against women, and in the Draconian sanctions that guard it, the myth-cult speaks with one unconflicted voice: women are dangerous, polluting, and contemptible. And yet, seen more deeply, the myth-cult is remarkable precisely because it is one of the *most vivid* cultural manifestations of internal ambivalence of which we are aware. Much of this ambivalence is suggested by the central rituals and myths of the cults, which, amid the welter of gender-inflected ideas, are the most overt expressions of the polarity that underlies and energizes the entire system. In counterpoint to their professed disdain of women, the men impersonate women by "procreatively" generating initiates, imitating female reproductive physiology, and endorsing myths of the female origins of the cults. From this perspective, the fear, secrecy, sadism, and vigilance are what they seem to be, but also more: an expression of the *need* for women and *identification* with them. The myth-cult stakes a claim to masculinity, but it does so in ways that are problematic and deeply conflicted.

Moral ambivalence has a second and more poignant dimension for the men: they are intimately dependent upon the women they reject. While aggressively asserting their manhood, the men compromise basic, primary relationships with their daughters, sisters, mothers, and wives. These relationships must endure if the society is to survive, but they must do so in the face of intense misogyny. We regard this dilemma as the critical fault line in every myth-cult. The way it is played out between individual men and women constitutes a major portion of the moral life of the community and, we believe, explains the fragility of the institution and its occasional rapid demise (see below).

The moral ambivalence inherent in the myth-cult is seldom addressed in the literature. We believe this to be the case because such ambivalence will only rarely be culturally recognized. An open expression of the contradiction of love and antagonism would challenge the rightness and inevitability of the myth-cult, which like all brittle, heavily defended formations, cannot be directly assailed. Resistance to the cult, when it appears, occurs at the margins of public culture. For example, in the Tukuna story cited above, of the women forced to eat their daughter and sister without showing grief, we find implicit recognition that primary relationships are in conflict with the cult. Why else would one wish to weep at the cannibalistic destruction of a woman who violated the flutes? On occasion, however, the evidence for moral ambivalence is more direct. Such is the case of the Mehinaku, where one myth directly addresses the issue. We will find evidence of the same dilemma among the Ilahita Arapesh, where the inherent contradictions of the cult led to its ultimate demise.

THE MEHINAKU: THE COEXISTENCE
OF PHALLIC AGGRESSION AND LOVE

Gang rape among the Mehinaku of women who violate the men's house has not happened for perhaps 50 years. But it has occurred far more recently among other culturally similar tribes in the Upper Xingu region, and it remains a constant threat in the Mehinaku village today. Rape is part of a larger pattern of misogyny, which includes secrecy associated with the men's cult, relatively stringent taboos associated with menstruation, beliefs that female sexuality is dangerous and causes illness, deprecatory female stereotypes, and informal jokes and jeers directed toward women (see Gregor 1985).

Coexisting with this pattern of misogyny is genuine attachment between many spouses and between male and female kin. The most dramatic cultural manifestations of affection and love between men and women are found in mourning practices, which require a full year in seclusion for the bereaved spouse, and an extraordinary pattern of extramarital sexual relationships that proliferate lifelong, as well as casual, liaisons between the men and women of the community (see Gregor 1985). More subtle are a host of indications that husbands and wives really care about each other, including anxiety during prolonged separation and overt expressions of concern and affection. To a greater extent than is true among many cultures with men's institutions in Amazonia and Melanesia, Mehinaku gender relationships are truly bimodal. Men and women are joined by common interest, mutual affection, and kinship at the same time they are separated by antagonism and fear. Perhaps it is for this reason that the Mehinaku possess a well-elaborated myth, the only one of which we are aware in the literature, that directly challenges the public culture of the men's cult.

The Myth of Pahikyawalu

"Pahikyawalu" means, literally, "she who is covered with feces." The narrator of the myth, the Mehinaku chief, explains the title:

> This is a myth of a woman of Ancient Times. Hers is not a pretty name, it is not a name by which we greet people. It is a name from ancient times, because this woman was covered with feces, because she ate feces. Pahikyawalu committed a great crime. Decorating herself as a man ["She made a penis from a stick and wore it under her belt"], she slipped into the men's house at night and played the flutes. The men were amazed to hear her.
> "Who is that person playing?" asked all the men in their hammocks. "Ah, what a beautiful song that is. Is it the Song Master? No, he is asleep in his hammock." And they asked the others [the next day]: "Was it you?"
> "No, I was sleeping. Was it you?"
> "No, I stopped earlier."
> "Then who was that person?"
> Pahikyawalu's husband discovered the impersonation: "Oh," he said to her, "you are like garbage; it is men who [play the flutes], not women."
> The husband went to the plaza and denounced his wife to the village. But the men were too angry to rape her.
> They didn't want to have sex with her. They wanted to see her die in the grave. They wanted to bury her. They wanted her to suffer. "Yes, let her die, let her be buried," said the husband. Her real husband said that!

Together the husband and the men of the village dug a hole for Pahikyawalu in the center of the village. One of the men, her lover, participated, but he did not want her to die, yet he knew that the other men would be angry if he did not participate. The miserable, worthless husband spoke in front of the men's house: "So much the better, so much the better, good, great, it is good that she is dead!" For ten days Pahikyawalu lived in her hole in the ground, covered with her own feces.

At last her lover came to dig her up, because he was really her lover. She was dear to him, and that is why he wanted to help. He dug down into the earth until he came to her. Oh, it was so smelly, so disgusting. She was smeared with feces all over her body, but he was not disgusted by her. She was his lover. In the middle of the night he carried her in his arms to the stream. He washed her with soap. He rinsed her with water.

He took Pahikyawalu to another tribe, where she prospered and became beautiful. Her husband, now alone and without a wife, came to long for her. That husband, the one who had buried her, *he* went to get her!

Pahikyawalu went with her husband to return to the Mehinaku, but on the way through the forest he asked to have sex. First, she insisted, he must cut down a honey tree and reach inside to get the hive:

"Go inside, crawl in, get in, put your head in so that we can get all of the honey-juice," she said. He went inside the log, the fool.

"It is further in, further in. Go deeper, go further, go all the way in. Go in all the way!"

She took her husband's feet and pushed him all the way into the log. The honey got into his mouth and eyes! There was so much honey. He breathed in the honey: "Aka, aka, aka! . . . " He drowned in the honey, he died in the log! Here were his feet. . . . Here was his head. . . . He died in there.

"So much the better, so much the better," she said. I have revenged myself, I have gotten you back! You buried me in the ground and therefore I have gotten you back. It is good that you have died, oh it is good to pay you back!" And then she lectured her dead husband's ghost: "Don't you haunt us, don't you come back to us. You are not a spirit. When rain falls in the future [and the honey drips from the tree] say, 'Uru . . . uru . . . uru.' Everyone will [know you are there] and say, 'Alas, sadness and pity for you!'"

At one level Pahikyawalu is the woman that every man must be vigilant against. She assumes the most important of all male prerogatives—playing the sacred flutes—and does it better than all of the village men: "Ah, what a beautiful song that is. Is it the Song Master?" The narrator adds that it was "frightening and mysterious to hear her play." Her violation of the men's house raises the question as to whether the differences between men and women are flimsy cultural creations, as the myth of matriarchy also suggests. Women can assume male roles as easily as they can slip into their clothes. That the men were "too angry" with Pahikyawalu to rape her suggests that her breach of gender boundaries sexually incapacitated them, in effect, rendered them impotent. With the symbolic efficiency that is myth's forte, the episode condenses the idea—not unique to the Mehinaku—that male dominance depends on a workable penis, which in turn depends on the preservation of masculine sanctuary (Tuzin 1997).

These considerations explain why Pahikyawalu provoked rage and sadism: "the men wanted her to suffer." But standing against this anger are the primary relationships that bind men and women together. The husband, who leads the others against Pahikyawalu, is described as "miserable and worthless" and is killed. The narrator exults with her in delight over his demise. The lover, who rescues her from her living burial, is rewarded with a beautiful wife. Pahikyawalu, despite her confrontation with the men and her degradation, is idealized as "very beautiful, with broad strong thighs and her hair down her back."

The story of Pahikyawalu is a resolution of the fundamental dilemma of the cult. The rules of the men's cult are uncompromising and cruel, and they demand conformity, so much so that in the myth the lover was afraid to oppose the men's rage: "He did not want her to die, but he knew that the other men would be angry." The myth thereby pits a cruel law against the passion of lovers, the inherent mutual dependence of the genders, and the common humanity of men and women. We know that the dilemma is a real one, for despite the pressure to enforce the tradition of gang rape there are Mehinaku men today who are like the lover of Pahikyawalu. One of them directly confronts the tradition of assaulting women who see the flutes:

> No! I don't think this is good. Only in the past was this good. It was those headless, faceless idiots of long ago, of mythic times, that did this. It was the sex fiends of ancient times. I feel sympathy for a woman who has seen the flutes. A man who is a good man does not participate in raping her. If he is a good man he says to her, "I am sorry that it happened; alas for you!" A man who does not feel pity is a sex fiend, an unbathed, headless fool.

THE DEMISE OF A CULT: THE ILAHITA ARAPESH

Every men's cult is built, to a greater or lesser degree, on the same quicksand of moral ambivalence as that of the Mehinaku. Supported by secrecy and intimidation, they fly in the face of primary relationships between men and women. Perhaps for this reason, in both Melanesia and Amazonia, the cults are brittle—often shattering in the face of pressure from the outside.

Among the Ilahita Arapesh, the *Tambaran*, an elaborate men's cult, possessed many of the features we have described, including a secret "myth of matriarchy," ritual executions of women who transgressed the cult, and severe beatings and genital mutilations of initiates. As among the Mehinaku, the cult coexisted with daily relationships between men and women that reflected a measure of affection and concern as well as a normative sense that husbands and wives must care for and support one another (Tuzin 1982, 324). Nonetheless, the cult persisted and even managed to resist outside pressures for about

forty years of exposure from Christian missions and the Australian administration. Then, starting in the mid-1970s, the cult began to wither under the influence of various "modernizing" developments. Suddenly, in September
1984, the cult collapsed. The final moment came when, by prearrangement,
a number of men in their ritual prime announced to the women that the cult
had been a pack of lies from the beginning: the spirits did not materialize during the great conclaves; their "voices" were merely sound-making devices operated by the men; their gargantuan appetites for feast foods were, in truth,
the men's own; the violent exclusion of women had been a shameful deception.

Why did the men do it? Why did they kill something that was, in effect,
already dead? Why did they voluntarily surrender a masculine advantage
that had served them well for generations? Ostensibly, the men acted in
order to rid the village of what they now believed to have been an institution ruled by Satan—this in order to permit a great millenarian Event to
occur. At a deeper, cultural level, however, the men's act remedied a moral
dilemma that had troubled them ever since they adopted the Tambaran,
probably around the 1880s (Tuzin 1982). This dilemma centered on the
contradiction between ritual and domestic values. The guilty secret was
that the men's punishing claim to ritual supremacy—and, by implication,
the legitimacy of masculinity itself—rested on an illusion, a lie. In addition
to its various behavioral expressions (Tuzin 1982, 1997), the dilemma was
enshrined in a nonsecret myth that fantasized masculine dependence and
vulnerability.

In brief (see Tuzin 1980, 1–8 for full text), the story of Nambweapa'w goes
as follows:

The First Man was walking along when he heard the unusual sound of laughter
coming from nearby. He went to investigate and, from hiding, saw a group of cassowaries bathing in a pond. Having removed their skins, they had become beautiful
women. The man secretly stole the skin of the one he most fancied, so that later,
when the cassowary-women emerged to resume their skins, the one he had chosen
could not find hers. This led to the man's taking her home with him, where he
tricked her into piercing herself to create her external genitalia. They began their
married lives together. Her name was Nambweapa'w.

Man and wife advanced to old age, producing a long line of alternately sexed
children, who later in the story intermarried and became the ancestral parents of all
the world's peoples. The firstborn, a son, was the ancestor of the Ilahita Arapesh.
The father would take the older children to the garden, while the mother stayed
home to care for the youngest; then, the next day, the parents would reverse roles.

The youngest child, also a son, was about six years old when he discovered that
his father kept a cassowary skin in hiding, this after the father had donned the skin a
few times to frighten the youngster into ceasing his crying and whining. The next day,
in exchange for some coconut tidbits that the boy cried for during meal preparation,
he revealed this secret to his mother, who reacted by putting on the cassowary skin

and running back to her natural home in the forest. Before finally leaving, however, she instructed her children on how they were later to join her.

Accordingly, after some months they followed her, taking their old father with them. They hid him under a taro leaf at the prearranged meeting place. Namb-weapa'w went to them. After ordering the children down from the trees, she told her sons to take up their spears so that they (and their sisters) could come with her. But she noticed that there was one unclaimed spear remaining. She identified this as belonging to her husband, and, finding him crouched under the leaf, used it to crush his head.

Nambweapa'w's magic provided effortless abundance, a life in which death and pain and sorcery were unknown. This edenic existence was lost, however, when her children—all but the youngest—violated the one food taboo she had imposed. She punished them by turning herself into a wallaby and tricking the innocent, youngest son into killing her with a spear. Before she died, she revoked her sustaining magic and ordained that life thereafter would have pain and drudgery and death. The youngest son scolded his siblings. In a blaze of moral indignation, he was swept away by a sudden flood—to America, "as we now know," where he fathered the white race, and whence he will someday return with Nambweapa'w's magic.

This tale was not only a "charter," it indicated to the men how they could bring about the desired millennial Event and, in effect, recover Nambweapa'w's magic. Exposing the Tambaran's secrets was tantamount to "returning the cassowary skin," restoring to women their natural autonomy and power, thus opening the way to the edenic existence lost so long ago. The Tambaran was the repository of masculine identity, the champion of misogynistic rhetoric and deceit; destroy it, and all good things would follow.

What actually did follow was nothing like what the men anticipated and is the subject of a different study (Tuzin 1997). For now, it is enough to observe that the issue of masculine insecurity, deceitfulness, and existential uncertainty was traditionally recognized, and that it was expressed as an anxious need to protect the secrecy, and therefore existence, of the men's cult. And, just as the fear of death can become so great as to drive the sufferer to suicide, so the Ilahita men's fear that their secrets might be exposed to the women drove them in the end to commit the act of revelation themselves.

THE MEHINAKU, THE ARAPESH, AND THE AMBIVALENCE OF GENDER

The Arapesh and Mehinaku cases illustrate the intensity of moral ambivalence for those who participate in men's cults. In both societies the misogynist culture of the cult stands in stark opposition to quotidian life, in which the genders may be affectionate and supportive. As we read the literature of men's cults in Amazonia and Melanesia, we find that this pattern appears in many of the cultures of the area, except in the most intense cases of separation and antagonism of the genders, such as the Sambia and Mundurucú.[20] We believe that this dichotomy of official culture and daily life is itself a defense mechanism. The cult, with its dreamlike misogynistic imagery, encapsulates men's fears and provides them with a physical "sanctuary" (Tuzin 1997). Here in the clubby warmth of the men's house, by the very act of being apart from women, they stake out a claim to masculinity. Their obsessive vigilance and the policing of the boundaries are not to keep women from forcing their way in; the men know that the women understand the consequences and will stand clear when the flutes are blown. What the barriers, the secrecy, the aggression, and the vigilance do is to shore up an insecure sense of the masculine self and allow some expression of the primary-process impulses that underlie the cult—all without hopelessly compromising daily life. In this sense, the pattern is an example of "splitting," a relatively primitive defense mechanism first identified by Karen Horney, by which the individual deals with extreme ambivalence, as in cultures that divide women into "whores" and "virgins" (e.g., Gilmore 1996). In this instance, however, the splitting goes well beyond what Horney had in mind. The symbolic bifurcation of daily life and the myth-cult cleaves not only the image of women but also the physical community, the society, and the culture—all comprehensively riven between gender worlds. The balance is not an easy one, and as both the Mehinaku myth of Pahikyawalu and Arapesh history attest, it is accomplished at high social cost.

INTERPRETATION: VARIATIONS, PHILOSOPHIES OF GENDER, ORIGINS, AND COLLAPSE

A project in cross-cultural comparison naturally searches for similarities and in the process submerges potentially significant differences. Our examination of men's cults has been selective and has generally not dealt with the variations among them. We have, for example, taken little account of the varying intensity of the cults, which differ among themselves in the violence of their initiations, the degree of terrorization of women, the extent and significance of secrecy, and other critical dimensions. In this volume, Hill (Chapter 3) and Hugh-Jones (Chapter 11) examine men's cults that are clearly more muted than many of those cited above. Hill, who deals directly with the issue of variation, interprets some aspects of the cults as showing the interdependence of men and women; such a view is not inconsistent with our "ambivalence" model, though it does emphasize one pole over the other. Hugh-Jones, working from a "relational" perspective developed by Marilyn Strathern, goes further, however, to suggest that the myth-cults are philosophies, or "meditations," that are not so much about compensatory masculinity as they are "a reflection on the nature of the bodies of men and women." Rejecting, in part, his earlier, more psychological interpretations of Barasana symbolism, Hugh-Jones now suggests that gender complementarity and even similarity is the crucial relation, not gender opposition. We err in taking the cult too literally, he avers, because the Barasana themselves do not. Their attitude may be more like that of congregants at a Catholic mass who symbolically drink the blood and eat the flesh of Christ.[21] Few would argue that this says a great deal about the inner life of the participants. What is salient about the Barasana myth-cult, according to Hugh-Jones, is that they see the genders and their sexual biology as reflecting larger themes of the *similarity* of men and women in their common humanity.

What does one make of this interpretation, so skillfully presented by Hill, Strathern, and Hugh-Jones? When does the myth-cult graduate from raw primary-process thought to philosophic meditation? From our perspective, *never*—or at least *almost* never. Any "philosophy" incorporating the elaborate fantasies of men's cults is bound to have at least some emotional significance for those who perpetuate it. In fact, the philosophy of common humanity, to the extent that it is accurately deduced by a relational perspective, may itself be a way of containing the terror that the cult unleashes. The aggression and fear is so inherently painful that we would anticipate a reaction formation and an effort to "undo" the frightening world that it generates. What better mask than the obsessively intricate symbols, the arcane secrets, and the supernatural justifications that constitute cult knowledge? The anthropologist who would interpret this symbolic world as a positive philosophy is encouraged by the androgynous images (such as those associated with male procreativity and the ambiguity of genitalia) that are so pronounced in the symbolism of the cults. Looking at the cults in their most positive light (as most anthropologists are prone to do), what emerges is a reflection about gender and the commonality of male and female.

How might one adjudicate this matter? For us the most reasonable external measure of the extent to which the cults are philosophy or primary process is the degree to which they motivate action. Why would a philosophy espousing the common humanity of men and women also direct adherents to kill and rape their female kin, to force their children into unwelcome homosexual relations, to evulse their sons' teeth, to wrap them in ant frames, and to whip them and even kill them if they violate cult secrets? If the cults are mainly meditations about the commonality of male and female, why do they not say so and be done with it? Granted, all human conduct is overdetermined and has a hermeneutic dimension; but surely the *activities* of the cults are hard-edged realities. For us, the cults are in a land beyond the boundaries of relativism that no philosopher can wholly chart. We are not far in our position from Roger Keesing, who comments on male initiation practices in Melanesia: "I, for one, find the systems described here to be expressions of cruelty, inhumanity, oppression, and error, as well as cultural creativity" (1982, 37).[22] We need the insights of psychology and especially that of personality dynamics to explain the emotional content and the remarkable regularities in men's conduct in such different cultures.

But what if the cult rarely or never impels the men to take aggressive action against women and novices? Such is the case of the contemporary Barasana and the Kukwai described by Jonathan Hill in Chapter 3. In his book describing Barasana initiation, Hugh-Jones (1979) does not describe the whippings and beatings of novices that characterized the cultures of the northwest Amazon in the earlier part of the twentieth century. Jonathan Hill also informs us that the ant frames and other exquisite tortures of initiates have faded among the northern Arawakan people he has studied, gradually eroded by the impact of acculturation. We may thereby propose a continuum of cults based on an altogether different principle from those suggested by Whitehead ("kinship" vs. "clanship") or Allen (the prominence of men's initiation rituals). Our gradient is instead based on the salience of men's rage and fear, which we regard as the psychodynamic engine of the ideas associated with the cults. At one end are cults in full flower, in which men's terror and phallic aggression are fully embodied in ritual and conduct. Representative examples would include the Arapesh and the Sambia in Melanesia and the Mundurucú in South America. At the other end are cults like those of the current Barasana and the Kukwai, where such impulses are distanced from the participants and safely encapsulated in myth and symbol. These symbols, we may presume, once had their roots in the raw earth of sexual angst, but they are now airier formations, whose shape may be profitably examined with more intellectualized approaches. The transition corresponds, at a cultural level, to what "secondary revision" of dream content accomplishes for the individual. Just as a report of a dream conceals that which is emotionally threatening, so may religious systems (including those of the West) tidy up primary-process thought and evolve away from the emotional intensity of their origins.

THE ORIGIN OF THE CULTS

At the outset of this chapter we suggested that men's cults and their similarities in Melanesia and Amazonia are one of the great riddles of human cultural history. How could such parallel worlds develop in such geographically and historically separated regions? What could account for the resemblances of myths, hyperphallic cult objects, elaborate symbolism based on sexual imagery, mutability of gender, male procreative fantasy, the fragility of the masculine self, the uses of secrecy, the pattern of vigilance and obsessiveness, the terrorization of novices, and the phallic aggression toward women and consequent projective identification?

For us, the most persuasive answer comes from psychoanalysis and is perhaps best articulated in a brief paper by Robert Murphy (1959) on the Mundurucú men's cult. Murphy pointed out that the psychological roots of the cult draw on the universal emotional conflicts associated with the Oedipus complex. The simultaneous fear of women and antagonism toward them and the associated myths of matriarchy are reflections of the dark side of the family romance. Since the Oedipus complex is universal, Murphy wondered, "why are we not all swinging bullroarers?" (1959). His answer is that men's cults appear to flourish in social environments where the unity of groups of men and groups of women is not blurred by competing modes of role alloca- tion such as derive from political hierarchy or kinship (see Fisher [Chapter 6] and Descola [Chapter 5]). The small horticultural societies of Amazonia and Melanesia fit this description. In this environment men are unified by collec- tive labor and, especially, the defense of their communities. In Amazonia, women are also brought together in the communal processing of root crops. As a consequence, the division of men and women assumes extraordinary (by cross-cultural standards) social importance. This is fertile ground for the fluo- rescence of ideologies predicated on sex and gender, the embodiment of per- sonal symbols in public life, and the development of the myth-cult.

We may approach the problem in a different way, beginning with the sym- bolic images recurrent in Amazonian and Melanesian ritual ideology. If, as we propose, gender in these societies is anguished by moral contradictions, it fol- lows that the psychological gains bestowed by these ideas are, so to speak, worth the candle of discomfort. Although it goes without saying that these traditions are transmitted through cult initiation procedures, bush schools, folklore, and the like, the appeal and believability of these often fantastical ideas may be seen to rest on proclivities acquired in childhood. What is it, then, about childhood in these two regions that might account for their dis- tinctive similarities?

The intense, isolated relationship with the mother in infancy (see above) is part of the answer. But we may look in middle childhood, also. In brief, drawing upon an earlier study by one of the authors (Tuzin 1990), we pro- pose that part of the answer may lie in the scale and vitality of children's— especially boys'—groups in sedentary, tropical, tribal horticultural societies. Settlement and subsistence conditions are such that while girls in middle childhood are able and required to participate in subsistence activities, prac- tically from the time they can walk, boys at the same age are typically unable to perform heavy or dangerous men's work, namely, hunting, the clearing of forest, and the defense of the community. If the sexual division of labor is marked, as it would be in societies of these regions, given that the exigencies of food-getting favor the bifurcation of male and female responsibilities from an early age, little boys would not be called upon to assist their mothers, es- pecially if they are encouraged to remain separate from women to the great- est extent possible.

Such an arrangement establishes boys in a social world both actively and pas- sively separated from that of women, most significantly the mother, and not yet that of men. Cultural propositions are transmitted intergenerationally, but to an extent perhaps uncommon in, say, hunter-forager and pastoral societies,[23] a good deal of knowledge is also transmitted *intragenerationally,* within the relatively autonomous community of boys, where seemingly minor differences in age can produce inordinate differences in prestige and authority. Not only the mode of transmission but the types of knowledge involved, consisting of childish understandings about matters of sexuality, mystery, taboo, and danger, could dynamically foreshadow the style and content of adult imagination. Further enculturation in adolescence and adulthood might mitigate (or exacerbate) some of these earlier understandings, but the basic cognitive and emotional orientation acquired by children *from* children appears to persist and to influence the psychocultural functioning of adult institutions, men's cults in particular.

DEMISE OF THE CULTS AND MORAL AMBIVALENCE

The death of the Arapesh men's cult and the transitions that have marked those of the Barasana and Lakolai are by no means unusual. In many parts of the world men's cults are on the wane. Even where much of traditional culture otherwise persists, rape, violent initiations, and men's secrets have slipped away. There are surely many reasons. The decline of warfare is unquestionably critical, as illustrated by the Sambia, who initiated their last group of young men back in the 1970s. The decline of group life and the individualizing effect of external economic systems seems to have been instrumental in the end of the Mundurucú cult and others. The union of men, unsupported by the need for coordinated military action and fragmented by the impact of cash economies, could not endure.

But often, as in the case of the Arapesh, the demise of the cults is as much due to their internal flaws as to external pressure. Even in the instance of the Mundurucú, perhaps Amazonia's most rigid myth-cult, external pressures impinged on the villagers more as "choices." They could gain access to trade goods and live with their wives and work as rubber tappers, or they could remain at home and maintain the myth-cult. Many chose to leave for reasons that one might assume were not strictly economic.

In fact, the cults are fragile, if dark, flowers. The myths, rituals, and sexualized objects that constitute them are frightening acts of imagination, drawn from painful fears, wishes, and conflicts. The fantastical elaborations are in their way among the most remarkable of human creations, but they are ultimately out of joint, disconnected from the realities they claim to read, and subverted at every turn by positive relationships with mothers, sisters, wives, and daughters. As such, adherents are beset by nagging doubts and moral qualms. Among the Arapesh, even while the Tambaran was in full flower, this uncertainty was experienced as guilt and foreboding, and upon its death, as severe metaphysical disorientation. Among the Mehinaku, where the cult still lives, individuals voice their doubts ("it was those headless, faceless idiots of long ago, of mythic times, that did this") and the myth of Pahikyawalu expresses the villagers' collective anguish. Ultimately, the cults rest on the quicksand of moral ambivalence, and, as events proved among the Arapesh, their existence is precarious.

In all of this, there is a broad lesson both about the nature of the human condition and how we understand it. As social scientists we are trained to withhold moral judgment and to understand conduct primarily within its cultural context. This position has in many ways been salutary for anthropology. But it has also underwritten a relativism so extreme as to forgo not only judgment but also a search for what is general in the human experience. Men's cults, by exhibiting striking resemblances in Melanesia and Amazonia, respectively, broaden our focus. They encourage a shift in attention from cultural differences to core similarities, in this case of the psychology of the cult and its members, and more generally the psychology of gender. It is at this level that one finds the fears, anxieties, and yearnings that generate the cult, its fantastic symbols, and the far-reaching moral consequences for men and women. The comparative perspective, the basis of this volume, thereby takes us well beyond specific cultural contexts toward broad understandings of who we are as human beings.

NOTES

The authors are indebted to the Wenner-Gren Foundation for making this chapter possible. We are especially appreciative of the many suggestions of Dr. Volney Gay, a practicing psychoanalyst, who is also a professor in Vanderbilt University's departments of Religion, Anthropology, and Psychiatry.

1. In South America, men's cults of the kind that we will describe occur in four regions, including the northwest Amazon, the Upper Xingu, the upper Tapajos River, and, outside of Amazonia, in the Tierra del Fuego. In Melanesia, such cults are reported principally in the Sepik, Papuan Gulf, Eastern Highlands, and Mountain Ok regions of mainland New Guinea; the off-lying islands of New Britain, New Ireland, and the Duke of York group; the Solomon Islands; and Vanuatu.

2. As fantastic as this idea may seem, it is not inconceivable. Roger Keesing, in the context of Melanesian men's cults, speculates that the myth-cult is very ancient: "These forms of male cultism are very old. . . . My guess is that these systems developed under either hunting-gathering or hunting-horticultural regimens" (1982, 15). Other widespread religious ideas and practices may enjoy great antiquity. In *Muelos, a Stone Age Superstition about Sexuality*, for example, Weston LaBarre (1984) persuasively documents a set of ideas about body imagery that may well have their roots in the Paleolithic.

3. The myths from diverse regions within Amazonia and Melanesia are very similar on this point; we are aware of only a few instances in which the flutes or cult instruments were discovered or invented by men (see Gewertz 1988, 109).

4. As Hays (1988) puts it, in examining the Amazonian myths, Melanesianists look at these tales with a sense of déjà vu.

5. Interestingly, the myth, touching so deeply on gender issues, is itself a projective screen for the unwary anthropologist. Hence in Bamberger's interpretation (1974, 280), the myth is "but a tool used to keep woman bound to her place" and suggests a path toward liberation: "to free her we need to destroy the myth." The context for understanding the myth, however, is not contemporary gender politics or Western feminism but the men's cult in which it blossoms.

6. The Arapesh myth of the penis as a meandering trickster (Tuzin 1972) pairs almost identically with the Mehinaku myths of Kapukwa and the wandering vagina (Gregor 1985). See also Murphy and Murphy (1974, 100) for other Amazonian variants.

7. We recognize that the Shipibo did not have formal men's institutions, even though they had beliefs and practices associated with the myth-cult. Their practice of clitoridectomy is the only instance we are aware of in the Amazonian and Melanesian literature. It is striking that the ideology of clitoridectomy for the Shipibo fits much better with the men's myth-cult than that of sub-Saharan Africa, where the justification is in terms of sexual modesty and decency.

8. The familiar classical myth of the Amazons, in which masculinized women cut off their left breasts to facilitate archery, may make use of some of the same elements and themes of the detachability of organs and the mutability of gender.

9. "Papua New Guineans live in a gender-inflected universe in which the polarities of male and female articulate cosmic forces thought to be located in the human body; indigenous theories of human reproduction contain within them an implicit recipe for social reproduction" (Lindenbaum 1987, 222).

10. Note that the image is nearly identical to the Melanesian example of the bullroarer, cited just above.

11. To be "beltless" (*mowantalutsi*) in the Mehinaku dress code is to be naked.

12. The Yahgan of Tierra del Fuego are well south of Amazonia but possessed an intense and exceptionally well-documented men's cult that parallels many of the others in both Amazonia and Melanesia.

13. What Michael Jackson reports for the Karunka of northern Sierra Leone could apply as well to many societies of Amazonia and Melanesia (and Australia), hinting that the parallel elaborations marking the latter regions are, in part, anchored in more widely occurrent social and psychological imperatives. The "work" of the cult, Jackson was told, was "to keep men and women separate" (1977, 220). "Some informants confessed," continues Jackson (p. 221), "that within the cult 'there isn't really very much, though for the women it is awesome.' The secret objects themselves are far less significant than the principle of secrecy and the mystical powers which they symbolise. The betrayal of cult secrets leads not only to the punishment of the offender . . . , it also threatens the social order. For, 'if women have no respect for men then the principles of manhood will be as nothing.'"

14. For an especially dramatic South American example, see the illustrations of the Yurupuri flutes and trumpets from the northwest Amazon in S. Hugh-Jones (1979).

15. See Tuzin (1984) for an analysis of the sonic qualities of such instruments and their impact on the listener.

16. See Dundes (1976) for a somewhat different but persuasive interpretation, which sees the bullroarer as merging symbols of the male phallus with the anal birth of initiates. The association of the bullroarer with men's secret rituals around the world (see Lowie 1920) is in and of itself remarkable and suggests how well adapted it is as a part of the material

culture of men's cults. It expresses power and procreativity, while it intimidates the women, who are the uninitiated.

17. Hence Meigs (1984, 134) notes that Hua claim that if the women saw the flutes, "they would ridicule men for the stupid ruse by which they maintain their power."

18. The contaminating quality of the flutes can also affect women. Hence among the Desana, when the women touched the flutes and then their own bodies, "suddenly hair grew on their pubis and under their armpits, places that previously had no hair" (Reichel-Dolmatoff 1971, 169–170).

19. We are in debt to Volney Gay for this observation.

20. Herdt reports that men's and women's relationships are never comfortable, and that men fear women's genitals, which are "hot." The Mundurucú case, as reported by the Murphys, also suggests that the antagonism of the cult is carried on between individual men and women.

21. Stephen Hugh-Jones suggests this analogy (personal communication).

22. The vehemence of Keesing's remark is unusual in the literature even though often informally articulated by colleagues who have worked with men's cults. Although anthropology as a value-free science is in many ways laudable, the commitment to relativism produces an active bias against the study of ethical values (and moral ambivalence), especially in small-scale cultures (Tuzin 1982, 325).

23. For reasons discussed in Tuzin (1990), the *inter*generational transmission of cultural knowledge tends to be most pronounced in societies at the scalar extremes: the smallest, because of settlement size and subsistence regimes; the largest, because of formal educational institutions.

FOURTEEN

Reflections on the Land of Melazonia

Thomas A. Gregor and Donald Tuzin

How can we explain the compelling similarities between various sociocultural features indigenous to Melanesia and the Amazon? Along what dimensions might they be studied? Are the similarities "real," or merely artifacts of method or even imagination? More broadly, how can we construct a comparative method that could encompass cultures separated by half a world of space and at least 40,000 years in time? Separately and in aggregate, the preceding studies shed light on these questions. Most of them focused on the interregional comparison in the context of specific societies or relatively circumscribed ethnographic themes or theoretical models. As in all good ethnographic analysis, the devils were in the details—but so were the angels, and they are now known to us. In these remaining passages, then, we step back from the specific contributions and consider the case in a more general fashion. Our intention is to reflect from our own perspective on what we described in the introduction as the imaginary land of Melazonia.

In large part the Amazonia-Melanesia similarities consist of, or are traceable to, the limited possibilities imposed by conditions of tropical rainforest adaptation. Thus, many societies in both regions display the following characteristics: subsistence systems based on swidden horticulture and supplemented by fishing, hunting, and foraging; a pronounced sexual division of labor; dispersed settlements rarely containing more than a few hundred inhabitants; an egalitarian ethos disfavoring heritable rank, let alone stable social, political, or economic hierarchies; social relations based on marriage and kinship alliances, along with other forms of gift exchange; descent groups nonexistent or of weak corporate constitution, with flexible membership rules; warfare and raiding as the normal state between enemy and stranger groups; and elaborate ritual and mythical traditions, often centered on concepts of the body, procreativity, and secret men's cults. Of these parallels, the last-named (i.e., the sources and applications of ritual and mythic images) appear less derived from material circumstances. Precisely for this reason, such interregional symbolic resonance presents itself as more interesting and challenging than the previous, seemingly more expectable similarities. After all, what is there about a common ecology that could also predict myths of matriarchy or a preoccupation with bodily symbols? And yet, the parallel symbolic constructions are woven into the material fabric of life. To us they appear to be inextricably bound, implying that there is a functional linkage between the two. We will return to this relationship in a moment.

The studies presented here gain analytic leverage by examining the interregional comparison chiefly through the lens of gender. Although gender is currently of major anthropological interest, and although gender is as good a topic as any for analytically "controlling" the comparison, these were not the principal reasons for choosing it as a theme. For us, the gender focus of this volume is compelling on at least two general grounds. First, gender bridges the ontological gap between material and symbolic worlds by simultaneously anchoring itself in biological sex and cultural ideology—the two of which are brought together in the course of psychosocial development. Second, as a biocultural hybrid, gender penetrates and suffuses multiple existential domains and thereby structures emotion, cognition, ideation, and social behavior.

This leads to another, more specific justification for the focus on gender. To an unusual extent, as our contributors make clear, the societies and cultures of Amazonia and Melanesia are "gender-inflected" (Lindenbaum 1987). That is to say, in both regions differences between males and females are commonly used as a model for the organization of other differences occurring in the areas of social action, cultural ideology, perceived nature, and the cosmos. The differences may be complementary, oppositional, or downright adversarial; they may be biological facts of life, psychologically projected fantasies, or cultural constructions; they may lodge in the public arena or in the recesses of private imagination. Though the particular contours and contents of the inflection vary according to local circumstances, as shown by the essays in this volume, through it all can be seen the dangerous, procreative, erotic, sometimes disguised, and always ambivalent play of gender distinctions. For the cultural anthropologist, this characteristic is markedly present in the general Amazonia-Melanesia comparison. It is, indeed, a hallmark of both cultural regions and provides a secure basis for the comparisons we have initiated.

Of course, all societies are gender-inflected to some extent. "Male"/"female" distinctions are commonplace metaphors in the West, and in the East gender figures prominently as an organizing principle in, say, Hindu (especially Tantric) religion and cosmology and in the folk traditions of Buddhism (e.g., Spiro 1997)—to name only two examples. But such traditions utilize many other templates as well. In archaic states, kingdoms, and modern industrial societies, political and religious hierarchies, economic and occupational diversity, race and ethnicity, and other formations are ample sources of metaphors for generating and expressing meaningful differences. What distinguishes Amazonia and Melanesia from virtually all other regions is the relatively exclusive reliance on gender contrasts for general symbolic work, from which follows the fact that gender inflections are more *intense* in those regions than in others (e.g., Astuti 1998; Busby 1997b). While elsewhere competing with many other organizing principles, in Amazonia and Melanesia gender shares the field with few rivals.

This is not to say that alternative principles are altogether missing. With respect to Amazonia, we would cite Fisher (Chapter 6), who maintains that at least among the Kayapo, gender is to a degree interwoven with age categories. Viveiros de Castro (1992) looks to predator/prey relationships as a significant organizing template for many Amazonian cultures, and Descola (Chapter 5) minimizes the significance of gender and substitutes affinal relationships as the model for Amazonian symbolism. We are appreciative of these efforts; there is surely room for a multiplicity of analytical approaches. But we are also somewhat skeptical, in that the coupling of human biology and symbolism creates a powerful psychological reality for many peoples of Amazonia, as in Melanesia. It is not the construct of the analyst but *the lived experience* of the individual. The proof of this pudding is demonstrated by both the literature and the success of our authors in framing their gender-based comparisons. Further, we note that the main alternative—the current rage among interpretive ethnographers in both regions—is itself so suffused with gender significance as to be hardly distinguishable from it. Hence, the body—its parts (head, vagina, breast, penis, nose), substances (blood, bone, hair, semen, milk), and processes (birth, growth, aging, death)—permeate native ideas about masculinity and femininity and are the vital constituents of the social and psychological person.

This merging with bodily phenomena is a clue to gender's primordial character, hence its close proximity to some of the most primitive imaginings of all—primitive, that is, in the life of the individual and in the life of the species. As just noted, with increasing scale and complexity, societies develop new expressive needs and new symbolic resources for servicing them; gender inflections persist but are overlaid and obscured by novel meanings drawn from more rarified areas of experience. Along this trajectory our own society has reached the point where, in some circles, gender distinctions and inflections are actively suppressed and denied, on the theory that they are an unwelcome legacy of an archaic ("patriarchal") past that can be expunged by political action, the law, and the civil courts. Whether or not this ultimate postmodern solution is attainable, or whether it too will succumb to the law of the return of the repressed, the idea does underscore the anachronistic aura of gender inflectedness in a society that has (or *thinks* it has) outgrown its need for primordial significances of its own.

Under the existential constraints enumerated earlier, traditional societies in Melanesia and Amazonia are at a level of scale and complexity particularly conducive to the prominent gender reckoning addressed in this volume. To the extent that other regions—for example, west and central Africa—contain societies of similar type, gender-inflected ideas and institutions, such as men's organizations, occur there as well (e.g., Jackson 1977). In most such cases, however, the cultural prominence of gender is muted by the immediate or nearby presence of countervailing political and symbolic formations, such as ranked lineages, chiefdoms and kingships, and all that goes with them.

Our own Western societies make the point in a particularly effective way. In general, industrial cultures operate through a multiplicity of principles: the marketplace and its pressure for economic rationality and the organizing principles of religion, political affiliation, race, and social class. But this is not to say that we are so different from the tribal peoples of Amazonia and Melanesia. The striking parallels of male ethos in tribal cultures and Western men's clubs, fraternities, and barracks show that we all struggle with similar primal problems. The difference is to be found in the degree to which private symbols intrude themselves into the public domain and become a major template for organizing social life (see Murphy 1959; Kroeber 1923, 126; Gregor 1985). In Western culture there are only scattered islands and promontories of gender sovereignty, and they are beleaguered fortresses, newly threatened by the rising tide of public scorn and litigation. In many societies of Melanesia and Amazonia, however, Gender is still King.

If, according to our argument, the scale of the societies in our comparison is necessarily not overly great, neither is it overly small. For the effects examined in this volume to occur, a certain "critical mass" is generally required. Without a sufficient size of sex *and age* cohorts, gender cannot be fully cognized; there are simply not enough persons of similar life station to motivate, enact, or propagate a sense of solidarity on the basis of gender alone. As described by Lee (1979), among the !Kung San of the Kalahari Desert in Southern Africa, men identify themselves as caring husbands, responsible fathers, skilled hunters, effective healers, respected elders—but hardly ever simply as *men*. In a fascinating comparative study Patricia Draper (1976) describes how settled !Kung, living as cattle herders in large settlements, have developed marked gender categories that contrast strongly with the relatively undifferentiated nomadic !Kung. In Melanesia we have a similar historical divergence of the Mountain Arapesh, made famous by Margaret Mead (1935) for their purported absence of gender distinctions, and their close linguistic cousins, the Ilahita Arapesh, whose gender inflections are extreme even by New Guinea standards, brought about by the latter's sudden increase in settlement size and social complexity.

With demography as a background, there are a number of theories that reasonably connect gender inflectedness to the division of labor and to socialization. In many of the societies of Melanesia and Amazonia the social groupings not only are the right size for homogeneous gender cohorts but also actively encourage their formation. The need for defense, which is so prominent in both regions, brings men together *as* men and contrasts them with women. This is fertile ground for the growth of an intense (and often anxious) ideology based on sex and gender differences (Murphy 1959), as well as the mutual reliance and complementarity seen by some of our contributors. Similarly, both regions follow similar paths of early socialization, in which children enjoy an extended and even lush relationship with the mother only to experience a relatively painful separation when they are replaced at their mother's breast, in her hammock or bed, and on her hip by a younger sibling. This pattern may itself rest upon the protein-deficient root crops that are the staple in both regions and the consequent need for prolonged lactation (see Whiting, Kluckhohn, and Anthony 1958). In any event, the long period of intimacy with the mother and the separation from her poses precisely the kinds of issues implied by men's cults: extreme ambivalence toward women and anxiety and preoccupation with issues of sex and gender.

In our essay (Gregor and Tuzin, Chapter 13), we hazarded an additional account of why the societies of the two regions support men's cults or other strongly gender-inflected institutions. In brief, tropical-horticultural societies typically support a substantial group of coresidential youngsters (especially boys), flourishing largely outside the tuition or surveillance of adults. This occurs because men's work (gardening, hunting, and warring) is either too heavy or too dangerous for boys to participate in, whereas girls typically assist in women's work (foraging, crafts, and child care) from an early age. These conditions are right for a considerable amount of cultural knowledge to be transmitted *within* the "society" of youths, a process of *self*-enculturation during a period of life characterized by intense, anxious curiosity about sexual and gender-oriented things, with major implications for identity formation and the internalization of beliefs. These learning circumstances would have feed-forward effects precisely supportive of the gender-inflected practices, colorful ritual and mythic traditions, and secret men's cults these boys stand to inherit as adults.

None of these explanations is flawless. The Australian Aborigines and the Yahgan of the Tierra del Fuego in South America are anomalous, in that they are band-level hunter-foragers whose cultural approach to gender resembles that of Melanesian and Amazonian village horticulturalists. On the other hand, the explanations do make headway in synthesizing social, cultural, and psychological variables around the question of how gender comes to be hypercognized and widely inflected, how it remains so over structural time, and why it is more salient in certain kinds of societies than in others. In the immediate context of this volume, the explanation also helps to account for why the Jívaroan Achuar (Descola, Chapter 5), with their tiny settlements, are decidedly less preoccupied with gender than are, say, cultures of the northwest Amazon—though, as Descola's data demonstrate, they hardly ignore it.

For reasons that bear both on their general similarities to one another and on their mutual emphasis on gender and its inflections, Amazonia and Melanesia occupy the same middle range of cross-cultural societal variation. They are large enough in scale to have sufficient sociocultural *matériel* for the metaphoric elaboration of gender differences, yet small enough to retain close connection with existential realities of a more primordial character. Gender "speaks" with special clarity to those primordial concerns, for it is deeply implicated in feelings and understandings about personal and sexual identity, the body, procreation, and power. The Amazonia-Melanesia studies developed in this volume not only confirm and refine this appreciation; they disclose ways in which gender, its inflections and preoccupations, can come to permeate the ideas, institutions, and subjective experiences common to entire cultural regions—and beyond.

More broadly, the studies speak to the power and versatility of the comparative method. As Boas rightly perceived, the Victorian "comparative method" was unacceptably Procrustean in that cross-cultural comparisons were manipulated in order to verify the doctrine of a universal, unilineal sequence of cultural development. The critique was important and timely, but it had certain unfortunate long-term consequences. First, it discredited (or placed impossible demands upon) comparison *as such*, thus precluding (or continually obstructing) the emergence of anthropology as a humanistic science. Second, the Boasian critique discredited the search for universals of human experience and culture, thus leaving cultural anthropology ill-equipped, intellectually and methodologically, to incorporate eventual (especially late twentieth century) discoveries in psychology, evolutionary biology, neuroscience, and genetics, all of which operate comfortably at the interface of universal and particular humanity. Finally, it fostered—as a supposed alternative to universalism—the doctrine of cultural relativism, which, carried to its logical conclusion, glorifies the very incomparability of cultures. Such cultural insularity is, in our view, a fantasy, but it has contributed to what has become a very real intellectual insularity among cultural anthropologists, and on the part of anthropology vis-à-vis important allied disciplines; this insularity—or, if you will, fragmentation or lack of common cause—underlies the malaise or postparadigmatic sense of crisis one detects in current anthropology.

This volume will not undo all of these consequences, but the authors and editors hope that it will open new and more positive ways of thinking about cross-cultural—indeed, cross-regional—comparison. Unlike the Victorian notion of the same name, the comparative method celebrated here is not monolithic; even less is it Procrustean. Rather, as this collection demonstrates, comparison is a method that is highly adaptable to local empirical circumstances, particular theoretical aspirations, and even differing epistemological stances. The comparative method is proven to be, in fact, a basket of strategies, all of which share the methodological characteristic of guiding inquiry to higher levels of generality. Crucially—because the process is intrinsic to the comparative method—these generalizations reflect back upon, and confer a deeper understanding of, the phenomena originally in question. In its noblest aspect, however, the comparative method illuminates that which transcends specific cultures and regions and broadly encompasses the human condition. If this volume is entitled to any claim of success, it is because human experience, even in cultures separated by immense gulfs of time and space, is built on similar realities. These constitute the bedrock of the land of Melazonia that, thanks to the efforts of the contributors to this volume, is beginning to come into view.

REFERENCES

Albert, Bruce. 1985. "Temps du sang, Temps des cendres: Represéntation de la maladie, système rituel et espace politique chez les Yanomami du sud-est (Amazonie brésilienne)." Ph.D. dissertation, Université de Paris X.

Allen, Bryant J. 1976. "Information Flow and Innovation Diffusion in the East Sepik District, Papua New Guinea." Unpublished Ph.D. thesis, Australian National University.

Allen, Bryant, and Stephen Frankel. 1991. "Across the Tari Furoro." In E. L. Schieffelin and R. Crittenden, eds., *Like People You See in a Dream: First Contact in Six Papuan Societies*, pp. 88–124. Stanford: Stanford University Press.

Allen, Michael R. 1967. *Male Cults and Secret Initiations in Melanesia*. Melbourne: Melbourne University Press.

———. 1998. Male Cults Revisited: The Politics of Blood and Semen. *Oceania* 68:188–199.

Altenfelde Silva, Fernando. 1950. O Estado de Uanki entre os Bakairi. *Sociologia* 12:259–271.

Apo, Moge. 1986. "Magendo No. 1 Village, East Sepik Province." In Anon., ed., *Marriage in Papua New Guinea*, pp. 139–151. Boroko: Law Reform Commission of Papua New Guinea.

Århem, Kaj. 1983. *Makuna Social Organization*. Uppsala Studies in Cultural Anthropology, 4. Stockholm: Liber Tryck.

———. 1990. "Ecosofia Makuna." In F. Correa, ed., *La selva humanizada. Ecología alternativa en el Trópico húmedo colombiano*, pp. 105–122. Bogotá: Instituto Colombiano de Antropología.

———. 1996. "The Cosmic Food Web: Human-Nature Relatedness in the Northwest Amazon." In P. Descola and G. Pálsson, eds., *Nature and Society: Anthropological Perspectives*, pp. 185–204. London: Routledge.

Ariss, Robert. 1992. Foucault in the Highlands: The Production of Men in Papua New Guinea Societies. *The Australian Journal of Anthropology* 3:143–149.

Arlow, Jacob A. 1961. Ego Psychology and the Study of Mythology. *Journal of the American Psychoanalytic Association* 9:371–393.

Asea, Mana. 1986. "Iki Village, Western Highlands Province." In Anon., ed., *Marriage in Papua New Guinea*, pp. 76–84. Boroko: Law Reform Commission of Papua New Guinea.

Astuti, Rita. 1998. "'It's a Boy,' 'It's a Girl!' Reflections on Sex and Gender in Madagascar and Beyond." In M. Lambek and A. Strathern, eds., *Bodies and Persons: Comparative Perspectives from Africa and Melanesia*, pp. 29–52. New York: Cambridge University Press.

Aufenanger, Henry. 1972. *The Passing Scene in North-east New-Guinea.* Collectanea Instituti Anthropos 2. St. Augustin, Germany: Anthropos Institute.

Baldus, Herbert. 1937. *Ensaios de Ethnologia Brasileira.* São Paulo: Companhia Editoria Nacional.

Bamberger, Joan. 1967. "Environment and Cultural Classification: A Study of the Northern Kayapó." Unpublished Ph.D. dissertation, Harvard University.

———. 1974. "The Myth of Matriarchy: Why Men Rule in Primitive Society." In M. Rosaldo and L. Lamphere, eds., *Women, Culture, and Society,* pp. 263–280. Stanford: Stanford University Press.

Banner, Horace. n.d. "Distinção de Classe entre os Indios Kayapo." Unpublished manuscript.

Barlow, Kathleen. 1985. The Role of Women in Intertribal Trade among the Murik of Papua New Guinea. *Research in Economic Anthropology* 7:95–122.

Barnes, J. A. 1962. African Models in the New Guinea Highlands. *Man* 62:5–9.

———. 1970. *Three Styles in the Study of Kinship.* Berkeley: University of California Press.

Barnes, R. H. 1987. "Anthropological Comparison." In L. Holy, ed., *Comparative Anthropology,* pp. 119–134. Oxford: Basil Blackwell.

Barth, Fredrik. 1975. *Ritual and Knowledge among the Baktaman of New Guinea.* New Haven: Yale University Press.

———. 1987. *Cosmologies in the Making: A Generative Approach to Cultural Variation in Inner New Guinea.* Cambridge: Cambridge University Press.

Basso, Ellen. 1973. *The Kalapalo Indians of Central Brazil.* New York: Holt, Rhinehart and Winston.

———. 1985. *A Musical View of the Universe.* Tucson: University of Arizona Press.

———. 1995. *The Last Cannibals: A South American Oral History.* Austin: University of Texas Press.

Bastos, Rafael. 1978. *A Musicolólogia Kamayurá.* Brasilia: FUNAI.

Bateson, Gregory. 1932. Social Structure of the Iatmül People of the Sepik River. *Oceania* 2:245–291, 401–453.

———. 1958. *Naven.* Stanford: Stanford University Press.

Beauvoir, Simone de. 1952 [1949]. *The Second Sex.* New York: Alfred Knopf.

Bellier, I. 1993. Réflexions sur la question du genre dans les sociétés amazoniennes. *L'Homme* 126–128:517–526.

Benedict, Ruth. 1959 [1934]. *Patterns of Culture.* Boston: Houghton Mifflin.

Berndt, Ronald M. 1962. *Excess and Restraint: Social Control among a New Guinea Mountain People.* Chicago: University of Chicago Press.

———. 1965. "The Kamano, Usurufa, Jate and Fore of the Eastern Highlands." In P. Lawrence and M. J. Meggitt, eds., *Gods, Ghosts and Men in Melanesia: Some Religions of Australian New Guinea and the New Hebrides,* pp. 78–104. Melbourne: Oxford University Press.

Bidou, Patrice. 1996. Trois mythes de l'origine du manioc (Nord-Ouest de l'Amazonie). *L'Homme* 140:63–79.

Biersack, Aletta. 1982. Ginger Gardens for the Ginger Woman: Rites and Passages in a Melanesian Society. *Man* 17:239–258.

————. 1984. Paiela "Women-Men": The Reflexive Foundations of Gender Ideology. *American Ethnologist* 11(1):118–138.

————. 1987. Moonlight: Negative Images of Transcendence in Paiela Pollution. *Oceania* 57:178–194.

————. 1995. "Heterosexual Meanings: Society, the Body, and the Economy among Ipilis." In A. Biersack, ed., *Papuan Borderlands: Huli, Duna, and Ipili Perspectives on the Papua New Guinea Highlands*, pp. 231–268. Ann Arbor: University of Michigan Press.

————. 1996. Word Made Flesh: Religion, the Economy, and the Body in the Papua New Guinea Highlands. *The History of Religions* 36:85–111.

————. 1998. "Horticulture and Hierarchy: The Youthful Beautification of the Body in the Paiela and Porgera Valleys." In G. H. Herdt and S. Leavitt, eds., *Adolescence in the Pacific Island Societies*, pp. 71–91. Pittsburgh: University of Pittsburgh Press.

————. In press. "Interpreting the Ipili Spirit Wife." In P. Bonnemère, ed., *Women in Male Rituals of Papua New Guinea*. Ann Arbor: University of Michigan Press.

Bloch, Maurice. 1982. "Death, Women and Power." In M. Bloch and J. Parry, eds., *Death and the Regeneration of Life*, pp. 211–230. Cambridge: Cambridge University Press.

————. 1986. *Blessing and Violence*. Cambridge: Cambridge University Press.

————. 1992. *Prey into Hunter: The Politics of Religious Experience*. New York: Cambridge University Press.

Bloch, Maurice, and Jonathan Parry. 1982. "Introduction: Death and the Regeneration of Life." In M. Bloch and J. Parry, eds., *Death and the Regeneration of Life*, pp. 1–44. Cambridge: Cambridge University Press.

Boas, Franz. 1940 [1896]. "The Limitations of the Comparative Method of Anthropology." In *Race, Language and Culture*, pp. 270–280. New York: Macmillan.

Boccara, G. 1996. "Des Reche aux Mapuche (16°–18° siècles). Ethnogenèse et identité dans le Chili central." Ph.D. dissertation, Ecole des Hautes Etudes en Sciences Sociales, Paris.

Bohlen, Joseph B., James P. Held, Olwen Sanderson, and Robert P. Patterson. 1984. Heart Rate, Rate-Pressure Product, and Oxygen Uptake during Four Sexual Activities. Part 2. *Archives of Internal Medicine* 144:1745–1748.

Bolton, Lissant. 1996. "A Subtle Difference: Lengwasa—A Woman's Title-Taking Ceremony on Maewo, Vanuatu." Unpublished paper delivered to the Anthropology Colloqium, Australian National University, July.

Bonnemère, Pascale. 1990. Considérations relatives aux représentations des substances corporelles en Nouvelle-Guinée. *L'Homme* 30 (2):101–120.

————. 1992. "Le casoar, le pandanus rouge et l'anguille: Différence des sexes, substances et parenté chez les Ankave-Anga (Nouvelle-Guinée)." Ph.D. dissertation, Ecole des Hautes Etudes en Sciences Sociales, Paris.

————. 1993. Maternal Nurturing Substance and Paternal Spirit: The Making of a Southern Anga Sociality. *Oceania* 64:159–86.

————. 1994. Le pandanus rouge dans tous ses états: L'univers social et symbolique d'un arbre fruitier chez les Ankave-Anga (Papouasie-Nouvelle-Guinée). *Annales Fyssen* 9:1–32.

————. 1996. *Le pandanus rouge: Corps, différences des sexes et parenté chez les Ankave-Anga (Papouasie-Nouvelle-Guinée)*. Paris: CNRS Editions/Editions de la maison des sciences de l'homme.

Bourdieu, Pierre. 1977 [1972]. *Outline of a Theory of Practice*. Cambridge: Cambridge University Press.

————. 1990 [1980]. *The Logic of Practice*. Cambridge: Polity Press.

Bourgue, François. 1976. Los caminos de los hijos del cielo; estudio sociotemporal de los Kawillary del Cananarí y del Apoporís. *Revista Colombiana de Antropología* 20:101–144

————. n.d. Fieldnotes.

Bowden, Ross. 1983. *Yena: Art and Ceremony in a Sepik Society*. Oxford: Pitt Rivers Museum.

Boyd, David J. 1991. "Fore." In T. E. Hays, ed., *Encyclopedia of World Cultures*, vol. 2: *Oceania*, pp. 62–65. Boston: G. K. Hall.

Boyd, David J., and Karen C. Ito. 1988. "Culture and Context: Reproductive Decision Making in Okapa District, Eastern Highlands Province." In N. McDowell, ed., *Reproductive Decision Making and the Value of Children in Rural Papua New Guinea*, pp. 45–70. Boroko: Institute of Applied Social and Economic Research.

Brain, James L. 1979. *The Last Taboo: Sex and the Fear of Death*. Garden City, N.J.: Doubleday.

Brandewie, Ernest B. 1981. *Contrast and Context in New Guinea Culture: The Case of the Mbowamb of the Central Highlands*. St. Augustin, Germany: Anthropos-Institut.

Brison, Karen. 1992. *Just Talk: Gossip, Meetings, and Power in a Papua New Guinea Village*. Berkeley: University of California Press.

Broch-Due, Vigdis. 1993. "Making Meaning Out of Matter: Perceptions of Sex, Gender and Bodies among the Turkana." In V. Broch-Due, I. Rudie, and T. Bleie, eds., *Carved Flesh/Cast Selves: Gendered Symbols and Social Practices*, pp. 53–82. Oxford: Berg.

Brown, D. J. J. 1979. The Structuring of Polopa Feasting and Warfare. *Man* 14:712–732.

Brown, Michael F. 1986. *Tsewa's Gift: Magic and Meaning in an Amazonian Society*. Washington, D.C.: Smithsonian Institution Press.

————. 1993. Facing the State, Facing the World: Amazonia's Native Leaders and the New Politics of Identity. In A.-C. Taylor and P. Descola, eds., *La Remontée de l'Amazone: Anthropologie et Histoire des Sociétés Amazoniennes*. Special issue of *L'Homme* 33(2–4): 311–320.

————. 1994. "Beyond Resistance: A Comparative Study of Utopian Renewal in Amazonia." In A. C. Roosevelt, ed., *Amazonian Indians from Prehistory to the Present: Anthropological Perspectives*, pp. 287–311. Tucson: University of Arizona Press.

Brown, Michael F., and Eduardo Fernández. 1991. *War of Shadows: The Struggle for Utopia in the Peruvian Amazon*. Berkeley: University of California Press.

Brown, Paula, and Georgeda Buchbinder, eds. 1976. *Man and Woman in the New Guinea Highlands*. Washington, D.C.: American Anthropological Association.

Brumbaugh, Robert C. 1980a. Models of Separation and a Mountain Ok Religion. *Ethos* 8:332–348.

————. 1980b. "A Secret Cult in the West Sepik Highlands." Unpublished Ph.D. dissertation, SUNY–Stony Brook.

————. 1990. "'Afek Sang': The Old Woman's Legacy to the Mountain-Ok." In B. Craig and D. Hyndman, eds., *Children of Afek: Tradition and Change Among the Mountain-Ok of Central New Guinea*. Oceania Monograph no. 40, pp. 54–87. Sydney: University of Sydney Press.

Bruner, Jerome S. 1960. "Myth and Identity." In H. A. Murray, ed., *Myths and Mythmaking*, pp. 276–287. New York: George Braziller.

Buchbinder, Georgeda, and Roy A. Rappaport. 1976. "Fertility and Death among Maring." In P. Brown and G. Buchbinder, eds., *Man and Woman in the New Guinea Highlands*, pp. 13–35. Washington, D.C.: American Anthropological Association.

Buchillet, Dominique. 1983. "Maladie et mémoire des origines chez les Desana du Uaupés." Unpublished Ph.D. dissertation, Université de Paris X.

Bulmer, Ralph N. H. 1965. Beliefs Concerning the Propagation of New Varieties of Sweet Potato in Two New Guinea Highlands Societies. *Journal of the Polynesian Society* 74:237–239.

———. 1967. Why Is the Cassowary Not a Bird? A Problem of Zoological Taxonomy among the Karam of the New Guinea Highlands. *Man*, n.s. 2 (1):5–25.

———. 1974. Memoirs of a Small Game Hunter: On the Track of Unknown Animal Categories in New Guinea. *Journal d'Agriculture Tropicale et de Botanique Appliquée* 21:79–99.

Burridge, Kenelm O. 1960. *Mambu: A Study of Melanesian Cargo Movements and Their Social and Ideological Background*. New York: Harper & Row.

———. 1969. *New Heaven, New Earth: A Study of Millenarian Activities*. New York: Schocken Books.

Burt, Ben. 1994. *Tradition and Christianity: The Colonial Transformation of a Solomon Islands Society*. New York: Harwood Academic Publishers.

Busby, Cecilia. 1997a. Of Marriage and Marriageability: Gender and Dravidian Kinship. *Journal of the Royal Anthropological Institute* 3 (1):21–42.

———. 1997b. Permeable and Partible Persons: A Comparative Analysis of Gender and Body in South India and Melanesia. *Journal of the Royal Anthropological Institute* 3 (2):261–278.

Butt, Audrey J. 1958. The Mazaruni Scorpion. *Timehri: The Journal of the Royal Agricultural and Commercial Society of British Guiana* 36:40–54.

———. 1960. Birth of a Religion. *Journal of the Royal Anthropological Institute* 90:66–106.

Byer, Curtis O., and Louis W. Shainberg. 1991. *Dimensions of Human Sexuality*. Dubuque: Brown.

Carneiro, Robert L. 1970. Hunting and Hunting Magic among the Amahuaca of the Peruvian Montana. *Ethnology* 9:331–341.

Carneiro da Cunha, Manuela. 1973. Logique du Mythe et de l'Action: Le Mouvement Messianique Canela de 1963. *L'Homme* 13 (4):5–37.

———. 1978. *Os Mortos e os Outros. Uma análise do sistema funerário e da noção de pessoa entre os índios Krahó*. São Paulo: Editora Hucitec.

Carsten, Janet, and Stephen Hugh-Jones, eds. 1995. *About the House: Lévi-Strauss and Beyond*. Cambridge: Cambridge University Press.

Chagnon, Napoleon A. 1968. *Yanomamö: The Fierce People*. New York: Holt, Rinehart and Winston.

———. 1992. *Yanomamö*. 4th ed. Fort Worth: Harcourt Brace Jovanovich.

Chapman, Anne. 1982. *Drama and Power in a Hunting Society: The Selk'nam of Tierra del Fuego*. Cambridge: Cambridge University Press.

Chaumeil, B., and J.-P. Chaumeil. 1992. L'oncle et le neveu. La parenté du vivant chez les Yagua (Amazonie péruvienne). *Journal de la Société des Américanistes* 78 (2):25–37.

Chaumeil, J., and J.-P. Chaumeil. 1977. El rol de los instrumentos de música sagrados en la producción alimenticia de los Yagua del Nor-Este peruano. *Amazonía peruana* 1 (2):101–120.

Chaumeil, J.-P. 1989. Du végétal à l'humain. *Annales de la Fondation Fyssen* 4:15–24.

————. 1993. Des esprits aux ancêtres. Procédés linguistiques, conception du langage et de la société chez les Yagua de l'Amazonie péruvienne. *L'Homme* 126–128:409–428.

Chernela, Janet. 1993. *The Wanano Indians of the Brazilian Northwest Amazon: A Sense of Space.* Austin: University of Texas Press.

Chodorow, Nancy L. 1978. *The Reproduction of Mothering: Psychoanalysis and the Sociology of Gender.* Berkeley: University of California Press.

Chowning, Ann. 1987. "'Women Are Our Business': Women, Exchange and Prestige in Kove." In M. Strathern, ed., *Dealing with Inequality: Analysing Gender Relations in Melanesia and Beyond,* pp. 130–149. Cambridge: Cambridge University Press.

Clark, Jeffrey. 1991. Pearlshell Symbolism in Highlands Papua New Guinea, with Particular Reference to the Wiru People of Southern Highlands Province. *Oceania* 61:309–339.

————. 1997a. "State of Desire: Transformations in Huli Sexuality." In L. Manderson and M. Jolly, eds., *Sites of Desire, Economies of Pleasure: Sexualities in Asia and the Pacific,* pp. 191–211. Chicago: Chicago University Press.

————. 1997b. "Imagining the State, or Tribalism and the Arts of Memory in the Highlands of Papua New Guinea." In T. Otto and N. Thomas, eds., *Narratives of Nation in the South Pacific,* pp. 65–90. Amsterdam: Harwood.

Clastres, Hélène. 1995 [1975]. *The Land without Evil: Tupí-Guaraní Prophetism.* Urbana: University of Illinois Press.

Clastres, Pierre. 1972. *Chronique des Indiens Guayaki.* Paris: Plon.

Clifford, James, and George E. Marcus, eds. 1986. *Writing Culture: The Poetics and Politics of Ethnography.* Berkeley: University of California Press.

Collier, Jane F., and Michelle Z. Rosaldo. 1981. "Politics and Gender in Simple Societies." In S. Ortner and H. Whitehead, eds., *Sexual Meanings: The Cultural Construction of Gender and Sexuality,* pp. 275–329. Cambridge: Cambridge University Press.

Collier, Jane F., and Sylvia J. Yanagisako. 1987. "Introduction." In J. F. Collier and S. J. Yanagisako, eds., *Gender and Kinship: Essays toward a Unified Analysis,* pp. 1–13. Stanford: Stanford University Press.

Conklin, Beth A. 1989. "Images of Health, Illness, and Death among the Wari' (Pakaas Novos) of Rondônia, Brazil." Unpublished Ph.D. dissertation, University of California at San Francisco and Berkeley.

————. 1995. "Thus Are Our Bodies, Thus Was Our Custom": Mortuary Cannibalism in an Amazonian Society. *American Ethnologist* 22 (1):75–101.

————. 1996. Reflections on Amazonian Anthropologies of the Body. *Medical Anthropology Quarterly* 10 (3):373–375.

Conklin, Beth A., and Lynn M. Morgan. 1996. Babies, Bodies, and the Production of Personhood in North America and a Native Amazonian Society. *Ethos* 24 (4):657–694.

Connell, Robert W., and Gary W. Dowsett, eds. 1992. *Rethinking Sex: Social Theory and Sexuality Research.* Melbourne: Melbourne University Press.

Cook, Edwin A. 1969. "Marriage among the Manga." In R. M. Glasse and M. J. Meggitt, eds., *Pigs, Pearlshells, and Women: Marriage in the New Guinea Highlands,* pp. 96–116. Englewood Cliffs, N.J.: Prentice-Hall.

Cook, Edwin A., and Denise O'Brien, eds. 1980. *Blood and Semen: Kinship Systems of Highland New Guinea.* Ann Arbor: University of Michigan Press.

Cook, Edwin A., and Susan M. Pflanz-Cook. 1988. "'Children Make Me Happy': Reproductive Decision Making among the Manga, Jimi District, Western Highlands Province." In N. McDowell, ed., *Reproductive Decision Making and the Value of Children in*

Rural Papua New Guinea, pp. 71–102. Boroko: Institute of Applied Social and Economic Research.

Crapanzano, Vincent. 1981. "Rites of Return: Circumcision in Morocco." In W. Münsterberger and B. Boyer, eds., *The Psychoanalytic Study of Society*, vol. 9, pp. 15–36. New York: Psychohistory Press.

Crocker, Christopher J. 1985. *Vital Souls: Bororo Cosmology, Natural Symbolism, and Shamanism.* Tucson: University of Arizona Press.

Crocker, William H. 1990. The Canela (Eastern Timbira), I: An Ethnographic Introduction. *Smithsonian Contributions to Anthropology*, no. 33. Washington, D.C.: Smithsonian Institution Press.

Crocker, William H., and Jean Crocker. 1994. *The Canela: Bonding through Kinship, Ritual, and Sex*. Fort Worth: Harcourt Brace.

Crockett, Patricia J. 1979. "Conception and Birth among the Makru-Mansuku." In N. C. Habel, ed., *Powers, Plumes and Piglets: Phenomena of Melanesian Religion*, pp. 54–67. Redford Park, South Australia: Australian Association for the Study of Religions.

Da Matta, Roberto. 1976. *Um Mundo Dividido: A Estrutura Social dos Indios Apinayé*. Petrópolis, Brazil: Vozes.

———. 1982. *A Divided World: Apinayé Social Structure*, trans. Alan Campbell. Cambridge: Harvard University Press.

Damon, Frederick. 1983. Muyuw Kinship and the Metamorphosis of Gender Labor. *Man*, n.s., 18 (2):305–326.

De Wavrin, Don de M. le Marquis. 1930. Simples Notes sur la Tribu des Jivaro. *Bulletin de la Société des Americanistes de Belgique* 4:5–21.

Deacon, A. Bernard. 1934. *Malekula: A Vanishing People in the New Hebrides*. London: Routledge.

Decrease Report. 1896. *The Report of a Commission of Enquiry into the Decrease of the Native Population*. Suva, Fiji: Government Printers.

Descola, Philippe. 1981. "From Scattered to Nucleated Settlements: A Process of Socioeconomic Change among the Achuar." In N. Whitten, ed., *Cultural Transformation and Ethnicity in Modern Ecuador*, pp. 614–646. Urbana: University of Illinois Press.

———. 1982. Territorial Adjustments among the Achuar of Ecuador. *Social Science Information* 21 (2):299–318.

———. 1992. "Societies of Nature and the Nature of Society." In A. Kuper, ed., *Conceptualizing Society*, pp. 107–126. London: Routledge.

———. 1993. Les affinités sélectives. Alliance, guerre et prédation dans l'ensemble jivaro. *L'Homme* 126–128:171–190.

———. 1994a. *In the Society of Nature: A Native Ecology in Amazonia*, trans. N. Scott. Cambridge: Cambridge University Press.

———. 1994b. "Pourquoi les Indiens d'Amazonie n'ont-ils pas domestiqué le pécari? Généalogie des objets et anthropologie de l'objectivation." In B. Latour and P. Lemonnier, eds., *De la préhistoire aux missiles balistiques: L'intelligence sociale des techniques*, pp. 329–344. Paris: La Découverte.

———. 1996a. "Constructing Natures: Symbolic Ecology and Social Practice." In P. Descola and G. Palsson, eds., *Nature and Society: Anthropological Perspectives*, pp. 82–102. London: Routledge.

———. 1996b. *The Spears of Twilight: Life and Death in the Amazon Jungle*, trans. Janet Lloyd. London: HarperCollins.

Descola, Philippe, and J.-L. Lory. 1982. Les guerriers de l'invisible. Sociologie comparative de l'agression chamanique en Amazonie (Achuar) et en Nouvelle-Guinée (Baruya). *L'Ethnographie* 87–88:85–112.

Descola, Philippe, and Anne-Christine Taylor. 1993. "Introduction." In P. Descola and A.-C. Taylor, eds., *La remontée de l'Amazone.* Special issue of *L'Homme* 126–128:13–24.

Deshayes, P., and B. Keifenheim. 1994. *Penser l'Autre chez les Indiens Huni Kuin de l'Amazonie.* Paris: L'Harmattan.

Devens, Carol. 1992. *Countering Colonization: Native American Women and Great Lakes Missions, 1630–1900.* Berkeley: University of California Press.

Didi, Boyope Kangie. 1982. Kuru Kopiaka, Goddess Cult in the Lower Kaugel Valley of the Tambul Sub-district, Western Highlands Province. *Oral History* 10 (1):5–43.

Didlick, A. M. 1968–1969. Kaintiba Patrol Report, No. 3. Waigani: Papua New Guinea National Archives.

di Leonardo, Micaela. 1991. "Introduction: Gender, Culture, and Political Economy." In M. di Leonardo, ed., *Gender at the Crossroads of Knowledge: Feminist Anthropology in the Postmodern Era,* pp. 1–48. Berkeley: University of California Press.

Douglas, Bronwen. 1989. Autonomous and Controlled Spirits: Traditional Ritual and Early Interpretations of Christianity on Tanna, Aneityum and the Isle of Pines in Comparative Perspective. *Journal of the Polynesian Society* 98 (1):7–48.

Draper, Patricia. 1976. "!Kung Women: Contrasts in Sexual Egalitarianism in Foraging and Sedentary Contexts." In R. Reiter, ed., *Toward an Anthropology of Women,* pp. 77–109. New York: Monthly Review Press.

Dreyfus, Hubert L., and Paul Rabinow. 1982. *Michel Foucault: Beyond Structuralism and Hermeneutics,* 2d ed. Chicago: University of Chicago Press.

Dumont, L. 1975. *Dravidien et Kariera: l'alliance de mariage en Inde du Sud et en Australie.* Paris: Mouton.

———. 1977. *From Mandeville to Marx: The Genesis and Triumph of Economic Ideology.* Chicago: University of Chicago Press.

Dundes, Alan. 1976. A Psychoanalytic Study of the Bullroarer. *Man* 11:220–238.

Dureau, Christine. 1993. "Mixed Blessings: Christianity and History in Women's Lives on Simbo, Western Solomon Islands." Unpublished Ph.D. thesis, Macquarie University.

———. 1998. "From Sisters to Wives? Changing Contexts of Maternity on Simbo, Western Solomon Islands." In K. Ram and M. Jolly, eds., *Modernities and Maternities: Colonial and Postcolonial Experiences in Asia and the Pacific,* pp. 239–274. Cambridge: Cambridge University Press.

Durkheim, Emile. 1965 [1915]. *Elementary Forms of Religious Life,* trans. J. W. Swain. New York: The Free Press.

DuToit, Brian M. 1975. *Akuna: A New Guinea Village Community.* Rotterdam: Balkema.

Dye, Sally. 1983. What Disrupts Bahinemo Marriage. *Working Papers in Melanesian Marriage and Family Life,* no. 6. Goroka, Papua New Guinea: Melanesian Institute for Pastoral and Socio-Economic Service.

Edmiston, Patrick, and Melenda Edmiston. 1989. *Alamblak Background Study.* Ukarumpa, Papua New Guinea: Summer Institute of Linguistics.

Eggan, Fred. 1950. *Social Organization of the Western Pueblos.* Chicago: University of Chicago Press.

Elliston, D. A. 1995. Erotic Anthropology: "Ritualized Homosexuality" in Melanesia and Beyond. *American Ethnologist* 2 (4):848–867.

Erikson, P. 1996. *La griffe des aïeux. Marquage du corps et démarquages ethniques chez les Matis d'Amazonie*. Paris: Peters.

Ernst, Tom. 1991. Onabasalu Male Homosexuality: Cosmology, Affect and Prescribed Male Homosexual Activity among the Onabasalu of the Great Papuan Plateau. *Oceania* 62 (1):1–11.

Errington, Frederick, and Deborah Gewertz. 1987. "The Remarriage of Yebiwali: A Study of Dominance and False Consciousness in a Non-Western Society." In M. Strathern, ed., *Dealing with Inequality: Analysing Gender Relations in Melanesia and Beyond*, pp. 63–88. Cambridge: Cambridge University Press.

————. 1988. "Myths of Matriarchy Re-examined: Indigenous Images of Alternative Gender Relationships." In D. Gewertz, ed., *Myths of Matriarchy Reconsidered*, Oceania Monograph 33, pp. 195–211. Sydney: University of Sydney Press.

Escobar, Arturo. 1999. After Nature: Steps to an Antiessentialist Political Ecology. *Current Anthropology* 40 (1):1–30.

Evans-Pritchard, E. E. 1940. *The Nuer*. Oxford: Clarendon Press.

————. 1965. "The Comparative Method in Social Anthropology." In E. E. Evans-Pritchard, *The Position of Women in Primitive Societies and Other Essays in Social Anthropology*, pp. 13–36. New York: Free Press.

Eyre, Stephen L. 1988. "Revival Christianity among the Urat of Papua New Guinea: Some Possible Motivational and Perceptual Antecedents." Unpublished Ph.D. dissertation, University of California, San Diego.

Faithorn, Elizabeth. 1975. "The Concept of Pollution among the Kafe of the Papua New Guinea Highlands." In R. Reiter, ed., *Toward an Anthropology of Women*, pp. 127–140. New York: Monthly Review Press.

Fardon, Richard. 1990. "Localizing Strategies: The Regionalization of Ethnographic Accounts." In R. Fardon, ed., *Localizing Strategies: Regional Traditions of Ethnographic Writing*, pp. 1–29. Washington, D.C.: Smithsonian Institution Press.

Faron, L. C. 1969. *Los Mapuche. Su estructura social*. Mexico: Instituto Indigenista Interamericano.

Fausto, C., and E. Viveiros de Castro. 1993. La puissance et l'acte: La parenté dans les basses terres de l'Amérique du Sud. *L'Homme* 126–128:141–170.

Feld, S. 1982. *Sound and Sentiment: Birds, Weeping, Poetics, and Song in Kaluli Expression*. Philadelphia: University of Pennsylvania Press.

Feldpausch, Tom, and Becky Feldpausch. 1988. *Background Study [Namia]*. Ukarumpa, Papua New Guinea: Summer Institute of Linguistics.

Ferguson, R. Brian, and Neil L. Whitehead, eds. 1992. *War in the Tribal Zone: Expanding States and Indigenous Warfare*. Santa Fe, N.Mex.: School of American Research Press.

Feyerabend, Paul. 1978. *Against Method: Outline of an Anarchic Theory of Knowledge*. London: Verso.

Fienup-Riordan, A. 1990. Eskimo Iconography and Symbolism: An Introduction. *Etudes/Inuit/Studies* 14 (1–2):7–12.

Fisher, William H. 1991. "Dualism and Its Discontents: Village Fissioning among the Xikrin-Kayapo of Central Brazil." Unpublished Ph.D. thesis, Cornell University.

Fitz-Patrick, David G., and John Kimbuna. 1983. *Bundi: The Culture of a Papua New Guinea People*. Nerang, Queensland: Ryebuck Publications.

Forge, Anthony. 1966. Art and Environment in the Sepik. *Proceedings of the Royal Anthropological Institute, 1965*. London: Royal Anthropological Institute, pp. 23–31.

———. 1967. "The Abelam Artist." In M. Freedman, ed., *Social Organisation: Essays Presented to Raymond Firth*, pp. 65–84. London: Frank Cass.

———. 1969. Moon Magic. *New Society* 355:87–88.

———. 1973. "Style and Meaning in Sepik Art." In A. Forge, ed., *Primitive Art and Society*, pp. 169–192. London: Oxford University Press.

———. 1990. "The Power of Culture and the Culture of Power." In N. Lutkehaus, C. Kaufmann, W. E. Mitchell, D. Newton, L. Osmundsen, and M. Schuster, eds., *Sepik Heritage: Tradition and Change in Papua New Guinea*, pp. 160–170. Durham: Carolina Academic Press.

Fortes, Meyer. 1959. *Oedipus and Job in West African Religion*. Cambridge: Cambridge University Press.

———. 1966. "Ritual and Office in Tribal Society." In M. Gluckman, ed., *Essays on the Ritual of Social Relations*, pp. 53–88. Manchester: Tavistock.

Fortune, R. F. 1939. Arapesh Warfare. *American Anthropologist* 41:22–41.

Foucault, Michel. 1978. *The History of Sexuality*, vol. 1: *An Introduction*, trans. Robert Hurley. New York: Vintage Books.

———. 1980. "The Confession of the Flesh." In M. Foucault, *Power/Knowledge: Selected Interviews and Other Writings 1972–1977*, pp. 194–228. New York: Pantheon Books.

———. 1988. "Technologies of the Self." In L. H. Martin, H. Butman, and P. H. Hutton, eds., *Technologies of the Self: A Seminar with Michel Foucault*, pp. 16–49. Amherst: University of Massachusetts Press.

Frayser, Suzanne G. 1985. *Varieties of Sexual Experience: An Anthropological Perspective on Human Sexuality*. New Haven: HRAF Press.

Freud, Sigmund. 1950 [1913]. *Totem and Taboo*. New York: Norton.

Gardner, Donald S. 1988. "Mianmin Women: Myth and Reality." In D. Gewertz, ed., *Myths of Matriarchy Reconsidered*. Oceania Monograph 33, pp. 144–169. Sydney: University of Sydney Press.

Garrard-Burnett, Virginia, and David Stoll, eds. 1993. *Rethinking Protestantism in Latin America*. Philadelphia: Temple University Press.

Geertz, Clifford. 1973. *The Interpretation of Cultures*. New York: Basic Books.

Gell, Alfred. 1975. *Metamorphosis of the Cassowaries: Umeda Society, Language and Ritual*. London: Athlone Press.

———. 1979. Reflections on a Cut Finger: Taboo in the Umeda Conception of the Self. In R. H. Hook, ed., *Fantasy and Symbol: Studies in Anthropological Interpretation*, pp. 133–148. London: Academic Press.

———. 1992. "Inter-tribal Commodity Barter and Reproductive Gift-Exchange in Old Melanesia." In C. Humphrey and S. Hugh-Jones, eds., *Barter, Exchange and Value: An Anthropological Approach*, pp. 142–168. Cambridge: Cambridge University Press.

——— 1999. "Strathernograms, or, the Semiotics of Mixed Metaphors." In Alfred Gell, *The Art of Anthropology*, ed. Eric Hirsch, pp. 29–75. London: Athlone Press.

Gerstner, Andreas. 1937. Zauberei bei den But-Leuten an der Nordküste Neuguineas. *Anthropos* 32:967–973.

———. 1952. Jagdgebräuche der Wewäk-Boikin-Leute in Nordost-Neuguinea. *Anthropos* 47:177–192.

———. 1953. Aus dem Gemeinschaftsleben der Wewäk-Boikin-Leute, Nordost-Neuguinea. *Anthropos* 48:413–457.

Gewertz, Deborah B. 1983. *Sepik River Societies: A Historical Ethnography of the Chambri and Their Neighbors.* New Haven: Yale University Press.

———, ed. 1988. *Myths of Matriarchy Reconsidered.* Oceania Monograph 33. Sydney: University of Sydney Press.

Gewertz, Deborah B., and Frederick K. Errington. 1991. *Twisted Histories, Altered Contexts: Representing the Chambri in a World System.* Cambridge: Cambridge University Press.

Giannini, Vidal I. 1991. *A Ave Resgatada: "A Impossibilidade da Leveza do Ser".* Dissertação de mestrado, Universidade de São Paulo.

Gillison, Gillian. 1978. "'There Is No Other Sweet Life': Perceptions of the Female Role in a New Guinea Society." Unpublished Ph.D. thesis, City University of New York.

———. 1980. "Images of Nature in Gimi Thought." In C. MacCormack and M. Strathern, eds., *Nature, Culture and Gender,* pp. 143–173. Cambridge: Cambridge University Press.

———. 1987. Incest and the Atom of Kinship: The Role of the Mother's Brother in a New Guinea Highlands Society. *Ethos* 15:166–202.

———. 1991. "The Flute Myth and the Law of Equivalence: Origins of a Principle of Exchange." In M. Godelier and M. Strathern, eds., *Big Men and Great Men: Personifications of Power in Melanesia,* pp. 174–196. Cambridge: Cambridge University Press.

———. 1993. *Between Culture and Fantasy: A New Guinea Highlands Mythology.* Chicago: University of Chicago Press.

Gilmore, David D. 1990. *Manhood in the Making: Cultural Concepts of Masculinity.* New Haven: Yale University Press.

———. 1996. "Sexual Imagery in Spanish Carnival." In W. Shapiro and U. Linke, eds., *Denying Biology: Essays on Gender and Pseudo-Procreation,* pp. 27–50. Lanham, Md.: University Press of America.

Ginsburg, Faye, and Rayna Rapp. 1991. The Politics of Reproduction. *Annual Review of Anthropology* 20:311–343.

Glasse, Robert M. 1968. *Huli of Papua: A Cognatic Descent System.* Paris: Mouton.

Glasse, Robert M., and M. J. Meggitt, eds. 1969. *Pigs, Pearlshells, and Women: Marriage in the New Guinea Highlands.* Englewood Cliffs, N.J.: Prentice-Hall.

Godelier, M. 1982. *La production des Grands Hommes. Pouvoir et domination masculine chez les Baruya de Nouvelle-Guinée.* Paris: Fayard.

———. 1986 [1982]. *The Making of Great Men: Male Domination and Power among the New Guinea Baruya.* Translated by Rupert Swyer. Cambridge: Cambridge University Press.

Godelier, Maurice, and Marilyn Strathern, eds. 1991. *Big Men and Great Men: Personifications of Power in Melanesia.* Cambridge: University of Cambridge Press.

Goldman, Irving. 1963. *The Cubeo: Indians of the Northwest Amazon.* Urbana: University of Illinois Press.

Gombrich, Ernst. 1982. *The Image and the Eye: Further Studies in the Psychology of Pictorial Representation.* Ithaca: Cornell University Press.

Good, Kenneth. 1991. *Into the Heart: One Man's Pursuit of Love and Knowledge among the Yanomama.* New York: Simon and Schuster.

Gorlin, Peter. 1973. "Health, Wealth, and Agnation among the Abelam: The Beginnings of Social Stratification in New Guinea." Unpublished Ph.D. dissertation, Columbia University.

Gow, Peter. 1989. The Perverse Child: Desire in a Native Amazonian Subsistence Economy. *Man,* n.s., 24 (4):567–82.

————. 1991. *Of Mixed Blood: Kinship and History in Peruvian Amazonia.* Oxford: Clarendon Press.

Gregor, Thomas A. 1977. *Mehinaku: The Drama of Daily Life in a Brazilian Indian Village.* Chicago: University of Chicago Press.

————. 1979. "Secrets, Exclusion and the Dramatization of Men's Roles." In M.L. Margolis and W.E. Carter, ed., *Brazil: Anthropological Perspectives,* pp. 250–269. New York: Columbia University Press.

————. 1985. *Anxious Pleasures: The Sexual Lives of an Amazonian People.* Chicago: University of Chicago Press.

————. 1990a. "Male Dominance and Sexual Coercion." In J. Stiegler, R. Shweder, and G. H. Herdt, eds., *Cultural Psychology,* pp. 477–495. Chicago: University of Chicago Press.

————. 1990b. "Uneasy Peace: Intertribal Relations in Brazil's Upper Xingu." In Jonathan Haas, ed., *The Anthropology of War,* pp. 105–124. Cambridge: Cambridge University Press.

Guddemi, Phillip V. 1992a. When Horticulturalists Are Like Hunter-Gatherers: The Sawiyano of Papua New Guinea. *Ethnology* 31:303–314.

————. 1992b. "We Came from This: Knowledge, Memory, Painting and 'Play' in the Initiation Rituals of the Sawiyano of Papua New Guinea." Unpublished Ph.D dissertation, University of Michigan.

Haddon, Alfred C. 1898. *The Study of Man.* London: John Murray.

Hage, P. 1981. On Male Initiation and Dual Organization in New Guinea. *Man* 16 (2):268–275.

Hames, Raymond B., and William T. Vickers, eds. 1983. *Adaptive Responses of Native Amazonians.* New York: Academic Press.

Hanson, F. Allan. 1982. Female Pollution in Polynesia. *Journal of the Polynesian Society* 91:335–81.

Harner, Michael J. 1962. Jívaro Souls. *American Anthropologist* 64 (2):258–272.

————. 1973. *The Jívaro: People of the Sacred Waterfalls.* Garden City, N.J.: Anchor.

Harris, Marvin. 1968. *The Rise of Anthropological Theory: A History of Theories of Culture.* New York: Thomas Y. Crowell.

Harrison, Simon J. 1982. Yams and the Symbolic Representation of Time in a Sepik River Village. *Oceania* 53:141–162.

————. 1985. Ritual Hierarchy and Secular Equality in a Sepik River Village. *American Ethnologist* 12 (3):413–441.

————. 1989a. Magical and Material Polities in Melanesia. *Man,* n.s., 24:1–20.

————. 1989b. The Symbolic Construction of Aggression and War in a Sepik River Society. *Man,* n.s., 24:583–599.

————. 1990a. "Concepts of the Person in Avatip Religious Thought." In N. Lutkehaus, C. Kaufmann, W. E. Mitchell, D. Newton, L. Osmundsen, and M. Schuster, eds., *Sepik Heritage: Tradition and Change in Papua New Guinea,* pp. 351–363. Durham: Carolina Academic Press.

————. 1990b. *Stealing People's Names: History and Politics in a Sepik River Cosmology.* Cambridge: Cambridge University Press.

————. 1993. *The Mask of War: Violence, Ritual and the Self in Melanesia.* Manchester: Manchester University Press.

Hauser-Schäublin, Brigitta. 1977. *Frauen in Kararau: Zur Rolle der Frau bei den Iatmul am Mittelsepik, Papua New Guinea.* Basel: Ethnologisches Seminar der Universität und Museum für Völkerkunde.

Hawkes, Kristen. 1978. Big-Men in Binumarien. *Oceania* 48:161–187.

Hays, H. R. 1964. *The Dangerous Sex: The Myth of Feminine Evil.* New York: Putnam.

Hays, Terrence E. 1988. "'Myths of Matriarchy' and the Sacred Flute Complex of the Papua New Guinea Highlands." In D. Gewertz, ed., *Myths of Matriarchy Reconsidered,* Oceania Monograph 33, pp. 98–120. Sydney: University of Sydney Press.

Hays, Terrence E., and Patricia H. Hays. 1982. "Opposition and Complementarity of the Sexes in Ndumba Initiation." In G. H. Herdt, ed., *Rituals of Manhood: Male Initiation in Papua New Guinea,* pp. 201–238. Berkeley: University of California Press.

Healey, Christopher J. 1988. Culture as Transformed Disorder: Cosmological Evocations among the Maring. *Oceania* 59:106–122.

Heider, Karl G. 1976. Dani Sexuality: A Low Energy System. *Man,* n.s., 11:188–201.

———. 1979. *Grand Valley Dani: Peaceful Warriors.* New York: Holt, Rinehart and Winston.

———. 1991. "Dani." In T. E. Hays, ed., *Encyclopedia of World Cultures,* vol. 2: *Oceania,* pp. 43–46. Boston: G. K. Hall.

Herdt, Gilbert H. 1981. *Guardians of the Flutes: Idioms of Masculinity.* New York: McGraw-Hill.

———. 1982a. Sambia Nosebleeding Rites and Male Proximity to Women. *Ethos* 10 (3):189–231.

———. 1982b. "Fetish and Fantasy in Sambia Initiation." In G. H. Herdt, ed., *Rituals of Manhood: Male Initiation in Papua New Guinea,* pp. 44–98. Berkeley: University of California Press.

———. 1984. "Semen Transactions in Sambia Culture." In G. H. Herdt, ed., *Ritualized Homosexuality in Melanesia,* pp. 167–210. Berkeley: University of California Press.

———. 1987. *The Sambia: Ritual and Gender in New Guinea.* New York: Holt, Rinehart and Winston.

———. 1993a. "Introduction to the Paperback Edition." In G. H. Herdt, ed., *Ritualized Homosexuality in Melanesia,* pp. vii–xliv. Berkeley: University of California Press.

———. 1993b. "Sexual Repression, Social Control, and Gender Hierarchy in Sambia Culture." In B. D. Miller, ed., *Sex and Gender Hierarchies,* pp. 193–211. Cambridge: Cambridge University Press.

Herdt, Gilbert H., and Fitz John P. Poole. 1982. "'Sexual Antagonism': The Intellectual History of a Concept in New Guinea Anthropology." In F. J. P. Poole and G. H. Herdt, eds., *Sexual Antagonism, Gender, and Social Change in Papua New Guinea.* Special issue of *Social Analysis,* no. 12, pp. 3–28.

Herdt, Gilbert H., ed. 1982. *Rituals of Manhood: Male Initiation in Papua New Guinea.* Berkeley: University of California Press.

———, ed. 1984. *Ritualized Homosexuality in Melanesia.* Berkeley: University of California Press.

———, ed. 1994. *Third Sex, Third Gender: Beyond Sexual Dimorphism in Culture and History.* New York: Zone Books.

Herdt, Gilbert, and Michele Stephen, eds. 1989. *The Religious Imagination in New Guinea.* New Brunswick, N.J.: Rutgers University Press.

Héritier, F. 1996. *Masculin/Féminin: La pensée de la différence.* Paris: Editions Odile Jacob.

Hiatt, L. R. 1971. "Secret Pseudo-Procreation Rites among the Australian Aborigines." In L. Hiatt and C. Jayawardena, eds., *Anthropology in Oceania: Essays Presented to Ian Hogbin,* pp. 77–88. Sydney: Angus and Robertson.

Hill, Jonathan D. 1983. "Wakuénai Society: A Processual-Structural Analysis of Indigenous Cultural Life in the Upper Rio Negro Region of Venezuela." Unpublished Ph.D. dissertation, Indiana University.

————. 1984. Social Equality and Ritual Hierarchy: The Arawakan Wakuénai of Venezuela. *American Ethnologist* 11:528–544.

————. 1987. Wakuénai Ceremonial Exchange in the Venezuelan Northwest Amazon. *Journal of Latin American Lore* 13 (2):183–224.

————. 1988. The Soft and the Stiff: Ritual Power and Mythic Meaning in a Northern Arawakan Classifier System. *Antropológica* 69:3–25.

————. 1989. Ritual Production of Environmental Relations among the Arawakan Wakuénai of Venezuela. *Human Ecology* 17 (1):1–25.

————. 1993. *Keepers of the Sacred Chants: The Poetics of Ritual Power in an Amazonian Society.* Tucson: University of Arizona Press.

————. 1994. "Musicalizing the Other: Shamanistic Approaches to Ethnic-Class Competition in the Upper Rio Negro Region." In A. Barabas, ed., *Religiosidad y Resistencia Indígenas hacia el Fin del Milenio*, pp. 105–128. Quito: Abya-Yala.

Hill, Jonathan D., ed. 1988. *Rethinking History and Myth: Indigenous South American Perspectives on the Past.* Urbana: University of Illinois Press.

Hill, Jonathan D., and Robin M. Wright. 1988. "Time, Narrative and Ritual: Historical Interpretations from an Amazonian Society." In J. D. Hill, ed., *Rethinking History and Myth: Indigenous South American Perspectives on the Past*, pp. 78–105. Urbana: University of Illinois Press.

Hobart, Mark. 1987. "Summer's Days and Salad Days: The Coming of Age of Anthropology?" In L. Holy, ed., *Comparative Anthropology*, pp. 22–51. Oxford: Basil Blackwell.

Hogbin, H. Ian. 1934–1935a. Native Culture of Wogeo: Report of Field Work in New Guinea. *Oceania* 5:308–337.

————. 1934–1935b. Trading Expedition in Northern New Guinea. *Oceania* 5:375–407.

————. 1970. *The Island of Menstruating Men: Religion in Wogeo, New Guinea.* Scranton, Pa.: Chandler Publishing Company.

Holmberg, Allan R. 1969. *Nomads of the Long Bow: The Siriono of Eastern Bolivia.* New York: Natural History Press.

Holy, Ladislav. 1987. "Introduction: Description, Generalization and Comparison: Two Paradigms." In L. Holy, ed., *Comparative Anthropology*, pp. 1–21. Oxford: Basil Blackwell.

Hook, R. H. 1979. "Phantasy and Symbol: A Psychoanalytic Point of View." In R. H. Hook, ed., *Fantasy and Symbol: Studies in Anthropological Interpretation*, pp. 267–291. London: Academic Press.

Hornborg, A. 1988. *Dualism and Hierarchy in Lowland South America: Trajectories of Indigenous Social Organization.* Uppsala: Acta Universitatis Upsaliensis.

Horney, Karen. 1966 [1932]. "The Dread of Woman." In H. M. Ruitenbeek, ed., *Psychoanalysis and Male Sexuality*, pp. 83–96. New Haven: College and University Press.

Houseman, Michael. 1988. Towards a Complex Model of Parenthood: Two African Tales. *American Ethnologist* 15 (4):658–677.

Huber, Peter Birkett. 1974. "Identity and Exchange: Kinship and Social Order among the Anggor of New Guinea." Unpublished Ph.D. dissertation, Duke University.

————. 1980. The Anggor Bowman: Ritual and Society in Melanesia. *American Ethnologist* 7:43–57.

Huber-Greub, Barbara. 1990. "Land in the Abelam Village of Kimbangwa." In N. Lutkehaus, C. Kaufmann, W. E. Mitchell, D. Newton, L. Osmundsen, and M. Schuster, eds., *Sepik Heritage: Tradition and Change in Papua New Guinea*, pp. 274–285. Durham: Carolina Academic Press.

Hugh-Jones, Christine. 1979. *From the Milk River: Spatial and Temporal Processes in Northwest Amazonia*. New York: Cambridge University Press.

Hugh-Jones, Christine, and Stephen Hugh-Jones. 1993. "The Storage of Manioc Products and Its Symbolic Importance among the Tukanoans." In M. Hladik, A. Hladik, O. Linares, H. Pagezy, A. Semple, and M. Hadley, eds., *Tropical Forests, People and Food: Biocultural Interactions and Applications to Development*, pp. 589–594. New York: The Parthenon Publishing Group.

Hugh-Jones, Stephen. 1979. *The Palm and the Pleiades: Initiation and Cosmology in Northwest Amazonia*. Cambridge: Cambridge University Press.

———. 1992. "Yesterday's Luxuries, Tomorrow's Necessities: Business and Barter in Northwest Amazonia." In C. Humphrey and S. Hugh-Jones, eds., *Barter, Exchange and Value*, pp. 42–74. Cambridge: Cambridge University Press.

———. 1993. "Clear Descent or Ambiguous Houses? A Re-examination of Tukanoan Social Organisation." In P. Descola and A.-C. Taylor, eds., *La remontée de l'Amazone*. Special issue of *L'Homme* 126–128:95–120.

———. 1994. "Shamans, Prophets, Priests, and Pastors." In N. Thomas and C. Humphrey, eds., *Shamanism, History, and the State*, pp. 32–75. Ann Arbor: University of Michigan Press.

———. 1995a. "Inside Out and Back to Front: the Androgynous House in Northwestern Amazonia." In J. Carsten and S. Hugh-Jones, eds., *About the House: Lévi-Strauss and Beyond*, pp. 226–269. Cambridge: Cambridge University Press.

———. 1995b. "Coca, Beer and Cigars: Meals and Anti-meals in an Amerindian Community." In J. Goodman, P. Lovejoy, and A. Sherratt, eds., *Consuming Habits: Drugs in History and Anthropology*, pp. 47–66. London: Routledge.

———. 1996. Bonnes raisons ou mauvaise conscience? De l'ambivalence de certains Amazoniens envers la consommation de viande. *Terrain* 26:123–148.

Huxley, Francis. 1957. *Affable Savages*. London: Rupert Hart-Davis.

Ingemann, Frances. 1997. "Ipili Dictionary." Unpublished manuscript.

Jackson, Jean E. 1983. *The Fish People: Linguistic Exogamy and Tukanoan Identity in Northwest Amazonia*. Cambridge: Cambridge University Press.

———. 1996. "Coping with the Dilemmas of Affinity and Female Sexuality: Male Rebirth in the Central Northwest Amazon." In W. Shapiro and U. Linke, eds., *Denying Biology: Essays on Gender and Pseudo-Procreation*, pp. 89–127. Lanham, Md.: University Press of America.

Jackson, Michael. 1977. *The Kuranko: Dimensions of Social Reality in a West African Society*. London: C. Hurst.

Jara, F. 1991. *El camino del Kumu: ecología y ritual entre los Akuriyó de Surinam*. Utrecht: ISOR.

Johnson, Patricia L. 1982. "Gainj Kinship and Social Organization." Unpublished Ph.D. dissertation, University of Michigan.

Johnson, Patricia L., and James Wood. 1991. "Gainj." In T. E. Hays, ed., *Encyclopedia of World Cultures*, vol. 2: *Oceania*, pp. 71–73. Boston: G. K. Hall.

Jolly, Margaret. 1987. The Forgotten Women: A History of Migrant Labour and Gender Relations in Vanuatu. *Oceania* 58 (2):119–139.

———. 1989. "Sacred Spaces: Churches, Men's Houses and Households in South Pentecost, Vanuatu." In M. Jolly and M. Macintyre, eds., *Family and Gender in the Pacific: Domestic Contradictions and the Colonial Impact*, pp. 213–235. Cambridge: Cambridge University Press.

———. 1991a. "Soaring Hawks and Grounded Persons: The Politics of Rank and Gender in North Vanuatu." In M. Godelier and M. Strathern, eds., *Big Men and Great Men: Personifications of Power in Melanesia*, pp. 48–80. Cambridge: Cambridge University Press.

———. 1991b. Gifts, Commodities and Corporeality: Food and Gender in South Pentecost, Vanuatu. *Canberra Anthropology* 14 (1):45–66.

———. 1994a. *Women of the Place: Kastom, Colonialism and Gender in Vanuatu.* Chur, Switzerland: Harwood Academic Publishers.

———. 1994b. "*Kastom* as Commodity: The Land Dive as Indigenous Rite and Tourist Spectacle in Vanuatu." In L. Lindstrom and G. White, eds., *Culture-Kastom-Tradition: Developing Cultural Policy in Melanesia,* pp. 131–144. Suva: Institute of Pacific Studies, University of the South Pacific.

———. 1996, "Devils, Holy Spirits and the Swollen God: Translation, Conversion and Colonial Power in the Marist Mission, Vanuatu, 1887–1934." In P. van der Veer, ed., *Conversion to Modernities,* pp. 231–262. New York: Routledge.

———. 1998. "Other Mothers: 'Maternal Insouciance' and the Depopulation Debate in Fiji and Vanuatu 1890–1930." In K. Ram and M. Jolly, eds., *Maternities and Modernities: Colonial and Postcolonial Experiences in Asia and the Pacific,* pp. 177–212. Cambridge, Cambridge University Press.

———. 1999. Another Time, Another Place. *Oceania* 69 (4):282–299.

———. 2001a. "Infertile States: Person and Collectivity, Region and Nation, in the Rhetoric of Pacific Population." In M. Jolly and K. Ram, eds., *Borders of Being: Citizenship, Fertility and Sexuality in Asia and the Pacific,* pp. 262–306. Ann Arbor: University of Michigan Press.

———. 2001b. "From Darkness to Light? Epidemiologies and Ethnographies of Motherhood in Vanuatu." In V. Lukere and M. Jolly, eds., *Birthing in the Pacific: Beyond Tradition and Modernity?* pp. 189–221. Honolulu: University of Hawaii Press.

Jolly, Margaret, and Martha Macintyre, eds. 1989. *Family and Gender in the Pacific: Domestic Contradictions and the Colonial Impact.* Cambridge: Cambridge University Press.

Jolly, Margaret, and Lenore Manderson. 1997. "Introduction." In L. Manderson and M. Jolly, eds., *Sites of Desire, Economies of Pleasure: Sexualities in Asia and the Pacific,* pp. 1–26. Chicago: University of Chicago Press.

Jolly, Margaret, and Kalpana Ram, eds. 2001. *Borders of Being: Citizenship, Fertility and Sexuality in Asia and the Pacific.* Ann Arbor: University of Michigan Press.

Jones, Barbara Ann. 1980. "Consuming Society: Food and Illness among the Faiwol." Unpublished Ph.D. dissertation, University of Virginia.

Jorgensen, Dan, ed. 1983. *Concepts of Conception: Procreation Ideologies in Papua New Guinea.* Special issue of *Mankind,* no. 14.

Josephides, Lisette. 1985. *The Production of Inequality: Gender and Exchange among the Kewa.* London: Tavistock.

Journet, Nicolas. 1988. "Les Jardins de Paix." Ph.D. dissertation, Université de Paris.

———. 1995. *La paix des jardins. Structures sociales des Indiens curripaco du haut Rio Negro (Colombie).* Paris: Institut d'Ethnologie.

Juillerat, Bernard. 1986. *Les Enfants du sang. Société, reproduction et imaginaire en Nouvelle-Guinée.* Paris: Editions de la Maison des Sciences de l'Homme.

———. 1992. "'The Mother's Brother is the Breast': Incest and Its Prohibition in Yafar Yangis." In B. Juillerat, ed., *Shooting the Sun: Ritual and Meaning in West Sepik,* pp. 20–124. Washington, D.C.: Smithsonian Institution Press.

———, ed. 1992. *Shooting the Sun: Ritual and Meaning in West Sepik.* Washington, D.C.: Smithsonian Institution Press.

Kaberry, Phyllis M. 1940–1941. The Abelam Tribe, Sepik District, New Guinea: A Preliminary Report. *Oceania* 11:233–258.

———. 1941–1942. Law and Political Organisation in the Abelam Tribe, New Guinea. *Oceania* 12:331–363.

Kale, Joan. 1985. "The Religious Movement among the Kyaka Enga." In C. Loeliger and G. Trompf, eds., *New Religious Movements in Melanesia*, pp. 45–74. Suva: Institute of Pacific Studies, University of the South Pacific and the University of Papua New Guinea.

Kaplan, Joanna Overingo. 1975. *The Piaroa, a People of the Orinoco Basin: A Study in Kinship and Marriage*. Oxford: Clarendon Press.

Karsten, Rafael. 1935. *The Head-Hunters of Western Amazonas: The Life and Culture of the Jibaro Indians of Eastern Ecuador and Peru*. Helsingfors, Finland: Centraltryckeriet.

Kasprus, Aloys. 1973. *The Tribes of the Middle Ramu and the Upper Keram Rivers (North-East New Guinea)*. St. Augustin, Germany: Anthropos Institute.

Keesing, Roger M. 1982. "Introduction." In G. H. Herdt, ed., *Rituals of Manhood: Male Initiation in Papua New Guinea*, pp. 1–43. Berkeley: University of California Press.

———. 1985. Kwaio Women Speak: The Micropolitics of Autobiography in a Solomon Island Society. *American Anthropologist* 87(1):27–39.

———. 1989. "Sins of a Mission: Christian Life as Kwaio Traditionalist Ideology." In M. Jolly and M. Macintyre, eds., *Family and Gender in the Pacific: Domestic Contradictions and the Colonial Impact*, pp. 193–212. Cambridge: Cambridge University Press.

Kelly, Raymond C. 1976. "Witchcraft and Sexual Relations: An Exploration in the Social and Semantic Implications of the Structure of Belief." In P. Brown and G. Buchbinder, eds., *Man and Woman in the New Guinea Highlands*, pp. 36–53. Washington, D.C.: American Anthropological Association,

———. 1977. *Etoro Social Structure: A Study in Structural Contradiction*. Ann Arbor: University of Michigan Press.

———. 1993. *Constructing Inequality: The Fabrication of a Hierarchy of Virtue among the Etoro*. Ann Arbor: University of Michigan Press.

Kensinger, Kenneth M. 1992. A Body of Knowledge, or, the Body Knows. *Expedition* 33 (3):37–45.

———. 1995. *How Real People Ought to Live: The Cashinahua of Eastern Peru*. Prospect Heights, Ill.: Waveland Press.

———, ed. 1979–1985. Working Papers on South American Indians, Vols. 1–7. Bennington, Vt.: Bennington College.

———, ed. 1984. *Marriage Practices in Lowland South America*. Urbana: University of Illinois Press.

———, ed. 1993–1998. South American Indian Studies, Vols. 1–5. Bennington, Vt.: Bennington College.

King, Ursula. 1995. "Introduction: Gender and the Study of Religion." In U. King, ed., *Religion and Gender*, pp. 1–38. Oxford: Blackwell.

Knauft, Bruce M. 1978. Cargo Cults and Relational Separation. *Behavior Science Research* 13 (3):185–240.

———. 1986. Text and Social Practice: Narrative "Longing" and Bisexuality among the Gebusi of New Guinea. *Ethos* 14 (3):252–81.

———. 1987. Homosexuality in Melanesia. *Journal of Psychoanalytic Anthropology* 10 (2):155–191.

———. 1993. *South Coast New Guinea Cultures: History, Comparison, Dialectic*. Cambridge: Cambridge University Press.

————. 1994. Foucault Meets South New Guinea: Knowledge, Power, Sexuality. *Ethos* 22 (4):310–438.

————. 1997. Gender Identity, Political Economy and Modernity in Melanesia and Amazonia. *Journal of the Royal Anthropological Institute* 3 (2):233–259.

————. 1999. "Bodily Images in Melanesia: Cultural Substances and Natural Metaphors." In B. Knauft, *From Primitive to Post-colonial in Melanesia and Anthropology*, pp. 21–88. Ann Arbor: University of Michigan Press.

Kroeber, A. L. 1923. *Anthropology.* New York: Harcourt, Brace.

Kyakas, Alome, and Polly Wiessner. 1992. *From Inside the Women's House: Enga Women's Lives and Traditions.* Burunda, Queensland: Robert Brown.

LaBarre, Weston. 1984. *Muelos, a Stone Age Superstition about Sexuality.* New York: Columbia University Press.

Lambek, Michael, and Andrew Strathern, eds. 1998. *Bodies and Persons: Comparative Perspectives from Africa and Melanesia.* New York: Cambridge University Press.

Langness, L. L. 1967. Sexual Antagonism in the New Guinea Highlands: A Bena-Bena Example. *Oceania* 37 (3):161–177.

————. 1969. "Marriage in Bena Bena." In R. M. Glasse and M. J. Meggitt, eds., *Pigs, Pearlshells, and Women: Marriage in the New Guinea Highlands*, pp. 38–55. Englewood Cliffs: Prentice-Hall.

————. 1999. *Men and "Woman" in New Guinea.* Novato, Calif.: Chandler & Sharp.

Laplanche, J., and J.-B. Pontalis. 1973. *The Language of Psycho-Analysis.* Translated by D. Nicholson-Smith. New York: W. W. Norton.

Laqueur, Thomas. 1990. *Making Sex: Body and Gender from the Greeks to Freud.* Cambridge, Mass.: Harvard University Press.

Latour, Bruno, and Steven Woolgar. 1986. *Laboratory Life: The Social Construction of Scientific Facts.* Beverly Hills, Calif.: Sage.

Lattas, Andrew. 1991. Sexuality and Cargo Cults: The Politics of Gender and Procreation in West New Britain. *Cultural Anthropology* 6 (2):230–256.

————. 1992a. Hysteria, Anthropological Disclosure and the Concept of the Unconscious: Cargo Cults and the Scientisation of Race and Colonial Power. *Oceania* 63:1–14.

————. 1992b. Skin, Personhood and Redemption: The Double Self in West New Britain Cargo Cults. *Oceania* 63:27–54.

Lawrence, Peter and M. J. Meggitt, eds. 1965. *Gods, Ghosts and Men in Melanesia.* London: Oxford University Press.

Layard, John. 1942. *Stone Men of Malekula.* London: Chatto and Windus.

Leach, Edmund R. 1968. "The Comparative Method in Anthropology." In D. L. Sills, ed., *International Encyclopedia of the Social Sciences*, vol. 1, pp. 339–345. New York: The Free Press.

Leavitt, Gregory C. 1990. Sociobiological Explanations of Incest Avoidance: A Critical Review of Evidential Claims. *American Anthropologist* 92 (4):971–993.

Leavitt, Stephen C. 1991. Sexual Ideology and Experience in a Papua New Guinea Society. *Social Science and Medicine* 33:897–907.

Lee, Richard B. 1979. *The !Kung San: Men, Women, and Work in a Foraging Society.* Cambridge: Cambridge University Press.

Leenhardt, Maurice. 1979 [1947]. *Do Kamo: Person and Myth in the Melanesian World.* Chicago: University of Chicago Press.

Le Guin, Ursula. 1992. *Dancing at the Edge of the World: Thoughts on Words, Women, Place.* London: Paladin.

Lemonnier, Pierre. 1990. *Guerres et festins. Paix, échanges et compétition dans les Highlands de Nouvelle-Guinée.* Paris: Editions de la Maison des Sciences de l'Homme.

———. 1991. "From Great Men to Big Men: Peace, Substitution and Competition in the Highlands of New Guinea." In Maurice Godelier and Marilyn Strathern, eds., *Big Men and Great Men: Personifications of Power in Melanesia,* pp. 7–27. New York: Cambridge University Press.

———. 1993. "Pigs as Ordinary Wealth: Technical Logic, Exchange and Leadership in Papua New Guinea." In P. Lemonnier, ed., *Technological Choices: Tranformations in Material Cultures since the Neolithic,* pp. 126–156. London: Routledge.

Lepowsky, M. 1993. *Fruit of the Motherland: Gender in an Egalitarian Society.* New York: Columbia University Press.

Levine, Harold Gary. 1987. "'Taboos' and Statements about Taboos: Issues in the Taxonomic Analysis of Behavior Restrictions among the New Guinea Kafe. In L. L. Langness and T. E. Hays, eds., *Anthropology in the High Valleys: Essays on the New Guinea Highlands in Honor of Kenneth E. Read,* pp. 45–72. Novato, Calif.: Chandler and Sharp.

Lévi-Strauss, Claude. 1969a. [1949]. *The Elementary Structures of Kinship.* Boston: Beacon.

———. 1969b. *The Raw and the Cooked.* Translated by J. and D. Weightman. New York: Harper & Row.

———. 1973. *From Honey to Ashes: Introduction to a Science of Mythology.* London: Jonathan Cape.

———. 1984. *Paroles données.* Paris: Plon.

———. 1985. *La Potière Jalouse.* Paris: Maspero.

Lewin, Esther, and Albert E. Lewin. 1988. *The Random House Thesaurus of Slang.* New York: Random House.

Lewis, Gilbert. 1975. *Knowledge of Illness in a Sepik Society.* London: Athlone Press.

———. 1980. *Day of Shining Red: An Essay on Understanding Ritual.* Cambridge: Cambridge University Press.

Lewis, Ronald K. 1988. "The Interrrelationship of Taboo and Kinship as the Cohesive Agent of Saniyo-Hiyowe Society." In M. K. Mayers and D. D. Rath, eds., *Nucleation in Papua New Guinea Cultures,* pp. 61–69. Dallas: International Museum of Cultures.

Lidz, Theodore, and Ruth Wilmanns Lidz. 1989. *Oedipus in the Stone Age: A Psychoanalytic Study of Masculinization in Papua New Guinea.* Madison, Conn.: International Universities Press.

Liep, John. 1991. "Great Man, Big Man, Chief: A Triangulation of the Massin." In Maurice Godelier and Marilyn Strathern, eds., *Big Men and Great Men: Personifications of Power in Melanesia,* pp. 28–47. New York: Cambridge University Press.

Lincoln, Bruce. 1989. *Discourse and the Construction of Society: Comparative Studies of Myth, Ritual, and Classification.* Oxford: Oxford University Press.

———. 1991. *Emerging from the Chrysalis: Rituals of Women's Initiation,* pp. 110–119. Oxford: Oxford University Press.

Lindenbaum, Shirley. 1976. "A Wife Is the Hand of Man." In P. Brown and G. Buchbinder, eds., *Man and Woman in the New Guinea Highlands,* pp. 54–62. Washington, D.C.: American Anthropological Association.

———. 1979. *Kuru Sorcery: Disease and Danger in the New Guinea Highlands.* Palo Alto, Calif.: Mayfield Publishing Company.

———. 1984. "Variations on a Sociosexual Theme in Melanesia." In G. H. Herdt, ed., *Ritualized Homosexuality in Melanesia,* pp. 337–361. Berkeley: University of California Press.

———. 1987. "The Mystification of Female Labors." In J. F. Collier and S. J. Yanagisako, eds., *Gender and Kinship: Essays Toward a Unified Analysis,* pp. 221–243. Stanford: Stanford University Press.

Lindstrom, Lamont. 1978. Cargo Cults, Sexual Distance and Melanesian Social Integration. *Canberra Anthropology* 1(2):42–58.

———. 1993. *Cargo Cult: Strange Stories of Desire from Melanesia and Beyond.* Honolulu: University of Hawaii Press.

Lipset, David Michael. 1984. "Authority and the Maternal Presence: An Interpretive Ethnography of Murik Lakes Society (East Sepik Province, Papua New Guinea)." Unpublished Ph.D. dissertation, University of California, San Diego.

LiPuma, Edward. 1981. Cosmology and Economy among the Maring of Highland New Guinea. *Oceania* 51:266–285.

———. 1988. *The Gift of Kinship: Structure and Practice in Maring Social Organization.* Cambridge: Cambridge University Press.

Lizot, Jacques. 1985. *Tales of the Yanomami: Daily Life in the Venezuelan Forest.* Cambridge: Cambridge University Press.

Lloyd, J. A. 1992. *A Baruya-Tok Pisin-English Dictionary.* Pacific Linguistics, Series C, No. 82. Canberra: Australian National University.

Lloyd, R. 1973. "The Anga Language Family." In K. Franklin, ed., *The Linguistic Situation in the Gulf District and Adjacent Areas, Papua New Guinea.* Pacific Linguistics, Series C, 26:33–111.

Losche, Diane B. 1982. "Male and Female in Abelam Society: Opposition and Complementarity." Unpublished Ph.D. dissertation, Columbia University.

Loving, Richard, and Aretta Loving. 1975. *Awa Dictionary.* Pacific Linguistics, Series C, No. 30. Canberra: Australian National University.

Lowie, Robert. 1920. *Primitive Society.* New York: Boni and Liveright.

Lowman, Cherry. 1973. *Displays of Power: Art and War among the Marings of New Guinea.* New York: The Museum of Primitive Art.

Lowman-Vayda, Cherry. 1973. "Maring Big Men." In R. M. Berndt and P. Lawrence, eds., *Politics in New Guinea: Traditional and in the Context of Change: Some Anthropological Perspectives,* pp. 317–361. Seattle: University of Washington Press.

Lukere, Victoria. 1997. "Mothers of the Taukei: Fijian Women and 'the Decrease of the Race.'" Ph.D. thesis, Research School of Pacific and Asian Studies, Australian National University.

Lukere, Victoria, and Margaret Jolly, eds. 2001. *Birthing in the Pacific: Beyond Tradition and Modernity?* Honolulu: University of Hawaii Press.

Luoma, Pirkko. 1981. *Something about the Urim Ideology.* Ukarumpa, Papua New Guinea: Summer Institute of Linguistics.

Lutkehaus, Nancy C. 1995a. "Feminist Anthropology and Female Initiation in Melanesia." In N. Lutkehaus and P. Roscoe, eds., *Gender Rituals: Female Initiation in Melanesia,* pp. 3–29. New York: Routledge.

———. 1995b. *Zaria's Fire: Engendered Moments in Manam Ethnography.* Durham: Carolina Academic Press.

Lutkehaus, Nancy, Christian Kaufmann, William E. Mitchell, Douglas Newton, Lita Oswmundsen, and Meinhard Schuster, eds. 1990. *Sepik Heritage: Tradition and Change in Papua New Guinea.* Durham: Carolina Academic Press.

Lutkehaus, Nancy C., and Paul B. Roscoe, eds. 1995. *Gender Rituals: Female Initiation in Melanesia.* New York: Routledge.

Macdonald, Mary N. 1991. *Mararoko: A Study in Melanesian Religion.* New York: Peter Lang.

MacDonald, Wendy. 1992. Cultural Values, Gender Relations and Social Change: Perceptions of Development in a Sepik Village. *Research in Melanesia* 16:61–78.

MacLean, Paul D. 1962. New Findings Relevant to the Evolution of the Psychosexual Functions of the Brain. *Journal of Nervous and Mental Disease* 135:289–301.

Manabe, Takashi, and Kazue Manabe. 1982. *Kwanga Anthropology Sketch: "Mami (A Type of Yam)" Reveals Dynamic Kwanga Social Structure.* Ukarumpa, Papua New Guinea: Summer Institute of Linguistics.

Mandeville, Elizabeth. 1979. Agnation, Affinity and Migration among the Kamano of the New Guinea Highlands. *Man,* n.s., 14:105–123.

Marshall, Leslie B., ed. 1985. *Infant Care and Feeding in the South Pacific.* New York: Gordon and Breach Science Publishers.

Matos Arvelo, Martin. 1912. *Vida Indiana.* Barcelona: Casa Editorial Mauci.

May, Patricia, and Margaret Tuckson. 1982. *The Traditional Pottery of Papua New Guinea.* Sydney: Bay Books.

Maybury-Lewis, David. 1967. *Akwe-Shavante Society.* Oxford: Clarendon Press.

———, ed. 1979. *Dialectical Societies: The Gê and Bororo of Central Brazil.* Cambridge: Harvard University Press.

McCallum, Cecilia. 1996. The Body That Knows: From Cashinahua Epistemology to a Medical Anthropology of Lowland South America. *Medical Anthropology Quarterly* 10 (3):347–372.

McDowell, Nancy A. 1975. Kinship and the Concept of Shame in a New Guinea Village. Unpublished Ph.D. dissertation, Cornell University.

———. 1988. A Note on Cargo Cults and Cultural Constructions of Change. *Pacific Studies* 11:121–134.

———. 1991. *The Mundugumor: From the Field Notes of Margaret Mead and Reo Fortune.* Washington, D.C.: Smithsonian Institution Press.

McKinnon, Susan. 1991. *From a Shattered Sun: Hierarchy, Gender and Alliance in the Tanimbar Islands.* Madison: University of Wisconsin Press.

McKnight, David. 1975. "Men, Women, and Other Animals: Taboo and Purification among the Wik-mungkan. In R. Willis, ed., *The Interpretation of Symbolism,* pp. 77–97. London: Malaby Press.

Mead, Margaret. 1935. *Sex and Temperament in Three Primitive Societies.* London: Routledge.

———. 1940. The Mountain Arapesh. II. Supernaturalism. *Anthropological Papers of the American Museum of Natural History* 37:317–451.

Meggitt, M. J. 1957. The Ipili of the Porgera Valley, Western Highlands District, Territory of New Guinea. *Oceania* 28:31–55.

———. 1964. Male-Female Relationships in the Highlands of Australian New Guinea. *American Anthropologist* 66:204–224.

Meigs, Anna S. 1976. Male Pregnancy and the Reduction of Sexual Opposition in a New Guinea Highlands Society. *Ethnology* 15:393–408.

———. 1984. *Food, Sex, and Pollution: A New Guinea Religion.* New Brunswick, N. J.: Rutgers University Press.

Menget, P. 1993. Les Frontières de la chefferie: Remarques sur le système politique du haut Xingu (Brésil). *L'Homme* 126–128:59–76.

Merrett-Balkos, Leanne. 1998. "Just Add Water: Remaking Women through Childbirth, Anganen, Southern Highlands, Papua New Guinea." In K. Ram and M. Jolly, eds., *Modernities and Maternities: Colonial and Postcolonial Experiences in Asia and the Pacific,* pp. 213–238. Cambridge: Cambridge University Press.

Metraux, Alfred. 1927. Le Bâton de Rythme: Contribution à l'étude de la distribution géographiques des éléments de culture d'origine Mélanésienne en Amérique de Sud. *Journal de la Société des Américanistes de Paris,* n.s., 19:117–122.

————. 1963. "Religion and Shamanism." In J. H. Steward, ed., *The Handbook of South American Indians*, vol. 5: *The Comparative Ethnology of South American Indians*, pp. 559–599. New York: Cooper Square.

Mimica, Jadran. 1988. *Intimations of Infinity: The Cultural Meanings of the Iqwaye Counting System and Number*. Oxford: Berg.

Mitchell, William E. 1978. *The Bamboo Fire: An Anthropologist in New Guinea*. New York: W. W. Norton & Company.

Moore, Henrietta. 1994. *A Passion for Difference*. Oxford: Polity Press.

Morris, Brian. 1987. *Anthropological Studies of Religion: An Introductory Text*. Cambridge: Cambridge University Press.

Morton, John. 1984. The Domestication of the Savage Pig: The Role of Peccaries in Tropical South and Central America and Their Relevance for the Understanding of Pig Domestication in Melanesia. *Canberra Anthropology* 7 (1–2):20–70.

Mosko, Mark. 1995. Rethinking Trobriand Chiefship. *Journal of the Royal Anthropological Institute*, n.s., 1 (4):763–85.

Murphy, Robert F. 1957. Intergroup Hostility and Social Cohesion. *American Anthropologist* 59:1018–1035.

————. 1958. *Mundurucú Religion*. Berkeley: University of California Press.

————. 1959. Social Structure and Sex Antagonism. *Southwestern Journal of Anthropology* 15:89–98.

————. 1960. *Headhunters' Heritage*. Berkeley: University of California Press.

————. 1961. Deviance and Social Control 1. *Kroeber Anthropological Society Papers* 24:55–61.

Murphy, Yolanda, and Robert F. Murphy. 1974. *Women of the Forest*. New York: Columbia University Press.

————. 1985. *Women of the Forest*, 2d. ed. New York: Columbia University Press.

Nadel, Siegfried F. 1952. Witchcraft in Four African Societies: An Essay in Comparison. *American Anthropologist* 57:661–679.

Nadelson, Leslee. 1981. "Pigs, Women, and the Men's House in Amazonia: An Analysis of Six Mundurucú Myths." In S. Ortner and H. Whitehead, eds., *Sexual Meanings*, pp. 240–272. New York: Cambridge University Press.

Nelson, Harold Edwin. 1971. "The Ecological, Epistemological and Ethnographic Context of Medicine in a New Guinea Highlands Culture." Unpublished Ph.D. dissertation, University of Washington.

Newman, Philip L., and David J. Boyd. 1982. "The Making of Men: Ritual and Meaning in Awa Male Initiation." In G. H. Herdt, ed., *Rituals of Manhood: Male Initiation in Papua New Guinea*, pp. 239–285. Berkeley: University of California Press.

Newton, Douglas. 1987. Shields of the Manambu (East Sepik Province, Papua New Guinea). *Baessler-Archiv* (N.F.) 35:249–259.

Nihill, Michael. 1989. The Bride Wore Black: Aspects of Anganen Marriage and Its Meaning. *Social Analysis* 26:65–90.

Nimuendajú, Curt. 1946. *The Eastern Timbira*. Berkeley: University of California Press.

————. 1950 [1927]. Reconhecimento dos Rios Içana, Ayarí, e Uaupés. Relatorio Apresentado ão Servico de Proteção ãos Indios do Amazonas e Acre, 1927. *Journal de la Société des Americanistes*, n.s., 39.

————. 1952. *The Tukuna*, vol. 45. University of California Publications in American Archaeology and Ethnology. Berkeley: University of California Press.

————. 1967 [1942]. *The Serente*, trans. R. H. Lowie. Los Angeles: Publications of the Frederick Webb Hodge Anniversary Fund.

Nordenskiöld, Erland. 1938. *An Historical and Ethnological Survey of the Cuna Indians.* Göteborg, Sweden: Göteborgs Museum, Ethngrafiska Audelningen.

Obrist van Eeuwijk, Brigit. 1992. *Small but Strong: Cultural Contexts of (Mal-) Nutrition among the Northern Kwanga (East Sepik Province, Papua New Guinea.)* Basel: Wepf.

O'Hanlon, Michael. 1989. *Reading the Skin: Adornment, Display and Society among the Wahgi.* London: British Museum Publications.

Ortner, Sherry B. 1974. "Is Female to Male as Nature Is to Culture?" In M. Rosaldo and L. Lamphere, eds., *Woman, Culture and Society*, pp. 67–88. Stanford: Stanford University Press.

———. 1990. Gender Hegemonies. *Cultural Critique* 14:35–80.

———. 1996. *Making Gender: The Politics and Erotics of Culture.* Boston: Beacon Press.

Ortner, Sherry B., and Harriet Whitehead, eds. 1981. *Sexual Meanings.* Cambridge: Cambridge University Press.

Paige, Karen Ericksen, and Jeffery M. Paige. 1981. *The Politics of Reproductive Ritual.* Berkeley: University of California Press.

Patterson, Mary. 1981. "Slings and Arrows: Rituals of Status Acquisition in North Ambrym." In M. R. Allen, ed., *Vanuatu: Politics, Economics and Ritual in Island Melanesia*, pp. 189–236. Sydney: Academic Press.

Peletz, Michael. 1995. Kinship Studies in Late Twentieth-Century Anthropology. *Annual Review of Anthropology* 24:343–372.

Perrin, M. 1983. *Le chemin des Indiens morts. Mythes et symboles guajiro.* Paris: Payot.

Philsooph, H. 1980. "A Study of a West Sepik People, New Guinea, with Special Reference to their System of Beliefs, Kinship and Marriage, and Principles of Thought." Unpublished Ph.D. dissertation, University of Edinburgh.

Picon, F. 1983. *Pasteurs du Nouveau Monde.* Paris: Editions de la Maison des Sciences de l'Homme.

Pollock, Donald K. 1993. "Conversion and 'Community' in Amazonia." In R. W. Hefner, ed., *Conversion to Christianity: Historical and Anthropological Perspectives on a Great Transformation*, pp. 165–198. Berkeley: University of California Press.

———. 1996. Personhood and Illness among the Kulina. *Medical Anthropology Quarterly* 10 (3):319–341.

Pongiura, Samuel Piasause Wompiampi. 1993. "Haiwohwie-Ninere Hrie-Hwori: Music for a Purpose: A Cultural Activity of the Yangoru, East Sepik Province Papua New Guinea." Unpublished B.A. thesis, University of Papua New Guinea.

Poole, Fitz John Porter. 1981a. "Transforming 'Natural' Woman: Female Ritual Leaders and Gender Ideology among Bimin-Kuskusmin." In S. B. Ortner and H. Whitehead, eds., *Sexual Meanings: The Cultural Construction of Gender and Sexuality*, pp. 116–165. Cambridge: Cambridge University Press.

———. 1981b. "Tamam: Ideological and Sociological Configurations of 'Witchcraft' among Bimin-Kuskusmin." In M. Zelenietz and S. Lindenbaum, eds., *Sorcery and Social Change in Melanesia.* Special issue of *Social Analysis,* no. 8, pp. 58–76.

———. 1982. "Couvade and Clinic in a New Guinea Society: Birth among the Bimin-Kuskusmin." In M. W. de Vries, R. L. Berg, and M. Lipkin Jr., eds., *The Use and Abuse of Medicine*, pp. 54–95. New York: Praeger.

Poole, Fitz John P., and Gilbert. H. Herdt, eds. 1982. *Sexual Antagonism, Gender and Social Change in Papua New Guinea.* Special issue of *Social Analysis,* no. 12.

Posey, Darrell. 1994. "Environmental and Social Implications of Pre- and Postcontact Situations on Brazilian Indians: The Kayapo and a New Synthesis." In A. C. Roosevelt, ed., *Amazonian Indians from Prehistory to the Present: Anthropological Perspectives*, pp. 271–286. Tucson: University of Arizona Press.

Pospisil, Leopold. 1958. *Kapauku Papuans and Their Law.* New Haven: Yale University Press.

Radcliffe-Brown, A. R. 1951. The Comparative Method in Social Anthropology. The Huxley Memorial Lecture for 1951. *Journal of the Royal Anthropological Institute* 81:15–22.

Ramos, Alcida Rita. 1995. *Sanumá Memories: Yanomami Ethnography in Times of Crisis.* Madison: University of Wisconsin Press.

Rapp, Rayna. 1993. "Reproduction and Gender Hierarchy: Amniocentesis in America." In B. D. Miller, ed., *Sex and Gender Hierarchies,* pp. 108–126. Cambridge: Cambridge University Press.

Rappaport, Roy A. 1968. *Pigs for the Ancestors: Ritual in the Ecology of a New Guinea People.* New Haven: Yale University Press.

Read, Kenneth E. 1951. The Gahuku-Gama of the Central Highlands. *South Pacific* 5 (8):154–164.

———. 1952–1953. Nama Cult of the Central Highlands, New Guinea. *Oceania* 23:1–25.

———. 1954. Marriage among the Gahuku-Gama of the Eastern Central Highlands of New Guinea. *South Pacific* 7:864–871.

———. 1955. Morality and the Concept of the Person among the Gahuku-Gama. *Oceania* 25:233–282.

———. 1959. Leadership and Consensus in a New Guinea Society. *American Anthropologist* 61:425–436.

———. 1965. *The High Valley.* New York: Charles Scribner's Sons.

Reay, Marie. 1988. "Man-Made Myth and Women's Consciousness." In D. Gewertz, ed., *Myths of Matriarchy Reconsidered,* Oceania Monograph 33, pp. 121–143. Sydney: University of Sydney Press.

Reddish, Paul, producer. n.d. *Guardians of the Flutes: The Secrets of Male Initiation.* London: Filmakers Library.

Reichel-Dolmatoff, Gerardo. 1971. *Amazonian Cosmos: The Sexual and Religious Symbolism of the Tukano Indians.* Chicago: University of Chicago Press.

———. 1973. *Desana: Le symbolisme universel des Indiens Tukanos du Vaupés colombien.* Paris: Gallimard ("Bibliothèque des Sciences Humaines").

———. 1975. *The Shaman and the Jaguar: A Study of Narcotic Drugs among the Indians of Colombia.* Philadelphia: Temple University Press.

———. 1996. *Yurupari. Studies of an Amazonian Foundation Myth.* Cambridge: Harvard University Press.

Reigle, Robert. 2000. "Kaapu Kak Sari: Sacred Music of the Nekeni." Unpublished Ph.D. dissertation. University of California, Los Angeles.

Renard-Casevitz, F.-M. 1985. Guerre, violence et identité à partir des sociétés du piémont amazonien des Andes centrales. *Cahiers Orstom* 21 (1):81–98.

———. 1991. *Le banquet masqué. Une mythologie de l'étranger chez les Indiens Matsiguenga.* Paris: Lierre et Coudrier.

Ribeiro, Berta. 1995. *Os Índios das Águas Pretas.* São Paulo: Editora da Universidade do São Paulo.

Rivière, Peter. 1969. *Marriage among the Trio: A Principle of Social Organisation.* Oxford: Clarendon Press.

———. 1984. *Individual and Society in Guyana: A Comparative Study of Amerindian Social Organization.* Cambridge: Cambridge University Press.

Robbins, Sterling G. 1982. *Auyana: Those Who Held onto Home.* Seattle: University of Washington Press.

Robertson, Alexander F. 1996. The Development of Meaning, Ontogeny and Culture. *Journal of the Royal Anthropological Institute*, n.s., 2 (3):591–610.

Robinson, Kathryn. 2001. "Government Agency, Women's Agency: Feminisms, Fertility, and Population Control." In M. Jolly and K. Ram, eds., *Borders of Being: Citizenship, Fertility and Sexuality in Asia and the Pacific*, pp. 36–57. Ann Arbor: University of Michigan Press.

Rodman, Margaret. 1987. *Masters of Tradition: Consequences of Customary Land Tenure in Longana, Vanuatu.* Vancouver: University of British Columbia Press.

Roe, Peter G. 1982. *The Cosmic Zygote: Cosmology in the Amazonian Basin.* New Brunswick, N.J.: Rutgers University Press.

Roheim, Géza. 1950. *Psychoanalysis and Anthropology.* New York: International Universities Press.

Rojas, Zolezzi E. 1994. *Los Ashaninka, un pueblo tras el bosque. Contribucíon a la etnología de los Campa de la Selva Central Peruana.* Lima: Pontificia Universidad Católica del Perú.

Rosaldo, Michelle, and Louise Lamphere, eds. 1974. *Woman, Culture and Society.* Stanford: Stanford University Press.

Roscoe, Paul B. 1989. The Pig and the Long Yam: The Expansion of a Sepik Cultural Complex. *Ethnology* 28 (3):219–231.

———. 1994. Amity and Aggression: A Symbolic Theory of Incest. *Man*, n.s., 29:49–76.

———. 1995a. "'Initiation' in Cross-cultural Perspective." In N. C. Lutkehaus and P. B. Roscoe, eds., *Gender Rituals: Female Initiation in Melanesia*, pp. 219–238. New York: Routledge.

———. 1995b. "In the Shadow of the Tambaran: Female Initiation among the Ndu of the Sepik Basin." In N. C. Lutkehaus and P. B. Roscoe, eds., *Gender Rituals: Female Initiation in Melanesia*, pp. 55–82. New York: Routledge.

———. 1995c. Of Power and Menace: Sepik Art as an Affecting Presence. *Journal of the Royal Anthropological Institute* 1:1–22.

———. 1995d. The Perils of "Positivism" in Cultural Anthropology. *American Anthropologist* 97 (3):492–504.

Rubel, Paula, and Abraham Rosman. 1978. *Your Own Pigs You May Not Eat.* Chicago: University of Chicago Press.

Rubin, Gayle. 1975. "The Traffic in Women." In R. R. Reiter, ed., *Toward an Anthropology of Women*, pp. 157–210. New York: Monthly Review Press.

———. 1992 [1984]. "Thinking Sex: Notes for a Radical Theory of the Politics of Sexuality." In C. Vance, ed., *Pleasure and Danger: Exploring Female Sexuality*, pp. 267–283. London: Pandora Press.

Sahlins, Marshall. 1985. *Islands of History.* Chicago: University of Chicago Press.

Salisbury, R. F. 1962. *From Stone to Steel: Economic Consequences of a Technological Change in New Guinea.* Parkville, Victoria: Melbourne University Press.

Sanday, Peggy. 1981. *Female Power and Male Dominance: On the Origins of Sexual Inequality.* Cambridge, England: Cambridge University Press.

Santos Granero, F. 1994. *El poder del amor. Poder, conocimiento y moralidad entre los Amuesha de la selva central del Perú.* Quito: Ediciones Abya-Yala.

Scaglion, Richard, and Richard G. Condon. 1979. Abelam Yam Beliefs and Sociorhythmicity: A Study in Chronoanthropology. *Journal of Biosocial Science* 11:17–25.

Scazzocchio, F. B. 1979. "Ethnicity and Boundary Maintenance among the Peruvian Forest Quechua." Unpublished Ph.D. thesis, University of Cambridge.

Schiefenhövel, Wulf. 1982. "Kindliche Sexualität, Tabu und Schamgefühl bei 'primitiven' Völkern." In T. Hellbrugge, ed., *Die Entwicklung der kindlichen Sexualität*, pp. 145–163. Munich: Urban and Schwarzenberg.

Schieffelin, Edward L. 1976. *The Sorrow of the Lonely and the Burning of the Dancers.* New York: St. Martin's Press.

———. 1981. "The End of Traditional Music, Dance and Body Decoration in Bosavi, Papua New Guinea." In R. Gordon, ed., *The Plight of Peripheral People in Papua New Guinea,* vol. 1: *The Inland Situation,* pp. 1–22. Cambridge, Mass.: Cultural Survival.

Schindlbeck, Markus. 1980. *Sago bei den Sawos.* Basel: Ethnologisches Seminar der Universität und Museum für Völkerkunde.

Schneider, David. 1976. The Meaning of Incest. *Journal of the Polynesian Society* 85:149–69.

———. 1980. *American Kinship: A Cultural Account,* 2d ed. Chicago: University of Chicago Press.

Schroeder, Roger. 1992. *Initiation and Religion: A Case Study from the Wosera of Papua New Guinea.* Freiburg: University Press Freiburg Switzerland.

Schurtz, Heinrich. 1902. *Alterklassen und Männerbunde.* Berlin: G. Reimer.

Seeger, Anthony. 1975. The Meaning of Body Ornaments: A Suya Example. *Ethnology* 14:211–224.

———. 1981. *Nature and Society in Central Brazil: The Suya Indians of Mato Grosso.* Cambridge: Harvard University Press.

———. 1987. *Why Suyá Sing.* Cambridge: Cambridge University Press.

Seeger, Anthony, Roberto Da Matta, and E. B. Viveiros de Castro. 1979. A construção da pessoa nas sociedades indígenas brasileiras. *Boletim do Museu Nacional, Antropologia,* n.s., 32:2–19.

Seger J., M. Godelier, L. Halle, P. Lemonnier, J. L. Lory, P. Roger, J. Ruffie, and D. Salmon. 1988. Red Cell Enzyme Polymorphisms in Papua New Guinea Eastern Highlands. *Gene Geography* 2:99–106.

Seymour-Smith, C. 1991. Women Have No Affines and Men No Kin: The Politics of the Jivaroan Gender Relation. *Man,* n.s., 26 (4):629–649.

Shapiro, Warren. 1989. The Theoretical Importance of Pseudo-Procreative Symbolism. *The Psychoanalytic Study of Society* 14:71–88.

———. 1995. Sex, Violence and "Cultural Constructionism." *Journal of the Royal Anthropological Institute* 1:625–626.

———. 1996. "The Quest for Purity in Anthropological Inquiry." In W. Shapiro and U. Linke, eds., *Denying Biology: Essays on Gender and Pseudo-Procreation,* pp. 167–189. Lanham, Md.: University Press of America.

Shapiro, Warren, and Uli Linke, eds. 1996. *Denying Biology: Essays on Gender and Pseudo-Procreation.* Lanham, Md.: University Press of America.

Shaw, R. Daniel. 1990. *Kandila: Samo Ceremonialism and Interpersonal Relationships.* Ann Arbor: University of Michigan Press.

Shoemaker, Nancy. 1995. "Kateri Tekakwitha's Tortuous Path to Sainthood." In N. Shoemaker, ed., *Negotiators of Change: Historical Perspectives on Native American Women,* pp. 49–71. New York: Routledge.

Sillitoe, Paul. 1979. Man-Eating Women: Fears of Sexual Pollution in the Papua New Guinea Highlands. *Journal of the Polynesian Society* 88:77–97.

———. 1980. The Art of War: Wola Shield Designs. *Man,* n.s., 15:483–501.

Silverman, Eric Kline. 1993. "Tambunum: New Perspectives on Eastern Iatmul (Sepik River, Papua New Guinea) Kinship, Marriage, and Society." Unpublished Ph.D. dissertation, University of Minnesota.

Simmel, Georg. 1950. "The Secret and the Secret Society." In K. H. Wolff, trans. and ed., *The Sociology of Georg Simmel,* pp. 305–371. New York: Free Press.

Sims, Andrew, and Anne Sims. 1992. *Ritual and Relationships in the Valley of the Sun: The Ketengban of Irian Jaya*. International Museum of Cultures Publication No. 30. Jayapura and Dallas: Cenderawasih University and International Museum of Cultures.

Siskind, Janet. 1973. *To Hunt in the Morning*. New York: Oxford University Press.

Spiro, Melford E. 1997. *Gender Ideology and Cultural Reality*. New Haven: Yale University Press.

Spriggs, Matthew J. T. 1985. "A School in Every District": The Cultural Geography of Conversion on Aneityum, Southern Vanuatu. *Journal of Pacific History* 20 (1–2):23–41.

Staats, Susan K. 1996. "Fighting in a Different Way: Indigenous Resistance through the Alleluia Religion of Guyana." In J. D. Hill, ed., *History, Power, and Identity: Ethnogenesis in the Americas, 1492–1992*, pp. 161–179. Iowa City: University of Iowa Press.

Steinbauer, Friedrich. 1979. *Melanesian Cargo Cults: New Salvation Movements in the South Pacific*, trans. M. Wohlwil. St. Lucia, Queensland: University of Queensland Press.

Steinfels, Peter. 1994. Female Concept of God Is Shaking Protestants. *New York Times*, May 14, A-8.

Stephen, Michele, ed. 1987. *Sorcerer and Witch in Melanesia*. New Brunswick, N.J.: Rutgers University Press.

Stewart, Pamela J., and Andrew Strathern, eds. 1997. *Millennial Markers*. Townsville, Queensland: James Cook University, Centre for Pacific Studies.

Stoler, Ann Laura. 1991. "Carnal Knowledge and Imperial Power: Gender, Race and Morality in Colonial Asia." In M. di Leonardo, ed., *Gender at the Crossroads of Knowledge: Feminist Anthropology in the Postmodern Era*, pp. 51–101. Berkeley: University of California Press.

———. 1992. Rethinking Colonial Categories: European Communities and the Boundaries of Rule. *Comparative Studies of Society and History* 13(1):134–161.

———. 1995. *Race and the Education of Desire: Foucault's History of Sexuality and the Colonial Order of Things*. Durham: Duke University Press.

Stoller, Robert J. 1974. Symbiosis Anxiety and the Development of Masculinity. *Archives of General Psychiatry* 30:164–172.

Strassman, Beverly I. 1997. The Biology of Menstruation in Homo Sapiens: Total Lifetime Menses, Fecundity, and Nonsynchrony in a Natural-Fertility Population. *Current Anthropology* 38 (1):123–129.

Strathern, Andrew J. 1970. The Female and Male Spirit Cults in Mount Hagen. *Man*, n.s., 5:571–585.

———. 1972. *One Father, One Blood: Descent and Group Structure among the Melpa People*. London: Tavistock.

———. 1976. Some Notes on the Cultivation of Winged Beans in Two Highlands Areas of Papua New Guinea. *Science in New Guinea* 4:145–152.

———. 1977. Melpa Food-Names as an Expression of Ideas on Identity and Substance. *Journal of the Polynesian Society* 86:503–11.

———. 1984. *A Line of Power*. London: Tavistock Publications.

———. 1996. *Body Thoughts*. Ann Arbor: University of Michigan Press.

Strathern, Andrew J., and Marilyn Strathern. 1968. "Marsupials and Magic: A Study of Spell Symbolism among the Mbowamb." In E. R. Leach, ed., *Dialectic in Practical Religion*, pp. 179–207. Cambridge: Cambridge University Press.

———. 1971. *Self-Decoration in Mount Hagen*. Toronto: University of Toronto Press.

Strathern, Andrew, and Pamela J. Stewart. 1998. "Melpa and Nuer Ideas of Life and Death: The Rebirth of Comparison." In M. Lambek and A. Strathern, eds., *Bodies and Persons: Comparative Perspectives from Africa and Melanesia,* pp. 232–251. New York: Cambridge University Press.

Strathern, Andrew, and Gabriele Stürzenhofecker, eds. 1995. *Migration and Transformations: Regional Perspectives on New Guinea,* ASAO Monograph No. 15. Pittsburgh: University of Pittsburgh Press.

Strathern, Marilyn. 1972. *Women in Between: Female Roles in a Male World: Mount Hagen, New Guinea.* London: Seminar Press.

———. 1979. The Self in Self-Decoration. *Oceania* 49:241–257.

———. 1981. Culture in a Net Bag: The Manufacture of a Subdiscipline in Anthropology. *Man,* n.s., 16:665–688.

———. 1988. *The Gender of the Gift: Problems with Women and Problems with Society in Melanesia.* Berkeley: University of California Press.

———. 1990. "Negative Strategies in Melanesia." In R. Fardon, ed., *Localizing Strategies: Regional Traditions of Ethnographic Writing,* pp. 204–216. Washington, D.C.: Smithsonian Institution Press.

———. 1991. *Partial Connections.* Savage, Md.: Rowman and Littlefield.

———. 1992a. *Reproducing the Future: Essays on Anthropology, Kinship, and the New Reproductive Technologies.* New York: Routledge.

———. 1992b. "Parts and Wholes: Refiguring Relationships in a Postplural World." In A. Kuper, ed., *Conceptualising Society,* pp. 75–104. London: Routledge.

———. 1993. "Making Incomplete." In V. Broch-Due, I. Rudie, and T. Bleie, eds., *Carved Flesh/Cast Selves: Gendered Symbols and Social Practices,* pp. 41–51. Oxford: Berg.

———. 1995. "Gender: Division or Comparison?" In N. Charles and F. Hughes-Freeland, eds., *Practising Feminism: Identity, Difference, Power,* pp. 38–60. London: Routledge.

———. 1998. "Divisions of Interest and Languages of Ownership." In C. Hann, ed., *Property Relations: Renewing the Anthropological Tradition,* pp. 214–253. Cambridge: Cambridge University Press.

Strauss, Hermann. 1990 [1962]. *The Mi-Culture of the Mount Hagen People, Papua New Guinea,* trans. and ed. B. Shields, G. Stürzenhofecker, A.J. Strathern. Pittsburgh: University of Pittsburgh.

Strong, Pauline Turner. 1996. "Feminist Theory and the 'Invasion of the Heart' in North America." In M. Harkin and S. Kan, eds., *Native American Women's Responses to Christianity.* Special issue of *Ethnohistory* 43(4):683–711.

Sullivan, Lawrence E. 1988. *Icanchu's Drum: An Orientation to Meaning in South American Religions.* New York: Macmillan.

Taylor, Anne-Christine. 1983. The Marriage Alliance and Its Structural Variations in Jivaroan Societies. *Social Science Information* 22 (3):331–353.

———. 1993a. "Les bons ennemis et les mauvais parents: Le traitement de l'alliance dans les rituels de chasse aux têtes des Shuar (Jivaro) de l'Equateur." In E. Copet-Rougier and F. Héritier-Augé, eds., *Les complexités de l'alliance: IV. Economie, politiques et fondements symboliques,* pp. 73–105. Paris: Editions des Archives Contemporaines.

———. 1993b. Remembering to Forget: Jivaroan Ideas of Identity and Mortality." *Man,* n.s., 28 (4):653–678.

Thorne, Tony. 1990. *Bloomsbury Dictionary of Contemporary Slang.* London: Bloomsbury.

Townsend, Patricia K. 1990. "Our Women Are Okay: Aspects of Hiyewe Women's Status." In Nancy C. Lutkehaus, C. Kaufmann, W. E. Mitchell, D. Newton, L. Osmundsen, and M. Schuster, eds., *Sepik Heritage: Tradition and Change in Papua New Guinea,* pp. 374–379. Durham: Carolina Academic Press.

———. 1995. "The Washed and Unwashed. Women's Life-Cycle Rituals among the Saniyo-Hiyowe of East Sepik Province, Papua New Guinea." In N. C. Lutkehaus and P. B. Roscoe, eds., *Gender Rituals: Female Initiation in Melanesia,* pp. 165–182. New York: Routledge.

Turner, Terence S. 1966. "Social Structure and Political Organization among the Northern Kayapo." Unpublished Ph.D. dissertation, Harvard University.

———. 1980. "The Social Skin." In J. Cherfas and R. Lewin, eds., *Not Work Alone,* pp. 112–140. London: Temple Smith.

———. 1995. An Indigenous People's Struggle for Socially Equitable and Ecologically Sustainable Production: The Kayapo Revolt against Extractivism. *Journal of Latin American Anthropology* 1 (1):98–121.

Turner, Victor. 1967. "Betwixt and Between: The Liminal Period in Rites of Passage." In V. Turner, *The Forest of Symbols,* pp. 93–111. Ithaca: Cornell University Press.

Tuzin, Donald F. 1972. Yam Symbolism in the Sepik: An Interpretative Account. *Southwestern Journal of Anthropology* 28 (3):230–254.

———. 1976. *The Ilahita Arapesh: Dimensions of Unity.* Berkeley: University of California Press.

———. 1977. Reflections of Being in Arapesh Water Symbolism. *Ethos* 5 (2):195–223.

———. 1978a. Politics, Power and Divine Artistry in Ilahita. *Anthropological Quarterly* 51:61–67.

———. 1978b. Sex and Meat-Eating in Ilahita. *Canberra Anthropology* 1 (3):82–93.

———. 1980. *The Voice of the Tambaran: Truth and Illusion in Ilahita Arapesh Religion.* Berkeley: University of California Press.

———. 1982. "Ritual Violence among the Ilahita Arapesh: The Dynamics of Moral and Religious Uncertainty." In G. H. Herdt, ed., *Rituals of Manhood: Male Initiation in Papua New Guinea,* pp. 321–355. Berkeley: University of California Press.

———. 1984. Miraculous Voices: The Auditory Experience of Numinous Objects. *Current Anthropology* 25 (5):579–589, 593–596.

———. 1990. "Of the Resemblance of Fathers to Their Children: The Roots of Primitivism in Middle-Childhood Enculturation." In L. Bryce Boyer and S. Grolnick, eds., *The Psychoanalytic Study of Society,* vol. 15, pp. 69–103. New York: Analytic Press.

———. 1992a. Sago Subsistence and Symbolism among the Ilahita Arapesh. *Ethnology* 31 (2):103–114.

———. 1992b. "Revelation and Concealment in the Organization of Meaning: A Methodological Note." In B. Juillerat, ed., *Shooting the Sun: Ritual and Meaning in West Sepik,* pp. 251–259. Washington, D.C.: Smithsonian Institution Press.

———. 1995. Art and Procreative Illusion in the Sepik: Comparing the Abelam and the Arapesh. *Oceania* 65 (4):289–303.

———. 1996. "The Spectre of Peace in Unlikely Places: Concept and Paradox in the Anthropology of Peace." In T. Gregor, ed., *A Natural History of Peace,* pp. 3–33. Nashville: Vanderbilt University Press.

———. 1997. *The Cassowary's Revenge: The Life and Death of Masculinity in a New Guinea Society.* Chicago: University of Chicago Press.

————. n.d. "*Sartor Resartus:* The New Guinea Micro-Evolution Project, 1959–1983 and After: A Comment." Paper delivered to the 93rd Annual Meeting of the American Anthropological Association. Atlanta, November 1994.

Txukarramãe, Megaron, and Mick Stout. 1990. "A expedição venatório dos Kayapó e animais importantes." In Darrell A. Posey and William L. Overal, organizers, *Ethnobiology: Implications and Applications*, vol. 1, pp. 227–241. Belém, Brazil: Museu Paraense Emílio Goeldi.

Urban, Greg, and Joel Sherzer, eds. 1986. *Native South American Discourse.* Austin: University of Texas Press.

Valentine, Charles. 1961. *Masks and Men in Melanesian Society.* Lawrence: University of Kansas Press.

van der Hammen, M. C. 1992. *El manejo del mundo. Naturaleza y sociedad entre los Yukuna de la Amazonia colombiana.* Bogotá: TROPENBOS.

Van Gennep, Arnold. 1981 [1909]. *Les rites de Passage.* Paris: Picard.

————. 1960 [1909]. *The Rites of Passage*, trans. M. Vizedom and G. Caffee. Chicago: University of Chicago Press.

Vance, Carole S. 1989. "Social Construction Theory: Problems in the History of Sexuality." In A. van Kooten Niekerk and T. van der Meer, eds., *Homosexuality, Which Homosexuality?* pp. 13–34. Amsterdam: An Dekker/Schorer.

————. 1991. "Anthropology Rediscovers Sexuality: A Theoretical Comment." In S. Lindenbaum, ed., *Anthropology Rediscovers Sex.* Special issue of *Social Science and Medicine* 33:875–884.

Verswijver, Gustaaf. 1985. "Considerations on Mekrãnotí Warfare." Unpublished Ph.D. dissertation, Rijksuniversiteit Gent, Belgium.

————. 1996. "Between Village and Forest." In G. Verswijver, ed., *Kaiapó Amazonia: The Art of Body Decoration*, pp. 11–25. Gent, Belgium: Royal Museum for Central Africa (Tervuren), Snoeck-Ducaju & Zoon.

Vicinus, Martha. 1982. Sexuality and Power: A Review of Current Work in the History of Sexuality. *Feminist Studies* 8 (1):136.

Vidal, Lux B. 1977. *Morte e Vida de uma Sociedade Indígena Brasileira.* São Paulo: Editora Hucitec.

Vilaça, Aparecida. 1989. "Comendo Como Gente: Formas do Cannibalismo Wari' (Pakaa Nova)." Master's dissertation, Programa de Pós-Graduação em Antropologia Social, Museu Nacional, Universidade Federal do Rio de Janeiro.

————. 1992. *Comendo Como Gente.* Rio de Janeiro: Editora UFRJ.

————. 1996. "Quem Somos Nós: Questões da Alteridade no Encontro dos Wari' com os Brancos." Unpublished Ph.D. dissertation, Museu Nacional, Universidade Federal do Rio de Janeiro.

Viveiros de Castro, Eduardo B. 1979. A fabricação do corpo na sociedade xinguana. *Boletim do Museu Nacional, Antropologia*, n.s., 32:40–49.

————. 1992. *From the Enemy's Point of View: Humanity and Divinity in an Amazonian Society*, trans. Catherine V. Howard. Chicago: The University of Chicago Press.

————. 1993a. "Alguns Aspectos da Afinidade no Dravidianato Amazônico." In M. Carneiro da Cunha and E. Viveiros de Castro, eds., *Amazônia: etnologia e historia indígena*, pp. 149–210. São Paulo: NHII-Universidade de São Paulo.

————. 1993b. La puissance et l'acte: La parenté dans les basses terres d'Amérique du Sud. *L'Homme* 33:141–170.

————, ed. 1995. *Antropologia do Parentesco. Estudos Amerindios.* Rio de Janeiro: Editora da UFRJ.

————. 1996. Images of Nature and Society in Amazonian Ethnology. *Annual Review of Anthropology* 25:179–200.

Waddell, Eric. 1972. *The Mound Builders: Agricultural Practices, Environment, and Society in the Central Highlands of New Guinea.* Seattle: University of Washington Press.

Wagenheim, Jeff. 1995. Among the Promise Keepers. *New Age Journal* (March/April), 78–81; 126–130.

Wagner, Roy. 1972. *Habu: The Innovation of Meaning in Daribi Religion.* Chicago: University of Chicago Press.

————. 1977. Analogic Kinship: A Daribi Example. *American Ethnologist* 7:71–85.

Wallace, Anthony F. C. 1969. *The Death and Rebirth of the Seneca.* New York: Random House.

Warry, Wayne. 1986. Kafaina: Female-Wealth and Power in Chuave, Papua New Guinea. *Oceania* 57:4–21.

Warus, Joseph. 1986. "Uma Village, Southern Highlands Province." In Anon., ed., *Marriage in Papua New Guinea,* pp. 47–62. Boroko: Law Reform Commission of Papua New Guinea.

Watson, James B. 1963. A Micro-Evolution Study in New Guinea. *Journal of the Polynesian Society* 72:188–192.

————. 1973. "Tairora: The Politics of Despotism in a Small Society." In R. M. Berndt and P. Lawrence, eds., *Politics in New Guinea: Traditional and in the Context of Change: Some Anthropological Perspectives,* pp. 224–275. Seattle: University of Washington Press.

————. 1977. Pigs, Fodder, and the Jones Effect in Postipomoean New Guinea. *Ethnology* 16 (1):57–70.

————, ed. 1964. New Guinea: The Central Highlands. *American Anthropologist* 66, part 2, special issue.

Watson, James B., and Virginia Watson. 1972. *Batainabura of New Guinea.* HRAFlex Books, 051–004, Ethnocentrism Series. New Haven: HRAF.

Webster, Hutton. 1907. *Primitive Secret Societies: A Study in Early Politics and Religion.* New York: Macmillan.

Weiner, Annette B. 1976. *Women of Value, Men of Renown: New Perspectives on Trobriand Exchange.* Austin: University of Texas Press.

————. 1988. *The Trobrianders of Papua New Guinea.* New York: Holt, Rinehart and Winston.

————. 1992. *Inalienable Possessions: The Paradox of Keeping-While-Giving.* Berkeley: University of California Press.

Weiner, James F. 1986. Blood and Skin: The Structural Implications of Sorcery and Procreation Beliefs among the Foi. *Ethnos* 51:71–87.

————. 1987. "Diseases of the Soul: Sickness, Agency and the Men's Cult among the Foi of New Guinea." In M. Strathern, ed., *Dealing with Inequality: Analysing Gender Relations in Melanesia and Beyond,* pp. 255–277. Cambridge: Cambridge University Press.

————. 1988. Durkheim and the Papua Male Cult: Whitehead's Views on Social Structure and Ritual in New Guinea. *American Ethnologist* 15 (3):567–573.

————. 1995. *The Lost Drum: The Myth of Sexuality in Papua New Guinea and Beyond.* Madison: University of Wisconsin Press.

Weiss, Florence. 1994. "Die Unterdrückung der Fraueninitiation: Zum Wandel des Ritualsystems bei den Iatmul." In B. Hauser-Schäublin, ed., *Geschichte und Mündliche Überlieferung in Ozeanien,* Basler Beiträge zur Ethnologie, Band 37, pp. 237–259. Basel: Ethnologisches Seminar der Universität und Museum für Völkerkunde.

Weiss, G. 1975. *Campa Cosmology. The World of a Forest Tribe in South America.* New York: American Museum of Natural History.

Werbner, Richard. 1989. *Ritual Passage, Sacred Journey: The Process and Organization of Religious Movement.* Washington: Smithsonian Institution Press.

————. 1992. "On Dialectical Versions: The Cosmic Rebirth of West Sepik Regionalism." In B. Juillerat, ed., *Shooting the Sun: Ritual and Meaning in West Sepik,* pp. 214–250. Washington: Smithsonian Institute Press.

Werner, Dennis. 1980. "The Making of a Mekranoti Chief: The Psychological and Social Determinants of Leadership in a Native South American Society." Unpublished Ph.D. dissertation, City University of New York.

————. 1984. *Amazon Journey: An Anthropologist's Year among Brazil's Mekranoti Indians.* New York: Simon and Schuster.

Whitehead, Harriet. 1986a. The Varieties of Fertility Cultism in New Guinea: Part I. *American Ethnologist* 13 (1):80–99.

————. 1986b. The Varieties of Fertility Cultism in New Guinea: Part II. *American Ethnologist* 13 (2):271–289.

Whitehouse, Harvey. 1995. *Inside the Cult: Religious Innovation and Transmission in Papua New Guinea.* Oxford: Oxford University Press.

Whiting, John W. M. 1941. *Becoming a Kwoma: Teaching and Learning in a New Guinea Tribe.* New Haven: Yale University Press.

Whiting, John W. M., Clyde Kluckhohn, and A. Anthony. 1958. "The Function of Male Initiation Ceremonies at Puberty." In E. Macoby, T. M. Newcomb and E. L. Hartley, eds., *Readings in Social Psychology,* 3rd ed., pp. 359–370. New York: Holt.

Whitten, N. E. 1976. *Sacha Runa. Ethnicity and Adaptation of Ecuadorian Jungle Quichua.* Urbana: University of Illinois Press.

Wilbert, Johannes. 1977. "Navigators of the Winter Sun." In E. P. Benson, ed., *The Sea in the Pre-Columbian World,* pp. 16–46. Washington D.C.: Trustees for Harvard University.

Williamson, Margaret Holmes. 1975. "Kwoma Society: Women and Disorder." Unpublished Ph.D. thesis, Oxford University.

————. 1990. "Gender and the Cosmos in Kwoma Culture." In N. Lutkehaus, C. Kaufmann, W. E. Mitchell, D. Newton, L. Osmundsen, and M. Schuster, eds., *Sepik Heritage: Tradition and Change in Papua New Guinea,* pp. 385–394. Durham: Carolina Academic Press.

Wood, Michael. 1982. "Kamula Social Structure and Ritual." Unpublished Ph.D. thesis, Macquarie University, Sydney.

Worsley, Peter. 1968. *The Trumpet Shall Sound: A Study of 'Cargo' Cults in Melanesia,* 2d ed. New York: Schocken.

Wright, Robin. 1981. "History and Religion of the Baniwa Peoples of the Upper Rio Negro Valley." Unpublished Ph.D. dissertation, Stanford University.

Yanagisako, Sylvia, and Carol Delaney. 1995. "Naturalizing Power." In S. Yanagisako and C. Delaney, eds., *Naturalizing Power: Essays in Feminist Cultural Analysis,* pp. 1–22. New York: Routledge.

Zillmann, Dolph. 1984. *Connections between Sex and Aggression.* Hillsdale, N.J.: Lawrence Erlbaum.

CONTRIBUTORS

Aletta Biersack has studied Ipili speakers since 1974. Her research on the Paiela and Porgera valleys of Papua New Guinea has been reported in many articles and book chapters. She is the editor of *Ecologies for Tomorrow: Reading Rappaport Today* (a "contemporary issues forum," *American Anthropologist* 101:5–112), *Papuan Borderlands* (1995), and *Clio in Oceania* (1991).

Pascale Bonnemère is a researcher at the CNRS. Among other writings, she is the author of a monograph on the Ankave-Anga of Papua New Guinea, *Le pandanus rouge* (1996), and has recently coordinated a volume on the implication of women in Papua New Guinea male rituals. Her most recent research concerns the Ankave system of food taboos as revealing modes of connection between persons through the life cycle.

Michael F. Brown is Lambert Professor of Anthropology and Latin American Studies at Williams College. He is the coauthor of *War of Shadows: The Struggle for Utopia in the Peruvian Amazon* (1991) and the author of *The Channeling Zone: American Spirituality in an Anxious Age* (1997).

Beth A. Conklin is Associate Professor of Anthropology and Religious Studies at Vanderbilt University. As a cultural and medical anthropologist, she focuses on the ethnography of native Amazonian societies, body concepts, personhood, cannibalism, and the politics of representations of indigenous peoples.

Philippe Descola prepared his doctorate under the supervision of Claude Lévi-Strauss after extensive fieldwork among the Jívaroan Achuar of Ecuador. His books include *Les idées de l'anthropologie* (1988), *In the Society of Nature* (1994), *The Spears of Twilight* (1994), *Nature and Society* (1996), and *La production du social* (1999). He is presently a professor at the Collège de France.

William Fisher is an associate professor at the College of William and Mary. His recently completed study of the effects of logging and mining on indigenous communities in the Amazon is entitled *Rain Forest Exchanges: Industry and Community on an Amazonian Frontier.* He was in residence at the University of Brasilia as a Fulbright Scholar in 2000.

Thomas A. Gregor is Professor and Chair of Anthropology at Vanderbilt University. His research centers on the tribal peoples of central Brazil; his theoretical interests include gender, psychoanalysis, and psychological approaches to culture. Professor Gregor is the author or editor of books on the Mehinaku Indians and the nature of peace and conflict, as well as the coproducer of ethnographic films in Brazil. He is currently engaged in research and publication on the anthropology of peace and nonviolence among the native peoples of South America.

Jonathan D. Hill is Professor of Anthropology at Southern Illinois University in Carbondale. He is editor of *Rethinking History and Myth: Indigenous South American Perspectives on the Past* and *History, Power, and Identity: Ethnogenesis in the Americas, 1492–1992* and author of *Keepers of the Sacred Chants: The Poetics of Ritual Power in an Amazonian Society.* He currently organizes the project "Comparative Arawakan Histories: Rethinking Culture Area and Language Family in Amazonia."

Stephen Hugh-Jones teaches social anthropology at the University of Cambridge. His field research on the Tukanoan-speaking peoples of the Colombian Vaupés region spans some 30 years. His research interests include ritual and mythology; architecture, kinship, and social structure; enviromental relations; food and drugs; and indigenous movements. His main publications include a monograph on initiation rituals, books that he has edited on barter and "house societies," and papers on history, shamanism, attitudes to animals, and ethno-education.

Margaret Jolly is Professor and Head of the Gender Relations Centre in the Research School of Pacific and Asian Studies, Australian National University. She writes on gender in the Pacific, the politics of tradition, exploratory voyages and travel writing, missions and Christianity, sexuality, cinema, and art. She is the author of *Women of the Place: Kastom, Colonialism and Gender in Vanuatu* (1994) and coedited *Family and Gender in the Pacific* (1989), *Sites of Desire / Economies of Pleasure: Sexualities in Asia and the Pacific* (1997), *Maternities and Modernities: Colonial and Postcolonial Experiences in Asia and the Pacific* (1998), and *Governing Bodies: State, Sexuality and Fertility in Asia and the Pacific* (2000).

Paul Roscoe is Professor of Anthropology at the University of Maine. His recent publications include "Amity and Aggression: A Symbolic Theory of Incest" (*Man*) and "War and Society in Sepik New Guinea" (*Journal of the Royal Anthropological Institute*). He is coeditor of *Gender Rituals: Female Initiation in Melanesia* (Routledge).

Marilyn Strathern is William Wyse Professor in the Department of Social Anthropology at the University of Cambridge and Mistress of Girton College. Her research interests are divided between Melanesian and British ethnography. *The Gender of the Gift* (1988) is a critique of anthropological theories of society and gender relations as they have been applied to Melanesia, while *After Nature* (1992) comments on the cultural revolution at home. Recent publications include the coauthored *Technologies of Procreation* (1993) and a collection of essays, *Property, Substance and Effect: Anthropological Essays on Persons and Things* (1999).

Donald Tuzin is Professor of Anthropology and founding director of the Melanesian Archive at the University of California, San Diego. His works cover various topics in social and psychological anthropology and include, most recently, *The Cassowary's Revenge: The Life and Death of Masculinity in a New Guinea Society* (1997) and *Social Complexity in the Making: A Case Study among the Arapesh of New Guinea* (2001).

NAME INDEX

SUBJECT INDEX

abstinence, sexual, 151, 158, 180. *See also* sexual avoidances

Achuar: belief in plant and animal "souls," 98–99, 102–103; collective residences of, 94; description of territory, 94–103; gardening myths of, 97–99; gender and kinship relationships, 91, 95–98; gender roles of, 96–98; head-hunting by, 95; hunting traditions of, 96–99; male domination over women, 99–100; marriage systems of, 95; origin myths, 102; and vision-seeking, 100–101

African studies, 335, 340

age and gender considerations, 115–117, 120–121, 125, 134–135

age categorization, 105

age grade, 139

alliance theory versus descent theory, 82–83

Amazonia: animals in, 246; body imagery in, 313–314; cosmologies in, 106–108, 111, 116, 122, 169; couvade in, 12; death and life rituals in, 143; descent traditions in, 245–246; ear-piercing in, 12; ethnography and ethnology researchers in, 6; flute playing in, 18; gender distinctions in, 9; gender imagery in, 138; gender-inflected societies in, 8; gender irrelevance to culture in, 10; gift exchange in, 250; kin relationships in, 10; male cults in, 13–14, 18; male initiation rituals in, 12, 13; male sexual avoidances in, 281–288; marriage systems, 246, 247; masculinity in, 297–300; parallels with Melanesian culture, 1, 123, 144–153, 167, 170–171, 309–313, 320, 337–343; postcolonial effects on gender politics in, 199–203; procreative symbolism in, 12–13; rebirth rituals by males in, 17, 19; reproductive beliefs in, 85; ritual transformation in, 151–153; seclusion rituals in, 151–153; self-concept in, 11–12; sexuality and mythology in, 9; sexual practices in, 297–300; social structures in, 106–108; social transition rituals in, 11. *See also specific cultures*

androgyny, 253, 262

Anga: male initiation rituals of, 19–31; origin myths of, 41; origins of, 18; and rebirth rituals by males, 17; social organization of, 19–20

animal and plant "souls," 98–99, 102–103

animal mythology, 111, 118, 122, 137, 251–252

animals, domestic, 113, 246

Ankave: birth reenactment by, 24; clans of, 21; description of territory, 21; dietary customs of, 21; food taboos of, 29; gender politics in, 192–193; gestation reenactment by, 24; and male initiation, 22; nose-piercing by, 22; origin myths of, 40; red-pandanus-rubbing by, 22–23; seclusion of mothers by, 30–31

anthropologists, cultural backgrounds and biases of, 92–93

Compositor:	Publication Services
Text:	10/12 Baskerville
Display:	Baskerville
Printer and Binder:	Sheridan Books, Inc.